Cream of the
KAPPAN

Cream of the
KAPPAN
1956-1981

Compiled and edited
by
Stanley M. Elam

𝕿

A Diamond Jubilee Publication of the
Phi Delta Kappa Educational Foundation

Cover design by Victoria Voelker

Library of Congress Catalog Card Number: 81-83808
ISBN Number: 0-87367-776-5
Copyright © 1981 by Phi Delta Kappa, Inc.,
Bloomington, Indiana
Printed in the United States of America

This anthology is dedicated to the two Phi Delta Kappa executive secretaries with whom I worked: The late Maynard Bemis (from 1956 to 1970), who almost literally gave his life to Phi Delta Kappa, and Lowell Rose, under whose administrative magic and exuberant good temper the organization continues to thrive.

The KAPPAN *would not have been the kind of journal I have sought to portray in this book had these leaders not given me friendship, encouragement, and support.*

Contents

Preface

Today is April 10, 1981. The sorting process is over. Thank heaven.

Between July 1965 and January 1981 I edited 239 issues of the *PHI DELTA KAPPAN*—all but eight of those published during the period.* Roughly 3,000 unsolicited manuscripts were published in those 239 issues. The articles were drawn from upwards of 25,000 offered for publication. Another 400 to 500 feature pieces were solicited, usually from established authors. This book thus represents a winnowing of articles, from 25,500 or thereabouts down to 49.

When I began skimming the 17 million words or so contained in 25 volumes of the *KAPPAN*, I was looking for the "40 best articles." That was my charge. This book was to have been titled *The Best of the KAPPAN, 1956-1981*, a sort of crown jewel for Phi Delta Kappa's Diamond Jubilee Year celebration.

It took fully 18 months for me to see how ridiculous my search had become. There are no "best" articles, I finally realized, only articles that, for different people at different times, may be instructive, entertaining, or—more rarely—inspirational. By the time this shaft of light penetrated, I had built a list of 143 articles I considered appropriate for the anthology. There was enough material for three volumes of this size. I was considering roulette to replace my increasingly flexible criteria of selection when the dawn broke and I took refuge in "editor's intuition," a euphemism for purely personal prejudice.

I recall the answer I used to give chapter audiences when they asked how material is selected for *KAPPAN* publication. "It's very personal," I said. "It depends a great deal on which side of the bed I get out of on the day final selections for an issue must be made." I quit giving that answer when I heard someone mutter, "He should have stayed in bed." (A disappointed author, no doubt.)

But it is perfectly true that for 25 years the *KAPPAN* reflected, essentially, the peculiar interests, preferences, and beliefs of one person: me. There was always, of course, a board of editorial consultants. I often asked for their advice, because I was often uncertain. And they were very helpful. But ultimately the decision to publish or not to publish was mine, and it was based on complex considerations that, in many instances, I would have difficulty in explicating. The same may be said of the choice of material for this book. In any case, I felt that the word "best" had no business in the title.

My first aim, as editor during the tumultuous quarter century of educational history just ended, was to identify and present, as beguilingly as possible, information and ideas that would be useful to a wide range of readers. Far more today than in 1956, *KAPPAN* readers represent leadership at every level and function of education in America—and to some extent in other continents. As I have sometimes

*The only interruption in my tenure was an eight-month sabbatical during which I filled in between Warren Syfert, *NASSP Bulletin* editor who retired in the summer of 1970, and Thomas Koerner, who took the position after I returned to Phi Delta Kappa in the spring of 1971. Donald W. Robinson was *KAPPAN* acting editor during my sabbatical.

found it necessary to explain to authors, the *KAPPAN* is edited for the reader, not for people who need publication credits. I have tried to apply that same rule to this book.

Some comment on the organization of this volume is in order. Educators are impressed by order and coherence, and well they should be. Order requires discipline, thought, and a certain talent for manipulation. At first I was determined that this book would display a clever organizational style. Thus I quickly eliminated "alphabetical by author's name." Dumb. Another clean but simple organizing principle I considered was the chronological. It had the attraction of promising a sort of history of educational ideas over this past quarter century. But in practice it would have been unrewarding, I think. Certainly the book would have been a failure as a history of educational ideas. One frequently applied selection criterion was: Is the article still sound and useful? That criterion would certainly have fought against the historical principle.

For a time I was fascinated with the notion of forcing the articles into an issues framework. After all, the *KAPPAN* has always dealt with issues. Six great perennial problems in education are encompassed in two questions: Who will teach what to whom and how? How will education be financed and controlled? I soon found, however, that a "miscellaneous" or "bifurcated" category kept growing. With the possible exception of "what to teach"—in a transition period like ours curriculum is all—"miscellaneous" turned out to be the biggest chapter. Finance was neglected, I found, not because it is unimportant as an issue (this year it is positively unnerving) but because most finance articles become badly dated within a short time. And if there is a more dismal topic than school finance, it is the history of school finance. I abandoned the issues idea on April 1.

A less artificial yet logical and useful organization had to be found. Should it, I asked, follow the haystack principle of a typical *KAPPAN*? After all, the book is less than three times the length of a single issue of the journal. Why not simply offer a haystack table of contents?

In the end I compromised. This book uses the "open classroom," "buffet," or "landscape architect" principle of organization. There are interest areas here and there. You will find large curriculum oases and little problem pits. To grace the background there are some noble trees (a Tyler, a Havighurst) and in the foreground flower gardens (a Lewis, a Knudson). There are entrees (a Gibbons, a Coleman) and desserts (a Cross, a Cunningham). There are exotic plantings (a Postman, a Rafferty even). In short, the book is, I hope, an attractive jumble—suggested by the mixed metaphors I have used—from which the discerning reader will select whatever appeals, and perhaps return again for refreshment or edification.

A word now about the introduction I have written for authors and articles. Every journal article has a history and a rationale. Sometimes editor/author correspondence heightens and reveals these, but unfortunately I have always followed a policy of round-filing author correspondence after a three-year grace period. So I have been corresponding with or phoning many of the anthology authors over the past month or so. I hope you find their comments as interesting as I did, and the author/topic updates informative.

Finally, I must express a conviction that grew and flourished with my work on this book. It is this: Very few professional roles could possibly be more rewarding than editorship of the *PHI DELTA KAPPAN* has been for me. It put me in daily contact with the people and the ideas that propel a great profession. It stimulated me to develop my own limited talents. I don't pretend that the tasks were all pleasant. There was the recurring necessity to reject the cherished work of dedicated colleagues—a wrenching experience akin to service on an execution squad. There were the unrelenting deadlines and the constant uncertainty about the adequacy of one's judgment. But the rewards have been almost overwhelming. The outpouring of good wishes since my retirement has been amazing and delightful. May I offer one representative letter?

> *I want to thank you for all that you contributed to my professional growth and understanding over the 25 years you served as editor of the* KAPPAN. *Your leadership made it the most important publication to enter my home. I have looked forward to it each month as a source of intellectual stimulation and have never been disappointed. It always conveys relevant and substantive messages in a highly readable fashion.*
>
> *I have felt close to you, although we have never met. Your influence on my life was so substantial that it seems as if we had a personal relationship.*
>
> *Thank you for all you have contributed. Now I'm looking forward to the promised book with memorable articles from past* KAPPANs.

> *W. Scott Westerman, Jr.*
> *Dean, College of Education*
> *Eastern Michigan University*

Now that's the kind of backtalk I like. Thank you, Dean Westerman. This is the book, and I hope you like it.

Stanley M. Elam

About the Editor: Stanley M. Elam

In early 1979 Stanley Elam was asked to compile this anthology for publication in 1981, Phi Delta Kappa's Diamond Jubilee year and Stan's twenty-fifth year as editor of the *KAPPAN*. The fraternity traces its origins to the formation of a study club for graduate students in education at Indiana University on January 24, 1906. Stan arrived at the new Bloomington, Indiana, Phi Delta Kappa headquarters in 1956 as the third full-time editor of the *KAPPAN*, which was founded in 1915.

As director of PDK publications as well as editor of the journal, Stan had little time to work on the book until he retired in December, 1980. And after that he was distracted by several urgent projects (including a failing effort to break 90 on the golf courses of Green Valley, Arizona, where he moved upon retirement). I began to get photocopies of articles he had chosen for the book long before I received an introductory chapter or a rationale for the choices he was making. When the introduction did come, I realized that there were certain gaps in it. It told the reader very little about Stan himself. This pleasant task has fallen to me.

Stanley Munson Elam was born in Illinois on the day Woodrow Wilson was inaugurated for his second term as President: March 4, 1916. He was the second son of Robert Lee and Alice Anderson Elam, whose families were mostly farmers and teachers. His mother died when Stan was 3, and his father never remarried. Stan helped operate a subsistence farm during his childhood and adolescence in the Twenties and through the Great Depression. He is grimly proud of the fact that few of life's necessities in those years came from the grocery store or mail-order house. Most of them were grown and processed at home. These conditions contributed to a hard-won discipline and self-sufficiency that characterized his later career.

Stanley and Cecil (the elder brother) showed early academic promise. Both were high school valedictorians; Cecil was graduated from Eastern Illinois University at Charleston (then a teachers college) with high honors, Stan with honors. Both of these young men earned a good part of their college expenses while in school, but Stan developed several extracurricular interests as well. He gravitated early to student publications, editing the college yearbook as a sophomore and the weekly *Eastern News* as a junior and senior. Blessed with a remarkable young adviser, Franklyn Andrews, who somehow coaxed excellence from students off the farms of southeastern Illinois, these publications won top honors in state and national competition for many years.

Stan married Elizabeth Jones, an Eastern Illinois University student, at the end of his junior year in college. It was a departure from convention in those days to marry while still a student, but, he reports, "Elizabeth improved my manners, broadened my intellectual interests, and perhaps even sweetened my disposition." Marriage also qualified Stan, in a year when less than half his class found teaching positions, for a high school principalship. In those years principals were married; teachers were single. Since Stan had taken care to meet state minimums for teaching English, history, government, economics, general science, biology, Latin, algebra, and geometry, he taught all of those subjects in his three years as teacher-principal at Jewett, Illinois. In a small system, versatility, not depth, was an advantage. Besides this, Stan drove the school bus, coached athletic teams, advised two student publications, directed a play, and—during the last two years—served as superintendent of schools. Through it all he maintained his interest in journalism. He even picked up small change as a downstate stringer for the *Chicago Daily News*.

By 1943, after two years as principal in a four-year high school at Willow Hill, Illinois, and a master's degree in school administration, Stan was ready to move up. He moved upstate. At Allerton, Illinois, he was a superintendent again but now taught only two classes a day. Coaches were scarce in wartime, however, and Stan soon found himself in charge of basketball, baseball, and track. By March he was burned out, to use the current phrase. He also felt that he was missing the great event of his lifetime, World War II. So he applied for and won a commission in the U.S. Naval Reserve. After lengthy training (including four pleasant months at Harvard University), he began drilling a 12-man communications team for the expected amphibious assault on the Japanese mainland. Two A-bombs changed those plans, and within six weeks Stan was rummaging through the rubble of Hiroshima. He spent six months of 1945-46 in Japanese occupation duty at Kure (near Hiroshima) before returning to his wife and young son in Illinois. Now a decision had to be made. Would he return to school work or seek a career in journalism? He was lucky. The week before starting a proferred newspaper job, he was offered an opportunity to combine education and journalism. For 10 years, then, he served as director of public relations and alumni services at Eastern Illinois University, his undergraduate alma mater. Prodded by Eastern President R. G. Buzzard, who was in the process of building the best-trained teacher education faculty in the country, Stan finished a doctorate at the University of Illinois, Urbana. Dean Willard Spalding and N. L. Gage helped tailor a program in education and mass communications for him, with courses under Wilbur Schramm, a pioneer in the latter field.

The Ed.D. in 1955 opened up new career vistas. Stan realized that dispensing the rosy mists of PR were not for him. But he liked the writing and editing. At Eastern he founded and edited one quarterly journal and took his turn editing a state college newsletter, *Education Today*. When the *KAPPAN* editorship vacancy was announced, he was ready.

Stan's career as *KAPPAN* editor began at age 40. He brought to the job a love of good literature, a respect for solid journalism, and a certain contempt for the thin gruel that sometimes passes for professional education writing. In his second *KAPPAN* editorial, for example, he mentioned reading an accumulation of several hundred unsolicited manuscripts, using these words: "I have been splashed with the froth of generalization and spotted with the flyspecks of statistical minutiae. I have been engulfed in Horatio Alger stories (for who's going to write an article titled 'How I Fell Flat on My Prat'?)" And he complained bitterly about 1) violations of good usage and mechanical errors, 2) use of pompous phrases to pad out thin ideas or make simple ones seem profound, and 3) inability to come to the point quickly. Those faults still plague much education writing.

A good deal of Stan's career as an editor has been devoted to the improvement of writing in the education field. It is one reason he became active in the Educational Press Association of America and served for two years as its president. He supported and helped develop the EdPress awards for excellence in educational journalism—and gained quite a few for the *KAPPAN*, including the top prize, the Golden Lamp for overall excellence, in 1977. He has participated in at least 20 seminars intended to improve the writing skills of educators, and continues to do so since retirement. "Had not Bill Van Til beaten me to it," Stan says, "I might have done a book on writing for professional publication. But Bill did it so well I have given up that ambition."

Of course Stan's major contribution was development of the *KAPPAN* into the leading general journal on education in America. I don't want to dwell on that, but perhaps a few statistics from Stan's last report to the PDK Board of Directors (July 1980) will suggest the magnitude of his accomplishment between assumption of the editorship in 1956 and his retirement in 1980:

Volume 38 (1956-57)	*Volume 61 (1979-80)*
384 small pages, 9 issues	736 large pages, 10 issues
93 major articles	188 major articles
3 regular features	13 regular features and departments; many photos, cartoons, sketches, and much use of color
No advertising	40 pages of display and classified ads
Circulation approximately 26,000, with fewer than 100 nonmember subscribers	Circulation approximately 132,000 with 17,300 nonmember subscribers producing gross income of approximately $170,000. (The nonmember subscriptions were increased to 25,000 after a campaign in the summer of 1980.)
One-member editorial staff	Four-member editorial staff
All composition and page make-up by printer	All composition and pages produced in-house
Request to reprint, 32; articles digested in *Education Digest*, 3	Requests to reprint, 937; articles digested in *Education Digest*, 9

When Stan solicited articles from 17 major figures in education for the January 1981 Diamond Jubilee issue of the *KAPPAN*, only one did not seize the opportunity to contribute. That would not have been the case in 1956. Authors now know that the best way to insure an audience of influential people in education is to publish in the *KAPPAN*.

I need say little more. There are 25 volumes of the *KAPPAN* to speak for Stan and his colleagues. This book, which Stan insisted on calling *Cream of the* KAPPAN, not *The Best of the* KAPPAN, as we originally suggested, may well take readers unfamiliar with the journal back to the stacks in their college libraries. They will generally find well-thumbed volumes of the *KAPPAN* there, for by the early Sixties it had become the most widely used journal in America for the induction of young people into the teaching profession. That it also ranks, according to a study reported in *The Reading Teacher*, as the journal most used in making school program changes is a tribute to the extraordinary skill, range, and devotion Stan and his editorial colleagues brought to the *KAPPAN*.

May 1, 1981   Derek L. Burleson
                                              Editor, Special Publications
                                              Phi Delta Kappa

I

The Education of an Editor

Introduction

The words "brash," "callow," and "uncertain" come to mind as I now read editorials written in my first two years as KAPPAN editor. The best that can be said of those early efforts is that I was aware of the problem. The KAPPAN, I knew, had not found its niche in the world of educational journalism. It lacked personality, identity, and focus. It needed a touchstone by which to test the quality and usefulness of available materials.

It was with this troubling knowledge that I attended a meeting of the KAPPAN editorial consultants in Detroit in the spring of 1968. It was a memorable meeting. Presiding was Sam Brownell, superintendent of the city's schools and a former U.S. commissioner of education. Among the consultants was my good friend from college days, Roy Wilson, then director of press and radio relations for the National Education Association. The three of us prepared a motion addressed to the Phi Delta Kappa Board of Directors. It recommended that the KAPPAN "deal with controversial problems, getting and setting forth all sides of issues important to education." The resolution passed and was approved by the PDK board. That fall my editorial asked, "What Are the Issues?" I quoted Irving Melbo of the University of Southern California as follows, "The ability to recognize issues is an art too often lacking among educational administrators. But perhaps the fault lies with the institutions which trained them, because no man can recognize issues if he has not learned to think in terms of issues. The simple truth is that great economic and social forces sweep over communities that are only half conscious of what is befalling them. Wise statesmen are those who foresee what time is bringing and endeavor to shape institutions and to mold men's thoughts and purposes in accordance with the change that is silently surrounding them."

Volume 40 of the KAPPAN (1958-59) began tentatively to identify and deal with what time was bringing to the schools, "letting personalities fall where they may." I set up a committee consisting of Theodore Brameld, Harl Douglass, Arthur H. Rice, Sr., and two classroom teachers, Chris Carnahan and Jack Fishleder, to help in this enterprise. That was the beginning of a continuing search. It is still the anchor of KAPPAN editorial policy.

Obviously, it is not easy to deal forthrightly with hot issues in a journal supported by people whose careers depend more on boat-steadying than on boat-rocking. I recall addressing a 1962 meeting of EdPress editors on the topic, "How to Treat Controversy and Keep Your Job."

The first real test of the PDK board's commitment to the policy it had endorsed came in the fall of 1961. Myron Lieberman and I had met by accident

3

that summer, and he asked me why no education journal had paid the least attention to "the most significant education development of the year." "What's that?" I asked. "It is the success of the United Federation of Teachers [Local 2 of the American Federation of Teachers, AFL-CIO] in forcing the New York City Board of Education to accept collective bargaining by teachers," he told me. "An election to choose a sole bargaining agent will be held late this fall. The choice will be between the NEA and the AFT."

I persuaded Lieberman to write about the coming election and to discuss the relative merits of the NEA and AFT as teacher bargaining representatives. When the manuscript arrived for the October issue, I realized that I would have to publish a contrary view. Lieberman (soon to be a candidate for the AFT presidency) ridiculed the NEA's capacity to serve as a bargaining agent. Fortunately, Robbins Barstow, an NEA field representative in Connecticut, agreed to respond to the Lieberman polemic in time to meet our November deadline, and as it turned out the election was not held until December. The AFT bought 5,000 reprints of the Lieberman article and the NEA bought 10,000 reprints of Barstow's as campaign literature. Apparently Lieberman was four times as effective, for the AFT won the election by a two-to-one margin.*

It happened that the October KAPPAN hit desks at NEA headquarters in Washington, D.C., while a board meeting was in session. Within a few days PDK Executive Secretary Maynard Bemis was getting telephone calls and letters from NEA officials around the country. So did some PDK board members. The gist of their messages: Stan Elam is either a fool or a dangerous radical and should not be editing an education journal. True to their commitment, PDK leaders ignored these criticisms.

Next February I met Mildred Fenner, editor of the NEA Journal (now Today's Education), in the breakfast line at the old Traymore Hotel in Atlantic City, long-time annual gathering place for the American Association of School Administrators. Mildred's greeting was, "Well, Stan, I guess you learned something this year."

I did, of course, but the NEA's education was just beginning. Eventually NEA leaders came to appreciate the accuracy of most of Liberman's observations in his article, "The Battle for New York City's Teachers," and reorganized to meet the AFT challenge.

In the mid-Sixties Phi Delta Kappa sponsored a series of summer institutes on collective negotiations at such institutions as the University of Pennsylvania, Harvard, the University of California at Berkeley, and Indiana University. Lieberman and I were usually the co-directors. In all, nearly 1,000 superintendents, teacher association leaders, school board members, and professors attended these institutes. The KAPPAN continued to cover collective bargaining issues and teacher militancy throughout the decade, publishing, in all, over 40 articles related to the topics. Lieberman became a regular contributor and eventually a KAPPAN consultant. He has contributed 28 articles, editorials, and reviews, besides serving as guest editor of three special KAPPANs

*For details of the NYC bargaining election, see Allan M. West, The National Education Association: The Power Base for Education (New York: The Free Press, 1980), pp. 51-57; also, Marshall O. Donley, Jr., Power to the Teacher: How America's Educators Became Militant (Indiana University Press in association with Phi Delta Kappa, 1976), pp. 46-55.

("*Big Business, Education, and Technology,*" *January 1967;* "*An Overview of Accountability,*" *December 1970; and* "*Education and the Feminist Movement,*" *October 1973). In fact, my good friend Bill Ellena, then associate executive director of the AASA and now superintendent of schools in Charlottesville, Virginia, once twitted me by referring to the PHI DELTA LIEBERMAN. But my judgment that Lieberman's views are generally pertinent, logical, well-informed, and sometimes even prescient has been confirmed by many other editors. His articles have appeared in* Harper's, *the* Saturday Review, *the* American School Board Journal, *and half a dozen other reputable magazines. He has also written a number of well-regarded books.*

Lieberman's "*Eggs That I Have Laid: Teacher Bargaining Reconsidered,*" *is reprinted here because it documents an almost complete reversal in some of the author's convictions. Lieberman's KAPPAN articles up to* "*Eggs*" *were all pro-bargaining. What caused him to change his mind? That is a topic worthy of a separate article. I would like to write it some day, after my education has been completed.*

Lieberman is now president at Educational Employment Services in Modesto, California.

In my early days as KAPPAN editor, style sometimes won out over substance in my choice of material. For example, I featured a flashy but empty piece titled, "*Ain't That a Pistol*" *(December 1956). It was written by Sydney Harris, the syndicated* Chicago Daily News *columnist (now with the* Sun Times*), who in those days liked to shock teacher audiences with his irreverent wit.*

Then I went overboard for Max Rafferty's work. At that time Rafferty was superintendent at Needles, California. He had co-authored a substantial textbook on school administration with Emery Stoops, the distinguished University of Southern California professor and a former PDK president. Rafferty had also been a candidate for the Phi Delta Kappa executive secretary position in 1956, when Maynard Bemis was chosen.

In all, I published eight Rafferty articles over a four-year period. They were colorful, explicit, and irritating or persuasive, depending upon one's ideological orientation. Several of them were so reactionary that I felt compelled to give equal space to progressives. For example, Robert Havighurst, the liberal University of Chicago professor who had established himself as an authority on adolescent development, responded to "*Cult of the Slob*" *with a mild and sensible piece titled* "*What to Do About the Tough, Hostile Boy*" *(December 1958).*

I think it was at the summer PDK board meeting in 1959 that the affable John Whinnery drew me aside. John was then president of Phi Delta Kappa and a prominent figure in the Association of California School Administrators. "*Stan,*" *he said,* "*a lot of us think you are overdoing Max Rafferty. He's not very popular in the profession out here, you know.*"

It was friendly advice, not censorship. We both knew that. And it wasn't until Max Rafferty ran for state superintendent of public instruction in California in 1962 that I accepted John's advice. Rafferty brought out a book titled Suffer, Little Children *that spring. It included all eight KAPPAN articles, but happily did not mention the KAPPAN. I reviewed the book as campaign literature, commenting that* "*as a statement of philosophy it is be-*

wildering and inconsistent. As a statement of program it is almost totally worthless, because it lacks specificity. But as campaign literature in a state at least outwardly in the throes of a conservative education revolution, . . . it may help bring Rafferty to the fore in a crowded field of candidates."

When Rafferty won the election I asked him for a brief statement of the goals of his administration. He replied as follows: "In light of your recent review of Suffer, Little Children, I suggest that you reprint [Samuel] Johnson's famous reply to one who had treated him as you have treated me: 'Is not a patron, my lord, one who looks with unconcern on a man struggling for life in the water, and when he has reached ground encumbers him with help? The notice you have been pleased to take of my labors, had it been early, had been kind; but it has been delayed till I am indifferent, and cannot enjoy it, till I am solitary, and cannot impart it, till I am known, and do not want it.'"

Rafferty's next appearance as a KAPPAN author was in October 1977, when at my invitation he wrote "Should Gays Teach School?" (he said NO!) as part of a special feature on the topic. He ended the piece with this not-very-subtle putdown of the editor: "Can't we really find something more important educationally to spend our time and energy on? If not, how about a rousing KAPPAN on 'techniques of defecation'?"

Rafferty left California for the more salubrious political climate of Alabama after he was defeated in a run for the U.S. Senate on the Republican ticket in 1970. He has been dean of the College of Education at Troy State University ever since, but expects to retire this year. He regularly airs his views on education in a syndicated column. It appears in some 100 generally conservative U.S. newspapers.

"Cult of the Slob" drew scores of letters to the editor, and Rafferty told me he received over 150. I include the article in this anthology not as a "cream" piece but as an illustration of my early attempt to change the somewhat stuffy, innocuous image of the KAPPAN. The article deals with one aspect of the problem of whom to teach. It is a problem that will always be with us.

Perceptive, tolerant, optimistic, liberal, gifted, hard-working, dependable, versatile, prolific. Those adjectives all suit the late Donald W. Robinson.

Robinson began writing for the KAPPAN in February 1960, with "Ideals for Tomorrow's Schools." In October of that year he began a column, "Scraps from a Teacher's Notebook," which was to appear more or less regularly for some 14 years. I was so impressed with his early work that I commissioned two articles, "The Conservative Revolution in California Education" and "The Teachers Take a Birching," and both were sparkling journalistic achievements. When the PDK board approved my request to employ an associate editor in February 1962, I had no hesitancy in recommending Robinson, who left the chairmanship of the social studies department at Carlmont High School in Belmont, California, to take the position that summer.

Robinson's background was amazingly varied. After an undergraduate degree at Harvard, he finished his doctorate at the University of Pennsylvania. He taught in Pennsylvania, Florida, Mississippi, Colorado, and California. A good deal of his work was at the college level, including stints in administration.

Robinson joined the staff of the National Association of Secondary School Principals in 1968, but returned to Phi Delta Kappa in 1970 as editor of special *publications and* KAPPAN *associate editor. He served as acting* KAPPAN *editor in 1970-71 while I was on sabbatical as interim editor of the* NASSP Bulletin. *Among Robinson's most notable achievements was development of the PDK "fastbacks," hugely popular booklets sponsored by the fraternity's Educational Foundation. Robinson retired in 1976 at age 65, but continued to serve Phi Delta Kappa. He was editor of the* KAPPAN *book review section until his death from cancer in September 1980. His last "Scraps" column— number 75 in the series—was titled "They Gave Me Two Months to Live." It appealed for more enlightened treatment of terminal cancer patients.*

Don Robinson and I taught each other much, but I probably got the better of the deal. His scope was protean. He did interviews, wrote editorials, planned specials, churned out features, reviewed books, and prepared his thoughtful column, all with equal facility and skill.

"Psychoanalysis and Education," reprinted here from the April 1962 KAPPAN, *illustrates Robinson's versatility. Esther, his widow, assures me it was written with no help from her, although as a psychiatric nurse she might well have given it.*

I am sorry Don is not here to enjoy this walk through past KAPPAN *pages.*

—SME

The Battle for
New York City's Teachers
by Myron Lieberman

*In Education as a Profession, published in 1956, Myron Lieber-
man said, "Should the trend toward collective bargaining in
public education become widespread, it is likely to necessitate
far-reaching changes in the NEA if that organization is to lead
the way toward professionalism." A test of NEA ability to adjust
may now be at hand, as 49,000 teachers prepare to select an
agent to bargain with the New York Board of Education. And
the AFT has in New York its best opportunity since 1919 to
challenge NEA leadership.*

The PHI DELTA KAPPAN *will welcome for publication
other competent analyses of the organizational and professional
problems posed by recent New York City developments.*

In June 1961 New York City's teachers voted 27,367 to 9,003 in favor of
collective bargaining by employees licensed by the superintendent of schools.
During the 1961-62 school year, the city's 49,000 teachers will vote on 1)
whether they favor a systemwide or divisional basis of representation; and 2)
what organization they wish to bargain for them. This vote is likely to be one
of the most important educational events of the 1960s. What follows is an
attempt to clarify the major issues involved. Despite their crucial importance,
these issues are not being clarified by the mass media, educational journals,
institutions of higher education, or the competing organizations.

The significance of the New York City collective bargaining election is to
be found in its potential impact upon the National Education Association
(NEA) and the American Federation of Teachers (AFT). At present the NEA
is by far the larger of the two organizations. On 31 May 1960 it enrolled about
714,000 members, 49% of the nation's total instructional staff. About 1,317,000
persons, or 93% of the total, were members of the 64 state education associations affiliated with the NEA, which maintains separate white and Negro associations in the South. While there are no reliable statistics on membership in
local associations, a majority of the nation's teachers are probably members
of the 7,135 local associations affiliated with the NEA.

In contrast, the AFT enrolls just under 60,000 teachers, about 4% of the national total. Since teachers generally join local and state federations simultaneously with membership in the AFT itself, the total number of teachers enrolled in local and state federations is very close to the total number of AFT
members.

For many years the two organizations have been in a membership stalemate. The proportion of teachers who are NEA members has increased
somewhat in the past 10 years, but not at the expense of the AFT. The latter
enrolls about the same proportion of teachers as it did 10 years ago. One way
or the other, the organizational election in New York City is likely to shatter
this stalemate.

As things stand, both NEA and AFT locals exist side by side in many communities. In a collective bargaining situation, however, it is very difficult to
keep the minority organization alive, especially if the employer bargains only

with the majority organization. Employees are reluctant to pay dues to an organization that cannot represent them. Over the long run, leaders of the minority organizations must join the majority organization or lose their collective influence. Thus the dynamics of collective bargaining favor the growth of the majority organization at the expense of the minority ones.

This is not so ominous for the AFT as might first appear. Although over-all it is much smaller than the NEA, its membership is larger in several major urban districts, such as New York City, Chicago, and Detroit. In some cases, the differences are quite striking. For instance, in New York City there were only 749 NEA members to at least 6,000 in the AFT in 1960-61. Should AFT locals in these central cities establish themselves as the bargaining agent for the teachers, the results could be disastrous to the NEA. Not only would it be shut out of key urban districts but it would be in real danger of losing the suburbs as well. We are only a few years away from metropolitan teachers' organizations, and the organization that prevails in the central cities will eventually prevail in the suburbs. The New York City election may indicate the direction in which teachers are likely to go.

In view of the three-to-one vote for collective bargaining, we can assume that most teachers will vote for some organization. They could, however, vote for 1) an organization not affiliated with either the NEA or the AFT; 2) an organization affiliated with the NEA; or 3) the United Federation of Teachers (UFT), which is the New York local affiliated with the AFT. Let us consider these three possibilities.

Despite the many weaknesses of the AFT and the NEA, and despite the fact that less than 25% of the city's teachers are currently enrolled in these organizations, I doubt whether any organization not affiliated with either can win. Certainly, the choice of such an organization would be almost as foolish as a vote for no organization at all. The effectiveness of a local organization depends in large part upon the effectiveness of its state and national affiliates. A local organization without such affiliates faces severe handicaps. For instance, the New York City teachers are affected in many ways by state and federal legislation. If they vote for an organization without state and national affiliates, they will have to finance their state and national program completely from local funds. The inevitable outcome would be inadequate representation or none at all at state and national levels. Similarly, purely local organizations cannot finance the research, service, instructional, and other activities needed in all communities but too expensive to be financed by an isolated local organization.

These conclusions are not invalidated by the current weaknesses of the NEA and the AFT. One reason is that these weaknesses are partly due to the massive nonparticipation in these organizations by New York City's teachers. But the decisive point is that under the present circumstances, at least, it is more realistic to work within existing national organizations than to start new ones. For this reason, we must analyze briefly the issues that divide the NEA and the AFT.

The major differences between the organizations concern administrator membership and affiliation with labor. The NEA has no constitutional restrictions on administrator membership. Although its affiliated locals are free to impose such restrictions, less than 10% of them do so. By contrast, the AFT has constitutional provisions prohibiting active membership by superintendents and permitting other administrators and supervisors active membership only under certain safeguards designed to prevent their domination of AFT locals.

The NEA takes the position that the exclusion of administrators is not appropriate for "professional" organizations. Local professional associations of doctors, lawyers, and dentists enroll all practitioners in a given area, hence so should those of teachers. It also contends that since administrators and teachers must work together, they should be in the same organization.

The Administrator Membership Question

Leading authorities in public administration clearly reject the NEA's view that top-level public administrators should be active members of organizations that represent public employees in matters of employment.[1] Most authorities in school administration either ignore the issue or advocate unrestricted administrator membership in teachers' organizations. However, one leading text in the field states that "The wise administrator will encourage teachers to develop strong local organizations among whose major purposes are the improvement of pay and of the working conditions of teachers. *It is probably undesirable for administrators to be members of such organizations.*"[2]

On this score the NEA's appeal to the practice of fee-taking professions is irrelevant. Fee takers do not stand in an employer/employee relationship with each other. For this reason there is no danger of employer domination of their local associations.

NEA literature on administrator domination has ignored the fact that the American Association of University Professors has an even stricter prohibition against administrator membership than does the AFT. It also ignores the relevant experience of engineers' organizations. Formerly, these organizations enrolled both employers and employees who were engineers by profession. During the depression, however, they were of little help to employee-engineers. Efforts to enlist organizational support along this line were frustrated by the active opposition of employer-engineers. Today, engineers and scientists who have a much higher level of training than teachers are enrolled in organizations that exclude administrative personnel from their ranks.

The NEA naturally denies the charge that it is administrator dominated, but the policies proposed by its leaders in New York City would have weakened the teachers more than anything proposed by the Board of Education itself. At a board hearing in November, Eric Rhodes, director of the New York City office of the NEA, urged that "no organization be eligible for nomination as bargaining representative unless it gives complete assurance that it will adhere to the law and that it will not call its members into strikes." Similar sentiments were expressed by other NEA leaders at this time.

The right to strike is an extremely important safeguard for most occupational groups. To tell your employer that you will continue to work no matter what he does—the practical significance of a no-strike clause without employee safeguards—is to encourage the very kind of employer behavior that produces strikes. Unless there is administrator domination or orientation, it is difficult to understand why the leaders of a teachers' organization would advocate that recognition as a bargaining agent be limited to organizations that undermine teacher bargaining power even before an election is held.

A "no-strike" policy is often advocated as professionalism. Actually, all major professional codes of ethics not only permit but require their members to withdraw their services under certain conditions. However, since doctors, lawyers, and other fee takers do not work for a single employer, there is no occasion for them to withdraw their services simultaneously. Thus, even if it were true that they do not strike (and it is *not* true), the reason has nothing whatever to do with the notion that strikes are unprofessional per se. The professions clearly accept the principles used to justify strike action by salaried employees.

Basically, unrestricted administrator membership is wrong because it leads straight to a totalitarian form of government. Employee organizations behind the Iron Curtain are too weak to protect either the public interest or the interests of their members. The reason is that these organizations are dominated by the employer—that is, the government.

Not Totalitarian in Intent but in Effect

NEA members are usually shocked to hear their membership policies described as totalitarian, since as individuals they abhor totalitarianism as much as do AFT members or anyone else. But policies that are not totalitarian in intent can be so in effect. The plain truth is that unrestricted administrator membership in employee organizations, whether the employees be public or private, professional or nonprofessional, tends to destroy the independence and integrity of the organization. Furthermore, this is so regardless of the personal characteristics of the administrator members.

The fundamental fallacy in much NEA thinking about administrator membership is the tendency to personalize the issue, to regard the exclusion of administrators from teachers' organizations as justified only if and when the administrators are "bad guys." Since no administrator regards himself as the kind of person from whom teachers need protection, none accepts exclusion when it is interpreted as a personal reaction. But the rationale for exclusion concedes—or at least I am willing to—that every school administrator is a decent, fair-minded fellow. As the saying goes, some of my best friends are administrators, including some who disagree with me on this issue. But for all their good intentions and sincere affirmations of dedication to teacher welfare, I contend that they have no business in an organization composed of teachers whom they must assign, promote, transfer, evaluate, dismiss, or otherwise control.

The arguments on this issue in education textbooks and courses occasionally reach the cliché level but rarely rise above it. A typical "rebuttal" to the AFT position on administrator membership is that since teachers and administrators must work together, they ought to be in the same organization—as if we do not cooperate and work every day with people not in our organizations, or as if belief in nonmembership for administrators is tantamount to belief in noncooperation with them.

Even the AFT has failed to recognize the pervasive influence of administrator domination in teachers' associations. This is partly due to AFT inattention to the NEA and partly to the limitations of the AFT's program. For example, the AFT pays little attention to certification. In this respect, it is an ineffective union. Effective unions have always paid considerable attention to job control, through such policies as the closed shop or the union shop.

"Certification" is merely a fancy name for job control, except that in education such control is not exercised by teachers' organizations.

A Conflict of Interest

In the abstract, most educators favor high certification standards. In practice, the superintendent frequently finds that he cannot hire a regularly certified teacher at the salary he is authorized to offer. Thereupon he writes to the state education department, requesting an emergency certificate for someone who does not meet the regular requirements. The superintendent cannot tell his school board: "I won't seek an emergency certificate because it's against the policy of my professional organization." He is employed to carry out the board's policies, not the organization's. *It is unrealistic to expect him to use his organizational influence to stop himself from hiring teachers with substandard qualifications.* Thus the teachers' associations do not really throw their strength into eliminating emergency certificates, because they are dominated by the superintendents—the group leading the charge on state education departments to issue emergency certificates.

Essence of Professionalism—or Nonsense?

Professional ethics is another important aspect of professionalization that has been corrupted by administrator domination of teachers' associations. Consider the following questions from the *NEA Journal*. Under the heading, "How Professional Am I?", an author asks:

> Do I refrain from adverse criticism of a colleague's method or work except when requested by a school official for the welfare of the school? . . .
> Do I talk things over with the administrator next above me? . . .
> Do I support the policies of my principal and superintendent? . . .
> Do I avoid criticism of my principal and superintendent in public? . . .
> Do I support the policies of my board? . . .[3]

Material like this, which equates professionalism with acquiescence to administrative direction, is professional nonsense. Yet this nonsense is taught to teachers and prospective teachers every year as the essence of professionalism. School administrators (and uncritical teachers) may regard acquiescence to their administrative policies as the essence of professionalism, but no serious student of the professions would do so for a minute. An occupational group that is not ready to resist administrative direction upon occasion has no claim to professional status.

Let us next consider the second major issue dividing the NEA and the AFT, i.e., teacher affiliation with labor. The NEA objects to such affiliation on the ground that teachers should not have any special obligations to, or be formally affiliated with, any particular segment of the population. The AFT position is that affiliation does not compromise teachers in any way but provides them needed support to gain their objectives.

The argument that teacher affiliation with national labor bodies compromises the teacher has been clearly repudiated by the test of experience and weight of authority. Teachers have been affiliated with labor since 1916. By this time, if teacher affiliation with labor tended to produce all the dire consequences attributed to it, the evidence should have been forthcoming long ago. Nevertheless, although NEA literature calls attention to the evils of affiliation, it does not cite actual cases where affiliation compromised a group of teachers. The evils are always assumed, not demonstrated.

Would Labor Affiliation Taint Teachers?

Some people believe that teacher affiliation with labor would embroil teachers in disputes of no direct concern to them and that it would encourage teachers to adopt unprofessional tactics supposedly characteristic of the worst unions. Paradoxically, experts in public administration favor affiliation of public service employees on precisely opposite grounds. They point out that the impact of affiliation is one of restraint, not encouragement to aggressive action. The relationships between the AFT and the AFL-CIO are a case in point. When the AFT became affiliated with the AFL in 1916, it was Samuel Gompers, the president of the AFL, not the teachers, who insisted that the AFT pursue a no-strike policy. True, some locals of the AFT have gone on strike over the years, but so have some locals of the NEA and some not affiliated with either the NEA or the AFT. This observer knows of no case wherein affiliation with labor was a causal factor in a teachers' strike.

The strike by the UFT on 7 November 1960 illustrates many of these points. Prior to this strike there was not a single public statement of support for it from the AFL-CIO, either in New York or Washington. In fact, it is public knowledge that some AFL-CIO leaders were opposed to the strike. When it ended, Harry Van Arsdale, head of the Central Trades and Labor Council in New York City, gave public assurances that there would not be another. The next day, these assurances were publicly repudiated by the president of the UFT.

In summary, the common belief, even among AFT members, is that the federation gets its militancy from the labor movement, but the evidence for this is dubious. It is more likely that the more militant teachers gravitate toward the AFT; affiliation with labor is probably a result more than a cause of their greater militancy.

The important question is not whether teachers have a right to affiliate with the AFL-CIO. It is whether affiliation is effective, or how it could be made more effective. These questions are ignored in the debate over whether teachers have the "right" to affiliate.

Many of the federation's staunchest supporters are the first to concede that it has never used affiliation to good advantage. On this score the New York City situation is a matter of the utmost interest. If the UFT wins the election, other AFT locals in large urban centers are certain to request collective bargaining elections in their communities. In some communities the effectiveness of AFL-CIO support may prove decisive in whether these elections are held. Of course, the AFT locals will still have the problem of winning the elections, but presumably they will not push for elections where their chances of winning are poor.

Suppose, as should and eventually will be the case, that organizations permitting unrestricted administrator membership are not eligible as bargaining agents. NEA locals are obviously not going to give the AFT a clear field in collective bargaining elections. On the contrary, we can expect NEA locals to limit administrator membership, embarrassing as this change may be. In these cases the choice of bargaining agent will boil down to one between AFT and NEA locals, both of which exclude top-level administrators. In my opinion this is how the competition will ultimately be joined, and it will pay us to consider the ramifications of this situation very carefully.

Local teachers' organizations need the active support of their state and national bodies. If the latter are administrator dominated, they are not likely to intervene in situations where the teachers are in conflict with the local administrators. This is not speculation. The history of the NEA and its affiliated state associations reveals that their intervention is more probable when teachers are lined up with their administrators than when against them. In other words, any effective solution to the problem of administrator domination requires that the problem be faced at the state and national as well as at the local level. A solution short of this is no solution at all.

An Inadequate Compromise for NEA

This point suggests that the potentialities for the AFT to make inroads on NEA membership are much greater than is commonly realized in either organization. Many local associations affiliated with the NEA maintain some restrictions upon administrator membership. In fact, it is quite possible that more teachers are members of NEA locals restricted to classroom teachers than there are members of the AFT. Given the interdependence of local, state, and national organizations, the affiliation of classroom teacher locals with state and national associations permitting unrestricted administrator membership clearly represents an inadequate compromise. The occasions when outside help is likely to prove decisive are just the occasions when the classroom teacher locals in the NEA are unlikely to get it.

AFT Potential for Absorbing NEA Locals

AFT national leadership has never considered the possibilities of detaching classroom teacher locals en masse from the NEA. However, its New York City leadership has already demonstrated the possibilities inherent in this approach. The UFT itself was formed by a merger of the New York Teachers Guild, the old Local 2 of the AFT, and a large body of teachers from the High School Teachers Association, which was affiliated with the NEA. Such mergers will not be confined to New York City if the UFT should win the forthcoming election.

Although the arguments most frequently advanced against the AFT have negligible merit, the federation is characterized by serious deficiencies as a professional organization. In general, it has had to devote so much of its resources to the struggle for existence that it has never developed the kind of program needed by the nation's teachers. Freedom from administrator domination is necessary to enable teachers to formulate a program. It is not a program or a substitute for one. Five years ago I wrote:

> Perhaps if the trend toward collective bargaining by organizations of public school teachers were to become very pronounced, the AFT would have its best opportunity since 1919 to challenge the leadership of the NEA. If this opportunity should present itself, the AFT would have to solve a number of basic organizational problems to take full advantage of it. It would have to find means of satisfying the subject matter interests of teachers. It would also have to develop programs in such areas as certification, accreditation, professional ethics, and teacher education, areas in which its in-

fluence at present is negligible. Only time will tell, however, whether or not the AFT will have such an opportunity and whether or not it will be able to take advantage of it.[4]

That opportunity is now at hand. One might argue that a single collective bargaining election does not constitute a trend, but consider this fact: New York City employs as many teachers as are employed by the 10 smallest states combined. But the number of teachers involved, impressive as it is, does not convey the full importance of the election. One outcome of it, regardless of who wins, will be increased participation by New York City teachers in national organizations. This will be particularly true if the UFT should win. In this observer's experience, the generation coming to power in the UFT constitutes the largest pool of outstanding teacher leadership to be found in any local organization of teachers in the country. The forthcoming election would be important in any case, but it would be much less so if it did not involve the organizational fate of so many teachers who are capable of national leadership.

It is probably too early to predict the winner of the election. The outcome will depend to some extent upon whether the elections are held on a divisional or a systemwide basis. Should the former prevail, the UFT would probably carry the junior high division and stand a good chance of carrying the high schools as well. The NEA appears to be stronger in the elementary schools.

Despite the fact that the NEA has traditionally favored a single all-inclusive organization to represent teachers in each community, many NEA leaders in New York City are advocating a divisional basis of representation. This may be an indication that they fear the outcome of any election to select a systemwide bargaining agent.

Although NEA membership is much smaller than AFT membership in New York City, many teachers who are not members of the NEA belong to one or more of the 15 city organizations affiliated with the NEA. NEA leaders assert that these organizations enroll more than half the city's teachers. Nonetheless, it is difficult to predict how they will vote in a showdown. Many of these organizations are of the paper type, with nominal dues and no full-time staff. By contrast, UFT members pay from $7.50 to $30 a year dues and their organization has an active year-around program.

UFT's Chances of Winning

The 27,367 to 9,003 vote for collective bargaining was a tremendous boost to UFT morale, since the UFT was the only major New York City organization that actively campaigned for collective bargaining. Nevertheless, the federation's chances of winning a systemwide majority are a matter of conjecture. It can be assumed that the overwhelming majority of the 9,000 teachers who voted against collective bargaining will also vote against the UFT in the organizational election. This bloc of votes equals or exceeds paid-up federation membership in recent years. It seems obvious, therefore, that teachers not in the UFT who voted for collective bargaining will decide the outcome.

Logically, most of these teachers should vote for the UFT. It would hardly make sense for them to vote for collective bargaining and then select a bargaining agent that is opposed to or does not understand collective bargaining.

But logic often has as little to do with teacher elections as with other kinds, and the outcome will be influenced by several factors that should be irrelevant to the choice of bargaining agent.

The Achilles heel of the NEA may not be collective bargaining itself but the association's poor record on other issues of considerable interest in New York City. In 1956 the New York City delegation to the NEA convention made an unsuccessful effort to stop the NEA's travel division from sponsoring tours from which Jewish teachers were excluded. This situation developed when certain Arab countries refused to allow Jewish teachers to be included in NEA-sponsored tours of these countries. Leading Jewish organizations, such as the American Jewish Congress, requested the NEA to cease sponsoring tours under these circumstances. The NEA took the position that the Arab countries, not the NEA, were responsible for the discrimination. By this logic, the NEA might as well hold its annual convention in Mississippi and contend that any discrimination against Negro delegates is due to Mississippians, not the NEA. During the past year or two the NEA appears to have seen the light on this issue, but the association's foot-dragging on it is widely known and resented. When the votes are counted, these tours may turn out to be the costliest ever sponsored by an educational organization in this country.

In 1961 the NEA finally got around to passing a resolution supporting racial integration in the public schools. On the other hand, the AFT has a good record in this area, as evidenced by its assistance to Negro plaintiffs in the segregation cases and the federation's expulsion of locals practicing segregation. A strong AFT vote in New York City might well force NEA leaders to conduct an agonizing reappraisal of association inactivity in implementing integration.

NEA strategy thus far has been aimed primarily at blocking or delaying collective bargaining elections, at least until association forces in the city become better organized. To my knowledge, no NEA-affiliated organization in the city has come out strongly for collective bargaining. Some have opposed it; others have stated that it is not objectionable if the teachers want it. Now that an organizational election seems certain, the pressure will grow on NEA leaders in the city to formulate a more positive program.

Undoubtedly, the huge membership of the NEA outside of New York City will be stressed, perhaps in terms like these: "We already have half the teachers in the country. Most of the others are members of affiliated state and local associations. If you disagree with our present policies, join these associations and try to change them. You can't be effective in an organization that enrolls only a small proportion of teachers throughout the state and nation."

This is a plausible argument, especially in an election designed to eliminate a multiplicity of competing organizations. However, in my opinion it is an argument with a built-in boomerang. Although both the NEA and the AFT are comparatively weak organizations at state and national levels, the reasons are not the same in both cases. The NEA already enrolls three times as many members as the American Medical Association, and its budget is larger than that of many powerful professional organizations. This strenthens the argument that its weakness is not due to lack of money or members but to administrator domination, *a weakness that by its very nature is unlikely to be remedied by more members or by internal reorganization.*

It is one thing to urge an organization composed entirely of teachers to change its policies on a particular issue. It is an altogether different thing to urge an organization to free itself from administrator domination by ejecting administrators from the organization. The very evils involved make it likely that only teachers prone to martyrdom will take the initiative on this issue and that few others, regardless of their convictions, will follow them. Administrator membership in teachers' organizations is like the camel's nose in the tent—once he's in, you can't get the critter out.

Regardless of what organization, if any, wins the election, it will be a landmark in the history of American education. By accepting bona fide collective bargaining, however reluctantly and belatedly, the New York City Board of Education is making one of the most important contributions to education ever made by a board of education in this country. Very soon, it will be up to the teachers of New York City to rise to the occasion. For better or for worse, they have an unprecedented opportunity to influence the course of American education in the 1960s.

---

1. See Morton Robert Godine, *The Labor Problem in the Public Service*. Cambridge: Harvard University Press, 1951, pp. 101-02.

2. Willard B. Spalding and Van Miller, *The Public Administration of American Schools*, 2nd ed. Yonkers-on-Hudson, N.Y.: World Book Company, 1958, p. 332. (Italics added.)

3. Grace I. Kauffman, "How Professional Am I?" *NEA Journal*, April 1950, p. 286.

4. Myron Lieberman, *Education as a Profession*. Englewood Cliffs, N.J.: Prentice Hall, Inc., 1956, p. 372.

Eggs That I Have Laid:
Teacher Bargaining Reconsidered
by Myron Lieberman

*Once a strong advocate of rights for teacher organizations equal
to those possessed by unions in the private sector, Mr.
Lieberman has now changed his mind. To compensate for the
inherent advantages of public employment, he says, teacher representational rights should be considerably reduced.*

In 1962 the first significant collective bargaining contract covering teachers
was negotiated in New York City. Since then, collective bargaining in education has developed nationally at an impressive pace. At least 32 states now
provide teachers with bargaining rights, and a growing majority of teachers
(60% or more) work pursuant to collective bargaining contracts. Membership
in teacher unions has increased enormously; simultaneously, dues therein
have been increased, so that the resources available to these unions may
even exceed $500 million annually. Since 60% to 80% of school budgets are
spent for personnel, virtually every aspect of education has been affected by
this dramatic shift to collectively bargained terms and conditions of employment.

Since 1962 collective bargaining has sometimes been sold to legislatures
and school boards on a "try it, you'll like it" basis. Others simply inherited bargaining as a fixture on the educational scene, just as its absence was taken for
granted in an earlier era. Regardless of how it is presented or experienced,
however, there is one crucial difference between the present situation and
that of the 1960s. Today we have a wealth of experience in teacher bargaining
to guide us. What was advocated or opposed in the 1960s on the basis of logic
or intuition or speculation or analogy can be tested today against a body of experience. Today there is no excuse for debating whether or how collective
bargaining in education differs from collective bargaining in the private
sector. The differences are real and important, and they justify this conclusion: Providing public employees collective bargaining rights similar to those
provided private sector employees is undesirable public policy.

In the 1960s the appeal to "equity" was the major public policy justification for teacher bargaining. Without bargaining rights, teachers, like other
public employees, are allegedly second-class citizens. Privately employed
guards can unionize and strike; publicly employed ones cannot. Bus drivers
for a privately owned company can strike; if the same routes were taken over
and operated as a public utility, the drivers could not bargain or strike.
Similarly, teachers in private schools can organize and bargain; those in
public schools cannot.

For the sake of argument, let us agree that teachers ought to have "equity"
with private sector employees. To assess the equity argument objectively,
however, we must consider all the crucial differences between public and
private sector employment, not just the absence of bargaining rights in public
education. Among these, perhaps the most important difference is that
teachers often play an important role in determining who is management. For
example, teacher organizations are frequently active in school board elec-

tions. In some situations they have a decisive influence upon who is elected. In contrast, private sector employees have no legal or practical role in selecting management, and it would ordinarily be futile for them to try to do so.

In some jurisdictions at least, the political influence of teachers upon public management has been extremely advantageous to teachers. This influence affects not only what is proposed, accepted, rejected, and modified, but the timing of concessions, the management posture toward grievances, and the extent of management support services for bargaining. Sometimes even the choice of management negotiator is subject to an unofficial but effective teacher veto.

It is easy to underestimate the impact of teacher political influence on teacher employment relations, because typically this influence has to be shared. Often, it is more veto power than "do" power. One should not be misled, however, by the fact that teacher-backed candidates do not always support the teachers—or may even oppose them on occasion. Such situations notwithstanding, the political dimension constitutes significant teacher advantages over private sector employment.

In this connection, teacher opportunities to influence the choice of state officials must also be considered. True enough, private sector employees have equal opportunities to influence or to elect such officials. The point is, however, that state officials seldom affect the context or substance of private sector bargaining. Typically, the governor of a state has no role in collective bargaining for private sector employees. Such bargaining is regulated by the National Labor Relations Board, a federal agency. On the other hand, the governor frequently plays a decisive role in whether there is to be public sector bargaining at all, and if there is, on such matters as the scope of bargaining, the nature of unfair labor practices, the relationship of bargaining to budgetary schedules, the impasse procedures, and the balance of bargaining power between the parties. In addition, governors often play a crucial role in substantive matters subject to bargaining. For example, the governor typically is the most important single individual in the annual aid-to-education controversy. Since states provide nearly half of public school revenues, the gubernatorial role is much more important to teachers than it is to most private sector unions. For teachers, as for other local public employees, the implications are obvious. Political activity at the state level pays the teacher a larger dividend than it does the factory worker or the farmer.

The fact that the National Education Association and the American Federation of Teachers are once again seeking to enact federal legislation providing bargaining rights for state and local public employees in no way negates the foregoing analysis. Obviously, if public employee unions can achieve their goals by one legislative enactment instead of 50, they will do so. As a matter of fact, while they are striving for federal and state bargaining laws, they are also seeking state legislative benefits on matters normally considered subject to bargaining. Every group has the right to use the ballot box to advance its interests; my point is only that the opportunity to do so is more advantageous to teachers than to private sector employees.

The political dimension of public sector employment works to the advantage of teachers in several different ways. For example, there is greater turnover in public sector than in private sector management. More important, private sector management tends to have a greater direct and personal stake in resisting unreasonable union demands. This is particularly apparent with respect to pension and retirement benefits. Public management frequently achieves bargaining agreements by excessively generous pension and retirement benefits. Such concessions may not require any immediate tax increase. Thus the management officials responsible for the agreement can be heroes to the public employees for being generous—and to the public for not raising taxes. Unfortunately, the practice saddles taxpayers with enormously expensive long-range commitments. Significantly, the tendency to "end-load" agreements this way has become evident in local, state, and federal agreements. It is difficult to see the equity in requiring private sector employees to provide retirement benefits for public employees that greatly exceed their own, but that is the present situation.

Another crucial point is that public management has less incentive than private management to resist union demands. If private sector management makes a concession that impairs the long-range profitability of the enterprise, that fact is reflected *immediately* in the value of the company. Thus, unlike public sector management, management in the private sector cannot avoid *immediate* accountability by agreement to excessive deferred benefits. Although these observations are subject to exceptions and qualifications, they reflect a significant teacher advantage over private sector employees.

The major disadvantage of public employees relates to revenue-raising and ratification procedures. Normally, the private sector employer can negotiate an agreement without public or political opposition. When the employer representative signs the agreement, the employer is bound. Raising revenue and ratification by a public agency can be more difficult, and the difficulties may serve as a brake on what management is willing to do. For example, a school board may be unwilling to face the opposition to higher taxes needed for justified increases in teacher compensation.

Nevertheless, even on this issue, teachers have some advantages. The school board's financial situation is known to the union, as is the board's room for maneuver. Indeed, teacher union representatives are sometimes more knowledgeable than school administrators about the district budget. My point is not to advocate secrecy in government, but merely to point out that teachers have an inherent advantage over private sector employees with respect to their information needs concerning employment relations.

Another tactical advantage of teachers is that they have very little, if any, obligation of loyalty to their employer. On the other hand, private sector employees are under some obligation not to damage the employer. In the context of a labor dispute, private sector employees can urge the public not to purchase the employer's product or service, but otherwise their rights to criticize the employer's product or service are limited in ways that do not apply to teachers. Again, I am not advocating restrictions on teachers' rights to criticize school boards and administrators. The fact is, however, that teachers enjoy legal rights to criticize their employers that exceed such rights in the private sector. Needless to say, this is an advantage over private sector employment, especially in view of the political dimension of teacher bargaining.

The fact that a public enterprise cannot move physically constitutes still another advantage of public sector employees. Again, although the employer's ability to move varies from industry to industry and within industries, the inability of school boards to relocate as a response to employee pressure is obviously advantageous to teachers. In the private sector, multinational corporations have even resisted unionization successfully by moving certain operations from one country to another. Sometimes the threat of doing so helps to moderate union demands. On the other hand, you cannot move the schools of Tucson to Mexico, for example, or even to the Tucson suburbs, in order to avoid excessive demands by Tucson teachers.

Another major advantage of teachers over private employees is that teachers are entitled to certain rights of due process even in the absence of a collective agreement or statutory protection. For example, where teachers have acquired an expectancy of reemployment, they may not be fired without due process. Note that this protection is grounded in the federal Constitution, not state statutory enactments. *Thus teachers without bargaining rights frequently have more protection against arbitrary and unjust employer action than do private sector employees with bargaining rights.* In fact, teachers sometimes have the benefit of an extensive system of statutory benefits that exceed the benefits negotiated in the private sector. In California teachers and teacher unions have the following benefits, among others, under state law:

1. Strong protection against dismissal or suspension
2. Ten days of sick leave, cumulative without limit
3. Right to due process even as probationary employees
4. Substantial notice before termination
5. Layoff rights
6. Military, bereavement, personal necessity, legislative, industrial accident, and illness leave
7. Sweeping protections in evaluation
8. Limits on district authority to reduce benefits
9. Protection against noncertified employees doing teacher work
10. Duty-free lunch periods
11. Right to dues deduction
12. Right to prompt payment of salary
13. Right to notice of school closing
14. Protection from legal actions for action in the course of employment
15. Protection from being upbraided, insulted, or abused in the presence of pupils
16. Limits on the work day and work year

In the private sector, collective bargaining is the means of self-help to these benefits; bargaining rights were not superimposed on them. Providing bargaining rights in addition to this vast complex of statutory benefits is not equity for teachers; it is *more than* equity by a wide margin. In the private sector, employees would presumably have had to make various concessions to get these benefits, if they got them at all. In California, as in many other states, the benefits existed prior to bargaining and no employee concession was or is required to achieve them. This is an enormous advantage to the teachers.

Theoretically, California could repeal all the statutory benefits just mentioned and the teachers could bargain from ground zero. For this reason, it may be argued that the existence of statutory benefits for teachers does not constitute an inherent advantage of public sector over private sector employees. In fact, however, even the legal possibilities are not so clear. In some states, such as New York, public employee pension benefits may not constitutionally be reduced by the state. Unfortunately, this fact did not seem to lessen the generosity of the legislatures, which must now grapple with the problem of funding public employee pension and retirement benefits that require alarming proportions of state revenues.

According to teacher unions, the most glaring inequity between public and private employment is the fact that in most states teacher strikes are prohibited. If we limit our analysis to the legal right to strike, and ignore the practical difficulties of enforcing penalties for illegal teacher strikes, there appears to be an inequity. Nevertheless, this inequity is more technical than practical, and the typical legislative remedy for it has added to the advantages teachers have over private sector employees.

First, we must recognize that teacher strikes are not an economic weapon for teachers. If they are an economic weapon at all, they favor management. The "loss of production" resulting from a teacher strike is hardly noticeable. Who can say, years or even months after the fact, what difference was made by a few days or weeks of schooling, more or less? From the standpoint of putting economic pressure on the employer, the loss of the right to strike in education is no loss at all. On the other hand, because teacher strikes are political, not economic weapons, not having the right to strike actually strengthens the political effectiveness of teachers. The public is not aware of the economic ineffectiveness of teacher strikes, while it tends to be sympathetic to the argument that something should be done to help employees who cannot strike.

Because teachers typically don't have the right to strike, state legislation usually prescribes considerable time for bargaining and for impasse procedures. As a result, school management often concedes more than it would in a strike settlement. After all, the longer management is at the table, the more it gives away. The concessions management makes to avoid protracted negotiations and impasse procedures are often much greater than the concessions it would make to avoid or settle a strike.

Legislatures ought to be concerned about the fact that too much time, not too little, is devoted to public employee bargaining. Instead of providing a minimum amount of time for bargaining, legislatures should consider a maximum. Teacher unions could still be amply protected against any lack of time due to inadequate management preparation, e.g., through the mechanism of unfair labor practices.

The emphasis on mediation and fact finding in public education has been very costly to the public for another reason, which is widely ignored. This emphasis has been a significant causal factor in teacher persistence in unreasonable demands. A teacher union that has had to settle or strike, and thereby expose its members to loss of income, will be more reasonable than a union whose options were either to settle or to invoke the statutory impasse procedures.

As long as the alternative to settlement is an impasse procedure, teacher persistence in unreasonable demands is only to be expected. In fact, the very existence of the impasse procedures often strengthens teacher determination to concede as little as possible, lest they weaken their position in the impasse procedure. Thus in remedying a legal inequity whose practical importance is vastly overrated, the legislatures have enacted impasse procedures that are more damaging to effective management than the legalization of teacher strikes would be.

The weakness of the equity argument is dramatically illustrated in cases where a board of education tries to discharge striking teachers after the board has bargained in good faith to impasse. In the private sector the employer has the right to replace strikers under these circumstances; "equity" would appear to justify a similar right for school boards. Nevertheless, striking teachers have successfully argued that they can be fired only pursuant to the causes and procedures set forth in the tenure laws. These procedures typically require a board hearing for each individual teacher; the practical implications are to make it impossible to fire striking teachers in many districts. We are thus treated to the hypocritical spectacle of teacher unions crying to the public about the inequitable absence of a teacher right to strike, while they urge their members to strike because it is practically impossible to discipline or fire striking teachers.

Let me turn next to the impact of collective bargaining upon pupils. There are at least four positions on this subject:

1. Teacher bargaining is good for pupils.
2. Teacher bargaining is bad for pupils.
3. Teacher bargaining has no visible impact on pupils one way or the other.
4. We don't really know what its impact is, and it wouldn't matter much if we did.

Theoretically, each of the four positions might have been valid at one time. In the 1960s we probably did not know enough to draw valid conclusions about the impact of teacher bargaining. Today, however, this agnosticism is not so defensible.

The proposition that collective bargaining is good for pupils has its origins in politics, not in education. Probably the most important single difference between private and public sector bargaining is the political dimension of the latter. Essentially, it is a contest for public opinion. Whoever can appear to be the defender and supporter of children has an enormous advantage in the struggle for favorable public opinion. For this reason teacher union propaganda is almost invariably couched in terms of pupil welfare.

Such appeals have a certain plausibility, but only because at some points teacher interests appear to coincide with pupil interests. For example, teachers want small classes, and small classes appear to be beneficial to students. Teachers want more preparation time, and who can be opposed to adequately prepared teachers?

Nevertheless, even if these teacher proposals were of demonstrable benefit to pupils—and usually they are not—they would not support the conclusion that teacher bargaining is an overall benefit to pupils. For one thing, we must also look at teacher proposals on issues where teacher interests conflict with pupil interests. For example, at least 10 times a year I have to negotiate on teacher proposals that teachers be dismissed in the afternoon when pupils are. A common variant on this theme is that teachers be dismissed when pupils are on Fridays and days preceding a holiday or vacation. Such proposals are hardly in the best interests of pupils. On the contrary, they are obviously in the interest of teachers to the detriment of pupils, as are many other teacher proposals.

In short, teacher interests sometimes support and sometimes conflict with the interests of pupils. When teacher interests can be made to appear as pupil interests, the teacher union will do its utmost to persuade the community that teachers are primarily interested in pupil welfare. Nevertheless, if teacher bargaining is not harmful to pupils, it is only because school boards do not agree to most teacher proposals at the table.

Actually, teacher proposals frequently generate more public support than they really deserve. To illustrate, consider most teacher proposals to limit class size. A wealth of research clearly invalidates the assumption that there is invariably a positive correlation between smaller classes and student achievement; but let us assume that the correlation exists. Assume also that teachers are successful in achieving limits on class size in negotiations. Nevertheless, it would be fallacious to conclude that bargaining has a beneficial effect upon students, or upon student achievement. After all, the practical issue is not only whether lower class size improves student achievement, it is whether the use of district funds to reduce class size is the most optimum use thereof. Pupils may need textbooks or physical security or a decent meal even more than smaller class size. The fact that such alternatives are typically ignored in negotiations helps to explain why most teacher arguments on the subject are nothing more than rationalizations of positions taken solely because they are in the interests of teachers. In saying this, I do not denigrate teacher self-interest or challenge the right to pursue it. My point is that, from the teacher point of view, pupil welfare is a secondary or even tertiary consideration in teacher bargaining.

Realistically and practically, why should it be otherwise? How can it be? The teacher union is legally and practically the representative of *teachers*. *Pupils* did not elect teacher unions to represent *pupils; teachers* elected them to advance the interests of *teachers*.

In this connection, the advent of collective bargaining clearly should end the controversy over whether teaching is a "profession." This controversy has been around for a long time, and most educators now consider it a semantic morass. Nevertheless, the issue has been definitely resolved by teacher bargaining—resolved in favor of the proposition that under collective bargaining teaching is not and cannot be a profession in the traditional sense. I say this even though I formerly advocated collective bargaining as a means of professionalization. What puzzles me now is not that I was mistaken but that my position was so obviously a mistake. At any rate, let me describe briefly the intellectual process by which I came to the erroneous conclusion that collective bargaining would be supportive of, or at least consistent with, professionalism.

Over 20 years ago I wrote a book titled *Education as a Profession*. In writing it, I defined a profession as an occupational group that, among other things, emphasizes the service to be rendered rather than the economic gain to the practitioners as the basis for the organization and performance of the service performed.

I then asked this question: What prevents teachers from achieving professional status as defined above? My answer was this: Teachers cannot achieve professional status because their organizations are weak. Their organizations are weak because they are dominated by employers, i.e., by school management. This domination is used to frustrate association efforts to "professionalize" teaching. Example: Superintendents desperately need teachers, hence their association influence is used to oppose efforts to raise certification standards.

My thought was that, under a system of collective bargaining, management would be excluded from teacher organizations. Such exclusion would enable the organizations to become more vigorous and effective advocates of the higher standards that administrators would not and could not support because of their position as management representatives.

In retrospect, part of the analysis was substantially correct. Collective bargaining brought about the exclusion of school administrators from teacher organizations, and these organizations became much stronger in the process. Unfortunately, another crucial consideration was overlooked. In representing teachers, a teacher union cannot be guided strictly or even primarily by public interest considerations. It must necessarily be guided by the interests of its members—interests basically adverse to the public interest.

On this issue the case is no different from a client's employment of an attorney. An attorney represents the client, not the public interest. This does not mean that there are no limits or constraints upon the representational function—but all of us expect our attorneys to act in our interests, whether we are suing the government, trying to stay out of jail, or seeking governmental approval to rezone a building.

Teachers frequently object to the proposition that their organizations are primarily oriented to teacher welfare. Nevertheless, this is not only the fact of the matter but it would probably be dangerous if it were not the case. For example, suppose a district desires to dismiss a teacher for alleged incompetence. If the teacher union were to be the judge instead of the teacher advocate, the teacher would be without effective representation. This would be a most undesirable outcome, since effective representation is so important in our society.

Paradoxically, teacher organizations would lose rather than gain support among *teachers* if the organizations adopted a public interest posture in fact as well as in rhetoric; at a rhetorical level there is no problem, because most teachers believe that what's good for teachers is good for the country. At least, I have yet to hear a teacher union assert that more money for teachers, shorter hours, smaller classes, lighter loads, and more teacher benefits generally are not also in the best interests of the community—and I'm not holding my breath.

Assuming that the previous analysis is substantially correct, what of it? What policies or actions does it suggest? Who should do what?

I am troubled by the foregoing analysis; I am troubled especially by the immense practical difficulties of doing anything constructive about it. Clearly, we cannot go back to the pre-bargaining days. For better or for worse, we have institutionalized collective bargaining or something like it in most states. The personnel and resources available to teachers and other public employee unions virtually insure the continuation of collective bargaining in the public sector. Thus the political influence of public employee unions—the same factor that gives them an undue advantage in bargaining— is also a major deterrent to remedial action at the legislative level.

Furthermore, it is useless to look to higher education for any help in this matter. Many institutions of higher education have departments that are supposed to study and analyze labor legislation. Unfortunately, the professors in these departments frequently moonlight as mediators, arbitrators, conciliators, and fact finders. To avoid jeopardizing their moonlighting roles, they avoid criticism of labor legislation generally, and especially of legislation that encourages and promotes the use of extended impasse procedures and grievance arbitration. On the contrary, they frequently promote such legislation, seeing no problem whatever in finding it in the public interest. The relationship is not necessarily conscious and deliberate. My point is, however, that the philosophy that what's good for General Motors is good for the country lives in these departments, as indeed it does in education generally.

As previously noted, the differences between public and private sector bargaining are not all favorable to public employees. In my opinion, however, most of them are, even though their practical importance varies from state to state. Clearly, the justification for public employee collective bargaining is much stronger in states like Mississippi, which have virtually no statutory benefits, than it is in states like California, which have very substantial statutory benefits. Paradoxically, however, bargaining has emerged first and foremost in the states where it has the least justification and has yet to emerge in many states where its justification is comparatively greater. It must be emphasized, however, that most of the advantages of public employment are ineradicable, regardless of the political jurisdiction involved. Short of disenfranchising public employees, we cannot eliminate their additional leverage on their employer through the political process. Similarly, the rights of public employees to due process are grounded in the federal Constitution, and it is not realistic to anticipate the elimination of these rights through the political process. If, therefore, equity is to be achieved, it must be achieved by adjusting the representational rather than the constitutional rights of public employees. To compensate for the inherent advantages of public employment, such adjustment should provide representational rights that are different from, and significantly less than, private sector bargaining rights.

The Cult of the Slob
by Max Rafferty

America's most volcanic school superintendent-author here puts in focus—in fact, he puts in a white-hot glare—one of the most nerve-racking and fundamental problems administrators face: What to do with the juvenile delinquent, given the purposes most of us have accepted for the schools and the compulsory education laws now universal.

> *Is this the Thing the Lord God made and gave*
> *To have dominion over sea and land . . .?*
> *—Markham*

We speak today of changes—desirable or necessary—in the high schools of the land. Gentlemen, I invite you to consider with me the case of the triumphant Slob.

He stands before us at this moment, unwashed and unregenerate. His hair is agleam and adrip with oil, kneaded behind into strange whorls and sinuosities. Below the ears and following the slack jawline, it descends in bristling tufts, and with an exuberance unknown since the more militant days of the late General Burnside. Hairiness, in fact, is the very badge and symbol of the Slob. He spends a considerable portion of his day coiling and matting, as the Mock Turtle did reeling and writhing.

Our Slob is apt to wear his clothing much as the ladies of Regency days flaunted their bodices—for purposes of revealing rather than concealing. His shirt is open to the fourth button, coyly baring naked flesh down even to the navel. Trousers are slick denim, buckled low upon the hips and hinting at an eager willingness to go even lower. Boots are standard Slob attire, as is the cheap leather jacket with "GENTS" or "ROADRUNNERS" blazoned luridly upon its back.

His stance approximates the so-called "debutante slouch" of a generation ago. His walk is an exaggerated, hip-swinging roll which harks back to the gait of the old salt-water sailor temporarily marooned on land. His talk is a modern thieves' jargon, relying strongly upon scarcely disguised obscenity and intelligible mainly to other members of the cult. His music is the monotonous and nerve-racking drumbeat of the primeval jungle.

If we were to overcome our instinctive revulsion long enough to institute a more intimate search of the Slob's person, we should find exotic treasure indeed. Aside from the miscellaneous and unprintable items of pornography that we may expect as a matter of course, we are bound to come upon several pieces of equipment that will cause even our experienced eyebrows to do a demivolt. I do not refer here to the ubiquitous switchblade knife, normally used to enforce terrorized quiescence upon the victim of a mass rape. Nor do I allude to the bicycle chain, commonly swung menacingly about the heads of smaller boys in order to collect protection money, nor even to the zip gun that lends a deadly note to the gang rumbles.

No, I have reference rather to the inked or tattooed device worn upon the hand or arm, strikingly suggestive of an unholy brotherhood of crime and startlingly reminiscent of the Mafia. I allude in passing also to such esoteric appurtenances as the razor-studded cap brim for slashing faces, and the shortened tire iron for breaking legs. Surely, such a walking chamber of horrors should at least cause us to pause for consideration.

I am reminded in this connection of the Duke of Wellington's comment when confronted with a somewhat similar situation. During the Peninsular Campaign, the Duke kept the sea-lanes to London sizzling with his insistent demands for reinforcements. After an interminable delay, the laggard troops arrived in Spain, but to everyone's horror they turned out to be jailbirds and sturdy rogues, the scourings of the London streets. As the Iron Duke sat glumly on his horse before the heights of Torres Vedras watching the clumsy recruits attempting to drill, an eager aide approached him.

"Tell me, m'Lord, d'ye think these blighters will frighten old Boney?"

The Duke regarded him grimly.

"I can't say about Boney, but by God they frighten *me!*"

I must confess that I am with the Duke in this matter. They frighten *me*.

Study Slobbism—in Self-Defense

It is these added refinements, these supererogatory icings on the cake of delinquency, that in my opinion constitute ample cause for our serious study of the Slob in any symposium on high school problems. In sober truth, and especially since educators have of late become prime targets of the Slob's more lethal aggressions, we are left with little choice other than to initiate an examination of Slobbism, if only out of self-defense.

After all, so long as the characters who lurched menacingly about our high school corridors and snarled defiantly at their teachers confined their activities to mere lurching and snarling, it was expedient for us to chalk up such behavior to "release of tensions" and "animal spirits," and to let it go at that. A good many of our abler instructors, it is true, dropped out of the business, unable or unwilling to assume the role of Frank Buck constantly challenging the carnivores, and some of the hardier souls who stuck it out were carried out feet first as the result of brushes with certain of their pupils whose tensions they had unwittingly helped to release. But minor bloodletting such as this was dismissed by school administrators as statistically inconsequential, and life in the Great American High School rocked and rolled along its accustomed path.

Until recently . . .

When, a few months ago, a junior-grade disciple of Slobbism toted his rifle to school for kicks and spent the better part of a half hour chivvying his startled principal from office to lavatory as the hot lead flew.

And a short time later, another junior high principal was so bedeviled and intimidated and just plain scared that he chose to solve his problems by jumping off a roof and spattering himself all over a playground, while the Slobs stood by and sniggered.

Then, just recently, the crash of shotgun fire added a touch of piquancy to the run-of-the-mill noises of a California campus as a sulky Slob blew the leg off an athletic director who had been unwise enough to intervene between the grinning gunman and a potential victim.

It may seem at first glance that these examples of Slobbism are excessively sanguinary, but simple assault and battery in the schools is, quite frankly, too common to talk about. Almost every edition of your favorite newspaper contains a matter-of-fact story about some schoolman who has been slugged or roughed up by a pack of punks. Such treatment is coming to be regarded as just another occupational hazard, ranking somewhere on the scale between simple writer's cramp and accumulation of chalk dust in the lungs. So long as this one-sided tong war took place outside the inner sanctum of the principal or the superintendent, we administrators were inclined to shrug it off.

Isolated instances, you know.

Or, "Mr. Jones brought it on himself, in a way. Had trouble establishing rapport."

But recent happenings have placed things in a somewhat different light. The zip gun sights have been raised, and Mr. Administrator is finding himself uncomfortably in dead center. His concern has ceased to be academic and is rapidly becoming personal. I can only assume that a good many of my colleagues, in the face of imminent stabbing or shooting, are going to revise their priority listings of significant high school problems to place Slobbism somewhere up near the top.

At least they will if they are as downright cowardly as I am.

School Not Battleground, Hunting Preserve

Even if schoolmen turn out to be heroes, however, it is still high time to concern ourselves seriously with the peculiar problem posed by this twentieth century version of *Homo neanderthalensis*. A school is neither a battleground nor a hunting preserve, and unless we address ourselves energetically to the solving of this puzzle, we are going to find ourselves increasingly beset within our ivory towers by baying bands of Slobs. So perhaps the mills of the gods, by grinding perilously near our persons, may compel us at last to take the action that the scandalous and pitiful plight of our normal, decent pupils, terrorized by these creeps, has so long demanded of us.

The old head-in-the-sand technique of minimizing or ignoring the size of the Slob in the hope that he will somehow get lost won't work anymore. It has been fashionable to say smugly that these are maladjusted boys, thrown up through no fault of their own from the modern maelstrom of wars, depressions, and broken homes. To this pious platitude is usually appended the magnificent *non sequitur* that, after all, these social deviates compose but a very small fraction of the total adolescent population. A similar observation, of course, might be made with equal truth about the cholera bacillus.

Let's Understand the Enemy

It is important that we understand our enemy. And it is an enemy we are talking about, not just a misunderstood by-product of the machine age. The Slob, or more important the whole institution of Slobbism, is the mortal adversary of Education.

Slobbism negates all the values we teach.

It convulses hysterically against all disciplines.

It derides morality in any form.

It persistently seeks out ugliness and filth in preference to beauty and decency, like the unlovely but irreproachable Biblical dog that insisted on returning to its vomit.

Above all, it takes pleasure in inflicting pain.

The Slob is thus the exact opposite of the gentleman, who is defined by Newman as one who never willingly inflicts pain. Our Slobbish citizen not only inflicts pain; he revels in it. The threatening note, the obscene phone call, the ravaging of women and children—these are the Slob's stock in trade. Indeed, it has been truly said that his sole interests are sadism, sex, and speed, in that order.

The Slob's mental processes are so rudimentary as to be almost non-existent, although a certain amount of animal cunning is sometimes to be found in his agile twisting and turning to avoid work and to remain out of jail. The brain, however, is not so much deficient as unused. It has been short-circuited by a constant succession of appeals to the emotions. The Slob is ruled by his passions. He warms easily to rage. He burns with lust upon the slightest pretext. He shivers, occasionally, with clammy fear. He is adrenal rather than cerebral, physical rather than mental.

He is, in short, the perfect antithesis of everything Education stands for. The paradox lies in the fact that he is also the product of Education. A dozen years ago, he was in our kindergartens. He went on our field trips to the bakery and danced around ribboned poles at our May festivals. Only yesterday he was studying "social living" in our junior highs. He has been tested and guided and motivated. It has cost the taxpayers, over a decade or so, several thousand dollars to produce a Slob. It hardly seems worth it, does it?

To wax classical for a moment, we may compare Education to old Cronus, who produced a numerous family only to find himself in his old age hunted down mercilessly and mutilated by his own children. This is a melancholy prospect indeed. Let us see if, from our knowledge of Slobbism, we can avert from our profession the fate of Cronus.

First, let us clear the ground by conceding in advance some of the more obvious trusims. Let us concede that the great majority of our high school pupils are as yet free from the grosser manifestations of Slobbism. We can agree, too, as to the essentially nonschool origins of the phenomenon. No one doubts the intricately complex causes that rub against each other long enough and intimately enough to produce the smolder or the flash of blind violence. But, when all this has been said, it does not follow that Education is absolved of all responsibility for the golems who stalk its halls.

Whose fault is it that no more exciting and rewarding goal than sheer sensuality has succeeded in capturing the imagination of these people? Hedonism, after all, is as old as the hills. Its lure was exploded before Christ. Surely Education can, if it tries, break in upon the sterile, revolving-door cycle of liquor and licentiousness.

Who is to blame for the pathological inability of these persons to concentrate for more than a few fleeting moments on anything less basic than feeding, fighting, and fornicating? Could it possibly stem from the kaleidoscopic and chaotic mishmash of canal-building, Hopi Indians, tomato growing, air transport, and steel puddling through which we have merry-go-rounded our pupils in recent years? Is it possible that we have produced a group unamenable to discipline simply because we have never insisted upon their mastering anything that required discipline to overcome?

It is barely conceivable that, by destroying the hierarchy of values that placed mastery of specific subject matter in a position of paramount importance, we have persuaded these already confused minds that nothing in life, including life itself, is of any particular importance. We have required them to go to school, but we have not required them to do any work. Instead, we have created special "courses" wherein they might sprawl and leer in company with one another, and where constructive learning is laughed out of court. To the Slob, life is a dirty joke, with school the cream of the jest and educators the buffoons.

We talk of change in the nation's high schools.

Here is a change that must be made, and soon, if we are to avoid destruction.

Socially Uneducable Must Be Excluded

One way or another, the Slob must go. Those of his ilk who have passed the point of no return must be excluded from our schools as socially uneducable, even as we exclude the unfortunate imbecile as mentally uneducable. And let no one challenge our right to take this step. The Slob is more dangerous to his classmates than a walking case of typhoid or tuberculosis. We have not only the right but the clear and positive duty to quarantine him. It is our shame that we have not done so sooner. What will become of him? When he has reached this stage, he has passed beyond our power to correct. He is no longer susceptible to Education. He has become a subject for criminology.

As Dr. Johnson said of the Scotsman, much may be done with the Slob if he be caught young enough. With a program of specific goals, scientific testing, understanding guidance, and consistent discipline, a school should be able to nip a great deal of Slobbism in the bud. If the school is fortunate enough to be located in a community where the police are alert, the courts tough, and the citizenry concerned, the cult of the Slob can be broken by the united action of all. Where such a happy combination of attitudes is not present, it becomes the positive duty of the school administration to work diligently within the community to produce it.

We have gone overboard on universal education. It has become a fetish instead of a logically considered objective. By our stubborn refusal to exclude clearly pathological cases from school, we are presently permitting this fetishism to work irremediable wrong upon the great majority of normal children whom we are exposing to this moral plague. It is my conviction that Slobbism is a highly contagious disease. It must be treated as such. Isolation and prophylaxis are strongly indicated.

Law cannot help the deliberate homicide. He defies it.

Medicine cannot help the would-be suicide. He rejects it.

Religion cannot help the hardened atheist. He disbelieves it.

Even so, Education cannot help the full-blown Slob. He loathes it.

It is a sorry tribute to our perspicacity as schoolmen that we have let this thing drift to the point where many of us have become quivering quarry in our own classrooms. I submit that it will be pointless and tragic folly for us and for our country if we stand dithering by while the throat of Education is slowly cut with a switchblade knife.

Psychoanalysis and Education
by Donald W. Robinson

Freudian theory pervades every field of modern thought, yet no one has ever fully charted its influence on education. Here Phi Delta Kappa's associate editor-elect traces some of the effects, suggests ways in which teachers can make best use of psycho-analytic theory, and cautions against pitfalls.

The Impact of Psychoanalysis on Our Culture

The influence of psychoanalysis on education is as indefinable as it is undeniable, because it has been indirect. Sigmund Freud wrote in 1909 that the purpose of education is "to enable the individual to take part in culture and to achieve this with the smallest loss of original energy." However, neither he nor the later analytic theorists have had very much to say about how learning takes place or about what should be taught or how it should be taught. They are primarily concerned with the emotions, while the teacher has traditionally been more concerned with the intellect. Relating the former concern to the latter is the task recently assumed by the psychologist.

Sigmund Freud is often mentioned, along with Charles Darwin and Albert Einstein, as one of the great creative thinkers of modern times. Like the others, he formulated a new way of looking at things that has profoundly altered the way we think about man and his relations to other men and to the universe.

His writings constitute a body of doctrine commonly called psychoanalysis, a doctrine based on the concepts of unconscious motivation, conflict, and symbolism. In this article the word psychoanalysis will refer to this theory of human behavior set forth by Freud and his disciples.

The profound influence of the theories that Freud presented in books and essays from 1888 to 1938, theories he personally introduced to this country in a series of lectures in 1908, has been especially felt in the fields of psychology, sociology, anthropology, psychiatry, and psychosomatic medicine.

Increasingly, this influence is extending to the nonacademic world. The growing stream of popular books, the evident Freudian approach by writers on child care and marriage counseling, the prevalence of Freudian allusions in popular literature and drama, and the appeal of analytic speculations about the cause of any human frailty or deviation, all confirm the fact that we cannot escape the influence of Sigmund Freud.

A leading psychologist who resists the Freudian influence nevertheless admits that "It would be difficult to overestimate the impact of Freud's thoughts on the thinking of our times, especially among the classes which may be considered as supplying the intellectual leadership for the nation."

The impact on the schools has been no less important. It is readily apparent in the current school jargon. Teachers are threatened. Students have guilt feelings, aggressive tendencies, frustrations. Teachers stand as parent surrogates, help students to recognize identification and projection and deal with anxiety and tension. These terms and the attitudes they represent are direct outgrowths of the concepts formulated by Freud.

The American Handbook of Psychiatry acknowledges the influence of psychoanalysis on education in these words, "In education there has been a continuous trend toward the introduction of mental health principles in schools and a greater acceptance of the principles of individual, familial, and social dynamics. The importance of a wholesome school atmosphere, leading the pupil to a greater security and a feeling of belonging, of worth, and of dignity, as well as the importance of the teacher/child and the teacher/family relationships have been generally recognized. Progressive methods of education have been studied in relation to mental health aspects, and such extensive projects as 'human relations' classes have been highly successful. Psychiatric attention is being extended to every school level, including colleges and universities."

The card catalogue in the education library of a typical state college contains, under the heading *Psychoanalysis*, over 200 book titles. Goodwin Watson reports that psychology textbooks published in the 1920s averaged four pages devoted to unconscious factors in motivation, while books published in the 1950s averaged 46 pages on the same topic. Texts published in the earlier period devoted an average of seven pages to mental hygiene, while the more recent books averaged 57. The trend is well established.

The reaction of teachers to this trend is naturally mixed. Younger teachers may accept the Freudian orientation more wholeheartedly because their exposure to it has begun earlier and they have not had to overcome a previously established viewpoint. Some teachers resist the whole psychological approach with a blunt insistence that "our job is to teach our subject; let the parents and the doctors take care of the emotional problems. The schools do too much psychologizing already." Others are responsive to the mental health approach, recognizing that establishing emotional health in the child will enhance his intellectual learning, but are unaware of the debt this approach owes to Freud and psychoanalysis.

The origins of this reluctance are easy to find.

Man will resist any new idea that seems to contradict notions long held and accepted as "true," especially such a notion as the complete freedom of man totally to control his actions by sheer "will power." Men have held so tightly to this illusion that it has seemed immoral to suggest, as Freud did, that a man's power to control his actions is limited by forces that he is normally incapable of controlling or even recognizing. We do not actually believe that a person can by sheer determination control his emotions, but we know that in our culture he is expected to do so.

A conscious determination to exercise control is necessary, but not always sufficient, for effective living. Anyone who has been the victim of blushing, stuttering, claustrophobia, forgetfulness, overeating, alcoholism, migrane headaches, insomnia, hypochondria, excessive worry, or any of a hundred other unconsciously induced torments will testify that will power, even when adroitly applied, is often not enough.

The early years are so dominated by the constant urging by parents to "try," to "control," and to "master yourself" that the ego is unable easily to admit defeat by conceding that we are unable by sheer will power to conquer the disability that plagues us. All people bear some degree of disability, whether it is a compulsive urge to talk or merely being ill at ease in certain situations. Fortunate are those who can adjust to their own idiosyncracies, accept them, and prevent them from becoming disabling or disqualifying.

Resistance to the full acceptance of Freudian analytic ideas is normal and often assumes one of these rational forms:

1. *That psychoanalysis reduces the self-reliance of man by encouraging him to find explanations in circumstances beyond his control.* (The answer is that the Freudian approach is to *discover* what influences may be beyond the individual's *conscious* control and to offer a method for bringing these, too, within his control. An extension of consciousness can lead to higher levels of self-control, based on self-knowledge. Psychoanalysis seeks to replace the question "Does man possess free will?" with "How *much* free will does he possess?," and then seeks to enlarge the area in which he can exercise free will by revealing to him the source of some of his problems.)

2. *That the Freudian doctrine is unverifiable and unscientific.* (This is partly true, but the fact does not reduce the effectiveness of analysis. It might be difficult to demonstrate that Christianity or democracy are scientific, but that does not reduce their usefulness. And the power of the unconscious *is* clearly demonstrable, as in posthypnotic suggestion.)

3. *That Freudian literature is filled with bizarre, if not obscene, over-emphasis on sex and sexual symbolism.* (The explanation is that the ever-recurring phallic and vaginal symbols are expressions of the powerful libidinal forces that eventually find fulfillment, if they are not thwarted, in heterosexual activity. Some persons find this symbolism repulsive because it violates the rigid code they were taught that one does not talk about sex except in hospitals and bars, because it is dirty. Is the dream symbolism suggested by Freud more bizarre than everyday occurrences such as blushing and stuttering are *without* an explanation?)

Novelists long before Freud knew and exploited the power of the unconscious and the compelling importance of libidinal drives. Scientists, too, had underlined the instinctive urge to reproduce or the inherent urge for race survival. It is inconceivable that such a powerful urge should not influence the lives of individuals, even beyond their specific sexual acts. In this light Freud's emphasis on sex (which he defines in a far broader way than mere genital associations) is normal and desirable.

A different kind of resistance is engendered in persons who have had the misfortune to gain their first impressions of analysis from charlatans, quacks, or incompetents. Every complex social or psychological theory inevitably becomes altered as it becomes popularized. As the ripples of information circle out from the original source they become ever weaker and more easily distorted. This is equally true of Deweyism, Christianity, psychoanalysis, or any doctrine. The farther the gospel is spread the less it resembles the preachings of the master.

Most people probably adopt new ideas by bits and snatches. With respect to psychoanalysis, some accept the concept of the unconscious while rejecting the notion of the sexual stages of development. Some accept the idea of dreams as concealed expressions of unconscious urges while scoffing at the Oedipus Complex. As a result, the popular notion of psychoanalysis, as of every complex system, becomes a mishmash of distortions, dilutions, and eclecticisms.

The aversion that many teachers display toward Freudian doctrines results largely from this kind of peripheral misconception. Extremists who associated themselves with Freudian thought as well as with the fringe group of ultra-progressives have given analysis an undeserved reputation for sanctioning the removal of all control and restraint from the child. Neither Freud nor any reputable analyst recommended the absence of controls.

It is not surprising that some of Freud's emancipatory discoveries, like some of Dewey's, became the vehicles for extremist movements of permissiveness. The early extremist works were published during the late Victorian era when a reaction against excessive authoritarianism was beginning and every possible scrap of evidence was marshaled in favor of the new spirit of freedom. Freud was aware of the unhappy effect of excessive repression and inhibition, as today he would be equally aware of the tragic consequences of insufficient control and direction of children. Both extremes are equally at variance with his theory and with the ideas of reputable analysts today.

The Influence of Psychoanalysis on Education

A generation ago the obstreperous youngster was described as acting up. Today he is diagnosed as acting out. If the effect of the psychological emphasis had been no more than to create a new terminology, it would not warrant our serious attention. Some partisans are certain that the psychological impact has rescued the schools from utter collapse, while others are equally convinced that the effect has been nearly disastrous.

The teachers of this country have welcomed the psychologists, though frequently unaware of their debt to psychoanalysis, and have eagerly attempted to incorporate their ideas into school practice. This is not surprising, since, with the extension of compulsory school attendance through high school, teachers have been unduly preoccupied with the problems of the emotionally disturbed students. Any new knowledge from psychology was welcomed if it promised hope of assistance in understanding and dealing with the mass of students who would once have been eliminated from school by virtue of their intellectual and emotional limitations, but who now must remain until graduation or until they reach age 16 or 17.

The direct influence of psychoanalysis on school curriculum is apparent and significant. Teaching units on mental health and sex education have been introduced and psychological testing has mushroomed in importance, as have guidance and counseling services. Important as these influences have been, we are not here concerned as much with them as with the overall changes in educational philosophy and the resultant effect on teaching methods.

Psychoanalysis and Progressive Education

Psychoanalysis has been frequently equated with progressive education. It has been extravagantly praised and vehemently damned for introducing the permissiveness that has so conspicuously marked our child-rearing in the past generation. It deserves neither the praise nor the blame.

Three brief quotations should help to clarify the analytic position:

Dr. Peter Neubauer says, in an article in *The Atlantic* in July 1961, "Freud pointed out that denial and conflict were as essential a part of the process of growth as gratification, and he never minimized the child's need for direction."

Anna Freud wrote, "The task of a pedagogy based upon analytic data is to find a *via media* between these extremes—that is to say, allow to each state in the child's life the right proportion of instinct gratification and instinct restriction."

Dr. Pearson, whose 1954 volume, *Psychoanalysis and the Education of the Child*, is probably the most comprehensive book on this subject, says, "Every individual must learn that he is affected by two fields of influence, the external world of sensory perception and the inner world of instincts. The influence of the latter far out-shadows the former and in case of conflict takes precedence. Both too much frustration and too much gratification will hamper the development of the ego."

Excessive authority neglects to train the youngster for emancipation from dependence on the parent figures. Extreme permissiveness in the early years fails to provide the needed authority figures whom the child can use as models in developing his own personality.

If this sounds like a truism known by every experienced teacher, it is. And one of the reassuring aspects of psychoanalysis is that it *does* confirm the common-sense wisdom of the best of human experience. Psychoanalysis, like education, has for its major goal the freeing of individuals for rational living, unhampered by the bonds of ignorance or emotional thralldom.

Dr. Pearson dwells at length on the importance for teachers of the reality principle. He says, "Every opportunity to test reality is useful in helping the child solve his intrapsychic conflicts. During the latency period there should be ample opportunities for unsupervised and unrestricted play so that each child may have the chance to work out his specific conflicts in the make-believe of play." Note that this is very different from suggesting that the child should never be supervised, directed, or corrected. It is interesting to note, as Lilli Peller reminds us, that the child often takes his play just as seriously as the adult takes his work.

Pearson continues, "In reality human life consists more of hard and tedious work than of pleasurable experience, and if the individual wishes to lead a pleasurable life he must develop the capacity to accept and adjust to reality—to the realities of the physical world, the needs and desires of other people in this world, and the customs and mores of the world in which he lives. Only when the individual has this capacity will he be able to attempt to change any part of the environment—the physical work, the other members of his social group, or the prevailing customs and mores."

It is recognized that a child is far more likely to attain a satisfactory adjustment to reality if he is exposed to teachers who operate from reality, for the child incorporates not only what the teacher teaches but all aspects of the teacher's personality.

If the teacher has an extremely rigid personality, or is sadistic, or is too inhibited, the child may incorporate some of this quality.

Pearson suggests that this may benefit the child if it happens to be the opposite of extreme parental traits, or harm him if it reinforces parental extremes.

Psychiatric Examinations for Teachers

It is self-evident today that emotional "maturity" is especially essential in a teacher. Pearson and many others urge that student teachers be required to undergo a period of direct psychoanalysis, and, where this is impossible, that applicants for teaching be screened by a rigid psychiatric examination.

It is tempting to speculate on the emotional stability of teachers. Dr. Shipley presents data from a 1948 study of admissions records at the Mayo Clinic showing that while 17% of the physicians admitted to the clinic were found to have emotional illness, 19% of the farmers, 30% of the dentists, and 36% of the lawyers and housewives, 55% of the teachers admitted were suffering from emotional illness! The assumption that teaching harbors a higher percentage of neurotics than other occupations is a popular one. Although it cannot be thoroughly proved or disproved, it can be supported by logical inference, based both on the emotional wear and tear of the job itself and on the attraction of teaching for persons emotionally reluctant to compete in the hurly-burly adult world.

It is just possible that the influence of psychoanalysis on our culture has helped to determine the type of person who tends to become a teacher. If the extreme traditional school with its "this hurts me more than that does you" spirit attracted and then aggravated the "hard" or sadistic personality, the newer, more "progressive" school may appeal to the "soft" or philanthropic personality. Although the analytic approach requires neither "hard" nor "soft" but reality-based teachers, still an indulgent school, spawned in a permissive community, may tend to recruit overly sentimental teachers, who in turn will extend the permissive atmosphere still farther.

At present no way exists to determine accurately how many teachers have unconsciously selected teaching as a solution for some deep-seated personal conflict, especially a conflict involving authority.

Analysts recognized this hazard among themselves and attempted some years ago a substantial study of the unconscious reasons why some analysts elected to concentrate in *child analysis*. Although the study was never formally completed, the evidence that was collected indicated three unconscious motives prompting the choice of child analysis. It is evident that these motives *might* operate equally in the choice of teaching as a career. They are:

1. Fear of overaggressive impulses toward adults, consciously controlled by feelings of marked inferiority with adults and feeling more comfortable with children.

2. Unconscious desire to get even with hated siblings by being in a position where they can control children.

3. Conscious or unconscious hatred of parents, expressed as a determination, "When I grow up I'll show you how children should be treated."

No implication is intended that unconscious motivations are necessarily bad, but they *can* be unfortunate if they are too intense, and especially if they are not recognized and understood.

Three Pitfalls Faced by the Analytically Oriented Teacher

Warnings should be advanced about three danger areas where the well-meaning teacher frequently errs in his efforts to promote mental and emotional health in his students. These three errors occur and are frequently cited by critics as failures of the psychological viewpoint.

The first of the three pitfalls is overemphasis on the developmental aspects of the child's personality at the expense of his intellectual development. Properly handled, teacher attention to the psychological problems of the child, with all of the interviews, tests, sociograms, play therapy, or whatever techniques are indicated, can be helpful in freeing the child from emotional blocks and in enhancing his ego so that he becomes a more effective learner as well as a happier person. If, however, so much time and attention is directed to the study of the psychological problems that too little is left for planning and directing the program of intellectual accomplishment, the child's education suffers. Perhaps there cannot be an overemphasis on emotional adjustment, but there can be an underemphasis on essential factual learning. Teachers are sometimes accused of overpsychologizing. This charge makes little sense as stated, for no teacher can know too much about the psychological problems of his students, but he *can* know too little or care too little about the learning that results from his instruction. If he goes overboard in his enthusiasm for psychology to the neglect of his subjects, he is justifying the charge that the schools are producing well-adjusted ignoramuses.

If the teacher's enthusiasm for helping the youngsters with obvious emotional problems leads to the neglect of the healthy average child, who also requires attention, he is derelict in his responsibility.

In addition to the general danger of overenthusiasm, a teacher who is familiar with analytic concepts is susceptible to *special* enthusiasms that can be harmful. One of these is the excessive interest and anxiety sometimes aroused in the teacher for the welfare of the problem student. For example, the teacher may know that the lonely child may be odd or queer and that the distance between queerness and schizophrenia may be short, and so may go overboard in his anxious efforts to help the child to socialize. The teacher, in his fear that the child may overdo fantasy or day-dreaming, may prevent the child from working or playing alone, when the child very much needs the constructive values that he can only find alone. This concern about children's day-dreaming has sometimes led to an overemphasis on togetherness that makes children almost incapable of remaining alone.

So long as interest in psychology and personality development of the child demonstrably contributes to the improvement of his intellectual performance, it will receive general support. When it becomes a movement to substitute the development of the personality for the development of the mind, it contradicts a long-held and deeply cherished notion of the purposes of education. When the concept of the power of the unconscious is overstated, it becomes in effect a kind of anti-intellectualism (or at least anti-academicism), that has been the target of recent attacks on the public schools.

The Teacher as a Behavior Model

A second and equally serious pitfall is neglecting to fulfill the child's need for a satisfying parent figure by being a "real person." The extreme progressive era encouraged the teacher to seek the background, to be inconspicuous and nondirective, so that the child might develop freedom, self-confidence, and initiative. Again common sense tells us that the advice might be an excellent antidote for extreme teacher domination, but that the opposite extreme can be equally unfortunate. Children at every stage need the teacher partly as a model of behavior after which to pattern their own conduct. The teacher who remains always inconspicuous provides no pattern. At the same time, on the strictly conscious level, students need teachers to tell them what they should learn and show them how to learn it—in short, to teach them.

Teachers who simply let children grow by self-expression are, it is true, avoiding the error of overdomination, but they are not teaching. It seems likely that a share of the apparent neurosis and insecurity today results from the fact that young people have had insufficient direction from adults. They have anxieties because they have not been given standards by which to measure their own conduct. A major function of the teacher is to lead. As a parent symbol he should afford the child the security that the child can derive from the knowledge that he is accepted as a loved child, even while he is corrected for his mistakes and is punished for his wrongdoing. The child seeks this security, both consciously and unconsciously, from the teacher's admonitions and examples. Without it he cannot learn as much.

Lilli Peller is referring to this function when she writes, "The teacher who puts herself on the child's level all the time, who encourages indulgence, who shows lavish admiration for any scribble—this teacher fails to inspire the child's wish to identify himself with her. Much as she tries to captivate the child's interest, she fails to get it. This does not imply that the so-called old-fashioned school has the most effective ways to promote learning and growth; it only indicates that conditions are more complicated than we thought." A school program must be geared to children's abilities and interests, but the child also expects the teacher to make demands and is disappointed when he receives no assistance from the teacher in dealing with his instinctual pressures. Teachers themselves retain enough of the childish need for parent figures that they frequently place the very concept of learning, or more often a specific new formulation of ideas, such as the Freudian concept, in a parent role. Their intellectual reaction to it is very much colored by their emotional reaction, which betrays a striking similarity to the manner of a child reacting to a parent, either prostrating himself completely to the new demands or rebelling violently against them. The role of the parent symbol is always present, and it is a role that the teacher cannot refuse to play.

Dealing with Resistance to Learning

The third weakness that sometimes comes into teaching with those who profess the mental health point of view is the failure to recognize the importance of resistance. Resistance to learning in the classroom is just as normal and inescapable as is resistance in the analyst's office. Man has a deep-seated human instinct to keep what is his own, especially his beliefs and feelings. Learning, if it is to be meaningful, must alter some cherished misconceptions of the learner, and these he will relinquish only slowly and reluctantly. Therefore, when certain of the progressive teachers interpret students' resistance to learning as unacceptable or as evidence that the learning situation has been badly planned, they are missing a major analytic point. If the learning is significant, some students *must* resist it and be unhappy about it. This does not make either the teacher or the lesson wrong. Teachers who feel that all learning must be gay and pleasant, almost to the point of being carefree and effortless, are denying the essence of learning. It would probably be an indefensible overstatement to assert that without discomfort and resistance no valuable learning can take place, but this statement is valid if we accept literally the popular dictum that the only learning that is truly worthwhile is that learning that results in changed behavior.

This proposition too can be tested by reference to adults. If we observe teachers or others discussing the relative merits of traditional versus progressive methods of teaching, it will soon become apparent that for most of them something more is involved than a rational desire to share viewpoints and discover the best way to teach. What is more powerfully though unconsciously involved is a resistance to having their notions of teaching challenged. The concept of resistance is as significant in learning as the notion of the parent image, and it should be thoroughly understood by the teacher.

It now becomes apparent that the three separate dangers inherent in the analytic approach all result in the same damage. The teacher who emphasizes the psychological approach at the sacrifice of subject matter, the teacher who neglects the role of the demanding parent figure, and the teacher who tries to eliminate or avoid pupil resistance are all playing into the hands of "easy learning" to the long-range disadvantage of the child.

The reader should, of course, beware of interpreting the three warnings as being pleas for a return to authoritarian methods, or for more homework for students, or for more attention to academic requirements, or any other prescription. If they are pleas at all, they plead for keeping psychological and intellectual goals in balance, for having the teacher understand his psychological as well as his academic role, and for recognizing the inescapability of student resistance to learning.

In exonerating Freud and psychoanalysis of responsibility for the errors and excesses of well-meaning but misdirected disciples, we do not intend to excuse the teachers who perpetrate the damaging excesses.

Analytic theory in the hands of incompetent teachers is dangerous, but no more dangerous than psychological ignorance in the hands of incompetents. Where there has been incompetent teaching by analytically oriented teachers, let us blame the incompetence, not the philosophy.

Summary

Despite the pitfalls, we must learn to make the best possible use of all the available tools and techniques that give promise of aiding in the herculean task of educating all the children of all the people. We must master the psychological contributions in order to improve the excellence of our intellectual accomplishments. And we need some other emphases in the school also. Excellence in imagination, in persuasion, and in artistic creativity are not to be scorned. The point is simply that excellence can seldom be attained by teachers who are unaware of their own emotional limitations and who stoutly resist self-knowledge by asserting that intellectual content is all that matters.

Psychoanalysis seeks for its followers the rational life, through the control and understanding of the emotions. Education too has as its goal the rational life and seeks to promote a way of life directed by reason rather than by emotion. The cooperation of education and psychoanalysis in the attainment of their common goal seems natural and desirable.

Teachers cannot be trained as psychoanalysts. They cannot attempt the reconstruction of pupil personality. Nevertheless, in dealing with emotionally deficient children, the teacher is compelled to make some effort to minimize the effects of the child's personality disorders, as well as to prevent their aggravation, if he or she is to have any hope of teaching the student.

Consequently, the teacher who is equipped with an understanding of the child's normal and abnormal behavior is more likely to succeed.

The master teacher who can recognize compulsions, fantasies, projection, identification, and other similarly emotionally dictated behavior can no more eliminate them than the master mariner can eliminate the adverse winds and tides. Neither would be called a master if he failed to recognize the adverse influences and guide his teaching or his navigation accordingly. It is important to have teachers who are analytically sophisticated as long as we have students who are immature and unstable. Otherwise, teachers in positions of authority over children who are unable to respond wholesomely will cause still more maladjustment. A few rare souls learn this without recourse to analysis, as they did before Freud began the systematic study of the unconscious. Unfortunately, still fewer of these rare souls find their way into public school teaching.

Analytic sophistication by teachers is obviously not the only need. Attention to mental health at every level is called for. Dr. Neubauer says, "Perhaps the greatest lag in the field of mental health is the relative lack of action to implement our conviction that emotional health and pathology are determined in early childhood. More than half of all hospital beds in the U.S. are occupied by mentally ill patients, yet there exist almost no institutional facilities for the emotionally disturbed preschool child. As long as we neglect the needs of the very young, we will continue to have a large population of adolescents and adults suffering from neurosis or the acuter forms of mental sickness."

The research need also is great and the present effort pitifully meager. Dr. Shipley quotes a 1959 report of the National Health Association to the effect that for every reported case of polio $216.84 is being spent for research; for every person hospitalized for mental illness $.01 is spent for research.

Four-fifths of all counties in the U.S. still have no psychiatric service whatsoever. Studies of school children indicate that from 7% to 12%—between two and four million—are in need of psychiatric treatment.

The mental health problem is immense. It is not the school's problem, but the school cannot escape responsibility for doing everything in its power to avoid aggravating it.

The various statements of the role of the teacher in handling this problem have this in common: They are all predicated on a continually increasing awareness and sophistication of psychoanalytic concepts. This is all that can be safely suggested, for psychoanalysis is not prescriptive.

Dr. Lawrence S. Kubie presents a convincing case for the importance of psychoanalysis to education in his introduction to *An Application of Psychoanalysis to Education*, by Richard M. Jones. Dr. Kubie reminds us of the necessity for making emotional maturation a part of the educational process by a continuous concern from kindergarten to university for making self-knowledge in depth part of the mainstream of education. He does not urge that teachers play at being analysts, but only that education take place in an atmosphere in which emotional disturbances can be recognized and resolved instead of being repressed and aggravated. He goes on to say:

The child's fifth freedom is the right to know what he feels; but this does not carry with it any right to act out his feelings blindly. This will require a new set of mores for our schools, one which will enable young people from early years to understand and feel and put into words all the hidden things which go on inside of them, thus ending the conspiracy of silence with which the development of the child is now distorted both at home and at school. If the conspiracy of silence is to be replaced by the fifth freedom, children must be encouraged and helped to attend to their forbidden thoughts, and to put them into words, i.e., to talk out loud about love and hate and jealousy and fear, about curiosity over the body, its products and its apertures; about what goes in and what comes out; about their dim and confused feelings about sex itself; about the strained and stressful relationships within families, which are transplanted into schools.

Dr. Kubie's plea, and it was Sigmund Freud's foremost plea, is for awareness. If teachers are aware of the deepest needs and feelings of their students, and if the students are encouraged to become aware of their own thoughts and feelings, far more effective learning will take place.

Traditionalists and progressivists stand together in abstract acceptance of the notion that the proper study of mankind is man. Increasingly, they are sharing the awareness that Sigmund Freud contributed greatly to this study and that teachers have much to learn from him that will make them better teachers by making their students better learners.

II
Basics

Introduction

*F*or the Diamond Jubilee issue of the KAPPAN (January 1981), Harold Shane prepared an article titled "Significant Writings That Have Influenced the Curriculum: 1906-81." Eighty-four curriculum professors took part in the survey from which he drew the article. Their ratings put Ralph W. Tyler's Basic Principles of Curriculum and Instruction (1949) in a tie with John Dewey's Democracy and Education (1916) for "most influential." Other authors in the top 10 were George S. Counts and Jerome Bruner. Examples of the writing of these three appear in this chapter, which I call "Basics" because the articles deal with issues of fundamental importance. They raise questions that every educator in a leadership position must wrestle with throughout his career.

For the March 1977 KAPPAN, Kevin Ryan et al. wrote a brief biography titled "Ralph Tyler: Education's Mr. Fix-It." The occasion was the Ohio State University PDK Chapter's first Distinguished Educator Award, given to Tyler a few months earlier. The article begins: "To students of education, he is the author of Basic Principles of Curriculum and Instruction, the preeminent textbook in the field. To teachers, he is a champion of their involvement in the development of what they teach. To the higher education community, he is the former dean of the University of Chicago's Division of Social Sciences and [founding] director emeritus of the Center for Advanced Study in the Behavioral Sciences at Stanford, California. To curriculum makers in agriculture, home economics, medicine, nursing, and public health throughout the world, he is one who has helped them find their own goals and discover reasonable ways of meeting them. To administrators, he is a man with a knack for making organizations go." In short, Ralph Tyler is a modern-day Renaissance man.

Here are some of the influential posts Tyler has held: director of evaluation for the famed Eight-Year Study of Secondary Schools (1934-42); director of the Cooperative Study in General Education, a project involving 22 colleges (1939-45); director of the examination staff of the U.S. Armed Forces Institutes (1942-53); chairman of the Exploratory Committee on Assessing the Progress of Education (1963-69), which planned the National Assessment of Educational Progress; acting president of the Social Science Research Council (1971-72); and vice-chairman of the National Science Board (1962-68). He has been visiting professor at a dozen universities, including Harvard, Virginia, Ohio State, and Texas.

The late George S. Counts was one of the legendary group who made Teachers College, Columbia University, the most influential teacher education center in America for decades. When I came to know him as a member of the PDK Commission on International Relations in Education, he had retired from Columbia and was teaching at Southern Illinois University, Carbondale, which assembled a number of elder statesmen in its School of Education. His first KAPPAN article during my tenure as editor was part of a series called "Classics Revisited," in which we asked educators to review their best-known works. Counts chose to review Dare the Schools Build a New Social Order? *under the title "Dare the School Build the Great Society?" and using the byline G. Sylvester Counts. He called himself a "very close relative" of George S. Counts. Like most of the other authors in this series, he stuck by the ideas expressed a generation earlier. I preferred to reprint "Should the Teacher Always Be Neutral?" in this anthology because it displays the humor and benign wisdom that made Counts a favorite among his students.*

Robert Ebel, professor of education and psychology at Michigan State University for many years, has written 10 articles for the KAPPAN *and served a four-year term as an editorial consultant. I have always found his work closely reasoned and logically compelling. "What Are Schools For?," the piece I chose to include here, brought more favorable mail to Ebel than any other article he has written. It also brought letters like this to the editor: "Hosanna! Someone has finally dared take a few whacks at the curriculum tree, which has begun to look like an overladen Christmas decoration." Of course, Ebel was not the first influential educator to suggest that the schools attempt too much. But not many authors say it so well.*

Ebel retired from Michigan State at the end of June 1981, after a career of extraordinary achievement. He was president of the American Educational Research Association when he wrote the article reprinted here, and had just completed editing the fourth edition of the Encyclopedia of Educational Research. *He continues to live in East Lansing, but says he will now do only the things he likes to do.*

Only one article by Jerome Bruner has appeared in the pages of the KAPPAN. *Among other reasons, I chose to reprint it here because Bruner is the lone "Classics Revisited" author who, upon deepening his study of education, found his "classic" (*The Process of Education*) faulty. Bruner, now visiting scholar in psychology and social relations on the arts and sciences faculty at Harvard, was director of the Center for Cognitive Studies there when he wrote the paper on which this article was based. It was delivered as a speech at the annual conference of the Association for Supervision and Curriculum Development in March 1971. In a sense, the speech ended the 10-year reign of curriculum structuralists whose ideas were popular after the Soviet Union orbited Sputnik I in 1957.*

John Goodlad, dean of the Graduate School of Education, University of California at Los Angeles, emerged in the Seventies as one of our most highly regarded contemporary leaders of educational thought. Since 1975 Phi Delta Kappa has published several articles under his byline, including a co-authored series on "A Study of Schooling," an ambitious project supported by the U.S. Office of Education and several major foundations, and a book, What Schools Are For *(1979). Goodlad continues to direct research for* /I/D/E/A/, *the education arm of the Kettering Foundation.* "Can Our Schools Get Better?" *won an award in 1979 from the Educational Press Association of America in the "learned article" category.*

—*SME*

Emphasize Tasks
Appropriate for the School
by Ralph W. Tyler

A student of the behavioral sciences identifies six kinds of learning best undertaken by the high school. Other kinds should be left to other agencies, he suggests.

The spectacular success of the American high school in the past half century is a major source of present difficulty. Because it has attracted a high proportion of American youth, because most high school students like the school and like the work they are doing there, and because high school graduates have learned things that easily differentiate them from those who have not attended high school, the public thinks of the high school as the logical institution to assume all the significant responsibilities for youth. Whatever the educational demand of the moment—driver education, elimination of juvenile delinquency, "air age" education, swimming and other sports, specific vocational skills—the American public views the high school as not only capable of assuming successfully almost any conceivable task of education or training but also as the proper agency to undertake any such job that seems important to some group. No clear basis that the high school can use in selecting the tasks it should undertake is commonly recognized in America.

Discussions of this problem are frequently confused by arguments regarding the values of learning to drive safely, of wholesome recreation, of appreciating the contributions of aviation, of learning to swim and to participate in other sports, and of acquiring specific occupational skills. These are not the primary issues facing secondary education. Many of the jobs the high schools are urged to do are worthwhile and many of them the schools can do effectively. The essential point to be made is that the total educational task involved in inducting youth into responsible adulthood is far too great for any one of our social institutions to undertake effectively. Only by the fullest utilization of the potential educational efforts of home, church, school, recreational agencies, youth-serving organizations, the library, the press, motion pictures, radio, television, and other formal and informal activities can this nation meet its educational needs. Modern society is highly complex and requires of its members knowledge, skills, attitudes, and practices of a range and level far beyond those required a generation ago. And yet a baby born today is indistinguishable from babies born at the birth of our nation. It is only through education—that is, through things learned after birth—that man becomes competent to live in a modern world rather than in a primitive culture. Hence, the educational task is a tremendous one that can only be met by the enlistment of all relevant resources. Failure to encourage and to help other institutions to bear part of the responsibility inevitably weakens our total social structure and reduces the effectiveness of our total educational achievements.

Encourage Other Educational Agencies

Yet this is what we do when we in the schools assume responsibilities that can be discharged by others. Reduced working hours give many adults time to teach driving, swimming, and the like. Churches and other institutions are seeking channels through which to serve youth. Many industries are able to provide on-the-job training. Few, if any, communities adequately utilize the educational potential available outside the school. Instead, they waste the precious resources of the school on jobs that others can do. It is clear that two things are necessary: We need to organize community understanding and leadership for a wide attack upon the total educational job, and we must clearly differentiate the educational responsibilities of the school from those of other agencies.

In identifying the tasks that are particularly appropriate for the school, its special characteristics need to be carefully considered. One major feature of the high school is the fact that its teachers have been educated in the arts and sciences. Frequently this characteristic is played down or overlooked because subject matter has often been viewed as dead material—a collection of items to be remembered but not a vital ingredient in life itself. Too frequently we have failed to identify the constructive role of the arts and sciences in education. Properly understood, the subject matter of these fields is not dead but can be the source of a variety of understandings, values, abilities, and the like that aid the student in living more effectively and more happily. The school should be drawing upon these resources to enrich the lives of the students. Our effort should not be to make the classroom more like life outside the school but to make life outside the school more in harmony with the values, purposes, and knowledge gained from the classroom.

This viewpoint emphasizes college and university education in the arts and sciences as a primary resource for the high school to use, but this is a valid position only insofar as the contributions of the arts and sciences are used as vital means of learning and not as dead items to recall. This can be done and often is. All of us can think of illustrations of the way in which each of the major fields of science and scholarship can provide things that open up avenues for living. In science, for example, the kinds of problems with which the scientist deals in seeking to understand natural phenomena and to gain some control over them, the methods scientists use for studying problems, the concepts they have developed for helping to understand the phenomena with which they deal, the data they are obtaining about various natural phenomena, and the generalizations they have developed for relating factors and for explaining phenomena—all these give us tools for understanding our natural world and for seeking to gain more control over it. They also give us a basis for continuing our own study and learning about natural phenomena long after high school.

The Uses of History

In history, to take another example, we find bases for understanding developments that take place over periods of time. History gives us methods for studying problems that involve the time dimension and the interrelations of political, economic, social, and intellectual life. History gives us concepts with which to think about and to understand social change. It gives us data and some generalizations. It can help the high school student to be at home in a world of change and development and to take an active, understanding role in this world.

The other subject fields can furnish similar examples of problems, methods, concepts, and generalizations so important in finding meaning and effectiveness in life. When we build the high school curriculum, the arts and sciences need to be treated as vital means of learning. They must be examined carefully for their possible contributions rather than viewed as matters of rote memorization. Furthermore, the education of teachers in these fields should be effectively utilized. All too often we have employed teachers in jobs that do not draw upon their education. The task of the school is partly defined by this important characteristic: the employment by the high school of teachers who are educated in the arts and sciences.

The School's Unique Resources

A second significant characteristic is the skill of the high school staff in facilitating the learning of students. By and large, teachers are effective in teaching. Their training and experience have been largely focused on it. In addition to these characteristics of the teaching staff, there are three other features of the high school to be considered in selecting appropriate educational tasks. The school has special types of equipment and facilities, such as libraries and laboratories. The arrangements of enrollment and attendance in the high school permit the organization of learning experiences over a considerable period of time. The high school has built a tradition commonly recognized and respected in the community. This tradition includes such elements as impartiality, objectivity, and concern for human values. These are very important characteristics not possessed in equal degree by other social institutions. The kinds of jobs the school undertakes should primarily be those that depend upon these characteristics, since they provide for unique contributions.

Considering these features of the school, several kinds of educational tasks are recognized as particularly appropriate. One of these has already been mentioned, namely, learning that is based substantially upon the arts and sciences. A second is the learning of complex and difficult things that require organization of experience and distribution of practice over considerable periods of time. A number of illustrations will quickly come to mind. Probably reading and mathematics are most commonly recognized as fields in which the basic concepts and skills require careful organization, beginning with simple materials and moving gradually to more complex matters over the years of elementary and secondary school. Clearly, this kind of learning is uniquely possible in the school rather than in the less well-organized conditions of other agencies.

A third kind of educational task appropriate for the school is to provide learning where the essential factors are not obvious to one observing the phenomenon and where the principles, concepts, and meanings must be brought specially to the attention of the learner. Thus the scientific concepts and principles that explain the growth and development of plants are not obvious to the observer of plants or even to an uneducated farm hand. The school can more effectively provide for this learning than can the home or the job.

Providing Out-of-Ordinary Experience

A fourth kind of learning appropriate for the school is where the experiences required cannot be provided directly in the ordinary activities of daily life. Geography and history are excellent illustrations of fields where daily life experience alone is not likely to provide sufficient insight into historic matters and matters relating to places far removed. If young people are to develop an understanding of history, it will require the attention of a specialized agency able to provide materials serving to give vicarious experiences and to organize them effectively. The same is true for geography. We cannot depend entirely upon the informal experiences of daily life to provide these kinds of learning.

A fifth kind of learning particularly appropriate for the school is that which requires more "purified experience" than is commonly available in life outside the school. Students may learn something of art, music, literature, or human relations from the examples commonly found in the community, but where these fall far short of the best, the students have no chance to set high standards for themselves. The school can provide examples for study and enjoyment that represent the best available.

A sixth kind of learning particularly appropriate to the school is that in which reexamination and interpretation of experience are very essential. Our basic ethical values are commonly involved in the daily experiences of youth. Questions of justice, fairness, goodness arise again and again on the playground, in the marketplace, and elsewhere. It is not likely, however, that sheer contact with these ideas will be enough to help the individual youth to develop values that are clearly understood and effectively utilized. The school can provide opportunity from time to time to recall these experiences, to examine them, and seek to interpret them, thus clarifying the meaning of values as well as helping youth to appreciate them more adequately. In the realm of ethical values this type of responsibility will be shared by the home, the church, and youth organizations, but in the realm of esthetic values it is probably true that only the school is likely to provide the opportunity systematically.

These six kinds of learning that are peculiarly appropriate for the high school ought to be strongly emphasized in its program in contrast to other learnings that can be provided by other agencies. There are, of course, educational jobs that are good in themselves but do not require the particular conditions that the school provides. When the school undertakes these tasks, it must either neglect other important things or attempt more than it can do well, spreading itself too thin, and not achieving as effective educational results as it should. Concentrating its efforts upon the educational job that the high school is uniquely fitted to undertake and encouraging other community agencies in their responsibilities will greatly raise the educational level of the nation.

Should the Teacher Always Be Neutral?

by George S. Counts

A foolish consistency is the hobgoblin of little minds.
—Ralph Waldo Emerson

In my later years (I am 80 this month) I always warn my students at the first meeting of a class by quoting an old English proverb: "Old men and far travelers may lie by authority." Since I am both, having visited 17 countries, I tell them to put a question mark after everything that I tell them. An old man can say that he remembers something very well, that it happened when he was in high school. Also, if a question is raised about some other country, he can say that he traveled all over that country in his own Ford automobile. To illustrate, I tell them that the only time I ever saw Abraham Lincoln on the television screen was when he read the Emancipation Proclamation and that I can still recall the image of that tall and lean man dressed in a long black coat and wearing the sideburns and beard of the "common man"! I am reminded here of an observation made by Oscar Wilde: "To give an accurate description of what has never occurred is not merely the proper occupation of the historian, but the inalienable privilege of any man of parts and culture."

This article is supposed to be a "response" to the very interesting and challenging essay by Joe Junell.* However, I shall merely attempt to write a few words relative to the subject of indoctrination and imposition in the educative process. My involvement in this issue emerged full-blown in a debate with John Dewey at a meeting of educators in February 1932. I defended the thesis that a measure of indoctrination is inevitable, although I rejected the proposition that anything should be taught as absolutely fixed and final and rather defended the idea of "imposition" as a basic and inescapable aspect of the process of rearing the young in any society. Of course I emphasized the point that I was not using the term in a pejorative sense but in its original meaning derived from the Latin verb, *imponere*, "to place on." A few weeks later I gave an address at a meeting of teachers in New York City. Present in the rear of the auditorium was John Dewey. When the time came for questions and remarks from the floor, the great philosopher stood up and said that he had checked the meaning of the word "indoctrination" in Webster's dictionary and discovered that it meant "teaching."

It is impossible to discuss the question under consideration without an understanding of the role of culture in the life of man. First of all, we must realize that every human being is born helpless, but with infinite potential in all directions. If left alone, he would quickly perish. But being born in a society with its cultural heritage he may rise above the angels or sink below the level of the brute. We can see this demonstrated throughout the ages and obviously in this twentieth century. Although every individual is unique, he is molded by his culture and thus becomes a human being.°° Quotations from

---

°Joseph S. Junell, "Do Teachers Have the Right to Indoctrinate?," *Phi Delta Kappan*, December 1969, pp. 182-185.
°°We must realize, however, that no two individuals are identical and that every individual responds to his culture in terms of his own unique character.

two very distinguished anthropologists are most appropriate here. Graham Wallas in his *Our Social Heritage*, published in 1921, wrote that "we have become, one may say, biologically parasitic upon our social heritage." Bronislaw Malinowski in the last of his great works, *Freedom and Civilization*, published after his death in 1944, said approximately the same thing in these words: "This brief outline of the cultural background of our problem in evolutionary perspective was given to show first and foremost that not a single human act, relevant to the science of man, occurs outside the context of culture." A distinguished British mathematician, H. Levy, in his *The Universe of Science* (1932) places the capstone on the argument: "*It* [our culture] *has inherited us.*" Consequently, the nature of the human being is dependent on the culture which inherits him. Here is the supreme imposition.

Since the origin of *Homo sapiens*, education, in both its informal and its formal aspects, has embraced the total process of inducting the young into a given society with its culture, its ways of acting, feeling, and thinking, its language, its tools, its institutions, its ethical and aesthetic values, its basic ideas, religious doctrines, and philosophical presuppositions. It is therefore not an autonomous process governed by its own laws and everywhere the same. This process begins at birth and continues on through the years. And we are beginning to realize that the preschool years, the period of infancy and early childhood, are by far the most important years in the development of the talents and the molding of the character of the individual. During my first trip to the Soviet union in 1927 I became acquainted with the Commissar of Education, Anatole Lunacharsky. One day when we were discussing the Soviet program of preschool education he repeated an old Russian proverb: "We can mold a child of 5 to 6 years into anything we wish; at the age of 8 to 9 we have to bend him; at the age of 16 or 17 we must break him; and thereafter one may well say, 'only the grave can correct a hunchback!'"

Without this imposition of the culture, as all of this makes clear, man would not be man, except in a biological sense—if he could survive. But the fact should be emphasized that cultures are extremely diverse. Consequently, a human being born and reared in one culture may differ greatly from one born and reared in another culture. I have often told my students that a person doesn't see with his eyes or hear with his ears, but with what is behind his eyes or behind his ears. And this depends on his native culture and his experience therein. This principle applies even to physical objects, such as the sun, the moon, and the stars. Obviously, the moon will never again be what it was before the flight of Apollo 11.

The language that is imposed on the child from the moment of his birth may well be regarded as symbolic of the culture. Lewis Mumford in his *The Myth of the Machine* (1968) demonstrates very clearly that in the evolution of man language has played a much greater role than the machine. Indeed, without language man would not be man. And of course we all know that there are many different languages. But the truth is not sufficiently emphasized that languages differ, not only in forms and sounds but also in values. One may well say that every language, in a sense, constitutes a world apart from others. The translation of one language into another is often difficult because the "same" word will differ in meaning from one language to another. A dictionary will be of some assistance but it will not solve all the problems. The basic idea in these observations is well documented in a great book entitled *The Poetry of Freedom* (1945), edited by William Rose Benét and Norman Cousins, which is a collection of poems from the major languages of the world. More than two-thirds of the volume, 554 of the 806 pages, is devoted to poems from the English-speaking peoples. And I know that the editors did everything they could to find appropriate poems from other languages. If they had chosen some other theme, such as worship of nature or military valor or romantic love, I am certain that the proportions would have been different. It is clear therefore that language constitutes a tremendous imposition on the individual. I have often told my students that, if we do not want to impose anything on the individual, we should not allow him to learn a language until he becomes 21 years of age and then let him choose the language he prefers.

A given society is always a bearer of a particular culture, and societies vary as their cultures vary. Consequently, an education that would be appropriate for one society might destroy another. After the first Sputnik soared into outer space in October 1957, the question was asked over and over again: Is Soviet education superior to ours? The answer, of course, is that the question makes no sense because the two societies are so profoundly different. However, if the question were presented in this form the answer would be different: "Does Soviet education serve the purposes of Soviet society better than our education serves the purposes of our society?" In this case the answer might be in the affirmative, since education for a democracy is far more difficult than education for a dictatorship.

This truth has been recognized through the ages. More than two centuries ago Montesquieu in his great classic, *On the Spirit of the Laws*, wrote that "it is in a republican [democratic] government that the whole power of education is required." The reason for this resides in the fact that such a government must rest on "virtue," which involves "self-renunciation" and is "ever arduous and painful." Also, it "requires a constant preference of public to private interest," and "to inspire such love ought to be the principal business of education." Thomas Jefferson, the father of our democracy, agreed with Montesquieu. In 1824, the year before he died, he wrote in a letter to a friend: "The qualifications for self-government are not innate. They are the result of habit and long training." Horace Mann, father of our common school, saw clearly the relation of education to social and political systems. In his Ninth Annual Report (1845), he warned the citizens of Massachusetts: "If there are not two things wider asunder than freedom and slavery, then must the course of training which fits children for these opposite conditions of life be as diverse as the points to which they lead." Finally, Herbert Spencer, in his *The Americans* (1892), issued the following challenge to our education: "The republican form of government is the highest form of government; but because of this it requires the highest form of human nature—a type nowhere at present existing." In spite of the unprecedented expansion of our schools in this century, we have obviously failed to develop the "form of human nature required." To have done so would have required a revolutionary form of imposition. Political liberty, with all of its demands on human nature, if it is to endure, is certainly one of the most extraordinary impositions on the mind and character of man in the entire history of *Homo sapiens*.

We must realize also that we are living not only in a very special kind of society but also in an age of revolution as wide as the planet. Henry Steele

Commager, in his *The American Mind* (1950), warned us that "the decade of the Nineties [was] the watershed of American history"—a watershed between an "America predominantly agricultural" and an "America predominantly urban and industrial." And Carl Bridenbaugh stated without equivocation in his inaugural address as president of the American Historical Association in 1963, "It is my conviction that the greatest turning point in all human history, of which we have any record, has occurred within the twentieth century." Thus, in view of the swiftness of social change, we may say that an education that may be appropriate for one generation may not be appropriate for another. We are consequently confronted today with William F. Ogburn's "cultural lag" and Alfred North Whitehead's generation gap. The fact is that since crossing the great watershed we have never sat down and considered seriously how our children and youth should spend their years in our urbanized and industrialized society. Also, with the reduction of the earth to the dimensions of a neighborhood, we have failed to sense that the age of tribalism and nationalism is closing and that a new age of internationalism is well over the horizon. The nature of the imposition must be radically altered.

A few words in closing about the school. We must realize that, whenever choices are made in the launching of a program, values are involved. This is obviously true in the shaping of the curriculum, the selection of textbooks, the giving of grades, the organization of social activities, the construction of a school building, the hanging of pictures and paintings on the walls of a schoolroom, and in the selection of a teacher. I have often told my students that, if we want to avoid imposing anything on our children, we should alter the architectural style of the building every day. Also, I call their attention to the fact that our arithmetic textbooks transmit to the younger generation countless social, political, and moral ideas—for the most part a white middle-class culture. And we know that our history textbooks, until very recently, practically excluded the Negro.

The need for developing the independent and critical mind in the members of the younger generation is implicit in much that I have written and is clearly a form of imposition. However, something more must be said. The student should not be encouraged to engage in criticism just for the sake of criticism. The truly critical mind is one of the most precious resources of a free society. At the same time such a mind should be highly disciplined. We should never disregard the basic thesis of Carl Becker in his *Freedom and Responsibility in the American Way of Life* (1945), one of the most insightful books in the literature of our democracy. That thesis is that with every right or freedom there goes a responsibility. The alternative is chaos and anarchy. The critical mind should be armed with knowledge and understanding, and perhaps with a modicum of humility and wisdom. Even a scientist must undergo and practice a severe discipline. He must practice the intellectual virtues of accuracy, precision, truthfulness, open-mindedness, and absolute integrity. The limits of freedom in the rearing of the child are thus expressed by Bronislaw Malinowski in his *Freedom and Civilization:* "We see quite clearly why the freedom of the child, in the sense of letting him do what he wishes and as he likes, is unreal. In the interest of his own organism he has constantly to be trammeled in education from acts which are biologically dangerous or are culturally useless." And Judge Learned Hand, one of our foremost students of jurisprudence, warned us: "A society in which men recognize no check upon their freedom soon becomes a society where freedom is a possession of only a savage few."

The big question, therefore, is not whether we should impose anything on the child in the process of education but *what* we should impose. In the swiftly changing world of the twentieth century we must certainly examine our cultural heritage critically in the light of the great and inescapable realities of the present age and the trends toward tomorrow. What this means, in my opinion, is to present to the younger generation a vision of the possibility of finally fulfilling the great promise of America expressed in the Declaration of Independence: "We hold these truths to be self-evident, that all men are created equal, that they are endowed by their Creator with certain unalienable Rights, that among these are Life, Liberty, and the pursuit of Happiness." Clearly, if science and technology can show us how to fly to the moon and circumnavigate the planets, we should be able to employ these powerful forces for bringing our practices into harmony with our historic professions.

A final illustration of the critical importance of the question of imposition in the rearing of the young in our democracy is clearly revealed in our treatment of the Negro down through the generations. Gunnar Myrdal, a renowned Swedish social scientist, in his great two-volume work, *An American Dilemma* (1944), issues a challenge that we can disregard only at our peril. In his first chapter, entitled "American Ideals and the American Conscience," he states: "America, compared to every other country in Western civilization, large or small, has the *most explicitly expressed* system of general ideals in reference to human interrelations." These ideals embrace "the essential dignity of the individual human being, of the fundamental equality of all men, and of certain inalienable rights to freedom, justice, and a fair opportunity." Our dilemma is the consequence of the great gap between our professed ideals and our practices. He adds, therefore, that "the treatment of the Negro is America's greatest and most conspicuous scandal, . . . America's greatest failure." And then he relates this condition to the subject of my article in the following generalization: "The simple fact is that an educational offensive against racial intolerance, going deeper than the reiteration of the 'glittering generalities' in the nation's political creed, has never seriously been attempted in America." Certainly a major problem confronting our program of education is the resolution of this *dilemma* in the shortest possible period of time. But to achieve this goal the teacher cannot be neutral and the essence of the traditional pattern of imposition in our culture must be reversed.

What Are Schools For?
by Robert L. Ebel

Perhaps, after all, they are where the young should learn useful knowledge.

When the history of our times is written, it may designate the two decades following World War II as the golden age of American education. Never before was education more highly valued. Never before was so much of it so readily available to so many. Never before had it been supported so generously. Never before was so much expected of it.

But in this eighth decade of the twentieth century public education in this country appears to be in trouble. Taxpayers are revolting against the skyrocketing costs of education. Schools are being denied the funds they say they need for quality education. Teachers are uniting to press demands for higher pay and easier working conditions.

College and high school students have rebelled against what they call "the Establishment," resisting and overturning regulations, demanding pupil-directed rather than teacher-directed education, and turning in some cases to drink, drugs, and delinquency. Minorities are demanding equal treatment, which is surely their right. But when integration makes social differences more visible, and when equality of opportunity is not followed quickly by equality of achievement, frustration turns to anger that sometimes leads to violence.

Surely these problems are serious enough. But I believe there is one yet more serious, because it lies closer to the heart of our whole educational enterprise. We seem to have lost sight of, or become confused about, our main function as educators, our principal goal, our reason for existence. We have no good answer that we are sure of and can agree on to the question, What are schools for?

It may seem presumptuous of me to suggest that I know the answer to this question. Yet the answer I will give is the answer that an overwhelming majority of our fellow citizens would also give. It is the answer that would have been given by most educators of the past who established and operated schools. Indeed, the only reason the question needs to be asked and answered at this time is that some influential educators have been conned into accepting wrong answers to the question. Let me mention a few of these wrong answers:

● Schools are not custodial institutions responsible for coping with emotionally disturbed or incorrigible young people, for keeping nonstudents off the streets or out of the job market.

● Schools are not adjustment centers, responsible for helping young people develop favorable self-concepts, solve personal problems, and come to terms with life.

● Schools are not recreational facilities designed to entertain and amuse, to cultivate the enjoyment of freedom, to help young people find strength through joy.

● Schools are not social research agencies, to which a society can properly delegate responsibility for the discovery of solutions to the problems that are currently troubling the society.

I do not deny that society needs to be concerned about some of the things just mentioned. What I do deny is that schools were built and are maintained primarily to solve such problems. I deny that schools are good places in which to seek solutions, or that they have demonstrated much success in finding them. Schools have a very important special mission. If they accept responsibility for solving many of the other problems that trouble some young people, they are likely to fail in their primary mission, without having much success in solving the rest of our social problems.

Then what is the right answer to the question, What are schools for? I believe it is that schools are for learning, and that what ought to be learned mainly is useful knowledge.

Not all educators agree. Some of them discount the value of knowledge in the modern world. They say we ought to strive for the cultivation of intellectual skills. Others claim that schools have concentrated too much on knowledge, to the neglect of values, attitudes, and such affective dispositions. Still others argue that the purpose of education is to change behavior. They would assess its effectiveness by examining the pupil's behavior or performance. Let us consider these three alternatives in reverse order.

If the schools are to be accountable for the performance of their pupils, the question that immediately arises is, What performance? A direct answer to this question is, The performance you've been trying to teach. But that answer is not as simple or as obviously correct as it seems at first glance. Many schools have not been primarily concerned with teaching pupils to perform. They have been trying to develop their pupils' knowledge, understanding, attitudes, interests, and ideals; their cognitive capabilities and affective dispositions rather than their performances. Those who manage such schools would agree that capabilities and dispositions can only be assessed by observing performances, but they would insist that the performances themselves are not the goals of achievement, only the indicators of it. A teacher who is concerned with the pupil's cognitive capabilities and affective dispositions will teach quite differently, they point out, than one whose attention is focused solely on the pupil's performances. And, if performances are not goals but only indicators, we should choose the ones to use in assessment on the basis of their effectiveness as indicators. Clearly, we cannot choose them in terms of the amount of effort we made to develop them.

But, if we reject performance goals, another question arises: What should be the relative emphasis placed on affective dispositions as opposed to cognitive capabilities? Here is another issue that divides professional educators. To some, how the pupil feels—his happiness, his interest, his self-concept, his yearnings—are what should most concern teachers. To others the pupil's cognitive resources and capabilities are the main concern. Both would agree that cognition and affect interact, and that no school ought to concentrate solely on one and ignore the other. But they disagree on which should receive primary emphasis.

In trying to resolve this issue it may be helpful to begin by observing that the instructional programs of almost all schools are aimed directly at the cultivation of cognitive competence. Pupils are taught how to read and to use mathematics; how to write and to express perceptions, feelings, ideas, and desires in writing, to be acquainted with history and to understand science. The pupil's affective dispositions, his feelings, attitudes, interests, etc., constitute conditions that facilitate or inhibit cognitive achievement. They may be enhanced by success or impaired by failure. But they are by-products, not the main products, of the instructional effort. It is almost impossible to find any school that has planned and successfully operated an instructional program aimed primarily at the attainment of affective goals.

That this situation exists does not prove that it ought to exist. But it does suggest that there may be reasons. And we need not look too far to discover what they probably are.

Feelings are essentially unteachable. They can not be passed along from teacher to learner in the way that information is transmitted. Nor can the learner acquire them by pursuing them directly, as he might acquire understanding by study. Feelings are almost always the consequence of something—of success or failure, of duty done or duty ignored, of danger encountered or danger escaped. Further, good feelings (and bad feelings also, fortunately) are seldom if ever permanent possessions. They tend to be highly ephemeral. The surest prediction that one can make when he feels particularly good, strong, wise, or happy is that sooner or later he is going to feel bad, weak, foolish, or sad. In these circumstances it is hardly suprising that feelings are difficult to teach.

Nor do they need to be taught. A newborn infant has, or quickly develops, a full complement of them—pain, rage, satiety, drowsiness, vitality, joy, love, and all the rest. Experience may attach these feelings to new objects. It may teach the wisdom of curbing the expression of certain feelings at inappropriate times or in inappropriate ways. And while such attachments and curbings may be desirable, and may be seen as part of the task of the school, they hardly qualify as one of its major missions.

The school has in fact a much more important educational mission than affective education, one which in the current cultural climate and educational fashion is being badly neglected. I refer to moral education—the inculcation of the young of the accumulated moral wisdom of the race. Some of our young people have been allowed to grow up as virtual moral illiterates. And as Joseph Junell points out elsewhere in this *KAPPAN*,* we are paying a heavy price for this neglect as the youth of our society become alienated, turn to revolt, and threaten the destruction of our social fabric.

This change in our perception of the function of the school is reflected in our statements of educational objectives. A century ago Horace Mann, Herbert Spencer, and most others agreed that there were three main aspects of education: intellectual, moral, and physical. Today the main aspects identified by our taxonomies of objectives are cognitive, affective, and psychomotor. The first and third elements in these two triads are essentially identical. The second elements are quite different. The change reflects a shift in emphasis away from the pupil's duties and toward his feelings.

Why has this come about? Perhaps because of the current emphasis in our society on individual liberty rather than on personal responsibility. Perhaps because we have felt it necessary to be more concerned with civil rights than with civic duties. Perhaps because innovation and change look better to us than tradition and stability. Perhaps because we have come to trust and honor the vigor of youth more than the wisdom of age.

*Joseph S. Junell, "The Limits of Social Education," *Phi Delta Kappan*, September 1972, pp. 12-15.

In all these things we may have been misled. As we view the contemporary culture in this country, it is hard to see how the changes that have taken place in our moral values during the last half century have brought any visible improvement in the quality of our lives. It may be time for the pendulum to start swinging back toward an emphasis on responsibility, on stability, on wisdom. Older people are not always wiser people, but wisdom does grow with experience, and experience does accumulate with age.

Schools have much to contribute to moral education if they choose to do so, and if the courts and the public will let them. The rules of conduct and discipline adopted and enforced in the school, the models of excellence and humanity provided by the teachers, can be powerful influences in moral education. The study of history can teach pupils a decent respect for the lessons in morality that long experience has gradually taught the human race. Schools in the Soviet Union today appear to be doing a much more effective job of moral education than we have done in recent years. This fact alone may be enough to discredit moral education in some eyes. But concern for moral education has also been expressed by educational leaders in the democracies.

Albert North Whitehead put the matter this way at the end of his essay on the aims of education:

> "The essence of education is that it be religious."
> "Pray, what is religious education?"
> "A religious education is an education which inculcates duty and reverence. Duty arises from our potential control over the course of events. Where attainable knowledge could have changed this issue, ignorance has the guilt of vice. And the foundation of reverence is this perception, that the present holds within itself the complete sum of existence, backwards and forwards, that whole amplitude of time which is eternity."[1]

If these views are correct, moral education deserves a much higher priority among the tasks of the school than does affective education. But it does not deserve the highest priority. That spot must be reserved for the cultivation of cognitive competence. Human beings need strong moral foundations, as part of their cultural heritage. They also need a structure of knowledge as part of their intellectual heritage. What schools were primarily built to do, and what they are most capable of doing well, is to help the student develop cognitive competence.

What is cognitive competence? Two distinctly different answers have been given. One is that it requires acquisition of knowledge. The other is that it requires development of intellectual skills. Here is another issue on which educational specialists are divided.

To avoid confusion or superficiality on this issue it is necessary to be quite clear on the meanings attached to the terms *knowledge* and *intellectual skills*. Knowledge, as the term is used here, is not synonymous with information. Knowledge is built out of information by thinking. It is an integrated structure of relationships among concepts and propositions. A teacher can give his students information. He cannot give them knowledge. A student must earn the right to say "I know" by his own thoughtful efforts to understand.

Whatever a person experiences directly in living or vicariously by reading or listening can become part of his knowledge. It will become part of his knowledge if he succeeds in integrating that experience into the structure of his knowledge, so that it makes sense, is likely to be remembered, and will be available for use when needed. Knowledge is essentially a private possession. Information can be made public. Knowledge cannot. Hence it would be more appropriate to speak of a modern-day information explosion than of a knowledge explosion.

The term *intellectual skills* has also been used with a variety of meanings. Further, those who use it often do not say, precisely and clearly, what they mean by it. Most of them seem not to mean skill in specific operations, such as spelling a word, adding two fractions, diagramming a sentence, or balancing a chemical equation. They are likely to conceive of intellectual skills in much broader terms, such as observing, classifying, measuring, communicating, predicting, inferring, experimenting, formulating hypotheses, and interpreting data.

It seems clear that these broader intellectual skills cannot be developed or used very effectively apart from substantial bodies of relevant knowledge. To be skillful in formulating hypotheses about the cause of a patient's persistent headaches, one needs to know a considerable amount of neurology, anatomy, and physiology, as much as possible about the known disorders that cause headaches, and a great deal about the history and habits of the person who is suffering them. That is, to show a particular intellectual skill a person must possess the relevant knowledge. (Note well at this point that a person cannot look up the knowledge he needs, for knowledge, in the sense of the term as we use it, cannot be looked up. Only information can be looked up. Knowledge has to be built by the knower himself.) And, if he does possess the relevant knowledge, what else does he need in order to show the desired skill?

Intellectual skill that goes beyond knowledge can be developed in specific operations like spelling a word or adding fractions. But the more general (and variable from instance to instance) the operation becomes, the less likely it is that a person's intellectual skills will go far beyond his knowledge.

Those who advocate the development of intellectual skills as the principal cognitive aim of education often express the belief (or hope) that these skills will be broadly transferable from one area of subject matter to another. But if the subjects are quite different, the transfer is likely to be quite limited. Who would hire a man well trained in the measurement of personal characteristics for the job of measuring stellar distances and compositions?

Those who advocate the cultivation of knowledge as the central focus of our educational efforts are sometimes asked, "What about wisdom? Isn't that more important than knowledge?"

To provide a satisfactory answer to this question we need to say clearly what we mean when we speak of wisdom. In some situations wisdom is simply an alias for good fortune. He who calls the plays in a football game, who designs a new automobile, or who plays the stock market is likely to be well acquainted with this kind of wisdom—and with its constant companion, folly. If an action that might turn out badly in fact turns out well, we call it an act of wisdom. If it turns out badly, it was clearly an act of folly.

But there is more than this to the relation of knowledge to wisdom. C. I. Lewis of Harvard has expressed that relation in this way:

Where ability to make correct judgments of value is concerned, we more typically speak of wisdom, perhaps, than of knowledge. And "wisdom" connotes one character which is not knowledge at all, though it is quality inculcated by experience; the temper, namely, which avoids perversity in intentions, and the insufficiently considered in actions. But for the rest, wisdom and knowledge are distinct merely because there is so much of knowledge which, for any given individual or under the circumstances which obtain, is relatively inessential to judgment of values and to success in action. Thus a man may be pop-eyed with correct information and still lack wisdom, because his information has little bearing on those judgments of relative value which he is called upon to make, or because he lacks capacity to discriminate the practically important from the unimportant, or to apply his information to concrete problems of action. And men of humble attainments, so far as breadth of information goes, may still be wise by their correct apprehension of such values as lie open to them and of the roads to these. But surely wisdom is a type of knowledge; that type which is oriented on the important and the valuable. The wise man is he who knows where good lies, and how to act so that it may be attained.[2]

I take Professor Lewis to mean that, apart from the rectitude in purposes and the deliberateness in action that experience must teach, wisdom in action is dependent on relevant knowledge. If that is so, the best the schools can do to foster wisdom is to help students cultivate knowledge.

Our conclusion at this point is that schools should continue to emphasize cognitive achievements as the vast majority of them have been doing. Some of you may not be willing to accept this conclusion. You may believe some other goal deserves higher priority in the work of the school, perhaps something like general ability to think (apart from any particular body of knowledge), or perhaps having the proper affective dispositions, or stable personal adjustment, or simply love of learning.

If you do, you ought to be prepared to explain how different degrees of attainment of the goal you would support can be determined. For if you cannot do this, if you claim your favored goal is intangible and hence unmeasurable, there is room for strong suspicion that it may not really be very important (since it has no clearly observable concomitants or consequences to render it tangible and measurable). Or perhaps the problem is that you don't have a very concrete idea of what it is you propose as a goal.

Let us return to the question of what schools are for, and in particular, for what they should be accountable. It follows from what has been said about the purposes of schooling, and about the cooperation required from the student if those purposes are to be achieved, that the school should not accept responsibility for the learning achievement of every individual pupil. The essential condition for learning is the purposeful activity, the willingness to work hard to learn, of the individual learner. Learning is not a gift any school can give. It is a prize the learner himself must pursue. If a pupil is unwilling or unable to make the effort required, he will learn little in even the best school.

Does this mean that a school should give the student maximum freedom to learn, that it should abandon prescribed curricula and course content in favor of independent study on projects selected by the pupils themselves? I do not think so. Surely all learning must be done by the learner himself, but a good teacher can motivate, direct, and assist the learning process to great advantage. For a school to model its instructional program after the kind of free learning pupils do on their own out of school is to abandon most of its special value as a school, most of its very reason for existence.

Harry Broudy and John Palmer, discussing the demise of the kind of progressive education advocated by Dewey's disciple William H. Kilpatrick, had this to say about the predecessors of our contemporary free schools and open classrooms:

> A technically sophisticated society simply does not dare leave the acquisition of systematized knowledge to concomitant learning, the by-products of projects that are themselves wholesome slices of juvenile life. Intelligence without systematized knowledge will do only for the most ordinary, everyday problems. International amity, survival in our atomic age, automation, racial integration, are not common everyday problems to which common-sense knowledge and a sense of decency are adequate.[3]

Like Broudy and Palmer, I believe that command of useful knowledge is likely to be achieved most rapidly and most surely when the individual pupil's effort to learn is motivated, guided, and assisted by expert instruction. Such instruction is most likely to occur, and to be most efficient and effective, when given in classes, not to individuals singly.

If the school is not held to account for the success of each of its pupils in learning, for what should it be accountable? I would say that it should accept responsibility for providing a favorable learning environment. Such an environment, in my view, is one in which the student's efforts to learn are:

1. guided and assisted by a capable, enthusiastic teacher;

2. facilitated by an abundance of books, films, apparatus, equipment, and other instructional materials;

3. stimulated and rewarded by both formal and informal recognition of achievement; and

4. reinforced by the example and the help of other interested, hard-working students.

The first two of these aspects of a favorable learning environment are unlikely to be seriously questioned. But perhaps a word or two needs to be said in defense of the other two. First, what of the need for formal recognition and reward of achievement as a stimulus of efforts to achieve?

In the long run learning may be its own reward. But the experience of generations of good teachers has shown that in the short run learning is greatly facilitated by more immediate recognition and rewards. This means words of praise and of reproof, which good teachers have used from ancient time. It means tests and grades, reports and honors, diplomas and degrees. These formal means and occasions for recognizing and rewarding achievement are built into our system of education. We will do well to retain them, to disregard the perennial advice of educational reformers that such so-called extrinsic incentives to achievement be abandoned—unless, of course, we are also willing to abandon excellence as a goal for our efforts.

Next, what of the influence of classmates in either stimulating, assisting, and rewarding efforts to achieve, or disparaging and ridiculing those efforts? In the experience of many teachers these positive or negative influences can be very strong. Of course a teacher's attitudes and behavior can tend to encourage or discourage learning. But much also depends on the attitudes the students bring with them to the class. If they are interested and prepared to work hard, learning can be productive fun. If not, learning is likely to be listless and unproductive.

There may be some teachers with a magic touch that can convert an uninterested, unwilling class into a group of eager learners. I myself have encountered such teachers only in movies or novels. Surely they are too rare to count on for solving the problems of motivation to learn, especially in some of the more difficult situations. For the most part, motivation to learn is an attitude a student has or lacks well before a particular course of instruction ever begins.

Going to school is an opportunity, and ought to be so regarded by all pupils. The good intentions that led us to enact compulsory schooling laws have trapped us. School attendance can be made compulsory. School learning cannot be. So some of our classrooms are loaded with youths who have no wish to be there, whose aim is not to learn but to escape from learning. Such a classroom is not a favorable learning environment.

The remedy is obvious. No upper grade or high school young person ought to be allowed in a class unless he wants to take advantage of the opportunity it offers. Keeping him there under compulsion will do him no good, and will do others in the class harm. Compulsory school attendance laws were never intended to create such a problem for teachers and school officials. Have we the wit to recognize the source of this problem, and the courage to act to correct it?

Let me now recapitulate what I have tried to say about what schools are for.

1. Public education in America today is in trouble.

2. Though many conditions contribute to our present difficulties, the fundamental cause is our own confusions concerning the central purpose of our activities.

3. Schools have been far too willing to accept responsibility for solving all of the problems of young people, for meeting all of their immediate needs. That schools have failed to discharge these obligations successfully is clearly evident.

4. Schools are for learning. They should bend most of their efforts to the facilitation of learning.

5. The kind of learning on which schools should concentrate most of their efforts is cognitive competence, the command of useful knowledge.

6. Knowledge is a structure of relationships among concepts. It must be built by the learner himself as he seeks understanding of the information he has received.

7. Affective dispositions are important by-products of all human experience, but they seldom are or should be the principal targets of our educational efforts. We should be much more concerned with moral education than with affective education.

8. Intellectual skills are more often praised as educational goals than defined clearly enough to be taught effectively. Broadly general intellectual

skills are mainly hypothetical constructs that are hard to demonstrate in real life. Highly specific intellectual skills are simply aspects of knowledge.

9. Wisdom depends primarily on knowledge, secondarily on experience.

10. Schools should not accept responsibility for the success of every pupil in learning, since that success depends so much on the pupil's own efforts.

11. Learning is a personal activity that each student must carry on for himself.

12. Individual learning is greatly facilitated by group instruction.

13. Schools should be held accountable for providing a good learning environment, which consists of a) capable, enthusiastic teachers, b) abundant and appropriate instructional materials, c) formal recognition and reward of achievement, and d) a class of willing learners.

14. Since learning cannot be made compulsory, school attendance ought not to be compulsory either.

Schools ought to be held accountable. One way or another, they surely will be held accountable. If they persist in trying to do too many things, things they were not designed and are not equipped to do well, things that in some cases cannot be done at all, they will show up badly when called to account. But there is one very important thing they were designed and are equipped to do well, and that many schools have done very well in the past. That is to cultivate cognitive competence, to foster the learning of useful knowledge. If they keep this as their primary aim and do not allow unwilling learners to sabotage the learning process, they are likely to give an excellent accounting of their effectiveness and worth.

---

1. In *The Aims of Education* (New York: The Macmillan Company, 1929).

2. C. I. Lewis, *An Analysis of Knowledge and Valuation* (LaSalle, Ill.: Open Court, 1946).

3. Harry S. Broudy and John R. Palmer, *Exemplars of Teaching Method* (Chicago: Rand McNally, 1965).

The Process of Education Revisited
by Jerome S. Bruner

*"I believe I would be quite satisfied to declare, if not a mora-
torium, then something of a deemphasis on matters that have to
do with the structure of history, the structure of physics, the
nature of mathematical consistency, and deal with them rather
in the context of the problems that face us."*

Ten years have passed since *The Process of Education* was published—a
decade of enormous change in the perspective and emphasis of educational
reform. I am torn between beginning my account as an archaeologist reconstructing that period by its products, or beginning with a message of revolutionary import. I shall moderate both impulses, begin with a bit of archaeology, and show how my excavations led me to a certain revolutionary zeal.

Let me reconstruct the period in which *The Process of Education* came
into being. Nineteen fifty-nine was a time of great concern over the intellectual aimlessness of our schools. Great strides had been made in many fields of
knowledge, and these advances were not being reflected in what was taught
in our schools. A huge gap had grown between what might be called the head
and the tail of the academic procession. There was great fear, particularly,
that we were not producing enough scientists and engineers.

It was the period shortly after Sputnik I. The great problem faced by
some of my colleagues in Cambridge at the time was that modern physics and
mathematics were not represented in the curriculum, yet many of the decisions that society had to make were premised on being able to understand
modern science. Something had to be done to assure that the ordinary decision maker within the society would have a sound basis for decision. The task
was to get started on the teaching of science and, later, other subjects. They
were innocent days. But beware such judgments rendered in retrospect. At
worst, the early period suffered an excess of rationalism.

The prevailing notion was that if you understood the structure of knowledge, then that understanding would permit you to go ahead on your own;
you did not need to encounter everything in nature in order to know nature,
but by understanding some deep principles you could extrapolate to the particulars as needed. Knowing was a canny strategy whereby you could know a
great deal about a lot of things while keeping very little in mind.

This view essentially opened the possibility that those who understood a
field well—the practitioners of the field—could work with teachers to produce new curricula. For the first time in the modern age, the acme of scholarship, even in our great research institutes and universities, was to convert
knowledge into pedagogy, to turn it back to aid the learning of the young. It
was a brave idea and a noble one, for all its pitfalls. It is an idea that still bears
close scrutiny, and we shall give it some later.

It was this point of view that emerged from the famous Woods Hole conference on improving education in science (the impetus and inspiration for
The Process of Education). No curriculum project in the first five years after

that was worth its salt unless it could sport a Nobel laureate or two on its letterhead!

The rational structuralism of Woods Hole had its internal counterpoise in intuitionism—the espousal of good guessing, of courage to make leaps, to go a long way on a little. It was mind at its best, being active, extrapolative, innovative, going from something firmly held to areas that were not so firmly known in order to have a basis for test. Of course, everybody knew that good teachers always have encouraged such use of mind. But perhaps good teachers were being driven underground by the prevailing literalism. . . .

At Woods Hole and after there was also a great emphasis on active learning, poking into things yourself, an emphasis on active discovery rather than upon the passive consumption of knowledge. It, too, derived from the idea that making things one's own was an activity that would get things structured in one's own way rather than as in the book. Some enthusiasts ran away with the idea of the "discovery method," that one should even discover the names of the constellations! It is a modest idea, but with profound consequences, some of which were not understood at the time—and we shall come back to it.

During the early Sixties, in various projects, it was discovered again and again how difficult it was to get to the limit of children's competence when the teaching was good. . . . No wonder then that we concluded that any subject could be taught in some honest form to any child at any stage in his development. This did not necessarily mean that it could be taught in its final form, but it did mean that basically there was a courteous translation that could reduce ideas to a form that young students could grasp. *Not* to provide such translation was discourteous to them. The pursuit of this ideal was probably the most important outcome of the great period of curriculum building in the Sixties.

With all of this there went a spirit and attitude toward students. The learner was not one kind of person, the scientist or historian another kind. The schoolboy learning physics did so as a physicist rather than as a consumer of some facts wrapped in what came to be called at Woods Hole a "middle language." A middle language talks *about* the subject rather than talking the subject.

I recall a dark day on Cape Cod, the day after the conference ended. It was raining. We, the steering committee, thought surely the whole enterprise had been wrongly conceived. We would end, we feared, by turning the educational Establishment against us and science. Then *The Process of Education* was published. It was acclaimed. I want to tell you about acclaim. Acclaim is very hard to cope with if you have business in mind. For once something is acclaimed it can be ignored in a noble way. The acclaim from which we suffered was that each reader-teacher picked the part he liked best and proclaimed it was exactly what *he* was doing! But the period of being acclaimed into impotence passed as new curricula began to appear.

Producing curriculum turned out to be not quite as we academics had thought. Something a bit strained would happen when one caused to work together a most gifted and experienced teacher and an equally gifted and experienced scientist, historian, or scholar. There was much to be learned on both sides, and the process was slow and decisions had to be made about the level at which one wanted to pitch the effort—the college-bound, the "average," the slum kid?

There were aspects of the undertaking that we had not counted on—mostly after the production. One was the problem of bureaucracy in education (the subject of an entire yearbook recently published by the ASCD), including the issues of adoption and distribution of materials, etc. A second was an even deeper problem: the training of teachers to use curricula. Both of these remain unresolved—the first constrained by fiscal difficulties, the second by the genuinely puzzling questions of teacher recruitment, training, and supervision. I cannot pretend to competence in this area. . . .

So much for the archaeology. What I should like to do now is shift to other matters more concerned with present and future.

The movement of which *The Process of Education* was a part was based on a formula of faith: that learning was what students wanted to do, that they wanted to achieve an expertise in some particular subject matter. Their motivation was taken for granted. It also accepted the tacit assumption that everybody who came to these curricula in the schools already had been the beneficiary of the middle-class hidden curricula that taught them analytic skills and launched them in the traditionally intellectual use of mind.

Failure to question these assumptions has, of course, caused much grief to all of us. Let me quote from the preface of a book I have just written, *The Relevance of Education:*[1]

> This book is built around essays written between 1964 and 1970, years of deep and tumultuous change. They were disturbing years. They had an impact in their own right, amplified by my increasingly strong involvement during the period with very young human beings. These were my "subjects" in experiments and observations. The contrast between the exterior social turbulence and the human helplessness I was studying kept imposing itself.
>
> The period of these essays is the period of the elaboration of youth culture, with its concomitant revolt against "establishment" schooling. It extends from Berkeley to Columbia, through the Harvard bust and the Sorbonne riots, to the Prague spring and summer, and the beginnings of the long and cruel winter that followed. In our own universities we have gone from the salad days of "new colleges" to the present "hard line" of so many faculties. The young began the period in political activism; then there was the sharp fire of a new extremism; now, in . . . early . . . 1971, it is a new disengagement.
>
> Through the turmoil and idealism of these years has run a theme of "naturalness," of "spontaneity," of the immediacy of learning through direct encounter. A distrust of traditional ways has brought into question whether schools as such might not be part of the problem—rather than a solution to the problem of education. American educational reform in the early Sixties was concerned principally with the reconstruction of curriculum. The ideal was clarity and self-direction of intellect in the use of modern knowledge.
>
> There were brave efforts and successful ones in mathematics and physics, in chemistry and biology, and even in the behavioral sciences. The faltering of the humanists at this time was puzzling, though it later became clearer. A revision of the humanities involved too many explosive issues, we were to discover.
>
> In the second half of the decade, the period of these essays, deeper doubts began to develop. Did revision of curriculum suffice, or was a more fundamental restructuring of the entire educational

system in order? Plainly, the origins of the doubt go deep and far back into the changing culture and technology of our times. But our ruinous and cruel war in Vietnam led many who would have remained complacent to question our practices and priorities. How could a society be so enormously wealthy, yet so enormously and callously destructive, while professing idealism? How wage a war in the name of a generous way of life, while our own way of life included urban ghettos, a culture of poverty, racism, and worse?

We looked afresh at the appalling effects of poverty and racism on the lives of children, and the extent to which schools had become instruments of the evil forces in our society. Eloquent books like Jonathan Kozol's *Death at an Early Age* began to appear.

It was the black community that first sought "free schools," freedom schools. They were to help black identity, to give a sense of control back to the community. Just as the civil rights movement provided models for social protest at large, so, too, the drive for free schools for the children of the black poor produced a counterpart response in the intellectual middle-class community. The revolt against the system very quickly came to include the educational Establishment. Generous-minded men like Ivan Illich and Paul Goodman, inveighing against the deadening bureaucratic hold of teachers and educational administrators, voiced a new romanticism: salvation by spontaneity; "dis-establish" the established schools. It was a view that, as we know, took immediate root in the "in" youth culture.

But if romanticism was solace for some, despair was the order for others. By the spring of 1970, when Elizabeth Hall, one of the editors of *Psychology Today*, asked me what I thought about American education at the moment, all I could answer was that it had passed into a state of utter crisis. It had failed to respond to changing social needs, lagging behind rather than leading. My work on early education and social class, for example, had convinced me that the educational system was, in effect, our way of maintaining a class system—a group at the bottom. It crippled the capacity of children in the lowest socioeconomic quarter of the population, and particularly those who were black, to participate at full power in the society, and it did so early and effectively.

It is not surprising then that this little volume, arranged roughly in chronological order, should begin with an essay that bears the title, "The Perfectibility of Intellect," vintage 1965, and end with one called "Poverty and Childhood," a product of 1970.

And so a half decade passed. By 1970 the concern was no longer to change schools from within by curriculum, but to refit them altogether to the needs of society, to change them as institutions. It is no longer reform but revolution that has come to challenge us. And it is not so plain what is the role of the academic in such an enterprise.

What would one do now? What would be the pattern at a Woods Hole conference in 1971? It would not be in Woods Hole, in that once rural, coastal setting. More likely, we would gather in the heart of a great city. The task would center around the dispossession of the children of the poor and the alienation of the middle-class child. In some crucial respect, the medium would surely be the message: the school, not the curriculum, or the society and not even the school. And in my view, through my perspective, the issues would have to do with how one gives back initiative and a sense of potency, how one activates to tempt one to want to learn again. When that is accomplished, then curriculum becomes an issue again—curriculum not as a subject but as an approach to learning and using knowledge.

The rest of what I have to say concerns these issues—of activating a learner, of giving him his full sense of intent and initiative.

Consider first getting people to want to learn something, how to make the learning enterprise sustained and compelling. In a recent article in the *Saturday Review*, I proposed that it is possible to conceive of a Monday-Wednesday-Friday curriculum covering the standard topics, and a Tuesday-Thursday and indeed Saturday way of doing things in which immediate and compelling concerns are given the central place—activism? Let them on Tuesdays and Thursdays prepare "briefs" in behalf of their views, make a case for things they care about. Let them prepare plans of action, whether they be on issues in the school, on the local scene, or whatever. What is important is to learn to bring all one's resources to bear on something that matters to you now. These are the times for the migratory questions that wander on long after their answers are forgotten, just because they are great questions. And there must be more time for the expressive elements—the encounters, the hates, the loves, the feelings. All this need not be antic, nor need it all be in the manner of presenting one's case. I have seen experiments using improvisational theater, drama, film, and the like to teach and to question history, projects in which one learns to construe events through different sets of eyes. To what an extraordinary extent do films and plays of the contemporary scene matter in this! Ionesco or Pirandello are not so much concerned with absurdity but with how not to be caught with the obvious. This is not something to be prescribed. But it can surely be explored how it is we are perplexed by the texture of the society in which we live.

An extraordinary, moving book called *Children of Barbiana* is about a contemporary Tuscan hill town in Italy. The children there had failed so many times in so many ways in school that they had given up generation after generation—consigned to unskilled labor. A priest came to the parish. He started a school in which nobody was to fail, a school in which it was expected that everybody had to pass. It was everyone's responsibility to see that everybody in the class mastered the lesson before anybody could go on to the next lesson.

A community is a powerful force for effective learning. Students, when encouraged, are tremendously helpful to each other. They are like a cell, a revolutionary cell. It is the cell in which mutual learning and instruction can occur, a unit within a classroom with its own sense of compassion and responsibility for its members.

These were matters we did not do enough with at Woods Hole. We did not think about mutuality because we were stuck on the idea of curriculum—in spite of the fact that our laboratories and our very curriculum projects were set up rather like communes!

Inevitably, somebody will ask, "Well, how are you going to grade them?" You might also ask, "How in the world are you going to grade all of these distinguished colleagues who write collaborative articles among themselves and their graduate students?

There is a group of high school girls in Concord, Massachusetts, who are tutoring in the local elementary school. Those who are acquainted with cross-age tutoring will know, as I discovered, the extent to which those who help are helped, that being a teacher makes one a better learner. But should it be such a surprise? Is this not what is meant by passing on the culture?

What we say of the peer group and the near-peer group holds for the different age levels within the society. For in some deep way, what is needed is the reestablishment of a "learning community" beyond formal school, which, as now constituted, is far too isolating. It is not just by removing the barriers between elementary and high school students or by establishing a lifetime relationship to one's college where one can return for sustenance and become part of a broader learning community again. M.I.T. pronounced a few years ago that an engineer's education is obsolete after five years, so he must be brought back to bring him up to date. Let him come back, yes, but let the price of admission be that he discharge his obligation then to those who are just beginning—teacher, tutor, guide, what?

Finally, I would like to explore, in the interest of relevance, whether we might not recapture something of the old notion of vocation, of ways of life, or to use the expression of so many undergraduates today, of "lifestyles." I am impressed with contemporary concern for lifestyles. I have just finished a term as master of Currier House, a Radcliffe-Harvard house, and I assure you of the genuineness of this concern. But I am appalled that it is rarely translated into what one *does* with a lifestyle, the kind of vocation and livelihood in which we can express it. Could it be that in our stratified and fragmented society, our students simply do not know about local grocers and their styles, local doctors and theirs, local taxi drivers and theirs, local political activists and theirs? And don't forget the styles of local bookies, aspiring actresses, or illegitimate mothers. No, I really believe that our young have become so isolated that they do *not* know the roles available in the society and the variety of styles in which they are played. I would urge that we find some way of connecting the diversity of the society to the phenomenon of school, to keep the latter from becoming so isolated and the former so suspicious.

Let me add one last thing not directly connected with *The Process of Education*, but a problem of the first order today. One cannot ignore it in talking of education. We shall kill ourselves, as a society and as human beings, unless we address our efforts to redressing the deep, deep wounds that we inflict on the poor, the outcast, those who somehow do not fit within our caste system— be they black or dispossessed in any way. If there is one thing that has come out of our work with the very young, it is the extent to which "being out," not having a chance as an adult, or as a parent, very quickly reflects itself in loss of hope in the child. As early as the second or third year a child begins to reflect this loss of hope.

When any group is robbed of its legitimate aspiration, it will aspire desperately and by means that outrage the broader society, though they are efforts to sustain or regain dignity. Inequity cannot be altered by education alone, another lesson we have learned in the past decade. The impact of poverty is usually transmitted through the school as well. It cannot be counteracted by words unless there are also jobs and opportunities available to express society's confidence in what is possible after school.

There must be ways in which we can think honestly of reformulation of the institutions into which our schools fit, as one integral part. Surely it requires that we redirect our resources, re-order our priorities, redefine our national effort, and come to terms with the fact that we have a deep and brutal racism in us—in all of us. We must learn how to cope with that. The young know it; they despise our failure to talk about it and our other difficulties. History may well side with them.

In the end, we must finally appreciate that education is not a neutral subject, nor is it an isolated subject. It is a deeply political issue in which we guarantee a future for someone and, frequently, in guaranteeing a future for someone, we deal somebody else out. If I had my choice now, in terms of a curriculum project for the Seventies, it would be to find a means whereby we could bring society back to its sense of values and priorities in life. *I believe I would be quite satisfied to declare, if not a moratorium, then something of a deemphasis on matters that have to do with the structure of history, the structure of physics, the nature of mathematical consistency, and deal with them rather in the context of the problems that face us.* We might better concern ourselves with how those problems can be solved, not just by practical action, but by putting knowledge, wherever we find it and in whatever form we find it, to work in these massive tasks. *We might put vocation and intention back into the process of education, much more firmly than we had it there before.*

A decade later, we realize that *The Process of Education* was the beginning of a revolution, and one cannot yet know how far it will go. Reform of curriculum is not enough. Reform of the school is probably not enough. The issue is one of man's capacity for creating a culture, society, and technology that not only feed him but keep him caring and belonging.

---

1. Anita Gil (ed.). New York: W. W. Norton, 1971.

Can Our Schools Get Better?
by John I. Goodlad

The answer is "possibly," says Dean Goodlad. But reconstruction and improvement will require a new vision and a supreme cooperative effort by enlightened citizens and professionals. Here are basic considerations.

The generally accepted goal of improving our schools may be chimeric. This is not to say that school improvement is impossible. But it is to suggest that, given the circumstances surrounding schooling today and what is needed to effect improvement, we—that is, our society—may not be up to it. Indeed, given certain of these circumstances and conditions, our schools may deteriorate, and dissatisfaction and disaffection may increase.

I do not personally accept the proposition that school improvement is an impossible goal. But I do not believe that our schools will be better simply by wishing them so or by trying harder to do much of what is now done. And my skepticism regarding many of our most popular beliefs about education and schooling and the practices stemming from them is such that I would more readily predict, from much of our effort, poorer rather than better schools for the future. But this need not be a self-fulfilling prophecy.

The argument for or against my major proposition revolves around a set of related propositions. I shall state several of these and then discuss each in turn. Instead of waiting to the concluding pages to make some positive suggestions for school improvement, I shall advance a position regarding each subproposition, indicating what I believe is required if solid progress in education and schooling is to be realized.

The Elements of Debate
Proposition One: The norm by which the performance of schools is now judged is entirely inadequate, from one perspective, and, from another, corrupts the educative process.

Proposition Two: The fixing of responsibility for improved performance according to the standards used inhibits the creative processes required for significant progress.

Proposition Three: Virtually equating education with schooling has so burdened the schools with responsibility that satisfactory performance, even if appropriate norms and standards of accountability were applied, would be exceedingly difficult to attain.

Proposition Four: The widely accepted assumption that schooling is good and more is better has resulted in an enlarged system that serves, as often as not, to deprive the educational process of the nourishing resources it needs.

Proposition Five: Although much of the support for our system of schooling has been derived from rhetorical principles exhorting individual opportunity, egalitarianism, and openness, in actuality the system is quite closed with respect to principles of operation other than those on which it has been built.

Proposition Six: The prevailing theories of change that take as their model factories and assembly lines simply do not fit the realities of schooling, and so funds usually accompanying their application only compound the cycle of failure and disappointment.

Proposition Seven: In spite of some self-congratulatory rhetoric to the contrary, education is still a relatively weak profession, badly divided within itself and not yet embodying the core of professional values and knowledge required to resist fads, special-interest groups, and—perhaps most serious of all—funding influences.

Partly as a consequence of what some of these subpropositions imply, schools are not now in charge of their own destinies. Many of the changes and adaptations they should have initiated by themselves are now being forced upon them by court and legislative action. And, unfortunately, many people outside of schools who think they know what will lead to school improvement are not uniquely blessed with the special insight and wisdom that would tell them what is required.

The Standard of Success

Over a period of more than 300 years, the American people have enlarged their educational expectations for schools. Beginning with narrowly academic and religious goals in the seventeenth century, they added vocational and social goals in the eighteenth and nineteenth centuries and goals of personal or self-realization in the twentieth. These goals now encompass a wide range of knowledge, skills, and values and a kaleidoscopic array of scientific, humanistic, and aesthetic sources of human enlightenment. Nearly all of our children spend eight or nine years in the place to which primary responsibility for achieving these goals is consciously ascribed. Most spend 12 or 13 years there; some spend 16 or 20 or more.

And yet we are content to use various combinations of the first six letters of the alphabet and two numbers, sometimes representing total scores and sometimes percentile rankings, as virtually the sole evidence for passing definitive judgment on the adequacy of an individual's or a school's performance. Large numbers of parents apparently suffer no pangs of conscience in withholding support and love or inflicting pain and humiliation purely on the basis of these letters and grades. Others bestow gifts and lavish praise on their achieving children with little thought to whether their marks were obtained with little effort, through cheating, or at the expense of peers, some of them friends and neighbors.

But neither these dissatisfied/satisfied parents nor their fellow citizen nonparents give much thought to whether the students' curricula were well-balanced, their interest and curiosity aroused, their talents unleashed, their creativity fostered, or their sentiments and tastes refined. Presumably, the almighty letter grade and the SAT score tell it all.

We smile wryly when a speaker repeats the cliché: Half the students will always be below average, and we can never have most of the students above the fiftieth percentile. But next day we're back in that old groove again, hard at work trying to get everyone above the mean. Clearly, by this criterion our schools never will be any better.

My subproposition, stated earlier, is that from one perspective the conventional achievement norm is an inadequate criterion of school success and, from another, it corrupts the educative process. If we are to use student outcome as a major measure of school and student performance—and I assume we will for a long time to come—then let us at least endeavor to appraise that performance in line with the four sets of goals for which our schools are responsible. This means developing and using tests geared to domains designated by these goals and not tests made up of often-irrelevant items designed to elicit 50% success and 50% failure—tests pitting student against student but telling us little or nothing about them or their schools.

But we must go far beyond such measurement into what is, surprisingly, little-explored terrain—namely, into qualitative appraisals of what goes on in schools. For the past several years my colleagues and I have been developing instruments by means of which to describe elements of the curriculum and teaching; to solicit administrators', teachers', students', and parents' views on aspects of schooling; and to compare and relate some of these data. The task is extraordinarily difficult—far more difficult than measuring student outcome. Perhaps this is why so little along these lines has been done. Our purpose is not to evaluate schools but to emphasize the necessity of assembling data on schools as a basis for determining their present condition and beginning a process of improvement.

It seems to my associates and me that how a student spends precious time in school and how he feels about what goes on there is of much greater significance than how he scores on a standardized achievement test. But I am not at all sure that the American people are ready to put a rather straightforward criterion such as this ahead of the marks and scores we worship mindlessly in much the same way our supposedly more primitive ancestors worshiped the gods of thunder and fire. And so it will be difficult for schools to get better and even more difficult for them to appear so.

Accountability

Adherence to norm-referenced standardized test scores as the standard for judging student, teacher, and school performance has led quite naturally to a stultifying approach to accountability. There is nothing wrong with the idea of being accountable—that is, being required to give an account. The problems and injustices in contemporary approaches to educational accountability stem from the fact that all the richness, shortcomings, interpersonal relations, successes, and failures are reduced to a few figures, much as one records profits and losses in a ledger book.

This is the familiar, linear, reductionist model that squares nicely with the manufacture of paper cups and safety pins and the basics of bookkeeping. During the past two decades it has been applied to the preparation of school administrators, teacher education, planning and budgeting processes, and, most recently, the progress and graduation of high school students. We are all familiar with accountability by objectives, competency-based teacher education, PPBS, and proficiency tests. The expectation in using all of these is that education in the schools will improve as a consequence, with higher test scores serving as the ultimate criterion. There is no evidence to date that any such improvement has occurred. Indeed, the evidence appears to be precisely in the opposite direction.

The irony here is that the decline in test scores often is blamed on those "soft and tender" educational innovations of the 1960s, not on these "hard and tough" approaches to accountability. Yet there is growing suspicion that the much-touted supposed reforms of the Sixties never occurred—they were, for the most part, nonevents. On the other hand, there is all around us evidence to the effect that accountability by objectives, PPBS, competency-based teacher education, and the like have dominated the scene for some time. Is it not time to consider seriously the proposition that this cult of efficiency has failed to make our schools more efficient? Is the time not overdue for seriously considering other ways of accounting for what goes on in the educational system and our schools?

How about these criteria, just for starters: How many students officially registered in high schools were today absent, for reasons other than illness, and walking the streets of New York, Detroit, Atlanta, Denver, and Los Angeles? Why? How many high school and college suicides, worldwide, last year, occurred as a direct consequence of grades or test scores? What schools have trouble keeping students home even when ill because they are so anxious to come to school? Or what about this school administrator's criterion: "I know this is a better school now because the kids don't throw up as often"?

And how about the accounting implied in the following questions: What legislators have checked lately to determine how their legislation affected school principals' paperwork, balance in the curriculum, parents' willingness to assist the school, or teachers' freedom to select methods and materials most suited to the needs and characteristics of their students? How recently, if ever, did the several dozen different kinds of specialists in your state department of education come together to determine what a secondary school would look like if all of their currently independent proposals came together in a single curriculum? How many school districts have adjusted their inservice education programs and credits so as to provide time and rewards for local school faculties seeking to improve the quality of life in their workplaces? How many researchers are moving from those studies of single variables in the learning process that have yielded no significant findings to those much more complex inquiries required for understanding school and classroom environments so that we might understand, also, how to improve them? And how many teachers have thought at least twice and then decided to keep their mouths closed before saying that educational research is a waste of time?

These and other accounting questions serve not only to suggest the breadth of responsibility we all must share in seeking to improve our schools but also the folly of concentrating the bulk of our time, energy, and resources on those ubiquitous test scores. Perhaps the greatest irony of all about the diploma mill is that even as we are regarding high grades with some awe, we don't know what they mean. My colleague, Robert Pace, pointed out some years ago that school grades predict school grades and not much else—not compassion, not good work habits, not vocational success, not social success, not happiness.

If misplaced emphasis were the only consequence of focusing narrowly on the accounting process, the subject would not warrant impassioned attention. But what arouses one's emotions are the many negative side effects already suggested, what is curtailed, and what is driven out. My guess is that those relatively low-level cognitive processes most easily measured and most emphasized in the current back-to-basics movement will show some improvement in test scores during coming years. But my further guess is that those more complex intellectual processes not easily measured will decline at an equal or greater rate.

And i am convinced that continuation along the impoverished curricular and pedagogical lines implied by "back to basics" would lead ultimately to educational bankruptcy in our schools, acceleration in alienation and drop-out rates, and in grades having even less relevance to life than they do now. But, fortunately, the weakness of schools demonstrated in their rhetorical zigging and zagging is also their saving grace. Just as the zig is becoming excessive, we start to zag. Regrettably, we often are out of sync—zigging when we should be zagging and zagging when we should be zigging—but that is a tale for another day.

We now need to turn *from* the reductionist process in schooling by which complex human goals and processes become measurable, relatively unimportant, and probably only remotely related to the important ideas with which we began. We need to turn *toward* learnings rich in opportunities to derive varied meanings and devise creative, individual approaches to understanding and problem solving. Robert Rosen, the distinguished theoretical biologist, suggests the contrast between what we do and what we should do:

> . . . [M]an has a biologically rooted need to engage in complex activities. . . . And it is the activities themselves which are [essential], not the ends which are supposed to be attained by them; these ends are the inessentials and the by-products. Somehow, we have gotten turned around so as to believe that, on the contrary, the ends are primary and the means secondary.[1]

More Is Better

Three of the propositions stated at the outset are so closely entwined that I shall group them for discussion purposes:

Three: The virtual equating of education with schooling has so burdened the schools with responsibility that satisfactory performance, even if appropriate norms and standards of accountability were applied, would be exceedingly difficult to attain.

Four: The widely accepted assumption that education and, therefore, schooling is good and more is better has significantly enlarged the system but has not improved the education provided by that system.

Five: Although much of the support for our system of schooling has been derived from rhetorical principles exhorting individual opportunity, egalitarianism, and openness, in actuality the system is quite closed with respect to principles of operation other than those on which it has been built.

As stated earlier, our schools are expected to address four sets of goals. Performing the educational function implied is demanding enough, especially when one realizes the potential for internal conflict in seeking to achieve these complex goals. Successful development of the free self, for example, is seen by many as sheer hedonism, interfering with the goal of responsible citizenship. But the other functions the school is expected to undertake virtually overwhelm the educational ones. They include at least the following:

1. The preservation of values and traditions thought to be central to the unification and welfare of previous generations. These interests are not al-

ways in the best interests of present and future generations, hence frequently interfere with their proper education.

2. The enhancement of values and traditions seen to be required by changing circumstances. Ecological studies are seen by some people as essential for schools, but long-term ecological considerations interfere with short-term economic ones.

3. Significant contributions to the solution of critical human problems. For example, school populations and professional personnel are shifted about to achieve desegregation, frequently making it more difficult for schools to achieve the stability they require for effective educational performance.

4. The performance of functions formerly perfomed by existing institutions or not yet assumed through the creation of new ones. With no accompanying changes in the resources, time, and regularities of schools and, often, no conscious internalization of the new functions, subsequent performance usually is less than satisfying.

It should not surprise us that schools receive few accolades for what they do in many new areas of responsibility. The behavior problems not dealt with in the home are not well dealt with in a school now, lacking what was once a home/school collaboration. The more schools take on, the more vulnerable they are to attack and criticism. Further, the more they take on, the fewer resources they have for and the less attention they give to their educational function. Ironically, the more they take on, the less other institutions assume responsibility for education.

In effect, we have the grandest faith in and expectations for education, accompanied by myopic concentration on a single institution in seeking fulfillment of these expectations. The pressures for increasing the educative role of other agencies and institutions are weak.

Meanwhile, our schooling-dominated educational system, like some stubbornly self-destructive dinosaur, seeks to adapt only by growing larger. It expands at the bottom by enlarging its feet, at the top by growing a longer neck, and sideways by expanding its girth. More is equated with good and still more with better. But before the system can congratulate itself for effecting these expansions, almost everyone is complaining that the schools are simultaneously declining in quality (the test scores are down) and costing more.

There are very few instances in our society of organizations increasing in size without increasing in complexity as well as in preoccupation with self-maintenance. Our educational system is, in functioning reality, an array of primary, secondary, and tertiary schools made systemic by a host of assumptions translated into rules and regulations for the operation of each unit. This system is held together by structural arrangements of such proportions that their maintenance consumes a large portion of the resources allocated to the whole. It becomes reasonable to seriously consider the possibility that making the system better, according to the principles by which it operates, actually makes the education provided worse.

In expanding our expectations for schooling, we shall almost invariably be disappointed unless we also broaden the criteria of evaluation. In expanding our definition of universal schooling, we raised the compulsory leaving age to 16 without significantly providing educational alternatives for a broader range of clientele. Now, decades later, some people are proposing a reduction in this age to 14 because many young people find little in school to attract them and disrupt those who have learned to adjust to the principles on which schools operate.

Similarly, we are taking more and more children of a younger age into the system and judging the success of this venture by how well these children perform on the conventional standards of achievement. We fail to ask what these children gave up in order to go to school earlier or how well the school is substituting for the declining role of parents. Nonetheless, on the scoreboard we chalk up another victory for universal education.

I am doubtful about all of this changing rapidly for the better through some kind of systematic, rational planning. But I do see signs of change, not necessarily portending only good things. It is not out of the question that the dinosaur will collapse because of its sheer weight and lack of mobility. Bills for sweeping voucher plans could and would pass in several states if it were not for uncertainty about the economic implications, some considerable worries about regulatory procedures (including those exercised by the bodies implementing the legislation), and fear that one dinosaur simply will be replaced by another.

Without fully realizing it, we may be at the end of an era. A new era will emerge in an evolutionary way and on a broken front. The view that small is good is affecting many aspects of our daily lives. Some responsible legislators are becoming aware of the fact that their good intentions, expressed in bill after bill—many of them underfinanced and most of them hopelessly tangled in regulations and procedures of accountability—are compounding the work of school personnel. It has been suggested by members of the California legislature that they declare a two-year moratorium on legislation pertaining to schools.

As more and more people become products of the system—especially the upper levels of the system—its values for personal advancement become less clear. As more people participate in the system, interest in virtues such as equal access declines. Only the most and least favored segments of the system fight for equality, the former because they are confident in their unequal status and the latter because they see the schools as still the avenue of access to social and economic equality. All the rest want the "best," not equal education. Consequently, support for one standard system declines and the desire for alternatives increases. Even if the alternatives differ from the conventional only in rhetoric rather than program, they weaken the system, and this is not bad. Unfortunately, the alternatives do not necessarily provide better education.

There are two very significant signs of our being at the end of one era, even if we cannot yet discern the character of the next. First, principles previously unquestioned or questioned only by "radicals" begin to come in for more serious, popular questioning. For example, it is possible for me to question here the very concepts with which most of us have spent our lives and not be regarded as particularly dangerous—indeed, many of you identify readily with what I am writing.

Second, the less tenable long-established principles come to be, the more intense the ceremonial rain dances by those who fear the personal consequences of new ones. That is, threatened groups and individuals try harder to do what gave satisfaction before, however inappropriate and outworn the behaviors may be. For example, it is clear that we should have established, long ago, firmer collaborative bonds between the schools and business and industry for the conduct of vocational education. The schools should not have shouldered this burden to the degree they did. In so doing, they failed to produce the gratitude they expected from the private sector; today, business and industry complain more than ever about the failure of schools to teach the basics. As a consequence of the gap between the two, new institutions and arrangements for bridging education and work are emerging. As if to proclaim that the old order changeth not at all, segments of the established school-related vocational education community have been increasing the intensity of their rain dances. This is a sure sign that the times are changing.

Toward New Models of Change

And now I shall weave together Propositions 6 and 7:

Six: The prevailing theories of change that take as their model factories and assembly lines simply do not fit the realities of schooling.

Seven: In spite of some self-congratulatory rhetoric to the contrary, education is still a relatively weak profession, badly divided within itself and lacking the necessary core of professional values and knowledge.

The model of change most commonly applied to educational improvement comes from the same root and stem as the criteria for success, models of accountability, and patterns of funding referred to earlier. All are part of a theory of rationality that calls for the precise delineation of goals to be accomplished, the use of goals to justify means, and the measurement of previously defined goals. Applied to the improvement of schooling, the model usually assumes an institution incapable of improving itself, an institution not devoid of goals, not with differing goals, but with inadequately defined goals. The model also assumes more intelligence outside of schools than in them and a relatively impotent, passive target group of personnel.

For brevity, let me pass quickly over these assumptions, which undoubtedly are causing some consternation in your mind now that I have made them explicit. Let me simply say that I think they are wrong and that the more one probes into schools as social systems and subcultures, the more firm one becomes in the conclusion that the model encompasses the problems of school improvement quite inadequately. At any rate, intense utilization accompanied by unprecedented funds has not produced the intended effects in the products.

Whether one explores past or present instances of schools achieving marked success in whatever they set out to accomplish, one comes out with a quite different picture from the above in regard to how success was achieved, however fuzzy and perplexing that picture may be. The elements in that picture appear to be at least the following:

1. The school as a unit has a great deal of autonomy in the system or is itself the total educational system for a given population of students in its community setting. One immediately thinks of Evanston Township High School or New Trier High School in an earlier era. The superintendent or principal was headmaster of a single school, relatively well paid and free to travel and participate as a person of importance on the national scene. Or one thinks of that handful (5%) of the all-black schools that produced 21% of the black Ph.D.s during one period of our history. Among them were McDonough 35

High School in New Orleans (California State Superintendent Wilson Riles graduated from it); Frederick Douglass High School in Baltimore; Dunbar High School in Washington, D.C.; and Booker T. Washington High School in Atlanta. Of course, many other factors were involved, but this is part of my point: The schools will not be improved by single interventions, however well funded.

2. The school has a sense of mission, unity, identity, and wholeness that pervades every aspect of its functioning—not just its interscholastic athletic programs. The people connected with it have a sense of ownership, of belonging to a special institution. "I teach at" or "I attend Union High" is spoken with a sense of pride. Currently, many aspects of American life work against such a school *Zeitgeist*. Consequently, achieving such a school requires extraordinary dedication, commitment, and hard work on the part of everyone.

3. The principal is central to the attainment of the kind of school implied. She or he, far more than any other person, shapes and articulates the prevailing ambiance and creates a sense of mission. In recent studies of schools effecting integration with some success, almost invariably the principal was identified as strategic. In the successful black schools referred to earlier, again the significance of the principal—his or her values, dedication, and strength—came to the surface. Almost invariably, too, the principal is a person with a strong sense of personal worth and potency, one who takes a position on issues and is not regarded as a pawn of the superintendent or of strong individuals or groups within the community.

4. The surrounding infrastructure is supportive. The superintendent recognizes the school as the key unit for change and improvement, encourages principals to be captains of their ship, works directly with them as often as possible rather than building a wall of central office administrators between them and himself, and supports them even while disagreeing with them. A significant part of the budget—the discretionary part—is built from the bottom up, with each school principal bringing forward plans projected several years into the future, plans developed collaboratively at the site level.

You will be thinking, "Of course, anyone can succeed in such an ideal setting." But this is to miss my point. Ideals are not given; they represent conditions to be achieved.

The school milieu and characteristics described will not in themselves assure high attainment in the academic, social, vocational, and personal goals set for our schools. But they do suggest some necessary but insufficient conditions generally neglected in society's efforts to improve schooling. And they certainly suggest the folly of employing simple panaceas designed to affect some small part of the instructional process. A school that is well along toward becoming a good place to work and study is the school that can take on virtually any project with reasonable expectations of success.

It goes almost without saying that much more is required for successful educational performance. But most of the rest lies in the classroom and is up to teachers. Again, however, the principal plays a key role in providing the support, encouragement, and resources required—the very conditions he or she requires for effective performance as a principal.

Basic to the principal's role in instructional improvement are at least two major kinds of understanding. First, the criterion of accountability for the principal is development of a comprehensive educational program—one that does not shift from one emphasis to another, neglecting the arts when "back to basics" is the popular slogan and stressing responsible citizenship only in time of national crisis. Second, the principal purges from his views of instruction any and all commitments to panaceas and simple solutions. We know now that no innovation or intervention consistently and unambiguously makes a difference in student outcomes. Successful teachers orchestrate 10 or more major contributors to learning in order to assist student progress. These include assuring that students understand directions before embarking on the task, maintaining momentum, keeping students involved, using positive reinforcement but not unrealistic praise, varying instructional techniques, alternating the length of learning episodes, providing regular and consistent feedback, and on and on. Teachers are more likely to engage in these arduous, demanding teaching techniques when what they do is known to and supported by the principal. Teaching, like administrative leadership, is a relatively lonely activity.

I have implied throughout that schools will be better if legislators, school board members, parents, and superintendents see themselves as responsible and accountable for enhancing the effectiveness, unity, and sense of mission of the single school. This may mean passing less rather than more reform legislation, reducing rather than increasing districtwide programs and demands, giving more rather than less autonomy to principals and teachers, and using contextual as well as outcome criteria as measures of successful performance. But, clearly, this does not mean that schools automatically will be better. Whether or not they will, even given the support implied, depends on the education profession, and one must ask, seriously, whether we are up to it.

We are a badly divided profession, with each segment perceiving only a part of the whole, lacking awareness of and commitment to the systematic, collaborative functioning required for significant improvement. Much of what I have said is threatening to many superintendents who see power as finite and the decentralization of it to the principals as undermining their authority. Many are more preoccupied with massaging the system than with assuring that resources and support get to the school ships at sea. They are more preoccupied with budgets, crisis management, and public affairs than with educational goals and programs. Relatively few have internalized, let alone articulated, the view that the prime measure of their success is the quality of life in the schools under their jurisdiction.

Far more threatened are those second- and third-level managers and supervisors who, not clear on their role to begin with, view increased autonomy and resources at the site level as restricting and delimiting their role even more. Their fears are not unjustified. I am convinced that education is improved to the degree that qualified personnel and instructional resources get close to students. As I said earlier, beyond a level of vital, priority need, adding highly paid personnel to the central office often makes education worse rather than better.

For principals, there is a certain stultifying protection in the ambiguity of the role. Being caught up in the demands of the district office and the routines of management, most of which could be done better and less expensively by someone else, the principal has no time for the development of programs and people within the school. This ambiguity conspires with status elements of the job to cause principals to play their cards close to their chests, making their lonely jobs even lonelier. Association with peers usually occurs through the conduct of interscholastic athletics and so tends to be competitive rather than collaborative. And yet principals long for collegial relationships with peers in settings where, perhaps with the help of a supportive colleague or university professor, they can explore openly the problems for which they were not prepared.

The departmental structure of high schools for both governance and program development violates most of what we know about policy development, chops up the curriculum into fiefdoms that make significant change all but impossible, and immobilizes the school in the face of pervasive problems such as violence and institutional erosion that cut across departmental lines. Teachers, in turn, are more tied to their disciplines and the teaching of content than oriented to the personal needs of children and youth, a situation reinforced by their professional associations and the prevailing system of accountability. The principals and teachers of elementary, junior high, and secondary schools rarely come together to examine the total educational programs for children and youth.

Teacher educators, for the most part, assume that teacher education begins and ends with the admission and graduation of students and has little or nothing to do with the school and classroom environments of teaching and learning and the role schools of education should play in their improvement. Too many researchers are preoccupied with research on single instructional variables that rarely account for more than 5% of the variance in student outcomes. Too few study the complex phenomena of schooling in their natural environment, developing the needed new methodologies instead of seeking to adapt the old.

One could go on and on in this vein, citing also the precarious nature of a large, divided profession constructed on the flimsiest base of core knowledge and professional beliefs. We have much to do together and little energy to waste on bemoaning the shortcomings of legislators, parents, and one another. We have met the enemy and he is us. What is challenging to me and, I hope, to you is that most of the paths we must walk are reasonably clear, blocked with debris at many places but visible nonetheless. And most of them are paths along which only you and I need walk to assure that a significant part of what is required to make our schools better will be accomplished.

Our schools can and should be better. But educators must take the lead, together, to make them so. Large numbers of parents and students are ready to join us, I believe, in making our schools, one by one, better places in which to live and work. The slogans for improvement are, for the most part, meaningless rhetoric. Our schools must be reconstructed, one by one, by citizens and educators working together. Nothing less will suffice.

---

1. Robert Rosen, "Do We Really Need Ends To Justify the Means?" *Center Report*, February 1976, pp. 29, 30.

III
The Light Touch

Introduction

*I*n lists of qualities that students find most attractive in their teachers, "sense of humor" is always a winner. Just as regularly, humor and satire get top ratings from KAPPAN readers who write "Backtalk" letters or respond to readership surveys. Thus the KAPPAN nearly always includes one or more light features per issue, and cartoons have become a fixture.

As Jonathan Swift demonstrated nearly three centuries ago, satire is perhaps the most effective form of polemic writing. One of the most versatile satirists to write for the KAPPAN is Ken McIntyre, the University of Texas professor and author of highly regarded works in school administration. Over two decades, McIntyre has skewered and roasted a variety of sacred cows in the pages of the journal. But because I could not bring myself to choose among them, I'm content merely to list a few of his contributions and urge the reader to look them up in the library. McIntyre lampooned certain group processes in "How to Make an Impression in a Discussion Group Without Actually Saying Anything" (March 1957) and "The Wonderful One-Hoss Cliché" (November 1959); the arrogance and naïveté of Admiral Rickover's education criticism in "The Trouble with Submarines" (April 1960); professorial pomposity in "The Art of Obfuscation" (December 1961); academic censorship in "How to Avoid Being Half Safe" (October 1962); doctoral dissertation style in "How to Write a Thesis Without Really Thinking" (November 1964); hypocrisy, discord, and other ills of higher education in "Higher Education in Lower Tonteria" (April 1966); and the pretensions of research in "Reuben's Plan: The Safe Way to Select Leaders" (December 1979).

Among my all-time favorite pieces of satiric writing is "Spreading the Benefits of Accountability," by Ray Cross, in the March 1976 KAPPAN. Cross turns out to be second-generation Ken McIntyre, because he did his Ph.D. in school administration at Texas when McIntyre was head of the Division of School Administration there. Cross greatly admired McIntyre's lampoons published in the KAPPAN.

At least as well as far lengthier serious pieces, "Spreading . . ." reveals the fatal flaw in accountability theory as applied to education: the impossibility of one person relieving another of his responsibility for himself. Interestingly enough, this little tour-de-force represents Cross's first attempt at writing satire.

Cross is now professor of educational administration at Corpus Christi State University. He is author of some 30 serious papers and articles, the latter achieving publication in such journals as the National Elementary Principal, the Journal of Educational Research, and Educational Leadership.

"*Nobody Calls Me Doctor*" *(May 1965) is one of those little gems that build the reputation of both author and editor. Several generations of doctoral students have resonated to this classic, and it has been a kind of touchstone in the life of its author, William E. (Bud) Davis. He made it the title piece in his first book (Pruett, 1972) and, after narrowly losing in a run for the U.S. Senate on the Democratic ticket in Idaho (in the year when Nixon demolished McGovern), he wrote a privately distributed booklet describing his fling at politics. The title was* Nobody Calls Me Senator. *A witty, vivid, and pungent account, it could well be a handbook for the amateur politician. When I told Davis I was planning to reprint "Nobody Calls Me Doctor," he wrote that he is now in the process of pulling together anecdotes from his most recent experiences in higher education. His wife suggests that it be titled* Nobody Calls Me. *Such a title would be totally misleading, however. Davis has been a university president for 16 years, 10 at Idaho State at Pocatello and six at the University of New Mexico, Albuquerque, his present position. Only 20 years ago he was teaching English and coaching football (an unholy alliance, he notes in his book) at Rapid City High in South Dakota.*

Unfortunately, I no longer have addresses for the author of "All Is Not Zip-a-dee-do-Dah in the Foreign Service" (October 1956), who called himself J. Orvis Quimby; for John Gauss, who submitted "Teacher Evaluation: Socrates" (January 1962); or for Rozanne Knudson, author of "Catcher in the Wrong" (October 1964). Mildred Fenner requested Quimby's address and invited him to write for the NEA *Journal. "Socrates" was reprinted so many times I lost track of the number. "Catcher" won a prize from* The Writer's Market *and became the title piece in an anthology of humor from the* KAPPAN *collected by Bill Turney, who later became president of PDK.*

For years, when depressed by certain aspects of my editorial work, I have turned to one of these three pieces to restore my perspective. So enjoy.

—SME

Spreading the Benefits of Accountability

by Ray Cross

I am a person who is not easily impressed. I left the TV and went to bed in the middle of the first moon walk; I never give Raquel Welch a second glance; and I greeted with a mere chortle the news that Strom Thurmond had fathered a child at age 72. So you can appreciate it when I say that I am impressed with the accountability movement in education.

High time, I say, that we started applying business principles to education. Right on, I say, to the no-nonsense approach that demands results from educators. No more of this preoccupation with inputs and process. No more faulting a student's heredity and background for the teacher's failure to bring him up to grade level.

So taken with accountability am I that I have recently tried to extend its application to other human services. Sort of spreading the benefits of accountability. So far, I've made two attempts. I'll describe them so as to encourage others to do the same.

Episode 1

The inspiration to spread the benefits of accountability first came to me when my neighbor, Max Flaccidham, was recounting one of his reveries. Max was sprawled in his recliner in front of the tube, so he told me, watching the Oakland Raiders and the Washington Redskins. Half asleep and into his fourth can of beer, he was watching 48-year-old George Blanda trot jauntily to the sidelines after kicking an extra point, when suddenly the injustice of it all hit him.

"Why," he mused, "am I not as good a physical specimen as George Blanda? There he is cavorting around the Oakland backfield, throwing passes and kicking 40-yard field goals. I'm only 44 and can't even walk to the refrigerator without breathing hard. Blanda is vigorous, lithe as a cat, flat-stomached; and I am listless and rotund, with a 42-inch girth. He defeats the Washington Redskins football team, and I can't even beat my 14-year-old daughter at Ping-Pong. On TV commercials he brags about keeping up with the younger players both on and off the field, and I. . . . Well, something's wrong."

Seizing the opportunity, I asked Max if he had a doctor. Max said he did, the same one for 10 years. "I see him once, sometimes twice a year."

"Max," I said, "it's time to hold your doctor accountable for your physical condition." I then proceeded to acquaint him with the fundamental principles of the accountability movement and what it has done for education. I pointed out that here was a chance to do the same thing for the medical field. He must confront his physician and demand results.

A week later I ran into Max at a pizza joint. He was ingesting his third slice of mozzarella, two empty cola bottles before him. I asked him about his confrontation with his doctor.

Max looked wan.

"The doc said it's too late for me to be like Blanda."

"Too late?"

"Yeah," said Max. "Doc says Blanda has spent most of his last 30 years doing calisthenics, running wind sprints, and bouncing off linebackers, while I've spent most of my last 30 years sitting in a chair and draped in a recliner."

"Didn't you point out that your work at the bank and the lifestyle in your family have fostered a sedentary disposition and that he should not blame *your* environment for *his* performance failure?"

"I told him all of those things," Max replied, "but he said like hell he was responsible. He told me I was 30 pounds overweight when I first came to him 10 years ago and had followed none of the diets he put me on and never did any of the exercises he suggested. I tried to tell him it was his fault about the diet and exercises for not making them attractive enough."

"Hey, that's a good comeback, Max," I said. "What did the doc say to that?"

"He didn't say anything for a while. He just stared at me with sort of a puzzled look. Finally, he did say that no matter how I dieted or exercised I would never look like George Blanda, because I just wasn't built like him."

I was aghast. "You don't mean he's blaming it on your heredity."

"I guess he was," said Max. "He said he's known both my parents for years and that they are short and dumpy, so what could I expect? He said it was foolish to think that I or even a small percentage of men in their forties could have the physique and stamina of Blanda. I told him I would settle for just being average in physique and endurance and that any doctor worth his salt should be able to make his patients average—sort of up to health level. He said I was being absurd."

"You must have laid into him for that," I ventured.

"I really did," Max said. "I said I was not at all satisfied with his explanation and that I was going to employ the ultimate sanction—getting another doctor."

"What did he say to that?"

"He said I should be sure to get one with psychiatric training."

Episode 2

I decided that if accountability is to be extended to other human services it will not be done by the likes of Max Flaccidham. I determined to take a hand in it myself.

My opportunity to do so was not long in coming. My target was the ministry.

Now, I have as great a respect for ministers as the next person. Not only does it take a special kind of person to become a man of the cloth, but ministers undergo a long period of training before entering a not-too-well-paid profession where they are called upon to help people, often under stressful conditions. However, clergymen tend to be as misguided as educators were before accountability. That is, they tend to think in terms of services rendered rather than results achieved.

I had my chance when I found myself seated across from our minister at a church dinner. After some small talk, I asked the Reverend if he had seen the newspaper report that crime had increased by 19% over the previous year, and didn't he wonder about the clergy's responsibility in this, their business being the morals of the nation. He responded patiently. He said indeed he did feel that the ministry had a responsibility for reducing the nation's crime rate, as did many other agencies and individuals in society.

"But," I said, "the churches are the institutions bearing primary responsibility for the morals of the people, and when the crime rate steadily increases from year to year, we must hold our spiritual leaders accountable."

"Furthermore," I continued, "look at other indicators of moral breakdown—drug usage, infidelity, juvenile delinquency. And what about Watergate! All of these can be laid directly to performance failure by the ministry."

The Reverend held on to his patience, although I had the feeling he wasn't taking me seriously enough. "You know," he replied, "we cannot force everyone to come to hear our sermons; much less can we exercise absolute control over their behavior."

"Ah," I countered, "if your sermons were sufficiently compelling, not only would people come but they would also be influenced. The point is that *you* must be held accountable for *their* behavior. You must stop judging your performance in terms of number of people attending services, number of sermons preached, increases in church membership, and the like. You must start assessing your contributions by results—the increase of virtuous acts and the decrease of sinful ones. Only in this way will you know how to become more effective in your ministry."

He was incredulous. "How will I find out about the virtuous and sinful acts of members of my congregation?" I acknowledged that he had something of a measurement problem, but I offered him my copy of Webb's *Unobtrusive Measures.*

"Maybe," I said, "our church could pioneer for accountability in organized religion. We could tie our church contributions to your success in sin reduction and virtue increase—sort of an effort to bring all members of the congregation up to virtue level. What do you think, Reverend?"

"I think I will pray for you," he replied.

I am becoming somewhat concerned about the imperviousness of other professions to accountability for results. However, I am not giving up. I have an appointment with the president of the local bar association next week. I see no reason why both prosecutors and defense attorneys can't win at least 80% of their cases.

Nobody Calls Me Doctor
by William E. (Bud) Davis

News Item—*In May and June of this year nearly 2,000
doctorates in education will be awarded by some 100 U.S. and
Canadian colleges and universities. Of this group more than
1,500 will be men, and of the men at least 80% will be members
of Phi Delta Kappa.*

"Congratulations, Doctor!"

I beamed. My graduate adviser, relieved that I had not seriously embarrassed him before his colleagues, grasped my sweaty paw and wrung it gleefully. "Congratulations, Doctor!"

The treasured phrase was repeated again and again as my examining committee passed in review—some smiling, some jesting, some looking as if they had just violated a sacred trust. I should care. I had their names on the dotted line. It was too late for them to renege.

"Congratulations, Doctor!"

I caressed the words. "Doctor Davis." What a grand sound! What alliteration! What dignity! What pomp! I repeated it to myself, much as a new bride surely must repeat her newly acquired last name. I strolled home, leaping easily from cloud to cloud and mouthing the magic formula. "Doctor Davis, Doctor Davis, Doctor Davis."

I was met at the door by my youngest daughter, who said, "Hi, Dad." Obviously, she hadn't gotten the word.

My wife, however, caught my victory smile. "Congratulations, Doctor!" she said. I shrugged modestly.

My young daughter looked amazed. "Is Daddy a doctor?"

"Well, almost," my wife explained.

"Barring a volcanic eruption between now and commencement," I joked.

My daughter obviously was still puzzled. "Does that mean he can take out my tonsils?"

"No, dear," my wife explained patiently. "He isn't that kind of a doctor."

"Then what kind of a doctor is he?"

"He's a doctor of education."

"Oh," my daughter replied, somewhat bored with the whole thing. "Daddy, can I have a nickel?"

Well, what can one expect from a mere child?

I began to wonder why, with all the smart people who had been awarded doctorates, none had come up with some simple method by which we might be identified. For example, like an Army colonel, we could wear some emblem on our shoulders, such as a flailed silver eagle (or a plucked pheasant). Or, like an admiral in the Navy, we could wear gold braid on the cuffs of our blue blazers. Like a German field marshal, we could carry a baton. Or if that seemed too pretentious, we could carry a swagger stick like a Marine Corps drill instructor. The embroidered letters "Ed.D." on the lapel would be too obvious, but surely some kind of lapel pin like a Rotary button would be appropriate.

Alas, even these moderate gestures are regarded as being in poor taste. I even discovered that it is deemed unethical to sign my correspondence with the appropriate *"Dr.* W. E. Davis." It is all right to have the degree, but not all right to let anyone know it. It was enough to make a doctor cry.

Friends still called me by my undistinguished nickname. Athletes still called me "Coach." Bills were still addressed to me as "Mister." The children still called me "Dad."

Even the campus newspaper kept referring to me by my antiquated title. In reviewing a conference, they stated that in attendance were: Dr. Jones, Dr. Smith, Dr. Barnes, and *Mr.* Davis.

It was all very frustrating.

But, by thunder, I decided that at least in one area I would insist upon being called "Doctor." I browbeat the secretaries until they complied. This went very well for awhile, until one day in my absence the president of the university called. (To protect the innocent, I shall refer to him as President White.) He asked, "Is Mister Davis there?"

My alert secretary answered. "If you mean *Doctor* Davis, *Doctor* Davis is not in. Whom shall I say is calling?"

"Well, when *Doctor* Davis arrives, will you please tell him that *Mister* White called?"

I decided to try the subtle approach. I quit referring to myself as Doctor Davis. Instead I made off-hand references to my training. I would drop little hints like, "Now when I was writing my doctoral thesis. . . .' Or, "I remember that book very well. When I was studying for my doctoral exams. . . ." This seemed to be working well, until some starry-eyed student asked. "Sir, when do you expect to get your degree?"

I've given up the battle on the home front. Just the other night I was sitting in front of a snapping fire, sipping a scotch and water (a very academic drink), listening to a little Rachmaninoff on the stereo (the cultural touch), and reading a learned publication (the continued pursuit of knowledge). My wife came in looking very fetching and with that come-hither glint in her eyes asked, "Shall we go to bed, Doctor?"

Blushing, I replied, "Aw, what the hell! Just call me Bud."

All Is Not Zip-a-dee-do-dah
In the Foreign Service
by J. Orvis Quimby

Africa
August 1959

My dear Phi:

It has come to my attention through your columns that 1,000 of your chaps are all atwitter at the prospect of doing an education hitch abroad.°

Before making firm commitments, best you alert these sports to the fact that all is not necessarily zip-a-dee-do-dah in the foreign service.

Take, for example, the simple matter of what transpires *before* one boards the ship or plane for a life of intrigue and adventure.

Unselfishly, and for the good of the corps, I offer myself as a case in point.

To give you the feel of it, recall the hardships suffered by traveling men in the past.

Traveling men of yesteryear developed heel spurs while switching and cajoling Hannibal's sleazy elephants over the Alps; took grapeshot through the groin and shoulder upon marching through Georgia with Sherman; snarled over raw fish entrails with Eddie Rickenbaker on the raft; and incurred the hernia assisting Col. Guinness in erecting the bridge on the River Kwai.

These tribulations dwindle to the proportions of a minor skin rash, however, when compared with the trauma and deep mental abrasions sustained by me upon making ready for a stint abroad.

The details are these:

Hark you back seven or eight months. At the time I was plying the trade of education consultant off the torpid southwest coast of Highway 66.

I remember it was following a routine curriculum committee meeting, wherein 14 of my crisp, leafy recommendations had been wilted by the group's priggish view that money and education are synonomous, that I scooted down the hall to the superintendent's office, barged in and blurted:

"Sir, in my three-year tenure not one of 322 recommendations has been passed upon, due to the sycophant business manager's zeal for clapping a lock on the petty cash drawer and gulping the key."

Heady with power, nostrils aflare, I pushed into deeper water.

"And, furthermore, unless major changes eventuate, I deem it necessary to gather my collection of curriculum guides and press on to more appreciative milieus—such uncontaminated frontiers as the interior of New Guinea, the wilds of Africa, the wastes of Antarctia, where education freebooters such as I can swashbuckle unencumbered and bring *real* education to the rank and file."

A trenchant pause ensued. Through the corridors, past the boiler room, out across the football field, one could hear the plaintive knell of a steeple bell. Decades slithered past. Civilizations rose and fell. Presently, outside the window, the clatter of ants, filing home from work, sliced the silence.

°One project of Phi Delta Kappa's Commission on International Relations in Education in 1959 was the compilation of a list of PDK members willing to accept foreign education assignments. It listed some 1,000 persons. —SME

The Super, white, then blue, then tomato-soup red, tunneled through a mountain of unsigned memos, overdue bills, parental threats, and unsavory clippings from the letters-to-the-editor column, and decreed thus:

"Captain Hornblower, hand over your sword! Sweep out your kiosk—after which, pause at the supply office for a final inventory. Your predecessor, a ne'er-do-well with forged credentials, got away with a typewriter, a steel file cabinet, 23 flagons of ink, and a dozen reams of prime onion skin."

With faded fedora in hand and lips pursed, I alerted sundrious placement authorities, penciled the want ads, and subsequently wheedled an education consultant berth with an overseas agency, signing on for a two-year stint in Africa.

Then I quaffed two fingers of Johnnie Walker, gathered my loved ones around the legs that once had stolen 46 bases in the Three-I League, and announced the change of course. The tidings wrought shrill cries and great wing flapping.

"Surely," wailed they, "we'll perish what without the advantages of Little League, frozen peas, television, green stamps, oboe lessons, and Sears financing."

In the grand tradition of Moses, I stood before the multitudes and rejoindered thus:

"Mark ye well! Far better to expire quickly, impaled upon the spear of an aborigine, than to founder slowly in the swamp of unfulfilled promises."

Having them gaffed, I staged a two-week workshop to allay all doubt. Each session was spiced with old, shredded Tarzan films and the scent of myrrh. For topping, I took to posing on the hearthstone in pith helmet and safari jacket.

In the end, they were drawn and quartered. Precise plans were laid for the great adventure.

The house sold within a month at a mere 20% loss. Nine dusty, rigorous trips were made to a rural military installation for health exams. A round of inoculations set off a bloodletting rebellion within our ranks. Nothing short of a cat-o'-nine-tails would bring the recalcitrants to heel.

Then a horde of coveralled packers, replete with crates and demolition gear, descended upon our little grey home in the West. For three days and three nights the air was rent with blasphemous oaths and the bludgeoning of select Chippendale and cherished credenzas.

Neighbors gathered at the windows, cheering lustily whenever the packers scored a point. A more enterprising, dull-normal youth sold lemonade.

At this writing, a rash of law suits are pending in the higher courts.

This interim was garnished with a flurry of special delivery letters and long distance phone calls to the agency as to who would pay the storage bill and where the hell were the airplane tickets. At my expense, an extra mailman and messenger boy were assigned to handle the excess traffic on our route.

Two weeks after we moved into a local motel, a courier appeared with a seven-page missive, chock full of curves. The most teeth-grinding was: Personnel files covering my pedigree and future hopes had been misplaced by a sloth-headed file clerk, and best I scrug over to Washington, pronto, for a new paint job.

At this point, God's second mistake took over the pitching, demanding to know what kind of high jinks were these and to fork over the remaining pages in the book of traveler's checks, as she was going to grandma's house in Indiana and not to communicate until the kinks had been smoothed from the labyrinth.

She, the four dwarfs, 29 assorted pieces of luggage, and a chrome-plated baby stroller faded into the morning haze.

In turn, with loins girded and 1,000 clam in the red, I pressed on to Washington, D.C., the Athens of the Eastern Seaboard, whither I was set upon by the niftiest cadre of phrase-makers south of Teachers College.

I was prodded into a bullpen with various other "specialists," each firmly convinced that his particular brand of tea was all the old world needed to cure its ills.

I was stripped in jig time of my princely, professional bearing and molded to the agency's "outline method of getting things done." Ofttimes a brief twinge of remorse and nostalgia rippled through the lower extremities and I yearned to return to the tweedy, slovenly, sedentary ways that set lesser men apart at Deadwell State Normal.

I was shunted and shuttled from one soothsayer's tent to the next. Within a matter of weeks I was plucked, neat and shiny, from the conveyor belt, complete with trench coat, snap-brim hat, pants and coat to match, button-down collar, striped tie, scotch-grain shoes, and an attaché case to replace the shopping bag I had come to love. All that was needed to qualify me for a floorwalker's position at the May Company was a carnation in the lapel and a thread-thin mustache.

There followed a brief twirl with the travel section. Books, charts, and maps were consulted. Polaris was shot and bearings taken. With uncanny accuracy, the travel experts scheduled me for not less than three 2:30 a.m. arrivals at remote, windswept ports of call. After a cursory investigation, I found that few if any of these spellbinders had ever been east of Hackensack.

Festooned on a 49-pound packet of passports, tickets, and literature on "how to get on in the agency," I was neatly bound into the womb position and thrust aboard the aircraft for New York City and a reunion with Mrs. Gulliver and her four Lilliputians, who arrived on the 7:15 from Chicago.

Thus began life in the foreign service.

And so, Old Phi, we have come full circle. In conclusion, might I lodge a minor suggestion. Before feeding 1,000 of your best education lancers to an international agency's "orientation grinder," best you ship them out to me for two weeks of intensive counsel.

Be warned. If you decline this liberal proposition, the sight of their consultant blood, running full in the streets of America, will be your eternal penance. I wash my hands of it.

And now I must roll myself in my leopard skin, snuff out the candle, and listen to the rhythmic throb of jungle drums, spiced by the clatter of passing Coca-Cola trucks. After all, Africa, don't you know, is a land of contrasts.

Fraternally yours,
J. Orvis Quimby

. . . And on the Other Hand

Mr. Quimby, in a letter not intended for publication—but he should worry, what with that ridiculous pseudonym—also says this:

"Life in the foreign service goes well. I recommend a two-year overseas tour of duty for every educator in America, if for no other reason than the fact that it gives occasion for counting one's blessings and alters one's perspective. As a 10-year man in education, I must confess that this is the most exciting and rewarding professional experience I have ever had. I hope to make it a career."

Teacher Evaluation
by John Gauss

TEACHER EVALUATION

TEACHER: Socrates

A. PERSONAL QUALIFICATIONS

	Rating (high to low) 1 2 3 4 5	Comments
1. Personal appearance	☐ ☐ ☐ ☐ ☒	Dresses in an old sheet draped about his body
2. Self-confidence	☐ ☐ ☐ ☐ ☒	Not sure of himself—always asking questions
3. Use of English	☐ ☐ ☐ ☒ ☐	Speaks with a heavy Greek accent
4. Adaptability	☐ ☐ ☐ ☐ ☒	Prone to suicide by poison when under duress

B. CLASS MANAGEMENT

1. Organization	☐ ☐ ☐ ☐ ☒	Does not keep a seating chart
2. Room appearance	☐ ☐ ☐ ☒ ☐	Does not have eye-catching bulletin boards
3. Utilization of supplies	☒ ☐ ☐ ☐ ☐	Does not use supplies

C. TEACHER/PUPIL RELATIONSHIPS

1. Tact and consideration	☐ ☐ ☐ ☐ ☒	Places student in embarrassing situation by asking questions
2. Attitude of class	☐ ☒ ☐ ☐ ☐	Class is friendly

D. TECHNIQUES OF TEACHING

1. Daily preparation	☐ ☐ ☐ ☐ ☒	Does not keep daily lesson plans
2. Attention to course of study	☐ ☐ ☒ ☐ ☐	Quite flexible—allows students to wander to different topics
3. Knowledge of subject matter	☐ ☐ ☐ ☐ ☒	Does not know material—has to question pupils to gain knowledge

E. PROFESSIONAL ATTITUDE

1. Professional ethics	☐ ☐ ☐ ☐ ☒	Does not belong to professional association or PTA
2. Inservice training	☐ ☐ ☐ ☐ ☒	Complete failure here—has not even bothered to attend college
3. Parent relationships	☐ ☐ ☐ ☐ ☒	Needs to improve in this area—parents are trying to get rid of him

RECOMMENDATION: Does not have a place in education—should not be rehired.

Catcher in the Wrong
by Rozanne Knudson

"He started talking in this very monotonous voice, and picking at all his pimples. I dropped about a thousand hints, but I couldn't get rid of him. All he did was keep talking in this very monotonous voice about some babe he was supposed to have had sexual intercourse with the summer before. He'd already told me about it a hundred times. Every time he told it, it was different."
—The Catcher in the Rye, Salinger

If you really want to hear about it, I lost my first teaching job in a row over the paragraph quoted above. I don't feel like going into too many details, cause the gory parts would give you about two heart attacks apiece. But anyway, there I was stuck in crummy Nowheresville, a teacher of English. I often wonder how I got through that year without losing my skin since I'd never had a class in sociology, psychology, education, or anything except about three thousand hours of literature—oh, and some neat geology courses. So I taught along all year and did a terrific job of making students want to read all the time—I really did—and got a hotshot reputation which fizzled out when we all read *The Catcher in the Rye* that spring. Then the dopey principal got around eight million telephone calls about how filthy, for Pete's sake, how obscene—obscene, can you believe it?—the book was and how dirty-minded anyone would have to be to teach it. So I was called to the office daily to defend myself and the book, and at first I was very polite and talked about artistic merits, sensitive portrayals of adolescence, possibilities for bibliotherapy (except I didn't know that was what it was called in those days—bibliotherapy, I mean), and all that jazz. After about a week I discovered what a Philistine I was engaging in conversation. All's he cared about were those creeps on the phone; and he finally said, "Miss Knudson, I'm going to be the next superintendent here, and I'm not gonna get hung up on some book about a dirty Jew-boy." I laughed. I roared. So I got the shaft that June, and my boss forthwith became prince of that godforsaken school district.

I had a royal pain about the whole thing the next years I taught and saw myself the victim of a huge plot. I wallowed around in martyrdom. Big deal. But last year, after a few doses of sociology, I began to see the whole fiasco in a tolerant way—in a new frame of reference, to quote about 76 sources; and now I'm ready to offer some solutions to this huge, hairy problem of dirty books in the public schools. You see, not just *The Catcher* is in the wrong these days. Moronic mothers jump on about any modern novel in paperback, and fathers seem to get sucked into the fight. But mostly mothers. They all forget, I suppose, that most dowdy standbys in every English class, like *The Scarlet Letter* and *The Return of the Native,* feature some mighty cool adultery and other sexy stuff. And I could show you some pretty wild scenes in even the Bible. But not right now.

It's all enough to make any good English teacher want to find out the routine on joining a convent or something, until she stops to think about sociology for a minute. Now me, I figure it goes down deep to two ways of looking at the school's job. One bunch of guys sees the school as a commonweal outfit just banging around to serve the public. These guys claim that they can leap around and pass out advice to teachers about choosing some books and burning others. Other guys preach that the school is set up more like a professional organization, you know, like doctors' offices, and you don't just waltz in and tell doctors what to prescribe, do you? Three years in these public schools has turned me about partly yellow, but I'm still gutsy enough to admit I favor the doctor's-office approach. I mean, after all, what good is a trained English teacher if she can't even pick a few lousy books for her kids? It makes me feel sad to know that the public often doesn't believe the advice we give them about reading *The Catcher* the way they believe their doctor's advice about catching disease. It kills me.

But lookit. Here's what we can do if we support my side. This works. I checked it all out. It's called the united-front ploy. All the English teachers on the school staff get together, see, and choose up the books they want to use. Now don't get me wrong. They don't need to flip and choose *Tropic of Cancer* or some other stuff just to show that they are big prescription writers. So they make this list of anything that they want to teach, excluding obscenity, and then ring in the principal and say, "See here, these are our choices and alternatives for reading this year." He relies on these well-educated specialists and commends their choices. He's a real prince. The superintendent loves his teachers and principals and knows they are real pros. He backs their choices of materials. He might even peep at the list to make a few suggestions, but he doesn't queer anything already planned. He is also a prince. Now the teachers shut their doors and teach *The Catcher*. The whole class is driven mad with desire to read and read. Soon the telephone rings in the principal's office.

"Madam," says our swinging principal, "your son is being treated to the very best literature we have available in this great democracy of ours. He is fortunate to have such an excellent teacher presenting this fine novel." He sighs.

"I'll call the superintendent," and she does, but to no avail. Tough luck.

"I'll call the school board," but they, too, support their professional staff and don't budge, not a lousy inch. No one commits suicide or anything, and the united-front ploy has saved *The Catcher*. It's all pretty cool.

But I'd like to apologize like a madman for not giving the opposition a word or two here. It's pretty depressing to admit, but, let's face it, if more than just an unorganized rabble element of the community raises up to bug the English teachers—like if half or more of the parents decide that *The Catcher* is obscene or something, then the profession will be forced to back down, because ultimately *the* people are always running things for you, and the majority wins in our country. Very big deal.

So that's all I'm going to tell about. I could probably go on and on about the clucks who heckle our schools and the jerks who make it to the principal occasionally, but that stuff doesn't interest me too much right now. I've found a sort of middle road. I really have.

IV

Critics, Criticism, and Leadership

Introduction

A rain of criticism falls ceaselessly on education in America, sometimes as a thunderstorm, sometimes as a gentle and even refreshing shower. As a long-time public relations practitioner in a teachers college, I was particularly sensitive to these atmospherics when I joined the Phi Delta Kappa staff in 1956. Like most dutiful readers of the literature, I was convinced of the therapeutic value of social criticism, including criticism of education. In fact, one reason I left public relations was a growing sense that the art, as I saw it practiced, had the long-term effect of weakening education rather than strengthening it.

Not until very recently, because of the nature of much current criticism, have I felt that we are in danger of losing the best features of the educational system that has prevailed in the U.S. and Canada for over a century, with its ideals of free access, equal opportunity, and instruction to achieve the common beliefs and understandings that make community possible. These are at the heart of democratic education. This is not the place for an essay on threats to democratic education, but my growing apprehension accounts for the fact that the KAPPAN began, in the past two years, to publish articles like those by Harold Hodgkinson and Ralph Tyler in this section. They celebrate what is right in U.S. education.

I begin with Paul Woodring's "A Second Open Letter to Teachers" (April 1978), because it spans a quarter century of criticism. I recall reading Woodring's first "letter" (in Harper's, July 1952) and discussing it with my professors at the University of Illinois, then a cauldron of conflict, what with historian Arthur Bestor and his protege, botanist Harry Fuller, on the same campus with excellent interpreters of John Dewey in the College of Education. To me, Woodring, while making no claim to profundity, was the essence of calm good sense then, and he seems so now.

Paul Woodring is also a master of educational writing, with over 200 publishing credits in journals that insist on good writing. This ability was a prime consideration in his appointment as first education editor of the Saturday Review in 1960, when Norman Cousins was beginning to make SR one of the most vital of the country's upper-middle-brow periodicals. Woodring had no prior experience in editing, but, he says, he seemed to be the only person acceptable both to Cousins and the Ford Foundation, which provided support for the SR education supplement. Woodring was education editor for six years and editor-at-large for another four.

Woodring has been a member of the faculty at Western Washington University, Bellingham, since 1939 and in 1964-65 was its interim president. He is now Distinguished Service Professor Emeritus. His Ohio State University doctorate (1934) was in psychology. He has won three Educational Press Association of America awards for editorials and a School Bell Award for "distinquished service in the interpretation of education." Among his books are Let's Talk Sense About Our Schools (1953); A Fourth of a Nation (1957); New Directions in Teacher Education (1957); and The Higher Learning in America: A Reassessment (1968).

Says Woodring, "Although some of my writing, particularly A Fourth of a Nation, has dealt with philosophical issues, I have never claimed to be an educational philosopher. I see myself as an analyst and interpreter of the educational scene, and since I have tried to reach a wider audience, my style has inevitably become somewhat journalistic. (I take some pleasure in recalling that William James was also accused of being 'journalistic.')"

The term "teacher burnout" was recently coined to describe the sense of frustration and failure that assails many teachers whose efforts yield few monetary, psychic, or social rewards. Florence Lewis, author of "Letter from an Angry Teacher," speaks for burned-out teachers everywhere. A long-time English teacher at Lowell High School in San Francisco, Lewis has been a regular contributor to the KAPPAN and a variety of other professional and popular journals (even Playgirl). I suspect that writing is a refuge for her, but I am also confident that her creative skills and dedication to teaching have inspired love of literature in several generations of Lowell High students.

In the spring of 1969 I was looking over some back issues of the KAPPAN and came upon two articles that appeared in November 1958: Admiral Hyman G. Rickover's "A Comparison: European vs. American Secondary Schools" and William W. Brickman's contemptuous comments on it titled "Rickover as Comparative Educator." It occurred to me that, in a sense, the antithetical claims of these two authors would soon be subjected to pragmatic testing. The National Aerospace Administration (NASA) was about to attempt landing a man on the moon. The next time I was in Washington, therefore, I visited NASA headquarters and talked with some of the program staff. They agreed to furnish names and addresses for some 200 astronauts and top scientists, engineers, and administrators in the Apollo program. I sent questionnaires to all of these NASA leaders. "The Schools Behind Masters of the Moon" is the result.

In scheduling the article for the September KAPPAN that year, we gambled and won. But by mid-July I was almost as nervous as astronauts Armstrong and Aldrin must have been before they danced on the moon. I flew to Cape Kennedy and stood near Walter Cronkite and Vice President Spiro Agnew on the morning of July 16. Then Apollo II blasted off with a roar I can still feel. Four days later we knew we could release our special KAPPAN with its wrap-around, four-color cover (borrowed from Look magazine) portraying 26 of the key figures in the project's success. The lead feature, 12 pages long, included the two sections reprinted here, plus an editorial and an interview with Robert Gilruth, a school principal's son who directed the NASA Manned Spacecraft Center at Houston. My editorial attacked "The Bitter Problem of Priorities" and included a slightly maudlin note about a 4-

year-old boy who died of malnutrition in Titusville, a few miles from Cape Kennedy, a day before the Apollo blast-off. Most of us remain ambivalent about the space program, even as the space shuttle succeeds so splendidly. I still rather like my closing paragraph: "Man's destiny is to unlock the secrets of the universe; perhaps, as Wernher Von Braun said after Apollo II, to become immortal by populating the stars. Will he do it so obsessively, oblivious to other claims upon his God-given talents and energy, that he loses his saving humanity?" We now have an answer to that question: No. (But we go on obsessively building engines of military destruction. Not just humanity but the human race is in terrible danger.)

Let me append a modern footnote to this discussion of Sputnik, Rickover, the schools, and NASA. Morton Kondracke, editor of The New Republic, *put it this way recently in the* Wall Street Journal: *"In one respect, it's too bad that the space shuttle performed flawlessly on its maiden flight, thereby reestablishing America's pre-eminence in space exploration. In 1957, when the Soviets sent Sputnik aloft, a frightened U.S. responded with the National Defence Education Act, pouring billions of dollars into training not only astrophysicists and space engineers but linguists, geographers, and social scientists. Even though we have a space shuttle and the Soviets don't, this country desperately needs to. devote its attention and resources again to improving the quality of education. Because we have a space shuttle and the Soviets don't, it's possible for the Reagan Administration to ignore our educational needs. . . ."*

Cheek by jowl with the space-age feature in the September 1969 KAPPAN was a piece by Ira Polley, superintendent of public instruction in Michigan, titled "What's Right with American Education?" Ten years later, in November 1979, we published Harold Hodgkinson's "What's Right with Education." Note the absence of a question mark in the latter title. For the KAPPAN, the Hodgkinson article marked the beginning of an era in which we have accentuated the positive. Hodgkinson was the right person to initiate it. As a former director of the National Institute of Education (which he saved from political annihilation), he had access to numerous research reports testifying to the success of education. Most of them had gained little or no attention in either the public or professional media. Several are cited in the Hodgkinson article reprinted here. With others, they form the basis of a half-hour slide-tape report that has been shown, with the cooperation of PDK chapters, to audiences throughout the U.S. over the past couple of years. Such reports are the profession's best answer to irresponsible criticism.

Ralph Tyler consented to write "The U.S. vs. the World: A Comparison of Educational Performance" for the Diamond Jubilee special KAPPAN, published in January 1981. This balanced view stands as a rebuke to modern-day Rickovers.

The Robert Havighurst discussion of educational leadership rounds out this section. We need leaders of all the types he describes if we are to respond successfully to the basic changes that are occurring in our society. "Educational Leadership for the Seventies" was the first Paul M. Cook Memorial Lecture, and was delivered at the 33rd Biennial Council of Phi Delta Kappa on 28 December 1971. Cook was the first executive secretary of Phi Delta Kappa, serving from 1928 until his retirement in 1956.

Havighurst himself is one of those protean figures who could have been a leader in any profession. He chose education, and by 1950 had written Developmental Tasks and Education, a work that established him as one of the seminal thinkers in the field. He is himself a prime example of the scholar-scientist leader he describes.

The KAPPAN was fortunate to have Havighurst as one of its editorial consultants from 1966 through 1975. I have never known an educator with a surer grasp of his subject or greater knowledge of current developments in it. Approaching 80, Havighurst continues to serve as professor of education and human development at the University of Chicago. His most recent KAPPAN contribution (among 13 during my editorship) was "Indian Education: Accomplishments of the Last Decade," written for the Diamond Jubilee issue.

—SME

A Second Open Letter to Teachers
by Paul Woodring

The wave of school criticism in the late Seventies resembles the wave that swept over America's schools in the early Fifties. What can we learn from that fact? The author of a famous 1952 Harper's article explains.

"By this late date it must be obvious to everyone engaged in teaching that a strong groundswell is running against us. Entire issues of popular magazines have been devoted to critical examinations of public education, each year more books are published which attack current educational practices, and in meetings of boards of education more and more voices are being raised demanding changes in the schools."

Although the above might well be the lead for an article published in 1978, actually it is the opening paragraph of my "Open Letter to Teachers," published in the July 1952 issue of *Harper's*. Then, as now, there were charges that the quality of education had deteriorated, that discipline was being neglected, that children were not learning to read, and that there were too many "frills" in the schools. Then, as now, the proposed remedy was a return to "basic education." And then, as now, the criticism could not wisely be ignored by educators, because the schools had some serious defects.

Anyone who now rereads the critical books of the Fifties—Arthur Bestor's *Educational Wastelands*, Albert Lynd's *Quackery in the Public Schools*, Bernard I. Bell's *Crisis in Education*, Mortimer Smith's *And Madly Teach*, or the slashing attacks of Admiral Hyman Rickover—will find much that sounds familiar. And we must admit that some of the weaknesses identified by those critics still exist. When Evan Hunter's *Blackboard Jungle* appeared in 1954 there were demands for immediate reforms, but since that time the shocking realities that Hunter portrayed have become evident in more and more big-city schools. Rudolph Flesch's *Why Johnny Can't Read*, published in 1955, became a best seller, even though it was never entirely clear just who Johnny was or how many Johnnies there really were. It seems obvious that some of the boys and girls of the generation accused by Flesch of being illiterate are now the middle-aged critics and defenders of the schools of 1978, yet the charge that children are not learning to read is heard as often today as it was 23 years ago. And it is true now, as it was then, that some are not learning. The difference is that we now excoriate dropouts, insist on keeping every adolescent in school, promote on an annual basis, and graduate boys and girls at age 18 regardless of what they have learned. But it was not the teachers who demanded this change; most teachers would be delighted to have some standards established and enforced.

Since it now seems clear that criticism of the schools comes in waves and that the wave of the late Seventies closely resembles that of the early Fifties, we ought to be able to learn something from the past. Unfortunately, most of the critics seem unaware of the history of educational criticism, while the current defenders of the schools seem reluctant to learn from the past. We continue to hear the same tired and ineffective responses to the same old charges.

Even in the best of times the public schools are highly vulnerable to criticism because of their visibility. At the end of each day children return home and report on the day's events. (Private boarding schools are much less vulnerable because their children go home less frequently.) If children are punished, the parents rise in wrath; but if misbehavior goes unpunished, the school is criticized for lack of discipline. If a school concentrates on the academic disciplines, it is criticized for turning out graduates without "marketable skills"; but if it concentrates on vocational training, it is criticized for neglecting the sciences, the humanities, and the arts. If it tries to do all of these things at once, it will be criticized for not taking time to do anything well. But the public school belongs to the people and reflects their views. If the educational philosophy of the school seems to vacillate—as it does—it is because parents are confused about what they want, and school boards reflect the parents' confusion.

Educators, however, must accept some responsibility for the criticism. Some school administrators seem as confused about the proper goals of education as are the parents, when they ought to be better informed and better able to state and defend their goals. Some seem more concerned about "public relations" and a smoothly operating organization than they are about educational quality. Some are reluctant to take a firm stand on anything. Some speak educational jargon rather than English. And some teachers infuriate parents by taking a "teacher knows best" attitude, even with intelligent and well-educated parents who are legitimately concerned about their children's welfare.

Some of the critics, while writing vigorously, reveal their ignorance. Columnists, reporters, and editors in a number of cities have expressed alarm over their discovery that 40%, 50%, or 60% of the children in their schools have test scores "below the national norm," apparently unaware that, because the word "norm" as used by test makers means only "average," half the children in the nation must always be below the norm (unless all have identical scores). Other writers make too much of the fact that pupils in private schools score higher on college entrance tests than do those in public schools, ignoring the fact that the more selective private schools avoid the problem of educating slow learners by not admitting them, something a public school cannot do.

The recent decline in scores on the Scholastic Aptitude Test (SAT), used as a basis for admission to college, is a cause for concern; but no one knows whether, or to what extent, teachers or schools are responsible for it. The recent report of the Wirtz Committee attributes the decline to a wide variety of factors, including everything from television to the higher divorce rate. Perhaps the deemphasis on standards for graduation has resulted in lower motivation, but I can find no evidence of any decline in the quality of teaching over the past 14 years. It is not at all certain that the students taking the tests today can reasonably be compared with the much smaller, and presumably more highly selected, group that took the test 14 years ago. In any case, as its name implies, the SAT is designed to measure scholastic *aptitude* rather than prior learning.

Two of the major targets of the earlier critics have disappeared from the scene since 1952. Many of the earlier critics focused their attacks on "teachers colleges," which, they maintained, taught "nothing but methods" and turned out teachers insufficiently prepared in the academic disciplines. These critics were a bit confused, because the teachers colleges provided more liberal education than the critics were aware of, and in any case the great majority of secondary school and a large minority of elementary school teachers were not and never had been products of teachers colleges. They were graduates of private liberal arts colleges and of public and private universities.

Since 1952 teachers colleges as separate, single-purpose institutions have just about disappeared from the American scene. The state universities that have grown out of the one-time teachers colleges—San Francisco State and Kent State are conspicuous examples—now offer a wide variety of programs, and candidates for teaching are in the minority. In these institutions the academic disciplines are not taught by professional educators but by specialists in the academic disciplines, and every future teacher gets the major part of his instruction from these specialists.

The second disappearing target was that vague complex of theories, attitudes, and points of view called "progressive education." In 1952 progressive education was the favorite whipping boy of the critics; today it is rarely mentioned. John Dewey, who was called "the father of progressive education" (though he denied the paternity and was sometimes highly critical of the excesses of the progressives), also gets much less attention today.

A generation ago, under the aegis of progressive education, many educators made the mistake of trying to accept full responsibility for the total development of the whole child, ignoring the fact that over the course of a year the typical child spends between 80% and 85% of his waking hours out of school—in the home, on the street, on the playground, or God knows where. Parents, rather than teachers, are responsible for these out-of-school hours and consequently for a large part of the child's development. As everyone ought to know by now, because of ceaseless repetition, it is estimated that between the ages of 6 and 18 a typical child spends about as many hours watching television as he spends in school. If this is true, television producers must accept a large measure of responsibility for the child's moral development. But, with today's programming, before he becomes an adult a child will witness thousands of brutal acts often perpetrated by the "good guy"—a cop, a private eye, or a secret service agent who was "only doing his duty" when he took it upon himself to dispense "justice" by physical violence in utter disregard of all of our national principles of justice. It is impossible for teachers to counteract the effect of this televised mayhem, and it is silly for anyone to say that it does no harm to a developing personality just because there is "no proven correlation" between television and crime. A child learns from all of his experiences, in and out of school, and watching televised brutality in living color is surely an experience.

Although the schools should do what they can to foster morality, the moral standards of children will never be very much better than those of the society around them. If a school is a "blackboard jungle," it is because the surrounding community is a jungle. The schools of New York, Chicago, and Detroit are among the most expensive in the nation, and their teachers are highly paid in comparison to teachers in small towns, even when allowance is made for differentials in the cost of living. It is doubtful that pouring federal dollars into these schools will do very much to improve them until the communities themselves become better examples of civilized life. The primary task is that of improving the community.

Outside the major cities the prospects for public education look much better. Rural schools, particularly those in the South, have improved notably over the past 25 years. The major criticisms directed against the schools do not fit the facts in the smaller cities and rural areas where most Americans live.

Despite all clichés about ours being an "urban nation," fewer than 10% of all Americans live in cities of over one million population, and the percentage living in such cities is declining. Fewer than 30% live in cities as large as 100,000. The notion that our entire nation has become "urbanized" results from the curious habit of the Census Bureau of counting every community of over 2,500 people as "urban." Even by that definition, 53 million Americans still live in areas classed as "rural," while another 100 million live in small cities or in suburbs where the schools are far more successful than those in the really big cities.

One underlying source of criticism is that educators have promised too much and the people have come to expect too much of public education. Unlike a private boarding school, which has custody of a child throughout the day and week, the public school is a day school in which the child is present for only a few hours a day for half the days of the year. Within these time limits the school should not try to do everything that needs to be done; it should concentrate on what it can do best and leave many responsibilities to the home and other social agencies. This is the strongest argument for "basic education," provided that we can come to agreement on what is basic. As of now there is no such agreement. Some of those who use the term speak only of the three Rs, but no informed person thinks that "readin', 'ritin', and 'rithmetic" can reasonably take up the full time of a child throughout 12 years of schooling. Others, including the spokesmen for the Council for Basic Education, would add many of the traditional academic disciplines: algebra, history, foreign languages and literatures, the various sciences, art, music, and perhaps philosophy. But other enthusiasts for basic education place the emphasis on morality, religion, and patriotism, while some would add vocational training to the list.

For those in search of a definition, a good place to start is the dictionary, which says that "basic" means "forming a base or basis—fundamental—serving as a starting point." Learning to read obviously is basic, because it provides the basis for learning about all other subjects and everything else that is in print. Writing provides one of the bases for communication. Arithmetic is basic to higher mathematics and the sciences. It is also necessary for anyone who must keep accounts or compute an income tax. It might be argued that a knowledge of history, economics, political science, and the physical and social sciences is basic to sound decision making in the voting booth. Vocational training is secondary rather than basic: It is an application of basic knowledge to a vocation, as when an auto mechanic applies the principles of physics to the repair of an internal combustion engine. Some school activities, such as those of a cheerleader or drum majorette, do not appear to be basic to anything, however much fun they may be.

But it is not at all clear that all the activities engaged in during 12 years of formal schooling can be or should be "basic." After a child has taken the first or fundamental steps—which are the basic ones—he should take the second, third, and fourth steps. Basic education is most obviously appropriate during the early years of schooling.

The American public school has been the victim of rising expectations without a comparable rise in performance. We must redefine and delimit our goals and make it clear to the people just what we can and can not accomplish.

Because of the rapid fluctuation in the supply-demand ratio for various kinds of work, no school, not even a vocational school, can safely promise that every graduate will find the kind of job for which he has been prepared. If he was narrowly trained, his specialty may not even exist 10 years after his graduation.

A school with a broader and more liberal program offers better preparation for long-range goals, but no school, however academic its orientation and however eagerly it embraces basic education, can guarantee that every graduate will be well informed and deeply interested in the things that matter most, or even that he will be able to read difficult books with understanding and write with clarity and force. No school can assure parents that their children will become virtuous citizens who are psychologically well adjusted. All it can promise—all that any educator ought to promise—is an opportunity to learn under favorable circumstances, with the help of a competent teacher and with a modest amount of essential equipment, including some good books. Whatever the program may be, however competent the teacher may be, *it is the child who must do the learning.* If this can be made clear to parents, their demands on the school may be modified, and perhaps they will accept greater responsibility for their own part in the child's education.

Letter from an Angry Teacher
by Florence Lewis

More than ever, the public school teacher is accused of "a simple failure to teach basic skills" and is responsible for "an attendant syndrome of failure which contributes to a student's low self-esteem." Also, we are told, teachers fail "to relate to, or communicate with, or respect students, especially low-achieving students, as human beings. . . ." Looming large in the shadow of these charges is a conviction in the community that "schools as social systems promote a life of conformity, authoritarianism, a certain rigidity, almost compulsiveness. . . ."[1] May I respond to these failures, one at a time? I have been a teacher for 20 years and it is my duty.

First, the simple failure to teach basic skills. How the hell can we teach basic, especially basic, skills if the kids aren't there, if, even on the elementary level, one of the symptoms of the slow learner is that he isn't there because his mother isn't there or his father isn't there and he can't get to school by himself because he's maybe 7 years old.

I know what the teacher is supposed to do. She is supposed to go find the kid every afternoon when she has finished her "busy-work" and sit down in the middle of the kitchen or the basement or the attic of the child's home or his commune and announce, "Here I am. I'm Bradley's teacher. Where is Bradley? I want to teach him his basic skills."

Am I making up a story? Nope, I am not. I used to do that when I was in my twenties, and once I went looking for "Robert" to tell Robert that I wanted to relate to him by teaching him a lesson or two at home, and I wanted to relate to his widowed mother by begging her to get Robert to school, and Robert had four big brothers, and I almost got myself raped. I know! I should have accepted that too and joyfully, but I wasn't with it. I liked Robert, though. He told me what a sweathouse was. He told me it was a whorehouse, not a place where you dry out cocoa beans.[2]

What about schools as social systems that promote a life of conformity, authoritarianism, a certain rigidity? I recall a real battle-ax of a teacher forcing, literally forcing, speech sounds out of marginal kids, those who had been damaged by rubella or meningitis and consequently had lost part of their vision, part of their hearing, and part of their "learning centers." They literally could not speak, and this old vulture was teaching them how. She knew how. Yes, she did, but the kids wanted to go to sleep or wanted to drift off in a world where they could dream whatever half-visions they desired; and I recall seeing one of these kids cry because the old bird had been relentless and compulsive, "anal" even; and I ran off into a corner and wept with the uselessness and cruelty of it all.

Several months later the kid for whom I had wept saw me out of the corner of her eye and in strangulated but proud tones she spoke my name and told me that she was going home to Fresno for Christmas. She got every single word out. I hugged her and kissed her and put her hand on my throat and lips as I said over and over again how happy I was. And she nodded her head in agreement and kept saying, "Yes, yes."

Now, this was a marginal kid. Most of our low-achieving students have

both their senses. Do you suppose that a little more drill, a certain rigidity, a certain compulsiveness about drill . . .? Nobody says you can't play games, but those of us who have had difficulty learning a skill or a concept recognize with gratitude the teacher or the aide or the parent who stood over us and said, "Do it again!" "Say it once more." "I'll show you again." "Now you do it."

I am not suggesting humiliation in front of the class. I am not suggesting a lockstep. I am suggesting believing enough in what you have to give to a kid and believing that the kid, no matter what his problems are, can learn the skill and enjoy a sense of accomplishment. If we are too afraid to hang in there, doesn't it suggest that we have no real faith in our ability to teach or the ability of the kid to learn?

That old vulture teacher taught another lesson. She taught kids that learning would come hard but *that learning there would be.* Our instant-breakfast kids, instant everything, want instant learning, and often the teacher who argues for patience and time is the new ogre. On the elementary level, the argument from a parent or foster-parent whose child is not learning to read is that it doesn't take more than "a minute" to learn that stuff, if the teachers were not so lazy about giving an hour or two for a few days each week every month. For the slow learner, the rigid, almost compulsive teacher may be the one who can break through. It's easier to go off in the corner and cry.

But after Robert and the deaf-blind child, what happened? Did I concern myself "with the life concerns of adolescents: sex, love, joy, self-doubt, fear, anxiety, pain, loneliness, belonging—all the issues"?

How can I teach literature if I do not teach understanding of the human condition? For 10 years I have been a practicing if not a card-carrying member of the English 300 Society, whose philosophy briefly stated is that good teachers revise the curriculum and exchange ideas and try team teaching in order to deal closely with these human concerns; and the cry is still, "Nothing goes on in schools." But a good history teacher will also be able to fire up his kids on those factors that make it impossible for human beings to live together, let alone love one another.

Concerning the specific charge of not dealing with sex and love and joy—and, finally, life: Only recently has it been just a little bit easy to introduce certain "controversial" texts in the classroom. Believe it or not, there are still places in California, swinging California, where the board will not let a teacher bring *Catcher in the Rye* into the classroom. Five years ago, in my home town, a teacher who wanted "to study" *To Kill a Mockingbird* was called a radical, and had he not been a member in good standing with the teacher union, his superintendent would have fired him. Ten years ago a bright young teacher in San Francisco wanted to use an article from *Harper's* entitled "Sex," or something like it. It was a bland article; it was pabulum, but one of the parents at the school where I was situated sprang a leak, and our stupid central office ordered the high school to remove *Harper's* from the shelves and never to order it again. The poor girl who had suggested the article as a reading assignment was badgered and hounded and called upon to testify on her purpose and to explain. I daresay this girl thought twice about anything coming into her classroom that smelled of life or sex. Witness not too long ago the California State Board of Education, under pressure of the fundamentalists, insisting that we present Darwinian evolution as theory. And more recently the Vonnegut book burning is a grim reminder that the teacher may be willing but the community may not.[3]

I have now responded to three charges of failure. The issue still looms large.

What can we do with the fact that so many of our kids can't even read and write their own language? And so many of them are turned on to drugs? I believe we must quit asking for miracles from the schools. The schools cannot undo the first five years of a home where a kid has never been spoken to, just shoved aside. I know of some little ones who had never sat in a chair until they came to kindergarten. They literally do not know "chair." The world of kindergarten is a trip to another planet. These kids won't be ready to read for several years, not in an establishment-type school. What's the answer? To get rid of the chairs? Or does the kid need a different kind of school where the first thing he gets when he comes to school is breakfast?

And how do you fill up the hole in a kid whose answer to life is drugs—because there is only the abyss without the drug? School is absolutely the worst place for him. Does that mean that we make over the school to fit those kids who need one-to-one therapy or Synanon? And for kids who must have immediate rewards so that any kind of discipline, like steady attendance, homework (what's that?), or even carrying a book to class is out of the question, even drugs are an immediate kind of reward. What can we do for him when he needs "input," but he cannot put out? What's the answer? You tell me, because all this kid ever cries is, "I'm bored, I'm bored."

My school has basic emergency procedures for drugs and other referral services, and some members of the staff, tireless and dedicated, listen to and rap with kids. But the help a really helpless kid needs is open-ended. A teacher who has skills to teach can't give a troubled kid the whole of his day, and some kids need that and more. A really troubled child can devour his counselor or his teacher, and then the cry begins that Mr. So-and-so or Ms. or Mrs. is neglecting papers, the other kids, the classroom. The teacher who does his thing well needs to remain in the classroom, not as an advertisement for rapping but for teaching. And there is no good teacher who doesn't listen to a kid. But he's also got to teach five classes, attend meetings during his lunch and prep periods—and these are meetings on ways to revise the curriculum or "start a remedial program for kids who are cutting." And so pile on him two or three or five kids who have to see him anytime they have to see him, and the poor girl or guy loses his/her marbles. The other day I saw one of my colleagues say very gently to a troubled kid, "Look, I have to go to the can. I'll be right out." Is that any way to live?

Perhaps it's time I delivered myself of some real answers. Everybody else has. Let's really accept the idea that public education is changing. O.K. It has to. It's a tired old man who gets up at 6 a.m., shaves, tries to look respectable, even jaunty. But he faces a losing battle. He has to teach skills, keep the garbage from overflowing the halls, try out new lifestyles, keep the toilets safe for elimination, improve the curriculum, feed kids a hot lunch, strive for ethnic balance, introduce venereal disease "relevantly" into family living courses, maintain buildings, keep the walls up, keep the ground down, teach drug education, keep the pushers out, teach driver education. Oh, he's a tired old man. So let's take him out and shoot him. Once and for all. And get rid of him as a damned scapegoat.

And let's get rid of 12 years in Southeast Asia and end the mentality that caused and nurtured the cold war. But it's the Vietnam war more than anything else that has caused us to question that rotten old man and the sort of lies he taught us when and if he taught us—which he didn't. So let's give the war a medal.

And let's get rid of living for the buck. And the automobile. And then we can get rid of driver education. And drugs won't cost so much money.

And while we are doing all of the above, let's make a lot of love, because some activity should take the place of war and driver education.

And let's teach the language of Watergate. It has all the forms of discourse. Hey, maybe we should take back the medals that we just gave to the war and shoot the war. The war really pushed drugs on us. And let's give medals to the tired old man and his swinging teachers who tried to keep the old man alive by stretching him in all directions.

Perhaps the key is the teacher, unintimidated and confident. Confident that he has something to teach, confident that he can do it well. Unafraid to ask for courtesy while he's "communicating" skills or ideas, unafraid to ask for help if a kid isn't ready to learn or if the teacher honestly feels he can't handle the situation or the kid; like the kid who has been throwing typewriters out of the window or threatening him with a knife. Unafraid to demand breathing time for himself; unafraid to demand a classroom and a teaching schedule that will enable him to spot a troubled kid or a sick one. He may not be able to relate to that kid, but he can find those who can.

And the other key is holding on to good teachers where they are most needed—at the elementary and secondary levels. Rewards like respect and money should not be scorned in a society that places so much value on money and power. But the real problem is once again identifying what a good teacher is. Suppose a guy is great for rapping but teaching the skills bores him. Suppose he loves kids, wants to be friends with them, and that's all. He's not turned on to teaching anything. He teaches love. Is love enough? Kids soon get bored with love in the classroom. Suppose we have a teacher who teaches the kids basic math or algebra and behaves like a refrigerator. The kids come in and sit down. And they need sweaters. Can kids learn from a cold teacher? Suppose the answer is yes. Should we melt down the teacher of algebra? The weather does get cold on occasion. What about the rap specialist? Do we teach him how to spell?

There is such a thing as accountability. A teacher has obligations to his subject matter too. But what subject matter, I hear you cry, in a world gone crazy with war and poverty, alienation and drugs? What subject matter? Oh, love, let us hold one another and connect, but the story of our days will fade away, and the Brave New World will come and Orwell's DuckSpeak too, and the guys on top, oh the guys on top, they will know that 2+2 once equalled four, and a play called *The Tempest* had a gal called Miranda.

The key is the teacher, not his failures but his valor. Not his apathy but his courage under fire, his guts, his determination not to lose his collective marbles. Let's give him a medal. And shoot the guys who write articles from the outside, looking in.

---

1. All quoted lines come from an article entitled "Is Drug Education Working," *Satur-*

day Review, December, 1972, which a good friend photocopied and left on my desk in the hope that I would spring a leak.

2. Putting aside the dubious joy of being raped, how was I responsible for Robert's low self-esteem or his syndrome of failure? I was willing, I was wanting, I was ready to relate, communicate with, respect him and his mom. His dumb brothers got in the way.

3. I refer to the North Dakota burning of *Slaughterhouse Five*.

The School Behind Masters of the Moon
by Stanley M. Elam

*In the late Fifties the Rickover breed of critic blamed U.S. edu-
cation weaknesses for Russia's early lead in the "space race."
Were post-Sputnik improvements responsible for the present
U.S. lead? Well, hardly. . . .*
*As the basis for this article, KAPPAN editors queried nearly
200 key figures in America's space effort.*

Ten years after astronaut-to-be Michael Collins graduated from St. Albans
School in Washington, D.C., Admiral H. G. Rickover gave the fiftieth anni-
versary commencement speech there on the topic, "Why European
Secondary Schools Are Superior to American."

That was in 1958. Rickover was already the darling of post-Sputnik education critics who fed a humiliated America its necessary scapegoat. In his address,[1] Rickover said, "The chronic shortage of good scientists, engineers,
and other professionals which plagues us is the result of inadequate pre-pro-
fessional education—of time wasted in public school which must be made
up later on." In a 16 February 1958 *This Week* article, Rickover said that
"rightly, Sputnik has been seen as a triumph of Russian education." In his
opinion, the Russians had no trouble turning out skilled professionals—three
times as many engineers as we did, for example.

Rickover warned America that "to maintain scientific and technological
leadership and *the modicum of culture necessary in a civilized society* [italics
added], we must get to work on the long-range task of reorganizing our
public schools so that they may give us the kind of people needed today,
where few problems can be solved by common sense and hard physical work
alone, but where the need above all is for well-equipped minds, 'adjusted' to
this scientific era in man's history."

The Rickover brand of criticism had its effect, as every educator knows. A
new era in American education began with Sputnik I. For example, within a
year after its passage in 1958, the National Defense Education Act had poured
a hundred million new dollars into improvements in the teaching of science,
math, modern languages, and the training of "highly skilled technicians."

Knowledgeable Americans now recognize, however, that Rickover was
wrong in much of what he said a decade ago. We are now at a new appraisal
point. Education is newly challenged, but the challenges are different. The
outcome of the unofficial but universally recognized "race to the moon" that
developed between the USSR and the United States in the Sixties was little affected by the hard line in education advocated by Rickover and the Council
for Basic Education, with its emphasis on math and science in American prep
schools. Although (as Robert Gilruth says in the interview that follows this
article) the scientists and engineers who put Apollo 11 astronauts on the moon
are young, they are not *that* young. For example, Michael Collins at 39 is
about two years older than the average for astronauts, all 53 of whom had
finished high school by 1958.

For the wealthiest and most technologically advanced nation in the world, success in space was simply a matter of adjusting national priorities. All that was required was the national will to mount a giant program. The scientific principles had already been established by such men as Tsiolkovsky, Goddard, and Oberth (see "The Three School Teachers Who Opened The Space Age," p. 123). Many of the basic inventions had been made; there was a convergence of technologies, in computers, fuels, metallurgy, astronautics, and a host of new fields.[2] Sputnik provided the motivation, in the cold war context, and President Kennedy gave the national will a specific goal.

Nevertheless, Admiral Rickover was perfectly correct in emphasizing the importance of a well-educated work force for an enterprise as demanding as putting a man on the moon. For the U.S. it required the labor of 300,000 to 400,000 people over a period of eight years. Neither America nor the Soviet Union could have achieved what they have without an educated citizenry, and the remainder of this article will present some facts about the education of key figures in America's space achievement.

In preparing to write on this topic, we soon learned that no one had gathered the pertinent facts. The Public Information Office of the National Aeronautics and Space Administration in Washington was willing to help, however, and supplied information about and addresses for 170 key NASA scientists, engineers, managers, and other specialists, as well as thumbnail biographies of the 53 astronauts in training at the beginning of this year. A brief questionnaire was developed and mailed in early July to the 170 key NASA personnel and about 30 others representing some of the major NASA contractors. It asked only for information about their contributions to the space effort, an outline of their formal schooling, and frank opinions on the importance of different phases of this schooling in their careers.

Although the questionnaires were sent only a week or so before the crucial Apollo 11 flight, nearly half of the recipients took time to fill them out. Our major conclusions and impressions upon reading the replies and the NASA biographies can be briefly stated:

1. The formal schooling of key people in America's space effort is enormously varied, but the vast majority of our respondents attended public elementary and high schools in the U.S. (Only the colony of Germans brought to America from Peenemuende were educated elsewhere.) In almost equal numbers, they are graduates of public and private colleges and universities and federally operated military and service institutions of all kinds. At least half of them have the master's degree and nearly one-fifth have earned the doctorate.

2. Many of the engineers and scientists report being influenced in career selection by their early school experiences. Sometimes it was a high school course, sometimes a teacher whose influence was decisive. Usually it was a combination of these and other influences.

3. Interestingly, in a period characterized by revolt against what universities have come to represent, our respondents were almost unanimous in their praise of their college and university preparation. Obviously, they were campus "squares," achievement-oriented, disinclined to criticism and negativism, eager to pry open the store of goodies available on nearly any college campus. They would not be out demonstrating if they were in school today; they would be slaving away in their labs and dorms to master a discipline.

4. Talent can crop up anywhere. While prestige institutions may attract a

disproportionate share of it, nevertheless it is worth noting that the 170 "key people" identified by NASA did their college work at 119 different U.S. and 16 different European institutions (the German contingent again).

Twelve institutions each figured in the preparation of five or more of the key people: the Massachusetts Institute of Technology, 15; the University of Michigan, 10; Darmstadt University (Germany), 9; the U.S. Military Academy (West Point), 8; the U.S. Naval Academy (Annapolis), 7; Auburn University, George Washington University, Georgia Institute of Technology, Harvard University, Purdue University, and Rensselaer Polytechnic Institute, each 6; and Virginia Polytechnic Institute, 5. The range of other *alma maters* is almost incredible. There are graduates of great state and private universities, of junior colleges, of teachers colleges. O. C. Jean, deputy director of the Aero-Astrodynamic Lab at the Marshall Space Flight Center, Huntsville, Alabama, took his B.S. in math, 1951, at Murphreesboro State Teachers College. There is one graduate of Howard College (now Samford University) of Birmingham. He is P. R. Bell, chief, Lunar and Earth Sciences Division, Manned Spacecraft Center, Houston.

Perhaps the best way of conveying the flavor and thrust of replies to the questionnaire is to quote directly some of the prominent respondents.

Rocco Petrone is already a legendary figure at the Kennedy Space Center in Florida, famed for his driving energy and insistence upon perfection. As director of launch operations, he is responsible for the management and technical direction of preflight operation and integration, test, checkout, and launch of all space vehicles, both manned and unmanned. A West Point graduate in 1946, he played on the great Academy football teams during the era of All-Americans "Doc" Blanchard and Glenn Davis (Mr. Inside and Mr. Outside). He took his master's and professional engineering degrees at MIT in 1952. Says Petrone of his school experience:

"I believe my formal schooling—especially my graduate level education—prepared me very well for the responsibilities I have carried out in the space effort. I must also state that one of the biggest contributions of my formal education has been to stimulate further on-the-job education by raising the questions: Why? How come? Are you sure? Etc."

Christopher Columbus Kraft, Jr. (one of the men cited by Gilruth in his *KAPPAN* interview as a major contributor to space success) is director of flight operations for the Manned Spacecraft Center at Houston. A graduate of public grade and high schools in Virginia, he took the B.S. in aeronautical engineering at Virginia Polytechnic Institute. As early as 1963, he won the NASA Distinguished Service Medal from the President of the U.S. and since then has received many other awards for creative scientific and organizational achievements. He says:

"A math teacher at Hampton High School, Mrs. Stevens, probably had greater influence on my selection of engineering than anyone else in my lower education career. At college, Professor Seltzer, head of the Aeronautical Engineering Department, was really the cause of my selecting aeronautical engineering in my junior year as my major. The military program at VPI probably had a great deal to do with shaping my character and career. I feel that I received a good education at VPI, mostly in learning how to use the tools of basic engineering. However, because of the period during which I attended college (the war years), I was poorly prepared to enter into the world of aeronautical research and development. Most of my education in this field was obtained on the job, and particularly from William H. Phillips, who was my immediate supervisor at NACA [predecessor to NASA]. My work in the Flight Research Division at NACA gave me excellent schooling in those elements required for the manned spaceflight program."

E. D. Mohlere is director of university affairs at the Marshall center in Huntsville. A graduate of various grammar schools in Illinois and of the Oak Park High School in the Thirties, he has a rather unusual combination of college degrees: a B.S. in military engineering at West Point and an M.S. in metallurgical engineering at MIT to go with a bachelor's in international relations at George Washington University. He says:

"The high school I attended was a particularly good one that laid heavy emphasis on communicative skills. This has served well. The school pursued a policy of firm discipline. At times it seemed oppressive . . . [but] now I value the policy. This is not to say that thought was regimented—not at all. Freedom of thought and disciplined thought processes or mechanics are compatible despite news to the contrary."

Richard J. Allen is one of only four among the NASA respondents whose entire early schooling was obtained at private schools (St. Mary's of Loretto Grammar School and High School and St. Bernard High in Alabama). He is a major contributor to the "Gemini Configuration Management System" and "principal implementer of design certification of Apollo flight and ground systems for manned earth orbital and lunar missions" as test manager, Apollo Test Directorate. Like other NASA engineers, he is loyal to his schools: "Elementary school provided excellent basic tools. . . . The key was discipline and practice and an uncluttered curriculum with outstanding devotion to teaching by several dedicated sisters. . . . High school provided basic disciplines . . . good study habits, large workloads, excellent language training (Latin in particular), good math basics and science." Speaking of his early college education (at Vanderbilt), Allen mentions professors who developed an appreciation in the student for a good hard day's work. A Mr. Glenn "brought home the point that a problem worked well without the right answer isn't worth a damn." Allen believes the school environment today is too cluttered with "nice to know" rather than "need to know" information. He suggests that "the personal stability, emotional maturity, and capability to judge and reason effectively, developed initially in college, provide the cradle in which the student will build his professional career."

George C. White is director, Apollo Quality and Reliability, with responsibility for establishing policies and auditing performance of manned space flight centers. He says:

"The importance of information gained in formal school diminished rapidly after the first two or three years out of school. [But] attitudes developed toward continued learning from work experience were of increasing importance. . . ."

Roderick O. Middleton, now Apollo program manager at the Kennedy Space Center, writes:

"I obtained an excellent classical background at Harvard, a broad spectrum of engineering courses at Ft. Bliss (aerodynamics, instrumentation, computer technology, statistical theory in damage analysis missile guidance technology, rocket theory and application, etc.) not available, to the best of my knowledge, at any single university during that time. . . . I am not certain that adequate depth is available in most courses today, or that sufficient emphasis is placed upon breadth of knowledge, to provide the best system engineers in quantity."

Ernst D. Geissler directs research and development for the Aero-Astrodynamics Lab at Marshall Space Flight Center in Huntsville. He took his B.S. and M.S. degrees in physics and math at the Technical University of Dresden, Germany, in 1939 and his doctorate in applied math from the Technical University in Darmstadt in 1951. He received NASA's Award for Exceptional Scientific Achievement in 1963. His remarks are perhaps characteristic of the German colony's reaction to our questionnaire:

"The importance of formal school consists primarily in 1) training for logical and independent thinking as a foundation for later scientific work (primarily in high school plus college), and 2) providing working knowledge of fundamental concepts and tools in mathematics, physics, and general engineering and their applications toward problem solution (primarily at colleges and universities). It is neither possible nor necessary that this training be closely focused on the particular problems encountered later in professional life. . . .

"It is my impression that formal training in this country right after the war was of uneven quality and did frequently emphasize learning rather than independent thinking. However, since the Sputnik time, education has much improved, and many universities and institutes of technology produce not only excellent scientists and engineers but carry on significant research in science and technology related to space flight. The effort of American education has thus become an excellent foundation for further progress in space."

Perhaps three or four times as many scientists and engineers work for corporations and universities with NASA contracts as work for NASA directly. It was impossible in the limited time available to us to locate and question many of them, but Roger McFall is one example. He is a Milford, Michigan, mechanical engineer who helped with Bendix Corporation research and development in the new discipline of fluidics. Fluidic systems replace electronics for nuclear environments associated with NERVA rocket engines. McFall is a public schools product and graduate of Michigan State University (B.S. in mechanical engineering, 1960). He took the M.S.E. at Arizona State University in 1966. He says:

"I developed an interest in physics and math in high school. Math teacher Ray Ellis of Chesaning was a strong influence. Aptitude tests taken at a preregistration summer conference at Michigan State caused me to decide to change my major from art to mechanical engineering. This was the most important single influence on my career. One important weakness in my educational background (and probably in that of many other small town people) is that I never had the opportunity to meet scientific or engineering personnel and therefore never knew what their jobs consisted of until after I left high school."

Only one NASA respondent, J. W. Herring, has no college training. Herring is deputy director of the Technical Services Office at the Marshall Space Flight Center. He writes:

"The lack of formal education above the high school level has made it difficult for me to perform certain phases of my work with maximum efficiency. With more formal schooling I could communicate much better with our scientists and engineers, could better understand their problems and requirements, and therefore could provide them with efficient and effective support."

We shall say little about the educational backgrounds of the 53 astronauts listed by NASA's Public Information Office; they are better known than are other "masters of the moon." However, it is interesting to consider that these men, all accomplished pilots with many hours of flying to their credit, have spent at least half their lives in school. Their early training (with the exception of Collins) was in public schools. Almost all of them have the master's degree and 14 hold earned doctorates. Two have a medical degree. The doctorates come from many different institutions: three from the California Institute of Technology, and one each from Yale, Stanford, Michigan, the Massachusetts Institute of Technology (moon-man Aldrin holds this one), California at Berkeley, Kentucky, Harvard, North Carolina, and the University College of Cardiff, Wales. Two of the astronauts were educated outside the U.S. Philip Chapman earned his high school diploma at Parramatta High School in New South Wales, Australia, and his B.S. at Sydney University. The M.S. in aeronautics and astronautics and the doctorate in instrumentation, however, came from the Massachusetts Institute of Technology. John Llewellyn, schooled in Cardiff, Wales, U.K., took the B.S. and the doctorate in chemistry from the University College of Cardiff. He entered the NASA program after serving as a post-doctoral fellow at the National Research Council in Ottawa, Canada, and as a research associate and professor at Florida State University.

For the masters of the moon and beyond, there is no goal, no authority, more worthwhile or more dependable than facts, no talent more precious than "know-how." These modern, pragmatic, "square" men of science demonstrate a solid respect for "useful knowledge," a loyalty to the job at hand, a devotion to thorough preparation. Neil Armstrong did not become an Eagle Scout by smelling flowers. The masters of the moon did their homework.

In the November 1967 *KAPPAN*, Harry Broudy wrote of "Art, Science, and New Values." One of many astute remarks he made in that classic piece was this: "Our possibilities have outrun our imagination, and we look to artists to conjure up images of life that would make these possibilities aesthetically interesting and some of them irresistible." Will the explorers of space become new models for young America, opening up a frontier that will engage the virile compulsions of the young? Will space provide an opportunity to develop new meanings for patriotism, courage, integrity? Is the dissenter with his vision of Che Guevara as hero now passé?

Another remark made by Professor Broudy applies. He said that "once technology makes social justice possible, we cannot get by with good intentions." An education that avoids the realities of the earth, an education fuzzily aimed at some future escape to other worlds, seems unworthy if not actually ridiculous. We may decide to continue producing the kind of men Admiral Rickover wanted, men "to maintain scientific and technological leadership and the modicum of culture necessary in a civilized society," but we must do much better than that. We must try to provide education for social reconstruction on an earth in dire need of it.

The Three School Teachers Who Opened the Space Age

Education and space exploration are today as inseparable as yin and yang; in odd ways history has bound them together. The three dreamer-inventors who showed man how to master space were all teachers. "It is curious that the Romanian Hermann Oberth, like Tsiolkovsky and Goddard, earned his living as a teacher; presumably the academic life gave all three men both the leisure and the training for their speculations," says the *Life-Time* Science Library book, *Man and Space, 1964,* upon which this note is based. The different origins of these men are clear proof that no one nation can claim the Space Age as its own.

KONSTANTIN TSIOLKOVSKY

Konstantin Eduardovich Tsiolkovsky was a deaf schoolteacher born in a small town south of Moscow in 1857. He was passionately interested in science as a boy and became obsessed with the problem of space travel. Though largely self-taught, he had a sound grasp of physics and mathematics. He was one of the first men to realize that the rocket provided a means of escaping from the earth. As early as 1898, he had derived the fundamental mathematical laws of rocket motion upon which the design of all space vehicles is based. In 1903— the year of Kitty Hawk—he published his main results and laid the foundation of astronautics. Moreover, he foresaw space exploration as part of a continuing social process that would eventually transform human life and spread it through the solar system. To advance his ideas he poured forth a stream of articles and wrote the remarkable *Outside the Earth*, a fictionalized account of his theories. When the first airplanes were staggering off the ground, he wrote about satellites, solar energy, "ether suits," the use of plants to provide food and oxygen on long journeys, and colonization of the planets. He even considered the problem of baths in weightless spaceships. His solution: centrifugal showers.

By the 1930s Tsiolkovsky was something of a Russian national hero; he received a state funeral when he died in 1935.

ROBERT H. GODDARD

Robert Hutchings Goddard spent most of his life as a physics teacher at Clark University, his *alma mater*, in Worcester, Massachusetts. Born in 1882, he read H. G. Wells's *The War of the Worlds* as a child. (He was often absent from school because of illness.) He also read *The Scientific American* and began thinking seriously of rocketry and space travel when he was 17. His 1919 pamphlet, "A Method of Reaching Extreme Altitudes," was a discussion of what we now call meteorological sounding rockets, to which he added a postscript pointing out that the same principle could be used to land a visible charge of flash powder on the moon. A few farsighted men (among them Charles Lindbergh) appreciated the value of his work. With small private grants he was able to continue experimenting through the Twenties and Thirties. In 1926, at Auburn, Massachusetts, he launched the first liquid-propelled rocket. In the long perspective of history, it may emerge as a more important flight than the Wrights' initial performance.

HERMANN OBERTH

The third pioneer of astronautics was Hermann Oberth, who published a book in 1923 whose title is translated as *The Rocket into Interplanetary Space*. He arrived at the same conclusions as his Russian and American precursors but went a good deal beyond them. He not only outlined theoretical designs of high-altitude research rockets and man-carrying spaceships; he also revived the idea of the large manned satellite or space station, which had been more or less forgotten since Edward Everett Hale wrote "The Brick Moon" for the *Atlantic Monthly* in 1870. Oberth's speculations started a chain reaction in Germany, inspiring actual experimentation. Little rocket societies sprang up in many countries: Germany in 1927 (Oberth became its president), Russia in 1929, America in 1930, Britain in 1933. Only in Germany and Russia, however, did the pioneer rocket men receive the financial and governmental support essential for serious progress. And their backers, it is hardly necessary to say, were interested strictly in military objectives.

What's Right with Education
by Harold Hodgkinson

Evidence of the success of the public schools and colleges is very clear, says the former head of the National Institute of Education. But we haven't done very well in explaining this success to the public.

Let's start with the problem: Compared with other professions, education is an easy mark for any journalist trying to scare people. This tendency caused William Grieder of the *Washington Post* to respond with a fierce commentary on his colleagues titled "Stop Knocking Our Public Schools."

By contrast, when we think of medicine we think of elaborate surgical techniques (which are good), not of Americans' health (which is very bad). We are now fourteenth in the world in infant mortality and losing; driving from Harlem to Forest Hills is to move from 41 infant deaths per 1,000 to 14. There are few nations in the world in which one can take a drive like that. Males in 18 other countries live longer than in the U.S. And in Los Angeles, when surgeons went on strike, the death rate went down!

Indeed, the damage done by doctors and lawyers is so extreme—burial or execution—that their professions seldom allow the public to see this information. (How many Americans *are* seriously damaged by lawyers each year?) Education is particularly vulnerable in this regard, as we must report data on every student-"client" for every day that person is being educated. That data is in the public domain. We have almost no facts on the performance of many of today's nonschool education programs in assisting youth—CETA and Job Corps, for example, and community-based programs.

The press is not necessarily hostile toward education; it's just that we hand them such excellent information on our failures. What follows is an attempt to correct that balance, to present evidence of the very real and solid accomplishments of America's schools and colleges.

Opinion Surveys

Any careful reading of the poll literature establishes several things:

Decline in American faith in institutions is not a new development. It began in 1967 and is linked to the pervasive effects of inflation on savings and the "American Way." Harris polls show that faith in the leadership of seven social and political institutions such as major business corporations, Congress, and medicine dropped an average of 24 percentage points between 1967 and 1972 (see Table 1).

Compared with other institutions, schools rate very high in the confidence of Americans. Proposition 13 to the contrary, one-third of all Americans would actually pay *more* taxes for improved services from schools, more than any other institution. Twenty percent would pay more for community colleges (see Table 2). Many people would be willing to pay for more research on the educational system and would *actually pay more taxes for better public schools.*

The most important indicator of improved quality of life for Americans is "achieving a quality education for my children."[1] Eighty-nine percent of all respondents to a 1976 Harris poll agreed on this point.

TABLE 1
HARRIS POLL SHOWING PERCENTAGE OF AMERICANS WHO
EXPRESS FAITH IN U.S. SOCIAL AND POLITICAL INSTITUTIONS,
1967 AND 1972

	% 1967	% 1972
1. Faith in leadership of major business corporations	55	27
2. Faith in banks and other financial institutions	67	37
3. Faith in the military	62	27
4. Faith in the Congress	41	19
5. Faith in the chief executive	41	23
6. Faith in the scientific community	56	32
7. Faith in medical doctors	73	61

Source: Social Education, March 1972.

TABLE 2
PUBLIC OPINION ON SUPPORT OF GOVERNMENT SERVICES

	% Would Cut	% Would Hold	% Would Increase
Recreation, parks	22.6	56.4	15.5
Police & fire	4.2	62.0	30.8(2)
Sanitation	5.9	75.1	11.6
Public schools	13.3	49.7	31.5(1)
Community colleges	16.5	55.9	20.0
Welfare services	61.6	25.4	8.8
Health & medical	15.6	48.1	30.8(2)
Streets & highways	18.5	59.5	16.3
Day care	24.0	46.6	20.3
Libraries	14.7	63.0	15.0
None of the services	20.0	3.8	29.0(3)

Source: Education Commission of the States, *Finance Facts*, February 1979.

Performance of the Education System

Openness of the System—We forget that as recently as 1950 only about half of all white students and a quarter of black students graduated from high school (so the school didn't need to worry about the "lower half"). Today 85% of whites and 75% of blacks complete high school. The "lower half" is now very much a responsibility of the public schools—and increasingly of the colleges as well.

The remarkable thing, as shown by a comparison of Indiana high school students in 1944 and 1976, is that academic performance is slightly better in 1976, even though today's scores represent a much wider range of student backgrounds than was the case in 1944.[2]

Access to college has increased markedly for women and minorities in the last decade. They now are present in college in about the numbers they represent in the population at large (see Table 3). And 1.5 million Americans over age 55 are in colleges and universities today, according to the American Association of Retired Persons (reporting on an institute on lifelong learning held in January 1979).

This diversity means that we need new ways of measuring achievement, as we move from meritocratic to egalitarian commitments. Today we must be able to affirm specific knowledge and skill gains for every student rather than rely solely on group means. "Every high school graduate must be able to

TABLE 3
COLLEGE ENROLLMENT BY SEX AND RACE, 1970-76

	1970	Percent	1976	Percent	Change
Black	520,000	6.5	1,100,000	9.9	+580,000
White	7,400,000		10,000,000		+2,600,000
Female	3,000,000	37.8	4,700,000	42.3	+1,700,000
Male	4,920,000		6,400,000		+1,480,000
Total students	7,920,000		11,100,000		+3,180,000

Source: Conference Board Report, December 1977.

read at least at the tenth-grade level" is the current requirement. Not long ago it was, "We only take the top 20%, regardless of performance level." Employers now rely on increasingly specific measures of actual job knowledge and skills, not educational degrees attained.

Some Success Stories

One of the best recent studies of schooling is *The Enduring Effects of Education*.[3] It tested 18,000 adults of a wide age range on 250 items of general and specific knowledge. The conclusion: The longer you stay in school, the more you know. A 60-year-old high school graduate knows more than a person of the same age who only completed elementary school. Schools teach people things, and these effects last.

Increased years of schooling for blacks have had a major impact on their earning capacity. A recent study has reported that although blacks still make less than whites for the same job, the gap is narrowing for black males; and black women now make 100% of white women's salaries. (Remember, however, that women still make less than men.) The major reasons for the improved earnings are increased number of years of schooling and improvements in the quality of education for black students, according to a Rand Corporation study.[4]

Literally thousands of communities have desegregated their schools without either violence or declines in student performance. Indeed, the Southeast, now better desegregated than most regions of the U.S., is showing marked improvement in tests of academic skill.

Our Knowledge Base: We Know What Works

Even though systematic study of the education system is relatively new compared with our efforts in agriculture (100 years of federal support) and medicine, we now have a very useful information base in education. For example, we know what correlates with learning, and we know the strengths of these various relationships. They range from race and social class to birth order, nutrition of the mother during pregnancy, region, body chemistry, parental occupations, etc.

It is startling, but probably the best way to eliminate major student learning problems would be to make sure that every pregnant woman in the U.S. had one prenatal exam and an adequate diet during pregnancy. Researchers estimate that this would eliminate 40% of later learning problems. (At the moment, Aid to Dependent Children support is only available after the mother has given birth, which is too late.) Just as cancer researchers have discovered important environmental characteristics that relate to susceptibility, so education specialists have discovered that people learn much better in some environments than they do in others, and that nutrition before birth establishes the ultimate size of the brain. (With poor nutrition *in utero*, the baby has a one-in-four chance of being 250 grams below the normal 1,400 grams in brain weight at age 6. Brain growth is basically completed by age 6—before we get children in school. This is why heavy emphasis is placed on the first four years of life in the USSR education system.[5])

To a unique degree, the performance of the education system is linked to the quality of family life, nutrition and child care, parental interest in schooling, etc. It is clear that a society gets the school system it deserves. As Urie Bronfenbrenner and others have pointed out, the amount of time American parents spend in non-TV activity with young children has dropped alarmingly in the last decade. This is "prime (educational) time" for families; it cannot be paid back when the children are past age 10. This is not to say that parents are *the* problem, only that when schools and families do work together, the results are uniformly positive.

We know the characteristics of successful reading programs. A variety of techniques can be successful, but only with a set of dimensions that define the program: Parent involvement and support, a principal who plays a leadership role, a "critical mass" of teachers who support each other, and local ownership of innovation are all vital. These statements are supported by several studies reported by the U.S. Office of Education.[6]

The Head Start Program—This section on our knowledge base would not be complete without some reference to new facts about the federal Head Start program. Head Start was part of the yearning of political forces in the liberal Sixties to reduce inequalities based on race and class. Assumptions regarding the scale of such programs and the time needed to show differences were naive (the Westinghouse evaluations of the impact of Head Start on schooling were completed before the children had completed even one year of school!). Now we know that these programs *do* produce real differences in children, but some of these differences are "sleeper" effects that don't show up until grades 3 and 4.

In a special session at the American Association for the Advancement of Science meetings in 1977, the first "sleeper" findings were announced, causing Bernard Brown to say, "The score is now 96 to zero in favor of the early childhood programs." He stated some constants:

> Programs involving home visits by program professionals showed the greatest gains. Combining preschool classes with home visits produced IQ gains of around 10 points; without home visits, six points. With home-*based* programs, only 1% of children needed special education by the fifth grade; without the program, 30% needed special classes.[7]

These findings, although spectacular, attracted no interest in the educational or commercial press, only being reported in *Science News*. In 1979 some new attention is being given: Congress has increased the Head Start budget to $735 million for 1980. But there is little excitement in the Carter Administration for this good news, even though the Head Start task was clearly as difficult educationally as getting a man on the moon was technologically. We simply no longer believe in social reforms as we once did, and even news of success falls on deaf (yet liberal) ears. Styles have changed, low profiles are the order of the day, and programs like Head Start are perceived as part of the past, not the future.[8] They work, but few people care. The influence of Arthur Jensen, Christopher Jencks, and others has taken its toll, and it is now often thought naive to assert that schools can alter social conditions and life chances. Yet the evidence is clear that when the environment of the school and the home work together, and the characteristics noted here are present, students *can* gain in performance.

Test Scores—Of all the issues involving the knowledge base in education, none is as explosive as the issue of testing—minimum competency testing, SAT score declines, and truth-in-testing legislation. Yet data on the issue are often presented in a one-sided or ridiculous way, exemplified in many newspaper stories suggesting that as many as 50% of American students are reading "below average." Any adequate review of the literature would report the following:

1. Reading scores on both comprehension and vocabulary have increased steadily over the past decade for the first three grades of schooling.[9] (We've worked very hard on the techniques of early reading, and here is the result: In nearly every school, students can sound out words and read simple sentences.) Reading scores begin to decline in grade 7, when the task is to handle larger units of material—paragraphs and chapters. We need to work on these later cognitive reading skills.

2. National Assessment of Educational Progress data suggest that students age 9, 13, and 17 know basic skills rather well, but they have trouble applying them in new situations.[10] Students know *how* to add and subtract but not *when*. They can read a 10-page report and retain facts but have trouble writing a tight précis in one or two paragraphs of their own prose. "Basics" in the sense of reading print and performing math operations are well learned; the problem is in critical thinking. We need to know more about these skills and their acquisition.

3. American students at age 14 do very well in comparison with students of other nations in reading. In science they do better than their counterparts in Britain, the Netherlands, and Italy but not as well as those in Japan and Germany. They do as well in math as Swedish youngsters but not as well as those in Japan or France (see Figure 1).

4. On the Scholastic Aptitude Tests over the past decade, score differences by sex are from four to eight times larger than any declines in mean score. The SAT verbal and math test profiles are quite unlike those of the ACT, even though both measure the same aptitudes with similar populations.[11] Test scores on these tests went up in the late Fifties, which they are not supposed to do. ("Aptitudes" are not subject to the same short-term changes as are achievement scores.) The increase in the Fifties and the decline in the Seventies (on a few tests, not on most) are a phenomenon with many causes, but certainly in the Fifties we were trying to reject large numbers of "baby-boom" students seeking college admission, while in the Seventies the system of higher education became much more diverse in terms of race, sex, and age. Tests are used in this larger sense in meritocratic or egalitarian ways; they are in no way culture-free.

It seems that both test results and reports from college faculty members

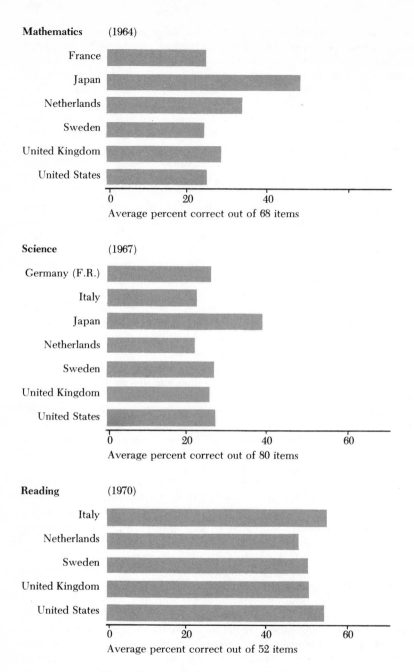

Fig. 1. International comparison of achievement

Source: Organization for Economic Cooperation and Development.

Reproduces Chart 5.03 in *The Condition of Education, 1977* (Washington, D.C.: National Center for Education Statistics, 1977).

assembled by Howard Bowen and John Minter indicate that in terms of *those who go on to college*, preparation for college by the public schools has not declined in quality.[12] (The only areas in which college faculty members report declines of significance are in math *reasoning*—not operational skills—and in writing, particularly précis and summary writing.) Given the fact that over 50% of high school graduates (and remember that 70% to 85% now graduate from high school) now try for further education, compared with the 10% to 20% in 1950 who entered postsecondary education, it is a remarkable achievement that American public schools are now doing for half of the school population what they used to do for only the top 10%.

Another interesting point is that graduate school admissions tests (the Graduate Record Exam, the Law School Admissions Test, and the Medical College Admissions Test) have not shown a pattern of serious decline during the decade, even as larger numbers from a wider sector of society have been taking the tests to move into the professions (see Figure 2). If the products of public schools were so bad, it is unlikely that colleges, no matter how superb, could compensate for the inadequacies, and very inferior graduate and professional school entry scores would be the logical result. Logical, but it has not happened.

A final point is that the *achievement* tests offered as a part of the SAT battery—tests of student knowledge in the standard academic areas of American history, biology, algebra, etc.—have shown no consistent pattern of decline over the decade. Certainly *achievement* scores should have fallen consistently if the public schools were failing. But they have not, even though a more diverse group is now taking the tests.

A summary of the college testing literature follows:

● Small declines on an 800-point test have been used by cynics to indicate that all is lost with American schools.

● There being no evidence from other countries to support a genetic hypothesis, we must assume that Americans *want* girls to do poorly in math and science and males to do poorly in verbal skills, especially poetry. (What a shame for the ancient Greeks, who believed that athletic and artistic prowess should go together!) Why is this so? When the test scores make clear how large these sex differences are in America, what are we educators to do?

● We need to work on the teaching of writing and math reasoning in the public schools.

● The U.S. does well internationally.

● Aptitude and achievement measures do not agree.

● Given the enormous diversity of high school graduates now taking college admissions tests compared with 1950, it would be reasonable to expect a 150- to 200-point drop on an 800- or 900-point scale test. The schools have risen to the challenge, preparing 50% of the high school population for college about as well as they did the top 10% to 20% in 1950.

Conclusion

Generally, we have now succeeded with an educational agenda, kindergarten through college, for the "top half." Some complain that a few of the top half today are not as good as the top 15% were three decades ago, but we have completed the agenda we were given and no one told us whom to

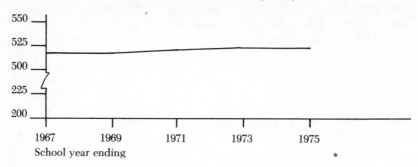

Law School Admissions Test (LSAT)

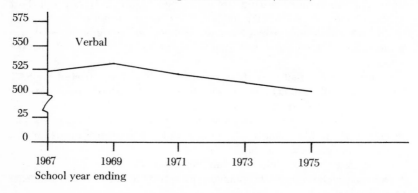

Medical College Admissions Test (MCAT)

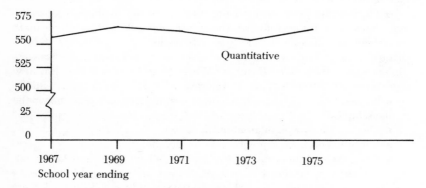

Fig. 2. Graduate school entrance test scores

Source of Data: Educational Testing Service, Association of American Medical Colleges.

Reproduces a portion of Chart 5.05, *The Condition of Education, 1977* (Washington, D.C.: National Center for Education Statistics, 1977).

TABLE 4
WHO IS LEARNING WHAT AND WHERE?

Agency	Number
Agricultural extension	12.0 million
Community organizations	7.4 million
Business and industry	5.8 million
Professional associations	5.5 million
Part-time college	5.3 million
City recreation	5.0 million
Churches, synagogues	3.3 million
College and university extension	3.3 million
Government services	3.1 million
Public school adult programs	1.8 million
Federal manpower programs	1.7 million
Armed forces	1.5 million
Graduate and professional	1.5 million
Trade unions	.6 million
Community education	.5 million
Free universities	.2 million
Total	58.4 million
In schools	12.4 million
Nonschool settings	46.0 million

Source: College Board, *New Directions for a Learning Society,* 1978, by Rex Moon.

neglect. No other nation has carried such a high percentage of its citizens so far.

In the next decade the agenda may well shift to the "bottom half." Many of the advocates of community-based education, CETA, and the Job Corps are zeroing in on the "lower half," with enormous amounts of funds and little in the way of performance data. Public school supporters are seldom included in meetings with Department of Labor and CETA-Job Corps personnel. Current debates on youth employment and reauthorization of certain vocational education legislation make clear how little influence the education establishment possesses, either in White House or congressional circles.

It is probably time for education organizations to begin to work together, as the Forum of Education Leaders is now doing. If the American Federation of Teachers, National Education Association, National Congress of Parents and Teachers, National Association of State Boards of Education, American Association of School Administrators, National Association of Elementary School Principals, and National Association of Secondary School Principals can meet together at the national level in order to explore areas of cooperation, it is time for local and state groups to do the same.

It is also clear that the functions of higher education are increasingly being performed by a variety of agencies—industry, the military, proprietary schools, museums, professional associations, etc. The College Board estimates that about 12 million people are studying in colleges and universities of the U.S., while 46 million adults are studying elsewhere (see Table 4). We must learn to collaborate with these new educational forces to improve coordination at the interfaces—local-state-federal, elementary-secondary-collegiate, and public-private-industrial-military.

Evidence on the success of the public schools and colleges is very clear, although seldom presented to the public. It is my thesis that all educational leaders are teachers regardless of their job. Teachers teach parents as well as students; principals teach the faculty, the PTA, and other community groups about the schools; and the superintendent teaches the board of education and city government. In terms of teaching the citizens about our school successes, we have not done well. The evidence is clear, and the time is most appropriate. If we are to call ourselves educational leaders, we must present our case, which is an excellent one, to the broadest spectrum of American citizens.

---

1. Harris Poll report, 8 November 1976.

2. Roger Farr and Leo Fay, *Then and Now: Reading Achievement in Indiana (1944-45 and 1976)* (Indianapolis: Indiana Department of Public Instruction, 1977).

3. Herbert Hyman, Charles Wright, and John Shelton Reed, *The Enduring Effects of Education* (Chicago: University of Chicago Press, 1975).

4. J. P. Smith and F. R. Welch, *Race Difference in Earnings* (Santa Monica, Calif.: Rand Corporation, 1978).

5. "Human Age and Brain Weight," *Unesco Courier*, January 1976, p. 20.

6. U.S. Office of Education, National Diffusion Network, *Summary of Reading Research* (Washington, D.C.: USOE/NDN, 1978).

7. As reported in *Science News*, 5 March 1977. See also *Summary: The Persistence of Preschool Effects* (Washington, D.C.: HEW, 1977).

8. See *Psychology Today* for September 1979, especially the interview by Maya Pines.

9. David Wiley, *Declining Achievement Scores: Do We Need to Worry?* (St. Louis: CEMREL, 1977).

10. *The Results of National Assessment* (Washington, D.C.: National Center for Education Statistics, 1977).

11. Wiley, op. cit.

12. Howard Bowen and John Minter, *Report on Private Higher Education* (Washington, D.C.: National Association of Independent Colleges and Universities, 1977).

The U.S. vs. the World:
A Comparison of Educational Performance
by Ralph W. Tyler

Cross-national data show that the U.S. educational system has been responsive both to societal change and democratic ideology. Schooling is available to a larger proportion of U.S. youth than is the case in other developed countries, yet the top 5% of U.S. young people attain the same high scores reached in nations where advanced schooling is reserved for an elite.

Only within the past 10 years have there been large-scale comparisons among nations of the educational attainments of their young people. In 1966 a consortium of research centers in 16 nations formed the International Association for the Evaluation of Educational Achievement, which has furnished comparative test results in six subjects.° Plans for a second round of cross-national testing are now being formed. The countries include most of those in Western Europe, Australia, New Zealand, Japan, Israel, and the U.S. These are modern, industrialized nations. Three of the others are developing nations: Chile, Iran, and Thailand. The subjects of the tests were reading, literature, mathematics, science, civic education, and a foreign language.

Achievement of Top 5%

One of the most surprising findings of the international evaluation was the fact that the average scores of the top 5% of young people completing secondary education in all the industrialized nations tested were approximately the same. This was not true for the three developing nations. Their average scores were much lower. These data suggest that the ablest students in an advanced country will attain a high level of achievement if the opportunity to learn a subject is available and if the society encourages such learning. But even the ablest students in the three developing nations did not achieve at a high level, possibly because the opportunities for learning these subjects were greatly limited and/or their societies did not encourage such learning.

Different Functions of Education

When making other international comparisons, it is necessary to keep in mind the different functions of education in the several countries and the different responsibilities assumed by different parts of the educational system of each country. In the U.S. three functions are expected of education: socialization, social mobility, and individual self-realization. In most of the other countries the public education system is not expected to aid individual self-realization, since it is hard to balance with socialization.

Socialization refers to the acquisition of the knowledge, skills, and attitudes required for effective participation in the society. It includes learning what is necessary to participate in the political life, in the economic life, and in the social institutions of the community. Because nations differ in what is expected of their citizens, the particular things to be learned also differ. How-

°*International Studies in Evaluation*, six vols. (New York: John Wiley; Stockholm: Almquist and Wiksell, 1973).

ever, even though countries differ in several important respects in their requirements for socialization, all modern industrialized nations seek to develop the ability to read and to use mathematics in handling quantitative
matters. That is, all modern nations seek to attain universal literacy.

Literacy

The international evaluation project included tests of reading, literature,
and mathematics. The average score of American 14-year-olds on the reading
comprehension test was 27.3, third highest of the 15 nations tested. In literature the average combined score for comprehension and interpretation for
American 14-year-olds was 16.5, exceeded only by New Zealand (18.7) and
Finland (17.2).

The 14-year-old students were selected for testing because, in modern nations, most children of that age are in school. Hence the test results can be assumed to give an approximate indication of the reading level of the entire age
group. For the older students this is not the case. At the time of the cross-
national testing program, the U.S. retained 78% of the age group through the
final year of secondary school, while Japan retained 70%, Sweden 65%,
Australia 29%, Hungary 28%, England 20%, Scotland 17%, New Zealand 13%, the
Netherlands 13%, and Germany 8%. These data indicate that the group tested
at the end of secondary school is much more select in most countries than in
the U.S. This should be kept in mind when reviewing the scores made by high
school students.

Reading results for the secondary school students are mixed. The average
comprehension score on the reading test placed the U.S. in the lowest third;
but on the literature test the average combined score on comprehension and
interpretation is exceeded only by those in four of the other nations. The U.S.
score is 21.9, New Zealand 26.8, England 26.4, Finland 23.8, and Sweden 23.3.
From these data it appears that the American education system enables
nearly three-fourths of our young people to attain a reading level that most
other nations only achieve with a very select group.

Writing is an aspect of literacy for which we have no cross-national comparisons. It is the only subject for which the U.S. National Assessment of Educational Progress (NAEP) has shown a consistent decline. Widespread use of
the telephone and the great amount of time spent by children in television
viewing mean that there is much greater emphasis on oral and pictorial communication than on writing. Furthermore, learning to write requires not only
practice by the learner but help in identifying writing difficulties and advice
on how to overcome them. That is, it requires more teacher time than most, if
not all, other subjects. For these reasons, declines in the proportion of young
people who write well can be expected unless special attention is given to this
subject. It is probable that there is a comparable decline in writing in other
modern nations, but no comparative data are available. Nonetheless, the importance of learning to write cannot be denied, even though a smaller proportion of students throughout the modern world are developing writing skills.
Several successful organized efforts in the U.S. to improve student performance in writing exemplify steps that can be taken to strengthen this aspect of
literacy. One such effort is being conducted by the Bay Area (California)
Writing Project, whose program is now national in scope.

Mathematics

The computational skills of arithmetic that are commonly taught in the elementary schools of the modern Western nations are acquired by a vast majority of children in these nations by age 14. In the case of the U.S., about 90% can add, subtract, multiply, and divide accurately with whole numbers. However, in all the nations tested, a smaller proportion of the children were able to apply these computational skills properly in solving the kinds of quantitative problems encountered in making purchases, in planning auto trips, and in computing taxes. Less than half of the U.S. children tested were able to apply computational skills to these kinds of quantitative problems. Among the advanced nations, only Japan's children made relatively high scores on such items.

In an earlier day children were commonly assigned chores involving the use of computation in constructing things, in making purchases, and the like. It was expected then that the school would teach children the computational skills, while these opportunities to use them outside the school would insure the development of problem-solving skills. This does not appear to be the case today. Schools and homes need to consider how best to allocate responsibility for providing practice in the actual use of the skills.

The scores made by secondary school students on tests of mathematics beyond arithmetic appear to reflect differences among the countries in patterns of course offerings, differences in the importance assigned to mathematics by national leaders, and the extent to which the secondary school seniors are a select group. The average mathematics score for American high school seniors was lowest among the nations tested. Israel, Japan, Germany, and France stood in the top third. It is likely that the high degree of selectivity accounts for the high scores in the other countries, but Japan retains 70% of the age group in the senior year. The performance of the Japanese students appears to reflect the great prestige in that country of engineering, science, and other fields involving mathematics. In the U.S. the top 5% of high school seniors make high scores in advanced mathematics. Should a larger proportion of high school students be encouraged to concentrate on this subject?

Political Socialization

A central task in the socialization of young people is the development of the knowledge, skills, and attitudes required to maintain the political system and to continue to adapt it to the changing conditions of modern life. The tests in civic education used in the international evaluation included tests of the students' understanding of their political system and their attitudes toward citizen rights and responsibilities in contrast to authoritarian control. For the 14-year-olds, the Federal Republic of Germany, Israel, and the Netherlands had the highest average scores on the tests of knowledge of the political system. Ireland and Italy, among the Western nations, had the lowest average scores, while the U.S. was in the middle group. For students completing the secondary school, those from New Zealand, Germany, and Sweden had the highest average scores, while Ireland and the U.S. were lowest.

In tests of attitudes toward democratic responsibilities in contrast to authoritarianism, the average scores for 14-year-olds did not vary much among the advanced nations, but this was not true for the secondary school seniors. The high averages (favoring a democratic system) were those of the students from Germany, Finland, Sweden, and New Zealand. Among the advanced nations, the U.S. and Ireland were lowest. NAEP data confirm the international finding that the least effective aspect of socialization in the U.S. is in citizenship.

In seeking explanations of the poor performance of U.S. students, we must assume that the age and stability of our political system is a partial factor. Perhaps our people take citizenship for granted and have little concern for its being well understood by the oncoming generation. Another important factor is the erosion of the opportunities for constructive learning of citizenship outside of school. If civic education is to be made more effective, it will be necessary for the school to reexamine contemporary conditions, to identify the kind of contributions that it is capable of making, and to encourage and support efforts of other community institutions, including the family, that have a part to play.

Economic Socialization

The effectiveness of an educational system in preparing its young people for work is not measured by the degree of unemployment in the nation. In the U.S. since 1930 there has rarely been a real shortage in peacetime of persons prepared to participate appropriately and constructively in the labor force. This is true in spite of the fact that there have been tremendous changes in the methods and conditions of work. Our economy demands a labor force composed largely of skilled technical and professional persons who have not only had education and training but are also flexible, i.e., able to learn new knowledge, skills, and attitudes as conditions require. But in spite of our nation's achievement in preparing the personnel demanded by our rapidly developing agriculture, industry, commerce, and services, there is still a large amount of youth unemployment. The U.S. has been least effective among the advanced nations in providing for a smooth transition of youth from school to work.

We can learn only a limited amount from the experiences of other nations in occupational socialization, partly because their more rigid class systems do not seek to provide a range of occupational options for most young people, partly because their means of moving from school to work involve greater responsibility on the part of employers and unions than has been acceptable in the U.S., and partly because, with the exception of Japan, the rate of occupational change has been much slower.

Socialization for Wise Consumption

In all societies citizens need to learn what is necessary for the wise consumption of limited resources. This is particularly important in the U.S., where the relatively large purchasing power of a majority of families has loosened the traditional constraints of limited income on consumption—constraints that in the past were quite confining for most families. Relative affluence often results in wasteful, harmful, and shortsighted consumption practices. To counteract this tendency, Americans need to develop the necessary understanding, disposition, and skills. The international evaluation group did not construct tests specifically to measure these things. However, the subject matter whose content is most relevant is probably science. In the U.S. science serves socialization in two ways. For some young people it is an important component of occupational education, because an industrial economy demands scientists, technologists, physicians, engineers, and other professionals who use scientific knowledge, skills, and attitudes. But the content of science is also an important component of the citizen's understanding of the natural world, of natural resources and their uses, and of the threats to humankind posed by pollution, by wasteful use of resources, and by technological destruction. In those nations where the expected role of citizens is to respect and trust the plans and actions of their leaders, science is primarily focused on contributing to occupational competence. In these countries most young people are not given an opportunity to learn science after age 14. Only those specializing in science are enrolled in secondary school science courses.

Keep this in mind in reviewing the results of the science tests in the international evaluation. For 14-year-olds, only Japan, New Zealand, and Hungary had an average score appreciably higher than that of the U.S. Only Belgium, the Netherlands, and Italy were appreciably lower. Scotland, England, Finland, Sweden, and the U.S. had approximately the same average scores. However, for students enrolled in the last year of secondary school, the results were different. Students in New Zealand and Japan had average scores far higher than the rest. In New Zealand only 13% of the age group continues through the secondary school, so the students tested were a very select group; but this was not true of Japan. The average science score of U.S. high school seniors was lower than all the modern nations participating in the evaluation except Belgium and Italy, but all the other nations except Japan have only a fraction of the age group completing secondary school. Before we consider explanations of the high average of the Japanese students, other relevant evidence should be reviewed.

In 1969-70 the NAEP included the field of science. Scores were relatively high, but by 1974, when a second assessment of science was conducted, they had dropped considerably. The report of the third science assessment shows that the decline has leveled off. At the time of the first assessment the American public was generally enthusiastic about the progress of our space program and other achievements in science and technology. But by 1973 reports of air and water pollution, the excessive use of natural resources, and the harmful by-products of modern technology had all influenced public opinion. Science was blamed for failing to protect the public interest, and its prestige had markedly declined.

Correspondence between public attitudes toward science and the average achievement of science knowledge by 17-year-olds suggests that public attitudes influenced the decision of many students to avoid science as a field of special interest and preparation. Public attitudes would seem to explain the high average score of secondary school seniors in Japan. Science still has high prestige there; the public believes that the remarkable economic development of Japan is based to a considerable extent on its mastery of science and its intensive use of technology.

What little comparative evidence is available indicates that most U.S. students, like those in other countries, are not acquiring the knowledge necessary for wise consumption. If they are to learn in science—and in other subjects—the knowledge, skills, and attitudes required for purposes other than occupational preparation, some new and concerted efforts will have to be made at the secondary school level.

Social Mobility

All societies that aspire to relative permanence must provide for social mobility. Adequate leadership cannot be obtained if it must be recruited only from children of the present leaders. The more power possessed by a family, the more difficult it is to motivate the children to work hard, to overcome obstacles, and to develop qualities of leadership.

The U.S. has long been recognized as a relatively open society in which there are a variety of opportunities for young people to rise in the social system, to assume leadership, to take on greater responsibilities, and to exercise power. Much of this is attributed to the educational opportunities more widely available in America than elsewhere. U.S. effectiveness in providing for social mobility is indicated by a study made in the 1950s of the social mobility of a probability sample of persons over 40 in the Midwest. This investigation found that approximately 50% of this group had risen in U.S. society; only 25% had fallen. No other nation has such a great degree of social mobility. This is indicated by another kind of evidence furnished by the international evaluation. In 1974, 14% of the secondary school seniors in the U.S. were from families of unskilled and semiskilled workers. In the Federal Republic of Germany, only 1% of the secondary school seniors were from families of unskilled and semiskilled workers; the comparable figure in England and the Netherlands was 5%, while the percentage for Finland, Sweden, and Hungary was about that of the U.S. Opportunities for higher education differ even more widely between the large European nations and the U.S. The evidence is clear that the U.S. is a more open society than the other large Western nations, but we have not yet reached the goal of equal educational opportunity for all.

Individual Self-Realization

An accepted part of democratic ideology is the right of the individual to be different and, in respects that do not threaten the stability of the society, to be a nonconformist. In the U.S. we pride ourselves on being a multicultural society, and we cherish individual uniqueness. Hence we expect our educational system to assist the individual young person in identifying and developing his or her unique talents and interests.

The international evaluation collected no data that throw light on the effectiveness of the education systems of the several nations in helping their youth toward fuller self-realization, nor does it measure the extent of educational opportunities furnished for this purpose.

In most of the other nations, however, the schools concentrate their attention on socialization, and the children of working-class parents have limited choices in what they study. The emphasis is on making an early occupational choice within limited possibilities, then preparing for this vocation. On the other hand, a stated goal of U.S. schools is to open up a range of options for children and to encourage them to explore various possibilities, postponing irreversible decisions until late in their schooling careers. There is little comprehensive evidence on the effectiveness of U.S. schools in this respect. It is a subject that deserves more adequate study.

In Summary

This review of cross-national data on educational achievement indicates that the U.S. educational system has clearly been responsive both to the rapid changes in society and to its basic democratic ideology. It has reached a larger proportion of its young people than almost all other nations, while its top 5% have attained the same high scores reached by nations that attempt to teach only a small fraction of their 18-year-olds. There are still problems to be solved, but the progress is encouraging.

Educational Leadership
For the Seventies
by Robert J. Havighurst

*This may be the decade of the administrator-leader (or social
engineer); the Whiz Kids have had their day.*

Is American education so bad that it must be abolished? Is the school dead, as
one writer has announced in the latest of the books attacking American education? Are we mutilating the minds of children in our schools, as another
author claims? Are our teachers stupid or malicious, or both, as another one
says? Must we have a radical and revolutionary change in our ways of
education that amounts to "deschooling society," as one of our Whiz Kids
argues?

I would not answer yes to any of these questions. But I do believe that
schools and colleges must change substantially in response to basic changes
going on in our society. We need leaders who will stimulate and direct change
in desirable directions.

The quickest way of changing an institution is to change its leadership.
This is the first of 14 propositions that constitute the final report of the New
York State Regents Advisory Committee on Educational Leadership.[1]

Phi Delta Kappa will publish a book this year titled *Leadership in American Education*, based on a symposium in March 1971. The National Society
for the Study of Education has produced a 1971 yearbook titled *Leaders in
American Education*,[2] built around the autobiographies of 11 persons who
were selected by a panel of educators as the most influential contemporary
leaders over 70 years of age.

Since about 1965 there has been a rapid turnover among the office-hold-
ing leaders of education. Many have resigned or retired prematurely. Others
have been forced out. This phenomenon has probably resulted from a
widespread uneasiness in America about the state of education. There is a
feeling that change is needed in the institution of education.

Who Are the Leaders?

In order to examine the problem of leadership, it may be useful to look
critically at our leaders. We can identify them by the positions they occupy,
or by asking people who the leaders are. The two different methods will
produce different names of leaders.

A list of 10 leaders was produced recently by Antioch College freshmen,
who were asked to respond to the question: What prominent human being
who has lived during the twentieth century do you most admire? The
freshmen of 1971 and also the freshmen of 1964 were asked this question, and
their first 10 choices were:[3]

1964		1971	
Rank	*Name*	*Rank*	*Name*
1.	Mohandas Gandhi	1.	Mohandas Gandhi
5.	Martin Luther King	2.	Martin Luther King

1964 (cont'd)		**1971** (cont'd)	
Rank	*Name*	*Rank*	*Name*
7.	Bertrand Russell	4.	Bertrand Russell
6.	Albert Schweitzer	6.	Albert Schweitzer
2.	John F. Kennedy	10.	John F. Kennedy
3.	Winston Churchill	3.	Malcolm X
4.	Franklin D. Roosevelt	5.	A. S. Neill
8.	Eleanor Roosevelt	7.	Ralph Nader
9.	Albert Einstein	8.	Caesar Chavez
10.	Woodrow Wilson	9.	Pablo Picasso

Comparison of the two lists shows how the immediate situation affects this kind of ballot. The 1971 list contains several radical innovators, who seem to have replaced several moderate leaders of the liberal Establishment.

The 11 persons featured in the NSSE yearbook, *Leaders in American Education*, were selected by a panel of judges from a list of about 30 men and women, all over 70 years of age. In choosing the names of the 30 "candidates," the NSSE committee had three categories in mind, namely:

Scholars—people whose principal claim to importance was their scholarly research and writing.

Leaders Through Ideas—people who promoted and clarified ideas that pointed to action.

Administrator Leaders—people who exercised power through administrative and managerial ability.

The panel of judges received a list of 10 or 12 names in each category and was asked for a preference vote, with the result that only one man was elected from the Administrator-Leader group, while equal numbers of Scholars and Leaders Through Ideas were elected.

The persons in the various categories were:

Scholars: Ruth Strang, Arthur Gates, John Brubacher, Sydney Pressey, and Robert Ulich.

Leaders Through Ideas: Carleton Washburne, George N. Shuster, James B. Conant, George D. Stoddard, and George S. Counts.

Administrator-Leader: William G. Carr.

This list was produced in 1968 and was limited to people over 70. Probably the selection procedure tended to favor people who have been influential through their writings.

The Leader in Action

For the purposes of this essay, I am going to define a leader as one who successfully stimulates and directs action in socially desirable directions.

The leader employs words, truth, and power to achieve his ends and can be judged on the quality of his use of these three instrumentalities. Depending on his emphasis on one or another of them, we can identify him as a prophet, scholar-scientist, or social engineer. Let us analyze the strength and weaknesses of these three types of leadership.

The Prophet. A prophet operating in the field of education has two very important and useful functions. He points the way toward new educational practices and policies; he serves as a gadfly, stimulating people to think

seriously about problems of education and seeing what is wrong with the contemporary forms of education.

Just now the prophets are relatively popular. They appeal to the unde-
fined frustration and discontent of thoughtful people who are convinced that
we should make sweeping changes in our society, including our educational
system.

It is important for students and practitioners of education to listen to the
prophets and learn from them. But we must remember that they are prophets
and not scientists. Their approach to truth is that of the prophet, not that of
the scientist.

It is also important to recognize the fact that there are false prophets as
well as true prophets. The distinction between the false and the true prophet
is not clear. It does not lie in his success or failure to predict the future—to
prophesy, in that sense of the word. It lies in his ability to grasp the social
reality and to interpret it to people in terms of their own needs and aspirations. It also lies in his ability to evaluate the possibilities for peaceful social
change under existing social conditions and to weigh these possibilities
against the possibilities of successful revolution with resulting improvement
in the society that emerges after the revolution. It also lies in the social and
ethical values he espouses.

I shall not try to label as true or false prophets the people I shall now name.
In discussing them critically, my primary concern is the extent to which they
use or usurp the role of scientist as a means of making prophetic utterances
and writings more influential. For the present-day prophet is almost sure to
attempt to combine his role with that of the scientist.

Categories of prophets operating now in the field of education are: 1) *conservative anarchists*—followers of Rousseau: Paul Goodman, John Holt,
Edgar Friedenberg, George Dennison; 2) *revolutionary anarchists*—Ivan
Illich, Everett Reimer; 3) *conservative oligarchists*—Max Rafferty; 4) *radical
pluralists*—Preston Wilcox.

Ivan Illich. Like other prophets, Ivan Illich is a man of intense moral
fervor, which shows itself frequently as a burning hatred of the social institutions of the affluent democracies and their attempts to influence and to "aid"
the poor and underdeveloped countries. Born in Central Europe, Illich grew
up in Vienna and became a Catholic priest. Emigrating to the United States,
he was assigned to a Puerto Rican parish in New York City. He served the
parish with such skill and devotion that he was sent to Puerto Rico, where he
became vice-rector of the Catholic University at Ponce. From that post he
left active service to the Church and moved to Mexico, where he founded the
Centro Intercultural de Documentacion in Cuernavaca, a center for study
and publication of sociocultural information about Latin America. Since
1967, the Cuernavaca center has held seminars and conferences and issued
publications aimed at radical reconstruction of educational procedures.

Illich's first speeches and writings on education in Latin America consist
of attacks on the schools and school systems as institutions maintained by
society for the benefit of middle-class families, while the great mass of the
population are deliberately limited to a few years of schooling and many of
them kept functionally illiterate.

In 1969 and 1970, Illich and his colleagues at Cuernavaca turned their attention to the educational system of the United States and argued for the "de-

schooling" of the American society.[4] They have worked out a theory of education that they believe can be applied both to underdeveloped countries and
also to the most highly developed countries. They would radically reduce
and limit the school system to brief periods of formal instruction in mental
skills, while the other aspects of education would be cared for informally by
other social institutions.

Underlying this program is a system of ethics that deserves consideration
by thoughtful people. It is a radical religious ethic that challenges the mate-
rialistic values of the modern democratic industrial societies. Illich charges
that the United States and other modern societies have created a "world
religion" of unending consumption of material goods. Its effect is to exploit
the natural resources of the world for the benefit of a relatively few people,
mainly the middle classes. Schooling is an element in the ritual of "unending
consumption" and is limited to a minority, while the majority are kept out by
the system of selection and exclusion that school systems always develop.

Thus the writings of Illich on education are a mixture of radical social
criticism (appropriate prophetic writing) with what purport to be scientific
analyses of the educational system in both South and North America. Illich
combines the roles of prophet and scientist in a most persuasive way for readers who are themselves predisposed to be hostile to the Establishment. His
writing consists of declarative sentences about education and society that
seem to refer to facts and which support his conclusions about the futility of
schooling as we know it today.

Yet these declarative statements—propositions about education in South
and North America—will seldom meet the criteria of scientific accuracy. To
one who has attempted to study education scientifically in South and North
America, as I have, Illich's propositions seem to be poorly substantiated. And
they are selected so as to support a preconceived set of conclusions.

As a gadfly, Illich is tremendously valuable. His moral insight and his pas-
sion for justice are badly needed by the people who hold power and influence in this society. As a scientist, he is a dismal failure. His knowledge is
severely limited, and he does not have a feel for the accurate description of
social reality. In a third role, as a social engineer, he is just now beginning to
show what he can do. His book titled *Deschooling Society* is worth reading,
though in my opinion it is weak in comparison with his purely critical writing.
The role of social engineer needs contributions from both the social scientist
and the prophet, and it is useful to have Ivan Illich and his associates at
Cuernavaca making their contribution.

The most popular prophets of today are anarchists. They want to reduce
the power of established government and established institutions, believing
that this would increase individual liberty for both children and adults. They
attack the existing order of things with great moral fervor and verbal facility.

Anarchists' Error: Elitism

The fatal error of the anarchists, as I see it, is their elitism. This characteristic appears to be relatively unconscious in Illich but conscious in most of this
group. A careful analysis of their proposals for education indicates that the
people who would profit if the anarchists' proposals went into effect would
be the *haves* rather than the *have-nots*. The people who are today living in
comfort and passing on to their children the material and intellectual advan-

tages of modern post-industrial society are the same ones best able to take advantage of greater individual freedom in choice of lifestyles, of ways of learning, and of ways of making a living. The poor, and those with the least verbal and technical skill, are least likely to profit from greater individual liberty unless anarchy is so complete that there is no "law and order" left, and everyone is free to plunder others as far as his brute strength will carry him. Institutions in a democratic society generally favor justice and opportunity for the poor, though these institutions need continual reform and remaking in a period of rapid social change.

The Scholar-Scientist. The scholar-scientist in the field of education has had the widest acceptance during the present century. With education a growing enterprise in a growing economy, and with psychology and sociology as the basic sciences of education, it was natural that people should look to the science of education for ideas to guide the growth of this institution.

The most effective ideas and theories developed by scientists were those concerning the learning process, the social development of the child and adolescent, the development of character and personality, and the functions of education in providing opportunity for social mobility. Research in cognitive development and in the reading process have provided the concepts on which primary schooling is based. There are many well-known names in addition to those appearing in the NSSE yearbook. John Dewey, Jerome Bruner, Ralph Tyler, Willard Waller, Jeanne Chall, Erick Erikson, Margaret Mead, and Lee Cronbach are a few of the names that come to mind.

The scientist is under obligation to seek the truth and to tell the truth as he sees it. Every proposition he states as a result of his work must be hammered out on the anvil of established facts. Any finding of potential importance is subject to testing and replication by other scientists.

The scholar-scientist sees problems and comes up with solutions. If his proposed solutions work, he becomes known as a leader.

Problems have arisen recently with respect to the education of minority groups and economically disadvantaged children, and with respect to the education of adolescents who are not likely to have middle-class careers. Also, problems have arisen concerning the place of the arts and humanities in education, problems that do not yield easily to the concepts and methods of twentieth century science.

Futhermore, the supposed objectivity and freedom from value prejudice of the social scientist has been challenged by able and acute critics within the social sciences. It is charged that social phenomena, especially in education, have been viewed through middle-class spectacles that screen out some important aspects of reality. In this connection, a group of sociologists have developed an approach to scientific method which they call *ethnomethodology*. Concerned especially with problems of communication between people of different sociocultural groups, they point out that middle-class and lower-class people use different languages or codes of meanings as well as different ways of understanding gestures, group situations, etc. The social scientist cannot get at the reality of what he is studying unless he becomes sensitive to these cultural differences of communication among the people he is studying.

I believe that the scholar-scientist will continue to exert important leadership as long as he maintains his search for truth, but the growing complexity of the social world and the changing problems it presents to education in the last third of the twentieth century will tax the resources and the methods of the scientist.

The Social Engineer. The administrator's leadership function is to use *power* effectively for the improvement of education. He is a social engineer in the sense that he applies men and materials through educational institutions to the improvement of society.

To be a leader, you must have followers and you must be going somewhere. Scholars tend to have readers but not followers. Prophets are usually lonely people with few followers.

Successful educational administrators are men and women of action who lead the way to improved concerted action by people who participate in educational systems.

We take the administrator for granted, in ordinary times, because he often administers an institution that runs by itself, once it is adjusted to the needs of the situation. But when the situation is as complex and rapidly changing as the contemporary one, institutions will break down unless they have wise and skillful administrators.

Bad Decade for Social Engineers

The 1960s were a bad decade for leaders in the role of social engineer. A number of very able ones worked at the role for a brief period and then retreated to the role of the scientist or to the more protected haven of the private philanthropic foundation. Others have been tough enough (or stubborn enough) to maintain the role—William G. Carr, Albert Shanker, Wilson Riles, Lloyd Michael. I would like to mention several superintendents of big city public school systems, but I am afraid the list would be broken by resignations before this essay appears in print.

The outcome of education in the 1970s rests on the shoulders of the administrator-leaders more than it does on the other categories of leadership. Faced with problems of divisiveness due to black, brown, and red power, the urban crisis, the welfare crisis, teacher militancy, student militancy, decentralization and local community control, unemployed youth, taxpayer resistance, and racial segregation, our leaders have at their disposal the ideas and knowledge of the scientists, the moral insight of the prophets, and the power of their office. Can they make an open-eyed and wise rather than blind use of their power?

A major handicap to responsible and constructive leadership will be the activity of the Whiz Kids. These are the men and women, generally very voluble, who go around saying, "Gee whiz, things are in an awful mess; let's start all over." The language is generally more profane and often obscene. Some of our Whiz Kids, in addition to some of the prophets named above, are Neil Postman, Ronald Gross, Peter Schrag, Herbert Kohl, and Nat Hentoff. According to these people, the schools are an utter failure for children of all social classes; they teach conformity to narrow middle-class conventionality; they mutilate children's minds; they destroy human freedom and dignity; they deny opportunity to the children of the poor.

The Whiz Kid usually has a panacea: some form of systems analysis applied to the educational process; private schools operated with vouchers from public funds; the open classroom; separate schools for children of the poor; a local school board for every ten thousand pupils.

Too often, the administrator has to cope with a divided school board or board of directors, which gives him very little freedom of movement and severely limits his use of the powers of his office.

This year may herald the beginning of a much better period. I believe that the administrator-leaders, if they keep their nerve and keep their eyes and minds open, will find it easier to meet the problems of the 1970s than it was to meet the problems of the 1960s. Some useful experiments have been carried on—among a greater number of zany ones. We have some successes and many failures to help us pick our way into the future. The Whiz Kids are wearing out their voices—and the attention of the public. Responsible leadership will be welcomed and supported by the people.

---

1. Board of Regents of the University of the State of New York, *Leadership for Education*, James A. Perkins, Chm. (Binghamton, New York, 1967).

2. National Society for the Study of Education, *Leaders in American Education*. Robert J. Havinghurst, Chm. (Chicago: University of Chicago Press, 1971).

3. Antioch College, *Antioch Notes*. Franklin A. Logan, Dean of Admissions, October, 1971.

4. Ivan Illich, *Deschooling Society*. (New York: Harper & Row, 1971).

V

The Anatomy and Dynamics of Change

Introduction

In the early Fifties I studied theories of socio-political change in a seminar led by B. Othanel Smith and William O. Stanley at the University of Illinois. I have been fascinated by the topic ever since, and that interest showed in the KAPPAN.

The first article in this brief section is drawn from a study directed by Smith. In 1971 the U.S. Office of Education asked him to take a brief look (there was a two-month deadline) at the subject of educational change. He invited Donald Orlosky to help with it. When the authors decided that their work would never see the light of day unless published in an education journal, Orlosky digested the 90-page report and submitted it to the KAPPAN. It was eagerly accepted, and "Educational Change: Its Origins and Characteristics" has become one of the most widely reprinted reports we have published. The editors still get requests for copies, a decade after the article first appeared.

Donald Orlosky, a former head of secondary education at DePauw University with a doctorate from Indiana University, joined Smith in 1969 as a professor of education at the University of South Florida, where the two have worked together on a number of projects. Orlosky and Smith co-authored Socialization and Schooling, *a book published by Phi Delta Kappa in 1975. (I'll have more to say about Smith in Section VI.)*

"The Lawn Party: The Evolution of Federal Programs in Local Settings" (November 1980) is drawn from the report of a major study conducted by the Huron Institute at Cambridge, Massachusetts. Eleanor Farrar is a senior research associate with the institute, John E. DeSanctis is a research associate, and David K. Cohen is its president. The research was funded by the National Institute of Education. The article is a condensed and revised version of "Views from Below: Implementation Research in Education," published in the Fall 1980 issue of the Teachers College Record, *which holds copyright.*

—SME

Educational Change: Its Origins and Characteristics
by Donald Orlosky and B. Othanel Smith

Insights from a study of major change efforts of the past 75 years

The purpose of this essay is to report a study of educational changes attempted during the past 75 years, examine the efforts to put these ideas into practice, rate the efforts to install them as successful or unsuccessful, attribute that success or failure to particular factors, and make recommendations to those who promote educational change. The changes selected are broad, macro-changes rather than narrow and specific changes. Also, many changes have been attempted during this period for which there is no record, but on the whole it may be assumed that the changes that are included in this account are of general significance.

Four categories were used to classify changes according to their degree of success or failure.° The symbols used and the descriptions for degrees of success were:

4—A change that has successfully been installed and has permeated the educational system.

3—A change that has successfully been installed and is sufficiently present that instances of the change are obvious.

2—A change that has not been accepted as a frequent characteristic of schools but has left a residue that influences educational practice.

1—A change that has not been implemented in the schools and would be difficult to locate in any school system.

Changes rated 3 and 4 were regarded as successes and changes rated 1 and 2 were regarded as failures. The changes were also classified according to the aspect of the educational system that was the focus of change. The symbols employed in this classification were: A—instruction, B—curriculum, and C—organization and administration.

Each idea for change was classified according to its origin. Some changes originated outside of the school setting and others arose within the field of education. The changes were classified as internal or external, using these symbols: I—internal origin, within the education field; and EX—external origin, outside the education field.

The fourth distinction made was between changes proposed recently and those proposed some time ago. Changes initiated after 1950 were regarded as recent; all others were listed in the pre-1950 era.

Table 1 provides an alphabetical listing by categories of the changes included in this report.

It is important to observe in Table 1 that a large number of changes (49) originated within the school system, compared with a small number (14)

°The authors independently classified the changes, then compared the results of their work. Agreement on the inside-outside dichotomy was 88%, for the post-pre 98%, for the success-failure categories 68% (no differences exceeded one scale point), and for the focus of the change, 72%. Differences were resolved on the basis of evidence that supported the rating.

originating from external sources. The schools initiated changes at a ratio of 3½ to 1, compared with individuals or agencies outside the schools. External changes were invariably in the areas of curriculum (eight instances) or organization and administration (six instances). The external ideas had a higher success percentage (93%) than the internal ideas (64%). These data suggest that when an idea has both outside group and school support, success probability is high.

It should not be inferred from the lower success rate of ideas originating within the field of education that ideas are likely to fail because of their origin. For instance, all efforts to alter instructional behavior originated within the education field, but it is notoriously difficult to change teaching habits. Also, the lower percentage of success is quite likely due to the fact that the professional literature reports a larger number of internal change attempts. Failures that originate outside of education are less likely to remain long enough to be recorded as an effort to change at the macro-level studied.

Changes were successfully implanted in instruction, curriculum, and organization and administration. None of these three categories was immune. Likewise, failures in all three areas suggest that each area had resisted changes or was unable to accommodate some of them. All of the successful changes in instruction came from within the education field, two-thirds of the changes in organization and administration originated within education, and half of the curricular changes came from within the field. Thus it appears that the public school is more responsive to change than is generally conceded.

Government influence was evident in such programs as Head Start, which required heavy financial support, and in compulsory attendance, where the legislative branch produced change through law.

The successful pre-1950 ideas usually involved school organization and administration. It appears to be easy to try and discard changes in curriculum and instruction, but when the machinery of organization and administration is modified, the change is relatively permanent.

It should be noted that there are factors and agencies not categorized in this analysis that bear on change and are influential in the determination of educational practice. They cannot be regarded as the basis for any particular change but affect the entire spectrum of educational practice. Four such factors within education are: 1) educational research, 2) school personnel (teachers, administrators, state departments, and university personnel), 3) educational commissions and committees, and 4) professional and extra-legal organizations. The elements outside of the field of education that should be taken into account include 1) state and federal constitutional requirements, 2) court decisions that rule on educational practice, and 3) pressure groups in society.

Planned change should be based on a combination of past experiences, current theories, and analysis of all aspects of the field of education. The conclusions that follow encourage such an approach and can serve as guides to those who promote educational change.

1. Changes in methods of instruction are apparently more difficult to make successfully than changes in curriculum or administration.

2. Changes in instruction are most likely to originate within the education profession. In no case in the past did a successful change in instruction come from outside of education. Changes in ways of teaching and organizing in-

TABLE 1
CHANGES LISTED ACCORDING TO DATE OF ORIGIN, SOURCE,
RATING OF SUCCESS, AND FOCUS OF CHANGE

Change	Post-1950	Source	Rating	Focus
Ability Grouping		I	3	A
Activity Curriculum		I	2	B
Adult Education		EX	4	C
British Infant School	X	I	3	B
Carnegie Unit		I	4	C
Community School		I	2	B
Compensatory Education	X	EX	3	B
Compulsory Attendance		EX	4	C
Conservation Education		EX	3	B
Consolidation of Schools		I	4	C
Core Curriculum		I	1	B
Creative Education	X	I	1	B
Dalton Plan		I	1	A
Desegregation	X	EX	3	C
Driver Education		EX	4	B
Elective System		I	4	B
Environmental Education	X	EX	3	B
Equalization Procedures		I	4	C
Extra-class Activities		I	4	B
Flexible Scheduling	X	I	2	C
Guidance		I	4	A
Head Start	X	EX	3	C
Home Economics		EX	3	B
Individually Prescribed Instruction	X	I	3	A
International Education		I	3	B
Junior College		I	4	C
Junior High School		I	4	C
Kindergarten		I	4	C
Linguistics	X	I	3	A
Look-and-Say Method		I	3	A
Media and Technology		I	4	A
Microteaching	X	I	3	A

struction are neither the result of legislation nor of social pressure, but rather are the outcome of professional wisdom and research. This is attributable partly to the fact that the teacher's behavior in the classroom is shaped by factors considerably removed from social concerns, partly to the stability of teaching patterns, and partly to the intellectual character of teaching about which the public has little information.

3. A change that requires the teacher to abandon an existing practice and to displace it with a new practice risks defeat. If teachers must be retrained in order for a change to be made, as in team teaching, the chances for success are reduced unless strong incentives to be retrained are provided.

4. Specific curricular changes such as the establishment of the elective system are often initiated from within the field of education. Successful changes in curriculum can originate either within the profession or from the outside. Neither point of origin monopolizes ideas for curricular change.

5. Curricular changes involving the addition of subjects or the updating

TABLE 1 (cont'd)

Change	Post-1950	Source	Rating	Focus
Middle School	X	I	3	C
Mid-year Promotion		I	1	C
New Leadership Roles		I	4	C
Nongraded Schools	X	I	3	C
Nursery Schools		EX	3	C
Open Classroom	X	I	3	A
Phonics Method		I	3	A
Physical Education		EX	4	B
Platoon System		I	1	C
Programmed Instruction		I	3	A
Project Method		I	2	A
Safety Education		I	4	B
School Psychologist	X	I	3	C
Self-contained Classroom		I	3	C
Sensitivity Training	X	I	2	A
Sex Education	X	EX	2	B
Silent Reading		I	4	A
Social Promotion		I	4	C
Special Education	X	I	4	B
Store Front Schools	X	EX	3	C
Student Teaching		I	4	A
Team Teaching	X	I	2	C
Testing Movement		I	4	C
Tests and Mesurements		I	4	A
Thirty-School Experiment		I	1	B
Unit Method		I	2	B
Unit Plan		I	2	A
Updating Curriculum Content		I	3	B
Visiting Teacher		I	2	A
Vocational and Technical Education ..		EX	4	B
Winnetka Plan		I	1	A

of content are more permanent than changes in the organization and structure of the curriculum. Efforts to change the curriculum by integrating or correlating the content, or by creating new category systems into which to organize the content, are made at great risk. Complete or considerable displacement of an existing curriculum pattern is not likely to be permanent even if the faculty initially supports the change. This can be attributed partly to cognitive strain on the faculty, partly to upsetting the expectations of pupils and consequent parental distrust, and partly to faculty mores that tend to become stronger when threatened by change.

6. Changes in the curriculum that represent additions such as new subjects or changes in the substance of subjects can be made most securely with support from legislation or organized interest groups. The failure of curricular changes to be permanent may be attributed either to lack of social support or to resistance to displacement of the existing curriculum pattern. If school authorities are successful in finding social backing for the addition of a

subject to a curriculum, the change can be made with little risk of failure. On the other hand, if social opposition is pronounced, the probability of the change not being made is very high, or if it is made, it is likely not to persist.

7. Efforts to alter the total administrative structure, or any considerable part of it, are likely to be unsuccessful.

8. Changes that represent additions or extensions of the educational ladder, such as junior college, are more likely to be lasting than changes that entail general modifications of the administrative organization, such as flexible scheduling.

9. The lack of a diffusion system will lead to abortive change. A change initiated in a particular school, in the absence of a plan for diffusion, no matter how loudly it may be acclaimed, is not likely to become widespread or to be permanently entrenched.

10. Changes that have the support of more than one critical element are more likely to succeed. Compulsory education, with legal, social, and educational support, did not have to overcome as much resistance as it would have if only educators had supported it.

11. Changes will be resisted if they require educational personnel to relinquish power or if they cast doubt on educator roles. Accompanying legislative, legal, and financial impetus increases the probability of success in such changes.

12. The weight of the cognitive burden is one of the significant factors that determine the permanence of a change. If the cognitive load is light, i.e., if not many people are required to learn many new facts and procedures, a change is more likely to persist than if the burden is heavy. The weight of the burden is proportional to the number of factors entailed in the change. For example, if the total administrative structure is the object of change, the chances for successful innovation will be low. The same observation can be made about changes in methods of instruction or curricular changes.

13. The initiation of change may come from a number of sources—professionals, social groups, government, and so on—and changes may arise from research, as in the case of ability grouping, or from ideologies, as in the case of the core curriculum, or from professional wisdom, as in the platoon system. The source of the change appears to have far less to do with its staying power than the support the change receives and the strain it places upon the school personnel. The core curriculum and creative education are constant drains on the time and energy of a faculty, and they consequently tend to disappear even though each may enjoy faculty support. On the other hand, international understanding tends to be more persistent as a curricular change. It requires far less time and energy of the teacher and has enjoyed no greater support from the faculty than either the core curriculum or creative education.

14. The federal government, as a change agent, will have optimum success if it takes certain facts into account. In the first place, the government acts in two ways. It passes enabling legislation empowering various federal agencies to do specified things to attain certain goals. In the second place, it acts through the courts to interpret laws, to establish norms, and to order certain actions by school officials. Programs of the U.S. Office of Education are based largely upon enabling legislation. In the development of its programs the USOE is subject to the same conditions of success as any other change

agent. For example, its efforts to induce changes in methods of teaching are likely to be less successful than efforts to change curriculum content or to extend or modify the educational ladder; its efforts are likely to be more successful if it has the support of commission recommendations, organized groups, and professional personnel.

The data set forth in this report are too broad to provide insight into the sort of situational analysis that successful change entails. More refined data can be secured by intensive case studies. A few well-chosen case studies can be made to explore the underlying variables whose manipulation and control can give a change agent greater assurance of success.

The educational system in a dynamic society cannot remain stagnant. We should expect changes to be proposed that will alter the school system, since the United States is undergoing rapid change. The idiosyncracies of a particular situation may not always conform to the patterns revealed in this study, but it is likely that an understanding of the characteristics of the changes proposed over the last three-quarters of a century will be helpful in the development of successful procedures in the installation of educational changes.

The Lawn Party: The Evolution of Federal Programs in Local Settings

by Eleanor Farrar, John E. DeSanctis, and David K. Cohen

Researchers have long tried to find out why federal education programs often fail to meet the goals set for them. The authors offer the "lawn party" hypothesis: A federal program is the occasion for a gathering, and the guests do pretty much as they please.

For the past 20 years, the failure of federal education reforms to achieve their intended outcomes has been a persistent puzzle. Researchers have offered a variety of explanations for this failure, but most answers have had one thing in common: the view that implementation is the second stage of a two-stage process that begins with policy formulation. Implementation is seen as the process of carrying out policy. We believe that the outcomes of many federal attempts to upgrade local schools can be better understood if implementation is viewed as a process of policy evolution, in which local participation modifies and sometimes completely reformulates a program's federal blueprint. "Policy"—which is at the outset usually only a set of broad and often diverse intentions or dispositions—changes and develops as the federal program is harnessed to local needs and priorities. Implementation is not the carrying out of a formulated policy but part of its evolution. And in that evolution—in certain circumstances or with certain programs—a multitude of local dispositions and actions are more important than the dispositions and actions of federal agencies.

Questions about implementation first came up in education research circles in reaction to the supposed failure of the Elementary and Secondary Education Act (ESEA) of 1965.[1] When sizable Title I grants to school districts appeared not to improve the achievement of disadvantaged youngsters, there were arguments over evaluation methodologies and politics. But it also seemed sensible to ask the next question: If students' test scores were not improving, was the money being spent as intended?

A series of federal audits and program reviews represented the first attempt to examine the local implementation of federal reforms. They concluded that there were two kinds of gross problems of implementation: First, federal money was being misspent; second, even when spent as intended, it yielded unimpressive results. In some cases no implementation of federal policy occurred because federal funds were indeed being used to supplant rather than supplement, or were spread too thin across all students to have any effect on target youth, or were spent on things quite unrelated to education. But why, in those cases where federal money was spent as intended, did the programs also fail to improve student achievement?

This question led to more elaborate efforts to evaluate program effectiveness. In the late Sixties such federal efforts as Follow Through and Head Start Planned Variation were to experiment with different "models" of early childhood education, to identify educational programs that "work." Evaluations of these efforts soon made it apparent that this was no easy task. Student outcomes suggested that many of these programs also did not work, and researchers began to suspect that perhaps the new models were not being used properly.[2] Therefore, in a new generation of implementation studies, they tried to weigh fidelity to original plans in terms of detailed program components.

These studies were beset by problems such as rater unreliability and lack of instrument sensitivity to model changes over time. Site visits revealed that the models in practice were even more complex than they had seemed on paper. Site interpretations of the models varied from time to time and place to place; even the developers' ideas about the models changed over time; and it was not clear whose standard of implementation should prevail. The studies showed implementation to be a tangle of unresolved problems, of competing political values in the change process.

These early audits and implementation studies shared a view of implementation as a center-to-periphery process: Programs initiated by central (federal) officials were expected to be "carried out" at the periphery (school districts). From this perspective, the implementation of many compensatory education programs, such as Title I and Follow Through, was often foiled by the district. This conception of implementation fit with other views popular in research circles at the time. Social scientists recommended that federal officials use a more scientific approach to program development and monitor local programs more vigorously[3]—implying that implementation is simply the systematic translation into practice of carefully formulated policy.

In the face of continuing reports of program failure and growing skepticism about federal social intervention, researchers for the first time began to ask whether federal expectations were always reasonable.[4] That question, while still considering states and local districts as the installers of federally conceived plans, carried the seeds of quite a different view. These seeds began to germinate in the Rand Corporation's Change-Agent Study (1974-78),[5] which emphasized the importance of local contributions to implementation. This study provided the next stage in the history of research on implementation. Rand researchers saw motivation, commitment, and a sense of local ownership as important ingredients in program success. This meant that there must be bilateral adjustments—"mutual adaptation"—between federal intentions and local wishes.[6] The study thus contained in embryonic form the idea of implementation as a continuous process of policy evolution. But it did not develop that notion. Paradoxically, while stressing the importance of local initiative, the Rand researchers still pictured implementation as the local installation of federal policy.[7]

These two views of implementation—as a linear (center-to-periphery) process or as a bilateral (mutually adaptive) process—have shaped most studies of federal education programs. In both views the federal program goals are the main criteria by which success is judged. With this perspective, evaluators have had to assume that federal programs are clearly specified. In reality, this is seldom the case. Giandomenico Majone and Aaron Wildavsky have pointed out that most policies and programs are not templates, but bundles of potentialities or predispositions waiting to be defined at the local level.[8] Federal school reform programs, for example, generally define a domain for action (such as education for the disadvantaged, or vocational training), and within that domain they may establish priorities (such as teacher training or student achievement). But such definitions and priorities leave room for a variety of legitimate interpretations.

Local school districts get little guidance in making those interpretations, because federal enforcement and compliance activities are generally weak. In reality, therefore, local education agencies have considerable autonomy to work their will on federal programs—with notable exceptions such as Title VI of the Civil Rights Act of 1964. No wonder, then, that studies based on a linear or a bilateral view of implementation have been hard put to explain the outcomes of federal education reforms.

We propose a perspective with more explanatory power: Implementation is actually a complex and continuous process of policy evolution. This perspective springs in part from the phenomenological view of policy expressed by Majone and Wildavsky, who argue that "attainment of a goal is a unitary process or procedure, not a double process of setting the goal and then devising an implementation plan." Majone and Wildavsky do not see implementation as an unanchored process of goal discovery, however. Rather, it is the development of the "capacities, potentialities, and other dispositional qualities of a policy idea."[9] Thus the implementation of a policy idea will vary for two reasons: First, not all the policy's many potentialities will be recognized, and second, any given idea will be interpreted differently in different settings.

The perspective of implementation as policy evolution also has roots in sociological thought—especially the work of Daniel Lortie and Karl E. Weick. Lortie has argued that there is low interdependence among organizational units in schools,[10] and Weick has suggested that school systems are "loosely coupled" and do not always function in a highly coordinated fashion.[11] Both notions imply that school systems lack a unified response to an external stimulus such as a federal program. Rather, different local groups are likely to perceive and seek to use the program in different ways. The so-called implementation process is not simply one of federal and school district managers struggling to reconcile two views of a program, but one in which various local individuals and groups bargain among themselves as much as with external agencies—or perhaps simply do as they please.

Seen in this fashion, the translation of federal programs to local settings does not resemble a precision drill team marching in order toward a specific goal, nor even an orderly bilateral negotiation. Instead, it seems more like a large lawn party. The federal program is the stimulus, the occasion for the gathering. But the party is only a temporary convergence. The guests (local administrators, teachers, board members, and parents) have larger and more lasting concerns awaiting them at home. Moreover, these guests do not attend for the same reasons. Some have come for the food, some to hear the music, some to talk with friends, some from a sense of obligation; and some aren't sure why they've come. And they have different ideas about what they want the party to be and what they hope to gain by attending it. For some the party is an escape from dull routine, for others a chance to cultivate business prospects; and many guests have never consciously identified their wants. Nor does each guest recognize what the other guests want. Each is relatively free to make of the party whatever seems most appropriate.

Within limits, guests thus create their own party—ranging from lively entertainment to a decorous, sedate affair—by developing some of the party's original potentialities and discovering others. Since this creation occurs over time and across a range of participants whose reactions are sometimes interactive and sometimes not, the lawn party, like implementation, is evolution. Local forces (the guests) are at least as important as federal intentions (the host) in determining the final form of federal policies and programs (the party)—and usually more so.

A good example is the test of education vouchers in Alum Rock, California, in the early Seventies. The U.S. Office of Economic Opportunity (OEO) sponsored the demonstration, hoping to discover whether competition for students would force schools to improve curricula and become more responsive to parents. But local participants had other priorities.

A major point of vouchers was to offer parents more options for their children. But Alum Rock parents did not seize the initiative. Instead, worried that children might not be able to attend their neighborhood schools, they negotiated a "squatters' rights" agreement whereby children already enrolled could continue to attend a given school. Parents also saw to it that every voucher school offered at least two alternative programs, so that children would not be forced out of a neighborhood school by the parents' distaste for an overly innovative or conservative program.

Alum Rock teachers for their part saw vouchers as a threat to job security. Thus they obtained an agreement that, if they left voucher schools for reasons associated with the demonstration, they would be given priority in assignments to other schools, or OEO would cover their salaries while they worked in the central office. This saved teachers from the threat of punishment by consumer preference. But once the program was under way, teachers began to realize that, along with some advantages and greater choice, vouchers also brought problems: more students, more planning, more meetings, more colleagues, more noise, more disruptions. They then changed the market aspects of the voucher scheme by seeing to it that each school was assigned an enrollment limit. This meant that less appealing schools would get the overflow of students, reducing the chances of failure all around.

Meanwhile, the superintendent used OEO funds to carry out his own agenda, a decentralization program that transferred more power to the principals. And these principals protected their new power from parental encroachment by refusing to publish comparative data that might encourage competition among schools.

From the federal perspective, then, Alum Rock is a story of program plans and priorities foiled by unanticipated local obstacles that produced major changes in the voucher design. But from the local view, vouchers provided the opportunity to accomplish a variety of things. Principals obtained more power, more money, and little competition, all of which they wanted. Parents were guaranteed neighborhood schools and some choice among programs, both of which they wanted. Teachers received the resources and the freedom to innovate and to teach as they preferred, along with job security. The superintendent made some progress in his efforts to decentralize authority in the district, and the federal funds kept his school system solvent.

Few of the Alum Rock participants paid attention to the voucher blueprint or the OEO's formal assessments of its implementation. If they measured success at all, it was not against central plans and priorities but against their own differing needs and desires. These local needs and desires, in fact, changed and shaped the federal initiative, much as guests shape a lawn party.

The same thing occurs when a federal program is installed simultaneously in several locations. Local needs and desires differ from place to place, so that the federal initiative is shaped somewhat differently by each locale. Since the federal initiative is usually only a general statement of themes, what happens at the local level can be described as variations on those themes. Some variations are less discordant than others, but virtually none is a single composition with everyone playing from the same score.

Experience-Based Career Education (EBCE) is a case in point. Like many federal education reforms, EBCE saw rigid high schools and bored adolescents as education's biggest problems. It sought to create an alternative program that would be more flexible and more relevant to students' future needs. Two general concepts guided the development of model EBCE programs by four regional educational laboratories in the early Seventies. First, the program was intended for all students—the college-bound as well as those planning to terminate schooling with a high school diploma. Second, EBCE sought to make education more relevant through a dual focus on academic skills and community-based exploration of potential careers.

Staff members at the four regional laboratories took these general concepts, interpreted them in light of regional needs and their professional backgrounds, and developed four somewhat different models. During the next four years, at a cost of more than $20 million, the program was implemented. Substantial evaluation efforts by the developers and by the Educational Testing Service concluded that the program was successful, both in teaching youths about work and in teaching the skills and social behavior deemed important for adulthood. Largely on that basis, EBCE was designated an exemplary vocational education program by the Joint Dissemination Review Panel and was made available for national dissemination with federal funding under the Vocational Education Act, Part D. By spring 1978 EBCE was operating in 42 states under three-year Part D grants and in about 100 districts with other funding. In record time it had become a national school and work program.

The implementation of EBCE was neither simply conceived nor simply executed; it was marked by negotiation, revision, and adaptation. Adaptation was rarely mutual, however. To meet local needs, school personnel did everything to the program models from fine-tuning to wholesale restructuring. In sites we visited, curriculum materials were revised or replaced, staff roles were redefined, program components were added or dropped, and student activities were redesigned. Model processes were also changed. Suggested sequences of project activities were altered to fit local practice, ready-made projects were revised to look like familiar classroom assignments, and much of the record keeping was reduced or eliminated altogether.

By comparison, schools and school systems made only minor accommodations for the program. Students were given permission to be out of the building during school hours, and in some districts a bus or van made extra trips to carry EBCE students to and from community placements. Most schools set aside classrooms and sometimes office space for the program, and such support services as mailing, copying, and separate telephone lines were often provided. But the changes were not profound and often they were not new. Schools and school systems changed much less than did the EBCE program design.

Teachers, of course, play a key role in determining the form of any education reform. Among EBCE teachers, we observed a diversity of views and interpretations of the innovation and a consequent diversity in programs. Some teachers saw EBCE as an opportunity to work closely with a few students. A West Coast science teacher, for example, became a half-time EBCE learning coordinator because this allowed him to work with small groups. "You get to know each student personally, get involved in their lives and their problems, and work things through with them," he explained. Not surprisingly, the EBCE program developed by this teacher and his colleagues heavily emphasized counseling.

Other teachers also showed a preference for small groups, but they turned their EBCE programs into academic tutoring sessions, playing down—and occasionally ignoring altogether—the career guidance and community exploration components. One teacher described his EBCE improvisation as "a one-room schoolhouse." He provided individual skills training for the full range of students, from those with learning disabilities to those who were academically talented. Meanwhile, teachers in a suburban EBCE program serving students with academic and behavioral problems set up a highly structured, individualized math and language skills program and postponed career exploration indefinitely. Although EBCE in this district gradually came to include some average and above-average students, the program itself remained largely unchanged.

Other EBCE programs reflected quite a different view; they emphasized career exploration and helped students find occupational placements, sometimes at the expense of the program's academic content. For example, an EBCE program director in a small Eastern city redesigned his job in order to spend much of his time in the community, recruiting sites and maintaining relations with resource people. He paid little attention to his few classes. "The students are only in the EBCE center for social studies and some sciences," he told us, "so we don't spend that much time with them." This variation, besides slighting the academic component, caused other faculty members to resent the director's flaunted freedom and to resist the EBCE program whenever possible.

There also were teachers who totally ignored EBCE's stated goals, using the program instead as a vehicle for reaching non-EBCE ends. One counselor had long been committed to developing a minority studies program in his high school but had received little support from colleagues or administrators. When the school district's administrators selected his school for EBCE as part of a magnet school desegregation plan, he enlisted as a part-time learning coordinator and began to work out his minority studies program under EBCE auspices. "My objective is to get a core group of students who would come into EBCE and pursue . . . cultural projects," he told us. In this case, district administrators had interpreted EBCE in terms of certain legal needs, and this staff member created a further variation on what was already a local improvisation.

Meanwhile, teachers not directly involved with EBCE had welcoming, hostile, or mixed reactions to the innovation—reactions that also helped to shape local programs. Some teachers in academic disciplines resisted EBCE as an attempt to water down the curriculum or as a threat to job security. The entire English department at one school opposed EBCE on the ground that it did not challenge students sufficiently. In this urban district, hard hit by declining enrollments, the teachers also blamed EBCE for drawing students away from some elective courses. They obstructed the program in several ways, describing it as an inferior track, assigning unusually demanding make-up work for classes missed because of EBCE, and marking students absent for participating in officially sanctioned out-of-school activities. Not surprisingly, some students refrained from joining EBCE, others dropped out, and student recruitment and program maintenance became a problem for EBCE staff.

Other non-EBCE teachers simply regarded the program as a nuisance. In one large suburban school EBCE was set up as a school-within-a-school for low-achieving, disruptive students. As an alternative on-campus progam it had considerable autonomy and few links to regular school life. Before the end of the first year, however, the social studies department, which shared a building with the EBCE program, complained to the principal that EBCE students were a source of disruption. The social studies teachers recommended that the program be moved to another building. EBCE staff members responded by persuading a widely respected teacher to join their program; they also persuaded the administration to designate EBCE as a regular school department. This helped legitimize the program for average and above-average students, who began to enroll. Thus the program survived, but it changed. Within four years the school-within-a-school serving a small subpopulation became an integrated department offering courses to all students.

If many non-EBCE staff members were hostile to the innovation, others welcomed it for providing a real service by meeting special student needs. One special education teacher viewed EBCE mainly as an alternative for "youngsters with just-below-average IQs who cannot make it in the regular classroom." In this school EBCE developed into a highly individualized remedial program to serve high-risk students who were not being helped elsewhere.

Other teachers welcomed EBCE because they could use it as a dumping ground for students with academic or behavioral problems. The staff of one program, established to serve "difficult" students, tried to recruit a better cross section in the third year, hoping to provide role models for less able students and more manageable conditions for themselves. But they had little success. Counselors continued to refer their problem students to the program, and classroom teachers said, "If you're not taking the problem youngsters, what good are you?" This program changed little, continuing to focus on academic and counseling components while ambitious early plans—such as long-term community placements—never materialized.

The concerns of administrators and school board members differed from those of teachers. In one community we visited, administrators tried to use EBCE to attract white students to an all-black school. Fearing a court order, they promoted EBCE to white students for its individualization, its flexible crediting and scheduling, and its difference from other school programs—all themes that were emphatically played in this local improvisation.

In a New England town, by contrast, the school board approved adoption of EBCE to curtail dropouts (and because it brought the district more than $100,000 in federal and state grants). Here the program evolved into an effort to keep marginal students in school long enough to get their diplomas. Another district in a particularly conservative state was more concerned with students who remained in school. There the school board adopted an academically oriented program tailored for above-average students.

In one small suburban school system a bare majority of the board approved a middle-level administrator's proposal to start an EBCE program, allowing him only a tiny budget. The result was a one-dimensional version of EBCE: A lone teacher spent one-fourth of her time in classroom activities with a handful of students, and career development was virtually ignored. Even this tiny program did not survive when the district's financial situation worsened after 18 months. Although one holdout board member spoke at length about how such a program might have helped his daughter, now floundering in college, the board voted to discontinue EBCE.

District administrators and school boards, like teachers, thus had varying views of EBCE. Some improvised on the innovation to solve nagging local problems ranging from desegregation to drop-out rates; others, more concerned with average student populations and conventional agendas, adopted EBCE as a mainstream program instead of an alternative. In either case, the program evolved from a particular configuration of interpretations.

For building principals charged with keeping a school running smoothly and keeping track of students, EBCE was often a source of irritation. One rural school principal, for example, told us that he was annoyed when students wanted to quit EBCE because they considered their job placements menial. What bothered him was "the enormous hassle" of reabsorbing these students into the regular program midway through the semester.

Other principals had nothing against the innovation per se but saw it as just one more program and one more headache. One principal let his faculty know that he was no friend of the program. Some teachers followed his lead, discouraging students from joining, disparaging those who did participate, and obstructing the program in other ways. Naturally, the program became an enduring source of controversy in this district.

Some principals were truly committed to EBCE's stated goals. One assistant principal told us that he wanted to insure that "every student in the high school has the option" of experiencing EBCE. Others saw it as a way to get problem youngsters out of school, where they could not disrupt classes. In one district the assistant principals in the middle and high schools had been pushing for an alternative program for alienated students. Here EBCE was shaped to this purpose. Some principals recognized the public relations value of a community-oriented program; they welcomed the exposure EBCE afforded their schools—and, by extension, their own careers. Others were grateful for the increased budgets, which helped them meet other needs.

EBCE thus turned out to be many different programs, developed by diverse groups and individuals improvising on a set of central themes. Such local divergence stems from the fact that school districts lack a simple, single purpose, and school district organization allows wide variation in what goes on in individual schools and classrooms. Instead of encouraging consensus around formal goals, federal intervention in local school districts tends to aggravate differences as teachers, administrators, and specialists interpret the program in terms of varied work realities and role requirements. *The difference between federal hopes and local action is not simply or necessarily the result of federal mismanagement or local obstinacy; it is due to differing and often contradictory local perceptions of a program and its purpose.* From our perspective, then, implementation is a misnomer. It is wiser to think of local installation of federal programs as a continuing process of policy making, during which various actors press their varied visions of policy.

EBCE is a particular kind of federal program, well suited to this interpretation. It was not mandated for a specific student population, nor was it intended to remedy a constitutionally defined inequity. Rather, it was made available to volunteering school districts by a combination of government and private agencies who had at their disposal no sticks and but a few carrots—some funds, but mostly recognition, free training, and free materials. The role of central authority is necessarily limited in such a program, and the influences at the periphery are consequently stronger. Thus "mutual adaptation" is more likely to occur among the elements at the periphery than between federal sponsor and local agency. But our interpretation of implementation as policy evolution is not limited to voluntary programs. The strong influence of local forces and the prevalence of mutual adaptation at the periphery seem typical of federal school programs. Even in categorical programs, where a strong federal role is possible in principle, there have been few instances in which federal directives authoritatively and uniformly steered local program development.

Our focus on program evolution in response to local diversity explains what was hard to explain in the inherited view: the persistent failure of local education agencies to do what is expected of them. In terms of evolution and organizational diversity, what once seemed irrational now seems natural and logical. But this raises new questions: How does one recognize good or successful implementation? Whose view of success should prevail?

Our answer is that there is no single, simple answer. A partial answer is to admit that there are varieties of success and that no single criterion can encompass them. Another but quite uncertain answer is to try to frame criteria for success in terms of processes, using such notions as problem solving to judge whether good things are happening. Yet another is to concede that no single intelligence can comprehend all the possible views of success, and to hope that helpful pictures will emerge out of diverse and divergent stories of implementation.

But if we can envision these and other solutions to the question of what constitutes successful implementation, it would be rash to imagine that we can pick the best one. For millenia human beings have examined their history, trying to assess the import of an action and the success of what was done. They have struggled to distinguish the important events and to identify what was important about them. They have tried to explain how men succeeded, how they failed, and why. These are the same issues that now bedevil students of federal program implementation. And there is no reason to believe that, in the study of federal program implementation, social scientists will solve these old and difficult problems.

1. For an account of the early evaluations of ESEA Title I implementation, see Milbrey Wallin McLaughlin's excellent study, *Evaluation and Reform* (Cambridge, Mass.: Ballinger, 1975). See also Jerome T. Murphy, "Title I of ESEA: The Politics of Implementing Federal education Reform," *Harvard Educational Review*, February 1971, pp. 35-63.

2. David K. Cohen, "The Value of Social Experiments," and Carol Lukas, "Problems in Implementing Head Start Planned Variation Models," in Alice M. Rivlin and P. Michael Timpane, eds., *Planned Variation in Education: Should We Give Up or Try Harder?* (Washington, D.C.: Brookings Institution, 1975).

3. See, for example, Egon G. Guba, "Development, Diffusion, and Evaluation," in Terry L. Eidell and Joanne M. Kitchell, eds., *Knowledge Production and Utilization in Educational Administration* (Eugene, Ore.: Center for Advanced Studies of Educational Administration, University of Oregon, 1968).

4. See, for example, Martha Derrick, *New Towns in-Town: Why a Federal Program Failed* (Washington, D.C.: Urban Institute, 1972); and Bernard Frieden and Marshall Kaplan, *The Politics of Neglect: Urban Aid from Model Cities to Revenue Sharing* (Cambridge, Mass.: MIT Press, 1975). Organizational theorists had already questioned the role of rationality in decision making, among them Charles E. Lindblom, Herbert Simon, and Richard M. Cyert and James G. March. Jeffrey Pressman and Aaron Wildavsky applied such notions in *Implementation* (Berkeley, Calif.: University of California Press, 1973), an account of the problems of implementing an Economic Development Administration program in Oakland. In education, the same ideas were used in Tyll Robert Van Geel's study, "Efficiency, Effectiveness, and Local School Systems: Will School Systems Adopt Planning, Programming, and Budgeting?" (Doctoral dissertation, Harvard University, 1972); McLaughlin's study of Title I, op. cit.; and Jerome T. Murphy's analysis of ESEA Title IV, *State Education Agencies and Discretionary Funds* (Lexington, Mass.: Heath, 1974).

5. *Federal Programs Supporting Educational Change*, 5 vols. (Santa Monica, Calif.: Rand Corporation, April 1975). This is a study of 29 planned change projects supported by four federal programs: ESEA Title III, ESEA Title VII, Vocational Education Part D Exemplary Programs, and Right to Read.

6. Rand Corporation, op. cit., vol. 1, p. 10.

7. Ibid., vol. 4 (abridged), pp. 3, 4.

8. Giandomenico Majone and Aaron Wildavsky, "Implementation as Evolution: Exorcising the Ghosts in the Implementation Machine," *Russell Sage Discussion Papers*, no. 2 (New York: Sage Foundation, 1978).

9. Ibid.

10. Daniel C. Lortie, *School Teacher: A Sociological Study* (Chicago: University of Chicago Press, 1975).

11. Karl E. Weick, "Educational Organizations as Loosely Coupled Systems," *Administration Science Quarterly*, March 1976, pp. 1-19.

12. David K. Cohen and Eleanor Farrar, "Power to the Parents? The Story of Education Vouchers," *The Public Interest*, Summer 1977, pp. 72-98. For more detailed accounts of the implementation of education vouchers in Alum Rock, see the published reports of the Rand Corporation (the evaluator of the Alum Rock program): Eliot Levinson, with Susan Abramowitz, William Furry, and Dorothy Joseph, "The Politics and Implementation of the Alum Rock Multiple Option System: The Second Year, 1973-74," *Analysis of the Education Voucher Demonstration, A Working Note*, May 1975; Stephen S. Weiner and Konrad Kellen, "The Politics and Administration of the Voucher Demonstration in Alum Rock: The First Year, 1972-73," *Analysis of the Education Voucher Demonstration, A Working Note*, August 1974; and Daniel Weiler, *A Public School Voucher Demonstration: The First Year at Alum Rock*, June 1974.

VI

The Uncertain Profession

Introduction

In the June 1977 KAPPAN we published the cartoon that appears on this page. It was ranked at the top among 50 unsolicited cartoons rated by KAPPAN consultants that spring. But it drew cries of pain and anger from many readers (mainly professors of education and their wives, as I recall), because it was seen as perpetuating an unfunny canard—one that in fact verges on libel. It should be obvious that for every person who fails as a teacher, goes back to school for an advanced degree, and gets a job as a professor of education, there are hundreds of bright, ambitious practitioners for whom an education professorship represents the peak of professional success. Just as teaching hospitals usually attract the best physicians, so teacher preparatory institutions generally attract the most apt students of education to their faculties.

Nevertheless, education is on the whole an immature profession, plagued by uncertainty, amateurism, and outright incompetence. A vicious cycle operates: Low status for public school teachers breeds low rewards, which drive out the "best and the brightest," which insures low status. These problems have been explored repeatedly in the KAPPAN. The articles in this chapter are representative.

"I couldn't do anything else, so I became a teacher. When I found out I couldn't teach, I became a professor of education."

Harry S. Broudy, who wrote "The Search for a Science of Education" for the Bicentennial edition of the KAPPAN *(September 1976), has frequently addressed this topic. And Harry Broudy is, as Maxine Greene once noted in a* KAPPAN *article, "a kind of culture hero in the world of education. His work in aesthetics and aesthetic education is but one facet of a professional life devoted to making things clear." Like Greene, I have always admired Broudy's writing, and was particularly fond of the wit with which he used to introduce issues of the* Educational Forum *when he edited that fine journal. A professor of educational philosophy at the University of Illinois (now retired), Broudy often makes his points with wry humor or epigrams such as this one: "Ignorance of educational history is the mother of innovation." Faddism— and innovation breeds faddism—is one more symptom of immaturity in the profession.*

I remarked in the editorial that introduced Richard B. Morland's classic piece, "The External Doctorate in Education: Blessing or Blasphemy?" (November 1973), that "in higher education the line between charlatanism and innovation often wavers and disappears." Also, I suggested that "few advances in knowledge or in educational practice are made without risk. Colleges tend to err on the side of caution, and they know it. Then guilty conscience helps the clever, greedy, and unscrupulous to rip off the system." These observations and Morland's article set off a debate in the pages of the KAPPAN *that still continues.*

In preparation for editing this book, I asked Morland to contribute background information. He wrote as follows:

> *My article on external doctoral degrees was adapted from a position paper I presented in 1973 to the Florida Council of Deans and Directors of Teacher Education. At that time several institutions in the state were conferring doctoral degrees upon candidates who spent a summer of study in rented facilities of various types and wrote dissertations at home. Another institution with no experience in professional education had launched two massive nationwide programs enrolling more than 1,500 students in Ed.D. programs. I thought it would be a matter of concern to educators for their highest professional degree to be awarded in such large numbers to persons who were not screened for admission by test scores or grade-point averages, who spent such limited time in formal study, who were not held to qualifying or comprehensive examinations, and who were subjected to so little control to insure that dissertations and practicums submitted were the students' own work.*
>
> *I did not intend to make a career of the stand I had taken on the external doctorates, but not a single week has passed since publication of the article that I have not had communications of one kind or another regarding these programs. Some of the earlier experiences were reported in my article titled 'On Growing Grapes in Greenland' (February 1975 KAPPAN).*
>
> *The thousands of words that have flowed since the article first appeared have generated much heat but little else. The questions I raised have not been addressed by professional associations, much less answered.*
>
> *In the meantime, the beat goes on. Today, the largest producers*

of the doctorate in education are the nontraditional institutions.°
What does this bode for the value of the degree? One need not
possess any type of degree to handle that question.

After taking his own doctorate at New York University, Morland joined
the staff of Stetson University in DeLand, Florida, in 1952 and has remained
there to the present. He is a former president of the East Central Florida
Chapter of Phi Delta Kappa and currently serves as an editorial consultant to
the KAPPAN.

One of the most engaging figures in American education is W. James
Popham of UCLA, a bumptious researcher/entrepreneur whose speaking
style makes him highly popular on the lecture circuit. He won the Distin-
guished Teaching Award given by UCLA's student association in 1967 and
followed it with a similar UCLA Alumni Association award and the Harvey
L. Eby Art of Teaching award in 1968. Popham manages to inject humor even
into his serious writing, and he has written over 200 research papers, nine
books, and numerous journal articles. His more than 20 filmstrip-tapes are
widely used in teacher education. He has directed the IOX, a Los Angeles-
based test development agency, for many years. He is a past president of the
AERA.

Interestingly enough, the Popham article reprinted here, "Teaching Skills
Under Scrutiny," is one of the most professionally unpopular I have solicited
for the KAPPAN. *Why? Perhaps R. Barker Bausell and William B. Moody,*
writing under the title, "Are Teacher Preparation Institutions Necessary?" in
the January 1973 KAPPAN, *found the answer. Reporting on the Popham*
study and their own research, they concluded that "teacher preparation as
provided by colleges of education does not result in increased student
achievement."

Knowing Popham's credentials, one would expect that a national commit-
tee studying teaching methods (it shall be nameless) would have been im-
pressed by Popham's research. It wasn't so. When I summarized Popham's
KAPPAN *piece at an opportune time in the committee's deliberations, back*
in 1972, no one commented. In fact, the committee acted as if I had belched in
church, ignoring the indiscretion.

Is Popham's research defective? Popham thinks not. (He has described
the study in greater detail in "Performance Tests of Teaching Proficiency:
Rationale, Development, and Validation." See the January 1971 American
Educational Research Journal.) *But Richard L. Turner, now dean of*
education at University of Colorado, contended in a KAPPAN *piece titled*
"Are Educational Researchers Necessary?" (January 1973) that the study is
indeed defective on at least three counts, which he specified. Turner con-
cluded: "In sum, Popham's study is not a fair test of the hypothesis that there is
no relationship between teacher preparation/experience and student per-
formance." (It is interesting that Turner was, I am told, one of the referees
who approved publication of Popham's AERJ piece noted above.)

As an admirer of both researchers, I remain neutral.

°Nova University alone has conferred nearly 2,500 Ed.D. degrees through its
external programs, 380 of them between 1 July 1979 and 30 June 1980.

Questions about teaching and teacher education like those raised by Popham led me to plan a special issue of the KAPPAN for October 1980. I persuaded B. Othanel Smith to guest edit it, partly because I had read and liked the manuscript for his book, Design for a School of Pedagogy. "Pedagogical Education: How About Reform?," reprinted here, is heavily based on the book, which is now available from the U.S. Government Printing Office.

Much of Smith's professional career has been spent in the examination of teaching and teacher education while teaching at the University of Illinois and the University of South Florida at Tampa. His leadership in these fields has been acknowledged by colleagues, who elected him president of the Philosophy of Education Society and the National Society of College Teachers of Education, as well as to offices in the AERA. The John Dewey Society's 1975 award and a citation from the National Teacher Corps are further testimony to the high regard in which Smith is held. Now, as a result of publication of his KAPPAN article, he has received the AACTE's award for excellence in professional writing.

For space reasons, I have not included comments on Smith's recommendations for reform in teacher education made in the same KAPPAN by several organization leaders: Thomas A. Shannon of the National School Boards Association, Warren G. Hill of the Education Commission of the States, Sharon Robinson of the National Education Association, Paul Salmon of the American Association of School Administrators, and David Imig of the American Association of Colleges for Teacher Education. All liked at least some of Smith's ideas.

One recent manifestation of the accountability movement in education has been a growing number of malpractice cases brought against teachers and school districts. Among the first—it was certainly the most widely publicized—was the suit Gary Saretsky analyzes in "The Strangely Significant Case of Peter Doe" (May 1973). When he wrote it, Saretsky was a research assistant at Phi Delta Kappa headquarters and a doctoral student at Indiana University. He is now program officer, Developmental Learning Opportunity Fund, New Jersey Department of Higher Education, where his concern for the Peter Does of education is at the center of his professional activity. He says, "Here in New Jersey, the only state to mandate a statewide College Basic Skills Placement Test for freshmen, 68% of entering students tested lack proficiency in reading and writing and 54% lack proficiency in computational skills. I'm sure a similar, if not worse, situation exists in other states."

To date, no plaintiff has won a malpractice suit in education. However, Eugene Connors, in a book published this year by Phi Delta Kappa under the title Educational Tort Liability and Malpractice, predicts that we are nearing the day when the courts will rule against a school defendant.° If so, the plaintiff's arguments are likely to parallel those of Susanne Martinez in the Peter Doe case; the judge and milieu will have to be different.

—SME

°So does James Leary in a new book, Educators on Trial. "If malpractice suits continue their present pace," he says, "they will become the most powerful influence on education in the 1980s."

The Search for a
Science of Education
by Harry S. Broudy

*Reincarnated, a U.S. citizen of 1776 would find the world in-
explicable—except in an elementary classroom. Why so little
change in the schools? A philosopher of education explores the
question here, using John Dewey's essay, "The Sources of a
Science of Education" (1929), as a starting point.*

A citizen of 1776 seeing the gang plows, planters, and huge combines on our
great prairie farms would be astonished. Factories turning out mountains of
goods by machine would also amaze him, as would jet planes, automobiles,
and modern hospitals. He would find communication by telephone, radio,
and television incomprehensible. Not only would he be confounded by the
size and complexity of the various operations, but he would be mystified by
the technology embodied in them. As for the scientific concepts that
rationalized this technology, they would be stranger to him than alchemy.

But if our '76 citizen walked into an American elementary schoolroom, he
would recognize quite readily what was going on. A teacher would be trying
to impart the skills of reading, writing, and ciphering plus the rudiments of
geography, history, and a few other subjects to 25 or more young pupils. (Of
course, the content of some of these subjects might amaze him.) He would see
large slates on the wall, and many books rather than a few. Some visual aids
he would understand readily, but not a console for television or computer-
aided instruction (in the unlikely event that he encountered one in the
ordinary classroom). By and large, neither the technology of contemporary
instruction nor its rationale would mystify him, certainly nowhere near so
much as the equipment used for lighting, heating, and air conditioning the
school building. Despite its size and scope, schoolkeeping is still a cottage industry.

Growing Corn and Growing Children

A prominent congressman, noted for his interest in education, not long
ago asked a conference of educational pundits why colleges of education did
not serve their clientele as do colleges of agriculture or engineering. He noted
that colleges of agriculture employed 1) scientists in chemistry, genetics,
mathematics, and economics; 2) technologists who invented or perfected
methods of planting, fertilizing, cultivating, harvesting, and marketing a
wide variety of crops; of breeding, feeding, and marketing livestock; and 3)
extension specialists who delivered help to the farmer in every phase of his
operation, from planting to filling out income tax forms.

Why, the legislator wanted to know, could not colleges of education,
employing the same types of personnel, deliver remedial services to the classroom door? Why could they not revolutionize instruction as colleges of agriculture have revolutionized farming? Why, we may all ask, is an educational
establishment that boasts of a giant research effort and a training program
that has staffed the schools with nearly three million teachers and administrators so continuously criticized for its inefficiency? Why, indeed, are the

problems so tediously the same, generation after generation? Why, in short, could the American citizen of 1776 find so much that is so familiar in the schools of 1976?

I shall not attempt to reconstruct the learned answers given by the educators to the congressman's questions; roughly, they were of two sorts. In one it was argued that teachers and administrators either did not know about or were unwilling to apply the available findings of research to teaching, curriculum, school organization, and finance. They pointed to the wealth of theories, studies, and projects wherewith one could document every discussion on every educational topic. And in fact the variety of teaching models on the market is so great that it is difficult to keep track of them. Nor has there been a dearth of educational innovations, although their theoretical soundness and usefulness often have been judged by the size of the grants they command and the publicity they enjoy. Most of them have emanated from the brightest and best in the college of education confraternity.

These responses elicited two other questions: First, what sort of scientific enterprise is it in which so many different theories continue to flourish side by side, seemingly invulnerable to refutation by argument or test? Where are the disciples of Karl Popper in educational research?[1] Second, why do teachers and administrators, beleaguered by critics from all sides, pass up possible rescue missions grounded on scientific research findings? The latter question was especially embarrassing, because the allegedly "stupid" or "foot-dragging" teachers and administrators had been trained by professors of education, presumably with the help of the research they were now accused of ignoring.

It has been suggested that teachers do not pick up on research as quickly as do farmers because the teacher's income is not seen as directly tied to productivity (i.e., learning) as is the farmer's. The farmer sees a new technique producing more profit for his neighbor, and so he readily adopts it. Furthermore, it is pointed out that a new technique in teaching requires more work for the teacher and may be perceived as a threat to well-established habits. There is little doubt that these factors are real and potent, and they deserve a far more extended discussion than is possible in this article. Aside from the thorny problem of determining and measuring productivity in teaching, there is a difference between using research and employing techniques that claim to be based on research. Even farmers, we are told, in the early days of the land-grant colleges had little faith in professors of agriculture. The research had to be translated into a technique that obviously worked to increase production before farmers took the professors seriously. Teachers, as a rule, are not confronted with such obviously successful techniques, although they are often asked to believe that research has assured such success.

Professors of education sometimes explain inadequate utilization of research by noting that the delivery of research findings in education is not the same as in agriculture, engineering, or medicine. Medicine and engineering have a layer of practitioners who have studied the basic theory of the disciplines contributing to their professional fields in their preservice training. Professional journals keep them apprised of developments in basic and applied research; periodic institutes inform them of the latest developments in both theory and practice. The dirt farmer probably does not correspond to the engineer and physician in this respect, unless he is a graduate of a college of agriculture. The extension service delivers the results of science and technology directly to the farmer in the field.

In the public school establishment, a strong cadre of professionals who have had preservice training corresponding to that of an engineer or physician does not exist. The strictly professional content of the ordinary preservice program for the teaching certificate is so meager that it is taken for granted that the moment the teacher enters on the first job he/she will require the ministrations of an inservice rescue squad. It is a bit like turning out automobiles that can make it on their own power only to the customer's door and forthwith have to be towed to the repair shop. Inservice study may supply something like the preservice training in other professions, but so varied are the inservice programs for teachers that it is difficult to generalize on their effects.

Research in education is communicated to other researchers either by doctoral study or through meetings that are rarely attended and journals that are rarely read by the practitioners in the field. Professors of education tend to think of themselves as theorizing about and occasionally designing the service that might be rendered to teachers and administrators, rather than as delivery agents. If delivery of the service, socially useful as it is, does not require a high order of theoretical competence, it will be downgraded by the professoriate, who tend to judge quality in terms of intellectual caliber and guild status rather than by social utility alone. In this the professor of education is not much different from professors of engineering, law, and medicine; but if the practitioner in education is more like the dirt farmer than the practicing engineer, then colleges of education do need good extension specialists.

The other reason offered to our prominent congressman for the lack of direct help to practitioners by the research-training establishment went something like this: Educational science does not generate the kind of empirical generalizations from which a powerful technology and definitive rules of practice can be derived.

So while one group of pundits was telling the congressman that there was plenty of good research if only the workers in the field would use it, another group was telling him that the workers in the field did not use research findings because they were not very useful. The legislator, therefore, could be pardoned for being puzzled. If the research was good, why was it not being used? If not good, why maintain an expensive research establishment?

Discussions such as these raise the perennial question about the nature and possibility of a science of education. The question is philosophical, but it has very practical reverberations. Moreover, some of the reverberations are anomalous, almost paradoxical. If a science of education really were to give us a theory from which we could derive rules that would enable schools to control learning, as the farmer can now control his crops, how would we react to it? At least one psychologist, B. F. Skinner, who claims that operant conditioning is a scientific theory that can do something very much like this, has had to listen to some harsh comments about himself and his theory.[2]

My own impression is that the congressman was really asking about a technology that would produce desired results efficiently. Whether it was science-based or not was incidental, although the success of science-based technology in agriculture and the existence of the educational research establishment naturally influenced him to pose the question in this form.[3] These hopes, one must confess, are not likely to be fulfilled, not because educational researchers are incompetent or lazy, but rather because the desired results are not analogous to the ear of corn that meets certain specifications or the automobile that travels so many miles on a gallon of gasoline. "Growing corn" and "growing children" are not analogous expressions, one reason for not taking the teacher-gardener metaphor too seriously. The goals of education (as distinguished from a particular school activity) are not this or that behavior, this or that habit or disposition, but a style of life for a whole person. None of the professions we have been holding up as models is responsible for such a totality of results. The structure of the good life may be constant, but the constellation of action, thought, and feeling consistent with this structure varies for each individual. There may not be a technology for producing virtue and happiness.

There is no factor in human welfare that American public schools refuse to embrace in their mission: genetic variations, skin color, economic and social injustice, emotional maladjustments—all must and will be taken into account. In assuming responsibility for such holistic, indeterminate outcomes, schools are promising far more than they can possibly do; the promise is a tribute to their good intentions rather than to their good sense. No science or combination of them can bail out such indiscreet hospitality. Science and science-based technology can help education only to the degree in which its mission is narrowed, objectified, and its results are publicly identifiable. Insofar as such reduction is resisted—and resistance there is—the very possibility of a science of education becomes problematical.

A Science of Education and 'Educational Science'

Considerations of this sort persuaded John Dewey nearly a half century ago to interpret educational science in a way that differs markedly from the positivistic empirical model that has worked so brilliantly in the physical sciences and their applications in agriculture, medicine, and engineering.[4]

The gist of Dewey's argument runs somewhat as follows:

1. Quantification as used in the physical sciences is hard to come by in psychological phenomena.

> Nor have we as yet any . . . general hypotheses in the light of which to know *what* we are measuring and by which we can interpret results, place them in a system, and lead on to fruitful indirect measurements. . . . The lack of an intellectually coherent system is a positive warning against attributing scientific value to results merely because they are reached by means of recognized techniques borrowed from sciences already established and are capable of being stated in quantitative formulae. Quantity is not even the fundamental idea of mathematics. (pp. 26, 27)

2. Repeatedly, Dewey points out that scientific laws as such do not yield rules of practice.

> No conclusion from scientific research can be converted into an immediate rule of educational art. For there is no educational practice whatever which is not highly complex; that is to say, which does not contain many other conditions and factors than are included in the scientific finding. (p. 19)

He cites the example of school administrators converting the biological finding that girls between the ages of 11 and 14 mature faster than boys at the same ages into the rule that boys and girls should be taught separately (p. 18). A current example is the translation of the fact of individual differences into prescriptions of individualized curricula for each pupil.

3. The data of an educational science, he holds, should come from educational phenomena and problems, and the conclusions should be tested by their educational consequences . (p. 33)

4. "Sciences already developed to a fair state of maturity are the sources from which material is derived to deal intellectually with these problems" (p. 35). Dewey does not regard the human sciences of psychology, sociology, and their kindred disciplines as being developed to a fair state of maturity, but they do provide the educator with findings that operate indirectly.

> Actually, he [the practitioner] employs the scientific results as intellectual tools *in* his empirical procedures. That is, they *direct his attention*, in both observation and reflection, to conditions and relationships which would otherwise escape him. (p. 30)

He warns against "attempting to extract from psychology and sociology definite solutions which it is beyond their present power to give" (p. 42).

5. Dewey distinguished scientific findings of psychology, sociology, and statistics from "educational science." To become educational science, they have to be transformed into "attitudes and habits of observation, judgment, and planning of those engaged in the educative act" (p. 32), i.e., when used "to make educational functions more intelligent." (p. 33)

6. Finally, he denies that social conditions determine educational objectives as the social sciences would have us believe. "Education [not educators] is autonomous and should be free to determine its own ends. . . . For education is itself a process of discovering what values are worthwhile and are to be pursued as objectives." (p. 74)

It is not surprising in the light of these observations that Dewey included among the sources of a science of education the philosophy of education, the experience of teachers and administrators, and disciplines such as psychology, psychiatry, and the social sciences. There is no intrinsic educational science content.

For Dewey, it would seem that educational science is thinking systematically about educational problems so that practitioners are more intelligent and more aware of what they are about (pp. 75, 76). This is a far cry from the theory/technology/application route found in agriculture, engineering, and medicine.

Although I find little in Dewey's analysis of the situation with which to take serious issue, it should be remarked that, for Dewey, science, scientific thinking, being intelligent, growth, and life itself all manifest the structure of the complete act of thought, with which most educators became familiar in his *How We Think*. Briefly, the complete act of thought (CAT) begins with a predicament in which action is blocked and leads to closer observation of the ruptured situation; a problem is defined that relates the predicament to its relevant contexts; known generalizations suggest hypotheses (ideas) about the causes and remedies of the difficulty; consequences of the hypotheses are exfoliated in thought; and, finally, a test is devised (an act of some sort) that confirms or disconfirms the prediction. Thus blocked action incites thought, which, if conducted properly, restores continuity of action. Doing and knowing are united in intelligent action. It is no exaggeration to say that this formulation of the CAT is the most comprehensive educational generalization of the last 100 years. It is a design for instruction, democratic action, morality, and, above all, growth as the progressive reconstruction of experience.[5]

Hence we can understand why about all Dewey really expects from the various scientific disciplines is a change in the attitude of the educator so that he is made open to new possibilities, new hypotheses; so that he can approach educational problems in a more liberal spirit and with constructive imagination (p. 58). Furthermore, we can understand why education, being of the same structure as good thinking and of growth and life itself, can generate its own norms and not rely on opinion polls or social conditions to discover them.

It is fair to say that in recent years education has relied on economists, sociologists, and psychologists for much more than the broadening of horizons and stimulating hypotheses. They have been hired to "study" education, and these studies have been used as bases for policy prescriptions, not merely for transforming scientific findings into what Dewey called "educational science."[6]

The identification of science, intelligent action, and the good life as the progressive reconstruction of experience by intelligence is a brilliant generalization, but it covers too much. First, it blurs the difference between highly developed, empirical, experimental disciplines such as physics or chemistry and hypothetico-deductive thinking in general. But not all good thinking is scientific, and not all good thinkers are scientists. When the possibility of a science of education is under discussion, the point is whether or not a science-like system of concepts, laws, and modes of inquiry can be hoped for that will explain, predict, and perhaps afford control of educational phenomena. To say, as Dewey did, that an intelligent stance toward problems of education stimulated by findings from the special sciences constitutes an "educational science" avoids the main issue. It might be less confusing to say that a philosophy of education exhibiting the structure of hypothetico-deductive thinking is possible, but not a science of education in the ordinary meaning of science.[7]

Second, universalizing the CAT tends to equate all cognition with the mediational processes of inference. But, as will be noted, there are constants in thought as well as the flow of inference between them; there is a cognitive component in the immediate; sooner or later, that out of which a construct is constructed must be cognized in terms of its own properties.

Third, Dewey's account of "educational science" makes it appear that any thoughtful educator, by being alert to the deliverance of the special sciences, can frame hypotheses and test generalizations concerning the problems of education. Today this is no longer likely. Knowledge about the economic, social, political, and technological factors that affect the goals and practices of the schools has become the domain of highly specialized disciplines. Yet the study of these disciplines does not automatically translate itself into the context of educational problems, so that the translation itself becomes a field for advanced study and training in the graduate school of education, and the results of the translation constitute the content of the professional studies in the preparation of educational personnel.

It goes without saying that even after the contexts of problems of education are constructed with some sophistication and rigor, prescriptions for action may require procedures and technologies that do not flow from adequate interpretation or understanding of the problems. Arguments for or against bilingual education in the public schools, for example, tell us little about how to teach English as a second language. For that matter, we are still arguing about the proper technology for the teaching of reading English as the first language.

The professions of agriculture, engineering, and medicine have done better with technology than with the social contexts in which the technology is to be applied, but they too are coming to realize what education should never have forgotten: namely, that ultimately the context in which professional problems arise and are dealt with is life itself—the totality of contexts. For the other professions consideration of the totality may seem peripheral, supplementary, and postponable; for education it must always remain central; it can be bracketed only temporarily and never for very long.

Illumination and Efficiency

A full-blown science of education, therefore, comprises two tasks. The first is a rigorous assessment of contributions from the special sciences and other disciplines for their relevance to building illuminating contexts for educational problems, and could be assigned to or assumed by the various foundational studies in the history, philosophy, sociology, psychology, anthropology, and economics of education. The second task is to translate or derive from various scientific findings procedures and technologies that would help solve educational problems. To whom is this latter task to be assigned? We do have a class of educational workers who might be called technologists, e.g., those who devise programs and apparatus for computer-aided instruction, or the practitioners of behavior modification techniques. Some of the techniques are invented by teachers in the classroom, and some are devised and taught by professors of education in methods courses. Some are consciously related to findings in some discipline or some combination of them; some are grounded in commonsense pragmatics; and some are no more than plausible hunches. It is in the articulation between these two tasks that the analogy to agriculture, medicine, and engineering breaks down.

For either use of educational science—foundational or technological—the problems of education will have to be stabilized with respect to taxonomies, terminologies, and modes of inquiry. In this respect the field of education is in a prescientific, pre-paradigmatic stage. It is virtually impossible to find consensus—explicit or implicit—on problems, theories, approaches, and criteria. The current enthusiasm for individual differences and unlimited options symbolizes the chaotic state of the art, as well as the embryonic state of the science. A science of which a basic generalization is that there can be no generalizations is strange science indeed.

The meager supply of educational technology based on a strong scientific base should not blind us to the possibilities of improving the efficiency of school operations by using available technology where it makes sense to do so. Nor should the philosophical nature of context building, so necessary to illuminate the nature of educational problems, influence us to downgrade its dependence on correct assessments of social and psychological reality, that is, on facts arrived at by scientific procedures.

The problem-solving, inferential character of the Complete Act of Thought tended to denigrate the factual basis for thinking. Rote learning and fixed habits were decried as rigid, as antithetical to thought as acting from impulse. Yet all thought uses concepts, rules, and operations that do remain constant—at least during a particular act of thought. Chlorine as a chemical element has a structure and properties that are given and constant; there are number *facts* without which arithmetical operations become clumsy. A fact can be questioned and thereby turned into a hypothesis, but then other facts that are not questioned are used to think about it. The thinking process always has some content, and when the content is embedded in a discipline, it is not available without some formal study of that discipline. The findings of economics, history, chemistry, and other disciplines cannot, as a rule, be plucked out of manuals and textbooks by consulting the index. But many progressive schoolmen, impressed with the importance of the process of good thinking, saw in Dewey's treatment of it an excuse to by-pass systematic study of subject matter. Accordingly, the quality of many school activities that stress thinking—projects, discussions—suffers from the low quality of the content the pupils bring to it. Quality of thought is measured not only by the correctness of its logical form but also by the correctness of the facts and hypotheses with which the process is carried on.

In the study of education there has been a laudable respect for fact as a basis for the discovery of law-like generalizations about teaching and learning, the curriculum, and the organization and management of schools. There is no lack of data on student populations, expenditures, or characteristics of this or that sample population of pupils, just as we have countless correlational studies that somehow accumulate without being cumulative. These data and studies are important, but we are not so fortunate with respect to data about the expectations the public or publics have with regard to school: about the role of the school in the complex of other social mechanisms. Perhaps our lack of solid information about these deeper layers of thought and expectations on the part of the clients of education explains why microstudies do not have the impact and import that they ought to have.

Some of these data can and should be supplied by the empirical methods of the social sciences, e.g., sociological and psychological studies about the relations of the school to the community, to various ethnic groups, social stratification, and the like. Yet there is a curious slippage between such studies and the interpretation of them. For example, we are living through a decade of proclamations that the public schools are a disaster. Educational writers, culture observers, and intellectuals on both the New Left and the Old Right all point to the public's unhappiness with the schools and draw the conclusion that the public is eager for alternatives, deschooling, open schools, return to basics, abandonment of basics, voucher systems, and dozens of other "innovations." But the Gallup polls published by Phi Delta Kappa have quite consistently indicated that the interview sample did not give the public schools a disaster rating, and that they did not share the perceptions of the schools attributed to them by the educational journalists. We have here a good example of the way political and philosophical ideology shapes the social reality it purports to describe. Even more mischievous is the peculiar ignorance displayed by some of the innovators with respect to the constraints under which schools have to operate in the society, especially in a society such as ours.

Yet there is a limit to the usability of empirical findings for educational prescription. For science, social or physical, seeks laws about what exists and not about what ought to be. Polling techniques to ascertain attitudes can get no further than what the interview sample answers in response to questions. Even when the pollster asks the respondent about his ideals, aspirations, and values, the answer he gets is all he can certify as fact. Whether the respondent meant what he said or understood what he said—and what he might have said had other questions been asked—must be left to conjecture. And this conjecture can rely on previous conjectures only in a very limited way, because human beings with imagination can conjure up possibilities so tenuously connected with actuality that they raise havoc with probability. This is why, even after the social sciences have helped ascertain the relevant facts, the philosophical, historical, and many other contexts of educational problems have to be explored and reexplored in every epoch before the goals, ends, or objectives can be assessed. Dewey was allergic to separations of means from ends and therefore balked at assigning goals and ends to philosophy and means to science and resisted allotting the study of educational goals to the social sciences and instructional means to psychology. But clearly the kind of inquiry that ferrets out and interprets the public's aspirations in terms of life outcomes of schooling is not the same as that used in devising arrangements that would satisfy these aspirations.

Perhaps the most glaring example of the gap between scientific findings and educational prescriptions is to be found in the sequence of events from the 1954 *Brown* decision by the U.S. Supreme Court on segregated schools down to the recent conclusion that social problems can't be solved by "throwing money" at them. In the *Brown* case the conclusion that "separate" cannot be "equal" was attributed to the sociologists and psychologists; but that schools *ought* to be equal is not a sociological finding or even a psychological one. It is based on a principle of social justice reflecting the moral convictions of the writers of the Constitution, although not all of them would have welcomed its application in the *Brown* case. The sociological and psychological findings were used to justify court-ordered busing in order to achieve desegregation. The results substantiated Dewey's dictum that it is extremely dangerous to jump from scientific findings to school policy. Yet, when sociological findings later confirmed the failure of the busing prescription, an equally abrupt leap was made to the principle (or excuse) that throwing money at this and kindred problems will not solve them. Scientific findings warranted neither of the prescriptions for educational policy.

Science gives us clues as to what probably is the case; and if it has available well-established empirical laws, it can make highly reliable predictions as to what would follow if this were the case. At present the social sciences, including economics, are far from being reliable guides either to the network of facts that constitute our social problems or to the consequences of any solution that might be attempted. Nevertheless, this is no warrant for abandoning scientific inquiry into human affairs. Science helps us mark the bounds of the possible beyond which no man or institution is morally obliged to go, but it also envisions potentialities that may create new fields of obligation. For science-based technology enhances human power, and new power may lame our excuses for not tackling the problems of poverty, disease, discrimination, and other forms of social injustice. Out of the complex of facts about the social reality as delivered by the empirical sciences and the other contexts needed to portray the total social reality—the human reality—the educator extracts prescriptions for educational policy and strategy. So although educators should refrain from looking to the sciences for rules of procedures or the principles of policy, they should not give up on the resources of empirical science too soon.

The Paradox of the Unwelcome Miracle

Suppose, *mirabile dictu*, it were announced that a project funded by the Department of Health, Education, and Welfare had discovered a variety of pills that would teach Johnny to read, spell, fill out income tax forms correctly, achieve any SAT score his parents might choose, and adopt any set of wholesome values the school board might specify, including respect for schooling. Here would be a triumph of educational technology that ought to gladden the hearts not only of Johnny's parents but the hardheaded tribes of accountabilists.

What reception would such an announcement receive? We can conjecture that the first reservations would come from Johnny's parents. First, they would like to know what else will Johnny learn if he takes the pill? Second, who decides which pills Johnny is to be given? Third, when can Johnny go off the pill? The first question comes back to Dewey's observation about the complex effects of any learning experience; the second bares our major concern with social engineering—who watches the engineers? The third is the most crucial of all: because Johnny is supposed to become a human being who engineers himself—a subject, not merely a manipulable object.

The notion of an individual's determining himself is uncongenial, not to say antithetical, to positivistic science. Science does not deal with individuals but with classes, species, and groups in terms of their essential and common properties. Individual differences may be interesting, but they have to be omitted from consideration in formulating scientific laws. But positivistic science goes further and denies any break in the causal chain. Skinner is consistent, it seems to me, in wanting to translate all language about freedom of the will into behavioral chains, causally determined.[8] To be sure, there is a way of construing freedom so as not to make it incompatible with determinism, but this involves acknowledging that the ability to deal with ideas (rather than with the physical realities that the ideas represent) in some sense frees the thinker from the causal nexus of physical events. But this view is itself suspect for a positivistic view of science and for a behavioristic conception of mind.[9]

Theories aside, it is a fact that the same human mind can conceive diametrically opposed theories about the nature of the human mind; whatever the ultimate decision on the nature of mind will be, it is to be doubted that B. F. Skinner's mind and that of John Dewey will have turned out to be fundamentally different in their essential structure.

The very same sort of mind that can conceive of a completely determined universal causal order can also conceive of a moral order in which what ought to happen becomes a reason for and sometimes a cause of what does happen.

This is an order of being in which the individual's acknowledgement of a moral law, in Kant's terms, becomes a self-imposed demand to act in accordance with that law. That men are in some sense machines and that they are in a more important sense not machines are both the declarations of mind. To yearn for a science that would give us perfect control of learning and to reject its use for that purpose, if it were found, is quite the human thing to do.

This ambivalence provides a cue for thinking about the science and technology of education. If there is a sense in which man is a machine or in which he behaves in a machinelike fashion, it may be quite possible and desirable to regard him in that sense. But this does not commit us to regard him merely as a machine and to exclude from educational thought all the ways in which he is not a machine.

It is nothing against personhood, humaneness, and individuality that some of our behavior is mechanical, rote, and uniform. Learning the multiplication tables by rote is a fairly mechanical procedure, whether done by recitation in unison under the direction of a live teacher or by pressing keys on the console of a computer. It is the nature of the task, not of the taskmaster or the performer, that makes it mechanical, prespecifiable, predictable, controllable, and measurable. Some tasks should be performed without taking thought (*pace* John Dewey), and reciting the multiplication tables is one of them; spelling ordinary words is another, and so is solving algebraic equations. A good way of not becoming a creative, intelligent person is to be intelligent and self-conscious about everything, everywhere, and at all times.

For such reasons I do not cringe at the thought of using an electronic technology to make the teaching of facts, principles, application of rules, and certain skills—that is, didactics—more efficient and more economical. Poor technology in didactics probably has done more to make the whole classroom experience mechanical drudgery than any other single factor, and I would regard the inspired teaching of spelling, arithmetic, and reading as a wasteful use of inspiration. A science of education that yielded a technology for efficient didactics would leave time and talent for other forms of teaching for which live teachers behaving like inefficient machines never seem to find time. It could also revolutionize the organization of schooling, so that it might be carried on in small neighborhoods rather than in huge congregations. It might change the mix of school personnel from more than two million alleged "professionals" (paraprofessionals with an A.B. degree) to a mix of 10-15% professional and 85-90% paraprofessionals (without A.B. degrees).

I am less optimistic about the prospects of science-based technology's revolutionizing or materially altering the conditions under which nondidactic teaching can take place. Developing the skills and habits of critical thinking, problem solving, learning by discovery, and group and individual therapy that correct emotional maladjustments of pupils, teachers, and parents—these are not directly amenable to technological solutions, because it is a unique constellation of behaviors with which we are concerned and not discrete performances. Apropos of this, we are told that there are now more than 130 approaches to psychological therapy vying for disciples. Furthermore, it is difficult to conceive of a theory, scientific or otherwise, that would reconcile the diverse ideologies that guide the therapists. It follows almost by definition that the more holistic our concern with the pupil or the educational process, the less reliable are studies that "show that" for educational prescriptions, because the better the studies are scientifically, the narrower their targets are likely to be. One day, perhaps, the social scientists will do a study "that shows" precisely that.

Concluding Unscientific Postscript[10]

If by a science of education one means a source of generalizations that enable the educator to construct with some system and rigor the psychological, historical, societal, and biological contexts of educational problems, then in principle at least such a science is possible. Such a science would be useful, as Dewey pointed out, for the interpretation and understanding of the problems of schools and pupils, but it would not necessarily, or even usually, yield rules of practice or tests of practice. Context-building theory does not guarantee the kind of prediction and the possibility of control required by efficient schooling or social engineering. Theory and technology that might give schooling this sort of control is meager, although behavior modification based on theories of conditioning makes claims to being that kind of theory. This theory, as well as any other that promised highly efficient control of the teaching/learning process, would be resisted by its alleged beneficiaries on the ground that it would be incompatible with the conception of the human essence—individuality, freedom, creativity. Nevertheless, this human essence is quite compatible with the existence of aspects of behavior that are mechanical, uniform, and prespecifiable, and to use technology to teach these types of behavior more efficiently does not make them or the user inhuman or nonhuman.

Part of our confusion about the potentialities for a science of education comes from mistaking an analytical theory for an empirically established one. An analytical theory gives a plausible account or classification of phenomena. For example, most theories about stages of development, including that of Piaget, are illuminating in that they put us on the alert for phenomena and hypotheses that otherwise we might ignore; they give us a way of interpreting events. There are many such developmental designs, and they live and flourish because there are enough human variations to provide exemplification for all of them—if one analyzes the data in a certain way. But the moment we try to build a curriculum or try to treat individual pupils in terms of these stages we find that the range of individual variations seriously limits their usefulness. Illumination is not control, although in some genius's mind it may lead to inventing means of control.

Illumination serves its purpose if it clarifies what the school can and cannot control. Failure to understand the social reality of schooling has trapped the schools into promising to alleviate crime, the use of drugs, parental ineptitude, pollution, the loss of identity, and kindred social and psychic ills. Good social science should help us assess potentialities more realistically, just as good history and philosophy should inhibit administrators from trying to treat pupils as products of mass-production machine industry.

Illumination and clarification by way of analytic theories of schooling and teaching, moreover, are the best defense against the improper use of the findings of empirical science in education, that is, against unseemly haste in adopting technological solutions and no less unseemly rejection of them. That such illuminating theories will come from the general wisdom of the race or even from the academic guilds in the colleges of liberal arts and sciences seems unlikely, although during the Sixties much money and journalistic ink were expended in trying to convince the public that specialized training and expertise in this kind of educational science were unnecessary.[11] Until the empirical sciences provide the pedagogical pills—and perhaps just when they do—the foundational, analytic science of education is our best hope.

Finally, whatever the social and physical sciences can contribute to the technology of schooling and whatever history, philosophy, psychology, and any other humanistic study can contribute to the construction of the contexts of educational problems, to be effective the enlightenment must be shared by administrators and teachers. Such enlightenment cannot be delivered in a handbook for teachers and in a three-day leadership conference for school administrators.

To acquire what Dewey called educational science, teachers and administrators have no alternative to studying the various ancillary disciplines well enough to understand their import for schooling. School personnel, if they are really professional, are not in the position of the farmer who can take the results of science and technology from the extension expert without understanding the rules and prescriptions being urged upon him. This is the difference between a professional and a paraprofessional.

So we conclude on the odd note that without a guild of professional teachers and administrators, a science of education based on any interpretation of the term will be ineffective, but that without a field of study that concerns itself in a systematic and rigorous way with the problems peculiar to education, there probably cannot be a profession of teaching.

1. Karl Popper, *The Logic of Scientific Discovery* (New York: Basic Books, 1959). Chapter X, "Corroboration, or How a Theory Stands up to Tests," is reprinted in Harry S. Broudy, Robert H. Ennis, and Leonard I. Krimmerman, eds., *Philosophy of Educational Research* (New York: John Wiley and Sons, 1973), pp. 280-307.

2. Especially in response to his *Walden Two* (New York: Macmillan, 1948) and *Beyond Freedom and Dignity* (New York: A. A. Knopf, 1971). Cf. Noam Chomsky, "The Case Against B. F. Skinner," *New York Review of Books*, December 30, 1971, pp. 18-24; also Michael Scriven, "The Philosophy of Behavior Modification," in C. E. Thoresen, ed., *The Seventy-second Yearbook of the National Society for the Study of Education*, Part I (Chicago: National Society for the Study of Education, 1972). For a systematic exposition of his views, see B. F. Skinner, *Science and Human Behavior* (New York: Macmillan, 1953). Selected readings on behaviorism can be found in Chapter 11, *Philosophy of Educational Research* (see fn. 1).

3. "Rural America was astonished that professors would presume to tell farmers how to farm, and at first their doubts were justified," said André and Jean Mayer in "Agriculture, the Island Empire," *Daedalus*, Summer, 1974, p. 89. Teachers and administrators, on the contrary, would like to be told, but don't trust what they hear.

4. *The Sources of a Science of Education*, Kappa Delta Pi Lecture (New York: Liveright, 1929).

5. I am informed by my colleague, Joe R. Burnett, that Dewey dropped the expression "complete act of thought" from the second edition of *How We Think*, and that nowhere in later works does he make inquiry so mechanical and fixed as it seems in the first edition. Nevertheless, it seems fair to say that the CAT as formulated in the first edition did become the paradigm of inquiry for many of the writers on education. A detailed discussion of the Kelley/Kilpatrick debate on the conception of science and a

science of education was presented in a paper, "Science vs. Philosophy in Education," presented by Ron Szoke of the University of Illinois at the AERA's annual meeting in Washington in 1975.

6. For example, the studies of Coleman, Moynihan, and Jencks.

7. Cf. *Philosophy of Educational Research* (fn. 1), pp. 254-78, for articles dealing with the hypothetico-deductive method in science.

8. Certainly Skinner, whose views probably represent our most "scientific" theory of human behavior, tries very hard to disabuse us of such notions as free will, and of a self that is anything more than the sum of the behaviors that have been systematically reinforced by the environmental forces acting upon him. But since all of our notions, including those of truth, according to Skinner, are the products of selective reinforcement, why the deterministic view of the universe should be more true than the indeterministic one is hard to account for on the basis of the theory itself. For the purpose of this article, the philosophical truth of free will, the autonomous self, the moral self, or their opposites is less important than the *fact* that the clients of the school and of the educational establishment phrase their assessment and expectations in these terms. If they are illusions, as Skinner would have us believe, their effects at least are real. A man acting on the illusion that he can jump over the moon nevertheless acts and thereby intervenes in the causal chain of events.

9. For example, cf. Gilbert C. Ryle's *The Concept of Mind* (London: Hutchinson's University Library, 1949). Whether reasons we give for our actions can become causes is a debated issue in ethical theory.

10. The name of an essay by Sören Kierkegaard.

11. I refer to the efforts of J. B. Conant and others to parcel out the work of colleges of education to its various parent disciplines.

The External Doctorate in Education: Blessing or Blasphemy?
by Richard B. Morland

Suddenly, one new institution in Florida, through its external program, is about to produce more education doctorates—1,600 in three years—than the three largest traditional producers. Here is a trenchant analysis of this questionable development.

Once upon a time the graduate student had to pack his meager earthly belongings into the old jalopy and move into a garage apartment near the university to work for his doctor's degree in education. If he was lucky, he had an assistantship at $1.75 an hour grading 100 freshman papers a week, a task that had to be squeezed in between his own studies and emptying the diaper pail. There was no other way. At least two years had to be spent in residence with nose to the grindstone, or at least buried in microfilm readers. The beleaguered graduate student prepared for his qualifying examinations, rolled with the punches in highly competitive seminars, withstood critical appraisals from very demanding professors, and went to the library to dig, dig, dig. He spent at least another year researching his problem and usually another writing the dissertation; sometimes he would rewrite it endlessly.

But all of this business of doctoral candidates having to play Sisyphus is no longer necessary. "New thinking" has not only removed the rock, it has leveled the hill as well. This has to be the greatest triumph of mind over matter since Heracles tricked Atlas. For hidden in the thrust for "new, exciting, innovative, relevant programs responsive to the times" is the nontraditional or external degree. It comes in various sizes and shapes, but always possesses the magical ingredient: It enables the graduate student to obtain his doctorate without leaving his job or the comforts of his own home.

The Nontraditional Idea

Acceptance of the idea that college degrees can be earned without attendance at a university is no fad. Off-campus programs are already having a tremendous impact on higher education. A report issued last year by the Educational Testing Service states that there were then from 1,000 to 1,400 nontraditional programs in colleges and universities, most of them two years old or less. The editor of this monograph, John Valley, points out the difficulty in even compiling an interim report: "the sheer volume of new developments."[1] ETS had to create its Office of New Degree Programs to handle the flood of inquiries.

To give direction to these new programs, the College Entrance Examination Board and ETS received a grant from the Carnegie Corporation to establish the Commission on Non-Traditional Study. The work of this blue-ribbon panel of 26 educators, chaired by Samuel B. Gould, is reported in three hardback books.[2] The focus of these several essays, as well as the many others appearing in the literature in higher education, is postsecondary education. The authors present a convincing case for college programs that would capitalize on the community resources, experiences, and potentials of certain neglected groups who have so much to gain from college-level work.

Little discussion, however, is centered on the types of program that culminate in the Ph.D. or Ed.D. degree for those who are already established and even identified as "education leaders." This article is concerned with some implications flowing from the nontraditional programs inaugurated by new universities that award the doctor's degree in education. The basic idea of external programs is a noble one and should be encouraged. It is also one that should not be contaminated by fostering questionable practices under the name of innovation and experimentation.

Three Examples

In order to raise some basic questions, three of these new universities located in Florida—Nova University of Ft. Lauderdale, Laurence University of Sarasota, and Walden University of Naples—are presented as examples of functional programs that have attracted much attention across the country. Of the three, Nova's program is by far the most comprehensive and best developed. Its degree requires three years as opposed to one year for each of the other two. Nova is also the only one that is accredited by the regional association. Laurence and Walden have been issued only temporary licenses to operate by the Florida Board of Independent Colleges and Universities, a body created by the state legislature in 1971 to change Florida's image as "a mecca for diploma mills."[3] The board, served by C. Wayne Freeberg as executive secretary, is already responsible for closing 17 institutions that were awarding Ph.D.s and Ed.D.s.

Building programs on their interpretation of the nontraditional idea, these three universities have much in common. Each takes a strong stand against established doctoral programs, asserting that they fail to meet the needs of the practitioner in education. A new and different kind of graduate education is advocated to free the student from the rigidity, obsolete requirements, and hidebound traditionalism that characterize typical doctoral programs. Their literature is rife with expressions such as "dynamics of flexibility," "breakthrough programs," "mission-oriented," "change agents," and "humanizing the educational process." Next to "innovative," the most popular adjective in their educational rhetoric is "meaningful." One of Walden's announcements, for example, reads:

> Walden University has developed an innovative Doctoral Program aimed at the educator who wants to affect [*sic*] a positive social change in society. We are looking for individuals who . . . have the desire and courage to attempt a meaningful alteration. . . . Logical analysis, research, and meaningful application are what we are after. . . . Prerequisites are: Master's Degree, nine hours of advanced credit, and three years [of] experience. There may be instances where meaningful life experiences can be recognized and accepted in lieu of academic prerequisites.[4]

Novelty and the necessity to expand one's horizons are also key concepts. Laurence has run a series of newspaper advertisements using historical incidents to demonstrate the difficulty the world has in accepting something new. Ptolemy and Copernicus are featured in one of these ads, all of which are capped with this intriguing truism: "Acceptance of a new idea is a painful experience to a closed mind."[5]

One indicator of closed-mindedness, apparently, is the belief that one has

---

Nova's Reaction

September 28, 1973

I appreciate the opportunity afforded me today to see Mr. Morland's article in galley. Since only one day remains prior to your publication deadline, I am responding briefly by wire. Historically, genuinely meaningful reforms in education, the operative rather than the merely rhetorical, have generated resistance or outright hostility. The Nova education program, approved as it has been by the regional accrediting agency and a number of state agencies, and involving many of the nation's leading education scholars and practitioners, still has created heated controversy.

Phi Delta Kappa, committed to the advancement of educational theory and practice, has decided to provide a professional forum for the public debate of essential issues in the preparation of educational leaders. Obviously, the Nova program is a part of this debate. We are confident that under the auspices of Phi Delta Kappa this debate will be informed and dispassionate. Certainly we must insist that we make the case for Nova's program alone and for no other institution. The article entitled "The External Doctorate in Education: Blessing or Blasphemy?" has the overtones of a polemic. It is impossible to deal with all its misstatements outside of the total context. Therefore we would appreciate your informing your readers that we would be happy to furnish complete information on any or all points regarding the Nova program upon request.

Abraham S. Fischler
President, Nova University
College Avenue
Fort Lauderdale, Florida 33314

---

to spend full time in study to acquire the knowledge and skills expected of one holding the highest degree in his profession. Each of these new universities emphasizes the fact that full-time study is not necessary. There is no need to leave the job or to lower one's standard of living to earn the coveted degree. The July 1972 brochure of Nova University (now discarded) was titled "How To Earn Your Doctorate Without Giving Up Living." Laurence claims that its program eliminates the "emotionally wrenching experiences" of extended residence work.[6] The current Walden catalogue echoes the theme: "Residency requirements, as required by the older, more rigidified institutions, pose a financial nightmare for candidates. [Our requirements] make sense in that they are realistically meeting the modern educator's needs."[7]

Precisely what these needs are, other than a degree as quickly as possible, is not spelled out, but there is no barrier to your joining the club if you hold the master's degree. This, plus some experience as a teacher, is about all that is required. The applicant does not have to present a specific academic average for his undergraduate or master's work, nor the GRE or other test scores. Examinations and tests seem to be dirty words for these innovative institutions. Noticeably absent in their requirements are entrance examinations, qualifying examinations, comprehensive examinations, or even course examinations. Even though there are no proficiency tests to measure your aptitude or skills in composition, you better know how to sign your name to a check. Nova charges $1,500 (in advance, please) for each of the three years the student is matriculated, plus the costs for two different trips to Ft. Lauderdale to attend the five-day institutes. Much of this, however, is tax deductible, and if you can qualify for veterans' benefits, Uncle Sam helps with the tab. Walden's costs come to $2,600 plus expenses for the required month in Naples. More than one-half of this is for the privilege of writing your dissertation at home. Laurence's charges are about the same as those for Walden.

Nova University

Although the three Florida institutions under examination adhere to the same basic philosophy on external degrees, there are major differences in the mechanics of the programs, especially between Nova and the other two. Nova, a private institution, was opened in 1966 as a graduate research university offering only the Ph.D. degree in the environmental sciences, social sciences, and behavioral sciences. It awarded four earned Ph.D. degrees and two *honorary* Ph.D. degrees in 1971.[8] (According to Lee Porter, the last time the Ph.D. was given away for a song was in 1937 when Bing Crosby received an honorary Ph.D. from his alma mater.[9]) Twenty-one students were enrolled full time. Nova had no endowment income and no programs in teacher education. Yet it was accredited by the Southern Association of Colleges and Schools in 1971 to embark on programs that would produce approximately 1,600 Ed.D. degrees within three years.

The love affair between Nova and SACS that resulted in its accreditation-in-advance is a story in itself. Not a single one of Nova's "clusters"* had commenced operation and the Ed.D. degree was not even mentioned in the catalogue. Just about every standard in the books—qualified resident faculty, financial resources, facilities, library resources, no credit through correspondence, three graduating classes, etc.—was set aside to accommodate Nova and others of its kind to follow. What this action did show is that the wheels of bureaucracy can be greased to get things done if there is the will and the power to sustain it. In brief, SACS's Standard IX, which governs special activities, was rewritten after the 1970 annual meeting and was formally adopted on December 1 during the 1971 meeting. Nova was admitted to membership on the same day. According to SACS's published proceedings, the new Standard X, which actually governs graduate programs, has never been officially adopted.[10]

Nova University sponsors two different types of off-campus programs. The first is the National Ed.D. Program for Educational Leaders. At present it has 27 clusters in 15 different states with from 25 to 32 students enrolled in each. Thirty-two additional clusters are in the planning stage. The students, most of whom are school administrators, meet once a month in seminars to work on their practicums and to participate in discussions led by "national lecturers" of considerable eminence who are flown in from their home campuses for the day. The participants are "responsible for the mastering of eight fields of competence": supervision, curriculum development, finance,

---

*Groups of 25 or more doctoral students concentrated in a given region.

educational policy systems, evaluation, resources for improving schools, managing the school, and technology and systems management. Just how this mastery is to be demonstrated is not clear. There is no mention of comprehensive or oral examinations of any type. The 1972 brochure called for "competency" examinations. This was changed in the 1973 brochure to "substantive" examinations.[11]

The requirements for the practicums, however, are delineated in some detail. Each student must complete four practicums: one "mini" of short duration that focuses on a relatively simple problem, one "midi" that addresses itself to two of the required fields, and two "maxi" practicums, one of which is done during the second year and one during the third year. Some of this work is done in groups. The student submits his work to the home campus for criticism in accordance with a published timetable. The cluster coordinators, most of whom are county-level administrators and supervisors in the local school district, "are not expected to get involved in the substantive work of the practicums." Neither can help be expected from the national lecturers. The participants are admonished "not to write directly to the lecturers for information or help for their practicums." All inquiries are to be directed to the director of practicums in Ft. Lauderdale.[12]

In addition to these requirements, the participant must attend two different institutes in Ft. Lauderdale that meet for four and one-half days. These all-day work sessions are led by nationally known authorities in their respective fields. In both of its programs, Nova has been able to attract top professional talent to serve as consultants, institute leaders, and lecturers.

The second Nova program, the Ed.D. Program for Community College Faculty, now has 27 clusters in 13 different states and Puerto Rico. The design of this program is quite similar to that for "educational leaders." The participant enrolls in six core modules, each carrying nine semester hours of credit, during the first two years. His final year is spent in two different specialization modules, and he must present a dissertation "that must meet the standards of the on-campus prototype."[13]

The cluster coordinator for the community college program is usually a member of the faculty in one of the community colleges in the area. All coordinators hold earned doctorates. The coordinator's role is much the same as that of the leaders program coordinator. He serves as the business manager, administrative leader, and "adviser, ally, and ombudsman to the participants."[14]

Assessment of the student's work is based on peer evaluation, self-evaluation, subordinate evaluation, and "superior evaluation" through reports that are filed at the end of each three-month period. The students also attend one-week institutes in Ft. Lauderdale annually in two of the three years they are enrolled in the program.

Nova's off-campus program has captured the imagination of practicing educators across America, and it has gained considerable support from acknowledged leaders. There is no reason to doubt that it will be able to carry through with its plans to develop additional clusters. With 50 clusters already operating and 32 scheduled to begin in the near future, Nova will have approximately 2,400 Ed.D. candidates in its two programs by 1975. Since the attrition is quite small, about 2,200 doctorates should be awarded every three years. This will mean that Nova will be producing more doctorates in education than the combined total of the three universities in the U.S. that presently award the greatest number of Ed.D.s and Ph.D.s in education (Indiana University, Michigan State University, and Ohio State University). According to the latest (1973) report of the National Center for Educational Statistics, only 13 universities conferred more than 100 doctor's degrees in education in 1971.

Laurence University

Laurence University of Sarasota is not to be confused with Lawrence University of Appleton, Wisconsin. The differences are much greater than the substitution of "u" for "w" in the spelling. Whereas Wisconsin's Lawrence is 125 years old, Florida's Laurence commenced operations in the summer of 1970. It awarded 93 Ed.D. and Ph.D. degrees in education the following summer.

Doctoral programs are available in general education, educational counseling, and higher education. The students are required to spend five weeks in residence in Sarasota, where they attend class from 9 a.m. to 5 p.m. five days a week. Six different courses are taken during the summer session, for which students receive 12 semester hours of credit. During the school year candidates register for 14 hours of Dissertation/Project Guidance. The dissertation is written in or near the candidate's home town under a field adviser who has been approved in advance by the institution. If his dissertation is accepted, the candidate returns to Sarasota the following summer to defend an abstract of it before a group of his fellow students and one adjunct faculty member. This fulfills all of the degree requirements.

The middle name of the founding president, Charles L. Palermo, provides Laurence University with its name. Originally located in the Sarasota Motor Hotel, its library holdings totaled 6,500 titles when the first doctorates were conferred. Included among these were 1,050 college catalogues and 1,700 dissertations on microfilm. Most of the old college textbooks, anthologies, and fiction, according to *Newsday*, are labeled "Property of Charles Laurence Palermo."[15]

Laurence's commencement has all the trappings of splendor, with grand marshals, flowing robes, gold tassels, and doctoral hoods. Laurence even has an alma mater song, the first stanza of which goes as follows:

> Come pilgrims traveling on the road
> In search of grails of truth.
> We find in Laurence what we seek.
> All hail thee, red and black.

These pilgrims do indeed know what they seek, and the applications pour in from all over the country. Nineteen different states plus Canada and Puerto Rico were represented in its first graduating class, 95% of whom lived farther than 1,000 miles from Sarasota. The demand for admission is so great that the administration had to announce that the size of the next entering classes "will be strictly limited to 250 new students per class."[16] If Laurence is successful in producing this many doctorates in education each year, it will be second only to Nova.

At present Laurence University is in limbo pending settlement of problems with the Florida Board of Independent Colleges and Universities over its license. This has not deterred the administration from carrying forward plans for expansion. President Palermo has moved to California to start a branch near Santa Barbara, and a new president has been brought in to direct the operation in Sarasota.

Walden University

About 120 miles south of Sarasota on Florida's lower west coast lies Naples, the home base for Walden University. Chartered in 1970 as a profit-making institution, Walden received its first students the following summer. Seventy members of its first class were awarded Ph.D. and Ed.D. degrees in education in 1972. The second class of 162 students, two-thirds of whom were 40 years of age or older, commenced their work during the summer of 1972. Thirty-three different states were represented in this class. This past summer approximately 150 students reported to the Cove Inn in Naples as the first step toward the Walden doctorate.

Walden's program is quite similar to that of Laurence University. The student enrolls in a summer session of four weeks, receiving 10 semester hours of credit for completing courses in foundations, research design, and thesis development. He then returns to his home town to write the dissertation under an approved field adviser. Fourteen hours of credit are awarded for this work. If his thesis is accepted, he receives his Ph.D. or Ed.D., depending on the nature of the dissertation, the following summer. There are no qualifying examinations, competency examinations, oral examinations, or defense of the dissertation.

The summer school faculty at Walden includes several educators with national reputations. The credentials of its field advisers, as with Laurence, are also quite impressive. None of the three institutions discussed in this article is lacking in the names of prominent educators to give prestige to their doctoral programs.

Walden sees its programs as "an opportunity to energize our minds and psyches so that positive personal results appear."[17] How this is accomplished in a summer session of four weeks and a year writing the dissertation while holding down a full-time position is not explained.

Some Questions

So many questions are raised by the prospect of an avalanche of doctorates in education obtained through external programs that all I can do here is list a few of them: 1) Are the programs described in this article truly non-traditional? 2) Are these institutions serving a constituency that cannot be served by established institutions? 3) What is involved in the production of a scholar? 4) Are libraries, facilities, and a resident faculty essential to the preparation of those seeking the highest degree in the profession? 5) Is scholarship a necessary component for the doctorate in education? 6) Why are the external doctoral programs only in the field of education and not in the arts and sciences? 7) What will be the taxpayer's reactions to paying salary increases if hundreds of persons in public education obtain their doctorates through external programs? 8) Are there dangers in the use of the Ph.D. by those who may go into other fields, such as marriage counseling, where there are no specific qualifications for licenses?[18] 9) How can experimentation and alternative programs be encouraged without destroying standards? 10) Should professors lend their names and the prestige of their institutions to programs of questionable quality? 11) What criteria are to be used to approve programs in teacher education where all or most of the work is done off campus? 12) What modifications need to be made in accreditation standards? 13) What do these nontraditional programs mean to the future of the education profession?

Some Answers

Because of space limitations, I can discuss only the first and last of these questions. The purpose of the nontraditional idea, as set forth by the Gould Commission, is to enable persons to achieve degrees, diplomas, or other credentials without the necessity of accumulating credits garnered through class attendance and the completion of particular courses. The payoff is in what one knows and in the ability to demonstrate competence. Nowhere is this demonstration apparent in the programs of the three institutions described in this article. Instead, the student merely completes courses or modules as traditional in their descriptions as anything found in the graduate catalogues of the universities they criticize.

There is no check on aptitude, knowledge, or competence. There is no check to insure that the student does the work himself. Unwittingly, these doctoral programs, built on correspondence courses and dissertations written under persons the institution never sees, could be generating as many ghost-writers as Ed.D.s.

Nova's program has many attractive features, and the established programs can benefit by studying carefully some of the things Nova is doing. But I would have much more respect for the program if Nova came out forthrightly with a statement something like this: "We expect our candidates to demonstrate a mastery of eight fields in professional education. When you can do this, come to Ft. Lauderdale and show us." There is no need to delay this demonstration for three years, if competence is the criterion. This is the basic principle of viable external programs. When the person can deliver, he is entitled to whatever accrues from that which he seeks. The University of London has been awarding external doctorates on this basis since 1836. London, however, is seldom mentioned as a paradigm, for the obvious reason that its degree requires the candidate to pass the most rigorous of examinations. Programs of the Nova-Laurence-Walden type are noticeably lacking in examinations of any sort.*

For the reasons given above, I submit that the nontraditional programs described in this article are nontraditional only in the sense that they have eliminated the extended residency requirement and other requirements associated with programs of rigor. They are what could be called "mini-traditional programs." Each requires a residency of some duration. The structure of each program is broken down into semester hours. Each requires the completion of particular courses, some of which hardly qualify as advanced courses. Each requires a dissertation. What is unique about writing a dissertation that matches "the on-campus prototype" or submitting four term projects? Defending the dissertation abstract before one's peers is unique, but it contributes little to the advancement of scholarship or to convincing others of the worth of the degree. These new institutions also award traditional

*Morland has stated to me that he regrets this statement in the original article. It should have specified "*entrance* examinations." —SME

degrees. To be consistent, they should create their own degrees and build their own reputations instead of borrowing from that which they disown.

The final question asks what these nontraditional programs mean to the future of the education profession. Many things. First, established schools of education must take a long, hard look at their own programs to see what they can incorporate from nontraditional programs that would reach the scores of professional educators who are now neglected. The irony of Nova's program is that, in almost every instance, there is a major university within commuting distance of the cluster it has established. In many instances this institution is in the same city. What Nova, as well as Laurence and Walden, has demonstrated is that there are literally thousands of experienced educators who are eager to undertake advanced graduate study if the opportunity is provided. Obviously, many of these people cannot meet admissions standards at established universities and should not be in doctoral programs. A sizable proportion can qualify, however, and they deserve the chance. Very little use is being made today of competence examinations in graduate programs of teacher education. Recognition of this principle alone would open the doors to those who are converging on unknown institutions for want of any other alternative.

Second, individuals must speak out whenever and wherever they find an erosion in academic standards. In his warning to those considering nontraditional programs, Stephen K. Bailey uses the analogy of "four serpents in a basket of shiny apples" to present some of the dangers. The first is the "serpent of academic shoddiness."[19] New graduate programs that make gratuitous motions toward scholarship should not go unchallenged. The stakes are too high to permit this.

Third, professional associations must use the collective influence of their memberships to see that standards are built into nontraditional programs, not for the purpose of preserving the traditional, but to insure that the recipient possesses the intelligence, knowledge, and competence universally associated with the highest earned degree. In a very real sense, the great intellectual train robbery is taking place before our very eyes. The Ed.D., which has always been emblematic of scholarly attainment, will have assumed an entirely different meaning in less than 10 years if the wholesale production of doctorates from schools-without-scholarship goes unabated. The sheriff to stop the heist of the train must be the education profession itself. As Frank G. Dickey and Jerry W. Miller point out, the privilege of self-governance carries with it the responsibility for policing its own activities and organizations.[20] In Florida, it is taking a government agency to do the work the education profession should have been doing all along.

Fourth, steps must be taken to see that these new graduate schools of education are accountable to those agencies in their respective states that license teachers. The three institutions discussed in this paper carefully avoid this, contending that the certification requirements vary too much from state to state. Their programs would be inhibited, they claim, and the freedom to experiment stifled if they had to meet the standards set forth by the state department of education. This is patently false. All states encourage flexibility through the "program-approval approach." What the claim actually means is that these schools do not want their programs inspected. If the degrees they are giving to teachers and administrators entitle them to advance in rank, the university should be held to the same standards as similar institutions in the state.

Finally, college administrators and professors who have previously looked with indifference or condescension on accrediting standards and agencies must take an active role in these agencies. Accreditation is the best and the most effective means of insuring that only programs of substance and quality are recognized.

To summarize, my concern is primarily with the product, not the process. There is no single route to the doctorate, and certainly various alternatives should be explored. But there should be some assurance that at the end the candidate possesses the knowledge and skills expected of one holding the highest degree that can be earned in the profession. The nontraditional degree can be a blessing if it is the catalyst for overhauling and reforming traditional ways in which the doctorate has been conceived. It can signal the end of the Ed.D. as a symbol of scholarly achievement if there are no standards to insure that it means just this.

1. John R. Valley, *Increasing the Options: Recent Developments in College and University Degree Programs* (Princeton: Educational Testing Service, 1972), p. 2.

2. Samuel B. Gould and K. Patricia Cross, eds., *Explorations in Non-Traditional Study* (1972); Gould, ed., *Diversity by Design* (1973); Cyril O. Houle, *The External Degree* (1973). All published by Jossey-Bass, San Francisco.

3. *Report of the State Board of Independent Colleges and Universities: Calendar Year 1972* (Tallahassee: State Board, April 10, 1973).

4. Walden University poster, fall, 1971.

5. *The Laurence University Leader: An Official Publication of Laurence University*, vol. 2, no. 1, November, 1971, p. 12.

6. Laurence University, *Graduate Bulletin 1972-73*, p. 7.

7. Walden University Institute for Advanced Studies, *Catalogue 1973-74*, p. 5.

8. W. Todd Furniss, ed., *American Universities and Colleges*, 11th edition (Washington, D.C.: American Council on Education, 1973), p. 36.

9. Lee Porter, *Degrees for Sale* (New York: Arco, 1972), p. 140.

10. See *Proceedings of the 77th Annual Meeting, Southern Association of Colleges and Schools*, December 10-13, 1972, pp. 42-48.

11. Cf. Nova University, *How To Earn Your Doctorate Without Giving Up Living*, July, 1972, p. 1, and *A New Alternative: The National Ed.D. Program for Educational Leaders*, April, 1973, p. 2.

12. "Practicums in the Nova University," 1972, pp. 18, 19.

13. Nova University, *Ed.D. Program for Community College Faculty*, Ft. Lauderdale, Fla., 1973, p. 5.

14. Ibid., p. 4.

15. *Newsday*, November 5, 1972, p. 13.

16. *The Laurence University Leader*, p. 18.

17. Walden University, *Catalogue 1973-74*, p. 6.

18. The problem of fraudulent degrees in psychology and psychotherapy is much greater than in education. See *The National Observer*, May 5, 1973, pp. 1 ff.

19. American Association for Higher Education, *College & University Bulletin*, March 15-April 1, 1972, pp. 2-3.

20. Frank G. Dickey and Jerry W. Miller, *A Current Perspective on Accreditation* (Washington, D.C.: American Association for Higher Education, November, 1972), pp. 55-60.

Teaching Skill Under Scrutiny
by W. James Popham

Results of a recently reported series of investigations reveal that experienced teachers may not be significantly more proficient than "people off the street" with respect to accomplishing intended behavior changes in learners. In three separate replications, groups of experienced teachers were unable to out-perform nonteachers in bringing about specified changes in learners. This article will 1) summarize those investigations[1] and the rationale underlying them, 2) consider the generalizability of the results, and 3) offer recommendations for altering an unacceptable state of affairs in the teaching profession.

A Measure of Teacher Effectiveness

The research reported here stemmed from an attempt to isolate a readily usable indicator that could be employed to assess a teacher's instructional skill. Anyone who has followed the search for a satisfactory measure of teaching proficiency must conclude that this area of inquiry may well represent one of the most high-investment/low-yield activities of our field. For over 70 years researcher after researcher has tried out such devices as administrator ratings, pupil ratings, systematic observations, and student performance on standardized tests. With few exceptions, the results have been thoroughly disappointing. Briefly, let's see why.

Ratings of teaching skill, whether supplied by administrators, pupils, or a visiting mother-in-law, are notoriously inaccurate. The administrator-rater looks in on Mrs. Jones's class and, if he sees her engaging in those splendid techniques he employed during his own marvelous moments as a classroom teacher, Mrs. Jones gets a good rating. Pupils may rate an instructor positively because he is a lenient grader or because he has a good sense of humor. In other words, ratings of teaching proficiency are based on highly variable conceptions of what constitutes good teaching. One rater's "dynamic" teacher is another's "unorganized" failure. That these variably derived and often unreliable ratings of teaching skill do not correlate well with most measures of pupil achievement should not surprise us.

Another widely used index of teaching effectiveness involves the use of systematic observations of the teacher's classroom practices. Employing more or less systematized check sheets, someone observes the teacher in action and derives an estimate of the teacher's skill based on the degree to which certain process variables are present (for example, frequency of teacher questions, pupil talk, etc.). The problem with the observation approach is that it is so process-focused that the observer rarely moves to the logical follow-up question: "What happens to pupils as a consequence of the teacher's using these processes?" The chief problem for proponents of observation-derived estimates of teaching skill stems from the clear evidence that widely divergent instructional tactics can be used to promote identical instructional goals. For one teacher a nondirective approach may be ideal, while another teacher might find a highly directive approach preferable. Yet, because of their idiosyncratic personalities, prior experience, and other variables, both teachers' approaches may be equally effective. Thus, while observational techniques may be helpful to a teacher for analyzing his instructional activities, they should not be employed as an index of teacher effectiveness. The correlation between instructional process and results in learners is not strong enough.

The third most widely used measure of teaching skill is pupil performance on standardized tests. But since standardized tests are designed chiefly to discriminate among learners,[2] not necessarily to indicate the degree to which identifiable skills have been mastered, they have not provided us with sufficiently sensitive estimates of how much progress pupils have made with a given teacher. An even more important reason for eschewing standardized tests is the fact that different teachers have markedly different emphases, even in the same course. One geography instructor will emphasize topography, another will stress natural resources. Given the grossness of standardized tests to begin with, such instruments cannot accommodate teachers' differential emphases.

Teaching Performance Tests

In an effort to provide a more defensible approach to the measurement of teaching skill, a series of investigations initiated at UCLA in 1964 resulted in the development of the *teaching performance test*, a heretofore untried vehicle for assessing instructional proficiency.[3] This approach is predicated on the assumption that the chief reason for a teacher's existence is to promote beneficial changes in learners. While we may expect a teacher to perform other functions, perhaps the most important role of the teacher is to modify learners so that they possess more knowledge, employ it more skillfully, cope more satisfactorily with their environment, and in general function as more humane members of a perilously threatened world society. One crucial ingredient of the teacher's skill rests on this ability to change learners. A teaching performance test measures such ability.

Briefly, teaching performance tests avoid the measurement problems arising from different teachers' pursuits of different objectives. This is accomplished by asking teachers to achieve the same objectives, yet permitting them to employ their own pedagogical preferences in doing so. By holding instructional goals constant, it becomes possible to contrast teachers with respect to their skill in accomplishing identical goals. Procedurally, a teaching performance test is carried out as follows:

1. The teacher is given one or more explicit instructional objectives (and, preferably, a sample of the measurement procedure used to assess each objective), plus any necessary background information related to the objectives.

2. The teacher is given sufficient time to plan an instructional sequence to accomplish the objective.

3. The teacher then instructs a group of learners in an effort to have the learners achieve the objective.

4. At the conclusion of the instruction the learners are measured with respect to the objectives, their performance providing an estimate of the teacher's instructional skill.

Development and Validation

As the chief focus of a four-year investigation at UCLA, three teaching performance tests were developed in the field of social science, electronics, and auto mechanics.

The social science performance test dealt with the topic of social science research methods and consisted of 13 specific instructional objectives measured by a 68-item posttest. The electronics performance test treated basic power supplies and contained 23 instructional objectives measured by a 47-item posttest. The auto mechanics performance test dealt with carburetion and possessed 29 instructional objectives measured by a 99-item posttest. In addition, all three performance tests contained a set of resource materials which could be used in planning an instructional sequence to accomplish the objectives. All materials associated with each of the performance tests were reviewed during development by a number of practicing teachers and other subject matter experts. In addition, each test was subjected to several field trials before the final versions were assembled.

In deciding on a reasonable approach to validate this method of assessing teacher effectiveness, a construct validation strategy was selected. Considering the nature of the requirements of teaching performance tests, it seemed that these tests ought to be able *at least* to distinguish between grossly disparate groups such as credentialed, experienced teachers and those who were neither credentialed nor experienced. In other words, if one were to ask a group of experienced teachers to complete a given performance test, in contrast to a group of people off the street, the experienced teachers ought to markedly outperform their inexperienced counterparts.

To test this validation hypothesis, suitable numbers of teachers and non-teachers were recruited in the Southern California region. After several months of recruiting and establishing administrative arrangements, 13 high school social science teachers, 16 high school and junior college electronics teachers, and 28 high school and junior college auto mechanics teachers were chosen to participate in the research. Identical numbers of nonteachers were also located. For the social science performance test, state college students were selected who were social science majors or minors but who had never taught or completed any professional education course work. For the auto mechanics test, garage mechanics served as the nonteachers. The nonteachers for electronics were television repairmen and electronics industries workers.

All three performance tests were subjected to validation contrasts in school situations involving 2,326 public school students. Although there were slight differences in the three tests, the general procedure required that each participating teacher have at least two sections of an appropriate class. One of these classes was then randomly assigned to the nonteacher, while another was randomly assigned to the regular teacher. Approximately two weeks prior to instruction, both the teacher and the nonteacher received the objectives for the performance test and the resource materials. Each was directed to plan a short unit of instruction to accomplish the objectives. No restrictions regarding instructional tactics were imposed; participants were asked only to achieve as many of the objectives as they could in the time available. Nine instructional hours were allowed for the electronics and auto mechanics test, four hours for the social science test.

On a prearranged date both the teacher and the nonteacher commenced instruction. At the close of the instructional period a member of the project research staff administered the posttest, previously unseen by teacher and nonteacher participants, to all pupils. In addition, a brief affective questionnaire was administered to students regarding their feelings about the subject matter of the unit.

Results

Contrary to prediction, the experienced teachers did not markedly outperform their inexperienced counterparts on any of the three teaching performance tests. Although there were slight differences in favor of the teachers, none reached statistical significance. Posttest results are presented in Table I, using average classroom means as the analysis unit.

In addition, analyses of students' responses to the anonymous questionnaires revealed no significant differences between the teacher and nonteacher groups. In short, no reliable differences favoring the experienced teachers were found. Why?

TABLE 1
POSTTEST RESULTS FOR TEACHER AND
NONTEACHER CLASSES

Test	Subjects	No.	Mean°	% Correct
Social science	Experienced teachers	13	33.4	66.8
	College students	13	32.3	64.6
Auto mechanics	Experienced teachers	28	48.0	48.5
	Tradesmen	28	46.7	47.2
Electronics	Experienced teachers	16	23.9	51.9
	Tradesmen	16	23.1	50.2

°Means of auto mechanics and electronics were adjusted by analysis of covariance for pretest differences.

An Interpretation

Although space limitations preclude an examination of possible methodological defects that might contribute to these results, there appear to be no readily available loopholes by which we can explain away the nonsignificant outcomes. A more straightforward explanation is available. *Experienced teachers are not particularly skilled at bringing about specified behavior changes in learners.*

We should not be surprised that teachers are not skilled goal achievers. Certainly they have not been trained to be; teacher education institutions rarely foster this competence. Nor is any premium placed on such instructional skill after the teacher concludes preservice training. The general public, most school systems, and professional teacher groups rarely attach special importance to the teacher's attainment of clearly stated instructional objectives.

For further corroboration of this interpretation, one needs only to speculate on the typical intentions of most public school teachers. They wish to cover the content of the course, to maintain classroom order, to expose the student to knowledge, and so on. Rarely does one find a teacher who, prior to teaching, establishes clearly stated instructional objectives in terms of learner behavior and then sets out to achieve those objectives. Only recently, in fact, do we find many teachers who are even familiar with the manner in which instructional objectives are stated in measurable form.

But while it may be true that experienced teachers in general—and there are obviously notable exceptions—are not particularly proficient in promoting learner attainment of specified instructional objectives, this is a *totally unacceptable* state of affairs. Every profession worthy of the name derives its professionalism precisely from the fact that its members possess a special expertise not present in non-members of the profession. Lawyers can prepare legal briefs. Surgeons can perform operations. Accountants can balance financial reports. People off the street can't do these things. But do teachers bring anything to bear on an instructional situation other than a general education, native intelligence, reasonable dedication, and borrowed teaching tricks? These attributes will permit a teacher to get through the school day, and a number of pupils will undoubtedly learn something. But contrast our current educational situation with the enormous dividends we might be getting if members of the teaching profession possessed really unique capabilities to promote desirable behavior changes in learners.

Corrective Action

What can be done to improve this situation? How can teachers become more skillful in accomplishing their major classroom mission? One general trend offers the promise of improvement along this line: specifically, the increasingly widespread support of objective-based instruction and, more broadly, the concept of educational accountability.[4] Rather than attending almost exclusively to instructional *process*, where innovation is applauded for its own sake irrespective of what happens to learners, American educators are beginning to get concerned about *outputs* of the system. More and more we see educators trying to take responsibility for what happens to the learners under their tutelage. Frequently, such accountability strategies are organized around measurable instructional objectives. To illustrate, the Instructional Objectives Exchange,[5] a nonprofit educational corporation, currently receives over 5,000 orders per month for its collections of measurable instructional objectives. Even assuming that many of these objectives collections never leave the educator's bookshelf, their widespread circulation attests to the fact that many educators are becoming far more attentive to results than to process.

A more specific and direct approach can be taken to augment instructional skill. We can provide teachers with what any instructional psychologist would consider a critical ingredient for modifying one's behavior; that is, we can provide teachers with *practice* in doing what we want them to do. First, we must amass a sufficient number of short-term teaching performance tests, perhaps involving instructional periods of no more than 15-30 minutes. At least one commercial firm is now distributing such teaching performance tests,[6] and I hope more agencies will soon be developing them.

By employing commercially available performance tests or by constructing their own, both inservice and preservice teacher educators can arrange for a series of teaching performance test clinics. To illustrate how such clinics might work, we can consider an inservice example. A departmental faculty—English, for instance—might meet once per week after school for a one-hour session. At the beginning of the hour, as his colleagues observe, one teacher would carry out a previously planned 15-minute lesson with a half dozen randomly selected learners. After the learners had been posttested on their attainment of the objectives, and ideally also on their affective responses to the teaching, they would be dismissed and the staff would clinically analyze the teacher's instruction. The analysis should be *non-punitive* in nature, for the focus must be on improving the instructional skills not only for the "teacher of the day" but for all those present. Furthermore, analysis of the teaching must be based on results displayed by the learners, not on the observers' personal preferences. If the learners achieved the objectives, what aspects of the instructional plan seemed to contribute? If the objectives were unachieved, what alternative tactics might have been used? The main thrust of the clinic strategy is to make public a teacher's instructional decision making and, obviously, to share demonstrably effective teaching tactics among colleagues. During subsequent weeks other teachers can take their turns completing the same or different teaching performance tests. As always, the post-lesson clinical analyses would stem from observed results with learners.

Comparable applications, of course, can be designed for preservice teacher education programs. Indeed, as a vehicle for assessing the adequacy of a teacher education program, such performance tests have considerable utility. If, for example, a preservice credential program cannot demonstrate that its candidates are far more skilled on such performance tests than they were when they commenced the program, then program modifications are clearly in order.

A Crucial Component

The ability to bring about specified behavior changes in learners is by no means the only dimension to consider in evaluating a teacher. One can readily imagine an instructor who was quite skilled in changing specified learner behavior yet grossly deficient in a number of personal and ethical categories. Even so, however, it may not be an overstatement to assert that the skill necessary to bring about intentional changes in learners should be considered a necessary but not sufficient attribute of the high-quality teacher. In view of research results such as those reported here, the teaching profession clearly must initiate schemes without delay whereby its members acquire this essential skill.

---

1. For a more extensive account of this research see W. James Popham, "Performance Tests of Teaching Proficiency: Rationale, Development, and Validation," *American Educational Research Journal*, January, 1971, pp. 105-17.

2. R. Glaser, "Instructional Technology and the Measurement of Learning Outcomes: Some Questions," *American Psychologist*, vol. 18, 1963, pp. 519-21.

3. I am indebted to the San Diego City Schools and several Orange County school districts for their cooperation in this project.

4. See, for example, the recently published volume by John D. McNeil, *Toward Accountable Teachers*, New York: Holt, Rinehart, and Winston, 1971.

5. Box 24095, Los Angeles, California 90024.

6. Vincent Associates, P.O. Box 24714, Los Angeles, California 90024, distributes a series of teaching performance tests plus filmstrip-tape programs regarding how to build and use such tests.

Pedagogical Education: How About Reform?
by B. Othanel Smith

*Our system for educating teachers must be thoroughly over-
hauled. That is the basic premise of this special* KAPPAN. *Mr.
Smith advocates a series of steps that would lead to truly professional schools of pedagogy. Officials of five major associations comment on his plan.*

Let's face it: Colleges of pedagogy will in all probability never overhaul their
programs if each college is to do it alone. There are too many hurdles, too
much disparity among institutions, too much institutional jealousy, too much
divisiveness and lethargy among faculties, too much fear, and too much in-
eptness in the leadership. It is likely, of course, that one or two institutions will
blaze a new path. But will others follow? Well, maybe. We won't know until
some college really does it. It is more probable, however, that only forces
broader and more powerful than those of a single college can ever break
through these barriers and restraints to bring about a new day in pedagogical
education. These forces will be political as well as professional, external to
colleges and universities, and guided by a new coalition of professional and
lay organizations and their leaders.

Before going further, let me make clear that this article is not an apology
or an alibi. Colleges of pedagogy have made significant contributions to
public education. Fifty years ago the average teacher, especially in small
towns and rural areas, had little more than two years of college work, and
many had only a high school education or less. Today the minimum requirement for admission to teaching is a bachelor's degree, and about one-third of
the nation's teachers hold a master's degree or more. Teachers have more
academic knowledge, better understanding of human development, more
positive attitudes toward children, and more competence in the procedures
and techniques of teaching than teachers of any other period of our history.
All of this has come about because of the elevation of pedagogy to a university study and the accumulation of research knowledge about teaching and its
underlying disciplines.

At the same time, demands upon teachers for more academic learning and
pedagogical knowledge and skill multiply as diversity among pupils
increases, as parental concern about the conduct of schools and the quality of
teaching becomes more acute, as legal aspects of teaching become more
complex, as every social malady is converted into an educational problem, as
school and classroom disruptions become more severe, and as knowledge—
academic and pedagogical—accumulates even more rapidly. All of these
conditions, and more, make teaching increasingly complex and place a heavy
burden upon schools of pedagogy to meet the growing need for more
thorough preparation of school personnel.

These new requirements, to say nothing of the old ones only partly met,
can be satisfied neither by tinkering with the programs and facilities of
pedagogical schools nor by inservice programs, no matter how brilliantly
conceived, planned, and executed. Make no mistake about it, adding a course
here and a course there, reshuffling academic requirements, screening candidates for admission, integrating methods courses and student teaching, or

adding an internship will have little effect upon the ability of teachers to cope with demands upon them now made by the growth of knowledge, new social conditions, and a consumer-oriented public that knows what it wants only in general and abstract terms. Nothing short of thorough overhauling of pedagogical education will do.

Where Teachers Are Educated

Pedagogical education is provided by an assortment of nearly 1,400 institutions, of which some 40% are private senior colleges with fewer than a thousand students and with a mere handful of pedagogical instructors. The remaining 60%—about 800 institutions—are of varying descriptions and quality. These schools, like the senior colleges, are neither associated in a single organization nor accountable to any common agency for the quality of their product. Only the state in which they reside has jurisdiction over their programs. Naturally, such a loose collection of institutions can do nothing, save by chance, to advance whatever coincidental interest they have.

These 800 institutions are a mixed bag of private universities, newly created state universities, old-line state universities, universities recently evolved from teachers colleges, and independent schools of pedagogy. The hope for effective pedagogical education lies among these institutions, yet their colleges of pedagogy are powerless to act except alone and even then under crippling constraints. Whatever improvements they make individually seldom coincide and never add up to a new collective program.

Internal Obstacles to Reform

Leaders of colleges of pedagogy are confronted by formidable if not impenetrable barriers. Some of the more serious obstructions are internal, a fact that has led some critics to assert that colleges of pedagogy have only themselves to blame for their plight.

Fear of losing tenure runs deep in pedagogical faculties since enrollments have fallen off. Even in the best of times, colleges of pedagogy are fiercely competitive in their quest for students. Any proposed change in program is always scanned for its effect upon enrollment. A faculty member will think of how the change will affect his or her classes; a department chairman will measure the change against its effects upon courses and enrollment, and the dean will do likewise for the college as a whole. When it appears that a change might depress enrollment, it is not unusual for someone to say, "If they don't come here, they will go elsewhere. So what is gained?" Of course this is a reasonable reaction, and it underwrites the impotence of colleges to lift themselves individually.

One of the most baffling and stubborn constraints upon reform is the absence of common beliefs. Much can be said for differences in fundamental ideas. They can be animating influences pushing a faculty toward intellectual growth. But there is a limit to their benefits. When differences rend the fabric underlying community of thought, the basis of rationality is torn asunder; mutual stimulation among the faculty is stymied and the possibility of institutional reform is blocked.

Proponents of open education, basic education, competency-based education, social reform education, futuristic education, humanistic education, scientific pedagogy—you name it—divide college faculties into rival camps, afflicting them with schisms comparable to what would exist in medical schools were their faculties made up of chiropractors, osteopaths, shamans, and faith healers along with physicians and surgeons. In this medley of orientations, doctrines, and opinions, it is next to impossible for a faculty to agree upon anything resembling fundamental change in its program. Professors typically agree to tolerate their differences so long as each can go his or her own way, in the belief that these cleavages constitute the conditions of creativity and change. This is a strategy of wallowing in confusion with false hope.

Related to these cleavages is another set of internal restraints. Pedagogical study is treated as if it were general education. This is evidenced in the tendency to adjust instruction and standards of evaluation to the student's level, a practice justifiable perhaps in a liberal arts program when individual development is the goal, but reprehensible where the welfare of a profession's clientele is at stake.

Further evidence is found in the fact that pedagogy is considered to be an academic rather than a clinical study. Except for student teaching that is carried on almost entirely by public school teachers, pedagogical courses are taught by lecture/discussion, with the study of textbooks the primary learning activity. This practice is reinforced by faculty commitment to graduate study geared to erudition and ultimately to research competence rather than to competence in either teaching or the training of teachers.

Moreover, many if not most courses are added to the college curriculum to satisfy the interests of instructors, although their value to teachers is often rationalized by objectives to which the courses do not lead. The criterion of instructor interest is appropriate for academic departments, but leads in a professional school to a multiplicity of courses having little content or relevance to the work of the professional. Some colleges offer more than 600 courses, the great bulk of which are there because of instructor interest or the pressure of ambitious departments rather than because they relate to the job requirements of teachers.

External Hurdles to College Reform

To the foregoing must be added certain external barriers. Money talks in colleges of pedagogy no less than in other colleges, but it speaks in a whisper. The support of pedagogical education is at a level inadequate for general college education. And this will be so as long as present state and university policies of financing the preparation of school personnel continue. Colleges of pedagogy in public universities are almost everywhere financed from state appropriations based upon full-time equivalent students (FTES). As a rule, universities prorate their appropriations among colleges, but not strictly by the FTES principle. Some colleges with low head counts may nevertheless be allocated funds in excess of what the FTES formula would require, and colleges with high head counts may, by the same token, receive smaller allocations.

In the years when registration in colleges of pedagogy were high, part of their productivity was used to finance colleges with low enrollments. Funds thus generated were used to maintain or even to improve the status of other colleges instead of colleges of pedagogy. The university administration typically sees this policy as a stabilizing influence across colleges and departments. Some deans of pedagogy look upon the policy as a mixed blessing: a boon when enrollments are drastically dropping and a penalty when they are up and rising.

Over the years, productivity of colleges of pedagogy has been high, so that generally speaking they brought more funds into the university than they received. But this is petty compared to the fact that the FTES policy locks the college program into a mode of instruction appropriate to erudition rather than to clinical training. Prospective teachers, and those on the job as well, require a great amount of laboratory experience as they study exceptionality, pedagogical psychology, methods and curriculum, evaluation, and the social aspects of schooling. For laboratory work a 10:1 student/instructor ratio is a maximum, but it is a ratio unlikely to obtain under the FTES policy.

Some accommodation of this formula to the requirements of clinical study in pedagogy could be made, as in fine arts at some universities, were it not for the bias of university culture against pedagogy as a professional study. It is easy to remember that universities reluctantly admitted pedagogy as a discipline, at first only for secondary teachers and even then as an academic rather than a clinical study. It is unlikely that academic deans would trim the FTES formula to fit the needs of clinical pedagogy.

Moreover, the university reward system, as everyone knows, is stacked against the clinical instructor. Universities on the whole justify themselves by their contributions to accumulated knowledge and their preparation of those who wish to devote themselves to that end. Naturally, faculty members who prove themselves most apt at research and scholarly productivity garner the lion's share of recognition and financial reward.

It is not so generally known, at least beyond academic circles, that prestigious members of pedagogical faculties also adhere to and support this system of rewards and its underlying conception of pedagogy as a graduate discipline. No one can seriously entertain the notion that pedagogy can be advanced without research and scholarship. However, this should not be taken to mean that pedagogy is or should be a graduate study, except for the few who are inclined toward research and scholarly work. How to accommodate both the clinical and research components of pedagogy within the context of academic mores and policies is a question that defies answer.

The Static Years

Failure to deal with the foregoing impediments, many of which are the creation of the colleges themselves, has brought stagnation to pedagogical education. During the last 50 years, when knowledge was increasing by leaps and bounds, the basic pedagogical program remained practically unchanged. The sequence of courses established in the Thirties—introduction to education followed by social foundations, educational psychology, methods courses, and practice teaching—remains substantially unchanged today. To be sure, practice teaching has been moved from the university to the public schools, some changes have been made in the content of educational psychology, slight modifications have been made in methods courses, and so on. But these changes have made no difference in either the amount of time devoted to pedagogical study or methods of instruction and training. Pedagogy is still taught as an academic study, and, while practice teaching has a touch of reality, it is still conducted with a minimum of direction by public school teachers and with practically none by university instructors. That this static condition of pedagogical institutions should have obtained during the period when all sorts of so-called innovations were being devised and urged upon the schools by professors is, to say the best, peculiar.

Government Takes Over

The failure of the colleges to take matters into their own hands and to do something about their programs creates a vacuum into which state and federal governments are moving in response to public dissatisfaction with schools and teachers. Governmental actions are splintering pedagogical education—some of it drifting into teacher centers, some into state departments, some into Teacher Corps projects, and some into either private or school workshops. The remainder is in colleges and departments of pedagogy where it is disjointed, part of the work being on campus and part in the public schools.

More and more, the tendency is for state and federal legislatures to lay down directions, policies, programs, and even curricular content, which in turn are interpreted and transformed into regulations by bureaucratic agencies. They are staffed with persons who know little about pedagogical education and whose experience in it is even less.

However, departments and agencies are merely the instruments for carrying out the will of legislative bodies. These bodies, as already indicated, are daily becoming more concerned about the quality of school personnel and the effectiveness of the public schools. As they prepare legislation for the improvement of schools and institutions of higher education, however, the real barriers to the improvement of pedagogical education are overlooked. This is partly attributable to the fact that members of the legislature are poorly briefed and little time is provided for in-depth discussion of the issues and problems of pedagogical schools.

It must be remembered, also, that the problems of pedagogical education are but a fraction of the total range of issues with which legislators must deal. Then, too, they have no expertise in educational matters and must depend upon briefings by their staff and consultation with elements of their constituents. Legislators are poorly disciplined in the collection and use of knowledge. They constantly substitute for expert knowledge their own opinions, beliefs, and information fed to them through various pipelines from their constituents. While this is true in nearly every domain of legislative concern, it is especially true in pedagogy, for the knowledge base of pedagogy is still little known and ill-appreciated.

Their staffs are ill-informed about, and inexperienced in, the professional education of school personnel. In addition to all of this, legislators are continually running for reelection. This consumes a large part of their time and energy, for they must keep their ears tuned to the folks back home as well as to the problems and issues of state. Then, too, legislation depends as much upon strategic obfuscation (to borrow an expression from the late T. V. Smith), trade-offs, and cloakroom deals as upon consideration of relevant knowledge and societal values.

The domain of legislative activity is in matters of value and policy, but these matters are best attended to when they are suffused with scientific knowledge. Unfortunately, outstanding pedagogical researchers and scholars, to say nothing of practitioners, all too often give conflicting information. And it is not uncommon to run into cases where scientific judgments are influenced by emotions. When spokesmen for pedagogy state judgments with certainty that they can support only with the weakest of probability (if at all), and when they give conflicting testimony on the same issue, all research evidence and testimony are likely to be thrown into disrepute. Legislators have enough difficulty in reconciling differences in values and notions of policy, without having to confront these issues with conflicting evidence from pedagogical practitioners, scientists, and scholars.

In this morass, federal education agencies have been less than helpful. But the new Department of Education can be useful without becoming involved in legislation simply by establishing communication with the colleges. Federal investment in research centers and laboratories has had little effect upon teacher training institutions. Their faculties know very little about the research of these federal agencies, and what they do know is more a subject of discussion than a means of improving the education of teachers. While neglect of this research is to be attributed in part to college faculties, it is mostly due to the federal agencies themselves, particularly the National Institute of Education (NIE). These agencies have repeatedly skirted the colleges, going directly to the public schools. The NIE, for example, has recently promoted and supported efforts to change school practices through dissemination and diffusion of research findings directly to the schools. The colleges of education, where some 200,000 teachers are produced each year and where the largest pool of trained personnel for the interpretation and application of research to educational practice is to be found, were thus almost completely circumvented. Furthermore, the faculties of these institutions carry on programs of inservice preparation unequaled in their scope and depth by those of any other set of institutions or agencies. One can only wonder how much better recent state education laws might have been and how much advancement could have been made in the education of teachers at both pre- and inservice levels had avenues of communication between NIE and the various laboratories and centers it supports been established and maintained with the colleges of pedagogy.

Toward a Way Out

Is there any way to replace the present hodgepodge of institutions now offering work in pedagogy with genuine professional schools? Some authorities think that it is impossible, at least in the foreseeable future. Many others are settling for a little change here and a little there as state legislatures become impatient and act. Just now the possibility of a fifth year of teacher education is riding high. Legislated as an internship, it entails little or no change in the campus program or modification of state and university policies now controlling and financing colleges of pedagogy. These minor changes are viewed as progressive steps. But toward what? There is no goal, no picture of pedagogical education toward which such changes count as steps.

Nevertheless, more than this can be attained in the near future if leaders of the profession unite to establish professional schools through legislation in state after state. But we cannot count on legislation to this end if legislative bodies are left to their ordinary counsel and to the conflicting views and pressures of the profession. We need a coalition of leaders, a coalition whose sole purpose is to see that legislative bodies are properly informed, advised, and influenced with respect to preservice pedagogical education.

Whatever the differences among various professional organizations—the American Association of Colleges for Teacher Education, the American Educational Research Association, the American Federation of Teachers, the National Education Association, and others—arising from organizational interests and ambitions, these differences should not lead them to be at odds about the preparation of school personnel. For it is to the benefit of all of these organizations, whatever their particular goals and persuasions, that preservice education be raised to the level of effectiveness and credibility to which the responsibilities and significance of the profession entitle it. The teaching profession will come into its own when its members are highly prepared at the preservice level, and when they can point with pride to colleges of pedagogy as the institutions from which they come and to a few such colleges as famous institutions where the highest quality of training and research are being practiced.

The various professional organizations have been, and largely continue to be, preoccupied with inservice education. This is understandable in terms of the concern of school administrators and supervisors with upgrading teachers. But preoccupation with inservice education is not understandable as an approach to the problem of raising the professional level of teaching and of improving the public image of the profession itself.

For a solution to the twin problems of how to improve both pedagogical education and the public image of the profession, inservice education is the wrong way to go. In the first place, it is a mammoth task in which the numbers are simply overwhelming. There are over two million teachers, of whom approximately two-thirds hold only a bachelor's degree. The resources for increasing their level of performance are totally inadequate. College faculties are largely used in preservice programs and would be almost completely absorbed in that function were the programs adequately developed. Experienced teachers, however well prepared, have neither the time nor the energy to assist with inservice training functions. And it hardly need be added that teaching loads and collective contracts allow little time for teachers to exchange tricks of the trade, let alone engage in serious study.

For another thing, colleges of pedagogy in the U.S. are now producing some 200,000 teachers per year, and within another five years may be turning out nearly as many as they were before the slump began. In each five-year period one million new teachers are added to the ranks. The output of ineffective preservice programs adds up to a stream of ill-prepared teachers greater than any inservice program can possibly cope with, even a program more extensive than anyone is ever likely to see.

What is the way to go? The first step, indeed the necessary first step, is to organize the leaders of the professional organizations and selected leaders of the colleges. The purpose should be to develop a meeting of minds with respect to the issues and problems of preservice education and the role of these organizations in dealing with the issues and problems. Probably the first order of business would be for the leaders to learn to work together and to build a measure of trust among themselves. The deliberations of this group would, one hopes, lead to the creation of a commission on preservice pedagogical education—a commission of prestigious laypersons and leaders of the pedagogical profession—to prepare a comprehensive plan and a strategy for creating professional schools of pedagogy.

Although the commission should consider all the conditions affecting pedagogical schools, it should be concerned primarily with the external conditions that prevent their conversion into truly professional institutions. These external conditions are frame factors that shape the structure and operation of pedagogical schools, and they apply universally, irrespective of the idiosyncratic differences from school to school. They are always present, regardless of the school's setting, its age, its faculty, or its standing. If these frame factors are modified—formulas by which schools of pedagogy are financed, time requirements for degrees, instructor/student ratios, autonomy in relation to state and federal departments of education, accreditation policies and procedures, and licensing policies and procedures—it would then be possible for colleges of pedagogy to deal with internal conditions and thereby to reform their programs, modes of instruction, admission policies, and evaluation of student progress.

In addressing the external factors, the commission need not start from scratch. They have been dealt with extensively in four recent studies: *Educating a Profession*, by Robert B. Howsam, Dean C. Corrigan, George W. Denemark, and Robert J. Nash; *Studies of Knowledge Production and Utilization Activities in Schools, Colleges, and Departments of Education*, by David L. Clark and Egon G. Guba; *The Case for Extended Programs of Initial Teacher Preparation*, by George Denemark and Norma Nutter; and *A Design for a School of Pedagogy*, by B. Othanel Smith, Stuart H. Silverman, Jean M. Borg, and Betty V. Fry.

Although the first two of these studies were issued four years ago and the other two in the last six months, they have been seriously addressed neither by teacher training institutions nor by organizations concerned with the problems of pedagogical education. These studies deal with the frame factors that cut across all pedagogical institutions as well as conditions within institutions that impede the development of adequate programs of pedagogical education.

It should be the first responsibility of the commission to come to grips with the issues raised by these reports and to deal with the frame factors over which single institutions can exercise little if any influence. It is here that the first steps toward the improvement of pedagogical education must be taken, for unless these frame factors can be constructively modified it is unlikely, indeed apparently impossible, that pedagogical schools can be transformed into genuine professional institutions.

Since these frame factors are embedded in state and federal laws and regulations, in policies of university boards of control and local boards of education, in court decisions, and in the policies of accrediting agencies, the commission will doubtless explore the legal and political dimensions of the conditions that now preclude the reform of pedagogical schools.

Anyone familiar with the special interests and competitiveness of professional organizations, with the tendency of pedagogical faculties to believe that it is creative and progressive for each college to do as it pleases, and with the delays and conniving of public office need not be told that the route suggested will be next to impossible to negotiate. The major hurdles are, first, to secure enough cooperation and agreement among professional groups to establish and maintain a coalition and, second, to create a movement that can be sustained long enough to see the program phased into legislation and institutionalized. To accomplish this it will be necessary for the professional leadership of each state to organize itself for collective action in order to inform the public and mobilize political forces to support legislation consistent with the work of the commission.

The upshot of all of this is that our professional organizations, whatever their differences, must now dedicate themselves cooperatively to the cause of public education as it is reflected in the colleges that prepare those who are to be the models, companions, guides, and instructors of our children and youth for almost a quarter of their lifetimes. Now is the time. Both the public and state governments are in the mood to act constructively. But they are floundering. They need leadership from the profession. If the leadership cannot put itself in order, the constructive mood of legislative bodies will evaporate. It is not unlikely that a decade of punitive legislation will then be ushered in, and the chances for significant advancement of teaching as a profession will have been lost for at least a generation.

The "four recent studies" Smith mentions as basic documents for his proposed commission are available as follows:

Howsam et al., Educating a Profession, was published in 1976 by the American Association of Colleges for Teacher Education, but is now out of print. It may be ordered from University Microfilms, attn. Books on Demand Program, 300 N. Zeeb Rd., Ann Arbor, MI 48106, paper $23.30, cloth $28.30. Both the Clark/Guba study and the Denemark/Nutter work can be obtained from ERIC. *Studies of Knowledge Production* . . . is ERIC: ED 139 805, price 98 cents; *The Case for Extended Programs* . . . is ERIC: SP 015 395, but coauthor George Denemark will send you a copy for $1.25. Address him as Dean of Education, University of Kentucky, Lexington, KY 40506. The Smith et al. book is available from the Superintendent of Documents, U.S. Government Printing Office, Washington, DC 20402. The stock number is 017-080-02098-0. (Editor's note in "Pedagogical Education: Time for Reform?")

The Smith Family   By Mr. and Mrs. George Smith

The Strangely Significant
Case of Peter Doe

by Gary Saretsky

An 18-year-old high school graduate is suing the San Francisco schools for one million dollars because he can't read. The concept has excited the interest of many people, from school reform advocates to comic strip artists.

> **"The Peter Doe *case is simply a forerunner of an effort on the part of parents to bring to focus, through the judicial system, attention upon the fact that the schools, the educational systems of this society, have failed to provide the Peter Does of this country the kind of education to which they're entitled."***
> **—Susanne Martinez, attorney**
> **for the plaintiff**

Four years ago, then Associate Commissioner of Education Don Davies provoked us to inquire: What are public schools accountable for? Four months ago, a suit was filed in San Francisco Superior Court that provoked us to inquire: What are public schools *legally* accountable for? Four days ago (9 March 1973) lawyers and education officials were provoked, at a Mayflower Hotel conference in Washington, D.C., to inquire what avenues of legal redress are available to those injured when the schools do not meet their responsibilities. They also asked: What are the implications of such actions for the future of public education?

The subject of the March conference was the *Peter Doe* case, a suit which accuses various California and San Francisco Unified School District education officers and employees of negligence, misrepresentation, breach of statutory duties, and constitutional deprivation of the right to education. (See pp. 220 and 221 for a summary of the facts and legal contentions in *Peter Doe*.)

A New Legal Strategy

The evening prior to the conference a group of interested lawyers conferred on a revision of the Peter Doe complaint and discussed courtroom strategy. All of them have been associated with precedent-setting cases establishing educational policy on equal opportunity, equal access, equitable financing, and student/faculty civil rights.

Their early discussions of other precedent-making decisions such as *Brown* v. *Board of Education* (1954), *Hobson* v. *Hansen* (1967), and *Serrano* v. *Priest* (1971)[1] highlighted the crucial problem, that the legal rights of *access* and *opportunity* serve only to open the schoolhouse door. Inside, the school may yet be impoverished, incapable of teaching basic skills, injurious to children's emotions, or irrelevant to children's needs.

The dialogue quickly went beyond the specifics of the case and led to the founding of a new legal strategy for education reform, one that would use the judicial process not only to hold the public schools legally accountable for the results of the educational process but would change the legal status of education from a privilege to a right.

Susanne Martinez, Peter Doe's attorney, began the conference the next

morning with the Peter Doe story and summarized the arguments she will use
in court. The next four speakers, Frederick McDonald (Educational Testing
Service), Judge Haskell C. Freedman (National Organization for Legal Problems in Education), Thomas Green (Syracuse Educational Policy Research
Center), and Harry Hogan (director of governmental relations, Catholic University) probed into the problems and difficulties to be surmounted, the
dilemmas to be faced, and the whole range of beneficial or devastating
consequences of the court's intervention.

The vigorous dialogue among the major speakers and the 60 other lawyers
and education officials in attendance returned repeatedly to the questions:
How can a court specify complex standards for learning? How can anyone
determine who is responsible for meeting these standards in public education?

Legal Strategies

Two fundamental legal approaches were explored. One was the constitutional route, which would claim deprivation of a "right" to education; the
second, less revolutionary route would be through common, tort, and statutory law. The constitutional approach, as described by Martinez, would seek
to impose an absolute responsibility for the "product" through extension of
the due process and equal opportunity clauses in the federal Constitution and
analogs that appear in state constitutions.

The constitutional approach has been successful in overcoming barriers to
equal access, equal opportunity, and equitable allocation of resources. The
issues in *Peter Doe*, however, are far more complex. Furthermore, the Supreme Court's *Rodriguez* decision, stating that education is not a right explicitly guaranteed by the federal Constitution, now casts a pall over the possibilities of such an approach through the federal courts.

The constitutions of most states, however, do speak specifically of education. This approach is therefore more likely to be pursued in the immediate
future.

A more traditional approach—lawsuits seeking a remedy for an individual—were also discussed. Among them: negligence suits, contending that
"reasonable care" was not exercised by the defendants in their instructional
duties; suits claiming misrepresentation of student progress on report cards,
in interviews with parents, or in the awarding of a diploma; suits contending
that school boards and/or state departments of education failed to carry out
their statutory duty; and suits charging breach of implied contract. As the
Peter Doe case indicates, all of these contentions may be made in one lawsuit.

A suit seeking a declaratory judgment was still another alternative approach mentioned by Harry Hogan. This approach does not require the court
to provide a remedy or to prescribe educational standards. All it asks of the
court is a declaration of the rights of the student or a legal opinion on the point
of law involved.

The education community had been forewarned that a case similar to
Peter Doe's would soon appear on the court dockets. In 1970, Stuart Sandow
published the reactions of 200 scholars, lawyers, educators, and legislators to
a fictitious event in which a father successfully sued his local school for fraud,
claiming that his son's diploma has no value, since his son could barely read.[2]

A year later Don Stewart's *Educational Malpractices: The Big Gamble in*

Our Schools came out, describing possible grounds for educational malpractice suits and encouraging such suits as a means of improving educational
practice.[3] More recently, James Mecklenburger and I predicted the linking
up of the militant consumer movement with the educational reform movement. In addition to cases such as Peter Doe's, we forecast possible class
actions against schools of education, state certification agencies, publishers
of educational materials, and teacher organizations and school boards when
the latter two agree to contracts that preclude the adoption of more effective practices.[4]

Defense Strategies

The education community has in fact evidenced a great deal of apprehension that suits as described above might be brought against the schools. The
professional journals have been replete with philosophically, theoretically,
and psychometrically elegant defenses against education being brought to
account. Legal journals, however, have carried no comparable arguments.
What, then, are the legal defenses that might be utilized by education
agencies and their employees? One obvious defense to a constitutional challenge would be to cite the March Supreme Court decision in *Rodriguez* v. *San
Antonio Independent School District*, which stated in part: "Education, of
course, is not among the rights afforded explicit protection under our federal
Constitution. Nor do we find any basis for saying it is implicitly so protected."

Two initial defense actions, to be anticipated as a response to the other
forms of lawsuits, would be the filing of a demurrer and entering of a claim of
sovereign immunity. The demurrer would simply contend that, even if all the
facts are true, they do not constitute a sufficient reason to rule in favor of
those bringing the suit. Sovereign immunity, sometimes called "governmental immunity," would posit that the plaintiff has no legal right to sue without the permission of the governmental agency, permission that is unlikely to
be granted.

State constitutions, statutes, and regulations often use vague or imprecise
language in prescribing the duties of education agencies. A common example
is, "The schools will provide a thorough education." A defense would attempt
to capitalize upon this vagueness simply by claiming there is, in fact, no duty
expressed by law or statute.

In instances where such language is more specific, or is interpreted as
indicating a duty, the defense would raise the issue of causality, claiming that
there is insufficient evidence to support a conclusion that the plaintiff's situation (i.e., his reading deficiency) is a result of anything that the defendant did
or did not do. Undoubtedly the Coleman Report and the Jencks study of inequality, as well as studies of the superior impact of hereditary over environmental factors, would be cited in such a defense.

The possibility of counter suits against parents and perhaps even against
the students themselves would be considered as a defensive action, to deter
the initiation of a suit or to mitigate the consequences of any of the above-
mentioned forms of litigation.

Possible Court Decisions

Any speculation as to what the actions of a court might be in such litigation
must first acknowledge the possibility that the court will take no action at all.
We have pointed out elsewhere that

. . . courts are reluctant to pursue fundamental issues in education where theory is complex, data is meager, and solutions thorny. Courts may claim that they lack competence and refer the issue back to local officials or state legislatures, since these governmental agencies exist to deal with these issues.

In some states "hold safe" laws would prevent cases being brought against school practitioners. In many states the right of citizens to sue any governmental agency or employee is denied or severely limited by law.

Since courts are already overloaded, unable to bring cases to quick and speedy trial, the addition of school-related cases to the court dockets might be denied because the courts are already too overburdened.[5]

A court may, of course, concur with the defense positions described above. If, on the other hand, the court finds itself in agreement with one or more of the plaintiff's contentions, it is faced with the difficult problem of prescribing a remedy for a very complex situation. A class action seeking a declaratory judgment, however, would reduce the magnitude of the decision facing the court both in terms of addressing the question of causality and the need to prescribe a remedy.

The possibility of a decision favorable to the plaintiff is thus greater in such an instance.

Consequences of Court Decisions

The consequences of such cases may be contrary to what was anticipated when the litigation was initiated. Certainly the loss of any one such action might work against the overall movement to reform education. Reactions to the *Rodriguez* decision, for instance, have characterized the decision as a major setback within both the legislative and judicial movements for educational reform.

A significant amount of educational self-reform has been initiated to avoid the incursion of the courts and the legislatures into basic educational policy making. The plaintiff's loss of such a suit would remove an important stimulant that has spurred certain reluctant agencies to initiate some innovative and successful plans and programs.

On the other hand, decisions finding that education agencies have failed to carry out their statutory duties might result in only a minimum accommodation on behalf of that agency, not improvement in the educational process. The reaction might be, What can be done to insure avoidance of a future suit filed on similar grounds?

Harry Hogan, one of the conference participants, discussed the possible counterproductive consequences should the court provide for a monetary remedy. He said, "The theory is that this is an effective way to accomplish change. It is based upon what criminal law calls deterrent efficacy, the theory that if this defendant has to suffer the payment of a damaging penalty other prospective defendants will be deterred and will behave in a socially more acceptable fashion. The difficulty here, of course, is that the plaintiff's victory might have just the opposite result. It might encourage litigation. If Peter Doe here makes anything like a million dollars because of his inability to read, he provides for others like him a short route to becoming a financial success. This strategy would therefore produce a socially undesirable result.

Regardless of that consideration, you would have the imposition of a tremendous cost upon the educational system which would inevitably result in the diversion of money from educational goals to the satisfaction of damages paid to this particular individual."

Implications for Education

The implications of using the courts to determine educational policy and to set standards are both threatening and encouraging. On the one hand, we are placing very fundamental questions—those more appropriate to the legislative arena, which is open to the public and the education profession through the campaign and election process and committee hearings—in the hands of "a few wise men" whose judgment is circumscribed by legal arguments or interpretations of a constitutional nature. On the other hand, in instances where we are not seeking specifications of standards and remedies, or financial damages, the courts can provide a means of bringing to the attention of the public, the legislature, and the educational community at large very precise problem areas to which their skills and knowledge should be addressed.

A Caveat

As an advocate of certain very fundamental changes in public education, I had high expectations for this conference and the prospects of a legal strategy of educational reform. But as I listened to some of the legally sophisticated but educationally essentialist and simplistic theories and arguments, I experienced a foreboding, worrisome fear of the "thalidomide effect," that the consequences of the "legal cure" might be far, far worse than the illness presently besetting public education.

Fortunately, the courts have sought expert testimony in areas where they lack specific knowledge. It is incumbent upon us then to seize this "opportunity" irrespective of its origin, not to obfuscate nor philosophize, but to demonstrate that education is a profession willing to set standards and, furthermore, willing to be held accountable if those standards are not met.

---

1. *Brown*—The Supreme Court prohibited de jure racial segregation in schools; *Hobson*—Washington, D.C., schools were required to equalize resources; *Serrano*—The California Supreme Court ruled that the quality of a child's education should not be determined or limited by the financial resources of his home community.

2. Stuart Sandow, *Emerging Education Policy Issues in Law: Fraud* (Syracuse, N.Y.: Syracuse University Research Corporation, 1970).

3. Don Stewart, *Educational Malpractices: The Big Gamble in Our Schools* (Westminster; Calif.: SLATE Services, 1971).

4. Gary Saretsky and James Mecklenburger, "See You in Court?" *Saturday Review*, October 14, 1972, pp. 50-56.

5. Ibid., p. 50.

A Summary of the Facts and Legal Contentions in Peter Doe°

The following is a brief summary of the facts and legal contentions in *Peter Doe* v. *San Francisco Unified School District*, as of 9 March 1973:

On 20 November 1972 an action was filed in San Francisco Superior Court against the San Francisco Unified School District, its Board of Education and superintendent of schools; the State Department of Education, its Board of Education; the state superintendent of public instruction; and 100 defendants alleged to be the agents or employees of public agencies.

The plaintiff is an 18-year-old Caucasian male high school graduate. His IQ as determined by the San Francisco School District is normal. During the course of his 13 years in the San Francisco public schools, he maintained average grades, never encountered any serious disciplinary problems, and maintained regular attendance. He advanced year by year through the public school system until he was awarded a high school diploma. At various points throughout his school career his parents expressed concern over his apparent difficulty in reading. They were repeatedly assured that he was reading at the average level and had no special or unusual problems.

Shortly after high school graduation, the young man was examined by two private reading specialists. Both indicated that he was reading at approximately the fifth-grade level. Since these tests, he has engaged in private reading tutoring and has made "significant progress" in improving his reading level.

The complaint contends that "Peter Doe"—his name is being concealed for obvious reasons—has been deprived of an education in the basic skills of reading and writing as a result of the acts and omissions of the defendants. Nine distinct legal grounds are cited to show the school district's liability. It is claimed that the defendants:

1. should be held liable in that they negligently failed to provide the plaintiff with adequate instruction, guidance, counseling and/or supervision in basic academic skills and negligently failed to ascertain accurate information as to plaintiff's educational progress and abilities (*general negligence*);

2. falsely represented to the plaintiff's parents that he was performing at or near grade level in reading and writing and was not in any need of special or remedial assistance, whereas the plaintiff was, in fact, performing drastically below grade level and in great and severe need of special assistance (*misrepresentation*);

3. violated relevant provisions of the California Education Code charging school authorities with the duty of keeping parents accurately advised as to the educational progress of their children, and that without such accurate information plaintiff's parents were unable to take any action to protect their minor son from the harm suffered (*breach of statutory duty*);

4. violated relevant provisions of the California Constitution and Education Code charging defendants with the duty to educate plaintiff and other students with basic skills of reading and writing (*breach of statutory duty*);

°Source: Youth Law Center, San Francisco, California.

5. violated relevant provisions of the California Education Code providing that no pupil shall receive a diploma or graduation from high school without meeting minimum standards of proficiency in basic academic skills (*breach of statutory duty*);

6. violated provisions of the California Education Code requiring inspection and revision of curriculum and operation of the schools to promote the education of pupils enrolled therein (*breach of statutory duty*)

7. violated relevant provisions of the California Education Code requiring school districts to design the course of instruction to meet the needs of the individual pupils (*breach of statutory duty*).

Another cause of action contends that:

8. by the acts and omissions of the defendants, their agents and employees, the plaintiff has been deprived of an education guaranteed by the United States Constitution and the laws and constitution of the State of California (*constitutional duties*).

The suit also contends that:

9. the State Board of Education and its agents and employees failed to properly discharge their statutory duties, including promulgating a minimum course of instruction to meet the needs of pupils, minimum standards of proficiency for graduation from high school, and administration and supervision of the educational system in California (*breach of statutory duty*).

The complaint contends that as a result of the acts and omissions of the defendants, the plaintiff: 1) has suffered a loss of earning capacity because of his limited ability to read and write; 2) is unqualified for any employment other than the most demeaning, unskilled, low-paid, manual labor which requires little or no ability to read or write; 3) has suffered mental distress, pain, and suffering; and 4) that said injuries and damage will result in his general damage in the sum of $500,000. The complaint asks that punitive damages of $500,000 be assessed against the defendants *in addition to* the general damages and the costs of private reading tutoring and court costs.

VII
British Imports

Introduction

*F*or nearly a decade, KAPPAN authors described, discussed, and argued the benefits and drawbacks of open education, an import from Great Britain. What is it? Is it a fad? Is it only for certain kinds of youngsters? Can all teachers employ it successfully? I like all of the articles we published, but none better than "So You Want to Change to an Open Classroom" (October 1971), by Roland S. Barth. At the time, Barth was principal of the Angier School in Newton, Massachusetts. This year he is a senior lecturer in the Harvard Graduate School of Education.

While the burgeoning popularity of back-to-basics seems largely antithetical to open education, the latter survives and flourishes in many schools. A fastback published by Phi Delta Kappa in 1972, Vito Perrone's Open Education: Promise and Problems, still sells well. It is PDK's all-time best seller among 168 fastbacks published to date; nearly 50,000 copies of this classic have been distributed.

Another recent education import is the teacher center idea. Stephen K. Bailey's November 1971 KAPPAN article, "Teachers' Centers: A British First," was the first mention of the new development in KAPPAN pages. While there was already considerable interest in this new approach to inservice education, at least among federal government officials, the 1971 article by Bailey, then professor of political science and educational administration at Syracuse University, helped propagate teacher centers throughout the U.S. Bailey underscored the importance of having teachers directly involved in and responsible for their own inservice education, to the dismay of certain U.S. Office of Education staff people, graduate deans of schools of education, and school board members. Teacher control is now inherent in federal legislation supporting teacher centers. There are about 90 government-funded centers today, and perhaps 300 that receive no federal money. The centers have been called "demilitarized zones where the battle-weary can trade ideas, confess their failings without fear of rebuke, and freshen up their skills" (Newsweek, 27 April 1981).

Since submitting this KAPPAN article, Bailey has written a book for Phi Delta Kappa under the title, The Purposes of Education (1976). He is now Francis Keppel Professor of Educational Policy and Administration at Harvard, having left the vice presidency of the American Council on Education, where he served from 1973 through 1977. He continues as president of the National Academy of Education.

In a recent communication Bailey says, "All of us look forward to the comprehensive summary of the British teacher center experience to be published by the National Foundation of Educational Research in England and Wales."

—SME

So You Want to Change
To an Open Classroom
by Roland S. Barth

*My telephone clangs incessantly these days and my mail box
bulges with letters. The great majority of calls and letters
request advice, materials, and information dealing with open or
informal education. Apparently Joseph Featherstone opened a
Pandora's box when he wrote his tantalizing articles in* The New
Republic *a few years ago; and Charles Silberman's* Crisis in the
Classroom *has virtually turned the box upside down and
scattered its contents across the nation.*

*Where do we go from here? What can we tell the hundreds
of excited and enthusiastic teachers who suddenly want to move
along more open lines? Do we begin moving furniture around?
Putting blocks in the corridor and buying cuisenaire rods?*

*To understate the case, this kind of activity may be a bit
premature. A wiser procedure may well be to stop a moment
and give serious thought to exactly what it means to become an
open or informal teacher. What* does *one believe about children? About knowledge itself? About the learning process? Are
these beliefs really compatible with a move toward open education? Should they be appraised and reappraised before one
plunges blindly ahead?*

*Roland Barth thinks so, and I concur. His article should help
each of us to conduct such a reappraisal, however agonizing it
may be.*

—Vincent Rogers, chairman,
Department of Elementary Education,
University of Connecticut; author-editor,
Teaching in the British Primary School

Another educational wave is breaking on American shores. Whether termed
"integrated day," "Leicestershire Plan," "informal classroom," or "open education," it promises new and radical methods of teaching, learning, and organizing the schools.[1] Many American educators who do not shy from
promises of new solutions to old problems are preparing to ride the crest of
the wave. In New York State, for instance, the commissioner of education,
the chancellor of New York City schools, and the president of the state
branch of the American Federation of Teachers have all expressed their intent to make the state's classrooms open classrooms. Schools of education in
such varied places as North Dakota, Connecticut, Massachusetts, New York,
and Ohio are tooling up to prepare the masses of teachers for these masses of
anticipated open classrooms.

Some educators are disposed to search for the new, the different, the
flashy, the radical, or the revolutionary. Once an idea or a practice, such as
"team teaching," "nongrading," and (more recently) "differentiated staffing"
and "performance contracting," has been so labeled by the Establishment,
many teachers and administrators are quick to adopt it. More precisely, these
educators are quick to assimilate new ideas into their cognitive and operational framework. But in so doing they often distort the original conception

without recognizing either the distortion or the assumptions violated by the distortion. This seems to happen partly because the educator has taken on the verbal, superficial abstraction of a new idea without going through a concomitant personal reorientation of attitude and behavior. Vocabulary and rhetoric are easily changed; basic beliefs and institutions all too often remain little affected. If open education is to have a fundamental and positive effect on American education, and if changes are to be consciously made, rhetoric and good intentions will not suffice.

There is no doubt that a climate potentially hospitable to fresh alternatives to our floundering educational system exists in this country. It is even possible that, in this brief moment in time, open education may have the opportunity to prove itself. However, a crash program is dangerous. Implementing foreign ideas and practices is a precarious business, and I fear the present opportunity will be abused or misused. Indeed, many attempts to implement open classrooms in America have already been buried with the epitaphs "sloppy permissivism," "neoprogressive," "Communist," "anarchical," or "laissez-faire." An even more discouraging although not surprising consequence has been to push educational practice further away from open education than was the case prior to the attempt at implementation.

Most educators who say they want open education are ready to change *appearances*. They install printing presses, tables in place of desks, classes in corridors, nature study. They adopt the *vocabulary*: "integrated day," "interest areas," "free choice," and "student-initiated learning." However, few have understanding of, let alone commitment to, the philosophical, personal, and professional roots from which these practices and phrases have sprung and upon which they depend so completely for their success. It is my belief that changing appearances to more closely resemble some British classrooms without understanding and accepting the rationale underlying these changes will lead inevitably to failure and conflict among children, teachers, administrators, and parents. American education can withstand no more failure, even in the name of reform or revolution.

I would like to suggest that before you jump on the open classroom surfboard, a precarious vehicle appropriate neither for all people nor for all situations, you pause long enough to consider the following statements on pages 228-232 and to examine your own reactions to them. Your reactions may reveal salient attitudes about children, learning, and knowledge. I have found that successful open educators in both England and America tend to take similar positions on these statements. Where do you stand?

Most open educators, British and American, "strongly agree" with most of these statements.[2] I think it is possible to learn a great deal both about open education and about oneself by taking a position with respect to these different statements. While it would be folly to argue that strong agreement assures success in developing an open classroom, or, on the other hand, that strong disagreement predicts failure, the assumptions are, I believe, closely related to open education practices. Consequently, I feel that for those sympathetic to the assumptions, success at a difficult job will be more likely. For the educator to attempt to adopt practices that depend for their success upon general adherence to these beliefs without actually adhering to them is, at the very least, dangerous.

At the same time, we must be careful not to assume that an "official" British or U.S. government-inspected type of open classroom or set of beliefs exists that is the standard for all others. Indeed, what is exciting about British open classrooms is the *diversity* in thinking and behavior for children and adults—from person to person, class to class, and school to school. The important point here is that the likelihood of successfully developing an open classroom increases as those concerned agree with the basic assumptions underlying open education practices. It is impossible to "role play" such a fundamentally distinct teaching responsibility.

For some people, then, drawing attention to these assumptions may terminate interest in open education. All to the good; a well-organized, consistent, teacher-directed classroom probably has a far less harmful influence upon children than a well-intentioned but sloppy, permissive, and chaotic attempt at an open classroom in which teacher and child must live with contradiction and conflict. For other people, awareness of these assumptions may stimulate confidence and competence in their attempts to change what happens to children in school.

In the final analysis, the success of a widespread movement toward open education in this country rests not upon agreement with any philosophical position but with satisfactory answers to several important questions: For what kinds of people—teachers, administrators, parents, children—is the open classroom appropriate and valuable? What happens to children in open classrooms? Can teachers be *trained* for open classrooms? How can the resistance from children, teachers, administrators, and parents—inevitable among those not committed to open education's assumptions and practices—be surmounted? And finally, should participation in an open classroom be *required* of teachers, children, parents, and administrators?

Assumptions About Learning and Knowledge[3]

Instructions: Make a mark somewhere along each line which best represents
   your own feelings about each statement.

Example: School serves the wishes and needs of adults better than it does
the wishes and needs of children.

strongly agree	agree	no strong feeling	disagree	strongly disagree

Assumptions About Children's Learning

Motivation

Assumption 1: Children are innately curious and will explore their environment without adult intervention.

strongly agree	agree	no strong feeling	disagree	strongly disagree

Assumption 2: Exploratory behavior is self-perpetuating.

| strongly agree | agree | no strong feeling | disagree | strongly disagree |

Conditions for Learning
Assumption 3: The child will display natural exploratory behavior if he is not threatened.

| strongly agree | agree | no strong feeling | disagree | strongly disagree |

Assumption 4: Confidence in self is highly related to capacity for learning and for making important choices affecting one's learning.

| strongly agree | agree | no strong feeling | disagree | strongly disagree |

Assumption 5: Active exploration in a rich environment, offering a wide array of manipulative materials, will facilitate children's learning.

| strongly agree | agree | no strong feeling | disagree | strongly disagree |

Assumption 6: Play is not distinguished from work as the predominant mode of learning in early childhood.

| strongly agree | agree | no strong feeling | disagree | strongly disagree |

Assumption 7: Children have both the competence and the right to make significant decisions concerning their own learning.

| strongly agree | agree | no strong feeling | disagree | strongly disagree |

Assumption 8: Children will be likely to learn if they are given considerable choice in the selection of the materials they wish to work with and in the choice of questions they wish to pursue with respect to those materials.

| strongly agree | agree | no strong feeling | disagree | strongly disagree |

Assumption 9: Given the opportunity, children will choose to engage in activities which will be of high interest to them.

| strongly agree | agree | no strong feeling | disagree | strongly disagree |

Assumption 10: If a child is fully involved in and is having fun with an activity, learning is taking place.

| strongly agree | agree | no strong feeling | disagree | strongly disagree |

Social Learning

Assumption 11: When two or more children are interested in exploring the same problem or the same materials, they will often choose to collaborate in some way.

| strongly agree | agree | no strong feeling | disagree | strongly disagree |

Assumption 12: When a child learns something that is important to him, he will wish to share it with others.

| strongly agree | agree | no strong feeling | disagree | strongly disagree |

Intellectual Development

Assumption 13: Concept formation proceeds very slowly.

| strongly agree | agree | no strong feeling | disagree | strongly disagree |

Assumption 14: Children learn and develop intellectually not only at their own rate but in their own style.

| strongly agree | agree | no strong feeling | disagree | strongly disagree |

Assumption 15: Children pass through similar stages of intellectual development, each in his own way and at his own rate and in his own time.

| strongly agree | agree | no strong feeling | disagree | strongly disagree |

Assumption 16: Intellectual growth and development take place through a sequence of concrete experiences followed by abstractions.

| strongly agree | agree | no strong feeling | disagree | strongly disagree |

Assumption 17: Verbal abstractions should follow direct experience with objects and ideas, not precede them or substitute for them.

| strongly agree | agree | no strong feeling | disagree | strongly disagree |

Evaluation

Assumption 18: The preferred source of verification for a child's solution to a problem comes through the materials he is working with.

| strongly agree | agree | no strong feeling | disagree | strongly disagree |

Assumption 19: Errors are necessarily a part of the learning process; they are to be expected and even desired, for they contain information essential for further learning.

| strongly agree | agree | no strong feeling | disagree | strongly disagree |

Assumption 20: Those qualities of a person's learning that can be carefully measured are not necessarily the most important.

| strongly agree | agree | no strong feeling | disagree | strongly disagree |

Assumption 21: Objective measures of performance may have a negative effect upon learning.

| strongly agree | agree | no strong feeling | disagree | strongly disagree |

Assumption 22: Learning is best assessed intuitively, by direct observation.

| strongly agree | agree | no strong feeling | disagree | strongly disagree |

Assumption 23: The best way of evaluating the effect of the school experience on the child is to observe him over a long period of time.

| strongly agree | agree | no strong feeling | disagree | strongly disagree |

Assumption 24: The best measure of a child's work is his work.

| strongly agree | agree | no strong feeling | disagree | strongly disagree |

Assumptions About Knowledge

Assumption 25: The quality of being is more important than the quality of knowing; knowledge is a means of education, not its end. The final test of an education is what a man *is*, not what he *knows*.

| strongly agree | agree | no strong feeling | disagree | strongly disagree |

Assumption 26: Knowledge is a function of one's personal integration of experience and therefore does not fall into neatly separate categories or "disciplines."

| strongly agree | agree | no strong feeling | disagree | strongly disagree |

Assumption 27: The structure of knowledge is personal and idiosyncratic; it is a function of the synthesis of each individual's experience with the world.

| strongly agree | agree | no strong feeling | disagree | strongly disagree |

Assumption 28: Little or no knowledge exists that it is essential for every-one to acquire.

| strongly | agree | no strong | disagree | strongly |
| agree | | feeling | | disagree |

Assumption 29: It is possible, even likely, that an individual may learn and possess knowledge of a phenomenon and yet be unable to display it publicly. Knowledge resides with the knower, not in its public expression.

| strongly | agree | no strong | disagree | strongly |
| agree | | feeling | | disagree |

---

1. For a fuller description of this movement, see Roland S. Barth and Charles H. Rathbone, annotated bibliographies: "The Open School: A Way of Thinking About Children, Learning and Knowledge," *The Center Forum*, Vol. 3, No. 7, July, 1969, a publication of the Center for Urban Education, New York City; and "A Bibliography of Open Education, Early Childhood Education Study," jointly published by the Advisory for Open Education and the Education Development Center, Newton, Mass., 1971.

2. Since these assumptions were assembled, I have "tested" them with several British primary teachers, headmasters, and inspectors and with an equal number of American proponents of open education. To date, although many qualifications in language have been suggested, there has not been a case where an individual has said of one of the assumptions, "No, that is contrary to what I believe about children, learning, or knowledge."

3. From Roland S. Barth, *"Open Education,"* unpublished doctoral dissertation, Harvard Graduate School of Education, 1970.

Teachers' Centers: A British First
by Stephen K. Bailey

Effective change comes from teachers, not from their critics or superiors.

Ever since DeWitt Clinton called America's attention a century and a half ago to the British infant schools as worthy of emulation, this country has derived policy nourishment from educational experimentation in the United Kingdom. In the 1960s the British open school received particular attention, serving as a basis for many of the reforms featured in the writings of distinguished American educators—including especially Charles Silberman's *Crisis in the Classroom.*

Perhaps the most significant potential British contribution to American education, however, is only now being identified and discussed: the development of teachers' centers. British experience with these centers, at least in their present form, is a matter of three or four years only. But the idea is so simple, so obvious, so psychologically sound, as to make one wonder why teachers' centers have not dotted the educational landscape for decades.

Teachers' centers are just what the term implies: local physical facilities and self-improvement programs organized and run by the teachers themselves for purposes of upgrading educational performance. Their primary function is to make possible a review of existing curricula and other educational practices by groups of teachers and to encourage teacher attempts to bring about changes.

Stimulated by a working paper on school-leaving age prepared by Britain's Schools Council[*] in 1965, and by a variety of ad hoc study groups and curriculum-development committees in the middle sixties, teachers' centers have mushroomed in the past half decade. Today there are approximately 500 centers located throughout England and Wales, over half with full-time leaders. The centers vary greatly in size, governance, scope of work, and the quality of tea and biscuits, but most of them are engaged in exciting and profoundly significant educational activities.

The underlying rationale for teachers' centers may be stated succinctly in terms of three interlocking propositions: 1) Fundamental educational reform will come only through those charged with the basic educational responsibility: to wit, the teachers; 2) teachers are unlikely to change their ways of doing things just because imperious, theoretical reformers—whether successions of Rickovers or Illiches or high-powered R & D missionaries from central educational systems—tell them to shape up; 3) teachers will take reform seriously only when they are responsible for defining their own edu-

---

[*]The Schools Council is an independent body with a majority of teacher members. Its purpose is to undertake, in England and Wales, research and development work in curricula, teaching methods, and examination in schools, and in other ways to help teachers decide what to teach and how. The council is financed by equal contributions from the local educational authorities on the one hand and the Department of Education and Science of the national government on the other.

cational problems, delineating their own needs, and receiving help on their own terms and turf.

The more these intertwining propositions buzz around the brain, the more apparent their validity becomes. In the United States, for example, we have developed in the past several years a slew of educational R & D centers, Title III supplementary centers, and educational laboratories, each in its own way designed to discover and disseminate new educational truths. Most of these centers and laboratories have done important work. But the impact of this work upon continuing teacher performance (and pupil performance) in the classroom has been miniscule. And well before federal largess was directed toward inducing educational reform through a trickle-down theory, many state and local education departments and teachers colleges had developed curriculum-improvement supervisors charged with being "change agents" through workshops and inservice training. But the initiative was almost always from the bureaucrat or the educrat, rather than from the teachers themselves.

Few professionals have suffered more painfully or seriously from "being done good to at" than teachers. In spite of the fact that they are the ones who work day in and day out on the firing line, the definition of their problems, of their roles, of their goals, always seems to be someone else's responsibility: supervisors, parents, college professors, textbook publishers, self-styled reformers, boards of education, state and national education officials.

What the teachers' center idea does is to put the monkey of educational reform on the teacher's own back.

And they love it!

When teachers find out that they have their own facility where they can exchange ideas, learn from each other, receive help as they see fit, munch bread and jam and drink tea without the interruption of a bell or buzzer, they come alive. New ideas come from old heads, and the new tends to be sounder because the heads are experienced.

How does a teachers' center work?

Let us look at an example.

One British teachers' center in a county borough of roughly 60,000 population emerged from a "new math" project sponsored in 1966 by the Nuffield Foundation. The deputy headmaster, a mathematician, provided "crash courses" for teachers from both primary and secondary schools. From a very successful crash course experience, participating teachers urged continuation and extension of the general activity. The deputy headmaster agreed to serve as secretary of a committee of elected teachers, and each school in the area was asked to nominate members. The cooperation of the chief education officer in the district was sought and he sent a representative from his staff.

The Schools Council report on this prototypic development (SC Pamphlet No. 1, 1969) says: "It was clear that the local teachers felt a need to come together to widen their experience and share ideas, not only in 'inservice' training but in the wider area of curriculum reform. It was clear also that, such was the interest, they would be prepared to spend some of their own time on this."

Adequate physical facilities for the new teachers' center were found in the form of an empty old primary school. The local education authority allocated

750 pounds for improvements. The facilities finally included a curriculum workshop for mathematics and science, a lounge, a small library, and the beginnings of a film collection. A part-time assistant acts as keeper of the schedule and as building superintendent. The program itself, however, is entirely teacher-initiated and controlled.

The Schools Council report on this particular center is studded with illuminating phrases:

• "The center's first task will always be to stimulate and draw together local initiative."

• "[Policy remains] . . . firmly in the hands of the teacher committee."

• "The whole concept of a teacher's job is getting more complex . . . and the more complex it gets, the more necessary it will be to mobilize the expertise of the teachers."

• "The teachers are asked to suggest the program of activities ['The committee is anxious to know the type of course you desire. Suggestions should be forwarded to the secretary. . . .']."

• "Any group of teachers may use the building in and out of school time, for projects and meetings. All you have to do is book ahead."

• ". . . making locally relevant any innovation, from whatever source, which commends itself to teachers in the area."

• "It is important that the center reflect local teacher opinion about the curriculum and test ideas locally generated. . . ."

These give the spirit and flavor of the entire teachers' center movement. But the fact that initiative is local and is from the teachers themselves does not preclude valuable relationships with local educational authorities, with representatives of the national Schools Council, with nearby teachers colleges and universities. The centers' committees facilitate such relationships, but on a basis far healthier than has often obtained in the past. Gone are the traditional deferential attitudes and the superciliousness that have so frequently marked "workshops-organized-for-teachers" by educational reformers in official or academic-status positions.

What are the activities? In the teachers' center noted above, programs have included, during school time: Nuffield Junior Maths (six meetings), junior science (six meetings), decimalization and the school (one day), infant environment (six lectures), maladjusted children (four lectures), and athletic coaching for schools (three days).

Typical after-school programs were: lecture/demonstration on understanding numbers, nine weekly meetings and discussions on how children learn, three lectures and workshops on visual aids, gymnastics and dance display, and devising a humanities course for leavers (those not planning further academic work beyond school-leaving age).

The teachers' center also promotes and provides exhibits of new textbooks, programmed instruction, audiovisual aids, homecrafts and handicrafts, and student art. Promotional and informational activities (bulletins, newsletters, posters, etc.) are disseminated to keep all teachers and other interested people in the area informed about programs and exhibits. After-school experimental classes on family life, adolescent identity crises, and community problems are undertaken with selected students.

But reports on the activities of a single center should not suggest a rigid format for all such centers. The key to the success and the enthusiasm associated with the teachers' center notion is control by *local* teachers. In consequence, center facilities and programs vary widely, depending upon the definition of need constructed by the local teacher-controlled center committees working intimately with local center leaders or "wardens." Some centers limit their curriculum investigations to a particular field like math or science; others attempt a wholesale review of the adequacy of an entire curriculum by grade or age; others have a strong social emphasis; still others feature outside lecturers and exhibits of new materials. Many centers feature formal in-service training courses; others stress informal workshops; still others provide facilities for self-study. Some centers are primary school oriented; others draw heavily from secondary schools. Some attempt to draw in students, parents, supervisors, professors of education, and others directly related to the educational process; others keep such types at arm's length and relish the sense of teacher autonomy and the sense of dignity that come from self-directed accomplishments.

Tactfully, in the background, are the supporting services of the Schools Council: studies, reports, curriculum R & D, conferences, etc. The council leaders, including their distinguished staff of field officers, are exquisitely sensitive to the importance of teachers' centers being locally operated and defined. The field officers of the Schools Council are themselves teachers loaned for short periods of time only to the itinerant functions of the Schools Council.

For the first time, local teachers are not low on the totem pole. They are prime movers in reforming an inevitably sluggish system. The reforms are not imposed by the arrogance of ministries, authorities, supervisors, or academicians. The reforms emerge from the teachers' own experiences and creative impulses. Through the field officers of the Schools Council and through the outreach of the local leadership of the teachers' centers, important educational innovations from whatever sources can be scrutinized and tested; but, once again, this is done on the teachers' own terms and turf.

Who pays? Local education authorities and, through contributions of time and materials, the teachers themselves. Capital improvements, major equipment and facilities, and basic operating costs come from the education committees of local authorities. But without significant inputs of time and talent (as well as marginal voluntary donations to help defray the costs of social food and beverages), teachers' centers could not exist—at least in their present form.

Depending on the size of the center, annual budgets may run from a few to thousands of pounds. In some cases, where teachers' centers agree to serve as area distribution headquarters for educational A-V materials, their local-authority budget may be sweetened substantially.

Experience with the center idea is still meager. But their stunning proliferation is testament to their meeting a felt need among teachers and among those who understand the futility of attempts to reform British education without the teachers being directly and importantly involved.

In 1970 the Schools Council sponsored three national conferences on teachers' centers in the United Kingdom. A total of 300 people attended. The liveliness of discussions and debates was indicative of the variety of opinions, experiences, and goals that inform the teachers' center idea. The conference spectrum ranged from the total enthusiast to the cynic.

Among the most insistent questions raised at the conferences were the following:

● How many of the center activities should be on an "in-school" as against an "after-school" basis?

● Should the "wardens" or "leaders" of the centers be part-time or full-time? And how should they be selected and trained? Is a new kind of profession emerging (i.e., teachers' center wardens)?

● Should teachers' centers encourage membership from those who are nonteachers?

● Should teachers' centers concentrate special attention upon the evaluation of, and experimentation with, new educational technology?

● How can more teachers be induced to use the centers—especially the apathetic who need the centers the most?

● What are the best methods for spreading the word of experts or even of "Charlie Jones's" good ideas?

The greatest problem seen by all members was the demand of development work on the time and energy of teachers. Although some of the work is presently done during school hours, much of it takes place after 4 p.m. The financial and logistical problems associated with this central issue are at the heart of the possibilities for long-range success and survival of teachers' centers in Britain.

Even at their best and most creative, teachers' centers are still tentative. New regional linkages and national information networks will surely be needed to supplement local insights and resources. At the moment, there is an inadequate flow of information about what is going on in other centers and areas; and extant knowledge and research directly related to locally defined problems is inadequately collected and disseminated. The Schools Council is sponsoring a series of regional conferences this coming year in order to address many of these issues.

But the basic concept remains structurally and psychologically sound, and our British cousins have good reason for being enthusiastic.

Fortunately, the idea is beginning to catch on in the United States. Don Davies, acting deputy commissioner for development in the U.S. Office of Education, is actively promoting the notion of a major network of local teachers' centers. Leaders in both the National Education Association and the American Federation of Teachers have shown considerable interest in the teachers' centers concept.

Would it not be wonderful if, after years of telling teachers what to do and where to go, American educational savants and officials suddenly discovered that the only real and lasting reforms in education in fact come about when teachers themselves are given facilities and released time "to do their own thing"? Perhaps in the not too distant future, following the pioneering experiment voted by the Unity, Maine, School District for the fall of 1971, a four-day week for teachers in the classroom will be standard. On the fifth day, the teachers will be in their teachers' centers, rapping about their common problems, studying new ways to teach and to understand students, imbibing a Coke or Pepsi, talking shop over billiards, and cheerfully allowing management to check off dues, parts of which will be assigned to defray the operating costs of the federally or state-funded teachers' center facilities. Linked through regional associations, informed by the R & D activities of a National Institute of Education, teachers' centers could form the essential but presently missing link between innovative ideas and pupil performance in the classroom.

VIII

The Decay
of
Urban Education

Introduction

*T*he next four sections deal with issues and problems that have been among the most troublesome for education leaders since I became editor of the KAPPAN in 1956. In one quick count, I noted 724 articles dealing with urban schools, discipline, testing, and desegregation in the 25 volumes I have skimmed. Thus we have averaged nearly 30 articles a year on these topics. The nine reprinted here are little more than a sampling.

In 1969 William J. Gephart, for many years director of PDK's Center for Evaluation, Development, and Research, suggested that I ask Luvern Cunningham of Ohio State University to write for the KAPPAN. As an OSU graduate, Gephart had heard of the unique program that took Cunningham, then dean of the OSU College of Education, into a black ghetto school to gain a better understanding of problems encountered there. "Hey, Man, You Our Principal?" was the result. The value of this article lies chiefly, I think, in the vividness and immediacy with which Cunningham tells his story. I recently asked him to reflect on the experience from the perspective of 12 years. (Cunningham is now Novice G. Fawcett Professor of Education at OSU.) Here is his response:

> 'Hey, Man . . . ,' has been reprinted more than a dozen times. It produced considerable mail, most of which tended to validate its description of an urban junior high.
>
> Not all urban schools or school districts are disasters; far from it. Nor were they then (1969). But the bright spots are tarnished by deeply troubled places. The good programs and the fine schools attract little media attention. Or when they do, our citizens are preoccupied with other matters. As a society, we have allowed the negative media blitz to wash out our faith.
>
> The problems of urban schools have remained much the same over the intervening years. The school about which the article was written is gone now, a victim of declining enrollments, and the wrecking ball. The school system is in convulsion. Devastating labor problems have arisen, including a lengthy teacher strike a year ago. The school district flirts with bankruptcy day by day. Court-ordered desegregation mangles its spirit, as decisions go up and down the appellate elevators of justice.
>
> The boys and girls have a few friends at the State House, none at city hall. The board is impotent, absolutely. It is a system adrift. And there is nothing in the works to make it better.
>
> From my perspective, personnel policies at state and local levels are the chief villains. There is no positive relationship between bar-

241

gained contracts and what happens in classrooms. Most of the planning and administrative energy goes into adult problems, not those of children and youth. And there is no receptivity or spirit for fresh thinking about personnel policy alternatives.

One constructive change would be to move collective bargain-in to the state level, liberating local school officials to tend to education problems. Other Western cultures would never allow work stoppages to jeopardize the life chances of young people. Ohio 'boasts' of the longest teacher strike in history in one of its districts. We have made tragedy a matter of policy.

I urge that the education professions in each state join in an intensive review of personnel policies. The focus should be at the state level. Such an analysis should not be hurried, nor should it be narrow. Policy regarding salaries, long service leaves, and other fringes should be examined. So should bargaining practices, absenteeism, recruitment, and retirement.

These are leverage points. These are the openings for real improvement. Otherwise, we will be wringing our hands with even more desperation a decade hence.

Taking a more abstract, theoretical view of the ills of urban education than did "Hey, Man . . .," Daniel U. Levine wrote "Concepts of Bureaucracy in Urban School Reform" for the February 1971 KAPPAN, a special issue that he himself planned. He writes that articles in this issue by Richard Lonoff and Seymour Fleigel "are still the best short descriptions anywhere of successful inner-city schools."

Director of the Center for the Study of Metropolitan Problems in Education, University of Missouri at Kansas City, Levine has devoted most of his professional career to the study of urban education. He served as a consultant to the research team whose work resulted in the publication, Why Do Some Urban Schools Succeed? The Phi Delta Kappa Study of Exceptional Urban Elementary Schools *(1980).*

Levine was a KAPPAN editorial consultant for eight years. Many of the 24 articles and reviews he has written for the journal were solicited during that period in the Sixties and early Seventies. Had space permitted, we would also have reprinted here his "The Segregated Society: What Must Be Done" (January 1969), which, like "Concepts of Bureaucracy . . . ," is an original and powerful article.

—SME

Hey, Man, You Our Principal?
Urban Education as I Saw It
by Luvern L. Cunningham

*Last May 12 principals from a Midwest city system exchanged
positions briefly with a number of professors and administrators
from the College of Education, Ohio State University. The idea
grew out of long-time collaboration between the city system and
Ohio State in the preparation of teachers.*

*Through design or chicanery, the dean of the OSU College
of Education, who had volunteered for the exchange, was assigned to what is generally regarded as the most difficult school
in the cooperating system. He frankly confesses that the experience was a revelation—a useful one, however, and in this report
he tells about it as he saw it.*

*At the request of administrators in the cooperating system, its
identity is withheld.*

This is a report. It is as objective as I can make it. The remarks that follow are
based on a few days' experience as principal of an inner-city junior high
school—a problem-saturated place.

I want it known that although what I say here is critical, it is not intended
to be critical of any person or group of persons. But it is an indictment of us
all—educators and laymen, critics and the criticized.

The notion of an exchange cropped up out of the woodwork. Someone
had an idea that this would be a good thing to do. The big-city people agreed
and we agreed and so we were off and running. We didn't have the luxury of
much advanced planning time. Had we had a chance to contemplate the
event in Columbus (in the peace and quiet and solitude of the ivory tower),
we could have lost our courage and copped out on the whole deal. We didn't
have that time, so we did appear at our respective schools at the appointed
hour, Monday, May 5. On that fateful morning (like little kids going to kindergarten) we picked up our pencil boxes and marched off to the schoolhouse.

I arrived at about 7:45 a.m. I had read about the city's riots in 1966 and I
knew it was near here that they had started. I was aware too that this was a
junior high that had been having its share of trouble. I knew that the faculty
had walked out in January in protest of school conditions. Most of the faculty
stayed away for two days, saying that this school was an unfit place in which
to carry on professional activity.

My first several minutes as the new helmsman were exciting, to say the
least. I walked in through the front door and introduced myself to the regular
principal's secretary. She was most cordial and smiled knowingly. I think she
chuckled to herself, thinking that this guy is really in for an education. If those
were her feelings she was quite right.

I walked into the office and was about to set my briefcase down. I looked
up and there must have been 20 faces, most of them black, all around. And
others were coming through the office door. Some were students, some were
faculty members with students in tow, others were clerks who wanted me to
make some monumental decisions about events of the day.

They weren't even in line. They were all just kind of standing around there competing for attention. And to make life more exciting a little black fellow with a flat hat and a cane about two feet long came up to me. He whipped that cane around on his arm and stuck it in my stomach and said, "Hey, man, you our principal?" I began thinking longingly of Columbus and said, "Well, no, I'm not. But I'm here for a week and I am going to be taking his place." I was backpeddling and trying to think of some answer that would make sense to this eighth-grade student.

A number of youngsters who were crowding around were just curious; others had problems. One was a girl who had recently been released from a correctional institution and was under court order to come back to school. She was there for an appointment, but she didn't want to come back to this or any other school. She was openly hostile, asking harshly that she not be made to come back. I had no file. I didn't have any background on this young lady. I was unprepared to make a decision. So instead of displaying administrative genius, I said, "Would you sit down over there and I'll talk to you later." She sat—head down, sullen, oblivious to the confusion surrounding us. It was an hour before I got back to her problem.

There was tragedy and comedy. A teacher who was obviously disturbed about something had a very attractive 16-year-old-girl by the hand. She came in and said, "I understand you're the new principal, Mr. Cunningham. Look at that skirt. Look at that mini-skirt. It's entirely too short. Just look at that thing. I think we ought to send her home. Aren't you going to send her home?"

She turned to the girl and said, "Is your mother home?" The girl said "No." "When will she be home?" "Well, she'll be home about 6:15 tonight."

The teacher turned to me and said, "We can't send her home." Then she marched the girl over in front of me, rolled that brief skirt up several inches and said, "Look at that, it's got a hem in it. It's got a hem in it that long. We ought to be able to take that hem out. Let's go back to the classroom." I didn't have a chance to say a word.

In the meantime other kids were still clustered around. They had their own brand of problems, so I said, "Would you go and wait outside the office please and come in one at a time?" They kept coming in with their questions, some that I could answer, most that I could not.

When the first bell rang and the students had to go to their homerooms, faces disappeared, the corridors cleared a bit, and there was an atmosphere of temporary calm. I was able to sit down and try to get my bearings. It was an inauspicious beginning, to say the least.

Let me comment a bit about Lester Butler. Lester was assigned to the principal's office. His responsibility was to be available during free periods for phone calls, delivery of messages, and any other tasks that might appropriately be handled by an eager, intelligent seventh-grader. After quiet had been established in the office on that first day, he gave me a quick tour of the building. He took me to the obvious places like the library, the auditorium, the gymnasium, and special classrooms, but he also pointed out the nooks and crannies, the special recesses, the hideaways of the old structure. With his special brand of radar, he was able to track me down and bring messages to me during the week when I was about the building. We became unusually fine friends.

This junior high school building is old. The oldest part was built 65 years ago. It has had two additions. Despite its age, the building has been re-furbished from time to time; it was painted and the windows were in. It's not particularly unattractive from the inside, but as a structure to house education it's a nightmare of inefficiency. Traffic patterns are unbelievable. You have to go upstairs to get downstairs. You go upstairs across a kind of plateau and down the other side to reach another part of the building. The arrangements for science and home economics facilities, as well as classrooms housing other particular specialized aspects of the curriculum, do not accommodate decent traffic patterns. When the bell sounds and classes pass, it is a wild place. It's wild in between times, too, for that matter.

The absentee rate is very high. Of the nearly 1,800 enrolled, between 350 and 400 were absent every day. Where they were no one really knows. There was no apparent relationship between my presence and the absentee rate; that's the way it is every day. During my first day a counselor took me in his car and just criss-crossed the neighborhood. He wanted to point out the housing, the neighborhood, the fact that the streets were crowded with humanity just milling around. It was a warm week, the first week in May. People were outside. Kids of all ages were all over. There appeared to be as many youngsters on the street as there were in the elementary school and junior and senior highs.

Ironically, everybody shows up during the lunch period. The lunches are partly financed with federal funds and the youngsters are admitted to the lunchroom by ticket. Kids who are truant get into the building (despite door guards) and into the cafeteria. They have something to eat and then melt into the community.

The building is a sea of motion—people are moving about all the time. Adults (teachers, teaching assistants, observers, student teachers, door guards, other people who get in through the doors despite the guards) and students are in the halls all the time. Some of the students have passes to go somewhere, given by somebody; but most students are just there. Those who don't have passes have excuses. As a newcomer seeing all of this motion, what should I have done? Should I have gotten tough? Should I have tried to shout them back to class? Should I have threatened such and such? Or should I have turned my head and let them go on about their own purposes? I turned my head.

When I was in my office students would come in with all sorts of questions, grievances, or requests for excuses. Apparently the pattern in the building is that if you can't get a hearing for your complaint anywhere else, you end up in the principal's office. I had a steady flow of customers.

The school has 85 teachers. There is a high absence rate each day among teachers too. They fail to show up for many reasons. The teacher absentee numbers (while I was there) would range from 11 to 14 per day. If you have a faculty of 85 and 14 teachers fail to show (and you don't get substitutes), you have to make some kind of ad hoc arrangements quickly to handle the crises. Each day three to five substitutes would appear and they would be assigned quickly to cover classes. But they were not enough. Furthermore, there was little relation between the substitutes' teaching fields and their assignments. The first priority is to put live people in classes to maintain some semblance of order.

The youngsters, as I said, were in motion. I had the feeling that I was walking on a live volcano. Classes were often noisy and rowdy. Fights and squabbles broke out frequently. Fights between girls occurred about five to one more often than fights among boys. But the fights among the girls were often over boys. The adult population was on pins and needles from the time the building opened in the morning until school was out at 3:30 in the afternoon. Everyone hoped to make it through the day without large-scale violence.

The day is organized around eight periods. Students have a number of free periods, during which time they are assigned to study halls. Some go to a large auditorium; others go to classrooms with teachers assigned to study hall duty there. Large numbers congregate in the cafeteria on the ground floor for "study." The cafeteria accommodates around 300 youngsters. Teachers are reluctant to supervise the cafeteria study halls. When they do, it is with fear and trembling. The place is noisy. Kids move around despite the efforts of several teachers to keep them seated. They shoot craps. Some play other games. There is bickering and fighting. Kids pick up chairs and fling them across the room at one another. It's dirty and hot.

The whole building is hot, because the custodians cannot shut off the heat. It is the only way to provide hot water for the lunch program. So they keep the stokers going to have hot water for the federally subsidized lunches. Everybody complains about it: the principal, the assistant principals, the teachers, the students, and the PTA.

The lunchroom study halls are unbearable. The undermanned custodial staff is unable to keep the table tops clean; a slimy film covers them. They are neither attractive for eating nor for study purposes. Because of the danger of intruders coming in off the streets, the major cafeteria emergency exit has been nailed shut. Teachers asked the principal to have the custodians do this. The custodians refused because of fire regulations. In desperation the principal himself nailed it shut. Each day he lives in fear that a fire will break out and students will be trapped. Large numbers might not get out through the narrow passageways that serve as entrances and exits. Thus a measure taken to protect the teachers could lead to another type of disaster.

We called the police only once during my stay. It was different at another junior high school where my colleague Lew Hess served as principal. At night following his first day, a fire bomb was thrown through his office window. It was a dud and didn't go off. On his last day three fire bombs were thrown inside the building and they did go off. The police and fire department had to be summoned each time.

On the second day, in a classroom study hall right across from my office, a young boy was late. His name was Willy Denton. He was about a minute and a half tardy and his excuse was that he had been next door signing up for a special program of summer employment. The study hall supervisor had obviously had a hectic morning. As Willy entered the room a few words were exchanged. The supervisor grabbed Willy, put a hammerlock around his neck, kind of choked him, and wrestled him out into the corridor. The noise attracted other kids. Immediately there were about 40 students as well as door guards right around the teacher and Willy. Willy got free for a moment but the supervisor caught him again, this time grabbing him by the shoulders. He shook him against the lockers and that was like whomping a big bass drum. The sound reverberated around that part of the building and more people came. The supervisor got a fresh hammerlock on Willy, dragged him over to my office, threw him in and across to the other side, and said, "Take charge."

I suppose that I turned whiter in that sea of black, but I took charge. I closed the door and asked Willy to sit down. All of a sudden another teacher opened the door about six inches and shouted, "Willy's got a good head on his shoulders," slammed the door, and left.

It was about 12 noon. The period had just started. There were nearly 35 minutes until Willy was to go to another class. So Willy and I just talked. I didn't think that lining him up for swats would make much difference. He was livid. If he had been white he would have been purple. He was furious, and so we just sat and talked.

We talked about what he liked and what he disliked. I asked him if he had worked last summer, since he was going to be employed this coming summer. He said that he had. I asked where and he said, "I worked in a church." And he added, "You know I teach Sunday School." I asked how old his class members were and he said, "Well they're about the same age as I am." "How many do you have?" "About 15, and sometimes I teach on Saturdays too." "Do you like to teach?" He said, "Well, it's okay. But boy those first Sundays my stomach just kind of turned around and I didn't know what I was doing. But it's better now. Like last Sunday, did you hear about that plane that was shot down in Korea? You know, we just talked about that. I sat down and we talked about that."

It was clear that Willy loved what he was doing in Sunday School. He liked math too, and he planned to go to high school. But he was so angry at that study hall supervisor. He trembled for several minutes; he just couldn't get control. We talked through the balance of the hour till the bell rang. I sent him on to his next class sans swats.

The PTA leaders came in to meet with me on Wednesday. They shared their definitions of the school's problems. I held a faculty meeting on Thursday. And I was amazed at the similarity between faculty and parent sentiments on the issues facing the school.

The teachers, by and large, are a very dedicated lot. Many of them are young; some of them are coming out of MAT programs. Despite their youth, they, like the rest of the faculty, are tired, disheartened, even despondent. But they don't want to fail.

One of the teachers was shot 10 days before I arrived on the scene. He missed his lunch break and went across the street to get a coke and a bag of potato chips. Coming back he was held up on the street and shot with a pellet gun. He came back into the building and walked into the principal's office with his hand pressed against his side. Blood was spewing between his fingers and he said, "I'm shot, I'm shot, I'm shot." The principal called an ambulance and got him to the hospital. But he was back teaching while I was there, with the pellet still in him. He hadn't had time to have it taken out. He was going to the hospital that weekend to have the bullet removed.

I tried to visit classes and meet teachers. As I became known around the building, it was rather like walking down the hall and being attacked by aardvarks. Teachers would come out, grab me by the arm, pull me back into the teachers' lounge or their classrooms, and say, "Let me tell it like it is here." Every one of them had deep feelings for the school and for the kids, but an inability to define the specific changes that would make a difference. Their intense desire to solve the school's problems, mixed with overwhelming despair, is one of the powerful impressions that remains with me as a consequence of those days.

In many ways it is an overmotivated but underprepared staff. As one young fellow who came in March said, "This is an overpeopled and understaffed school. We've got lots of special people running around under federal grants doing their particular thing. But they don't fit into any kind of mosaic that has meaning for solving the problems of the school."

Many teachers have the too-little-and-too-late kind of feeling. No one is apologetic about it. There is no sense of humiliation about being assigned to the school. But most of them want to get out, because they feel that it is an absolutely hopeless situation, that they can't afford to spend whatever psychic energy they have in fighting a losing battle. Even though they are emotionally committed to the place, they still want to leave. So the turnover rate is high. Some youngsters had had several different teachers in some of their classes since the beginning of the year.

After the early chaos of my first morning, I was able to visit a class being taught by a Peace Corps returnee. She was a young woman with an MAT degree. She had two adults with her in the room assisting with the youngsters. And it was pandemonium. She was trying to teach social studies. She was obviously searching desperately to locate something that might motivate or have some interest for 15 seventh-graders. Her Peace Corps assignment had been in Africa, so she was showing slides of how people construct thatched cottages there. It was something she knew about first-hand—she had been on the scene. But the kids tuned her out. They were making funny remarks and fighting.

One of the other adults in that room was a young man, a practice teacher who had arrived that morning. He had already been slugged twice by students before my 11 a.m. visit. I talked with him later in the week, trying to find out whether he was going to give up or stick around. I had to admire his tenacity. He was going to stay; he wasn't going to be licked by that set of events.

During the lunch hour a group of seventh-grade teachers who were cooperating in a transitional program (transitional from the sixth grade into junior high) were meeting for a planning session. I was invited to sit in. The young Peace Corps returnee came in with a tear-stained face. She just couldn't manage her situation. She didn't know what to do. She had to go back and face those classes that afternoon and the next day and the next. She had been advised by the principal and by others to turn in her chips and move to another school. But she just wouldn't do it. She had been fighting it since September, facing failure all year long, but she just would not give up. Others like her were having similar experiences.

The curriculum at this junior high is archaic, outmoded, irrelevant, and unimportant in the minds of the kids who are there. The faculty has agreed for the most part that this is true. But no one is able to design a pattern of change that will remedy or act upon all of the deficiencies that are so prominent in the program of studies. Because of the way the building is constructed (room sizes, locations, and the like), they are locked into an eight-period day. There just are not enough classrooms to handle a six-period organization.

Furthermore, there is ambiguity about who is responsible for curriculum reform. Everyone wants change, but no one knows how to achieve it.

They were administering the Stanford Achievement Test the week I was there. Large numbers of kids couldn't read it. Many couldn't even read the name of the test. Some of them would mark all of the alternative responses; some wouldn't mark any; some would just casually draw pictures on the test; some would stare; others would raise their hands and ask for help from those who were monitoring the testing.

A few teachers raised the question with me, "Why test?" It is a good question. Or why use that kind of testing for youngsters in a junior high school like this one? Apparently standardized testing is a systemwide requirement that may have had historical significance and is continued merely because no one has considered not doing it.

As I have said, most of the teachers' energy goes into control. I found few classrooms where I could say with any confidence that there was excitement relative to learning. The only place where I saw interest and motivation and product was in home economics, which enrolls both boys and girls. In other areas interest and motivation appeared to be near zero. It seems to me that the traditional school "subjects" have to be very carefully analyzed in terms of some relevance criterion.

We toss that word around a great deal—relevance. It's in everybody's language. It has reached cliché status more rapidly than most similar words in our professional jargon. Nevertheless, there is some meaning there.

When I ask myself what would be relevant to the young people at this school, I reach an impasse very quickly. It is hard to know what is relevant. Certainly it ties to motivation. If we were insightful enough to know what the prominent motivations are among such young people, then maybe we could organize a program of studies in keeping with interest areas. The program might look quite unlike the traditional subject-centered arrangement in these schools.

I mentioned earlier the "leakage" of the building, both inside out and outside in. The staff walkout in January 1969 took place because the school was an unsafe place in which to teach. The Board of Education responded by putting guards at the doors. The measure was to protect teachers and students from a range of intruder types. It was also to control students coming in and going out during the day. The guards have helped a bit in keeping invaders out of the building, but this move hasn't solved the pupil "leakage" problem. An outsider (or an insider for that matter) will cause a disturbance at one of the doors. Door guards come quickly from their posts to help out, leaving their own stations unattended. Other kids will then open the unprotected doors and run out or run in, whichever suits their fancy.

Administrators and teachers resort to corporal punishment. The chief vehicle for control is the swat system. The teachers worked out a scheme to improve control following the January walkout. Teachers volunteer to help with discipline in the "gym balcony," a little area overlooking the gymnasium. During free periods kids who have misbehaved, for whatever reason, are brought there. They queue up outside, both boys and girls, waiting to be swatted. Teachers take their turns up there in the gym balcony. Similar disciplinary lineups occur outside of the office doors of the three assistant principals, who have paddles or razor straps hanging from their belts. If they need to use them in the corridors, they do.

Disciplinary cases are brought first to their door. If they or the principal are too busy, in juvenile court or at home with a case of nerves or whatever it might be, then the students go to the gym balcony to get their swats. Afterward they go back to class or study hall or library or get out of the building.

I didn't administer corporal punishment. I don't know whether I was psychologically capable of it. I don't think I could have forced myself. Teachers on a few occasions brought students to my office. One teacher just threw them in, saying "Take charge" and leaving.

There doesn't seem to be any intrinsic motivation, any way of appealing to the interest of pupils to stay and learn. So everyone (adults and students) adjusts to the corporal punishment routine. No one likes it; no one wants it. Teachers hate it; the principals hate it. But they have no other alternative. They have not been able to discover any better control measure.

And now about death. There is an astonishing callousness about death among the students here. One of them had been killed a few days earlier. He was shot in a car wash down the street. I have mentioned the shooting of the teacher; fortunately that did not end in death. There were other shoot-outs in the neighborhood ending in fatalities. Lester Butler, on my first day, sought an excuse to attend a funeral. I asked for particulars. He said, "It's for my friend's father. He was killed a week ago. He was shot right outside the school. I want to attend the funeral. I'll come right back after it's over." I wrote the excuse.

Lester described the event without emotion, with placidness, with matter-of-factness. Death is a part of life here. Life is filled with its own brand of violence. Its violence is routine. It is not necessarily racial. It is grounded in hate which feeds upon itself. It is cancerous and spreads and spreads and spreads.

The cancer of hate is latent within the student body. You sense its power. You sense its presence and the prospect for its release at any moment. You do not know when it will burst forth and cascade around you. It is everywhere; it is nowhere. Lester sensed that the school was a powder keg. He would even try to describe it to me in his own way.

In many ways life at this junior high is a charade. People go about the business of routine schooling. Teachers laugh and smile. They walk through the corridors ignoring the rowdiness. They try at times, half-heartedly, to establish a bit of order. The administrators take the problem more seriously; they shout and cajole and urge and plead. The counselors do their thing. They talk with students. They describe worlds of glitter and gold. The students squirm and stare and ignore. The counselors' cubicles, tucked away here and there, are temporary refuges from the storm.

I was impressed with the door guards. They try. They understand the charade. Many of them have played the game for a lifetime. They represent well the male image. They are for the most part young, strong, handsome. They are on the side of the angels. That is, they try to support the purposes of the school. They work closely with teachers and administrative officials. They do their job. It involves keeping hoodlums off the street out of the building, avoiding physical encounters but not turning away from them. There is no training for their positions. They must exercise amazing discretion every minute of the day. Most of them have little formal education. But they have established a bond with the professional staff that is harmonious and marked by mutual respect. Each day I issued up a silent prayer of thanks that they were there.

What to do about this school? And other similar junior highs in other places? An archaic building, a largely uncaring community, an irrelevant program of studies, a student population that is out of hand, an unprepared, overpressured staff, a sympathetic but essentially frustrated central administration, a city that wishes such schools would go away. A proposal from the staff and administrators was to burn the school down. Destroy it. Get the symbol out of the neighborhood. This was more than a half-serious proposal.

Short of that, what can be done? This question haunted me during my stay. What could be done? Only a few feeble proposals occurred to me.

I would argue for complete building-level autonomy. The principal and faculty should run the show without concern for other places. They should be allowed to organize the program of studies without adherence to districtwide curriculum guides and the like. The principal should be free to select his own faculty without reference to certification. He should look for talented people anywhere and everywhere. They could be found across the street or across the nation. The principal should build his own budget and make internal allocations in terms of the faculty and staff's definition of need.

More radically, I would ask that the principal be given complete control over time. That is, he should be able to open and close the school at will. If in his judgment events are getting out of hand, he should have the power—indeed be expected—to close the school down for a day, a week, or a month. During the time the building is closed, all of the adults in the school, in cooperation with students and community leaders, should focus on the problems that are overwhelming them. They should develop a problem-solving ethos. They should include genuine and substantial neighborhood participation. They should zero in on questions one by one, work them through and seek solutions. The state, the city, and the central school administration should support but not interfere. What is required in schools like these is a set of solutions. There is no justification for keeping the building open simply to observe the state code.

The staff should be kept on during the summer. Give them an air-conditioned retreat; allow them to plan for the year ahead. Work on the program of studies, work on motivation, work on community linkage, work on patterns of staffing, work on everything.

It occurred to me that it might be wise for the boys and girls to be separated—have boys' schools and girls' schools. There are some research data to support this recommendation. I remembered a study in Illinois that I directed a few years ago. There we tried to discover the impact of segregated learning on achievement. We examined a small district where youngsters were feeding into one junior high school out of white schools, black schools, and integrated schools. We were interested in such factors as pupil alienation, attitudes toward schooling, and achievement in the traditional subject fields. We discovered some significant differences, but the overwhelming difference was how boys responded to the learning environments in contrast with how girls responded. The boys were getting the short end of the stick on most things.

Systems should depress the emphasis on attendance. I would even support abandoning compulsory education for this part of the city. Emphasize programs of interest and attractiveness; deemphasize regimentation. Much of the faculty's energy goes into keeping kids in school. And once in school, keeping them in class. Why fight it? Jettison the pressure toward control. Enroll students on the basis of interest only. Such policies violate the rich American tradition of education for everyone, but why carry on the charade? Why?

Again I want it understood that I came away from this school with profound admiration and respect for the regular principal, the three assistant principals, the several counselors, the many teachers, and the many special staff members, as well as the central administration. And I came away with respect for the students. The adults in the building are struggling feverishly. They are dedicated. They are, in their own way, in love with the school. But they are shell-shocked, exhausted, and desperate. They need help but they are not sure what kind of help. And I am not sure. I have advanced a few notions, but they need careful scrutiny and considerable elaboration.

It is clear that we have no experts in this sort of urban education anywhere. The most expert may be those professionals who are there every day engaging in the fray. But they are reaching out, and it is for this reason that some kind of liaison with universities and other sources of ideas is critical. Refined, umbilical relationships need to be developed. We are just scratching the surface at Ohio State. No one has *the* answer. Anyone who thinks he has is a fool. At best there are only partial answers—pieces of a larger mosaic that could at some point in the future fit together in a more productive fashion than today's mosaic.

There are many schools in America like the one I have described. We don't want to admit it, but there are. And all of us who bear professional credentials must carry that cross.

Such educational institutions are an indictment of presidents and senators; of justices and teachers; of governors and legislators. It is ludicrous the way we behave. Our pathetic politicians, wailing and wringing their hands, spouting platitudes and diatribes. They advance shallow excuses. They say that bold acts will not find favor with unnamed constituencies. And we educators stand impotent, frightened, disheveled in the face of such tragedy.

Concepts of Bureaucracy
In Urban School Reform
by Daniel U. Levine

The public school is a social system established to deliver good education to the students who attend it. Without quibbling about the definition of "good" education, let us assume that one major component is a minimal level of academic skills needed to compete successfully for rewarding employment. By this measure, many urban schools are unequivocally failing.

At another level of generality, most people would agree that a major goal of the public school is to teach students skills and attitudes needed for learning outside the school and for living satisfying lives as adults. Without implying that the schools in and of themselves can be held solely responsible for solving all the critical problems of urban society, it would be ludicrous to argue that most urban schools are succeeding in preparing students to live wisely and well in the bright new world (or, if you prefer, the new dark ages) of metropolitan complexity; to wit: dropouts, copouts, throwouts, flunkouts, tuneouts, and freakouts littered all over the metropolitan landscape.

Thus, whatever else one may say about them, urban schools today generally are not functioning as outstandingly effective delivery systems in terms of some of their major purposes.

Roots of the Problems

To understand why urban schools frequently are not delivering adequate education, it is best to begin by recognizing that they are bureaucratic institutions in the classic meaning of the term as defined by Max Weber and other nineteenth-century sociologists. That is, both within the school and within the larger educational system of which it is a part, roles are defined impersonally, numerous rules and expectations are codified to fit each role within a hierarchy of other roles, and fitness to fill a role is defined with reference to technical training and previous experience thought to be necessary to carry it out properly.

So far so good: The urban school is conceived in an effort to use rational planning and technical competence in the task of educating masses of citizens in an urban society. Where did it all go wrong?

Basically, the urban school, as it is now organized and operated, is a victim of the same forces and problems that are generating failure in other rational bureaucracies such as hospitals, social welfare agencies, industrial corporations, the military, and municipal service departments; it is not just in education that reformers are concerned with improving the structure and performance of urban delivery systems. Among the most important of these problems are *institutional complexity and overload, goal displacement, deficiences in communications and decision-making processes,* and *social and psychological distance between client and institution.*

This listing is not offered as an exhaustive catalogue of all the logically exclusive dysfunctions that rational bureaucracy is heir to, but it does call attention to some of the critical issues that reformers must specifically take into account in endeavoring to rebuild and revitalize urban schools.

Institutional complexity and overload refers to the tendency for institutions to be ineffective when their internal structures are too complicated to allow for adequate communications, or when the external frameworks in which they function are rendered inoperable by having too large a burden placed on them. In other words, the growing complexity of industrial society tends to make existing organizational structures and networks obsolete. Part of the problem is that a message retranslated 10 times is likely to be considerably more garbled than one transmitted directly to its recipient. Or, as was illustrated in the recent telephone crisis in New York City, the volume of messages may simply overwhelm available communications channels, making it necessary to tear out much of the existing system and replace it with new subsystems more adequate for the load.

Similar difficulties arise because multiplying the layers of complexity that exist in an organization tends to increase the number of points at which vested interests can counter organizational goals. In part, a complex institution becomes more vulnerable to dysfunctions merely because there are more places where things can go wrong—just as one comma out of place in a complicated computer program was responsible for the failure of a multi-million-dollar space probe.

In addition, adding layer upon layer to the organizational structure of modern society leads the individual to perceive the structure and his experience in it as artificial and unreal. Whether exemplified in the curriculum of the school, which becomes further and further removed from daily life, or in the impersonal humming of the Corporate State's computers, the by-products of complexity become too abstract to be believed. The result, as Ortega y Gasset prophetically foresaw in *Man and Crisis*, is an exploding rejection of institutions and the philosophic presuppositions that undergird them. The whole complex structure begins to totter and topple under its own weight.

Associated with the problems of institutional complexity and overload are those of *goal displacement* in the operation of large-scale rational bureaucracies. Since bureaucratic organizations have been established to impose a degree of order on an otherwise unplanned and chaotic environment, there is a certain drive toward permanency and self-perpetuation at the heart of rational bureaucracy. When the goal of self-perpetuation begins to outweigh other purposes, we have one type of goal displacement. A second type occurs when staff members become more concerned with or adept at retaining their positions than with furthering the organization's stated goals. An example of the first type of goal displacement is the museum or art gallery that evaluates itself in terms of the number of people who pass through its turnstiles. The administrator who devotes much of his time to making his unit look good to his superordinates is an example of the second. It must be emphasized that goal displacement is not so much a result of the dishonorable intentions of human beings as of institutional tendencies toward regularizing the organization's resources and services. Donald J. Willower has illustrated some of these tendencies in education as follows:

> The age-grade placement of students, the division of the curriculum into subjects in company with the all-important schedule that parallels this division, and the classroom arrangement itself, are forms of routinization that speak to the massive logistics of

educational organization. They make the enterprise more manageable; that is, they function to channel, order, and regularize the manner in which the organization attends and processes its clients.

At the same time, such routinization reduces the likelihood of instruction geared to variations in client characteristics, since procedures that accommodate unusual or unique client requirements are apt to be disruptive.

A quite tangible routinized structure is found in the report card, perhaps the most common formal communication of the school to its patrons. An important feature of this document is that it calls attention to student defects, not to those of the school. No one is ever informed that a student is not up to par because he had the misfortune to draw a poor teacher, or because the curriculum is indifferent or unsuitable. In consequence, the organization is protected and the responsibility for barren performance is placed squarely on the client.[1]

Since an organization is most likely to be deflected from its reasons for existing when pertinent information on what is really happening is not available to decision makers and clients at the right time, *deficiencies in communications and decision-making processes* are closely related to the phenomenon of goal displacement. Many interrelations between inadequate communications, uninformed decision making, and organizational dysfunctioning are vividly illustrated in a series of essays by the British writer C. Northcote Parkinson, as well as in anecdotal records of urban schools such as Bel Kaufman's *Up the Down Staircase.*

One major impediment to communications and decision making that already has been mentioned is the simple multiplication of hierarchical levels without corresponding adjustments to insure that the right information flows up and down the hierarchy to the right people at the right time. The most obvious immediate response to this problem is to reduce the number of hierarchical levels at which communications can be slowed or distorted and to allow for more fluidity in locating decision-making authority at differing levels in accordance with types of decisions to be made. When adequate adjustments are not made, institutions often continue to function largely as they did in the past, even though the environment has changed drastically and has outdated many of their operational rules and regulations.

Social and psychological distance between client and organization not only contributes to poor communications within an organization but also increases the likelihood that the organization will serve goals other than that of providing services to its clients. When the people who staff an organization and the people it serves have divergent values and personal histories, staff members and clients may not view the claims and expectations they press upon one another as legitimate and acceptable. Without a modicum of shared social experience and common psychological space between staff and clients, role incumbents may tend to place personal interests such as tenure in the job over the interests of clients, and clients may be unwilling or even unable to utilize the institution's resources as they were intended to be used. Thus, reduction of social and psychological distance between school personnel on the one hand and students and parents on the other is imperative if urban schools are to become more effective institutions. This problem seems to be growing as critical in predominantly middle-income schools as it already has become in low-income schools in the inner city.

Perhaps the most logical way to reduce social and psychological distance between organizations and their clients is to increase the clients' participation in decision-making processes within an organization. Although the term "participatory democracy" recently has become something of a slogan, it is a concept that can do much to help rebuild and reinvigorate urban schools. Participation of clients, as well as wider participation of employees in decision-making processes, can help to make an organization seem less complex and can contribute to the beneficial flow of information and feedback; in both these ways participation can enhance an institution's legitimacy and minimize tendencies toward goal displacement.

The difficulties involved in overcoming bureaucratic dysfunctioning should not be minimized. For example, reducing the number of hierarchical levels and providing for more client and staff participation in decision making easily generate new forms of goal displacement and additional communications distortion. The introduction of technologically advanced communications processes and equipment may increase the psychological distance between clients and staff or between staff members at different levels of the organization. Thus gains in one direction frequently seem to entail losses in other directions, and reform-minded administrators end up confronting what may turn out to be almost insoluble dilemmas. The problems of rebuilding urban schools are not about to be solved through the application of a few glib generalizations.

Much more could be said about any or all of these themes and their implications for urban schools. The December 1970 issue of the *KAPPAN*, for example, was devoted to the specific topic of accountability, which is intimately tied to the larger topic of organizational dysfunctioning in the schools. Many variations on these themes can and should be explored in redesigning educational programs as well as in theory and research on urban education. Decentralization, community control, performance contracting, voucher plans, and other topics could be fruitfully examined at length in terms of the concept of bureaucracy. The focus in this issue, however, is on the rebuilding of the urban school as an institution, and these related topics are introduced only incidentally as they bear on the focus. It is apparent that new ways of looking at and organizing bureaucracies are needed if urban schools are to grapple successfully with the myriad problems that beset them on all fronts. Several such perspectives selected from among the many that might be included in a longer article are reviewed in the next section.[2]

New Perspectives on Bureaucracy

One useful way to highlight differences between newer and more traditional approaches to bureaucratic organization is to distinguish, as Berton H. Kaplan does, between rational, efficiency-oriented bureaucracy and "development" bureaucracy.[3] The latter, according to Kaplan, is an organization whose major concern is with development, as contrasted with an overbearing emphasis on efficiency. This does not mean, of course, that development bureaucracies are unconcerned with efficiency; obviously, the question of utilizing resources ecomonically cannot simply be ignored. What the term does suggest is that some organizations have as their predominant goal the "management of change—that is, the direction of efforts to alter the basic pattern(s) of a way of life"—rather than a more direct focus on the attainment of predetermined output goals.[4]

Organizations that must put emphasis on development before it is possible to make much progress in satisfying efficiency criteria include those in which paramount importance is attached to socialization of clients into new roles. Socialization goals are overriding when the organization is not in a position to achieve its output goals because it is not able to work effectively with its clients. Examples cited by Kaplan include organizations functioning in environments in which social disorganization and disintegration are widespread and organizations heavily constrained by "enduring child-rearing frustrations, motivational problems, learning problems, problem-solving inadequacies, etc."[5] Urban schools, it should be evident, are (or should be) particularly good examples of development bureaucracies inasmuch as their first imperatives are to socialize students in productive learning roles and to reduce incongruence between client and institutional expectations. It is easy to conclude that this in turn requires a more "client-centered" approach, but to leave the matter at that is harmful, because doing so allows the naive to conclude that problems can be solved simply by being humane to clients (e.g., love and respect the child and give him something called "freedom"). The thesis of this article and indeed of this issue of the *KAPPAN*, however is that the real challenge is to reorganize and reform existing organizations so that institutional structures and processes achieve the goal without relying solely on the good intentions of professionals or other staff personnel.

Orion F. White has spelled out some of the implications of this position for administrative structures within bureaucratic organizations. He argues cogently that a client-centered orientation is most likely to be achieved and maintained by allocating authority to roles in accordance with "functional necessity." Authority relations, in this type of organization, are "lateral instead of vertical," and staff relations are specifically organized in accordance with the principle of "non-dominance." Structurally, such an organization "operates with overlapping administrative roles, in that one person may be over another in one functional area but under him in another area."[6] The primary purpose of these adjustments is to make it less likely that traditional efficiency criteria and rigid hierarchies will obscure the "helping relation" and lead to segmental treatment of the client.[7]

Eugene Litwak and Henry J. Meyer have carried this type of analysis still further in an important theoretical paper titled "A Balance Theory of Coordination Between Bureaucratic Organizations and Community Primary Groups."[8] Litwak and Meyer begin by rejecting the notion that bureaucracies (such as the school) and primary groups (such as the family) should be viewed as "alternative means for the achievement of most goals." They admit that bureaucracies and primary groups (such as the family) should be viewed as "alternative means for the achievement of most goals." They admit that bureaucracies and primary groups have "unique social functions" and characteristics that make them "incompatible" and even "antithetical" in some respects, but they also believe that the two kinds of social units must perform complementary functions if there is to be "optimal" social control and goal achievement. Hence they conclude that there should be "close communication between these two forms of organizations" and that one of the major tasks of organization theory is to select the most suitable "coordinating mechanisms" to achieve proper balance.[9]

Although the argument in Litwak and Meyer's paper is subtly developed at much greater length, for the purposes of this essay it is sufficient to emphasize implications pertinent to the topic of rebuilding urban schools. Of special interest are their conclusions concerning 1) organizations "confronted with deviant families or neighborhood groups" and hence in need of "some mechanism of coordination that permits communication over social distance"; and 2) organizations "confronted by both distant and supporting primary groups" and hence in need "of a range of coordinating mechanisms."[10] The inner-city elementary school with a particularly alienated constituency probably comes closest in education to fitting the first situation; the comprehensive urban high school is a good example of the second.

In the first situation, Litwak and Meyer conclude, emphasis should be placed on 1) working with local opinion leaders in the client community; 2) delegating functions as much as possible to associated groups with presumably better access to primary units among clients; 3) a "settlement-house" approach that locates physical facilities and services in the client community and makes change agents available to work there; and 4) a "detached-expert" approach that gives professionals in the organization "relative autonomy" to participate directly in the affairs of external primary groups.[11]

In the second situation, emphasis should be placed on selecting a situationally appropriate mixture of the coordinating mechanisms described above plus traditional rational-bureaucratic coordinating mechanisms such as 1) sponsorship of voluntary associations bringing organization personnel and clients together in a formal setting (e.g., PTAs); 2) utilization as a "common messenger" of an individual who is regularly a member of both the organization and the primary group (e.g., the child); 3) utilization of formal authority as a "basis for communicating with external primary groups"; and 4) employment of mass communications media as a means to influence primary groups.[12]

The final point in Litwak and Meyer's paper is one it would pay us well to keep in mind in education. After noting that some organizations have a better base than others for linking to the community, the authors point out that "*if an organization is not self-conscious about its coordinating mechanisms*" (italics added), then it will tend to communicate with primary groups using the common messenger and the opinion leader mechanisms, because these mechanisms develop informally and require little or no initiative from the organization.[13] This is precisely, of course, what has happened in education: Most public schools have relied on the child and on a few visible, presumably influential, persons in the community for communications with constituent primary groups. That abdicating responsibility in this way has led to the bankruptcy of many urban schools is hardly open to question.

Comments and Conclusions

The material in the first section of this article suggests that efforts to reform urban schools should: 1) aim to rebuild them as less complex institutions and/or equip clients and staff with better ways to handle institutional complexity; 2) reduce social and psychological distance between clients and the institution, particularly by increasing student and parent participation in decision making; and 3) provide specifically for additional information feedback in every aspect of the operation of the school.

The material on concepts of bureaucracy suggests that 1) urban schools should place major emphasis on gaining the cooperation of their clients rather than first using traditional efficiency criteria to allocate institutional roles and assess institutional processes; 2) this type of client-centered, service orientation is most likely to be achieved and maintained when authority is allocated laterally rather than hierarchically and organizational structures are experimental and fluid rather than fixed and permanent; and 3) urban educators should self-consciously select a situation-specific mixture of outreach-type as well as traditional communications mechanisms to coordinate the work of the school and the external primary groups whose cooperation is required to achieve the goals of education.

Some related points that should be made concerning the rebuilding of urban schools in general and inner-city schools in particular are:

1. Making authority relations in a school or school district less "vertical" in order to place certain necessary decision-making powers and responsibilities in the hands of staff members who work directly with clients has little to do explicitly with "democratic" administration (whatever that is). As Fiedler has shown in an important but frequently ignored study on leadership, situations that are highly problematic for an organization create a need for administrators who supply relatively "structured" leadership.[14] To put it mildly, urban schools today are highly problematic institutions.

2. For this reason, outstanding administrative leadership is by far the most important variable necessary for successful reform in urban schools. Successful inner-city schools invariably have particularly outstanding building administrators who absolutely refuse to engage in bureaucratic games of any sort.[15]

3. The critical importance of the building principal is closely linked to the cherished dream of individualization of instruction. On the one hand it is an obvious truth that instruction for disadvantaged students cannot possibly be successful without individualized diagnosis and prescription of students' strengths and weaknesses. On the other hand it is also a truism that individualized instruction has seldom been achieved in schools anywhere in the United States. One thing that outstanding inner-city administrators have in common is that they organize their schools so that methods and materials actually are utilized to individualize instruction and then insist that nothing—but *nothing*—will be allowed to prevent achievement of this goal. Visitors to their schools can expect to hear of such incidents as the following two reports from unusually successful schools:

> "My teachers were supposed to be attending a districtwide workshop that summer, but we found they could not achieve anything in these large groups, so I pulled them out and brought them back to the school to work in small groups on planning for the next year."

> "Our excellent new programmed reading materials were not working very well, mainly because teachers and aides had no space to work together on planning or to meet with students individually or in small groups. So the principal increased class size—the central office never found out—in order to free space for this purpose."

4. Much of the principal's leadership in establishing lateral authority relations can be discussed in terms of what he does to provide each party (i.e., teachers, students, parents) with a firm power base in school decision making. Once each group is in a position to stand up and say, "I know from direct experience that the way we are doing things is not working and I insist it be changed," the orientation in the school becomes one of solving problems rather than keeping the lid on or sweeping them under the rug. In a successful inner-city school, in other words, "End the nonsense" is the operating theme not just of the principal but of every interest group.

5. Urban schools should be built up of (or broken down into) small, relatively autonomous operating units. It is not important whether functional units are referred to as "houses," "grade levels," "families," "mini-branches," or some other term, as long as authority and responsibility are located primarily at the unit level and units are supplied with the resources and supporting services necessary to carry out their tasks.

6. The crucial factor in making use of promising practices from another school is to make sure that the organizational structure of the receiving institution is designed to implement the innovation effectively. For example, the receiving structure must be modified to insure continuous feedback across hierarchical levels, to minimize psychological distance between staff and clients, and to maintain a client-centered service orientation. Otherwise, promising practices borrowed either eclectically or as a total package from outside sources are not going to make very much difference.

7. Urban schools are not going to be rebuilt as effective institutions unless we first sweep the deck of existing organizational structures and practices that constitute fundamental obstacles to the attainment of educational goals. As Morris Janowitz points out in the following article, specialists and technologists have a vital and indispensable part to play in reforming urban education, but piling more specialists and new technologies on top of an already overloaded institutional structure will compound rather than alleviate our problems. What all this boils down to is the old rule of first things first—and the first priority in urban education is to introduce new concepts of organization and bureaucracy that emphasize the creation of authentic institutional communities, so that specialization and technique are not plugged into essentially dysfunctional vessels.

Emphasis in most of the following articles is placed on the difficult practical problems encountered in building or rebuilding an institution and on the crucial decisions made in solving them. In describing specific problems involved in implementing effective programs in urban schools, the authors show how the concepts reviewed in this article are being applied in different ways in different schools. I hope this combination of conceptual analysis and practical examples will prove useful for teachers and administrators impatient to rebuild their own schools.

1. Donald J. Willower, "Educational Change and Functional Equivalents," *Education and Urban Society*, August, 1970, p. 392; see also Alan Schick, "The Cybernetic State," *Trans-Action*, February, 1970, pp. 15-26.

2. Examples of other perspectives that it was not possible to include in this article include Warren Bennis's writing on post-bureaucratic, temporary organization and Kenneth Parsons's analysis of needs-cycling organizations.

3. Berton H. Kaplan, "Notes on a Non-Weberian Model of Bureaucracy: The Case of Development Bureaucracy," *Administrative Science Quarterly*, December 1968, pp. 471-83.

4. *Ibid.*, p. 472.

5. *Ibid.*, p. 482.

6. Orion F. White, Jr., "The Dialectical Organization: An Alternative to Bureaucracy," *Public Administration Review*, January-February 1969, p. 38.

7. *Ibid.*, pp. 36-37.

8. Eugene Litwak and Henry J. Meyer, "A Balance Theory of Coordination Between Bureaucratic Organizations and Community Primary Groups," *Administrative Science Quarterly*, June 1966, pp. 31-58.

9. *Ibid.*, pp. 36, 58. In effect, Litwak and Meyer reject the arguments of social analysts such as Everett Riemer and Ivan Illich who suggest that noncognitive goals should have little place in the schools, since they are more effectively achieved in primary group settings (*Alternatives in Education, 1968-69*. Cuernavaca, Mexico: Central Intercultural Documentacion, 1970) and of psychologists like J. M. Stephens (*The Process of Schooling*. New York: Holt, Rinehart and Winston, 1967) who believe that schooling in modern educational bureaucracies is too far removed from real life to be effective in interesting more than a minority of the young in abstract academic studies. Although there is no space in this essay to weigh all the arguments for and against these points of view, it at least can be said that unless existing educational bureaucracies are significantly transformed, and unless this rebuilding includes new mechanisms for coordination and communication with primary groups in the urban community, observers such as Riemer, Illich, and Stephens probably will be proved right by default.

10. *Ibid.*, pp. 51, 52.

11. *Ibid.*, pp. 39, 42, 52, 53.

12. *Ibid.*, pp. 40, 41, 50, 53.

13. *Ibid.*, pp. 57.

14. Fred A. Fiedler, "A Contingency Model of Leadership Effectiveness," in L. Berkowitz, ed., *Advances in Experimental Social Psychology*, vol. 1 (New York: Academic Press, 1964).

15. Russell C. Doll, *Variations Among Inner City Elementary Schools* (Kansas City, Mo.: Center for the Study of Metropolitan Problems in Education, 1969).

IX
Discipline

Introduction

As every well-informed educator knows by now, the public annually tells us, via the Gallup polls published in the KAPPAN, that discipline is the most serious public school problem. Only once in the first 12 polls was another problem given first rank. That was in 1971, when "how to pay for the schools" topped the list. (Interestingly enough, discipline ranks a poor second to school financing [33.2% vs. 62.2%] among members of Phi Delta Kappa polled with the same question in 1980).

I have chosen Edward A. Wynne's "Behind the Discipline Problem: Youth Suicide as a Measure of Alienation" (January 1978) from a score of candidates to head this section. It was an anchor piece in a special KAPPAN titled "The Problems of Discipline and Violence in American Education."

More than most authors, Wynne gets behind the symptoms and searches for causes of the behavior that school authorities consider unacceptable. Thus he would suggest that we worry more about the sources of John Hinckley's alienation than about ways of punishing him.° Wynne's recommendations consider the schools as a system; we won't get far, he believes, by limiting our attention to classroom gimmicks and the cookbook approach to discipline problems.

A social psychologist with training in law, Wynne brings a remarkable dedication as well as an unusual background to his subject. He is in fact so intensely concerned with elements in modern society that account for discipline problems in the young that he has founded a journal, Character, to pursue the inquiry begun in his KAPPAN article. Now three years old, Character appears to have won an audience. It continues to attract foundation support. Wynne edits and publishes the journal with the help of his wife, while serving as professor of education in policy studies at the University of Illinois, Chicago Circle.

Another Wynne article, "Looking at Good Schools," was chosen for publication in the January 1981 Diamond Jubilee KAPPAN.

The other article in this section discusses appropriate responses to student misbehavior in an era when teacher authority is severely circumscribed. The

---

°Aside from the lesser job specifications, why do we now have so many young Americans who are more ambitious to assassinate a President than to be one? If we get an answer to that question, and understand it, perhaps we will have a key to curriculum reform.

author, Thomas R. McDaniel, is director of the M.Ed. program at Converse College in Spartanburg, South Carolina, and head of its Division of Education. Just turned 40, he has already contributed to some 25 educational journals and has given dozens of workshops on such topics as school discipline and school law. (Another McDaniel article for the KAPPAN, "The Teacher's Ten Commandments," was a strong candidate for this anthology, but, because it deals with recent changes in law, it may soon become dated.)

Problems with classroom control are the most frequent cause of failure among fledgling teachers. Can teacher preparatory courses based upon works like those of Wynne and McDaniel help them significantly? This remains an open question. But it is quite possible that "discipline" will someday become a respectable academic discipline.

—SME

Behind the Discipline Problem:
Youth Suicide as a Measure of Alienation
by Edward A. Wynne

*In this profoundly disturbing article, Mr. Wynne sets himself
four tasks: 1) to show how Americans are failing to integrate the
individual and his social institutions, 2) to analyze the dis-integrating effects of modern formal education, 3) to discuss the
consequences of youth alienation, and 4) to suggest what correc-
tives educators may apply.*

There is a widespread public perception that "discipline" is the major problem facing modern education. It has been so listed in eight of the nine annual
Gallup Polls of public attitudes toward the schools taken between 1969 and
1977. However, the professional literature on education does not fairly reflect
this fact. Discipline is not ignored as a topic, but it is apparently not a matter
of high concern.

Ironically, there is a great deal of scientific data that amply support the
public's view of the primacy of discipline—or lack of it—as a problem. True,
these data do not deal directly with trends in student conduct while in school.
They do, however, reveal a number of long-range trends toward increasing
disorder, anger, and despair among American adolescents. Essentially, these
data reveal certain adolescent conduct and attitudes that can be characterized as symptomatic of increasing youth alienation. While not all of this alienation is reflected in acts of "indiscipline," it is understandable that laypersons
should use the nontechnical term "discipline" to articulate their sense that
something is profoundly wrong with many children and adolescents.

The data not only portray increased alienation, they also raise important
questions about the continuing vitality of American society. After all, that
vitality ultimately depends upon the ability of adult-operated institutions
such as schools to rear children and adolescents to become effective and competent adults. The data suggest that the proportion of youths maturing into
such competence may be steadily declining.

This article will present relevant data about contemporary youth alienation and offer an interpretation and prescription. Unfortunately, data
showing trends cannot always be current. The basic facts are collected
through elaborate counting systems, and there is necessarily a time lag in reporting and publication. Still, in view of the long-term, incremental patterns
disclosed, one would have to be extremely optimistic to suppose that up-to-
date data would reveal dramatic reversals.

Data About Youth Conduct

Between 1950 and 1975 the annual suicide rate of white youths between
the ages of 15 and 19 increased 171%, from 2.8 deaths for each 100,000 to 7.6.[1]
No other age group had so high a rate of increase. During these same years the
overall white suicide rate increased by only 18%. (See Figure 1.) Obviously,
the 15-to-19 suicide rates are not yet as high as the rates for older groups. In
the past, younger persons, embedded in family life, have always had lower
suicide rates than older persons. However, in our era we are confronting the

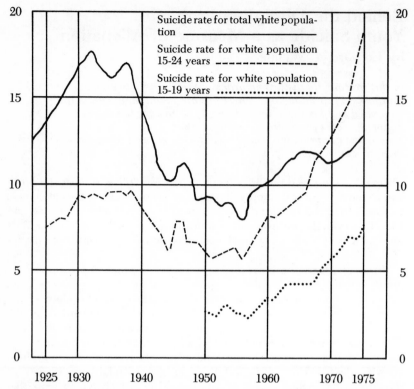

In order to portray long-range trends, the above chart displays national
suicide rates for three age groups: 1) the total white population, 2) white
males aged 15 to 24, and 3) white males aged 15 to 19. Suicide data are not
conveniently available for the 15 to 19 age group before 1950, hence the rate
for that group has only been graphed for 20 years. Note that increases in rates
for the 15 to 19 age group have been an important element in the dramatic
upward shift in the long-term pattern of suicide rates for the 15 to 24 age
group.

Fig. 1. Suicide rate for selected groups—U.S., 1925-75
(Rates are for 100,000 members of population in specified age groups)
Sources: Department of Health, Education, and Welfare; Public Health Service; National Center for Health Statistics

phenomenon of a somewhat stabilized adult rate, while the youth rate continues to climb. And the fastest rate of climb is among the youngest group,
those age 15 to 19. As the graph demonstrates, the increase in adolescent
suicides was relatively steady and incremental. The gradualness of the increase suggests that it was not directly related to the major political and social
upheavals of the period. For instance, the rate of climb during the allegedly
quiescent late 1950s was about the same as the rate of climb during the turbulent late 1960s.

Suicide statistics are a reliable measure of comparative changes in the suicide rate. The tabulations reflect the judgments of thousands of local health officers and coroners as to cause of death. Sometimes these individual judgments are incorrect. However, there is no reason to believe that the basic random pattern of "incorrectness" that prevailed years ago is not still in operation today.

The absolute number of youths involved in the increase is, fortunately, comparatively small. We have perhaps 3,000 to 4,000 reported suicides a year among whites aged 15 to 19. This is a minute fraction of our youth population. But the "problem" has immense symbolic and indicative significance. For each identified adolescent suicide, we undoubtedly have other suicides not identified as such, attempted suicides that are not tabulated, and youths who suffer from serious anxiety or depression but do not attempt suicide. Hence the 171% increase represents a concurrent 171% increase in general depression among our young people. This increase has occurred at a time when naive observers would infer that American youths, especially those from white families, "never had it so good."

There have also been increases in the rate of death by homicide among white males aged 15 to 19. In 1959 the rate was 2.3 such deaths per 100,000 members of the group. That rate steadily increased, so that by 1969 it was 4.9; by 1975 it was 8.2.[2] This represents a greater than 200% increase over 26 years. During the same period no other age group had a comparable increase in its homicide rate. The highest previous homicide rate for white males aged 15 to 19 during the twentieth century was 5.2 in 1919. (Incidentally, the rate for black males in the same age group started from a much higher base, and it also has been rising; but between 1969 and 1975 the black rate began to decline. In 1975 it was 47.8. In general, the black suicide rate is lower than the white rate.)

Like the suicide rate, the homicide death rate probably measures other events, albeit indirectly—e.g., woundings, beatings, threats, and the stimulation of profound fear. There is every reason to believe that such increased crimes against the young have generally been committed by their peers, i.e., other white male adolescents.

There is evidence of increased drug use by the young. In 1971, 30% of all college students surveyed in a national sample reported having used marijuana within 30 days of the survey; in 1970, 28% of a similar sample reported such use. And this use and experimentation sometimes include other, more powerful drugs. Seven percent of the respondents in the 1971 sample reported having used cocaine.[3] Again, two successive surveys of national samples of "youths" (no ages were given in the report) conducted in 1972 and 1974 asked respondents about their use of five illegal drugs. The 1974 respondents reported higher levels of usage for all five drugs than did the 1972 respondents.[4] A 1975 report of the National Institute on Drug Abuse also concluded that "there is no indication of any recent decline in the annual prevalence of any drug, with the possible exception of psychedelics."[5]

We do not have statistics about the national level of youth drug use before the late 1960s. Thus the issue of long-term trends in drug use is complicated. However, we do have some trend statistics from the late 1960s onward. The most thorough statistics cover San Mateo County (California) students for every year from 1968 to 1976.[6] San Mateo is an affluent suburban county. It is recognized as having relatively intense drug use and is, therefore, not typical.

TABLE 1
PERCENTAGE OF MARIJUANA USE AMONG MALE SAN MATEO COUNTY,
CALIFORNIA, HIGH SCHOOL STUDENTS FOR THE PERIOD 1968 TO 1976

	One or more uses in past year		Ten or more uses in past year		Fifty or more uses in past year	
Year	Grade 9	Grade 12	Grade 9	Grade 12	Grade 9	Grade 12
1968	27	45	14	26	na	na
1969	35	50	20	34	na	na
1970	34	51	20	34	11	22
1971	44	59	26	43	17	32
1972	44	61	27	45	16	32
1973	51	61	32	45	20	32
1974	49	62	30	47	20	34
1975	49	64	30	45	20	31
1976	48	61	27	42	17	30

Source: San Mateo County, Department of Public Health and Welfare, *Summary Report, 1976, Surveys of Student Drug Use* (San Mateo, Calif.: Department of Public Health, 1976).

Still, there is evidence that trends originating in California tend to spread. For example, the 1968 San Mateo levels represent current rates of adolescent marijuana use in many communities. The statistics thus provide a potential forecasting indicator. The San Mateo statistics on marijuana use among certain high school grades are set out in Table 1.

These statistics reveal a stabilization of use at a comparatively high level of intensity. Other tabulated San Mateo data reveal steady increases in student use of a variety of drugs. Nationally, it is also significant to recall that arrests of males under age 18 for narcotics law violations increased 1,288% between 1960 and 1972.[7]

There are also statistics on increased use of alcohol by youths. The San Mateo survey reported that the percentage of seventh-grade boys who had begun drinking during the previous year increased from 52% in 1969 to 72% in 1973. This increase is consistent with equivalent increases reported in other surveys in Duval County, Florida, and Toronto, Ontario. And this adolescent drinking is not simply tasting. In 1974, 23% of a national sample of youths between the ages of 13 and 18 reported being drunk four or more times during the past year.[8]

The increase in drug and alcohol use is obvious evidence of the growing drive for speedy gratification among the young—and of an effort to avoid or escape the environment around them. Incidentally, since much of that environment consists of their peers, the statistics might also imply that some adolescents are finding each other's company less and less pleasant without the support of drugs or alcohol.

The use of cigarettes has also increased among the young. Typical data disclose that between 1969 and 1975, in a national sample of females aged 13 to 17, the proportion of respondents who smoked a pack or more of cigarettes a day rose from 10% to 39%.[9]

Changes in the area of youth sexual relations have been significant. Between 1950 and 1975 the estimated number of illegitimate births for unmarried white females, aged 15 to 19, went from 5.1 per 1,000 to 12.1.[10] Technically, illegitimacy is measured by an entry on a birth certificate—either "married, and to whom" or "unmarried." For many years nearly all births in America have been registered, and the entry "married" goes on the certificate only if the particular married male is designated. Thus the "estimated" statistical shift is an accurate indication that increasing proportions of females are having babies without being married; the statistics represent a change in the conduct of successive groups of young males and females.

This increase in illegitimacy has occurred during a period characterized by increasing availability of contraceptives, abortion, and sexual information. Presumably, the increase means that young males are more willing to get females pregnant, that young females are more willing to risk (and accept) pregnancy, and that both females and males feel less responsibility for burdening infants with the handicaps of being born into a one-parent family consisting of a young and vulnerable mother.

Another pertinent sex-related change has been the spread of venereal disease among the young. Between 1956 and 1974, reported cases of gonorrhea (per 100,000 members of the 15 to 19 age group) rose more than 200%, while syphilis increased 100%.[11] These increases were associated with an increased availability of medicines, treatment centers, and appropriate preventive information. Obviously, the increases reflect a growth of casual (or promiscuous) sexual relations and in irresponsible attitudes among sex partners, who feel little concern for "protecting" one another.

Some national trend statistics are available on delinquency. Between 1957 and 1974 the number of delinquency cases per 1,000 persons aged 10 to 17 disposed of by American juvenile courts rose from 19.1 to 37.5.[12] Throughout the period, the proportion of status offenses (e.g., running away and other noncriminal conduct) to criminal acts (e.g., shoplifting, robbery) added together to calculate total delinquency remained relatively constant. Drug cases were a significant but not central element in the increase. There are also statistics for increased antisocial conduct in schools. One survey reported that, in the national sample of schools studied, assaults on teachers increased 85% between 1970 and 1973. During the same period the number of weapons confiscated from students by authorities in the schools surveyed rose by 54%.[13]

We should also consider the student unrest, building takeovers, and other youth disorders of the late 1960s and early 1970s. Occasional student disorder has always been a fact of American history, but the most recent wave involved a higher proportion of youth and took more destructive forms. For example, during 1969 and 1970 more than 8,000 bomb threats, attempted bombings, and bombings were attributed to student unrest.[14] In 1970 nine of the top 16 FBI most-wanted persons were youth activists, their crimes including murder, bank robbery, and bombing.[15] I shall discuss the significance of this particular form of disorder in more detail later.

I have presented data on a variety of self-destructive and other-destructive acts committed by adolescents from all races and social classes. In any particular year one measure may go up and another down. But if we were able to develop any system of accumulating and weighing these measures, such a system would, I believe, reveal a steady increase in these acts of alienation. And wherever comparable statistics are available, the data reveal that the rate of increase in youth alienation is greater than the rate for adults. Obviously, we must look at these acts cumulatively rather than discretely. We

TABLE 2
HAVERFORD COLLEGE, SAMPLE MMPI ITEMS FOR THE
CLASSES OF 1948 THROUGH 1968

Item	*Percent "Yes"*							
	1948-49	*1952*	*1956*	*1960*	*1961*	*1965*	*1967*	*1968*
When I was a child I didn't care to be a member of a crowd or gang..........	33	35	35	38	49	58	19	47
I could be happy living all alone in a cabin in the woods or mountains	23	28	34	38	33	35	42	45
I am a good mixer.........	77	49	48	63	60	58	38	43
I like to go to parties and other affairs where there is lots of loud fun	65	56	55	53	44	40	38	40
At parties I am more likely to sit by myself than to join in with the crowd	23	35	40	27	44	38	47	50
My worries seem to disappear when I get into a crowd of lively friends	71	69	73	68	58	65	56	55
If I were in trouble with several friends who were equally to blame, I would rather take the whole blame than to give them away...	63	56	50	57	47	43	33	45
When a man is with a woman he is usually thinking about things related to her sex ...	29	37	15	27	35	28	36	43
I enjoy reading love stories	55	49	35	25	44	30	18	25
I like dramatics	80	74	73	75	60	73	67	65
I would like to be a singer .	51	47	37	36	33	38	31	23

shouldn't make alcohol the issue one year, suicide the next, and so on. A segmented approach robs us of the chance to recognize the more general and shocking totality: Our children and adolescents are increasingly engaged in killing, hurting, and abusing themselves and others.

Statistics on Changes in Attitudes

Not surprisingly, changes in youth conduct have been accompanied by changes in adolescent attitudes. Some trend data are available.[16] Between 1948 and 1968 successive freshman classes at Haverford College in Philadelphia took the Minnesota Multiphasic Inventory (MMPI), a short-answer test that measures attitudes. Table 2 reports a sample of statistics derived from the student answers. The numbers listed for each item represent the proportion of students who answered "yes." Clearly, these data are not up to date, but they do help us to understand shifts in youth attitudes over a considerable part of the last quarter century and constitute the most complete longitudinal study available. When we consider more recent data later, a consistent relationship between the changes that occurred among the Haverford students and those revealed in current polls will become apparent. Finally, if we are concerned with interpreting the deeper meaning of the campus unrest of the Vietnam war period, the Haverford students represent a classic group of student militants—articulate, upper-middle-class, status-conscious. It is easy to recognize an overall attitudinal trend in their shifting answers. Essentially, the successive classes of students became less sympathetic to cooperative and group activities; more and more, they evinced attitudes consonant with withdrawal from contact or cooperation with others.

This increase in withdrawn attitudes among students was coupled with an apparent simultaneous increase in their self-centeredness. Between 1948 and 1968 the proportion of Haverford students who thought they could work great benefit to the world if given a chance rose from 40% to 66%, while the proportion of these 17-year-olds who thought they knew more than experts rose from 20% to 38%. It is not clear how these increasingly withdrawn and introverted students could render such benefit without human interaction or acquire the experiences incident to becoming so knowledgeable.

Other statistics about youth attitudinal trends show that the Haverford patterns are representative of trends displayed by successive cohorts of late adolescents on other college campuses. Attitudinal tests were administered to students at Dartmouth College in 1952 and 1968 and at the University of Michigan in 1952 and 1969.[17] Several similar questions were asked of all students queried at both colleges. For example, they were asked whether "human nature is fundamentally more cooperative." Agreement declined from 66% and 70%, at Dartmouth and Michigan respectively, to 51% and 55%. Another question asked whether "most of what I am learning in college is very worthwhile." Agreement declined from 67% and 74% respectively to 58% and 57%. Again, these students were asked to identify the private and public institutions (e.g., school, church, family) to which they felt related. The number and intensity of summed identifications declined from 296 and 259, respectively, to 269 and 206. In other words, successive groups of students have felt less and less relationship to the world. They have become increasingly *alien*-ated.

We also have the 1969 and 1973 Yankelovich youth surveys.[18] Unfortunately, they do not replicate questions asked in the Haverford, Michigan, and Dartmouth studies, nor do they cover precisely equivalent groups of adolescents. Still, I contend that they show a continuation of the trends toward egotism and withdrawal. Among the college students surveyed in Yankelovich's national samples, the importance of "privacy" as a value increased from 61% in 1969 to 71% in 1973. At the same time, the respective importance of "religion" and "patriotism," two values that stress the individual's obligation to extrapersonal concerns, declined from 38% and 35% to 28% and 19%. The two surveys also showed a continuing pattern of gradual dissemination and acceptance of the views of college youths among noncollege youths. In general, the views disclosed in the surveys demonstrate an enlargement of expectations about the rights of students and citizens and a lessening of expectations about the responsibilities of these same persons.

It is true that some of the period covered by the Yankelovich surveys encompassed the Watergate episode. Readers may deduce that this sorry national experience was an essential cause of the trend toward withdrawal. This interpretation is significant, because if Watergate was the "cause," and if Watergate was a transitory phenomenon, then we might expect youth attitudes to return to more healthy earlier patterns. However, the more long-range attitude trend statistics already presented suggest that the trend toward withdrawal long antedated Watergate. For example, between 1949 and 1952 the first shifts toward withdrawal were already appearing in the Haverford statistics. And over the next 20 years, as more and more Americans became prosperous, as poverty declined, as the status of blacks generally improved, and as large-scale international war was avoided, those students (plus those at Michigan and Dartmouth) became increasingly alienated.

The preceding data about trends toward increasingly individualistic and withdrawn youth attitudes are also supported by the diverse studies summarized by Dean Hogue in an analysis of the shifting values of college students over the past 50 years. Obviously, many of the measures used by Hogue to describe such trends are relatively imprecise. Still, the cumulative effect of the variety of data he has collected is highly persuasive.[19]

Increasingly, withdrawn attitudes have appeared among students during an era when the adult society has been dedicating increasing proportions of its economic resources to help the young. Thus, between 1950 and 1972 per-pupil daily expenditures in public schools increased by 170%, measured in constant dollars (to allow for inflation), while the national average pupil/teacher ratio (combining both elementary and high schools) declined from 25:1 to 21:1. It would seem that students were given more than ever before but liked their status—and, implicitly, the givers—less.

There are also significant cross-cultural statistics about the attitudes of American children. The statistics were developed in a contemporary international study of youth interaction patterns in six cultures.[20] Five of the cultures represented underdeveloped or primitive environments. The sixth group of students was composed of children in a New England community. A common rating scale was used by observers in all locations to evaluate youth conduct on the dimension of altruism versus egotism. In all, 134 children between ages 3 and 6 and between ages 7 and 11 were observed in the study. Approximately 9,500 interacts were indentified. When the median level of altruistic conduct was treated as 50%, the American children, with a level of 8%, scored as the most egotistic. The next lowest group was a tribe in India, with a level of 25%. The number of children involved was small. Still, the dramatically high level of egotism among the American children, compared with that of children in non-Western cultures, suggests that the data may justify comparative generalizations about the overall level of egotistic conduct among American youths or youths from industrial societies.

What the Changes Mean

The preceding statistics invite analysis. But the analysis must be put in an appropriate framework. The statistics do not tell how any particular youth will act, since the proportions of youths afflicted with dramatic forms of character deterioration—suicide, violent crimes, alcoholism—are fortunately small. In general, the statistics are not decomposed into socioeconomic classes, although some of the changes (e.g., student unrest, drug use, evidence of withdrawn attitudes) are clearly common among upper-middle-class youths. Despite the rather dramatic nature of some of the conduct trends disclosed, relatively little longitudinal research is available concerning the socioeconomic status of the youths involved in certain acts (e.g., suicide) 10 and 20 years ago in comparison with the status of the youths involved at present. Still, the statistics that are available provide an important, albeit imperfect, tool for forecasting general trends affecting youths and younger adults and for interpreting significant elements of youth conduct.

The rising suicide rate, in particular, while it directly involves a small number of youths, may provide a vital clue to the possible causes of the spread of alienation. In the late nineteenth century the French sociologist Émile Durkheim identified that rate as an important index of social cohesion and vitality.[21] He discovered that in European societies suicide was more prevalent among Protestants than among Catholics, urbanites than rural persons, the affluent than the middle and lower-middle classes, unmarried adults and childless married adults than married adults with children, males than females, and persons in the liberal professions than laborers and tradesmen. In other words, people were shielded from suicidal impulses because of the communal intensity of their religion, the stability of their life patterns, the predictability of their aspirations, the intensity and complexity of their social commitments, the focus of their responsibilities, and the tangibility of their work products. All of these shields were forces that placed human beings in complex but predictable patterns of human relations that moved toward identifiable goals.

Suicide is not so much the outcome of "pressure," but *pressure without social support*. Suicide does not automatically mean that a person has not been loved or cared for. It probably does mean that he was not needed by others in an immediate, tangible fashion. "Needed" should be understood in the sense we imply when we say we need the first-string member of an athletic team, the paper delivery boy, the only secretary in a small office, or the only wage earner in a family. The person needed must be obviously relied upon by others, and his absence should create a disruptive and foreseeable gap. In this light, it is understandable that one of the highest suicide rates is that of middle-aged bachelors and one of the lowest is that of married women with children; yet which of these two groups is subject to the greater pressure? Indeed, the most "pressured" status is that of being left without apparent and immediate responsibilities to help others. It is nice to know we are loved, but essential to know we are needed.

In effect, suicide is a measure of the extent to which a given modern society has succeeded or failed in integrating its citizens and its institutions. If that level of integration is low, suicide will increase, because people will be self-centered and lonely, and they will crumple under the inevitable tensions that life generates. Less self-centered persons will withstand such pressures better, because they will be tied to social systems that provide them with demands as well as help. Thus suicide is a measure of both individual self-centeredness and the efficacy of a society's integrating institutions. Evidently, both our adolescents and the institutions around them are increasingly tending to fail that test.

The other statistics already cited provide additional evidence of the growth of patterns of extreme individualism and even selfishness among adolescents. Thus it is often selfishness that promotes delinquent acts: the injuring or threatening of others or stealing from them. It is selfish to destroy public property made by the money and sweat of others in order to make one's point or to release one's frustration. It is selfish to become pregnant—or to make someone else pregnant—and bring into the world a child who will not receive the emotional support of a stable family.

We should also recognize that much of this adolescent antisocial conduct does not float around in space; rather, it descends onto tangible victims—most of them also adolescents. For instance, adolescents have the highest rates of crime victimization.[22] The victimization rate in 1974 (per 1,000 members for each age group) was 122 for 16- to 19-year-olds, 64 for the total U.S. population. In other words, adolescents were twice as likely to be victimized—usually by other adolescents. The most frequent crimes committed against the young were larceny and rape. And of course most of the despised drug pushers who sell drugs to young users are other adolescents, trying to earn money to buy motorcycles, maintain cars, or dress in expensive or flashy clothes.

The shifts in youth attitudes, as well as conduct, are also consonant with a growth of self-centeredness. For example, a common belief of mature adults is that it is right for a group member—one who is himself equally at fault—to take blame for his fellows. We call such an attitude loyalty or fidelity. In the Haverford questionnaire this measure of potential fidelity declined from 63% to 45%. It may also represent a selfish (or self-centered) attitude when students at public colleges, where 60% to 70% of the costs are borne by taxpayers, describe the world as largely uncooperative. Without the cooperation and sacrifices of others—not only their parents, but all citizens—the students would not be given most of the cost of their education.

But Durkheim was concerned with more than self-centered conduct. He also hypothesized that alienated persons would be excessively inclined toward loneliness, withdrawal, and self-destruction. The use of drugs, alcohol, and cigarettes is often associated with such attitudes. The same sense of inadequacy is implied by the responses to the attitudinal questions that suggest increasing drives toward isolation as reflected in the growing emphasis on privacy as a personal aspiration.

It is clear that the statistics demonstrate the increase of self-centeredness and loneliness among the young. Apparently, people expect more and more from society, but are simultaneously less and less willing to participate. Who, then, will be left to do the giving?

Durkheim's general analysis about dis-integrating social structures has obvious applicability to a variety of modern phenomena that increasingly surround our youths and young adults. These phenomena, while they also affect adults, have special significance for younger persons, since the younger a person is, the higher the proportion of his life has been spent in modern environments. Conversely, the older a person is, the less likely it is that his formative years were spent surrounded by modern phenomena. Table 3 indicates a variety of modern phenomena that affect our young and suggests the specific effects they have on human interaction, the attitudes taught by such effects, and the supporting evidence that discloses the attitudes.

Schools are simply one of the modern phenomena affecting the young. But schools are uniquely focused on the young and have been absorbing increasing proportions of the time of children and youths; and modern formal education at all levels, from preschool to higher education, is also highly dis-integrating. These education systems:

1. Segregate the young from adults except for their immediate family and teachers, a highly restricted class of adults.

TABLE 3
Modern Phenomena (A) That Affect Human Interaction (B), and
Thus Teach Attitudes (C), Plus Statistics That Demonstrate
Visible Patterns of Character Change (D)

A. Phenomena	B. Effects on Human Interaction	C. Attitudes Taught	D. Supporting Statistics
1. Technology	1. Lessening in frequency of intense human interaction	1. Less willingness to accept deferred gratification	1. Increase in youth suicide, illegitimacy, delinquency, drug and alcohol abuse, and self-centered attitudes
2. Urbanization and suburbanization	2. More frequent peripheral contacts	2. Loneliness (and latent anger and resentment)	2. Public perception that discipline is number one education problem
3. Affluence	3. Segregation among age groups	3. Ineptness in talking to strangers and adults	3. Statistics on declining public faith in important institutions, both public and private
4. Decline of youth work roles	4. Healthy adult role models less available for the young	4. Instability and exploitiveness in personal relations	
5. Large institutions	5. Less pressure on the young to learn and display maturity	5. Low levels of loyalty and increased disaffection from society	
6. Mass media	6. Less willingness to demand cooperation or loyalty from the young, or to ask them to display respect for traditions and symbols of the society	6. Fear of serious commitment	
7. Rationality and individualism		7. Greater willingness to hurt others	
8. Important and legitimate institutions and interest groups having a stake in the continuation of current "unhealthy" trends			

2. Segregate the young from contact with youths not in their immediate age range.

3. Segregate the young from contact with youths of different ability levels or from different socioeconomic classes.

4. Segregate the young (after elementary school) from persisting intense contacts with individual members of their age group, since students are frequently shuffled from one group to another to meet the needs of rational scheduling.

5. Deprive the young (in departmentalized schools) of intimate contact with individual faculty members.

6. Place the young in environments where they have few occasions to participate in the dramatic, collective release of strong emotions.

7. Fail to encourage young people to participate in cooperative work efforts.

8. Compel the young to work on projects unrelated to proximate social and economic needs.

9. Deprive the young of the chance to receive relatively immediate, tangible, commonly valued reinforcements (e.g., money, punishments, or pats on the back) in exchange for their efforts.

All of these patterns have continuously intensified over the past 20 to 30 years. School and college attendance has increased and has been prolonged. Schools and school districts have become larger, more bureaucratic, and more controlled by forces outside the purview of local parents, teachers, and administrators. Teaching has become more departmentalized and subject-focused. Extracurricular activities have evidently declined in importance, and school activities have been increasingly segregated from local community life. While pupil/teacher ratios have improved (at great economic cost), modern institutional structures encourage teachers to have brief contacts with many different groups of students; they often restrict students to transitory relationships with large numbers of fellow students. Oftentimes, the responsibility for relating emotionally to students has been taken away from teachers—the adults with whom students spend most of their time—and assigned to "specialists," e.g., counselors and social workers. The present system seems scientifically designed to teach students how not to handle intimacy and, consequently, how to fear and flee from it. But wholesome intimacy is essential to a satisfying life.

Thus far I have presented objective evidence of changes in the nature of 1) adolescent conduct, 2) the attitudes of many adolescents, and 3) our social systems in general and school organization in particular. I have also tied these diverse changes together in a logically related pattern. In the absence of convincing evidence to the contrary, we should assume that distressing youth conduct will continue and increase unless we change the social systems and schools that relate to our young. This analysis of the relationship between contemporary formal education and youth alienation is not essentially novel. A number of reports have presented similar conclusions; the general direction of my recommendations shares some of the emphases of these writings.[23]

Consequences of Youth Alienation

The growing trend toward youth alienation raises the central question of social continuity. Is our society rearing adults who can keep the country going? In the end, the survival of any society depends on its ability to create successive groups of mature adults (i.e., young people who are socialized to adulthood within the society) who are committed to the continuity of its major traditions. Those traditions include the production of goods and services to sustain the young, the aged, and the ill; the maintenance (through taxes and military service) of a necessary defense establishment; the persistence of a decent level of public order; and the commitment of citizens to constructive community and political activities to sustain the country.

The modes of satisfying such traditions are mutable, and they necessarily include adaptations. However, widespread and continuing commitment to the central themes of those traditions is imperative. In other words, a country can "work" only so long as the people in it care about one another as well as about themselves. And that attitude we call caring is both taught and learned. Without such commitments to the whole society, adults of productive age may fail to provide adequately for the emotional and physical needs of the young or the old; society may not maintain an appropriate level of defense; public disorder may pollute social life with fear or make social contacts so unpleasant that we adopt cellular modes of existence; or community and political activities may be abandoned to irresponsible and incompetent leaders/followers and thus be governed by short-sighted egotism. These disastrous outcomes can be the product of excessive personal cynicism, withdrawal, anger, selfishness, and social incompetence among our youths and adults.

As adolescent alienation has increased, so also have signs of alienation among older Americans. The suicide rate, again, invites attention. Essentially, the statistics have always revealed that young males (between 20 and 40) have higher suicide rates than do adolescent males (between 15 and 19). The higher young adult rates are presumably due to factors such as the shifting pressures around young people as they mature, leave their families, and enter into more impersonal environments. In the past 10 to 20 years both the adolescent and the young adult rates have been rising, although the adolescent rate has been rising more rapidly. Presumably, part of the cause for the young adult increase has been the growing proportion of alienated adolescents who carry their increasing fragility forward into adulthood. Another relevant phenomenon is the rising divorce rate, especially among younger married persons. While the steady increase has been a long-term rise, the alienating developments affecting adolescents are also long-term trends. And it is not surprising that increasingly anxious and insecure young adults are less able to make and keep judicious commitments—to make marriages that work. And when those marriages break up, children are often left to be reared by one parent. Thus again the personal actions (and shortcomings) of anxious persons affect the lives of others.

We should also look at collective age-group attitudes as well as the conduct of individuals. Attitudinal surveys of adult Americans have found evidence of increasing dissatisfaction with many important public and social institutions. The most careful analysis of these attitudinal statistics undertaken so far—covering the period 1968 to 1972—concluded that the group between 21 and 24 years of age, the youngest age group consistently surveyed, evinced a comparatively high level of distrust of government.[24] The only two groups with higher levels were age 50 to 59 and over 70. Perhaps one cause of this estrangement is not the inadequacy of government per se but the inappropriate socialization of the young. In other words, governments—as well as marriages—can be in trouble if they are held to unrealistically high standards because certain citizens seek to assuage their emotional anxieties by finding villains.

At this point let us return to the phenomenon of student unrest during the Vietnam war. Many adults see this unrest as simply a dramatic response to wrong actions by the government. I can consider here only certain limitations of this interpretation. Many acts of the students involved breaking the law, destroying property paid for by others, disrupting classes, disturbing bystanders, and even injuring (on certain occasions, killing) innocent parties. Of course the violators often offered subtle and elaborate explanations of their transgressions. But how many criminals fail to offer excuses? Is it surprising that articulate and educated persons offer more elaborate justifications? Perhaps it is equally significant to realize that, in general, the violators—as revealed in the statistics presented above—were lonely, filled with unrealistic confidence in their judgment, and members of an age group displaying an increasing disposition to engage in a wide variety of antisocial and self-destructive acts. Is it not conceivable that, for the great majority of the actors—the mass that made the demonstrations feasible—the unrest was largely an excuse for the release of latent aggression and the dramatic satisfaction of a variety of starved emotional needs? Of course the unrest eventually subsided, but this is not necessarily evidence that the underlying emotional causes have been satisfied; other measures of youth alienation have continued to show increases despite the end of the war. And perhaps, if another vehicle—real or apparent—as "good" as the war appears, we may have further collective outbreaks among the alienated.

Whether our society, at this time, is uniquely immoral or bad is hard to say—although I do not believe so. Governments will always be imperfect, like all human institutions. But I would contend that many people are applying higher standards to judging this country than ever before in its history. The application of such standards inevitably gives the judges many occasions for expressing anger, and it provides noble-sounding excuses for the display of what would ordinarily appear as selfish and unstable conduct. We cannot ignore this line of analysis as offering one explanation for much of the social dissatisfaction of our times.

Schools are not the only cause of this distressing situation, nor can they be expected to provide a full remedy on their own. The attitudes and conduct of their students reflect the forces that pervade their families, homes, and neighborhoods. Still, school managers do have some choices. Schools not only reflect students' attitudes; they can either try to constructively change those that are harmful or they can intensify them. Unfortunately, the structure of the modern school seems to encourage—almost aggressively—many modern phenomena that are particularly harmful to the young. As a result, the school cannot but aggravate the disabilities the students pick up outside its walls.

What can be done by educators to correct this situation? Essentially, we must strive to change the nature of human interaction in our schools. At the same time, we must increasingly remind the larger society of the limited power to effect change possessed by any one institution. We must also remind the society of the changes that are equally imperative in other social institutions besides schools—businesses, government agencies, neighborhoods, courts—if the challenge of adolescent alienation is to be met. Some of these other necessary changes will occur largely in noneducational contexts, but many will require these extra-school institutions to change their own relationships with schools. Meanwhile, in schools, educators must change or modify the school-related phenomena that cause the current forms of interpersonal isolation. Of course not all desired changes can be attempted at once. Most will occur incrementally and take many years to complete. And different patterns of change will be appropriate in different schools and communities. Still, some general directions can be indicated. Table 4 suggests the trend of such changes.

Many of the proposals presented here are not novel. Still, there may be a special value in seeing them presented in an integrated fashion and in a format that suggests their relationship with other in-school and societywide patterns.

TABLE 4
DESIRABLE SCHOOL CHANGES

School Change	*External Evidence of Change*
1. Less reliance on technology	1. Less use of busing, television, computers, national exams, elaborate lab and sports equipment
2. Fewer ties to typical urban and suburban patterns	2. Neighborhood schools; schools that discourage family geographic mobility; schools that encourage more long-term enrollment (K-8 versus K-6)
3. Lower economic costs, especially to general public	3. Students and families doing in-school chores and fund-raising to lower school costs; decline in average number of years of school attendance
4. Less bureaucracy	4. Greater authority given to building principal; teacher salaries and advancement dependent on less formal criteria; more genuine school decentralization; less subject specialization by teachers; more personalized grading of students
5. Smaller educational units	5. Smaller school buildings, or the division of schools in larger buildings into genuine subschools
6. Less rationality and individualism	6. More emphasis on school spirit, character development, honor codes, extracurricular activities, service, good discipline, and patriotism
7. More opposition to the current status quo in education	7. Increasing proportion of public and/or private schools that closely reflect the perspectives of average parents (i.e., the majority that is most worried about discipline as compared to other, better-organized groups tied to the status quo); emphasis on voucher systems, direct fees from parents, and other devices to heighten impact of parent values.

Some readers may wonder if the changes presage a drift toward a narrow parochialism. As an answer, let me mention the communities in which six of the last seven presidents of the U.S. were raised: Independence, Mo.; Abilene, Kans.; Stonewall, Tex.; Whittier, Calif.; Grand Rapids, Mich.; and Plains, Ga. Evidently, being raised in a small-town environment is not so disabling as cosmopolitans might imagine. Indeed, such a background may even be a source of reassurance to adults who eventually end up dealing with modern complexity. This is why "roots" are so often seen as a precious resource. It may be that, after leaving adolescence, young adults can advance their socialization to adulthood by such means as joining the armed services, attending a university, or otherwise being "broadened." But this broadening perhaps occurs best after a firm and localized foundation has been laid.

One may also wonder about the feasibility of creating more localized institutions, given the many powerful trends toward homogeneity and nationwide institutional structures. Obviously, the question cannot be answered easily. Still, child-rearing systems in all societies have always been somewhat isolated from the total social process. For instance, the family does—and must—create some form of wall or shield to constrain the child's experience. In addition, most cultures prohibit children from participating in or witnessing certain activities. Perhaps we can recognize the need to devise other walls—this time around schools. Such walls should cause schools to become less reflective of the impersonality and bigness that often pervade adult institutions. In other words, perhaps we can create schools that provide more supports for the young (while subjecting them to appropriate demands) until they are ready for more difficult challenges.

Of course one cannot predict whether educational changes of this sort will occur on a large scale over the next five to 20 years. It is simple enough to identify the many sources of resistance to them. However, in spite of such resistance, the pressures for the changes are really very powerful. The data that have been presented imply that present institutional situations are a source of steadily increasing social disorder and suffering. We can predict that, eventually, growing proportions of adults will wonder how the most powerful nation in the world can continue to function with an increasingly erratic and unstable electorate. Indeed, in the perspective of history, all too often large nations have crumbled not so much from raw external attack as from failure to rear mature adult citizens and leaders who knew how to work together. After such internal erosion, the society became inviting prey for an external enemy or some power-seeking group of demagogic revolutionaries. But in many ways such decadent societies were already "dead" before their visible downfall. The immediate problem, for America, is that the longer it takes us to get seriously started toward constructive change the longer it will take to reverse the current trends. It is like flying a jet airliner: After the controls have been moved so as to cause the plane to turn, it may still fly several miles before the turn appears to begin. We have built up a great deal of social momentum. How much persisting damage must be done to our social fabric before the effects of improvement begin to show? And how will the effects of that additional damage affect the lives of all of us?

1. U.S. Department of Health, Education, and Welfare, Public Health Service, personal communication, 1977; Public Health Service, *Mortality Trends for Leading Causes of Death, 1950-1969* (Washington, D.C.: U.S. Government Printing Office, 1974).

2. U.S. Department of Health, Education, and Welfare, Public Health Service, personal communication, 1977.

3. U.S. Department of Justice, Law Enforcement Assistance Administration, *Sourcebook on Criminal Justice Statistics, 1973* (Washington, D.C.: U.S. Government Printing Office, 1973).

4. U.S. Department of Justice, Law Enforcement Assistance Administration, *Sourcebook on Criminal Justice Statistics, 1976* (Washington, D.C.: U.S. Government Printing Office, 1977), p. 436.

5. U.S. Department of Health, Education, and Welfare, National Institute on Drug Abuse, *Marijuana and Health, Fifth Annual Report* (Washington, D.C.: National Institute on Drug Abuse, 1975), p. 63.

6. San Mateo County, Department of Public Health and Welfare, *Summary Report, 1976: Surveys of Student Drug Use* (San Mateo, Calif.: Department of Public Health, 1976).

7. U.S. Department of Justice, *Crime in the United States, 1972* (Washington, D.C.: U.S. Government Printing Office, 1972), p. 124.

8. U.S. Department of Health, Education, and Welfare, Public Health Service, *Second Special Report on Alcohol and Health*, preprint ed. (Rockville, Md.: National Institute on Alcohol Abuse and Alcoholism, 1974), p. 128.

9. Daniel Yankelovich, Florence Skelly, and Arthur White, *A Study of Cigarette Smoking*, vol. 1 (New York: Yankelovich, Skelly, and White, 1976), p. 36.

10. U.S. Department of Health, Education, and Welfare, Public Health Service,

Trends in Illegitimacy, U.S., 1940-56, Series 21, No. 15 (Washington, D.C.: U.S. Government Printing Office, 1968), and U.S. Department of Health, Education, and Welfare, National Center for Health Statistics, *Monthly Vital Statistics Report 25*, No. 10, Supplement, December 30, 1976.

11. U.S. Department of Health, Education, and Welfare, Health Services Administration, *Approaches to Adolescent Health Care in the 1970's* (Washington, D.C.: U.S. Government Printing Office, 1975), p. 12.

12. U.S. Department of Justice, *Sourcebook, 1976*, op. cit., p. 572.

13. U.S. Senate, Ninety-fourth Congress, First Session, Preliminary Report, Committee to Investigate Juvenile Delinquency, *Our Nation's Schools* (Washington, D.C.: U.S. Government Printing Office, 1975), p. 4. For similar conclusions about in-school crime in one state, see Task Force on the Resolution of Conflict, *Conflict and Violence in California's High Schools* (Sacramento, Calif.: California State Department of Education, 1973).

14. President's Commission on Campus Unrest, *Report* (Washington, D.C.: U.S. Government Printing Office, 1970), p. 387.

15. "Nine Radicals on Most Wanted List," *New York Times*, November 28, 1970, p. 13.

16. Douglas Heath, *Growing Up in College* (San Francisco: Jossey-Bass, 1968), p. 67.

17. Dean R. Hogue, "College Student Values," *Sociology of Education*, vol. 44, 1970, pp. 170-97.

18. Daniel Yankelovich, Inc., *The Changing Values on Campus* (New York: Pocket Books, 1973), and Daniel Yankelovich, *Changing Youth Values in the 70's* (New York: John D. Rockefeller 3rd Fund, 1974).

19. Dean R. Hogue, *Commitment on Campus: Changes in Religion and Values over Five Decades* (Philadelphia: Westminster Press, 1974).

20. John W. M. Whiting and Beatrice B. Whiting, "Altruistic and Egoistic Behavior in Six Cultures," in Laura Nader and Thomas W. Maretzki, eds., *Cultural Illness and Health* (Washington, D.C.: American Anthropological Association, 1973), p. 56.

21. Émile Durkheim, *Suicide* (New York: Free Press, 1951), p. 165.

22. U.S. Bureau of the Census, *Characteristics of American Youth: 1974*, Series P-23, No. 51 (Washington, D.C.: U.S. Government Printing Office, 1975), p. 29.

23. Urie Bronfenbrenner, "The Origins of Alienation," *Scientific American*, vol. 231, 1974, pp. 51-53; B. Frank Brown, *The Reform of Secondary Education* (New York: McGraw-Hill, 1973); James S. Coleman et al., *Youth: Transition to Adulthood* (Chicago: University of Chicago Press, 1974); National Panel on High School and Adolescent Education, *The Education of Adolescents* (Washington, D.C.: U.S. Government Printing Office, 1976); Frank Newman, *Reform in Higher Education* (Washington, D.C.: U.S. Government Printing Office, 1973); and Edward A. Wynne, *Growing Up Suburban* (Austin, Tex.: University of Texas Press, 1977).

24. Arthur H. Miller, Thad A. Brown, and Alden S. Raine, "Social Conflict and Political Estrangement," paper delivered at the 1973 convention of the Midwest Political Science Association, Chicago, May 3, 1973, pp. 44ff.

Exploring Alternatives to Punishment: The Keys to Effective Discipline
by Thomas R. McDaniel

Theoretical propositions bolstered by practical suggestions that teachers can incorporate into a repertoire compatible with their teaching styles and philosophies

Beginning teachers, and experienced teachers too, are acutely aware of the importance—and the difficulty—of maintaining good classroom discipline. The public, by declaring school discipline as the number one problem in American education in 10 of 11 Gallup polls to date, joins professional educators in the recognition of this major perplexity. Indeed, the most recent Gallup analysis (as reported in the September 1979 *KAPPAN*) points out that "one person in four names discipline as the most important problem" and that "either the public schools have found no way to deal effectively with this problem or the public is not yet aware of measures that are being tried." No wonder Rudolf Dreikurs and Pearl Cassel contend, "Presently our school system is in a dilemma regarding discipline. The controversy over punishment cannot be resolved unless we give teachers alternative effective techniques for dealing with children who misbehave and refuse to learn."[1]

Although the Supreme Court recently refused to agree that corporal punishment is a violation of the Constitution's Eighth Amendment prohibition of "cruel and unusual punishment,"[2] nearly all the extant research suggests that corporal punishment—indeed, any form of punishment—is unhelpful at best and at worst is absolutely counterproductive to good discipline. A panel of the American Psychological Association (APA) in 1972 asserted that "physical violence imprinted at an early age and the modeling of violent behavior by punishing adults induces habitual violence in children."[3] As early as 1938 B. F. Skinner found in animal experiments that punishments (or aversive stimuli) do no more than temporarily extinguish a response while creating fear and hostility in the process.

In spite of research, pronouncements by the APA and the American Civil Liberties Union (ACLU), and heavy liability to teachers who harm students through corporal punishment,[4] punishment continues to be the staple of disciplinary procedures in all too many schools. Corporal punishment has been banned in Poland since 1783, in the Netherlands since 1850, in France since 1887, in Finland since 1890, and in Sweden since 1958. Most Communist countries, including the Soviet Union, do not allow corporal punishment in public schools.[5] And yet in the U.S. 40 states authorize corporal punishment in schools while only Massachusetts and New Jersey disallow the practice by state law. Why does punishment continue to be used daily in American public schools? Tradition, increased school crime and violence, and the failure of school systems and teacher education programs to promote effective alternatives are the probable reasons. But there *are* alternatives.

Educational theory and research—drawing from various schools of thought, philosophies, and psychological perspectives—have provided teachers with a multitude of principles and practices that are superior to punishment in establishing good school and classroom discipline. These approaches require skill and perseverance but have the potential for creating positive relationships, cooperation, and self-discipline in students. While no more than a brief description is possible here, I encourage teachers to investigate these alternatives and incorporate into their disciplinary practices the approaches that seem most compatible with their teaching styles and personal philosophies.

The Behavioral Model—Techniques of behavior modification have grown out of operant conditioning experiments over the past few decades. The behavioral approach suggests that behaviors, whether in the cognitive or the discipline area, are shaped by principles of reinforcement. Both positive and negative reinforcement are more effective in developing "desirable" student behavior than is punishment. To use this approach the teacher should:

1. Catch the child being good and reward him. Many behavior problems result from a child's need for attention and his realization that teachers generally ignore behaving students in order to give attention to troublemakers. The squeaking wheel gets the grease. Reversing the process—by ignoring minor misbehavior to focus attention on cooperative children—is a lesson a class soon learns. The hardest part of this technique for the teacher is to be consistent, systematic, and doggedly patient. Rewards should immediately follow the behavior to be reinforced.

2. Establish rewards that children will work for and connect these directly to "desirable" behavior. Teachers can use questionnaires, classroom discussions, and observation of what children do in their free time (a technique called "premacking") to discover those things and activities children find rewarding. These rewards may then be paired with target behavior to strengthen motivation to behave appropriately. Food, toys, free time, trips, comic books, conversation breaks, special jobs, games—these are only a few of the reinforcers that an imaginative teacher can use as rewards.[6] For bigger rewards, use chips or markers as tokens that may, after accumulation to a specified number, be redeemed—as grocers use stamps of low monetary value to strengthen our tendency to shop at their places of business.

3. Praise desirable behavior in the classroom, using positive verbal and nonverbal responses. Research tells us that teachers do not use praise effectively and, in fact, use it far less than they *think* they do. One large survey in a public school system in Florida, for example, found that 77% of the teachers' interactions with children were negative in tone.[7] Teachers need to expand their verbal praise list beyond the conventional "good," "yes," "right," and "O.K." responses. They should work at such nonverbal reinforcers as smiles, nods, touch, attention, closeness, gestures, and eye contact. Instead of writing on the board the names of misbehaving students who are to "stay in" at recess, write names of the *best*-behaved students. With a noisy class, put a check mark in a column on the board after every five minutes of quiet and give the whole class five minutes of free time if they earn, say, five checks during the period.

4. Use "modeling" to teach appropriate behavior. Since children imitate behavior, particularly that of significant others such as peer leaders and teachers, teachers can exemplify the behavior they expect from students. When teachers try to talk over an undercurrent of classroom chatter, noisily walk around the room during a quiet-time seatwork assignment, come to class late and unorganized, and respond to "called-out" questions and

comments, they are modeling the very behavior they most despair of in students. Teachers should not only model the kind of behavior they expect from students but should use well-behaved, prestigious peers as group leaders or in paired seating arrangements in order to enhance their modeling value in the classroom.

5. Teach the cues that signal the approach of an expected behavior. Cueing can be one of the most effective techniques for eliminating situations that frequently result in punishment for children. While many teachers have developed—probably intuitively—a repertoire of cues, most teachers could benefit from a conscious, systematic, overt recognition that cues can be employed to create good behavior. A teacher may ring a small bell when it is time to change centers, turn the light switch on and off when it is time to put away laboratory equipment, stand before the class with a raised hand when attention is required, point to the lunch monitor when it is time to exit for lunch. But a creative teacher can go far beyond these obvious examples. In a restless and talkative class the students can be taught to cue the teacher that they know an answer by resting their heads on their desks. The teacher, of course, must then reinforce this behavior by recognizing a student who is giving the appropriate cue. Cues should be *explained* to students and *consistently* followed in the classroom.

6. Use negative reinforcement when a child's behavior is unacceptable. Unlike punishment, negative reinforcement allows the *child* to terminate an undesirable situation when he is ready to behave. The distinction may be slight, but it is important. Sending a misbehaving child to stand in the corner for "the rest of the period" is punishment; removing him from the group to a "time out" area "until he is ready to play by the rules" is negative reinforcement. In the first case a child can only reflect upon his sins, while in the latter he can decide to change his behavior and in so doing remove the mildly undesirable condition of solitary confinement. He is more likely in this negative reinforcement situation to develop positive behaviors, whereas punishment usually generates resentment and a desire for revenge.

Because behavior modification techniques can be powerful, teachers must be sensitive to the ethical implications[8] and the practical consequences[9] of this approach.

The Human Relations Model—The human relations approach to school discipline rests on a number of psychological theories, such as those developed by Carl Rogers, Haim Ginott, Thomas Gordon, and William Purkey. Those who look at discipline from a human relations perspective propose a number of strategies that supercede punitive measures. Emphasis is generally placed on communication, democratic processes, and personal interaction in the classroom. Practical application of theory suggests that the teacher should:

1. Treat students with respect and politeness. Ginott says, "A wise teacher talks to children the way he does to visitors at his home."[10] In what he calls "invitational teaching," Purkey says the focus is "on the teacher's belief system—that students are valuable, can learn, and are responsible for their conduct. The teacher communicates these beliefs within a framework of gentle but firm expectations for each student."[11]

2. Communicate effectively by describing rather than evaluating. Ginott says, "Sarcasm is not good for children. It destroys their self-confidence and

self-esteem. . . . Verbal spankings do not improve performance or personality. . . . When a child feels aggrieved, it is best to acknowledge his complaint and voice his wish. . . . 'Talk to the situation, not to the personality and character' is the cardinal principle of communication."[12] Instead of verbal punishment—what Ginott calls naming, blaming, and shaming—teachers should develop the language of acceptance, "congruent communication," and brevity of speech.

3. Communicate effectively by reflecting feelings. This is a counseling technique developed by Rogers. Gordon outlines a hierarchy of "communication facilitators"—passive listening, acknowledgement responses, door openers, and active listening[13]—that enhances this communication skill. The essential task for the teacher-as-listener is to clarify and restate what his students are saying, giving expression to underlying feelings that seem to be causing a student's anger, fear, or frustration. When a student challenges a teacher by saying, "I'm not going to take that stupid test now," a teacher using active listening would not respond by ordering, threatening, moralizing, or punishing; instead, he would reflect what he thinks is the student's underlying feeling: "You are afraid you are not going to do well." Such a response keeps communication open, avoids "put-down" messages, and avoids the usual power struggle in confrontations.

4. Communicate effectively by using "I-messages," a technique advocated by both Ginott and Gordon. The I-message allows a teacher to describe his own feelings—disappointment, fear, frustration—in such a way that students are not personally attacked or punished. It "avoids the negative impact that accompanies you-messages, freeing the student to be considerate and helpful, not resentful, angry, and devious."[14] These messages contain minimal negative evaluation of students and do not injure personal relationships. According to Gordon, the I-message has three components: a description of the *behavior* that bothers the teacher, a statement of the tangible *effects* of that behavior, and the *feeling* that the teacher consequently has. For example: "When you have your feet in the aisle [description of behavior], I am apt to trip over them [tangible effect], and I am afraid I will fall and get hurt [feeling]."[15] This kind of communication tends to strengthen human relations and reduces the conflicts and the roadblocks to communication that so frequently end in verbal or physical punishment for students.

5. Negotiate with students to establish rules of behavior and to find solutions to problems. William Glasser advocates the use of the classroom meeting to discuss and resolve community problems, and the "Glasser circle" is now used in many schools by teachers who are trying to involve students more responsibly in decision making. As Dennis Van Avery argues, "The process of learning responsibility can best take place between people who can really get to know each other. We need continually to be concerned about allowing small groups of young people to interact with responsible adults."[16] Gordon proposes a formal problem-solving process to deal with discipline and other shared problems in the classroom, a process that involves students in a democratic and creative way. The teacher defines the problem and facilitates a brainstorming of possible solutions (*all* are listed on the board), which are then evaluated. The class moves toward a consensus on the one solution that everyone—and that includes the teacher—is willing to try for a specified period of time.

Because the human relations approach requires an unusual range of skills and attitudes on the part of the teacher, a teacher's application of the techniques above should be developed carefully and patiently.

The Pedagogical Model—The pedagogical or preventive approach to discipline problems has grown out of research and practice. Obviously, this approach has been influenced by both behavioral research and humanistic theory—but the emphasis in the pedagogical model is on instructional practices and on specific interaction patterns involving students and teachers. There has been no shortage of advice to teachers about how to discipline; however, the focus here is on how to discipline without punishing. Among the selected principles to consider are those that argue that the teacher should:

1. Keep discipline problems from occurring by providing structured but varied lessons. When lessons are student-centered, provide for active learning, and promote student/teacher shared planning, a good deal of the boredom and frustration that create discipline problems can be eliminated. Teachers who design purposeful multi-activity plans, and do so by incorporating high-interest materials, are applying preventive discipline.[17]

2. Develop a repertoire of motivation techniques. Assigning projects to coincide with student interests, using "hands-on" learning experiences, making motivational statements, establishing rewards and prizes, providing for student choice wherever possible, employing instructional games, and showing personal interest in students and their educational accomplishments—all of these practices enhance student motivation. Of course it is also important for the teacher to show involvement in and enjoyment of the class activities, thus motivating by example.

3. Use voice control and distance management to keep the tone and pace of a class on target. A teacher should use the "soft reprimand" (rather than giving public attention to misbehaving students by using a loud reprimand), lower the voice and/or stop talking if an undercurrent of chatter develops (rather than trying to talk above the noise), employ pauses and voice inflection to assure voice variety. Moreover, the teacher should move *toward* individuals or small groups that are inattentive while moving *away* from students who are responding to a teacher's question. The teacher's proximity will tend to curtail inattention, while moving away from the responder will encourage him to speak louder and across a larger number of students included in the increased "stage distance."

4. Find natural or logical consequences for student misbehavior. Dreikurs, who argues for this approach to discipline in several of his texts, defines "natural consequences" as the "natural flow of events without interference of the teacher or parent. The child who refuses to eat will go hungry. The natural consequence of not eating is hunger." He defines "logical consequences" as "arranged or applied. If the child spills his milk, he must clean it up. In this situation the consequence is tied to the act."[18] If a child is late for class, asking him to make up the time at the end of the day is a logical consequence; having him copy pages from a dictionary is mere punishment. Because a child does not associate punishment with his action but with the punisher, he does not change his behavior or attitude. A natural or logical consequence teaches a student the rational reality of misbehavior. When a child is inattentive as an assignment is given, do not repeat it; when a student writes on his desk, require him to scrub the desk clean; when an instructional game

gets out of hand, call it off and return to less enjoyable routine work. But in each case be sure to stress the *connection* between the behavior and the consequence.[19] Natural and logical consequences make sense to the student and help him to learn from his mistakes.

5. Employ assertiveness training techniques when student compliance with requests is important. A teacher may occasionally need to be unusually clear and firm about a request to a misbehaving student, particularly when students are testing the limits of authority or are not convinced that a teacher means what he says. Frederick Jones describes this approach:

> Being assertive is the key. Assertiveness is 95% body language....
> First turn and face the child. If you're not willing to commit your body in that direction, don't expect the child to respond.... [P]ut an edge on your voice and say the student's name in a straight, flat tone. Next, make eye contact.... Lean toward him.... Very slowly walk right up to his desk so your leg is touching it; stand and look at the child. Don't say anything, don't hurry. By that time most kids will fold.[20]

In "assertive teaching" it is particularly important to stay with your request until you know you have made your point, repeating your position or request and refusing to be diverted or ignored. This is known as the "broken record" technique. Glasser's well-known "reality therapy" theory incorporates many assertive principles, such as "be committed.... Don't accept excuses. . . . Never give up."[21]

There are, of course, countless other pedagogical principles that can help the effective teacher to avoid confrontations and conflicts that may result in punishment and to find ways to deal with students in nonpunitive interactions.[22]

Because school discipline is a critical issue in education and society today, effective ways of creating healthy and happy classrooms must be an important concern of educators everywhere. It is unlikely that much constructive learning and teaching can be found where there is violence, disruption, apathy, and conflict between students and teachers. But it is also unlikely that we can expect administrative crackdowns on misbehavior, "get-tough" attitudes by school boards, or harsh punishment by teachers to create positive learning environments within school systems. The long-term solution to the school discipline crisis is a professional staff of educators—principals, counselors, and teachers—who can work competently and humanely with students and with instruction to find alternatives to punishment.

To accomplish these ends a concentrated, cooperative effort is essential. A few specific steps could move education into an action orientation to develop and disseminate effective disciplinary practices:

● *Recommendation 1.* Educational researchers should move quickly to design and evaluate models of classroom management that integrate the most attractive aspects of existing models (such as the three described in this article). These should be meta-theoretical models that draw from theory but point toward practice.

● *Recommendation 2.* Teacher education institutions should develop courses in classroom management for preservice and inservice teachers. These should include as much observation, microteaching, and simulation as possible. Emphasis should be placed on practical strategies in the classroom.

● *Recommendation 3*. School district personnel should create projects, perhaps in conjunction with universities, that are designed to involve teachers, principals, and supervisors in ongoing classroom and schoolwide experimentation with innovative methods and techniques of management and instruction.

● *Recommendation 4*. Professional organizations should emphasize classroom management by means of conferences and publications. Preventive discipline, home/school relations, motivation through subject matter, values education and the disruptive child, educational effects of punishment, causes of school violence—all of these need even *more* attention than they have so far received from the various associations of educators.

● *Recommendation 5*. Local, state, and federal levels of government should support efforts to get at the root of the discipline problem and to develop alternatives to punishment by providing funds for pilot projects and research at the various levels. Other forms of legislation and board action— e.g., to develop comprehensive discipline codes and policies, to create support services, and to establish consultant assistance to teachers and counselors—should be explored as well.

Clearly, these are interrelated enterprises and should be coordinated for maximum benefit. Sporadic efforts in all five areas can easily be found, but increased cooperative effort is now imperative. The problems of school discipline cannot be quickly solved with Band-Aid techniques and superficial hit-and-miss methods. Because the underlying causes of our more serious discipline dilemmas, particularly in the inner cities, cut deeply into the fabric of contemporary life, solutions depend ultimately on our ability to mend that fabric. Such a task belongs to the whole society, not to teachers alone. But teachers have a central role in the process. When teachers become skilled in the humane application of alternatives to punishment—those described here and others yet to be developed[23]—they can help schools become places where students live and learn in well-regulated liberty.

---

1. Rudolf Dreikurs and Pearl Cassel, *Discipline Without Tears*, 2nd ed. (New York: Hawthorn Press, 1972), p. 11.

2. The case, *Ingraham* v. *Wright* (1977), was decided on a split vote (5-4).

3. As quoted by Robert J. Trotter in "This Is Going to Hurt You More Than It Hurts Me," *Science News*, 18 November 1972, p. 332.

4. For some of these liabilities, see my "The Teacher's Ten Commandments: School Law in the Classroom," *Phi Delta Kappan*, June 1979, pp. 703-08.

5. Tobyann Boonin, "The Benighted Status of U.S. School Corporal Punishment Practice," *Phi Delta Kappan*, January 1979, p. 395.

6. Many recent texts in this area contain long lists of reinforcers along with explicit directions for scheduling rewards effectively. See, for example, J. Mark Ackerman, *Operant Conditioning Techniques for the Classroom Teacher* (Glenview, Ill.: Scott, Foresman, 1972); John and Helen Krumboltz, *Changing Children's Behavior* (Englewood Cliffs, N.J.: Prentice-Hall, 1972); Charles and Clifford Madsen, *Teaching Discipline: Behavioral Principles Toward a Positive Approach* (Boston: Allyn and Bacon, 1970); James Walker and Thomas Shea, *Behavior Modification: A Practical Approach for Educators* (St. Louis: C. V. Mosby, 1976); Charlotte Epstein, *Classroom Management and Teaching* (Reston, Va.: Reston Publishing Company, 1979).

7. Bertram S. Brown, "Behavior Modification: What It Is—and Isn't," *Today's Education*, January/February 1976, pp. 67, 68.

8. See, for example, Patricia Keir, "The Teacher as Behavior Engineer," *Educational Forum*, November 1977, pp. 111-17; and James D. Long and Virginia H. Frye, *Making It 'til Friday* (Princeton, N.J.: Princeton Book Company, 1977), Chap. 8.

9. See, for example, David L. Gast and C. Michael Nelson, "Time Out in the Classroom: Implications for Special Education," *Exceptional Children*, April 1977, pp. 461-64.

10. Haim Ginott, *Teacher and Child* (New York: Macmillan, 1972), p. 101.

11. William W. Purkey, *Inviting School Success: A Self-Concept Approach to Teaching and Learning* (Belmont, Calif.: Wadsworth, 1978), p. 57.

12. Ginott, op. cit., pp. 66-84.

13. Thomas Gordon, *TET: Teacher Effectiveness Training* (New York: Peter H. Wyden, 1974), pp. 61-64.

14. Ibid., p. 139.

15. Ibid., p. 144.

16. Dennis Van Avery, "Contrasting Solutions for School Violence," *Phi Delta Kappan*, November 1975, pp. 177, 178.

17. For other suggestions in this area, see my "A Stitch in Time: Principles of Preventive Discipline," *American Secondary Education*, June 1979, pp. 52-57. Also see Stanley A. Fagan and Nicholas J. Long, "Before It Happens: Prevent Discipline Problems by Teaching Self-Control," *Instructor*, January 1976, pp. 44-47.

18. Rudolf Dreikurs et al., *Maintaining Sanity in the Classroom* (New York: Harper and Row, 1971), p. 80. See also his *Logical Consequences: A New Approach to Discipline* (New York: Hawthorn Press, 1968) and *Discipline Without Tears* (New York: Hawthorn Press, 1972).

19. Don Dinkmeyer and Don Dinkmeyer, Jr., "Logical Consequences: A Key to the Reduction of Disciplinary Problems," *Phi Delta Kappan*, June 1976, pp. 665, 666.

20. Frederick Jones in "Instructor's Guide to Sanity-Saving Discipline," *Instructor*, November 1978, p. 64. See also in the same article the contribution by Lee Canter, "Be an Assertive Teacher," p. 60.

21. William Glasser, "Ten Steps to Good Discipline," *Today's Education*, November/December 1977, p. 61.

22. For some good practical suggestions, see Dudley Shearburn, "What to Do When You See Red!," *Teacher*, September 1977, pp. 90, 91; Marjorie L. Hipple, "Classroom Discipline Problems? Fifteen Humane Solutions," *Childhood Education*, February 1978, pp. 183-87; Dorothy Rathbun, "How to Cope in the Middle School Jungle," *Learning*, November 1977, p. 40 ff.; Leonard Burger, "Do You Referee When You Really Want to Teach?," *Instructor*, February 1977, pp. 55-58.

23. One new approach that has promise is transactional analysis. See Ken Earnst, *Games Students Play* (Millbrae, Calif.: Celestial Arts Publishing, 1972); Konstantinos and Constance Kravas, "Transactional Analysis for Classroom Management," *Phi Delta Kappan*, November 1974, pp. 194-97; and Joseph D. Purdy, "How to Win at Uproar," *Instructor*, August/September 1975, pp. 64-66.

X
Testing

Introduction

*M*inimum competency testing (for both students and teachers), truth in testing, bias in testing, IQ testing—all received their share of attention at the end of the Seventies. But no issue related to the subject got more ink in the popular press than the steady decline in Scholastic Aptitude Test scores after 1963. Respected researchers like Harold Hodgkinson (see his KAPPAN article in Section IV) scoff at the relatively modest declines in the face of the fact that over 50% of high school graduates now enroll in some form of higher education, compared to 10% to 20% in 1950. Also, Hodgkinson notes that up to 85% of all young people now graduate from high school. The percentage was much smaller before 1960. Hodgkinson is disturbed, not by the overall SAT declines, which we should expect, but by pronounced sex differences in test scores. "Do Americans want girls to do poorly in math and science and males to do poorly in verbal skills?" he asks.

Harold Shane is former dean of education and now University Professor of Education at Indiana University's School of Education. He is also one of the most prolific education writers in America, with over 450 publication credits. At the height of the SAT decline furor, he interviewed Willard Wirtz, an old friend who headed a College Entrance Examination Board panel charged with examining the decline. Shane's article, "The Academic Score Decline: Are Facts the Enemy of Truth?", appeared in the October 1977 KAPPAN shortly after the blue-ribbon panel released its 75-page report. The article is, I think, a model of interviewing technique, showing the power gained when the interviewer knows nearly as much about a subject as the interviewee.

In all, Shane contributed 41 articles, reviews, and interviews to the KAPPAN during my editorship. He gave invaluable advice as a long-term editorial consultant, both official and unofficial. KAPPAN editorial consultants are generally chosen for expertise in one area of education. Not Harold Shane. His contribution reminds me of a line from ancient Greek writing: "The fox knows many things; the hedgehog knows one big thing." Hedgehogs relate everything to a single central vision, to which they repeatedly return. Foxes have many different goals and look at the world from various perspectives. In literature, Dostoevsky was a hedgehog, Shakespeare a fox. In education we need hedgehogs and have them; we don't have enough foxes like Harold Shane.

Over the past decade education leaders have been attempting to restore *some balance in a society and a profession that have carried tests and testing to ridiculous extremes. No one should discount the value of scientific testing, which is one of the great achievements of modern educational psychology. But the proper uses and the limitations of testing are certainly not well understood by laymen; many teachers are almost as ignorant.*

Among the leaders whose concern about testing has led to effective action is Paul Houts, editor for 12 years of the prize-winning National Elementary Principal *and now director of a study of American high schools for the Carnegie Foundation. He was co-founder and vice president of the National Consortium on Testing, a coalition of 50 national educator and citizen groups concerned with testing. He edited* The Myth of Measurability, *a critical analysis of issues related to standardized testing. I am pleased to include in this volume his June 1976 article titled "Behind the Call for Test Reform and Abolition of the IQ."*

Arthur Whimbey's "Teaching Sequential Thought: The Cognitive-Skills Approach" was forced into this chapter because it was something of an orphan. I thought it deserved inclusion in the anthology. Certainly it gained a great deal of reader interest. And it is, after all, related to testing in several ways. For example, National Assessment of Educational Progress results suggest that pressures for more emphasis on such fundamentals as arithmetic computation have led schools to neglect an even more important fundamental: logical or sequential thought. Children in the elementary grades, according to NAEP data, are beginning to handle computation better than they once did, but have difficulty applying those skills in problem situations.

Are there particularly effective ways to teach sequential thought? Whimby says yes, and he gets support from observers like Fred Hechinger. Writing on "Basic Skills: Closing the Gap" in the October 1979 issue of Change, *Hechinger called attention to Whimbey's books,* Intelligence Can Be Taught *and* Problem Solving and Comprehension: A Short Course in Analytical Reasoning. *"Whimbey believes in the importance of systematic thought," Hechinger notes, "a process that can readily be acquired." Hechinger quotes John U. Monro, who resigned the prestigious deanship of Harvard College in 1967 to direct a remedial program at all-black Miles College in Alabama. According to Monro, the Whimbey method greatly improved black students' ability to perform mental tasks that are ordinarily associated with the idea of intelligence.°*

The Journal of Reading *for October 1980, in an article by Whimbey and others, reports gains of about 1.5 years on the Nelson-Denny and the equivalent of 100 points on the SAT among pre-college students at Xavier University (predominantly black) in Louisiana, after just five weeks in Project SOAR (Stress on Analytical Reasoning). SOAR uses Whimbey's "cognitive process instruction."*

—SME

°*A number of educators have asked where they can secure Albert Upton's series of workbooks titled* Think, *which Whimbey regards as effective in improving logical thinking ability in students ranging from fifth grade to college. The Upton materials are available from ISI-Think, 300 Broad St., Stamford, CT 06901.*

An Interview with W. Willard Wirtz:
The Academic Score Decline: Are Facts the Enemy of Truth?
by Harold G. Shane

The long-awaited report of the CEEB's blue-ribbon panel on SAT score declines appeared in late August. Mr. Shane probes the most sensitive areas of the report in this interview with the panel chairman.

After more than a decade of relative stability, academic performance of students in the U.S. began a steady decline in the early 1960s. Today Americans have data to imperil their illusions and intensify their fears about pupil progress. Achievement test scores have been falling for 14 consecutive years. One might almost say that the kids are on the skids, since there has been a consistent decline in aptitude and basic skills as measured by standardized tests.[1]

The interview with Willard Wirtz reported here sheds a good deal of light on this phenomenon. A former secondary school teacher, who subsequently taught law and then became secretary of labor (1962-69), Wirtz is now chairman of the National Manpower Institute. For the past two years he has served as chairman of an independent 21-member advisory panel charged with investigating the decline in Scholastic Aptitude Test (SAT) scores.[2] In late August the panel presented a summary of its findings, based upon 38 commissioned research projects, 27 of which are either available or in press.[3]

Shane: *Mr. Wirtz, let me begin our dialogue with a few background questions. I understand that the panel was commissioned by the College Entrance Examination Board (CEEB) and the Educational Testing Service, which cooperatively administer a 2½-hour examination designed to predict high school students' probable success when they go to college. About 1,500,000 juniors and seniors take the test each year. What is the CEEB's role, and how far back do SAT records go?*

Wirtz: The CEEB is one of the organizations that conduct college entrance examinations, along with the American College Testing program. This is only one of the College Board's functions, however. It's also interested in the overall relationship between secondary and postsecondary education and in various financial arrangements that will permit more young people to go on to college. Recently the CEEB has announced a renewed interest in continuing education, now called lifelong learning. The CEEB president is Sidney P. Marland, Jr., a former secondary school teacher and school superintendent, once a college teacher, and also a former U.S. commissioner of education.

The SAT is the most venerable of all tests of its kind, going back to the 1920s. It has been administered four or five times each year in a new edition.

S: *Was the advisory panel convinced that changes in the SAT—or lack of change—hadn't destroyed its validity?*

W: We can say with comparative certainty that an SAT score today means approximately what that score meant in any earlier year. The test is scored on a scale of from 200 to 800 and has two parts, verbal and mathematical, with separate scores for each. It was set up in 1941 to produce a mean score of 500 on each of these tests. From 1941 to 1963 SAT scores averaged around 500. As of 1963 they were still in that range. But since 1963 the average has been going down steadily. There has been a drop of 49 points in 14 years on the verbal part of the test and a drop of 32 points on the mathematical side.

S: *You say that scores have fallen a bit more each year, Mr. Wirtz. Has such a consistent, unbroken decline ever occurred before? Were there ups or downs, say, immediately after World War II or in the Fifties?*

W: There is nothing like the steady drop-off in scores of the last 14 years. In order to determine this, we went back 25 years. Between 1952 and 1963 those scores did fluctuate slightly from year to year; sometimes up, sometimes down. There was, by the way, an increase right after Sputnik I was put in orbit. We have assumed, without actually knowing, that this spurt reflected an increasing national interest in education. We were determined to catch up with the Russians. But there was no appreciable decline in SAT scores until 1964.

S: *Just how serious is a 49-point skid from 478 to 429 in the verbal section of the SAT? How catastrophic is the 32-point drop from 502 to 470 in mathematics?*

W: You used two terms, "serious" and "catastrophic." I think the declines are *not* catastrophic. But this is serious business. That's the phrase the panel has used. We have gone on to say that we think the drop in scores warrants the close attention of everybody in this country who is interested in education. At the same time, when the panel considered the whole picture we were surprised that the score decline wasn't *larger*. The past 15 years have been extraordinary ones in the history of this country.

S: *Why extraordinary?*

W: First, in the 1960s we made a conscious decision to see to it that a good many more young people stayed in high school and went on to college. We also did what we should have done long before: We eliminated some of the discrimination in admissions. And we got the school dropout rate down.

S: *I'm so interested in the topic I'm afraid I'll go off in all directions like a handful of spilled marbles. Let's return to a discussion of the causes of academic slippage. The advisory panel asserts that dwindling academic performance creates a serious situation "that warrants careful attention." Mr. Wirtz, what factor or factors, what changes before or since 1963, may have led to the aptitude score decline? Also, do the forces or conditions seem likely to continue to have as baleful or negative an impact in the future as they seem to have had in the recent past?*

W: Three time intervals should be considered. Between 1963 and 1970 there was a huge increase in the absolute number of students in the American educational system. In one year the total number of 18-year-olds jumped by over a million. That was the year 1964, the year the post-war baby boom hit the colleges. It also was the year in which SAT scores started down. So initially there was a huge educational problem because of the sheer increase in the number of young people. At that same time we decided to get rid of discrimination in access to educational opportunity. Because between 1965 and 1970 we decided to keep a good many more young people in school, some with lower grade averages in high school began to take SATs, because they planned on going to college.

S: *According to the panel report, between two-thirds and three-fourths of the academic score decline was attributable to changes in the composition of the test-taking population during this period. The college-bound student population included more of the economically disadvantaged, more women (who score lower on the math test), and more minority-group members. Do you feel that this caused part of the drop in scores?*

W: I prefer to look at it this way: The U.S. simply had not caught up with its emerging purposes. The country had not taken the steps that were necessary to successfully incorporate the changing composition of the test-taking population into the educational structure.

S: *You spoke of three periods of change?*

W: The second period was from 1970 to about 1975 or 1976. It was the period of sharpest score decline. Bear in mind that there was relatively little change in the composition of the test-taking group during the recent six-year interval of greatest decrease in SAT scores. There was some change, but it was a small factor, probably accounting for no more than a quarter, at most, of the continued decline.

S: *Then what other factors or changes do you perceive?*

W: During the Seventies there were a variety of forces, a combination of pervasive forces, to which we must give serious attention—particularly since they still are at work.

S: *I take it we are now approaching what the CEEB panel considers to be some of the basic, deep-rooted problems that have both contributed to and complicated score declines.*

W: That is correct, and the overall problem has many aspects. It includes the fact that we relaxed standards—learning standards—both in the schools and in society. It probably includes the fact that whereas young people had been taking a large number of basic courses a decade or more ago they now turned to a great many elective courses of one kind or another.

S: *Do I hear you condemning elective courses?*

W: Not at all! In the panel's judgment the difference is not between basic and elective courses. The difference is between courses that have a solid intellectual content and those that don't. And most particularly, in the panel's view, there has been an unfortunate erosion of the traditions of thoughtful reading and careful writing, a distinct decline in skill.

Beyond that there has been a relaxation of educational standards resulting in increased absenteeism, in questionable automatic promotions, in grade inflation, and in easier textbooks and related materials that seem designed to entertain rather than to educate. For one reason or another, as far as standards were concerned, our schools slacked off.

But it wasn't just the schools. For some years now there has been a problem in the family's declining participation in the learning process in this country. I would say there has been an array of basic changes.

S: *What data led the advisory panel to take a dim view of changes in family life?*

W: As recently as 10 or 15 years ago the number of young people in this country under 18 years of age who were living with fewer than two parents was only about 11%. The number has almost doubled since that time. Each year now an *additional* 300,000 young men and women under 18 live in families with fewer than two parents. The number of children in divorced families has doubled in the last 10 years. You begin to see the problem in broad perspective—and the extent of the effect it's going to have on education—when you realize that in many of the remaining two-parent homes both the father and the mother are working. Since TV is centered in the home, let me add that the years we are considering have also been the years of virtually universal television. By the time he is 16, the typical U.S. child has spent 10,000 to 15,000 hours in front of the tube. The full effect of this passive investment has yet to be assessed, but at the very least it has offered severe competition for the time that once was devoted to homework.

S: *So far you have touched on three "pervasive forces"—relaxed standards, mutations in family living, and the impact of television. Are there more on your list?*

W: We're also talking about a period in which those test scores were bound to be affected by what the panel has called a decade of distraction, a period in which a war was fought principally by these young people, a divisive war. It was a period of political assassination, particularly of their heroes. It was a period of rioting in the streets. It was a period of corruption of institutional stewardship in this country. It would have been very difficult for young people to place high on their list of personal priorities the goal of getting the highest possible scores on the Scholastic Aptitude Test during that period.

S: *Since you've come up to 1976 in your review, what is the third interval involved in score decline? Were you thinking of the present, or even of the future?*

W: I'm a little puzzled about this third period. I don't know whether it's a continuation of the interval of decline or whether it is a truly new era. In any case, for the past two years there has been relatively little decline in scholastic aptitude scores—much less than there was in the preceding two years. As a matter of fact, this year there is virtually no decline. Now whether this represents a pause or a turning point, it is still too early to say. But let me look ahead. In the near future I would suspect that there will be a change in academic performance, particularly because this country is now growing more and more aware of the problem. Not only through the educational system but in society as a whole we will begin to do things that ought to be done to repair and strengthen and revitalize both education in this country and the lifestyle of which it is a part.

S: *Could the interplay of the four factors you mentioned have created a synergism, a system in which the impact of the whole was greater than the sum of separate forces?*

W: I would say yes. While I'm not much of a believer in the "coincidence theory" of history, we've got to recognize that there has been an extraordinary confluence of forces in the last decade or two. It was strange, for instance, that the decision to extend educational opportunity in this country to so many more young people happened to coincide with the effects of a war, with a period of distractions of one kind or another in this country, and with a period of change in family lifestyles.

S: *Mr. Wirtz, although you probably have no hard data, let me ask the question: Since TV presumably has had a negative influence on homework and perhaps on academic performance, can it be that teacher effectiveness too has been impaired by the impact of the tube? May it not have made incursions into the time formerly put into careful preparation by teachers?*

W: I don't know why we should limit the question to teachers! The kids are doing just exactly what the American public is doing. The amount of time going into televiewing is not unique to children and youth. I assume that there have been effects that we still haven't fathomed. It's not easy to determine the extent to which television is taking over one role after another. In the report we've called it a substitute teacher and a surrogate parent. In answer to your question, I suppose the jury is still out in the question of whether TV has affected kids any more than it has adults, because it's just the kids who are taking tests. My guess is that it's had a great influence on all age groups and at every socioeconomic level.

S: *Do the developments you have inventoried as possible causes of score decline seem likely to be bottoming out? Or do you think that, say, rips in the fabric of the traditional family will create problems for a long time to come?*

W: Let me comment on the family, since you have singled it out—though I don't think it should be made a whipping boy. I know there are some critics today who are apocalyptic about the consequences of the breakup of the American family. I am more optimistic. Without being maudlin, I think that most of us would infinitely prefer taking a chance on being born into an average American family than into any other family in any place in the world. It is true that there is cause for concern because of changes in family lifestyles. But I disagree vehemently with those who see the family close to collapse. My answer to such doomsayers is a flat no. There will have to be adjustments to new lifestyles, and we need to adapt them to the whole learning process— but the panel's feeling on this was that the worst mistake would be to look on this situation as being one that warrants the apocalyptic commentaries that have been made on it. We're on the way up; the future still looks good.

S: *As I recall, advisory panel findings pointed out that declines on standardized tests have been greater at each successively higher grade level, beginning with grade 5. The panel also wrote that there were no such declines in grades 1-4. In effect, it would appear that, beginning in 1963, the longer pupils remained in school the poorer their academic performance became. Does this suggest that primary instruction is more effective than middle or high school teaching? Or do older children become increasingly demoralized by the turbulent environment of the schools in which drugs, vandalism, and violence sometimes play a part? As another possibility, could it be that that which is taught is less meaningful or less relevant as youngsters move into the higher grades?*

W: The trend you mention gave us a good deal of concern. By the time we finally reached some of the possible explanations for the decline after grade 4 we were also highly aware of the trickery of statistics.

It is not only true that there has been no decline in standardized test score averages through the first four grades; the decline is larger each succeeding grade, thus becoming greatest in grades 11 and 12.

Now let me suggest four possible explanations. One which immediately comes to everyone's mind is that teaching is less effective at the higher grades—that the longer kids stay in school the more ineffective teaching they get. Another possibility is that the aptitude tests are not as relevant at grades 11 and 12 as they are in earlier grades.

There are two other very interesting possibilities. First, those differences may very possibly reflect the increased school retention rate in this country.

When a larger cross section of our youth stays in school through the eleventh and twelfth grades, you get a population change at the upper levels that you don't have in the first four grades. Kids in the first four grades represent the same cross section today that they did 10 or 15 years ago, i.e., *all* in these age groups. At the eleventh and twelfth grades, we now enroll three-quarters of all the kids, whereas 12 or 15 years ago only about two-thirds of this age group stayed in school.

S: *And what's the other possible answer to worsening test performance?*

W: The CEEB panel discussions led to a very interesting area of conjecture. Perhaps scores are stable in the first four grades because TV is teaching these primary youngsters in very much the manner that they are taught in school during these first three or four grades. There's a close parallel between the kind of education that goes on in television and in the classroom. This isn't true at the eleventh and twelfth grades. There's a real disjuncture there. This interpretation illustrates the fact that you simply can't rely on statistics alone to analyze a situation of this kind.

S: *Do you think we should try to extend "Sesame Street" upward by re-designing the sets, scenes, and scripts for a more mature audience?*

W: Let's not take this matter lightly. The panel came to the conclusion that television is undoubtedly one of the contributing causes of score decline. The panel also concluded that TV and other mass media probably have the largest teaching potential that we know about today! Instead of trying simply to talk in terms of cutting down on the amount of televiewing, the thing to do is to have the community assume the same responsibility with respect to what is taught on television that it has always exercised with respect to what is taught in the schools. We think that the country could make television a master teacher. Television and education are badly out of kilter, and the stakes are probably higher than we so far have realized. TV has distracted today's youth from the kind of learning being measured in these tests. Yet television has infinite promise.

S: *Let me press further, Mr. Wirtz, with regard to statistical trickery in test scores. Is it possible that many students with high grades in secondary school simply don't bother to take the SATs because they're sure that they'll get into a college of their choice anyway?*

W: First, it is clear that there are now open admission policies in some universities. Other colleges of particularly high standing accept some of the more outstanding students on an early admissions basis. This helps to account for the fact that there has been a decline in the number of students repeating the SAT. Since second-test scores average 15 to 20 points higher, the early admissions policy, plus some open admissions, would have the effect you mention.

S: *Is there a profile of high achievers on the SATs?*

W: It would be difficult if not impossible to list the high scorer's characteristics. We do know these things: The higher scores tend to be made by children from families of higher socioeconomic status. With frequent exceptions, young people's scores parallel the educational attainment levels of their parents. There's an interesting correlation between the number of outside activities a student engages in and his or her test scores on the SAT. The more outside activities, the higher the scores. We have learned that those who take three or four years of foreign language will score as much as a hundred points higher, on the average, than those who take no foreign language. But I really must point out again the difficulties and ambiguities of the statistical approach. It may very well be that those with higher verbal ability take foreign language rather than that those who take foreign language display a high verbal ability on the SAT test. It is unquestionably true that there is a close parallel between high grades in high school and high scores on the SAT, but even here generalization is pretty dangerous.

S: *Many of the persons who will read this* KAPPAN *interview are practitioners. I think most of them would like to know what steps you would take if you were a superintendent of schools and concerned about reducing and then reversing present downward performance trends.*

W: Contrary perhaps to many readers' expectations, my first move as this hypothetical administrator would be to try to restore or to build anew the relationships between the teachers in the school and the teachers at home. I'm totally convinced that this has got to be a partnership arrangement. I'm totally persuaded that schools can do only part of this job and that the home, the family, has to do some more educating. That's why I would start by trying to develop a closer home-and-school alliance. There are those who would urge that we start being sterner and stricter about such things as attendance, promotions, the difficulty of teaching materials, and about holding kids to basics. I don't believe those short answers help. I'd settle for an alliance between family and school, with the thought and expectation that these problems have to be worked out on a community basis. It is a great mistake to count on the schools being able to do it all by themselves.

S: *In the CEEB report,* On Further Examination, *the panel identified "dispersal of learning activities," including a wide array of high school electives, as a possible contributive factor in academic score decline. Later the report says that secondary education should not be more rigid but "must become more diversified" without watering down the so-called "hard" subjects such as math, physics, and foreign language. It seems contradictory, Mr. Wirtz, to decry dispersal of learning, then defend flexibility and diversification. Can you elaborate a bit on this apparent paradox?*

W: I don't believe it's a paradox. I think it's a hard truth we must face up to. Let me illustrate. I expect that the panel report is going to be interpreted as attributing some of the score decline to the increased number of electives taken. That's only half true. What we're suggesting is that in the course of increasing the number of electives there's been a decline in the *standards* of these courses. Specifically, a good many high schools in the country have added courses in radio, television, and so forth. Thus a student can take a radio, television, and film course instead of basic English IV. Well, I believe that a good teacher can make a course in radio, television, and film just as demanding and just as stimulating as a good teacher can make a course in basic English IV—if basic English IV still includes what it did when I was teaching it: *Hamlet*, the evils of the split infinitive, and the iniquity of the terminal preposition! I like to think that as much hard thinking can be taught in connection with a subject that interests the student as can be taught in a subject that doesn't. The panel also concluded that if there is a single key to improvement, it is a return to the traditions of thoughtful reading and careful writing. And personally I'd emphasize the writing. I think writing is the sternest discipline there is—the best training instrument for thinking. The panel also suggests that it would be a great mistake to return to the basics without taking a good look at what the basics are—the basics common to the learning of children from different backgrounds with different interests.

S: *The committee report referred to the diminished motivation of youth. Would you speculate on this question? Perhaps this lack of motivation can be attributed to the increased personal security provided by welfare, unemployment benefits, minimum wages, and the like, which have become more numerous and generous since the 1960s.*

W: First, the panel does not talk simply about *youth's* motivation. Rather, it says at one point something like this: "It's perhaps most significant of all that during the past 10 years the curve of the SAT scores has followed very closely the curve of the entire *nation's* spirits, self-esteem, and sense of purpose." This is a pretty important point. I doubt that youths' motivations have declined much more than their parents' motivations have. Also, we talk pretty glibly about a *decline* in motivations when probably what is going on is a *change* in motivations.

S: *Could any lack of motivation be related to youth concluding that by 2000 A.D. there won't be enough affluence to go around? Why work if shortages, resource depletion, energy problems, and so on are going to force cutbacks in the standard of living and opportunities for economic gain?*

W: I find no basis personally, nor did the panel, for a conclusion that we're running out of opportunity in this country. Rather, we thought in terms of the prospect that, with the decline in natural resources, the future is probably more dependent than ever on the infinite development of the human resource. I expect that 10 or 20 years from now we'll be relying on a much more highly sophisticated, more highly trained generation of youth than we are today.

S: *Thus far, Mr. Wirtz, I've neglected an important question. After your two-year inquiry, do you think we should have standardized tests? There are some groups of professionals and other citizens who say that we should not. They doubt that we should test what we measure as intelligence. What do you regard as the future role of standardized testing?*

W: The panel recognized the extreme importance of this question, but also recognized that the limitations of our charge made it impossible to explore it. The panel did recommend that a comprehensive study be made of the function of tests in our society. I think most of us on the panel felt that this is less the Age of Aquarius than an Age of Accountability. There's going to be testing of one kind or another—standardized testing. I think most of us felt, too, that testing of this kind is probably a good thing to stimulate or restimulate a sense of commitment in this country to a standard of excellence. However, there is a danger in attaching too much significance to what all young people do at a particular point in their lives on a particular examination.

S: *How do you stand on the issue of so-called competency-based diplomas?*

W: I would not take a negative view of competency-based diplomas. I would, however, take a very dubious view of statutes now being passed in some states to prohibit promotion from one grade to another until an individual meets a statutorily prescribed standard.

S: *Back in 1968 I saw a first-rate performance of* Man of La Mancha *here in New York. Don Quixote, the central character of the play, had a great line.*

"Facts," he said, "are the enemy of truth."

Now here's my last question. May not the "facts" in the SAT score decline report hide an important "truth"? Does the decline not mirror the partial attainment of a long-standing American quest, a quest for greater equality of access to educational opportunity?

W: It's an interesting thing, Harold. One of the authors of this report must have seen that play! *On Further Examination* mentions that "figures may be enemy to the truth, because they tell only part of it." This prompted the panel to end its report thus: "It would be too bad if our concentration on the implications of a decline in the statistical averages on a set of standardized examinations should seem to ignore how incomplete a measure this is of either educational or broader human purpose."

While we've been asking why the scores on college entrance examinations have gone down, I think that T. S. Eliot's probing goes a good deal deeper. He says, "Where is the learning we have lost in information? Where is the understanding we've lost in knowledge? Where is the life we've lost in living?" And from the very beginning the panel had to keep reminding itself of the fact that we have been concerned with just *one* statistical measure of *one* set of competencies of only one minority part of American youth.

There are a great many values the SAT simply doesn't pretend to measure and can't possibly measure. That's the reason, basically, for the panel's call for a broader examination of whether we are measuring the things that ought to be measured.

The idea that nothing's right unless it can be proved is "true" only if you take the premise as the conclusion. There are many important things that can't be proved, things that statistics won't tell. And there's simply got to be broader attention given to whether we are—in education and in this whole society—putting the right emphasis on the right things.

---

1. For a detailed account, see Annegret Harnischfeger and David E. Wiley, "Achievement Test Scores Drop, So What?" *Educational Researcher*, March, 1976, pp. 5-12.

2. Advisory panel members, in addition to Willard Wirtz, included Vice Chairman Harold Howe II, Ralph W. Tyler, Ledyard R Tucker, Vivian H. L. Tom, Robert L. Thorndike, Barbara Thompson, Thomas F. W. Stroud, Rosedith Sitgreaves, Wilbur Schramm, Katherine P. Layton, Owen B. Kiernan, H. Thomas James, Matina S. Horner, Edythe J. Gaines, Frank W. Erwin, Bruce K. Ekland, Luis C. Cortes, Sandra A. Clark, and Benjamin S. Bloom.

3. The 75-page panel report, *On Further Examination*, just published, may be obtained for $4 from the College Entrance Examination Board, Publication Orders, Box 2815, Princeton, NJ 08540. Related CEEB studies are annotated in the report's appendix.

Behind the Call
For Test Reform and
Abolition of the IQ
by Paul L. Houts

*Use assessment as a tool for the education of all who need it,
not as an instrument for the exclusion of certain groups. That is
the point of current reform. To make the point, Mr. Houts re-
counts some of the ugly history of the IQ testing movement.*

Oliver Wendell Holmes once estimated that there were no more than 500
"civilized" people in the world. Unfortunately, history has left us no Holm-
esian definition of "civilized" on which to gauge the reasonablesness of his ap-
proximation, and to my knowledge no one has yet constructed a test to determine the degree to which we have become civilized. (We may be thankful for
certain blessings.) For some time now, however, through testing devices, we
have attempted to measure a similarly broad and complex human quality
called "intelligence." Moreover, we have accepted the results of these tests
with great seriousness, allowing them to wield a pervasive and, in many cases,
enormously damaging effect on the lives of children. One might well ask
how, as a nation, we have gotten ourselves into such a situation and how, if at
all, we are to get out. A little background here may be helpful.[1]

As students of psychology well know, the first usable intelligence test was
developed in France by Alfred Binet and Theodore Simon in 1905. Binet had
been asked by the French commissioner of instruction to develop a testing
procedure that would identify those students whose academic aptitude was
low enough that they might benefit from placement in special schools. The
original Binet test, then, was considered a practical diagnostic instrument;
Binet never intended to make a distinction between "acquired and congenital
feeble-mindedness." But the test was the first "successful" attempt in a long
series of efforts to develop mental tests, and it soon came to be accepted as a
test of intelligence. Evidence shows that Binet himself was not happy with
this state of affairs; as late as 1909, he was challenging and criticizing the mis-
use of his test by psychologists.

Alfred Binet died in 1911, and the task of revision was transferred to Stanford University. The Binet scale worked poorly in California; the results were
quite different from those in Paris. Binet's test was, therefore, revised for use
in this country by Lewis Terman of Stanford University. With that revision,
the Stanford-Binet test came to occupy an increasingly important position in
the American educational, psychological, and even political landscape.
Surely Binet himself would have been alarmed at the intent of this American-
ized version of his test. To quote Terman:

> ... [I]n the near future intelligence tests will bring tens of thousands
> of these high-grade defectives under the surveillance and protec-
> tion of society. This will ultimately result in curtailing the reproduc-
> tion of feeble-mindedness and in the elimination of an enormous
> amount of crime, pauperism, and industrial inefficiency. It is hardly
> necessary to emphasize that the high-grade cases of the type now so

frequently overlooked are precisely the ones whose guardianship it is most important for the state to assume.[2]

There seemed to be little doubt in Terman's mind as to who the defectives were likely to be. He found that a low level of intelligence (IQs in the 70 to 80 range) "is very, very common among Spanish-Indian and Mexican families of the Southwest and also among Negroes. Their dullness seems to be racial, or at least inherent in the family stocks from which they come."[3]

It is easy to be shocked and chilled by the overt racism of these words, but I think it is almost impossible to understand how such notions as the measurability and heritability of intelligence passed into almost mystical acceptance without looking at the historical climate of the times.

Bureaucratic societies have always found it necessary to categorize or classify people for certain purposes. But during the later part of the nineteenth century and particularly during the early part of the twentieth century, Darwinism had a strong hold on the thinking of America. It was an age that believed in fostering the "preservation of Favored Races in the Struggle of Life" (to use Darwin's own words). The popular catch phrases of Darwinism—"survival of the fittest" and the "struggle for existence"—offered an instant philosophical pegboard on which Americans, and American conservatives in particular, could hang a doctrine of laissez faire and a determination to maintain the current economic and social structure. The British philosopher Herbert Spencer was one of the first Darwinists to enjoy a considerable vogue in this country. But it was perhaps William Graham Sumner of Yale who was the most influential social Darwinist in America, and we need only read Sumner to understand how forcefully the theory of Darwinism could be applied to social and political arenas:

> Let it be understood that we cannot go outside of this alternative; liberty, inequality, survival of the fittest; not liberty, equality, survival of the unfittest. The former carries society forward and favors all its best members; the latter carries society downwards and favors all its worst members.[4]

To this philosophical context, add two important historical events: the great immigration to America (which had assumed massive proportions by the turn of the century) and World War I. Both of these events had a profound impact on this country in many ways, and, not incidentally, both helped to carry forth into popular acceptance the use of IQ tests.

Until 1921, no numerical limitation was placed on immigration to this country. But certain controls had begun as early as 1875: By the early part of the century, as great waves of Italian, Polish, Russian, and Jewish immigrants began reaching this country, the public, faced with more "exotic" types than the English, Scandinavian, and German immigrants it had been accustomed to, began to raise serious questions about some form of "quality control." In fact, even the "enlightened" Henry George was writing, as early as 1883, "What in a few years more are we to do for a dumping ground? Will it make our difficulty the less that our human garbage can vote?"[5] Such groups as the Boston-formed Immigration Restriction League were an indication of the intense antiforeign sentiment that was sweeping the country. Would the new immigrants undermine our political and social system? It was a persistent question, and concern continued to mount. Not coincidentally, in 1912 the

Public Health Service invited Henry Goddard to Ellis Island, where he administered the Binet test to immigrants, with an eagle eye out for detecting
the feeble-minded before they might enter the country.

In his extraordinary work, *World of Our Fathers*,[6] Irving Howe paints a
vivid picture of the hardships of the voyage that led to the immigrants' arrival
at Ellis Island, not to mention the confusion and disorientation they experienced as they were "processed." Moreover, all shared the terrible fear of
being deported, of being sent back. Given the circumstances, it is surprising
that more were not, in fact, deported; although, as Howe points out, "It is a
sad irony, though familiar to students of democratic politics, that under relatively lax administrations at Ellis Island, which sometimes allowed rough
handling of immigrants and even closed an eye to corruption, immigrants had
a better chance of getting past the inspectors than when the commissioner
was a public-spirited Yankee intent upon literal adherence to the law."[7]

The feeble-minded or mentally defective were marked with an *x* and
returned to their native shores or wherever they might find a home. In 1917
Goddard reported that "the number of aliens deported because of feeble-
mindedness . . . increased approximately 350% in 1913 and 570% in 1914. . . ."[8]
Who were these feeble-minded? Goddard's test results showed that 83% of the
Jews, 80% of the Hungarians, 79% of the Italians, and 87% of the Russians ar-
riving at Ellis Island were "feeble-minded."[9]

All of this might seem an ugly but irrelevant bit of American history were
it not for the fact that it illustrates cogently how, from an early point on, we
began to allow the notion of intelligence as a racial characteristic to creep into
our national psyche. But it would take World War I to bring the intelligence
test into full national prominence.

At the outset of the war, Robert Yerkes, then president of the American
Psychological Association, proposed a mass intelligence testing of draftees.
The military accepted the proposal, and as a result the now-famous Army
Alpha test was developed. The tests were originally designed to help in the
placement of the draftee, but, in fact, the test results were little used.

After the war, however, an analysis of the scores of approximately 125,000
draftees was made, and the results were published in 1921 by the National
Academy of Sciences. Not surprisingly, correlations were again made
between intelligence rating and race; and again, the Latin and Slavic groups
fared poorly. But the draftees in general didn't score as high as the psychologists felt they should, and the result was a general alarm that the intelligence
of Americans was declining. Lothrop Stoddard, writing in "The Revolt
Against Civilization," sounded the alarm when he wrote that "the *average*
mental age of Americans is only about 14," a curious conclusion when one ex-
amines the question of how the average adult intelligence could be less than
the average adult intelligence.

One of the few voices raised in protest over such conclusions was that of
Walter Lippmann, who, in a remarkable series of articles published in *The
New Republic* (and answered by Lewis Terman),[10] engaged the entire issue
of intelligence testing. Lippmann was quick to point out the intrinsic flaw in
the dogma of IQ: "Because the results are expressed in numbers, it is easy to
make the mistake of thinking that the intelligence test is a measure like a foot
rule or a pair of scales. . . . But intelligence is not an abstraction like length and
weight; it is an exceedingly complicated notion which nobody has as yet

succeeded in defining." Lippmann went on to warn that, "if the impression takes root that these tests really measure intelligence, that they constitute a sort of last judgment on the child's capacity, that they reveal scientifically his predestined ability, then it would be a thousand times better if all the intelligence testers and all their questionnaires were sunk without warning in the Sargasso Sea."

Unfortunately, little attention was paid to Lippmann's warning. He was regarded merely as a cranky critic of the tests. In fact, dazzled by the apparent success of the Army Alpha test, schools and colleges and organizations quickly seized on psychological testing as a useful and convenient device for sorting students. The development of achievement testing soon followed, and by 1929 more than five million tests were being administered annually.

Finally, although it may seem ironic in an age when the cultural and racial bias of the tests is much debated, I think it is important to note that the tests were perceived during the early years to be an egalitarian and objective way to select students, particularly for college admission. As Ralph Tyler has observed, "objective tests . . . were of special significance for those young people who deviated from the social standards that were tacitly accepted by teachers and principals. The tests furnished a means by which such students could show educational attainments apart from their manners, their social behavior, and their family background."[11]

I have gone into this historical background of intelligence testing for two reasons. First, I think it's essential to an understanding of how the notion that each human being had a native intelligence—one that could be measured and that remained relatively constant from birth—passed from mere popular acceptance to a state of almost mystical belief, one that persists to our own day. The other reason is that while the validity of IQ testing has been debated for decades now, the IQ controversy has recently become more heatedly—if not ferociously—debated. New York, Washington, D.C., and Los Angeles have stopped the use of IQ tests in the schools, and the state of Massachusetts is currently considering such a step. In addition, there have been several new and notable contributions to the literature on the subject, which are likely to add fuel to the fire—Leon Kamin's *The Politics and Science of IQ* and Benjamin Fine's *The Stranglehold of the IQ*.

Though the books share a common topic, they could not be less alike. Kamin's book is a superbly researched and splendidly written study of how we have allowed politics to taint our science in the area of IQ, particularly in respect to the question of its heritability, and it deserves wide reading within the profession. On the other hand, Fine's book is directed to the layman, and of the two it will probably be the book most widely read by parents. Published posthumously, the book is somewhat marred by its loose organization and its lack of a trenchant and polished style. But Fine's arguments are well reasoned and in its major points the book is right on target. For these reasons, it should help to dispel a good many myths parents may hold about IQ and standardized achievement tests.

Still, the effect of either of these books, not to mention the plethora of journal articles currently in view, remains doubtful. One need only recall *The Tyranny of Testing*,[12] by Banesh Hoffmann, a book written with great wit and style and elegant in the clarity of its thinking. Hoffmann's powerful brief against the dangers of machine-scored, multiple-choice tests should have aroused public indignation, if not a national movement to reform the tests. It did not. Hoffmann's book was debated in the education and public press for a time, and Hoffmann himself publicly debated the testers. But *The Tyranny of Testing* was published in 1962; it was only a few years later that we experienced the advent of unprecedented major federal aid to education, and consequently a new raison d'être for an increased use of the tests: evaluation of the programs funded. Similarly, the accountability movement today gives further impetus to the use of standardized testing.

But in spite of the continued proliferation of standardized tests, IQ testing has run into some special problems of its own. Put on guard by the studies of the new social Darwinists—Arthur Jensen, William Shockley, and Richard J. Herrnstein—minority groups have become alert to how the tests can easily be turned into an "engine of cruelty," to use Walter Lippmann's description. Moreover, many educators and parents are beginning to realize what Fine points out—"that the IQ measures what the child has already learned, not his capacity to learn. . . . The IQ cannot tell you anything about a child's curiosity, his motivation, his inner thoughts, his ability to get along with people, his chance to become an active or responsible member of society, his role as a community or national leader, his creative abilities, or his contributions to mankind."

Most important, educators are increasingly becoming more aware of the illogic of attempting to measure something we cannot define, not to mention the illogic of attempting to place on a single scale human beings who possess a wide variety of talents and abilities. As Jerrold Zacharias has observed elsewhere, "people are complex—talented in some ways, clumsy in others; educated in some ways, ignorant in others; calm, careful, persistent, and patient in some ways; impulsive, careless, or lazy in others. Not only are these characteristics different in different people, they also vary in one person from time to time. . . . It makes no sense to represent a multidimensional space with an array of numbers ranged along one line."[13]

Furthermore, none of these arguments should leave out the basic flaws inherent in the multiple-choice, machine-scored format, as well as the often inaccurate, invalid, and misleading content of the tests themselves.

Fine argues that the long overdue moratorium on IQ testing should take "top priority in the nation's educational agenda." But how reasonable is it for us to expect that such a moratorium on IQ testing will come into being? There certainly seems to be a growing climate of opinion against the tests. There are, however, a number of problems that I believe persist in our discussions of both IQ and standardized achievement testing.

The first problem is that we continue to argue about how to "fix" the IQ tests. Our debate stays within what Sheldon White has called a curiously restricted kind of "magic circle." Thus we still read or hear arguments for building more "culture-fair" tests, or proposals to improve the accuracy of the tests. I have even heard questions raised about how we can improve the scores on IQ tests—hence in effect, I assume, asking how we can raise the "intelligence" of Americans. But all of these arguments rest on the belief that there is some single, measurable human capability called "intelligence." Only when we have discarded that notion will we be able to make real progress in getting rid of the tests.

Second, we continue to argue that, without IQ tests, we will be left without a means of designing a school program to meet the child's strengths and weaknesses. This presupposes that the IQ tests offer us different and more conclusive information than, say, any number of achievement tests. In reality, the IQ tests are in most respects indistinguishable from the achievement tests. The difference is that an IQ score is apt to hamper a child's educational development when it is perceived as some kind of final judgment on his or her ability, as it too often is.

Moreover, while IQ scores are ostensibly used for the purpose of making judgments about individuals, we seem unable to resist using the scores to make judgments about groups. In this connection, I propose that we put an immediate stop to the shameful business of inferring or drawing conclusions about racial characteristics on the basis of IQ tests.

It is not my purpose here to debate the merits of Allan Ornstein's recent article in these pages.° But I think a number of Ornstein's points perpetuate, though perhaps quite unintentionally, just these kinds of inferences, of which we have seen all too many.

In attempting to build a case against devising culture-fair tests, the author cites the invalidity of the Black Intelligence Test of Cultural Homogeneity (BITCH) as a measure of intelligence, a point with which few people would argue. But after criticizing the BITCH for relying on vocabulary ("The questions are limited to vocabulary, and are ambiguous, both too hard and too easy; indeed the test is irrelevant to the larger society"), Ornstein goes on to observe:

> If we are interested in IQ for what it predicts by way of academic (and, to a lesser degree, occupational) performance, our verbally oriented tests fulfill the purpose they are intended to serve. . . . Furthermore, nonverbal scores fail to reflect the full range of a child's mental abilities. One perceives and thinks in terms of language. The child who is deficient in language will have trouble dealing with perceptual tasks such as classifying, selecting, and arranging. Interestingly enough, the intellectual deficit among blacks as measured by present instruments is not restricted to verbal tests; nonverbal tests of intelligence show an equally large difference. Furthermore, if general intelligence scores are broken down into various component abilities by scoring subtests, minor differences appear in the size of difference by race. *The average black intellectual deficit is quite general and is not restricted to specific skills involving standard English.* (Emphasis added)

Quite apart from its questionable assertions about the value of verbal tests, the article rests on several assumptions with which I take issue. Perhaps the primary one is that, assuming agreement that intelligence is the ability to label, categorize, conceptualize, and problem solve (a doubtful assumption), current IQ tests measure these abilities adequately. A look at the tests should convince us otherwise. Another assumption implicit in Ornstein's argument is that IQ tests must be valid tests of intelligence, since they predict school achievement. Leaving aside the issue of how good the correlation actually is—itself open to debate—surely it is understandable that by observing how well a child solves a series of puzzles we can predict how well he will do on

° "IQ Tests and the Culture Issue," *Phi Delta Kappan*, February 1976, pp. 403, 404.

future puzzles. The ability to do well on tests predicts the ability to do well on future and similar tests. But does the ability to do well on IQ tests actually reveal something about innate intelligence? Ornstein appears to believe so. After using such false verities to establish that IQ tests do in fact measure intelligence, he delivers his coup de grace: "The average black intellectual deficit is quite general and is not restricted to specific skills involving standard English." While the wording of the statement might bear out the linguistic predictions of George Orwell, I don't think there can be any doubt of what Ornstein is saying.

Nor do I agree that *"The remedy is not the elimination of the test or alteration of skills demanded by the school, so that there will be no need for such tests, but the elimination of learning inequalities and social inequalities"* (emphasis in original). Getting rid of IQ tests in no way requires us to alter the skills demanded by the schools, unless by chance the skills are merely the raison d'être for the tests. Is the tail indeed wagging the dog? Nor does Ornstein seem to see that the tests themselves may be one reason for the learning and social inequalities he is so anxious to remove.

Third, we become hamstrung by the concern that if we do in fact abolish the current IQ tests, then we must find a substitute for measuring intelligence. If we once accept the idea that we cannot measure what we cannot currently define or understand, then we will stop trying to measure "intelligence" and move toward a major effort to improve our methods of identifying each child's unique talents and abilities and assessing our progress as educators in helping that child to develop them. By no means should this endeavor be confused with an attempt to measure intelligence. My point is that the broader, the more ill-defined, the more complex the concept, the more difficult it becomes to measure. For example, it is easier to assess with some degree of accuracy a child's ability to compute than to measure his "creativity." We need to concentrate on determining definable forms of ability and degrees of competency within key but specific areas, the latter to be determined by the education community and the public.

This will require a strong commitment from the profession to develop alternatives to the present tests, not to mention major commitments of funding from the foundations, government agencies, and the Educational Testing Service for the development of such assessment techniques.

The fourth critical problem is that we have come to think of the development of tests, of test construction, as a science, albeit as a rather arcane one. With its highly specialized and technical language, psychometrics seems inaccessible and incomprehensible to the majority of the education profession. This illusion that test construction is a highly scientific process has given rise to the belief that the tests themselves, therefore, must be an "accurate" measure of a pupil's capability or progress. If as a profession we are ever going to make any progress in developing more effective assessment procedures, we must be ready to subject the current tests to rigorous examination, which means that the current secrecy surrounding the tests must be removed.

A related problem is the argument that criticism of the tests by the profession stems from an unwillingness to be held accountable. I believe that teachers, principals, and administrators are perfectly willing to be held accountable, but *not* on the basis of such an inadequate and misleading measure of their performance. To quote researcher Gene Glass, "Aside from the irrelevance of much of the content of standardized achievement tests, their use in evaluating teachers is unfair. . . . Even if the validity and fairness objections to using standardized tests could be met, available evidence indicates that teachers' effects on pupils' knowledge cannot be reliably measured by such tests."[14]

If we persist in defining accountability on the basis of test scores, we will continue to encourage teachers to "teach to the tests" and thereby seriously skew our entire educational process. I think we need only examine the nineteenth-century British experience with payment by results to see the inevitable results of such a misconception of accountability. That practice had a profoundly malevolent effect on the English education system, and I believe that determining the effectiveness of educators on the basis of standardized test results will have no less injurious an effect on our own system.

In this respect, it may be worth noting that we have yet to have a definite legal ruling on the use of test results as a valid measure of teacher competence. The *Scheelhaase* case is often cited as such. (Scheelhaase was a nontenured teacher who was dismissed—on the superintendent's recommendation—on the basis of poor performance by her students on standardized tests.[15]) But, in fact, the court skirted the question of the tests' validity as an appropriate measure of performance and ruled that "The board was entitled to rely upon the recommendation and conclusions of its superintendent, notwithstanding the existence of strong opinion contrary to his, regarding the use of the ITBS or ITED tests as a tool for teacher evaluation. . . . Thus its decision, even though premised upon an apparently erroneous expert opinion, cannot be faulted as arbitrary and capricious. The board's mere mistake in judgment or in weighing the evidence does not demonstrate any violation of substantive due process."[16]

Finally, we currently hear the argument that, without the tests, educational standards will decline. But we must ask, Whose standards? The testing companies'? We see the same problem in education's current tempest in a teapot, the decline in test scores. There are many possible reasons for this decline, among them a more heterogeneous student population; the availability of more options at the high school level, with fewer students taking the "traditional" subjects the tests deal with; a new attitude toward the tests by the students; and not least the content of the tests themselves. Certainly more than a single factor is at work. But if the tests do indeed insure the maintenance of high educational standards, then we must wonder how effective they have been. If the current test score decline represents a lowering of standards and a decline in the quality of teaching, then this has occurred in spite of the fact that as a nation we administer over 200 million achievement tests each year. (This figure, incidentally, represents only about 65% of all educational psychological testing that is carried out.)

One further observation in this respect: Critics of the tests are often linked to those who want to kill the messenger bearing bad news. The problem, to my mind, is not that the news is bad but that it is so misleading, so open to misinterpretation, and often so erroneous. It is not what the news is telling us; it is what it is failing to report. Critics are objecting not to the concept of evaluation but to the quality of the data base. The current tests are far more useful for sorting and classifying students than for diagnosing individual learning problems, which is the area in which teachers and principals need the most help.

No one should interpret the current controversy over standardized tests as an effort to abandon assessment. Rather, it is an effort to develop assessment procedures that are more in keeping with a new set of educational and social assumptions that we as a society are working on: that the purpose of education is not to sort people but to educate them; that in a knowledge society we need to expose as many people to education as possible, not to exclude them from it; that human beings are marvelously variegated in their talents and abilities, and it is the function of education to nurture them wisely and carefully; and, not least, that education has an overriding responsibility to respect and draw on cultural and racial diversity. Assessment of students must begin to reflect that philosophy, and that is the true reason for the current call for test reform and an end to IQ testing.

---

1. For additional background, the reader may wish to refer to a number of sources from which this discussion was drawn, particularly Richard Hofstadter's *Social Darwinism in American Thought* (Boston: Beacon Press, 1955); Leon J. Kamin's *The Science and Politics of IQ* (Washington, D.C.: Lawrence Erlbaum Associates, 1974); Walter Lippmann's series of articles in *The New Republic* (October 25, 1922; November 1, 1922; November 8, 1922; November 15, 1922; November 22, 1922; November 29, 1922; and Lewis M. Terman's reply, December 27, 1922); and Sheldon H. White's "The Social Implications of IQ," *National Elementary Principal*, March/April, 1975, pp. 4-14.

2. Lewis M. Terman, *The Measurement of Intelligence* (Boston: Houghton Mifflin, 1916), pp. 6, 7.

3. Ibid., pp. 91, 92.

4. Hofstadter, op. cit., p. 51.

5. Irving Howe, *World of Our Fathers* (New York: Harcourt Brace Jovanovich, 1976), p. 51.

6. Ibid., pp. 26-63.

7. Ibid., p. 45.

8. H. H. Goddard, "Mental Tests and the Immigrant," *Journal of Delinquency*, vol. 2, 1917, p. 271.

9. H. H. Goddard, "The Binet Tests in Relation to Immigration," *Journal of Psycho-Asthenics*, vol. 18, 1913, pp. 105-7.

10. Terman, *The New Republic*, op. cit.

11. Ralph W. Tyler, *Perspectives on American Education* (Chicago: Science Research Associates, 1976), p. 29.

12. Banesh Hoffmann, *The Tyranny of Testing* (New York: Collier Books, 1962).

13. Jerrold R. Zacharias, "The Trouble with IQ Tests," *The National Elementary Principal*, March/April, 1975, p. 25.

14. Gene V Glass, "Statistical and Measurement Problems in Implementing the Stull Act" (Paper presented at Stanford University, October 12-14, 1972).

15. See Paul Tractenberg, "Legal Issues in the Testing of School Personnel," and Henry C. Johnson, Jr., "Court, Craft, and Competence," in the May 1976 *Phi Delta Kappan* for detailed discussions of *Scheelhaase* and other cases in the measurement of teacher competence.

16. *Scheelhaase* v. *Woodbury Central Community School District*, U.S. Court of Appeals, Eighth Circuit, 7-1067 (1973).

Teaching Sequential Thought:
The Cognitive-Skills Approach
by Arthur Whimbey

*The ability to proceed through a sequence of analytical steps is
the foundation of all higher-order reasoning and comprehension.
Mr. Whimbey offers practical suggestions for teachers trying to
develop problem-solving skills, regardless of the subject matter.*

A significant percentage of the students in an advanced education course at a
major university were unable to solve the following problem:

**What day follows the day before yesterday if two days from
now will be Sunday?**

Put your mind to work on this problem for a few minutes and you will see
that, in a sense, it couldn't be simpler. If two days from now will be Sunday,
then one day from now will be Saturday, so today must be Friday. Furthermore, if today is Friday, then yesterday was Thursday, the day before yesterday was Wednesday, and the day that follows Wednesday is Thursday. So the
answer is Thursday.

Obviously, creative leaps and abstract insights are not required for this
problem—just systematic, sequential thought. Yet that is a thinking pattern in
which many students are weak. Try this problem with some of your own
students—even weaker graduate students—and observe why they fail. You
will find that they are unskilled in breaking a problem into clear, sequential
steps.

Low-aptitude students frequently try to go from Sunday (the only day
named in the problem) directly to an estimated answer without taking the
necessary intermediate steps. They begin with Sunday, scan the relationships
between the days stated in the problem, then with one vague leap pick a day
that seems approximately where the relationships would lead. It is for this
reason that Benjamin Bloom and Lois Broder have characterized low-
aptitude students as "one-shot thinkers."[1]

Even when low-aptitude thinkers do succeed in using the second half of
the problem ("two days from now will be Sunday") to determine that today is
Friday, they frequently will not separate the second half of the problem from
the first half, set the second half aside, and work through the first half. Low-
aptitude thinkers are not skilled in organized, sequential attacks on information. Instead, they skip unsystematically back and forth through the entire
problem, reexamining information that is no longer pertinent and thus confusing themselves.

Academic Aptitude Viewed as a Cognitive Skill. The ability to proceed
through a sequence of analytical steps is the foundation of all higher-order
reasoning and comprehension. It is what psychometrists call "academic aptitude" or "intelligence." All complex abstractions, classifications, transforma-
tions, problem solutions, and applications of generalizations are products of
accurate, sequential thought. But many of today's high school and college students have not sharpened this ability sufficiently for even moderate success in

academic work. Weaknesses surface in all areas, ranging from mathematical problem solving to the comprehension of history. Consider this math problem:

Ten full crates of walnuts weigh 410 pounds, while an empty crate weighs 10 pounds. How much do the walnuts themselves weigh?
  a) 400
  b) 390
  c) 310
  d) 510
  e) 420

This question is interesting because it is not laced with specialized mathematical operations and concepts. All that is necessary for its solution is for one to spell out the ideas fully, one at a time. Although the correct answer is 310 pounds, a common answer is 400 pounds. This error is easy to rationalize. The weight of only one box rather than 10 boxes was subtracted from the total. However, the answers 420 pounds and 510 pounds are also selected regularly by low-aptitude high school and college students, and these are less easily rationalized.

In solving the problem, the total weight must be categorized into two components—the weight of the walnuts and the weight of the crates. Then the crate weight must be broken down into 10 subcomponents—the weights of the individual crates. This is shown in the following diagram:

10 lb.	10 lb.	10 lb.	10 lb.	10 lb.	10 lb.	10 lb.	10 lb.	10 lb.	10 lb.	Total, 410 lbs.
Walnut Weight: 310 pounds										

A person need not visualize this diagram. But he must conceptualize the total weight in this manner—i.e., he must sequentially spell out this break-down in his mind—before he begins any arithmetic. If he doesn't, yet is forced to come up with some answer, he may perform meaningless arithmetic operations. He scans the problem and picks up some numbers but then combines them in a way that does not correspond with the true relationships between what they represent. Thus he may take $410 - 10 = 400$, or $410 + 10 = 420$, or $410 + 10(10) = 510$.

All mathematics teachers have heard certain students complain that they know mathematics but can't do word problems. What they really mean is, they can do simple arithmetic but can't organize the facts of a problem in a way that allows them to use arithmetic operations appropriately. It goes without saying that knowledge of arithmetic without the ability to comprehend problems is of limited value.

Reading and understanding history appears superficially very different from mathematical problem solving. But let's examine this essay on Greek culture that a college student misinterpreted:

> Some scraps of evidence bear out those who hold a very high opinion of the average level of culture among the Athenians of the Great Age. The funeral speech of Pericles is the most famous indica-

tion from Athenian literature that [the cultural] level was indeed high. Pericles was, however, a politician, and he may have been flattering his audience. We know that thousands of Athenians sat hour after hour in the theater listening to the plays of the great Greek dramatists. The plays, especially the tragedies, are at a very high intellectual level throughout. There are no letdowns, no concessions to the lowbrows or to the demands of "realism," such as the scene of the gravediggers in *Hamlet*. The music and dancing woven into these plays were almost certainly at an equally high level. Our opera—not Italian opera, not even Wagner, but the restrained, difficult opera of the eighteenth century—is probably the best modern parallel. The comparison is no doubt dangerous, but can you imagine almost the entire population of an American city (in suitable installments, of course) sitting through performances of Mozart's *Don Giovanni* or Gluck's *Orpheus?* Perhaps the Athenian masses went to these plays because of a lack of other amusements. They could at least understand something of what went on, since the subjects were part of their folklore. For the American people, the subjects of grand opera are not part of their folklore.

The author's attitude toward Greek plays is one of 1) qualified approval, 2) grudging admiration, 3) studied indifference, 4) partial hostility, 5) great respect.

The student read this article without a time limit and was permitted to refer back to it freely as he answered the question. He chose alternative No. 1.

I asked him to explain his choice and he replied, "The article said that Athenians may have attended the plays because they had nothing better to do, not because they were good." Notice that, in the context of the article, the student's reply is more a comment on the Athenian people than a criticism of the plays.

I asked what else the article said and he replied, "Pericles may have merely been flattering the Athenians; their culture may not have been that outstanding." This second comment has almost nothing to do with the plays; it bears solely on the culture. The student had not formed a distinct picture of the author's opinion of Greek plays in contrast with his opinion of Greek culture.

What form does the successful reading act take? The first sentence of the Greek culture essay began, "Some scraps of evidence bear out. . . ." What can be gathered from this? It suggests that a proposition is about to be presented that is supported by only meager or weak evidence. The second part of the sentence presents the questionable proposition: The average level of Athenian culture was high.

Fully understanding this sentence involves sequentially interpreting and combining the two parts. But many college students I have tested failed to keep track of the first part. Instead, they took the sentence as an unqualified assertion that the average level of Athenian culture was high.

Continuing in the article, the next two sentences present evidence supporting the proposition about the culture—but then other evidence that discounts and neutralizes the support. In abstracting and integrating this information, the good reader begins formulating two categories in his mind: 1) evidence supporting the proposition that the cultural level was high and 2) evidence questioning the support.

The remaining sentences of the article praise Greek plays, but then question whether the plays truly reflect average Athenian taste. Thus the pattern continues of first presenting evidence seeming to support the proposition but then attacking the evidence.

Finally, at the end of the article, the reader comes to the question concerning the quality of the plays. Evidence on the plays, in this article, is a subset of evidence about the culture. The reader may trust his memory or review the article. Either way, he must now sort the material into two new categories: 1) evidence bearing on the plays, 2) evidence not bearing on the plays.

In short order the reader finds many reasons to support alternative No. 5—the author's attitude is one of "great respect." The only thing that remains is to make certain that none of the author's remarks can be classed under one of the other alternatives, e.g., "partial hostility." But the evidence is all one-sided; the author has nothing but superlatives for the plays.

Notice how the material in this article must be mentally sorted and categorized in forming generalizations about the author's views. In this sense, comprehending the history selection uses the same mental processes as those employed in solving the previous mathematics problem, in which the total weight was categorized into different parts. More than that, categorizing is simply one form of sequential construction of understanding—the same skill isolated in both previous problems.

Teaching Thinking in Every Class. As our examples have shown, thinking—at least to some degree—consists of definable mental activities. The cognitive-skills approach to teaching makes explicit in instruction the mental activities engaged in by successful thinkers as they comprehend ideas and solve problems.

Teaching thinking runs into a peculiar difficulty. Generally there are two phases to teaching any skill: 1) The skill is explained and demonstrated to the student. 2) The student practices the skill with guidance and feedback. For example, golf is taught by showing the novice how to grasp the club, how to place his feet, and how to move his arms and body as he swings. The novice watches the pro—he can even watch a slow-motion film of the pro in action— and in this way he can learn the pro's technique. Furthermore, the pro observes the pupil as he practices, he points out his flaws, and he shows him how to improve.

In contrast to playing golf, the activities of skilled reasoning are generally carried out inside one's head. This makes it difficult for a teacher to teach and for a learner to learn. To teach something, we would like it out in the open where both the teacher and student can see it. As it is, a beginner cannot observe how an expert thinks in analyzing complex ideas. And the expert has trouble demonstrating his technique to a beginning student.

One solution to this dilemma is to have both students and teachers think aloud as they work through ideas. Have them vocalize their thoughts as they analyze relationships, sort concepts, and form generalizations. Naturally, a person cannot put all the motions of his mind into words, any more than a map maker could show every bend and hill along a road. But research shows that he can exhibit enough of his thinking for someone else to follow his path through a problem or complex concept.

A new course offered by the Physics Department at the University of

Massachusetts, Amherst, illustrates how this approach is used in the class-room. To teach students to verbalize their thinking as they solve problems, the class begins with problems from a workbook titled *Development of Problem-Solving Skills for Vocational and Educational Achievement.* The problems require careful analysis but do not involve knowledge of physics or mathematics. Students are asked to think aloud as they work a problem. They then read a transcribed protocol of how a good problem solver (a graduate student or professional) responded to the same problem. Here is a sample problem and a response from a third-year medical student with an exceptional academic record:

Original Problem

If the word <u>sentence</u> contains fewer than nine letters and more than three vowels, circle the first vowel. Otherwise, circle the consonant that is farthest to the right in the word.

Problem Solver's Response

The problem solver (Pr.S.) read the entire problem aloud.	"If the word *sentence* contains fewer than nine letters and more than three vowels, circle the first vowel. Otherwise, circle the consonant that is farthest to the right in the word."
	I'll start from the beginning.
	"If the word *sentence* contains fewer than nine letters. . . "
The Pr.S. pointed to the letters with his pen as he counted. **The Pr.S. wrote <u>yes</u> over the sentence (see original problem).**	I'll count the letters in *sentence*. 1, 2, 3, 4, 5, 6, 7, 8. Let me check it. 1, 2, 3, 4, 5, 6, 7, 8. So it does have fewer than nine letters. I'll write the word *yes* above the problem. That way I'll remember it.
The Pr.S. resumed reading.	"and more than three vowels . . ."
The Pr.S. pointed with his pen as he counted.	1, 2, 3. Let me check that. 1, 2, 3. It contains exactly three vowels, not more than three vowels. I'll write *no* on the problem to remind me.
	"circle the first vowel."
	So I won't do that.
	"Otherwise, circle the consonant that is farthest to the right in the word."
	The consonant farthest to the right? Let me see. Which is my right hand? This is my right hand. O.K., so the last letter is the one farthest to the right. But the last letter is *e*. The next letter over is *c*. So it is the consonant farthest to the right. I'll circle the *c*.

After this introduction to the technique of thinking aloud, the class shifts to problems involving basic physics concepts. For example, this problem teaches graphing as well as the rudiments of acceleration.

Problem

A bicyclist sets out on a 10-mile trip. The first half of the trip is level, but in the second half he must go up and down two hills.

Sketch a distance versus time graph that is consistent with the above information.

Students work in pairs or small groups, learn each other's strategies of attack, and continually check for errors. The instructor circulates among the class, answering questions and raising points for discussion. The course is new and still developing, so its ultimate effectiveness is yet to be seen. However, students are very enthusiastic. Here are three typical remarks:

> "The largest value of the . . . lab is in its function of directing students' energies at understanding. Another important function . . . is emphasizing mathematics as a tool for understanding physics rather than as a stumbling block."
> "I feel smarter."
> "The arguments and the questions the people in the lab ask make you verbalize your ideas, and that makes them clearer. You can see why they are right or wrong."

Science teachers can get more details of the program by writing its originator, Jack Lochhead.[2]

Courses with similar orientations but in different subjects are being developed at other universities. Steven Bartlett teaches a class in the Department of Philosophy, Saint Louis University, in which he uses Rubinstein's *Patterns of Problem Solving*[3] as the assigned text, combining it with vocalized practice in philosophical reasoning.[4] Students gain an average of six IQ points on the California Test of Mental Maturity. Perhaps of more immediate importance, Bartlett finds that the effectiveness of vocalized problem solving shows up "in the subsequent ability of class members to independently develop careful analyses with respect to a set of related problems."

In the area of language learning, Celia Barberena at Bowling Green State University has devised an effective Spanish course for educationally deprived students. Working in pairs, students begin with booklets that guide them through all the mental steps necessary to understand and answer questions in Spanish with correct grammatical form. Subsequent booklets gradually delete the reasoning guideposts, allowing students to initiate chains of mental steps on their own. Strong student satisfaction with this format is reflected in comments such as, "It shows me how to learn Spanish." Furthermore, a comparison of test grades shows current averages in the A and B range, whereas classes in past semesters scored in the C and D range.

These applications of the cognitive-skills approach in teaching physics, Spanish, and philosophy have appeared within the last two years. However, back in 1960 the *New York Times* carried a front-page report of Professor Albert Upton's experimental English course at Whittier College in which the average IQ of 280 freshmen increased by 10.5 points. Classes met once a week in a large lecture session and three times a week in small problem-solving groups supervised by advanced students. Students worked increasingly difficult problems dealing with comprehension and reasoning in the use of language, and they took turns explaining their analyses to the remainder of the group. English instructors such as Eugene Brunelle at SUNY, Buffalo, who adopted Upton's method, confirmed his IQ gains under rigorous experimental conditions and found parallel gains on reading comprehension tests and Guilford creativity measures. The Upton approach has recently been incorporated into a series of workbooks titled *Think*, which can be used with students ranging from the fifth grade to college and extend in reading level down to functional illiteracy.

Naturally, we would like students to develop strong thinking skills early, so that they can profit fully from the remainder of their education. Norman Chambers, director of the school psychology program at Bowling Green State University, is showing elementary school teachers how to use vocalized thinking to diagnose and correct learning difficulties. First the teachers pair up and solve problems vocally for several sessions. Then each teacher works individually with a youngster who has been identified by the school as showing poor progress in some area. Through a combination of discussions with the youngster's classroom teacher, his classroom quiz performances, and informal and standardized tests, the difficulty is pinpointed. For different youngsters this has included weaknesses in overall reading comprehension, drawing inferences from pictures of stories, understanding fractions, performing multiplication, selecting suffixes for verbs, and interpreting math word problems. A series of exercises is constructed in the weak area, starting at a very easy level and gradually becoming more difficult. The exercises are obtained from published sources and class quizzes, or they may be devised by the teacher. Starting with easy problems, the teacher demonstrates vocalized thinking for the youngster, then asks him to try it. While some youngsters are initially shy about vocalizing, so far all of those in the program have picked up the technique quickly. Furthermore, teachers report that after only three or four sessions, even the youngest pupils become more conscious of the control they have over their own thinking activities, and they become more concerned about accuracy and thoroughness. Here is one teacher's summary of her work with 6-year-old Tony, who is about to enter the second grade but last year had difficulty with math story problems:

I had Tony tell me step by step how he went about solving the problem. At times I had him draw diagrams for problems he was having particular difficulty with. Tony didn't really enjoy this part of the process, because he is weak in the area of fine motor control. He does not write neatly and has a hard time drawing things. Because of this, he didn't want to illustrate the problems, even simply. Tony did appear to like discussing the problems orally.

Taking Tony through the problem-solving process helped him in the few sessions where we worked together. Through using the process, Tony now reads the problems more slowly and more accurately, gaining all the information instead of just bits and pieces as he had previously done.

Generally, the youngsters show modest but consistent gains in test scores. Nevertheless, all teachers in the program agree that the training must somehow be continued in the youngsters' subsequent schooling, or the new mental habits are likely to weaken and fade. One fourth-grade teacher has begun asking students to vocalize all of their thinking as they solve long division problems at the blackboard. Another teacher will try working with just five students at a time, engaging them in vocalized thinking, while the rest of the class is busy on an assignment supervised by the teacher's aide. But all teachers report having a new perspective on teaching. That is, they agree that there are definite mental activities underlying scholastic performances, and these activities should be explicitly taught.

Arthur Jensen opened his controversial 1969 *Harvard Educational Review* article with the statement, "Compensatory education has been tried, and it apparently has failed."[5] Though there are strong counter-arguments to this conclusion, perhaps there is also some truth. Perhaps we should move on from isolated compensatory programs to full-fledged cognitive education.

Jensen claimed that, while properly conceived compensatory education programs have brought about IQ gains among educationally disadvantaged students, in many cases the gains tended to fade after two or three years of traditional schooling. Jensen, in fact, provided a superb thumbnail sketch of the traditional classroom but found changing it "unimaginable."

> We have accepted traditional instruction so completely that it is extremely difficult even to imagine, much less to put into practice, any radically different forms that the education of children could take. Our thinking almost always takes as granted such features as . . . an active-passive, showing-seeing, telling-listening relationship between teacher and pupils. Satisfactory learning occurs under these conditions only when children come to school with certain prerequisite abilities and skills . . . [including the ability to] engage in covert "mental" activity, to repeat instruction to oneself, to persist in a task until a self-determined standard is attained—in short, the ability to engage in what might be called self-instructional activities, without which group instruction alone remains ineffectual.

In view of this sketch, it should not surprise us that, with educationally disadvantaged children, the traditional classroom starves the tender roots of better thinking planted by compensatory education. But the educationally disadvantaged aren't the only victims of traditional education. Basing his conclusions on several studies, physics professor Robert Bauman reports that only 40% of our high school graduates have developed the capacity for what Jean Piaget calls formal operational thinking, a prerequisite for much college work. Moreover, standard college courses have little effect on this skill.

But suppose every class from elementary school through college focused on cognitive processes, stimulating and nurturing precise analytical thought in the various content areas. Might not all students emerge with better minds for succeeding in today's technological world?

The scientific study of education is in its infancy. Rather than accept Jensen's bleak appraisal that the *active-passive, covert mental activity* tradition in education is unalterable, that we have exhausted all avenues for increasing sequential thinking skills and have proven the task impossible, it seems more reasonable to align ourselves with Bauman's position: "It is much too early to permit a definitive statement of what works and what does not work in teaching, or what we may expect and what is beyond our reach."[6] The cognitive-skills approach to curriculum appears to correct flaws we have discovered in some of our educational traditions.

---

1. Benjamin S. Bloom and Lois J. Broder, *Problem-Solving Processes of College Students* (Chicago: University of Chicago Press, 1950).
2. Address him at: Department of Physics and Astronomy, University of Massa-

chusetts, Amherst, MA 01002. Also, see Jack Lochhead, *The Heuristic Laboratory: Dialogue Groups* (Amherst, Mass.: University of Massachusetts, 1976).

3. Moshe F. Rubinstein, *Patterns of Problem Solving* (Englewood Cliffs, N.J.: Prentice-Hall, 1974).

4. Steven Bartlett, "The Use of Protocol Analysis in Philosophy," in *Metaphilosophy* (forthcoming).

5. Arthur R. Jensen, "How Much Can We Boost I.Q. and Scholastic Achievement?" *Harvard Educational Review*, Winter 1969, pp. 1-123.

6. Robert P. Bauman, *Teaching for Cognitive Development: A Status Report* (Birmingham, Ala.: Project on Teaching and Learning in University College, University of Alabama, 1976).

XI

Desegregation and Black Leadership

Introduction

Shortly after the Supreme Court's Brown decision of May 1954, Phi Delta Kappa established a commission on the problems of school desegregation. Its major achievement was publication of a handbook, Action Patterns in School Desegregation: A Guidebook, reporting successful desegregation efforts in school districts from nearly every state in the South. Some 12,000 copies were distributed; every school superintendent in 11 Southern states received a copy. Significantly, I think, the authors of this volume, Herbert Wey and John Corey, went on to distinguished careers in education in the South. Charles Foster, relatively unknown in Phi Delta Kappa before he proposed the commission, was later elected president of the fraternity.

The book was only the first of many PDK efforts to help excise the cancer of racial discrimination in the schools. KAPPAN editors joined wholeheartedly in the continuing struggle; I have counted 83 major articles, three special issues, and innumerable news items on desegregation and related topics in the journal. However, I have chosen only two such articles for this anthology. I hope that sometime—perhaps as early as PDK's 100th anniversary (2006)—a book can be published celebrating an end to racial discrimination in the schools and recording the part that Phi Delta Kappa played in that long-postponed day.

My editorial, "The Prime Goals of Desegregation/Integration Are Social Justice and Domestic Tranquillity" (April 1975), was written to introduce three desegregation-related articles. I thought that too many leaders were justifying desegregation on the ground that it would improve black achievement in school (which we all hope for), and that failure to reach that goal should not discourage the effort. There are other more important goals. Apparently the note struck in the editorial appealed to many other educators. The piece received the Educational Press Association's Larry Johnson award in 1975 for "best editorial" in the EdPress competition.

Bob Cole, my successor as KAPPAN editor, wrote "Black Moses: Jesse Jackson's PUSH for Excellence" for the January 1977 KAPPAN. Later, Jackson addressed Phi Delta Kappa's Biennial Council and was given a 10-minute ovation. The fraternity then sponsored several appearances by Jackson to carry the PUSH message to big-city schools. In 1978 the KAPPAN was chosen by the U.S. Office of Education to summarize results of a conference involving twelve hundred educators from 61 cities. Conferees explored ways of achieving excellence in the schools and examined the philosophy and ac-

complishments of Project EXCEL, the Chicago-based PUSH for Excellence effort. The Rev. Jackson gave the keynote address at that conference. It is reprinted here from the November special KAPPAN, as edited by Ben Brodinsky from a tape transcript.

Jackson has many critics in education today. Some of them fault him for what they regard as unsatisfactory follow-up of his evangelical speeches in support of PUSH objectives. Others object to Jackson's style. A few object to the message itself. For example, Barbara Sizemore, a black intellectual who was once superintendent of schools in Washington, D.C., wrote in the January 1978 KAPPAN:

"[PUSH] . . . has merit and could be productive. It has several faults, however. It fails 1) to deal with both sides of the reciprocal black/white relationship in America and 2) to call for changes in the system to correct the unequal status of blacks and their prior deprivation."

Notwithstanding these objections, it seems to me that Jackson's ideas are basically sound. The time is certainly here for a new era in the civil rights movement, and Jackson is one of its prophets.

—SME

The Prime Goals of Desegregation/Integration Are Social Justice and Domestic Tranquillity
by Stanley M. Elam

America's long history of dealing with minorities is filled with cruel ironies. For example, at the time our grandfathers accepted the principle of "separate but equal" schools for blacks, they believed that public education was the "great melting pot" of American diversity.

In 1954 the *Brown* decision offered us an opportunity to shake off a half-century of hypocrisy. Here was a chance to reduce the cultural differences that separate schools for the races can only magnify. But we have spent the past 21 years gaining small successes and suffering large defeats. It has been a frustrating experience for an impatient people.

In recent years we have begun to abandon the melting pot idea altogether. Unable to eradicate pluralism, we are embracing it. Bilingualism is in, and multicultural studies have been introduced in more than half of the nation's 16,000 public school districts.° The courts are backing and filling on desegregation cases, and the federal government, once active in the enforcement of civil rights legislation, seems to have adopted the vicious "benign neglect" philosophy. Even certain disillusioned black leaders are ready to trade desegregation for a new kind of "separate but equal" guarantee. Coretta King recently said (in commenting on the Boston busing controversy), "I believe that the critical challenge today is to ensure a good education for all"—an unexceptionable statement spoiled by her reference to "the futile shuffling of students from one school to another with scant prospect of a meaningful educational experience in either."

Are we coming full circle? Are we on the verge of abandoning desegregation/integration as unprofitable or unworkable?

The *KAPPAN* staff fervently hopes that this is not the case. We believe that 21 years is barely time to gear up for a social experiment of desegregation/integration's magnitude and potential. We believe that educators and other thought leaders must somehow teach the nation patience and persistence in pursuing this experiment. They must make clear what the stakes are. They must achieve some consensus not only on the goals of desegregation/integration but on the means as well. We believe that the main prize is *not* increased academic achievement for blacks, although no one yet knows what achievement gains full, widespread, successful desegregation/integration might produce. It seems to us that the essential goals are socioeconomic justice and—ultimately—domestic tranquillity. The alternatives are bigotry, racial strife, and the sacrifice of minority rights.

Properly conceived and well taught in a desegregated situation, multicultural studies, bilingualism, and human relations courses can build bridges of understanding and acceptance. These bridges *must* be built, if we believe in social justice. Building them will take every ounce of energy and creativity educators can muster.

°According to David E. Washburn, whose study, "Multicultural Education in the United States," will be summarized in a forthcoming issue of the *KAPPAN*.

The melting pot notion was too simplistic, we now know. In a free society, pluralism is as inevitable as it is desirable. But for the sociopolitical mechanism of community, state, and nation to work, the people must have certain common experiences, beliefs, and attitudes. The role of the school is to identify them and to guarantee them, so far as is possible, to all children, whatever their race, intelligence level, or socioeconomic condition.

The *KAPPAN* features articles on desegregation/integration. We don't fully agree with all of them. For example, we see no purely "educational" solution for racism that can bypass desegregated schools. If social justice is indeed a prime objective of this democracy, then every social and legal means of pursuing desegregation/integration must be employed in both school and society.

In Pursuit of Equity, Ethics, and Excellence: The Challenge to Close the Gap
by Jesse L. Jackson

The greatness of this generation will be determined by how well we deal with the needs of this day in light of where we need to go as a people. The failure of this generation would be to answer questions that nobody is asking.

Historically, we have been locked out, and our challenge has been to move in.

1954—*We moved in* to the right of equal educational opportunity (*Brown* v. *Board of Education*).

1964—*We moved in* to the right of public accommodations (Civils Rights Act).

1965—*We moved in* to the right to participate politically (Voting Rights Act).

1968—*We moved in* to the right to buy a house in any neighborhood (Open Housing Act).

The new challenge is to move *up*. Upward mobility is the issue. Our struggle has shifted from the horizontal to the vertical. It was difficult marching across the plains, but it will be even more difficult climbing the mountain, often without the help of a rope.

Too many young people in this generation have lost their appreciation for the historic shoulders upon which they stand. The Merediths, the Hunters, and the Holmeses excelled because they served the need of their generation by busting down the barriers to opportunity. They refused to allow death threats, demagogues, dogs, or fire hoses to stand in their way. It was a good fight to create opportunity. But the challenge of this generation is to match opportunity with effort. If this generation is to be great, it must keep these doors of opportunity open, walk through them, and conquer the tasks beyond opportunity.

We must EXCEL because we are behind. There is one white attorney for every 680 whites, one black attorney for every 4,000 blacks; one white physician for every 649 whites, one black physician for every 5,000 blacks; one white dentist for every 1,900 whites, one black dentist for every 8,400 blacks. Less than 1% of all engineers are black. Blacks make up less than 1% of all practicing chemists.

We must EXCEL because resistance to our upward mobility has increased. *Bakke* and Bakkeism have convinced white America, erroneously, that blacks are making progress at white expense. The mass media have conveyed to white America that blacks have gained too much too fast and have come too far in their quest for equality.

We must EXCEL because the sickness of racism, in too many instances, forces us to be superior in order to be considered average.

We must EXCEL because competition is keener. The exportation of jobs to the cheap labor base of the Third World; the increased competition in the world market from Japan, Western Europe, and the Middle East; and cybernation and automation have forced us to compete for jobs requiring greater knowledge.

We must EXCEL because of the joy and fulfillment that comes in the victory of conquering a task and doing it well against odds.

Our goal is educational and economic equity and parity. The goal is to close the gap between black and white, rich and poor, male and female. We are behind in the race, and the only way to catch up is to run faster.

What does EXCEL advise in this race to close the gap? EXCEL is neither conservative nor liberal but focuses on what is basic. And what is basic is that effort must exceed opportunity for change to occur. What is basic is that there is nothing wrong with our genes, but there is something wrong with our agenda. We must change our agenda if we are going to close the gap and catch up.

EXCEL seeks massive involvement and massive effort. Both tears and sweat are wet and salty, but they render a different result. Tears will get you sympathy, but sweat will get you change.

Let me share with you the broad, but basic, concepts and ideas in the EXCEL program.

Equity

Racism has forced the black liberation movement to spend most of its time and effort fighting for opportunity. Thus, in 1954, the *Brown* decision allowed us to use the leverage of the law to compete as equals. EXCEL is not a departure from that historic struggle; rather, it is an extension of and a quest for the fulfillment of the historic goal of educational equity and parity. EXCEL supports the foundation laid in the *Brown* decision but argues that we must go beyond the desegregation of our schoolchildren to the desegregation of power.

What do we mean by that? We mean that power has not been desegregated; the same people who were in charge of segregation are in charge of desegregation. Thus black children, black parents, and black educators have no protection. They have no ability to redress their grievances.

You ask what grievances? What protection is needed? Nancy L. Arnez of Howard University suggests this list: 1) loss of teaching and administrative jobs by blacks through dismissals, demotions, or displacement; 2) loss of millions of dollars in projected earned income; 3) loss of racial models, heroes, and authority figures for black children; 4) loss of cherished school symbols, emblems, and names of schools by black children when their schools were closed and they were shifted to white schools; 5) subjection to segregated classes and buses, and exclusion from extracurricular activities; 6) suspension and expulsion of disproportionate numbers of black students; 7) exposure of black children to hostile attitudes and behavior of white teachers and parents; 8) victimization by forced one-way busing policies and the uprooting of black children for placement in hostile school environments; 9) victimization by misclassification in special education classes and tracking systems; 10) victimization by unfair discipline practices and arbitrary school rules and regulations; and 11) victimization by ignorance of black children's learning styles and cultural, social, educational, and psychological needs.

The country's agenda relative to desegregation today is 1) to enforce the present law; 2) desegregate the power; and 3) complete the task of changing people's hearts and minds, not just their behavior and actions.

In addition, we are increasingly confronted with a new phenomenon in our large cities. White flight has left our cities nonwhite and poor. The issue now is not so much segregated schools but segregated school systems. Therefore, we must fulfill the letter and the spirit of the *Brown* decision through metropolitanwide desegregation.

Another impediment threatening to deny us equal educational opportunity is the lack of adequate and equitable funding for our schools. The tax rebellion symbolized by the Jarvis-Gann Initiative in California; the refusal of the voters to support school bond issues in Cleveland and Toledo, Ohio, and elsewhere; and the Packwood-Moynihan tax credit proposal in Congress threaten to create a three-tiered educational system—a suburban school system based on class, a private school system based on race, and a public inner-city school system based on rejection and alienation.

At present the nation is in the process of a massive prison-building campaign. But building more jails and incarcerating more people is an uneconomic, as well as unethical, proposition. It is unethical because it doesn't attempt to change the individual into a productive citizen. It is uneconomic to the extent that if a young man or woman goes to any state university in this country for four years it will cost $20,000. If he or she goes to the state penitentiary for four years it will cost $50,000.

Yes, education and employment cost less than ignorance and incarceration.

A third impediment is the use of tests to disenfranchise us. Competency tests, too often, are used in a punitive rather than a redemptive way. We support tests and testing, but tests must be used to detect and diagnose, not to delete and eliminate.

Finally, economic equity and parity must parallel educational equity and parity. We cannot educate in an economic vacuum. We can no longer tolerate a white high school dropout getting jobs denied to black and brown high school graduates. An unemployment rate for blacks that is twice that of whites has a negative influence on educational goals. It discourages whites from getting an education because they feel they can get jobs without it. It discourages blacks from getting an education because they feel that even with an education they will not get the jobs.

Ethics

Ethnic discrimination and an ethical collapse are impediments to excellence. If we are to lift ourselves out of this morass, we must shift our sights from the superficial to the sacrificial.

If we are to close the gap and catch up, we must do so by disciplining our appetites, engaging in ethical conduct, and developing our minds.

A steady diet of violence, vandalism, drugs, irresponsible sexual conduct, and alcohol and TV addiction has bred a passive, alienated, and superficial generation.

Morally weak people not only do not grow in personhood, they contribute to the politics of decadence. A drunken army cannot fight a war for information and close that gap. Minds full of dope instead of hope will not fight for the right to vote. We need a sober, sane, disciplined army to catch up. The challenge of this generation of adults is to regain the confidence of this generation's youth. Only by reestablishing its moral authority can the task be done, for if we reestablish moral authority—that is, our believability, our trustworthiness, our caring—we can then teach discipline, and our children will learn self-discipline.

Truth, like electricity, needs a conduit, a conductor through which to travel. The teacher is the conductor. If the teacher has a healthy respect for the child, the teacher can be a good conductor. But if that teacher has exposed wires and is rotten on race or ethics or character or caring, he will either blow a fuse or set off sparks that burn up a child's life.

Without sounding anti-intellectual, we must be clear that the issues of life flow from the heart, not the head. You cannot teach children against your spiritual will, using only your intellectual skill. You cannot feed children with a long-handled spoon.

The need for a moral and ethical foundation is the reason EXCEL argues for a written code of conduct for students. It is the reason EXCEL argues for character education versus mere IQ education.

EXCEL believes in IQ.

EXCEL believes in developing one's brain.

We are not trying to argue that we ought to substitute consecration for developing our minds. But we must know that on a scale of 10, intellect does not deserve eight points. There are other factors in life. Integrity and drive and commitment and concern above and beyond oneself count also.

Push for Excellence

Effort must exceed opportunity for change to occur. Opportunity must be matched by a superior effort, an urge to EXCEL, a will to learn. We are not so dumb that we cannot learn if we study; but we are not so smart that we will learn if we don't study.

The question that has been asked of me most often is, Why are you putting all of this pressure on the victim instead of the victimizer? Why are you letting the "system" off the hook? I'm not arguing that the victimizer is not guilty. I challenge the victimizer everywhere I go. But I know that if the victimizer is responsible for the victim's being down, the victim must be responsible for getting up. It is in the victim's self-interest to get up and go! It is precisely because the slave is in chains that he must run faster.

In this relationship between slave and slavemaster, I have never known of a retired slavemaster.

Our quest for excellence must be balanced between educating the head and the hand. We must know that 80% of our children graduating from high school are going to the world of work and only 20% to college—and less than that 20% graduate. We must balance our emphasis on a liberal education with vocational and career education. We must concentrate on these five basic steps: exposure to knowledge, repetition, internalization, development of convictions about subject matter, and application of knowledge.

We must move from educational existence to educational excellence. We must contrast the politics of the five Bs—blacks, browns, budgets, busing, and balance—with the five As—attention, attendance, atmosphere, attitude, and achievement. When the doors of opportunity swing open, we must make sure that we are not too drunk or too high or too indifferent to walk through.

We must have involvement from the 10 levels affecting education: the board, the superintendent, the staff administrators, the principals, the teachers, the parents, the pupils, the religious institutions, the mass media, and the broader community.

Students must sign pledges that they will study a minimum of two hours every evening with the radio, television, and record player off with no telephone interruptions or social visits. Parents must pledge to monitor their child's study hours, pick up their child's report card each grading period, and go to the school to see that child's test scores.

At the beginning of the year, the principal must give a "State of the School" address. It should clearly define educational goals, establish rules, set up expectations, and lay out a plan for achieving the goals by the end of the academic year.

Upon graduation, students must be given a diploma in one hand, symbolizing knowledge and wisdom, and a voter registration card in the other hand, symbolizing power and responsibility.

In religious language, we argue that for one to do less than his or her best is a sin. In secular language, we argue that the purpose of life is to develop one's potential to his or her highest capacity.

We must know that if we sow short-term pleasure, we will reap long-term pain. But if we sow short-term pain, we will reap long-term pleasure.

We must teach our children that if they can conceive it and believe it, they can achieve it. They must know that it is not their aptitude but their attitude that will determine their altitude.

Fight for equity.

Fight for ethics.

Fight for excellence.

We must not only close the quantitative gap but the qualitative gap as well. We must . . .

—close the gap with doctors, but doctors who are more concerned with public health than personal wealth;

—close the gap with lawyers, but lawyers who are more concerned with justice than a judgeship;

—close the gap with preachers, but preachers who will prophesy, not merely profiteer;

—catch up in journalism, but we need journalists who will ascribe, describe, and prescribe, not merely scribble;

—catch up in politics, but we need politicians who seek to be of service, not merely seek an office;

—close the gap and catch up in teachers, but we need teachers who will teach for life and not merely for a living.

Believe in yourself. Believe in your ability to close the gap.

Believe in our children. Believe in your ability to teach them and their ability to learn.

Believe in our parents. Believe that if they are consciously sought and planned for, they will participate.

Believe that life is not accidental, that it has a purpose, if you will but seek the way. Hold on. PUSH for Excellence. EXCEL! EXCEL! EXCEL!

I am somebody. . . .

XII
Solutions

Introduction

Solutions *is a pretentious title, isn't it? But I have gone along with Strunk and White's* Elements of Style. *It says: "Don't qualify too much." Otherwise, the section might have been titled "Valiant but Inconclusive Attempts to Solve Putative Problems."*

In the May 1974 KAPPAN *Harry Passow summarized and critiqued half a dozen recently completed major studies of the high school in America, including* Youth: Transitions to Adulthood, *the report of the Panel on Youth of the President's Science Advisory Committee—often called Coleman II after its chairman, James S. Coleman. The key ideas of that report were foreshadowed in Coleman's "How Do the Young Become Adults?," which first appeared in the December 1972* KAPPAN. *I have chosen it for this volume because it sets forth, more clearly than most writing on the topic, a rationale for a reorganized educative system toward which, I hope, we are now stumbling. (I wrote an editorial to introduce the May 1974 special that featured the Passow article. It was titled "Secondary Reform: An Idea Whose Time Has Come." I should have placed a qualifying question mark after that heading.)*

James Coleman has become America's most controversial educational sociologist, for at least two reasons: First, his research deals with questions that are close to the bone; and second, conclusions drawn from almost all research in the social sciences can be disputed with conclusions drawn from other research (or the same research).

Equality of Educational Opportunity *(1966), the first Coleman Report, dealt with the effects of school social/racial composition on academic achievement. Coleman was chosen to direct the massive research it reports because of his excellent sociological study of 10 Illinois high schools and his reputation as a master in applying mathematical thinking to sociological data. Although* Equality *was questioned and reassessed by many experts, the report was repeatedly cited in court to justify desegregation orders. A decade later, Coleman's analysis of trends in the largest central-city districts between 1968 and 1973 was cited by opponents of busing for desegregation, because it documented the "white flight" phenomenon. In an October 1975* KAPPAN *article, "Racial Segregation in the Schools: New Research with New Policy Implications," Coleman suggested the need for reassessing the means and goals of school desegregation. The article brought a storm of protest published in subsequent issues that year.*

Now, in 1981, Coleman has come forth with a study concluding that "stu-

dents learn more in private high schools than in public high schools," as the Associated Press summarized it. The AP added: "Coleman's research also shows that, although private schools enroll fewer minority students, their classrooms are less segregated than public school classrooms."

This report, too, brought noisy protests. Education researchers were particularly aroused. Lee Cronbach of Stanford said, "It's this sort of thing that gives social science research a bad name. The generalizations of the [new] Coleman Report are virtually meaningless." Cronbach said that if you ask a simple-minded question you get a "bumper-sticker" answer. In this case the bumper-sticker is "Private Schools Do It Better."

The new Coleman Report is already being used to support the tuition tax credit idea now being argued in Congress. Many education leaders regard tuition tax credits as the most serious threat to the principles of public education that has come down the pike since World War II.

Coleman has written five KAPPAN articles, beginning with "The Competition for Adolescent Energies" (March 1961). Three had to do with the desegregation theme. In my opinion, "How Do the Young Become Adults?," not those on problems of school desegregation, will fare best over time.

Few journal articles have started education movements, but Maurice Gibbon's "Walkabout: Searching for the Right Passage from Childhood and School" is one of them. Published in the May 1974 KAPPAN along with a tear-out card inviting reactions, its ideas were powerful enough to generate a PDK Task Force on Compulsory Education and Transitions for Youth; a news-letter, Walkabout: Exploring New Paths to Adulthood; a number of experimental programs across the country, many of which were reported in the newsletter; and a book, The New Secondary Education, written by Gibbons with the help of the above-mentioned task force and published by Phi Delta Kappa. "Walkabout . . ." won an EdPress award, was summarized in Education Digest, and was reprinted in eight books. I believe it is the most frequently requested article for reprinting in KAPPAN history.

Without question, the Walkabout idea was popular because secondary reform was an idea whose time had come. Unfortunately, the time was also ripe for an almost antithetical movement, back to basics, which Ben Brodinsky describes in the third article in this section. The economics of education and the country's conservative mood favor back to the basics, I fear.

What is the effect on the author of having written a compelling piece like "Walkabout . . ."? I invited Gibbons to comment.

"'Walkabout . . .' carried me through a crisis in my professional life. A group of us had conducted an experimental field experience for student teachers that was highly rated by participants but severely criticized by the university administration. It was a rough enough situation that I began thinking about better ways of spending my life. Then I saw the film Walkabout. It seemed a perfect metaphor for the program we developed. I wrote the article, rewrote it several times, then submitted it. I will never forget the first sentence of your response: 'Your article is one of the most seminal I have received in my years as editor of the KAPPAN.'

Many rewarding experiences followed publication, including the response of KAPPAN readers, chairmanship of the PDK task force, authorship of The New Secondary Education, *membership on the PDK Options for Youth Committee, and contact not only with the fine members of those groups but also with many other educators around the U.S. and Canada. One was Gary Phillips, then director of Learning Unlimited, a program in Indianapolis employing Walkabout activities. After several contacts, we decided to work together. During the two years Gary was a visiting professor at Simon Fraser University, we developed Walkabout into Challenge Education. Gary is now director of a Challenge Education Project for the Kettering and Lilly Foundations, while I continue our work here. I am deeply grateful to you, the KAPPAN, and its many readers for the support and opportunities that made these developments possible. 'Walkabout . . .' really did change my life.''*

Obviously, "Walkabout . . ." was the work of a creative professional with broad experience and interests. After four years of teaching elementary school and seven teaching secondary English (including a year in England as an exchange teacher), Gibbons entered university work. He is now a full professor at Simon Fraser University in Burnaby, B.C. He has published poems, stories (including one book), TV and radio scripts, and about 50 articles and five books on education. He also happens to be an accomplished wood sculptor, having held exhibits in such widely separated cities as Vancouver, B.C., and Sydney, Australia. He once spent a month as the only white apprentice sculptor in a village of East Africa.

"Back to Basics: The Movement and Its Meaning" was written for the March 1977 KAPPAN by Ben Brodinsky, a journalist and editor who has reported education trends for some 45 years. Since 1933 Brodinsky has published some 500 articles; written 2,000 newsletters (Education Summary, Educator's Dispatch, Teacher's Letter, *EdPress Newsletter); and edited as many as 32 news publications a month for Croft Educational Services (1945-70). Now semi-retired, Brodinsky is an officer in the Connecticut State Poetry Association and reads two or three original poems a month to the group. "Helps keep my nouns and verbs sharp," he says.*

At my request Brodinsky made these observations about "Back to Basics. . . .":

"Since the article hit the streets in March 1977, my phone hasn't stopped ringing. (Now you know that's not literally true, but it's impressionistically true.) The reaction to the article was immediate, profuse, and continuous.

Here are the hard facts as opposed to impressions:

Books and pamphlets: John C. Flanagan, best known for his Project TALENT, asked me to edit Perspectives on Improving Education *(Praeger) almost the same day the KAPPAN article came out; it was intended to catch the spirit of the basics movement.* Defining the Basics of American Education, *a PDK Fastback, is also a direct outcome of the original article.*

Speeches: Since March 1977 to the present, I have given 11 speeches before state and regional associations and faculties of school systems, all based on the article. I also spoke on the basics at programs arranged by four PDK chapters.

Workshops/seminars: I served as leader of sessions dealing with basics on four different occasions in Connecticut school systems.

Offprints: I haven't kept score, but requests for offprints addressed to

*me total about 20. Phi Delta Kappa has received many more. I am told it is the
'most widely quoted article on the subject.'*

    *Classroom use: At least 20 college professors have requested permission
to use the article in their education courses (and I suspect quite a few others
didn't ask).*

    Reprints in books, annuals, compilations of readings: Total to date: seven."

    *An article by Evans Clinchy and Elisabeth Allen Cody in the December
1978 KAPPAN ("If Not Public Choice, Then Private Escape") makes clear
some of the reasons why many people are dissatisfied with public education
today. Having performed the miracle of mass education, educators are now
confronted with the results of their labors: an adult population that is knowledgeable, questioning, and restive. These people want, among other things,
greater choice of curriculum, of teaching methods, of school atmosphere.
These are not necessarily anti-democratic desires, as Clinchy and Cody note.
And it is possible for public education to meet them. Solutions are being
found in systems like those of Minneapolis and Indianapolis, which the
authors describe.*

    *Clinchy and Cody told the Indianapolis story up to the fall of 1978. It is im-
portant to carry it a bit further. The 1978-79 school year plan to go districtwide with the option schools was vetoed by Judge Hugh Dillin as part of his
order to desegregate the schools. Nonetheless, IPS decided to attempt a small
pilot program in spite of the fact that the options could not be considered part
of the desegregation plan. Six options created as part of the pilot program
were highly successful and were continued the following year, intact except
for the Basics School, which was discontinued because the program was not
substantially different from the regular IPS program. The seventh option
mentioned by Clinchy and Cody was declared illegal by Judge Dillin. There
have been some location changes for better pupil access. The Montessori Program has been especially successful and has been expanded to three locations. The number of teachers was increased from two to 13 and further increases are likely. Observers report no evidence of "white flight." IPS also
operates four magnet school programs for secondary students, all alive and
well. They are the School of Performing Arts, the Career Center, Health Professions Magnet, and a Humanities Magnet Program.*

    *Educators in public schools are properly worried about the increasing
popularity of tuition tax credits and the voucher idea. The best place to
combat these threats may not be federal and state legislative chambers, however, but in the public school systems themselves. The challenge demands
great ingenuity and massive change.*

    *Evans Clinchy and Elisabeth Allen Cody are both senior partners in Edu-
cational Planning Associates of Boston. Clinchy is also a research affiliate of
the Department of Urban Studies, Massachusetts Institute of Technology.*

    *Mary Anne Raywid's article, "The First Decade of Public School Alterna-
tives," was written for a special issue of the KAPPAN (April 1981) guest-
edited by Vernon H. Smith of Indiana University. Smith introduced the
special with an editorial titled "Alternative Education Is Here to Stay." He
noted that by 1980 there were thousands of public alternative schools,*

whereas in 1970 there were only a few. "At least 90% of our large school systems provide alternative schools," he writes (Raywid says 80%). "and more than a third of the smaller systems provide them too." Smith believes that the best explanation of the popularity of alternative schools lies in the fact that they were providing local control by parents, students, teachers, and administrators at a time of growing federal and state control through the legislatures and courts. Raywid emphasizes other motives. In any case, the time has obviously come for expanded options in education. It is my hope that they can be supplied in public education without losing the democratic virtues that are America's special gift to the modern world.

Raywid directs the Center for the Study of Educational Alternatives at Hofstra University in Hempstead, New York, where she teaches. She has spearheaded a national Project on Alternatives in Education that, with the sponsorship of several major educational organizations, initiated a major venture this fall. The undertaking parallels the famous Eight-Year Study, which in the 1930s sought the reform of American high schools by means of a combined research-development effort.

Raywid's first book, The Ax-Grinders, *explored attempts of the political right to influence school policy and practice in the Forties and Fifties. She has examined educational criticism since then in such articles as "Illich as Stalking Horse" (1974,* Focus on Learning*) and "The Novel Character of Today's School Criticism" (1979,* Educational Leadership*). Her contributions to the* KAPPAN *include "The Great Haircut Crisis of Our Time" (December 1966). Raywid became a* KAPPAN *editorial consultant in January 1981.*

The final two entries in this section are both drawn from the June 1981 KAPPAN *(edited, of course, by my successor, Robert W. Cole, Jr.). They illustrate very nicely one of the gratifying characteristics of a periodical. Unlike a book, which must await a new edition for feedback to become available to users, a periodical benefits promptly from its readership. In this case, Herb Kohl and Joe Nathan, two educators prominently identified with the alternative schools movement, offer criticism of Mary Anne Raywid's basic article on the topic, and she responds. A long-time critic of traditional schools, Kohl has written several books, including the heavily autobiographical* Half the House *(E. P. Dutton, 1974). But he is more than a critic; he is a persistent creator of alternative schools. For several years he was connected with the Berkeley, California, Center for Open Learning and Teaching, a small, nonprofit group that developed schools and curricula, prepared teachers, and worked with parents and community groups. Now he directs the Coastal Ridge Research in Education Center in Point Arena, California. Nathan's experience, unlike Kohl's, has been chiefly in public alternative schools. He was for several years program coordinator of the famed St. Paul (Minnesota) Open School. In 1978 he shifted to the assistant principalship of the Murray Junior-Senior High School in St. Paul, his present position. Nathan is co-author, with Wayne Jennings, of two other notable* KAPPAN *articles: "Startling/Disturbing Research Supporting Educational Change" (March 1977) and "Educational Bait-and-Switch" (May 1978).*

—SME

How Do the Young Become Adults?
by James S. Coleman

*Our economic organizations must change radically to
incorporate the young and to serve as institutions for learning.*

It is important to ask, along with specific questions about how schools function, more general questions about the development from childhood through
youth to adulthood. Only by continuing to ask these more general questions
can we avoid waking up some day to find that educational institutions are
finely tuned and efficiently designed to cope with the problems of an earlier
day. Among the more general questions, we need to ask how it is that the
young become adults, and what are the current and changing roles of various
formal institutions in that development.

There are three formal institutions that are especially important in examining the changes that are occurring in the way youths are brought to
adulthood. One is the school, another is the family, and a third is the workplace. I will reserve the school till last, because changes in the other two institutions proceed from other causes without regard for their consequences
for the young, while schools are explicitly designed with consequences for
the young as their primary goal. Thus the family and the workplace—together with certain other aspects of society—form the environment within
which the school functions.

Changes in the Family
It is necessary only to give a quick overview of changes in the family's
function in bringing children to adulthood, because those changes have been
so great. Classically, the family was the chief educational institution for the
child, because he carried out most of his activities within it until he left it to
form his own. That juncture in life was his transition to adult status—the transition to economic self-sufficiency and family head. The timing of this transition differed widely from place to place and from one economic setting to
another. On an Irish farm, it may have been age 35 or even older. In an industrial city, it may have been 16 or even younger. But the transition to full adulthood has characteristically taken place when the former child married and
either formed a new household or formed a subhousehold within his parental
family.

The family has gone through two major transitions that sharply limit its
occupational training of the young. The first of these occurred when the
father went out to work, into a shop or an office, and thus began to carry out
his major productive activities away from home, behind the closed doors of
an organization. The second occurred when the mother went out to work or
otherwise stopped carrying out her major productive activities in the home.
Before the first transition, families contained the major productive activities
of society. Thus the young learned not only the whole variety of things that
one commonly associates with the family, they also learned their principal
occupational skills and functions—if not in the family, then structurally close
to it, in an apprentice relation.

For boys, this occupational learning within the family began to vanish as
the father went out to work in a shop or an office. For girls, it continued

longer, as they learned the mother's principal occupation: household work, cooking, sewing, child care. But by now in most families that second transition has taken place as well: The mother's principal occupation is no longer household work; that work now occupies little of her time and attention. She either goes out to work like her husband or occupies herself in other activities that do not require the aid of her daughters. Even child care is minimal, as family sizes have declined. As an economist recently stated, "The home closes down during the day."

Thus the family as a source of occupational learning has declined as it lost its place as the central productive institution of society. But as both adults have come to carry out their central activities outside the home, they have removed other functions from the home and family as well. Friends are drawn from occupation, and adult cocktail parties have replaced neighborhood or extended family gatherings in the social life of the husband and wife. Less and less does the husband's and wife's social life take place in a setting that includes children. Some leisure activities are still carried out as a family, so I don't intend to overstate the case. But the point is that as these large occupational activities of adults moved out of the home, they took others with them, leaving it a less rich place in opportunities for learning for its younger members.

Changes in the Workplace

Changes in the workplace, subsequent to its removal from the home into specialized economic institutions, have also affected the movement of the young into adulthood. The major changes have been away from small organizations to large ones; away from ad hoc informal hiring practices to formal procedures with formal credentials required of applicants; away from using children in secondary and service activities toward excluding them from workplaces under the guise of "protection"; away from jobs requiring low educational credentials toward jobs requiring more education; away from loosely organized occupational settings in which workers participated with varying schedules and varying amounts of time toward a rigidly defined "full-time job" with a fixed schedule and fixed time commitment.

All of these trends (apart from some very minor and very recent movements in the other direction in a few of these dimensions) have led the workplace to become less available and less useful to the young until they enter it as full-time workers at the end of a longer and longer period of full-time schooling.°

These changes in the family and in occupational institutions have led both to become less useful as settings where the young can learn. The young remain in the family, while the activities from which they could learn have

---

°There are some complications to these trends and some statistics which appear to go in the opposite direction. For example, the labor force participation rates for persons aged 16-21 enrolled in school increased between 1960 and 1970, from 35 to 40% for men and 25 to 36% for women. But this change reflects an increase in school-going by those who in 1960 would have been only working. The proportion of persons aged 16 to 21 enrolled in school was much higher in 1970 than in 1960. This increase was largely due to a lack of full-time jobs in the labor force for a greatly expanded age cohort. Thus for many people education became the full-time activity, and labor force participation was restricted to part-time or in-and-out work.

moved out; the activities from which the young could learn remain in work-places, but the young themselves have been excluded. This exclusion places youth more on the fringes of society, outside its important institutions. If one is young, it is difficult to get a loan, to buy on credit, to rent an apartment, to have one's signature accepted for any of the many things that are common-place for adults. The reason is simple: The young have no institutional base; they are a lumpen proletariat outside those institutions of society that are rec-ognized by other institutions and give legitimacy to those persons who are within them.

Before turning to changes in the school, it is important to note one central aspect of the learning that occurred in home and workplaces—and still occurs, though to a sharply reduced extent. It is learning that is variously called "incidental learning" or "experiential learning." It is learning by acting and experiencing the consequences of that action. It is learning through oc-cupying a role with responsibility for actions that affect others. It is learning that is recognized in colloquial parlance as taking place in "the school of hard knocks." It is not learning that proceeds in the way that learning typically takes place in the classroom, where the first step is cognitive understanding, and the last step—often omitted—is acting on that understanding.

Changes in the School

When the major educational functions were in the home, the school was an auxiliary and supplementary institution with two functions. First, for the small fraction of the population whose occupational destination was clerical or academic, it taught a large portion of the occupational skills: languages, mathematics, philosophy, history. Second, for the large majority, it taught the basic skills of literacy. Then, as the changes in family and workplace took place, the school began to take on two additional functions: first, to provide occupational training for the increasing fraction of occupations that seemed to require technical book learning (occupations ranging from engineering to journalism); and second, to perform some of the educational activities that were not occupational but had been carried out to differing degrees and often with indifferent success in the family, ranging from music appreciation to civics. In addition to these explicit and positive functions, the school began to carry out an important but largely passive function as well: to house the young while the parents were off in their specialized adult activities outside the home. This is the function often derogatorily described as the "baby-sitting" function of the school. As women come more and more into the labor force and desire to participate even more than they do, the demand for such baby-sitting agencies has increased, extending downward in age to day-care centers for the very young. And as occupational opportunities for the young have lessened, the baby-sitting function has extended upward in age, with universities and colleges acting as temporary holding stations on the way to adulthood.

This transformation of the schools in response to society has had a consequence that is important in considering the path to becoming adult. This is the massive enlargement of the *student* role of young persons, to fill the vacuum that the changes in the family and workplace created. The student role of young persons has become enlarged to the point where that role occupies the major portion of their youth. But the student role is not a role of taking action and experiencing consequences. It is not a role in which one learns by hard knocks. It is a relatively passive role, always in preparation for action, but seldom acting. In attempting to provide the learning that had earlier taken place through experiential learning in the home and at the workplace, the school kept the same classroom mode of learning that was its hallmark: It not only moved the setting of those learning activities from outside the school to within; it changed the method from learning through experience as a responsible actor to learning through being taught as a student. There are some exceptions, but the general pattern followed that of the classical school, in which a *teacher* was the medium through which learning was expected to take place. This replaced *action* as the medium through which learning had taken place in the family or the workplace. The student role, in which a person waits to be taught, became central to the young person's life.

The consequence of the expansion of the student role, and the action-poverty it implies for the young, has been an increased restiveness among the young. They are shielded from responsibility—and they become irresponsible; they are held in a dependent status—and they become unproductive. But even if we saw no signs of irresponsibility, stagnant dependency, and lack of productivity, the point would remain the same: The school, when it has tried to teach nonintellective things, does so in the only way it knows how, the way designed to teach intellective capabilities: through a teacher, transmitting cognitive skills and knowledge, in a classroom, to students.

Although the complex problems created by these changes cannot be solved easily, I believe it would be a step toward a solution if we began to conceive of matters a little differently. In particular, the problems become clearer if we wipe away the confusion between "schooling" and "education." Previously, it was natural that schooling could have been confused with education, for schooling was that part of the education of the young that took place formally and thus had to be planned for and consciously provided. But the larger part of education took place outside the school. The child spent most of his time outside the school; school was a small portion of his existence. It taught him to read and write and work with numbers, but the most important parts of education it did not provide: learning about work, both the skills and the habits; learning how to function in society; learning how to be a father or mother, husband or wife; learning to take care of others and to take responsibility for others. Because these things were learned informally, through experience, or at least without formal organization, they could be disregarded, and "education" could come to be identified with "schooling."

But much of this other education evaporates as work takes place behind closed doors and as the family is reduced as a locus of important activities. "Schooling" meanwhile continues to mean much the same thing that it did before, except extended in time: the learning of intellectual skills. Thus, although schooling remains a small portion of education, it occupies an increasingly larger portion of a young person's time, while the remaining portion of his education is *not* well provided by ordinary, everyday, unplanned activities. Consequently, if an appropriate reform of education is to be made, it must begin with this fact: Schooling is not all of education, and the other parts of education require just as much explicit planning and organization as does schooling.

Once this is recognized, then the way is paved for creation of a true educational system—not merely a system of schools but a system of education that covers nonintellectual learning as well. If one were to go too quickly to a possible solution or pattern for the future, he would see this as immediately leading toward a multitrack school system in which some young people concentrate on intellectual skills while others concentrate on "practical" or "mechanical" or "vocational" skills. But this pattern fails to recognize clearly the impact of the above separation of schooling and education: It is not only *some* young people who need the nonintellective portions of education, it is all. Thus it is not the *persons* who must be divided into different tracks to learn different skills; it is the *time* of *each* person that must be so divided. Further, the division is not merely a division between intellectual skills and vocational or practical skills. It is a division among a variety of skills, only some of which are intellectual or vocational.

Skills the Schools Can Teach

If I were asked to catalogue the skills that should be learned in the educational system before age 18, I would certainly include all these:

1. Intellectual skills, the kinds of things that schooling at its best teaches.

2. Skills of some occupation that may be filled by a secondary school graduate, so that every 18-year-old would be accredited in some occupation, whether he continued in school or not.

3. Decision-making skills; i.e., those skills of making decisions in complex situations where consequences follow from the decisions.

4. General physical and mechanical skills; i.e., skills allowing the young person to deal with physical and mechanical problems he will confront outside work, in the home, or elsewhere.

5. Bureaucratic and organizational skills; i.e., how to cope with a bureaucratic organization, as an employee, customer, or client, or as a manager or entrepreneur.

6. Skills in the care of dependent persons; i.e., skills in caring for children, old persons, and sick persons.

7. Emergency skills; i.e., how to act in an emergency or unfamiliar situation in sufficient time to deal with the emergency.

8. Verbal communication skills in argumentation and debate.

This catalogue of skills is certainly not all-inclusive, nor are all the skills listed on the same level of generality. They do, however, give a sense of the scope of what I believe must be explicitly included in education.

The Question of Organization

The next question becomes, How is this all to be organized? Or perhaps, How do we change the schools to do all this? But the second question puts the matter wrong. My principal point, and it is the central point of the educational pattern of the future that I envision, is that we do *not* attempt to have the schools do all this. Schools are prepared to do what they have done all along: teach young people intellectual things, both by giving them information and giving them intellectual tools, such as literacy, mathematics, and foreign languages. Schools are not prepared to teach these other skills—and the history of their attempts to change themselves so that they could do this shows only one thing: that these other activities—whether they are vocational education, driver training, consumer education, civics, home economics, or something else—have always played a secondary and subordinate role in schools, always in the shadow of academic performance. The mode of organization of schools, the fact that they are staffed by teachers who themselves have been measured by academic performance, the fact that they lead in a natural progression to more and more intellectually specialized institutions, the universities and then graduate schools—all this means that they are destined to fail as educational institutions in areas other than teaching of intellectual skills.

The pattern for the future, then, as I see it, is one in which the school comes to be reduced in importance and scope and time in the life of a young person from age 12 onward, with the explicit recognition that it is providing only a portion of education. This reduction would necessarily occur, because these other skills must be learned as well—many of them by experience and practice, some of them including a little admixture of teaching.

Where to Learn Other Skills

It then becomes necessary to ask just where these other skills would be learned. An immediate response and an incorrect one, I believe, would be to attempt to design specialized institutions to teach these things, as vocational schools were designed to teach occupational skills. It is incorrect because, if my arguments are correct, these activities are best learned not by being taught but by acting. Thus it is necessary to ask where the action is. The answer is clear: It is in those specialized economic institutions of society into which first men, then women, went out from the family to work. It is in the occupational institutions of society. Women have learned this through the social-psychological poverty of home and neighborhood and have deserted the home for these workplaces.

Thus this education can appropriately take place only in the economic institutions of society—in those organizations behind whose doors adults vanish while the child vanishes inside the walls of the school. Such education could not be hit-or-miss, merely placing a young person on the job or in an apprentice situation. It would be necessary to carefully lay out the skills that were necessary to learn, more carefully than I have done in the catalogue of eight skills I've listed, and to organize the young person's experiences in such a way that he learns these skills. This would involve, of course, more than one institution outside the school. And it would require brilliance both in conception and in execution if it is to work well in early days. For it involves nothing less than a breaking open of the economic institutions of society, from factories to hospitals, a removing of the insulation that separates them from the young, and giving them an explicit role in the education of the young.

How this would be done will differ from society to society. In the free enterprise capitalist economy of the U.S. it could probably best begin by providing the young with entitlements that could be redeemed by business and other enterprises that try to provide the appropriate learning experiences. In other countries it might better be done in another way. But the end result would be similar: The young would be integrated into the economic activities of society from a very early age, *without* stopping their schooling, but merely by stopping the dilution of schooling that has occurred in recent years. The economic organizations of society would necessarily change, and change radically, to incorporate the young—not to become schools but to become institutions in which work is designed not only for productive efficiency but for learning efficiency as well. The revolution necessary in society is, if I am correct, a revolution within these occupational institutions, from General Motors to government agencies, from business offices to airports.

A reorganization of education in this way would require, if it is to be effective, standards of performance and criteria to be met in the areas other than intellectual, so that the credentials of a young person would be far broader than those implied by the various diplomas and degrees that have been carried over in modified form from an early period. Some of the credentials would be based on performance tests such as those used in industries and skilled crafts today. Others would be based on performance ratings by supervisors and on letters of recommendation. For developing other criteria, inventiveness and imagination would be necessary. But the essential point is that those skills must be just as explicitly evaluated and must form just as much a portion of a young person's credentials as intellectual skills do today.

Other Implications

There are a number of important implications to this reorganization of the path toward adulthood. If we recognize that it requires an explicit breaking open of work organizations to incorporate the young, the most direct implication is an enormous transformation of these economic institutions. Their product would be not only goods and services to be marketed but also learning, the latter paid for from public funds as schools are today. They would become much more diversified institutions, no longer preserving the fiction that nothing but production occurs within them, but recognizing that much of adults' social lives and most of their time expenditures take place within them. Then it would be necessary to expand that recognition into explicit designs.

A less direct implication of this reorganization of education is that it would reduce the relationship between educational performance and family educational background or social class. In schools the pervasive power of testing on intellectual criteria—the only real criteria the school knows—exacerbates and emphasizes the inequalities of academic background that children bring with them to school. If education is appropriately defined to include these other equally important skills, then the artificially heightened disparity between students from "advantaged" and "disadvantaged" backgrounds will be reduced—but only, of course, if these other activities are carried out in their natural habitat, rather than in the school, which constitutes an uncongenial setting for them.

Finally, a still less direct implication of this reorganization of education is related to the current controversy about school integration through balancing of the races or social classes in school. That controversy, which reflects a real problem where residential segregation is pronounced—as it is in all large urban areas—cannot be solved as long as education is identified with a school building containing classrooms and teachers. It can be solved if formal education takes place largely outside the schools and in economic institutions; for, among all of society's institutions, it is the economic that are the least segregated by race; and it is in these that racial integration produces least friction, because it occurs in a setting with work to be done in an organized rather than anarchic structure of interpersonal relations.

The effect of such a reorganized system of education in integrating the society racially would not be accidental. It would arise because the reorganization would not be ad hoc, not a makeshift patching up of outworn institutions. The reorganization would recognize fundamental structural changes in society—the drying up of family functions and the specialization of economic activities—and ask where in such an emerging social structure is the appropriate locus for the young, if they are to have the opportunity for moving to adulthood. The answer, of course, is that the young belong where everyone else is, where the action is. They belong inside the economic institutions where the productive activities of society take place.

Walkabout: Searching for the Right Passage from Childhood and School

by Maurice Gibbons

A year ago I saw an Australian film called *Walkabout* which was so provocative—and evocative—I am still rerunning scenes from it in my mind. In the movie, two children escape into the desert-like wilderness of the outback when their father, driven mad by failure in business, attempts to kill them. Within hours they are exhausted, lost, and helpless. Inappropriately dressed in private school uniforms, unable to find food or protection from the blazing heat, and with no hope of finding their way back, they seem certain to die. At the last moment they are found and cared for by a young aborigine, a native Australian boy on his walkabout, a six-months-long endurance test during which he must survive alone in the wilderness and return to his tribe an adult, or die in the attempt. In contrast to the city children, he moves through the forbidding wilderness as if it were part of his village. He survives not only with skill but with grace and pride as well, whether stalking kangaroo in a beautiful but deadly ballet, seeking out the subtle signs of direction, or merely standing watch. He not only endures, he merges with the land, and he enjoys. When they arrive at the edge of civilization, the aborigine offers—in a ritual dance—to share his life with the white girl and boy he has befriended, but they finally leave him and the outback to return home. The closing scenes show them immersed again in the conventions of suburban life, but dreaming of their adventure, their fragment of a walkabout.

The movie is a haunting work of art. It is also a haunting comment on education. What I find most provocative is the stark contrast between the aborigine's walkabout experience and the test of an adolescent's readiness for adulthood in our own society. The young native faces a severe but extremely appropriate trial, one in which he must demonstrate the knowledge and skills necessary to make him a contributor to the tribe rather than a drain on its meager resources. By contrast, the young North American is faced with written examinations that test skills very far removed from the actual experience he will have in real life. He writes; he does not act. He solves familiar theoretical problems; he does not apply what he knows in strange but real situations. He is under direction in a protected environment to the end; he does not go out into the world to demonstrate that he is prepared to survive in, and contribute to, our society. His preparation is primarily for the mastery of content and skills in the disciplines and has little to do with reaching maturity, achieving adulthood, or developing fully as a person.

The isolation involved in the walkabout is also in sharp contrast to experience in our school system. In an extended period of solitude at a crucial stage of his development, the aborigine is confronted with a challenge not only to his competence but also to his inner or spiritual resources. For his Western counterpart, however, school is always a crowd experience. Seldom separated from his class, friends, or family, he has little opportunity to confront his anxieties, explore his inner resources, and come to terms with the world and his future in it. Certainly, he receives little or no training in how to deal with such issues. There are other contrasts, too, at least between the Australian boy and the urban children in the movie: his heightened sensory perception, instinct, and intuition, senses which seem numbed in them; his genuine, open, and emphatic response toward them in saving their lives, and their inability to finally overcome their suspicious and defensive self-interest to save his. And above all there is his love and respect for the land even as he takes from it what he needs; and the willful destruction of animals and landscape which he observes in disbelief during his brushes with civilization.

Imagine for a moment two children, a young native looking ahead to his walkabout and a young North American looking ahead to grade 12 as the culminating experiences of all their basic preparation for adult life. The young native can clearly see that his life will depend on the skills he is learning and that after the walkabout his survival and his place in the community will depend upon them, too. What meaning and relevance such a goal must give to learning! What a contrast if he were preparing to write a test on survival techniques in the outback or the history of aboriginal weaponry. The native's Western counterpart looks forward to such abstractions as subjects and tests sucked dry of the richness of experience, in the end having little to do directly with anything critical or even significant that he anticipates being involved in as an adult—except the pursuit of more formal education. And yet, is it not clear that what will matter to him—and to his community—is not his test-writing ability or even what he knows about, but what he feels, what he stands for, what he can do and will do, and what he is becoming as a person? And if the clear performative goal of the walkabout makes learning more significant, think of the effect it must have on the attitude and performance of the young person's parents and instructors, knowing that their skill and devotion will also be put to the ultimate test when the boy goes out on his own. What an effect such accountability could have on our concept of schooling and on parents' involvement in it!

For another moment, imagine these same two children reaching the ceremonies that culminate their basic preparation and celebrate their successful passage from childhood to adulthood, from school student to work and responsible community membership. When the aborigine returns, his readiness and worth have been clearly demonstrated to him and to his tribe. They need him. He is their hope for the future. It is a moment worth celebrating. What, I wonder, would an alien humanoid conclude about adulthood in our society if he had to make his deductions from a graduation ceremony announcing students' maturity: speeches, a parade of candidates—with readings from their yearbook descriptions—a formal dinner, expensive clothes and cars, graduates over here, adults over there, all-night parties, occasional drunkenness and sexual experience or flirtation with it, and spray-painting "Grad '74" on a bridge or building. For many it is a memorable occasion—a pageant for parents, a good time for the students. But what is the message in this celebration at this most important moment of school life and in this most important shared community experience? What values does it promote? What is it saying about 12 years of school experience? The achievement of what goals is being celebrated? What is it teaching about adulthood? How is it contributing to a sense of community? What pleasures and sources of challenge and fulfillment does it encourage the young to pursue? And if our alien humanoid could look into the students' deepest thoughts, what would he conclude about their sense of readiness to live full and independent lives, to direct their own growth, to contribute to society, and to deal with the issues

that confront us as a world—perhaps a universe—citizenry? I think his un-
prejudiced conclusions would horrify us.

In my opinion, the walkabout could be a very useful model to guide us in
redesigning our own rites of passage. It provides a powerful focus during
training, a challenging demonstration of necessary competence, a profound
maturing experience, and an enrichment of community life. By comparison,
preparation and trial in our society are incomplete, abstract, and impersonal;
and graduation is little more than a party celebrating the end of school. I am
not concluding that our students should be sent into the desert, the wilderness, or the Arctic for six months—even though military service, Outward
Bound, and such organizations as the Boy Scouts do feature wilderness living
and survival training. What is appropriate for a primitive subsistence society
is not likely appropriate for one as complex and technically sophisticated as
ours. But the walkabout is a useful analogy, a way of making the familiar
strange so we can examine our practices with fresh eyes. And it raises the
question I find fascinating; *What would an appropriate and challenging
walkabout for students in our society be like?* Let me restate the problem more specifically. What sensibilities, knowledge, attitudes, and competencies are necessary for a full and productive adult life? What kinds
of experience will have the power to focus our children's energy on achieving
these goals? And what kind of performance will demonstrate to the student,
the school, and the community that the goals have been achieved?

The walkabout model suggests that our solution to this problem must
measure up to a number of criteria. First of all, it should be experiential and
the experience should be real rather than simulated; not knowledge about
aerodynamics and aircraft, not passing the link-trainer test, but the experience of solo flight in which the mastery of relevant abstract knowledge and
skills is manifest in the performance. Second, it should be a challenge that
extends the capacities of the student as fully as possible, urging him to consider every limitation he perceives in himself as a barrier to be broken
through; not a goal that is easily accessible, such as playing an instrument he
already plays competently, but a risky goal that calls for a major extension of
his talent, such as earning a chair in the junior symphony or a gig at a reputable
discotheque. Third, it should be a challenge the student chooses for himself.
As Margaret Mead has often pointed out—in *Growing Up in Samoa*, for
instance—the major challenge for young people in our society is making decisions. In primitive societies there are few choices; in technological societies
like ours there is a bewildering array of alternatives in lifestyle, work,
politics, possessions, recreation, dress, relationships, environment, and so on.
Success in our lives depends on the ability to make appropriate choices. Yet,
in most schools, students make few decisions of any importance and receive
no training in decision making or in the implementation and reassessment
cycle that constitutes the basic growth pattern. Too often, graduation cuts
them loose to muddle through for themselves. In this walkabout model,
teachers and parents may help, but in the Rogerian style—by facilitating the
student's decision making, not by making the decisions for him. The test of
the walkabout, and of life, is not what he can do under a teacher's direction
but what the teacher has enabled him to decide and to do on his own.

In addition, the trial should be an important learning experience in itself.
It should involve not only the demonstration of the student's knowledge, skill,

and achievement, but also a significant confrontation with himself: his awareness, his adaptability to situations, his competence, and his nature as a person.
Finally, the trial and ceremony should be appropriate, appropriate not as a
test of the schooling that has gone before but as a transition from school learning to the life that will follow afterwards. And the completion of the walkabout should bring together parents, teachers, friends, and others to share the
moment with him, to confirm his achievement, and to consolidate the spirit of
community in which he is a member. Keeping these features of the walkabout
analogy in mind, let us now ask the question, What might a graduation ceremony in this mode be like in a North American high school?

The time is September. The place, a school classroom somewhere in the
Pacific Northwest. Margaret, a student who has just finished grade 12, is
making a multimedia presentation to a number of relatives, over 20 of her
classmates, several friends from other schools, some teachers, the mayor, and
two reporters she worked with during the year. Watching intently are a number of younger students already thinking about their own walkabouts.
Margaret has been thinking about this moment since grade 8 and working on
her activities seriously since the night the principal met with all the grade 10
students and their parents to outline and discuss the challenges. Afterwards
she and her mother sat up talking about her plans until early morning. She is
beginning with the first category, *Adventure*, which involves a challenge to
her daring and endurance. The film and slides Margaret is showing trace her
trip through the Rockies following the path of Lewis and Clark in their exploration of the Northwest. Her own journal and maps are on display along
with a number of objects—arrowheads and the like—which she found
enroute. The names of her five companions—she is required to cooperate
with a team in at least one, but no more than two, of the five categories—are
on display. In one corner of the room she has arranged a set of bedroom
furniture—a loft-desk-library module, a rocking chair, and a coffee-table
treasure-chest—designed, built, and decorated as her work in the *Creative-
Aesthetic* field. On the walls are photographs and charts showing pollution
rates of local industries that she recorded during the summer and used in a
report to the Community Council. The three newspaper articles about the resulting campaign against pollution-law violators, and her part in it, are also
displayed to give proof that she has completed the third category, *Community Service*.

Margaret, like many of the other students, engaged in a *Logical Inquiry*
that related closely to her practical work. Her question was, What structural
design and composition has the best ratios of strength, ease of construction,
and economy of materials? Using charts of the various designs and ratios, she
describes her research and the simple experiment she developed to test her
findings, and she demonstrates the effectiveness of the preferred design by
performing pressure tests on several models built from the same material.
After answering a few questions from a builder in the crowd, she shows how
the problem grew out of her studies in architecture for the *Practical-Voca-
tional* category. Passing her sketch books around and several summer cabin
designs she drew up, she goes on to describe her visits to a number of archi-
tects for assistance, then unveils a model of the summer camp she designed
for her family and helped them build on their Pacific Coast property. Slides
of the cabin under construction complete her presentation. A teacher asks

why she is not performing any of the skills she developed, as the challenge requires, and she answers that her committee waived that requirement because the activities she chose all occurred in the field.

As Margaret's friends and relatives gather around to congratulate her, down the hall Ken is beginning his presentation with a report on his two-month *Adventure* alone in a remote village in France where he took a laboring job and lived with a French family in which no one spoke English. The idea arose during a discussion of his proposal to travel when the teacher on his committee asked him to think of a more daring challenge than sight-seeing in a foreign country. A professor in modern languages has been invited by the school to attend the presentations, converse with him in French, and comment on his mastery. Later with his own guitar accompaniment, Ken will sing a medley of three folk songs which he has composed himself. Then, to meet the requirements of the *Community Service* category, he plans to report on the summer care program which he initiated and ran, without pay, for preschool children in the community. The director of the local Child Health and Welfare Service will comment on the program. Finally, Ken will turn to the car engine that stands, partially disassembled, on a bench at the back of the room. His *Logical Inquiry* into the problem, "What ways can the power output of an engine be most economically increased?" is summarized in a brief paper to be handed out and illustrated with modifications he has made on the display engine with the help of a local mechanic and a shop teacher. He will conclude his presentation by reassembling the engine as quickly as he can.

If we entered any room anywhere in the school, similar presentations would be under way; students displaying all kinds of alternatives they selected to meet the five basic challenges:

1. *Adventure:* a challenge to the student's daring, endurance, and skill in an unfamiliar environment.

2. *Creativity:* a challenge to explore, cultivate, and express his own imagination in some aesthetically pleasing form.

3. *Service:* a challenge to identify a human need for assistance and provide it; to express caring without expectation of reward.

4. *Practical Skill:* a challenge to explore a utilitarian activity, to learn the knowledge and skills necessary to work in that field, and to produce something of use.

5. *Logical Inquiry:* a challenge to explore one's curiosity, to formulate a question or problem of personal importance, and to pursue an answer or solution systematically and, wherever appropriate, by investigation.

We would learn about such *Adventures* as a two-week solo on the high river, living off the land, parachute drops, rock climbing expeditions, mapping underground caves, an exchange with a Russian student, kayaking a grade three river to the ocean, scuba-diving exploits, sailing ventures, solo airplane and glider flights, ski-touring across glaciers, a month-long expedition on the Pacific Crest trail, and some forms of self-exploratory, meditative, or spiritual adventures. We would see such *Aesthetic* works as fashion shows of the students' own creations, sculpture and painting, jewelry, tooled leather purses, anthologies of poetry, a humor magazine, plays written and directed by the author, a one-man mime show, political cartoons, a Japanese garden featuring a number of home-cultivated bonsai trees, rugs made of home-dyed fibers, illuminated manuscripts, gourmet foods, computer art, a rock group and a string quartet, a car body design and paint job, original films, a stand-up comic's art, tapes of natural-sound music, and a display of blown glass creatures.

In the *Service* category, students would be reporting on volunteer work with the old, ill, infirm, and retarded; a series of closed-circuit television hookups enabling children immobilized in the hospital to communicate with each other; a sports program for the handicapped; a Young Brother program for the retarded; local Nader's Raiders kinds of studies and reports; construction of playgrounds, hiking trails and landscaped parks; clean-ups of eyesore lots; surveys of community needs and opinions; collecting abandoned cars to sell as scrap in order to support deprived families abroad; shopping and other trips for shut-ins; and a hot-meals-on-wheels program for pensioners. In the *Practical* realm we might see demonstrations of finely honed secretarial skills, ocean-floor plant studies, inventions and new designs of many kinds, the products of new small businesses, a conservation program to save a locally endangered species, stock market trend analyses and estimates, boats designed and built for sale, a course taught by computer-assisted instruction, small farms or sections of farms developed and managed, a travel guidebook for high school students, a six-inch telescope with hand-ground lenses and a display of photographs taken through it, a repair service for gas furnaces and other home appliances, and a collection of movie reviews written for the local suburban newspaper. And we would hear about *Logical Inquiries* into such questions as: How does a starfish bring about the regeneration of a lost arm? What does one experience when meditating that he doesn't experience just sitting with his eyes closed? What is the most effective technique in teaching a dog obedience? How do you navigate in space? Does faith-healing work, and if so, how? How many anomalies, such as the ancient Babylonian battery, are there in our history and how can they be explained? What folk and native arts and crafts have developed in this area? What are the 10 most important questions man asks but can't answer? What is insanity—where is the line that separates it from sanity? and, What natural means can I use to protect my crops most effectively from disease and insects? All day long such presentations occur throughout the school, each student with his own place and time, each demonstrating his unique accomplishment, each with an opportunity to be successful in his own way.

At the end of the day the families, their children, and their friends meet to celebrate this moment. The celebration takes a variety of forms: picnics, dinner at a restaurant, meals at home—some cooked by the graduating students—and buffets that all guests help to provide. In some instances two or three families join together. The ceremonies are equally varied, according to taste and imagination; some are religious, some raucous, some quite quietly together. In each the student is the center of the occasion. Parents and guests respond to the graduate's presentation. Teachers drop by to add their comments. And the student talks about his plans for the future. Some may find ways to announce the young person's entry into a new stage of independence and responsibility, helping him to clarify and pursue his next life goal. To conclude, there may be a school or community celebration to which all are invited for music, singing, and dancing. The only formal event would be a presentation of bound volumes of the student's reports on their accomplishments to the principal and mayor for the school and the community libraries. My own preference would be to include, also, some ritual experience of the family being together at the moment of its coming apart, or some shared experience of life's mystery; perhaps a midnight walk or coming together to watch the dawn—the world beginning again, beginning still.

Far-fetched? I don't think so. It is true that Margaret and Ken appear to be exceptional students. So many colleagues identified them as atypical that I almost added a Charlie and Lucy of much more modest accomplishment. But it seems to me that our expectations are conditioned by student performance in courses. In fact, we have no idea what they may be capable of when the same energy and ingenuity that has gone into our system for teaching them subjects is transformed into a system for supporting their own development of their own potential. How far they can and will go along any particular path they choose may be limited, over the years, only by their ability to conceive of it as possible and our ability to confirm it. Besides, we are concerned here as much with depth as with range, as much with the quality of the students' experience as with the manifest products of their effort. One experience of true caring for another without expectation of reward, one experience of breaking through the confines of one's own believed limitations, one mystery unraveled, are the seeds of all later commitment and growth, and are worth cultivating with everything at our disposal. The purpose is not just to stimulate an impressive array of accomplishments but to enable students to find out who they are by finding out what they can do, and to confirm the importance of that most essential human work.

Nor is it far-fetched to think of schools adopting a program to accomplish these ends. The concept is flexible. Any school or community may adapt this proposal to its own circumstances by choosing different categories of achievement, different plans for preparation in school time, a different manner of demonstrating accomplishment, and a different kind of ceremony. The basic principles—personal challenge, individual and group decision making, self-direction in the pursuit of goals, real-world significance in activity, and community involvement at all stages of preparation and conclusion—can be accomplished in a variety of ways. It is true that a decade ago such a proposal was unthinkable. The importance of grades and the singular pattern of schooling for achieving them were so general it appeared impossible and impractical to break out of the system. Since the educational troubles of the Sixties, with the rise of a responsible radicalism and the appearance of a number of technological and humanistic alternatives, many schools have successfully broken from old patterns to search for forms of education more appropriate for our times.

Some innovators, however, have merely put old content into new programs—for instance, by translating courses into assignment sheets and letting the student work through them at his own pace. Some changes—in the freest of free schools, for example—eliminate all content and directive instruction, relying instead on the student's discovery of his own program. Unfortunately, such laissez faire approaches too often create a leadership and authority vacuum in the classroom, one that students are unable to fill. The approach suggested here reflects what many innovative teachers and administrators have pointed out to me: that real change does involve new freedom for students, but that independence must be combined with a vivid personal goal and a framework within which the student can pursue it. If we remove the structure of subjects, disciplines, courses, lessons, texts, and tests, it is essential that we develop superstructures that will support the student's efforts to create a structure of his own. Autonomy, like maturity, is not a gift but an accomplishment of youth, and a difficult one to attain. This walkabout proposal describes one possible superstructure. For students who are already developing elements of their own programs—in open area elementary schools and interdisciplinary secondary humanities programs, for example— an appropriate walkabout would provide a clear, long-term goal and open the way for the school and community to develop a support structure as the student's need for assistance in pursuing his goal intensifies.

Preparation for the walkabout challenge can be provided in various degrees of intensity, depending upon how committed the school staff is to creating a curriculum that focuses upon personal development.

1. It can be an extracurricular activity in which all planning and work is done during out-of-school time.

2. It can be one element of the curriculum that is included in the schedule like a course, giving students time for planning, consultation, and training.

3. It can be the core of the grade 12 program, one in which all teaching and activity is devoted to preparing for trial.

4. It can be the goal around which a whole new curriculum is designed for the school, or for a school-within-the-school staffed by interested teachers for interested students.

If the school is junior secondary—this concept can readily be adapted to elementary schooling, too—students and parents should be notified of the graduation trial upon entry in grade 8, perhaps by a single announcement with an accompanying descriptive brochure. Trial committees—including the student, the parents, and a teacher—should be organized for meetings, likely as early as grade 9, to guide the student's explorations of possible challenges, so that serious planning and the preparation of formal proposals can begin in grade 10. To make the nature of the walkabout vivid, the committee should involve students in a series of "Experience Weeks" during which they would be out of school pursuing activities, first of the school's design and later of their own design, as trial runs. During these early years the student could also benefit from association with "big brothers" in the school, older students in more advanced stages of preparation who can help their younger colleagues, with considerable benefits for themselves as well. The committee would also be responsible for helping the student make his own choices and find the resources and training necessary to accomplish them; and by their interest, they would also help the student to develop confidence in his decisions and commitment to his own goals. A survey of student plans during any of the senior years would give the staff the information necessary to plan the most useful possible training, which could be offered in mini-courses—one day each week, for instance—or in a semester or a year-long curriculum devoted to preparation for trial. If students were required to write a two-page report on each challenge, a collection of these reports could provide an accumulating resource for younger candidates as well as a permanent "hall of accomplishment" for graduates. In such ways the walkabout challenge could also become a real focus for training in such basic skills as speaking, writing, and use of the media. These are only a few of the ways this proposal can be implemented and integrated with other aspects of school life.

But colleagues and parents with whom I have discussed the idea raise a number of problems potential in the walkabout challenge. What about the inequality that exists between students who have great resources for such walkabout activities at home and students who have few resources at their disposal? What about the risks involved for students on their own in the city and the wilderness? What if competition among students to outdo each other drives them to traumatic extremes or failure? On the other hand, what if students don't want to be bothered? How can we account for differences in ability; that is, how can we distinguish the apparently modest accomplishment that is a severe challenge for one student from the apparently grand accomplishment which is actually a modest challenge for another? These are not fantasy what-ifs, but the real concerns of those who want to anticipate and eliminate as many liabilities as possible. They deserve consideration.

Such questions point to basic issues; motivation, risk control, support, and assessment. In each case resolution depends upon close communication and cooperation among students, parents, teachers, and other members of the community. Students will be motivated by the personal challenge, but it will be essential for all the adults to confirm the importance of these challenges by their interest, concern, and involvement. Counseling by the parent/teacher committees will be essential to help students to clarify their personal goals and to help them decide on activities that stretch, but do not threaten to break, their spirit. But, since this walkabout is a growth experience, I must emphasize that appropriate counseling must help the student to clarify *his* goals and should not be advice giving or demand making. Failure, except where health and safety are seriously threatened, can also be a growth experience for persons who have accepted responsibility for their decisions and actions.

When risk is involved, as in the *Adventure Challenge*, communication and cooperation between home and school will be extremely important. The risk and liability must clearly be the student's, accepted as such by him and his family. But the adults should then help the student to eliminate all unnecessary dangers from the adventure and to develop the knowledge and skills that will make him the master of the dangerous situation he is planning to enter. If his challenge involves scuba diving, for instance, they should be sure that his equipment is adequate, that he has received professional training and certification for free diving, and that he has arranged for a skilled companion to accompany him. The adult committee can also be of assistance in helping students to arrange for necessary resources, such as scuba-diving equipment, in order to equalize the support each of them has available. However, the student with too many readily available resources is as much a problem as the student with too few—in terms of this proposal, at least. A more appropriate solution to the support issue would make the acquisition of resources the student's responsibility, no matter how much was available to him from parents—earning money for equipment and courses, scrounging materials, finding economical ways to travel—so that any achievement is more clearly and completely his own.

A spirit of competition among students attempting to outdo each other could easily emerge. Of course, competition is already a driving force in schooling. The difference is that there is only one kind of contest and one way to win in school competition, and the basic finishing order is quite clearly established after 12 years—usually, after the first year. In the walkabout experience proposed here each student chooses goals and activities which are important to him. Each will be different. Comparison will be difficult and somewhat pointless, particularly if the adult/student committees maintain focus on the student's personal growth through challenging himself rather than others. Everyone can be successful. To be an appropriate part of this learning/growing experience, any assessment must be the student's own judgment of the quality and importance of what he has done. The responses of many people during trial will provide participants with feedback on their progress, as will the audience at their final presentations and the guests at the evening ceremonies. Marks, grades—any comparative evaluation—would be disastrous. The competition is with one's self, not others. The pride is in the confirmation of competence, not superiority. The satisfaction is in the recognition by others of what one has proven to one's self: "I can accomplish. I can become. And therefore I can look forward with hope and anticipation." In these ways the issues of motivation, risk, support, and assessment can be converted from potential problems to beneficial elements of the program.

If there are problems to overcome, the effort required will be repaid by a number of benefits for the student and for the school. The school—any concerned adult—can have no higher aspiration for young people than assisting them to develop a profound sense of their own worth and identity. To reach this state, the young must find their way through the stormy clouds of self-doubt until they win the higher ground of confidence where greater clarity is possible. Getting there requires autonomy, initiative, and industry; three aspects of competence essential in the quest for identity—personal accomplishments which cannot be given or demanded, only nurtured. I believe the trial described here provides a framework for nurturing such development. The individual can clarify his own values and his goals. He can make decisions about his own directions and efforts. He can explore his personal resources by testing them in action. Curiosity, inquiry, and imagination will take on new significance. He will see the uniqueness of his emerging accomplishments and abilities gain greater recognition than his adaptation to the norms of school and peer behavior. The student can learn to work intimately with a small group on a real and significant task, and can learn from them how his contributions are perceived. With goals clearly in mind, he will be encouraged to initiate his plans and see them through to fulfillment even though obstacles challenge his resourcefulness. And having reached these goals, he may take justifiable pride in the competencies he has developed as well as the things he has achieved. In schools where students are directed, dependent, and ultimately have no personal rights, such an opportunity to earn respect and dignity on their own terms would be a significant advance. Most important, the student will not only have begun to clarify his life goals through these challenges, he will have experienced the cycle by which life goals are pursued. His graduation can thereby be transformed from a school ceremony marking the end of one self-contained stage to a community celebration marking his transition to an independent, responsible life. It can be a celebration of a new stage in the flow of his becoming a person. The school also seems likely to reap a number of benefits from the walkabout challenge program: a boost to school spirit; an opportunity to establish a new, more facilitative relationship between staff and students; a new focus for cooperation with parents and the rest of the community; a constant source of information about what is important to students—and parents; a means of motivating and focusing learning for everyone, particularly younger, beginning students; a constant reminder of the relationship between education and living; and a device for transforming the nature of schooling to combine freedom and responsibility, independence and clearly directed effort. And most important, it will enable us to communicate to our younger generation how important their growth and accomplishment is to us. In fact, the success of this concept depends on that communication.

I am interested in the walkabout challenge because it promises what I most want for my own children. No one can give life meaning for them, but there are a number of ways we can help them to give life meaning for themselves. Central to that meaning is their sense of who they are in the scheme of things and their confidence that, no matter what the future holds, they can decide and act, that they can develop skills to be justifiably proud of, that they can cross the most barren outback with a certain grace and find even in simple moments a profound joy. I hope that by exploring what they can do and feel they will come to know themselves better, and with that knowledge they will move through today with contentment and will look forward to tomorrow with anticipation. I think a challenging walkabout designed for our time and place can contribute to that kind of growth.

Back to the Basics:
The Movement and Its Meaning
by Ben Brodinsky

A leading education journalist reports on manifestations of the latest conservative swing of the pendulum and identifies its potential for good and bad.°

There is a movement in American education that irritates some educators, baffles others, and raises high the hackles of still others. Its stirrings put many a school administrator and scholar on the defensive. It is usually led by parents, ministers, businessmen, and politicians. National in scope, it is weak in some parts of the country, strong in others. In some communities the movement makes itself evident through polite editorials or strongly worded resolutions by PTAs; but sometimes it shows teeth and muscle—and the results are bitter controversy, curtailed school funds, defeated bond issues, and, in at least one place (Kanawha County, West Virginia), violence and bloodshed.

In some instances the movement focuses on a single objective—drill in the three Rs; in others, on a wide range of aims—including patriotism and Puritan morality. "It certainly lacks conceptualization," one curriculum expert told me as we were discussing the movement's underpinnings, "and it seems to thrive without organized and identifiable leadership." When that leadership is assigned to the Council for Basic Education, its officials squirm. "There are those who infer that CBE is interested only in reading, writing, and arithmetic," says George Weber, a CBE spokesman, "but basic education, to us, is by no means limited to the three Rs. We want to promote instruction in the basic intellectual disciplines for all students." The CBE is a great friend of the arts, and this fact alone may disqualify it for leadership among those whose adamant cry is "Back to basics!"

What *do* back-to-basics advocates want? Since they have no spokesman, platform, or declaration of principles, we must fall back on a composite. Here is what, at various times and in different places, back-to-basics advocates have demanded:

1. Emphasis on reading, writing, and arithmetic in the elementary grades. Most of the school day is to be devoted to these skills. Phonics is the method advocated for reading instruction.

2. In the secondary grades, most of the day is to be devoted to English, science, math, and history, taught from "clean" textbooks, free of notions that violate traditional family and national values.

3. At all levels, the teacher is to take a dominant role, with "no nonsense about pupil-directed activities."

4. Methodology is to include drill, recitation, daily homework, and frequent testing.

5. Report cards are to carry traditional marks (A, B, C, etc.) or numerical values (100, 80, 75, etc.), issued at frequent intervals.

6. Discipline is to be strict, with corporal punishment an accepted method of control. Dress codes should regulate student apparel and hair styles.

°*Editor's Note:* No effort has been made to update the many specific illustrations and examples offered in this 1977 article.

7. Promotion from grades and graduation from high school are to be permitted only after mastery of skills and knowledge has been demonstrated through tests. Social promotion and graduation, on the basis of time spent in courses, are out.

8. Eliminate the frills. The *National Review*, a conservative journal, put it this way: "Clay modeling, weaving, doll construction, flute practice, volleyball, sex education, laments about racism and other weighty matters should take place on private time."

9. Eliminate electives and increase the number of required courses.

10. Ban innovations (a plague on them!). New math, new science, linguistics, instruction by electronic gadgets, emphasis on concepts instead of facts—all must go.

11. Eliminate the school's "social services"; they take time from the basic curriculum. "Social services" may include sex education, driver education, guidance, drug education, and physical education.

12. Put patriotism back in the schools. And love for one's country. And for God.

Such a list, read as a totality, would cheer only the most rabid protagonists of back to basics. It chills even the most conservative of educators. It brings out the defensive mechanisms in most professionals.

"Where is back? What is basic?" said one educator during an interview on the subject. He echoed two questions that usually come up in the back-to-basics controversy. From my notes, made during interviews with educators, here is a composite of the views of those who either reject the movement, join it grudgingly, or accept only a few of its tenets:

"Back to basics? Look, we're moving *forward* to basics. We're broadening our basics to teach children to think, analyze problems, make wise decisions, develop confidence in themselves. As for the three Rs, why return when we've never left them? . . ."

"We're not going to repeal the twentieth century and we can't hold back the twenty-first. We're not going to give up everything we've learned about children, teaching, and learning during the last 50 years. . . ."

"Nothing new, nothing new here. There had been cries for basics long before Socrates started teaching what he thought was basic. In this country, demands for fundamentals crop up every decade. . . ."

"I'm suspicious of easy answers and snappy slogans. Back to basics is a simplistic solution for complex educational problems. If we carry it out as a national policy, it will throw us back 100 years. . . ."

"What was basic yesterday is not basic today and won't be 10 or 15 years from now. What is basic to one group of people is not necessarily basic to another. One person's frills are another person's basics. . . ."

"We do need to get back to the basics, but it is essential that we first identify the basics we want to get back to. . . ." (These words, attributed to W. Ross Winterowd, professor of English, University of Southern California, have gained a kind of fame in the nationwide controversy.)

Finally, after such litany, there frequently came the troubled question, "What could spawn such demands in this year of 1976 after a hundred years of progress in education?"

A search for causes leads the investigator to such factors as nostalgia in the 1970s; the public's whetted appetite for accountability; the nation's periodic swing to conservatism; the high divorce rate and the disintegration of the family, leading to demands that the schools provide the discipline which the home no longer can; the excesses of permissiveness; and a bundle of causes in which Dr. Spock, TV, and creeping socialism are crammed into the same bag.

More realistically, the whys and wherefores of the back-to-basics movement can be found in these developments:

1. Parents, often at the behest of educators, have taken a larger part in school affairs. As they delve deeply into the task, they don't like, or don't understand, what they see. They try to reshape policies and programs in accordance with their views.

2. Blacks and Hispanics claim, rightly or wrongly, that their children are ignored or shortchanged with respect to instruction in basic skills. The ghetto has been a hotbed for the basics.

3. Over the years, teachers have been urged to focus on creativity, on humanistic objectives, on development of independent thinkers. It has not always been clear to the classroom practitioner whether these were to be in addition to, or instead of, mastery of the skills. Confusion of educational goals has opened the way for the single-minded advocates of the three Rs.

4. Employers have long complained that high school graduates do not make productive workers because allegedly they cannot read instructions on the job and lack ability in arithmetic. To the slogan, "Johnny can't read, write, or figure," *Forbes*, a journal for industrialists, added, "And Johnny can't work, either."

5. Colleges have also long complained that the typical high school graduate is unprepared for college. Consequently, colleges have had to lower their standards of admission and to resort to remedial courses in English, math, and science. College officials join in the clamor that the schools should do a better job of teaching fundamentals.

6. As proof of their complaints, employers and colleges cite the 12-year drop in national test scores, which allegedly show a decline in student achievement. When the Gallup poll asked a sampling of parents in 1975 what, in their opinion, was the reason for the dropping scores, 22% of the respondents said, "Courses are too easy; there is not enough emphasis on basics."

7. Partisans of the basics often revolt against a) the growth of *super*-professionalism in education and b) the proliferation of the school's services and activities. The charge is that, first, educationists have made the schools a theater for experimentation—more in their self-interest than in the interest of the children. The new report card, the new math, and the new textbooks have failed to improve the educational product, they tell us. "Educators keep on making changes for the sake of change," said a Pasadena critic during a recent battle over basics. The second charge is that the public schools have grown into huge bureaucratic machines, with overstuffed curricula and oversized staffs. The schools have taken on services and programs that belong to the home, the church, and social agencies—from serving breakfasts to giving the Pill to schoolgirls. The schools seek to hide their shoddy performance under a mantle of "professionalism" and by using cover-up lingo that makes no sense to the layman.

8. Finally, there is the financial crunch. It is cheaper to finance a bare-bones, stripped-down school program than the runaway programs of the past

decade. Such fundamentalist reasoning scores with taxpayers beset by inflation and rising school budgets.

Since back to basics covers a range of convictions and dogmas, some educators embrace some of them, even if they reject most of them. It is not uncommon to find schoolmen and -women enthusiastic for the cause. When Robert L. Brunelle took the post as New Hampshire's state commissioner of education in August 1976, he did so with a ringing call for a return to basics: "If you can't read, you can't learn anything." Scattered throughout the country are other educators who go along with fundamentalist concepts.

But to the probable surprise of basics hard-liners, educators counter simplistic demands for the three Rs with a new educational trinity: 1) minimal competency, 2) proficiency testing, 3) a performance-based curriculum.

Around these technical terms cluster aims and concepts toward which educators at state and local levels are working at a slow but increasing tempo. These include, in addition to emphasis on the three Rs, the development of life (or survival) skills—that is, competencies needed for personal growth and for successful existence as citizen, consumer, jobholder, taxpayer, and member of a family.

To achieve this double layer of skills, educators are looking to a curriculum based not on textbook facts but on standards of performance. To check whether the performance-based curriculum works, educators are turning to tests of proficiency. No student is to go from grade to grade or to graduate from high school unless he or she can prove, by test results, the mastery of a minimal body of skills and information. This is the direction in which American education is starting to move—but as one educator put it, "It's a slow rush." Many school districts, perhaps a majority, are making no move in this direction. They are waiting for a national pattern to develop or for state laws to push them into action.

Although more than four-fifths of the nation's school boards believe their schools should put greater emphasis on reading, writing, and arithmetic, according to a National School Boards Association survey, few boards have adopted policies to set into motion formal back-to-basics programs. NSBA officials who keep track of policy development in the nation's school districts have found less than half a dozen policy statements reflecting the fundamentalist party line. Why?

"Consider what it would mean to policy development to go all the way back to the basics as some partisans demand," said a school board member. "It would mean restructuring the board's policy statements on philosophy, goals, instructional program, discipline, homework, study halls, retention, promotion, graduation, report cards, counseling, extracurricular activities— to mention but a few topics. No board is about to do that."

What, then, *are* school districts doing?

Without bothering to rethink districtwide goals or philosophy, some school boards are permitting *some* of their schools to get on the basics track.

Seventeen schools in Philadelphia (including a middle and a junior high) have gone basic—meaning that the principals demand neatness and decorum and that teachers stress reading and mathematics and require regular homework. Parents, largely black or Spanish-speaking, wholeheartedly support these moves.

The Philadelphia schools are among about half a hundred in the country that have adopted back-to-basics practices. Others include the highly publicized Myers School, in Charlotte, North Carolina, the Hoover Structured School, Palo Alto; and the John Marshall Fundamental School, Pasadena.

The Council for Basic Education, as a service to the cause, keeps a monthly tally of such schools and is pleased to add new ones to the list. The CBE reports that under consideration for fall 1977 is the establishment of fundamental or traditional schools in Madison, Wisconsin; Mesa, Phoenix, and Scottsdale, Arizona; Montclair, New Jersey; Montgomery County, Maryland; and San Diego.

As a parallel service to the cause, the Education Commission of the States keeps tally of schools moving toward minimal competency testing. Among another half a hundred schools adopting this practice, it lists Craig, Alaska; Gary, Indiana; Cedar Rapids, Iowa; and Providence, Rhode Island.

Looking up and down the line of actions taken by the nation's schools, we find a range of efforts from cosmetic to regenerating.

Some school districts are applying the Madison Avenue solution, advertising widely that, "Yes, we have been, are, and will be teaching the basics," then putting the spotlight on any project or activity dealing with skills. District 66 in Omaha, Nebraska, spent nearly two years on just such an effort as one way of "talking back to the back-to-basics tiger."

Thus any existing Right-to-Read project (a Title I activity), remedial classes in language arts and math, or the reintroduction of phonics partly, wholly, voluntarily, or on a compulsory basis, is cited by school administrators as a return to basics.

A community, moderately satisfied with its traditional program and not under the spur of state law to do anything about basics, can get ahead of the school critics by a modest initiative. In May 1976, Superintendent James Kennedy of Manchester, Connecticut (population 50,000), decided on a pilot program to test the 650 tenth-graders in the system for proficiency in language arts and mathematics. Passing the test has not been made a graduation requirement, but, if the school board should make it so, students would be given opportunities during their remaining high school years to master the skills the tests require. Even so modest an effort has aroused the interest of many New England school officials to whom proficiency testing is still novel.

A shift of emphasis in regular activities often serves as a response to demands for basics. In Hartford, for example, Superintendent Edythe J. Gaines is restructuring the annual budget so that basics get top priority and a little bit more money than the year before. The budget Gaines presented to her board for 1976-77 was "priority oriented," she said, "toward 1) basic thinking skills in reading and other language arts, including applications . . . and 2) basic thinking skills in mathematics, including applications. . . ." The word "applications" is important, reflecting a determination to test students at regular intervals to see if they have mastered the skills.

When a school system gets a new superintendent—particularly if young, activist, and black—a dramatic shift toward the basics often takes place, not because of pressure groups but because the new educational leader wants it that way. This is what happened in Oakland when Ruth Love, who made Right-to-Read famous, arrived in the Bay city in November 1975. Love set up "an educational scoreboard" with specific goals and moved toward a tight schedule of completion. The top items (of a dozen or more) on Oakland's scoreboard are given by Superintendent Love as follows:

"Children who complete the third grade will be able to perform basic skills."

"A program of intervention will be provided for children who are or who fall one year behind grade-level expectations in basic skills.

"Graduates will possess the academic resources for higher education, advanced training, or a marketable skill."

Intervention strategies in Oakland may mean simply giving individual attention to students who need extra help, or requiring students to work in math labs, or assigning them to separate classes where they spend a full school day on reading and math. To assure that graduates "possess the academic resources" for post-high school work, Oakland requires students to pass proficiency tests in reading, writing, and computation.

In Salem, Oregon, under state mandate but with much local initiative, Superintendent William M. Kendrick and his staff have made the high school diploma the omega of the basic skills program.

"The traditional high school diploma has been based on two legs," says Kendrick, "attendance (seat time) and course requirements (exposure). . . . Now we've added a third leg—demonstrated performance."

Graduation from Salem secondary schools depends upon completing all of 35 "competency performance indicators" (CPIs). Grouped under "personal development," "social responsibility," and "career development," the CPIs, or skills a student must demonstrate before getting his diploma, include:

Read a 200-word article and answer questions. . . . Read and state three conditions of an apartment rental agreement. . . . Cite advantages and disadvantages of various credit plans. . . . Balance a checkbook. . . . From a list of 30 foods, select and describe a balanced menu for breakfast, lunch, and dinner. . . . Given a simulated paycheck stub, identify from five to seven payroll deductions. . . . Demonstrate knowledge of voting procedures. . . . Identify helpful and harmful effects of garden and household chemicals. . . . Prepare a job application. . . .

Salem's entire curriculum is being revised to focus on the 35 performance objectives. The elementary schools are expected to lay the groundwork for later success in the competencies. "This will bring our schools together with one objective—that of assuring each student a program which will allow him to acquire skills for survival in today's complex society," says Kendrick.

Florida is back-to-basics country—land of the much-touted Accountability Act of 1976. Not all Florida county school systems have been galvanized into action by the act. Polk County, for example, reported late in 1976, "We have started looking into our curriculum to see what changes need to be made to conform to the act." One change likely to be introduced in many Florida school systems is more classroom time for language and math. In Hillsborough County (Tampa) "a minimal time frame" for primary grades calls for more than 13 hours a week of teacher and pupil activity in reading and writing and five hours in math; similar time allotments are called for in the intermediate grades. Such schedules go a long way to satisfy those who claimed that the three Rs are being neglected in Florida.

Duval County (Jacksonville) public schools are pleasing back-to-basics advocates by using a test measuring whether the person has mastered the basic reading skills "necessary for survival in everyday life." Students are asked to demonstrate whether they can follow a recipe, understand a rental agreement, understand an appliance warranty, evaluate a charge account agreement, pick out bargains in a grocery ad, determine long-distance telephone rates, and acquire essential facts from an insurance policy. A number of Florida state legislators are impressed with the Duval test (similar to many others now in use in the U.S.); they want to make passing such tests part of graduation requirements for every public school student in the state.

When a school system bears down heavily on minimal competency, it need not narrow its curriculum. This is illustrated by the Denver public schools, which offer courses and services some might call "frills": the arts; health, psychological, and social services; film making; sex education; and bachelor survival for boys. Yet community pressure for basics has been relatively weak in Denver in recent years. This may be due to a simple action by former Superintendent Kenneth Oberholtzer: Some 15 years ago he persuaded his board of education to require that each high school graduate successfully pass tests in language, arithmetic, reading, and spelling. At that time the move was practically unheralded. For nearly a decade Denver stood almost alone as the major school system with such a requirement. Today the Oberholtzer move is hailed as an act of educational statesmanship and a "touchstone in the movement to assure proficiency in high school graduates."

State agencies have traditionally been weak in leading educational reform, leaving that role to the cities and wealthy suburbs.

This time it's different. State legislatures, state boards of education, and state education departments have leaped forward in the basics/minimal competency movement. The Education Commission of the States in Denver has tried hard to keep up with events. "It's a fast-moving scene," said Chris Pipho of the ECS. "Daily bulletins are needed to keep up with the action."

Some "bulletins" during 1976 reported the death of proposed legislation for minimal competency or performance-based programs in Arizona, Connecticut, Louisiana, Pennsylvania, and Tennessee—although planning for these purposes continued in their state departments of education.

One bulletin, flashed to the educational community after a quickie survey by the National Center for Educational Statistics in August 1976, reported that 22 states had no plans or activities for statewide standards to be used in developing performance-based curricula or for controlling promotion and graduation from public schools. In the 29 states that were planning (and this could mean anything from discussing a preliminary statement to drafting legislation) or doing something concrete, the chief concerns were: providing multiple opportunities to pass a required test of competence for progression through the grades and introducing new proficiency tests for high school entrance and high school graduation.

These are, of course, also the goals of the scores of bills introduced into state legislatures during the past two to three years. In a first phase, much of the legislation dealt with proficiency tests for high school entrance and graduation. Under pressure of school critics, bills in state capitols became broader in scope, as illustrated by Florida's catch-all Educational Accountability Act of 1976 and New Jersey's "Thorough and Efficient" Public School Education Act of 1975.

Although the Florida act is ostensibly concerned with accountability, the back-to-basics advocates are mostly interested in the provisions that mandate the testing of basic skills in grades 3, 5, 8, and 11. Students who do not meet minimum standards, by performance, must be given extra help or placed in remedial programs. The state will provide technical assistance (a term not clearly defined) to school districts where pupil deficiences are identified.

By 1 July 1977, Florida school districts will move pupils forward, grade by grade, on the basis of performance rather than on social promotion. By 1978-79, Florida districts will have to establish performance levels for high school graduation, in addition to the normal course requirements. Students unable to meet such standards must get "remediation" from their schools. Boards of education are authorized to award differentiated diplomas to correspond to the varying achievement levels of graduates.

The state of New Jersey mandates "thorough and efficient education"—a phrase whose vagueness still puzzles school boards. The law calls for each school system to develop a curriculum that contains "all elements of basic skills necessary to function in a democracy" and sets up checkpoints in the school program to make certain that students receive the kind of instruction they require.

Under a State Board of Education schedule, New Jersey's State Department of Education administered tests in October 1976 to grades 4, 7, and 10. The results went back to school districts in January. Students found in the low 20% bracket were given immediate attention. The statewide plan, for any student scoring below the 65% mastery level, goes into effect next September. Before this date, school districts must file in Trenton their basic skills improvement plans. What these are to cover and how they are to be put to work will worry New Jersey educators throughout the long summer of 1977. But as far as New Jersey State Education Commissioner Fred G. Burke is concerned, "Ours is the most comprehensive basic skills effort in the nation, because it will assure a learning program for every student with basic skills needs."

Equally sanguine about *their* plans are state officials in other parts of the country.

In Oregon, where taxpayers have condemned "worthless" high school diplomas for nearly a decade, school systems are now deep in programs raising and tightening high school graduation requirements. As first mandated by Oregon's State Department of Education in 1972, graduation depends upon a student's ability to master competencies in three areas—personal development, social responsibility, and career development (in addition, of course, to the usual credits for courses and attendance). Districts were given authority to develop their own performance indicators.

A 1976 revision of the state plan now allows districts to develop indicators for either the three previously mandated areas or to develop replacements for them. How the student is to demonstrate his competence to function as a learner, a citizen, consumer, and family member is up to the local board. Georgia officials said late in 1976 that they may adopt the Oregon plan.

California, where interest in basics is endemic, passed legislation in 1976 requiring student testing at least once during the seventh through ninth grades and twice between grades 10 and 11. For those failing to demonstrate minimal proficiency, the law provides teacher/parent conferences and remedial classes. No student will receive a high school diploma after June 1980 unless he passes the required proficiency tests.

New legislation in the state of Washington requires school districts to develop learning objectives in behavioral terms. State funds may be withheld from the local districts for noncompliance. Meanwhile, a standardized test was given in 1976 to all fourth-grade students in reading, math, and language arts. Results are now used by schools to compare children's achievement levels with those of other pupils in the district, the state, and the nation. Plans for remedial action remain to be developed.

Virginia's Standards of Quality Act of 1976 requires the State Board of Education to set up minimum statewide educational objectives and a statewide test in reading, language arts, and math—all this not later than September 1978. The high school diploma is also a point of concern in this state, because Greensville County, Virginia, is the home of Superintendent Sam Owen, who has become a hero among back-to-basics advocates because he "got tired of handing out rubber diplomas." Greensville County graduation requirements, although no different from those being adopted in other districts, have been publicized as models.

And so state actions continued throughout 1976 and into 1977. The plans that came into being were remarkably alike in purpose and in content. It was test and teach, teach and test—to assure competence in basic skills and the mastery of a minimal body of information thought necessary for graduation.

Among many state plans, only the time schedule was different. Missouri mandated its students to take tests starting 1 July 1977; Alabama, Massachusetts, and Vermont were working toward a fall 1977 deadline for the start of testing; New York State decided to require three new tests for graduation, effective in June 1980. Educators predicted that by 1984 (Orwell, can you hear?) nearly all the states will have incorporated minimal competency testing into promotion and graduation requirements. And then, what then?

What *will* be the outcome of the back-to-basics movement? "There is potential for some good and much harm," said one educator. Among possible beneficial effects is, first, the chance that during the next decade the public schools will produce a cadre of better readers and youths better skilled in computation—and possibly even in writing. Second is the possibility of restoring the authority of the teacher in the classroom, where it has been eroded by policies of pupil planning and pupil direction of school activities. Next: "The barnacles of multitudinous goals and activities may be stripped from school systems where they have fouled the curriculum," said a Maine superintendent, "and that would be to the good." Finally, even the most conservative of laymen may begin to value individualized instruction, since many of the remedial plans call for teaching on a one-to-one basis.

These possible advantages will be more than outweighed, according to concerned educators, by the growth of state power at the expense of the local school board. Many educators cite interference in local school board affairs and eventual total control by the state as strong possibilities. "We're moving toward state superboards of schools," one superintendent said.

Testing, testing, testing will spread to an extent hitherto undreamed of. School districts are feverishly looking for proficiency tests and are adopting them as soon as they can find them. The test-making industry is making plans to expand. "What worries me most," said a curriculum director, "is that we shall actually be asking teachers to teach to the test—a practice already condoned."

But the overriding worry of many educators to whom I spoke was the possibility that the public schools "are moving toward producing a generation of minimal mediocrity." By stressing mechanical skills of communication and computation, by denigrating the arts and creativity, by dehumanizing the learning process and placing it under rote and autocracy, American education, it is charged, will lose the great generating power that has kept the nation free, inventive, and productive.

If Not Public Choice, Then Private Escape

by Evans Clinchy and Elisabeth Allen Cody

The increasing popularity of tuition tax credits and the voucher idea should tell public school advocates something: that private and parochial education is powerfully attractive, and not always for anti-democratic reasons. A few systems—e.g., those of Minneapolis and Indianapolis—have begun to meet the competition.

About a year ago, the public schools of this country began to hear rumblings of what could turn out to be a large educational earthquake.

The source of these tremors was the sudden emergence of the idea of tuition tax credits, a move to channel large sums of money into the support of private and parochial schools. The most prominent of these moves was the Tuition Tax Credit Act of 1977, the Packwood-Moynihan Bill in the U.S. Senate, which would, in the version debated last summer, have allowed parents currently paying tuition in the nonpublic schools a credit on their federal income taxes of up to $250 per child per year, beginning in 1980. In an earlier version, the figure was $500 per child.

At first glance, the billion or so dollars this bill would have minimally made available every year to the parents of the five million nonpublic school children in this country seems small. After all, the total public education budget has reached $76.8 billion per year. Quite rightly, however, public educators saw it as the hobnailed boot in the door. The question is not so much the amount of money that would go toward the immediate support of those five million children. It is the precedent that would be set and the added inducement such aid offers to public school parents to abandon the public schools. Once this principle is established, public educators wonder where it will all end. Why not $1,000 or $2,000 per child? Why not a credit for whatever the full tuition may be?

Concerned public school people, again quite rightly, see the tax credit as a disguised and only slightly watered-down version of the voucher idea. Voucher plans would provide all parents with a set sum of money each year for each of their children, money that parents could spend at the school of their choice, public or private.

Voucher plans have been seen by their advocates as introducing a healthy dose of free enterprise competition into the educational system. Opponents tend to see them as ways for relatively rich parents and their private schools to get richer while the nation's poorer families and their public schools remain right where they are. Although there would be competition, it would be unfair competition, since the public schools must serve everyone who shows up at the door, while nonpublic schools can be and usually are selective.

While all of this may be true, none of the arguments against the tax credit plan made in Congress dealt with the basic issue. The question that should be causing the proponents of public education to search their collective soul is this: Why is it that the nonpublic schools are so attractive to so many people? Why, for instance, are the parents of five million children willing to pay their normal public school taxes and also carry the added burden of tuition in the nonpublic schools? Why does the leadership of the National Education Association and the American Federation of Teachers, again as instances, feel that large numbers of parents would quickly put their children into nonpublic schools if they were offered tuition tax credits?

There are many reasons for what could turn out to be a mass flight from the public schools. Some parents enjoy the social prestige that is still attached to the private college-preparatory school. Many parents, who are using the Catholic, Protestant, and Hebrew parochial schools, sincerely wish their children to have an education that is based on a specific set of religious values, a kind of schooling that the public schools are prohibited from providing. Still, other parents, both white and minoritiy, are using the nonpublic schools as a means of escaping the rigors, disruptions, and even the dangers of school desegregation. And there are undoubtedly an unknown number of parents who choose the nonpublic schools because such schools *can* be selective and therefore do not have to deal with the disruptive, the violent, and the educationally disabled students who must be dealt with in the public schools.

Yet even all of these reasons do not fully account for the public's increasing disaffection with its public schools or the suddenly increased attractiveness of the nonpublic schools. A much more telling and fundamental set of reasons is contained in the arguments put forward in support of private education and the tuition tax credit plan. These arguments also inadvertently spell out in some detail what the public education establishment will have to do in order to rescue the public schools from tuition tax credits and the threat of a mass exodus of its clientele.

Listen, for instance, to New York State's Senator Daniel Patrick Moynihan, writing in the April 1978 issue of *Harper's*:

> I take pluralism to be a valuable characteristic of education, as of much else in this society. We are many peoples, and our social arrangements reflect this disinclination to submerge our inherited distinctiveness in a homogeneous whole. . . .
>
> Diversity. Pluralism. Variety. These are values, too, and perhaps nowhere more valuable than in the experiences our children have in their early years, when their values and attitudes are formed, their minds awakened, and their friendships formed. We cherish these values, and I do not believe it excessive to ask that they be embodied in our national policies for American education.

Note also the arguments put forward by Vincent Post, president of the New York State Organization of Catholic School Parents, writing in the *New York Times*:

> There are on the other hand many parents who prefer a different learning environment for their children—different in being more or less structured, more demanding with concern for specific values: academic, aesthetic, athletic, or religious. . . . The public school cannot provide for the needs of all children and their families. It is healthy to maintain options that match the needs of people.

Observe the position stated by Robert Lamborn, executive director of the Council for American Private Education:

When I first came into the business of private education back in 1930, everybody told me I was foolish, that the private schools would be dead within 10 years. Now my feeling is that the social forces at work in this country are more favorable to private education than at any time since I've been around.

When I say social forces, I mean the increased value that is being placed by parents on options, on the right to choose according to their own consciences and their own educational philosophies. Many parents want smaller institutions, smaller schools where the clients have more of a say and a greater impact, institutions that are more responsive to what students need and parents want. These parents simply don't believe they can get this within the public setting. They feel that private schools give them the chance to retain all of their options, to make serious and thoughtful choices.

The wall seems covered with large and legible handwriting. What concerns an increasing number of parents—or at least many of the active, concerned parents who are the lifeblood of any public school system—is that they feel they have virtually no say, no control over what is going to happen to their children in the public schools.

Far too many parents far too often feel themselves to be at the mercy of a remote and unresponsive bureaucracy. They feel—and too often quite rightly—that the decisions about what the school system will be like, how it will be run, and what it will offer parents and children are made at levels far removed from the individual parent, child, and school. Parents are rarely if ever consulted about what they want for their children. They are rarely given any opportunity first to define and then to select the kind of schooling they want. Given little diversity and almost no choice within the public system, parents are pushed toward exercising the only choice they have, the choice of abandoning the public schools altogether.

That this should be the case is ironic. Indeed, it can be said that public education in this country is experiencing the bitter if inevitable fruits of its own past success. It was only about 125 years ago that this country decided to provide both the opportunity and, if possible, the reality of formal schooling to every child and young person, including eventually all the children who had always been benignly ignored by everyone—the poor, the foreign born, the physically and mentally handicapped. As recently as 1921 there were only 334,000 young people graduating from high school, or 17.1% of all the country's 17-year-olds. By 1975 the number had jumped to 3,140,000, 74.4% of the nation's 17-year-olds.

Despite all the criticisms that have been both justly and unjustly leveled against it, the American system of public education between 1850 and the present has undertaken and largely succeeded in accomplishing the most massive formal schooling effort in the history of humankind. The system has produced—or has been instrumental in producing—the most literate and well-informed people on earth.

In order to achieve this miracle, in order to provide schooling for so many people in so short a time at the lowest possible cost, the public education establishment borrowed—or had forced upon it—the organizational structure and many of the managerial techniques of the mass-production, assembly-line industrial corporation. The typical American school system became a vertically organized, hierarchical bureaucracy with all basic decisions made at the top and then passed down through the ranks to the workers and clients at the bottom.

As part of this structure, and in an effort to make sure that every child is treated both equally and efficiently, public educators have felt compelled to search for and impose a single, standardized, and largely uniform type of schooling throughout most school districts. Thus the structure of the system itself has come to dictate the basic policy of most school systems, the basic decisions concerning what the system will offer parents, and the identity of those who will be allowed to take part in the decision-making process. Only rarely does either an elected board of education or the top management—the superintendent and assistant superintendents—make decisions that substantially alter the operations of the established structure. The thinking of board members and higher-level management is controlled and constrained by their knowledge of what the structure will allow and not allow.

Having adopted this structure and performed the miracle of mass education, the public education establishment now finds itself confronted with the results of its labors. It is faced with an adult population of parents who are knowledgeable, questioning, and restive. Increasingly, they reject the autocratic operations of the system as being impossibly rigid, thoroughly undemocratic, and quite unable to respond to the diverse but legitimate demands that parents are making on behalf of themselves and their children.

What this new, highly informed breed of parents—and perhaps especially the young parents of the postwar baby boom generation—is in the midst of discovering is that there is no single, uniform, widely agreed-upon, indisputably "right" way to educate all children. They are discovering that the so-called experts, from academic theoreticians to practicing school administrators, simply do not agree on any one approach.

Many parents as well as teachers and other educators believe that children—or at least some children—will benefit most from a highly structured, traditional, or back-to-basics type of schooling. Still other parents and educators believe that children will benefit from a less structured or "continuous progress" type of schooling in which each child moves through the prescribed course of study at his own most appropriate speed. Still other parents and educators believe that children will benefit from a developmental type of schooling that sees children as the primary agents in their own intellectual growth and therefore gives children a role in deciding what the day-to-day activities of schooling will be.

What these parents are discovering is that they are asking for something—educational diversity and choice—that the present educational structure is simply not designed to provide. In this very fundamental sense, the existing structure is obsolescent, if not downright obsolete. It is not a structure that can easily or genuinely respond either to the legitimate educational demands of its clients or to the legitimate professional needs of its most important employees, the teachers. It is therefore not a structure that can easily adapt to or long survive the threat posed by the tuition tax credit and the enhanced attractiveness of the nonpublic schools.

Yet adapt it must. Instead of an autocratic, hierarchical bureaucracy in which decisions flow from the top down, we will have to develop a much more democratic structure in which the important decisions about what should happen to children in school are made only as the result of intensive consultation with both parents and teachers, only after parents have specified what kinds of schooling they wish for their children, and only after teachers have specified what type of schooling they feel most comfortable practicing.

These decisions will then flow up to the central administration and the board of education, whose job it will be to insure that the desired options are provided. Instead of an industrial, mass-production corporate structure, we will have developed what economist Peter Drucker describes as a model based upon "socialist competition." Under this arrangement the schools remain public and are therefore owned by and are open to everyone. But within that public structure the individual schools are responsive to the marketplace and reflect what the clientele wants. This does not mean that every parent is compelled to choose or must make decisions without the advice and assistance of educators in the system. One of the options offered would be the opportunity of not choosing, i.e., of having a child assigned to whatever school the professional educators believe is best for that child. A system of diversity and choice, however, does empower every parent who wishes to control his child's education with the right to do so.

Other pieces of the industrial model will have to be altered as well. Parents and teachers in optional schools, for instance, may want and need a considerable amount of autonomy, including the power to spend their own lump-sum budget and the possibility of being governed, at least in part, by a board made up of elected parents and teachers. Some optional schools may wish also to be quite small. Instead of one large school in each section of town, parents might prefer a group of smaller schools, each housing its own option. Or large schools may need to be broken down into smaller, optional subschools.

In the few places where a system of diversity and choice has been tried within a public school system, the results have been impressive. In 1971 the Minneapolis, Minnesota, school system launched a pioneering effort in educational options called the Southeast Alternatives project. Using a small part of the city (the southeast section, including 29,000 people), the school system offered parents and teachers a choice among four different kinds of elementary schools: traditional, continuous progress, British primary/integrated day, and a K-12 free school.

Before this experiment was put into effect, a poll of the parents indicated that only about 35% of them were "satisfied" with what the school system was then offering them. After four years of diversity and choice, the parent satisfaction level reached 85%. The Southeast Alternatives options plan has now been adopted as the basic structure of the entire Minneapolis school system.

What is perhaps even more impressive is that the offering of educational options is being used to desegregate the schools in that city. Each optional school has racial quotas guaranteeing that at no time can the minority enrollment in an option exceed that of the school system as a whole. Since this approach to desegregation appears to be working without all the furor and turmoil that normally accompanies desegregation, the parents in Minneapolis, even if they have to put their children on buses, evidently feel that the educational benefit their children receive at the end of the bus ride is well worth the rigors of the trip.

The idea of offering educational options is being carried somewhat further in Indianapolis, Indiana, where the school board is proposing to desegregate its entire first-grade through sixth-grade elementary school population of approximately 32,000 children by means of educational options. During the past year some 1,500 parents and teachers participated in an options-building process at open community meetings during which they collaboratively designed the different kinds of schools they would like to see offered in the Indianapolis public school system. This design process resulted in the development of six distinct educational options: a back-to-basics or fundamental school; a traditional school; a continuous progress school; a continuous progress school operating in open space (a building without interior walls or regular classroom spaces); a Montessori school; and a developmental or integrated-day school.

Since the idea of parents asking for and actually being able to choose the kind of schooling they want for their children is so new, a seventh option was added. The seventh option allows parents to request to have their child remain in his present school, if such is possible within the racial balance requirements of desegregation. If that is not possible, then the parents have an opportunity to choose to have their child assigned to a school which practices a philosophy similar to that of the school the child is presently attending.

It was expected that this seventh option might draw up to 90%, or even 95%, of parental choices the first time around. (The plan, of course, calls for parents to select or reselect schools every year as more and more people accustom themselves to the idea of making educational choices.) During last March and April the parents of first-grade through sixth-grade elementary school children went through the options selection process. It turned out that the expectation that 90% to 95% of the choices would be for option seven was overly pessimistic. About 22% (or the parents of more than 6,000 children) chose one of the first six options, while 78% chose option seven. What is even more remarkable is that each of the first six options was selected by equal numbers of white and minority parents. Each of the six options drew almost exactly 50% minority and 50% white enrollments, thus almost exactly replicating the white and minority percentages of the school system as a whole. This is powerful evidence to support the idea that there are no racial preferences for particular kinds of schooling—at least in Indianapolis. The teachers, as it turned out, were slightly more conservative than the parents. Eighty-three percent of them chose the type of school in which they are presently teaching.

The options plan in Indianapolis is scheduled for slow and careful installation. In September 1978, the school system set up pilot optional schools for parents who wished their children to start immediately in the school of their choice.° Parents—and particularly those parents who chose option seven— will have a chance to visit the pilot schools and observe the different options in actual operation. This next school year will also be used to enable parents, teachers, and administrators to begin planning the extension of the elementary school options into grades 7 through 12.

In the spring of 1979, if all goes well, parents will again be asked to make their selections for September of that year, when the full citywide options plan—and mandatory citywide desegregation—will be officially put into ef-

---

°As of October 1, the Indianapolis options plan is expected to proceed regardless of what Judge Hugh Dillin and the Third Circuit Court of Appeals do with respect to two-way busing for desegregation. Pilot programs for each of the options are in full swing. —*The Editors*

fect, if the federal courts agree to allow Indianapolis to proceed with deseg-regation.

One further small but interesting event has occurred in Indianapolis as a result of the school board's commitment to educational options. There has been significant interest on the part of parents whose children are either now in private and parochial schools or who now have preschool children but have assumed that those children would have to go to private and parochial schools. Nearly 100 such parents filled out options selection forms requesting that their children be placed in one of the new optional schools being created by the public school system.

This probably does not signal a mass exodus from the nonpublic schools back into the public schools. It does, however, raise the intriguing possibility that a system of diversity and choice within the public schools might work not simply to stem flight from the public schools but actually to begin to reverse that trend. If such turns out to be the case, the threat of tuition tax credits, voucher plans, and the possible collapse of public education could turn out to be not an earthquake but merely a timely incentive to encourage us to figure out better ways of operating public school systems.

The First Decade of
Public School Alternatives
by Mary Anne Raywid

The alternative school movement was conceived in the Sixties.
How well has it survived the ravages of the Seventies and
emerged into the present decade? Remarkably well, says Ms.
Raywid in explaining the origins and momentum of this major
force in U.S. schools.

Several histories have already been written about the alternatives *to* public schools that emerged during the 1960s. The free and freedom schools that thrived during that tumultuous decade have been liberally chronicled and interpreted. But these alternatives, which had their roots outside public education, soon inspired alternatives *within* it—and that history remains to be written. This article seeks to tell the story of the first decade of alternatives within U.S. public school systems.

A number of schools have been credited as the first public alternatives—Philadelphia's Parkway, which opened in 1969 after two years of dreaming and planning; Wilson Open Campus School in Mankato, Minnesota, which dates from 1968; and Murray Road in Newton, Massachusetts, and Harlem Prep, both of which got under way in 1967. Since then all of these programs have experienced many changes, and countless others have followed in their wake. The aggregate, after 10 years of steady growth and sharing, is a distinctive and fairly healthy movement. There are notable common roots, practices, and concerns.

The first alternative schools—those named above—were not alternatives in the present sense of the term. These early programs grew out of the educational humanism of the Sixties, which envisioned existing schools as cold, dehumanizing, irrelevant institutions largely indifferent to the humanity and "personhood" of those within them. Many early leaders in the alternative school movement were likely to be strident critics of government and society, as well as of education. They were opponents of the Vietnam war, or critics of America's materialism, or challengers of our scientific-technocratic ethos—or all of these. Anti-Establishment sentiment and rhetoric were legion; students in many early alternative schools were associated with what Theodore Roszak dubbed the "counter-culture" and Charles Reich later called "Consciousness III." For the most part, neither the staff nor the students in those schools saw themselves offering any mere *alternative* to the conventional way of keeping school; they were characteristically much less modest and guarded. Most viewed their programs as the kind of reform desperately needed by *all* education. Although the term "alternative" was used—especially in connection with Parkway—it seems to have been introduced to highlight the displacement of classrooms by other arenas for learning rather than to suggest that there might be a multitude of good ways of conducting school. This latter idea did not seem to emerge until the early 1970s, when a number of factors led to it.

First among these factors was the bad news that followed (and dimmed) the promise of the Sixties. It is important to remember that the Sixties were

not only a time of protest; they were also a period of tremendous sociopolitical optimism and of substantial growth in our expectations for education. The
long critique of schooling that began after World War II suddenly gave way
in the Sixties to a wide assortment of ideas, and these received extensive
help—literally billions of dollars—from private and governmental sources.
Team teaching, programmed learning, computer-assisted instruction, and
structured curriculum were among the more specific innovations; and the
open classroom, compensatory education, the middle school, and individualized instruction gained substantial followings as more broad-gauged
proposals. Huge foundations—Ford, Carnegie, Rockefeller—generously
supported the experimental programs, and so did corporations. In New York,
for instance, "street academies" were supported by the Chase Manhattan
Bank, Union Carbide, and IBM, as well as by foundation funds.

During the mid-Sixties President Lyndon Johnson's Great Society program declared a War on Poverty. Education was to be in the vanguard of the
battle. Government funds were made available to schools in unprecedented
amounts under several different programs of the Elementary and Secondary
Education Act (ESEA) of 1965. The Head Start program of Title I was aimed
at children of the poor, explicitly to offset the disadvantages to which they
were subject. The intent of these efforts was to equalize opportunity.
Simultaneously, other programs such as Title III, ESEA, were introduced
specifically to facilitate innovation and the development of alternatives for
other populations as well; among the results were such now well-known alternative programs as the St. Paul Open School and Quincy High School II in
Illinois.

Evaluation of all of these programs, however, resulted in the bitterly disappointing finding of "no significant difference." As the Ford Foundation
commented in evaluating its own grant program, perhaps the biggest thing to
come out of it all was the knowledge of what are *not* the significant variables.
The foundation wistfully concluded that we really don't know how to improve schools.[1] Several years later, an extensive analysis of education research confirmed that finding, concluding that we had yet to discover a single
variable that is consistently correlated with educational success.[2]

These lackluster findings effectively halted new efforts at innovation,
with some critics demanding a complete moratorium on innovation of any
kind.[3] Instead, attention returned to the alternatives idea of the Sixties. Educators took renewed interest in alternatives and options per se and in alternative *systems*. Such systems were the express target of the federal Experimental Schools Program in 1971, which enabled Berkeley and Minneapolis to
set up extensively differentiated educations to be available by choice.

Moreover, a voucher program originating in the U.S. Office of Economic
Opportunity sought to extend such choice to include private schools as well as
public among the options. (Ultimately no takers could be found; the sole
voucher site—Alum Rock in San Jose, California—consisted exclusively of
public school programs.) There was very little initial interest. Vouchers
bogged down over the political issue of shunting public funds to sectarian
schools and over the opposition of professional groups. Ultimately, it was a
proposal without a constituency.[4]

Yet the 1970s continued to give an increasing amount of emphasis to the
provision of alternatives to all youngsters and their families. By 1973 Mario

Fantini's *Public Schools of Choice* elaborated the concept and showed how to implement it.[5] The National Consortium on Options in Public Education, organized at Indiana University in 1971, quickly became an international consortium. Under the leadership of Robert Barr, Daniel Burke, and Vernon Smith, ICOPE soon became a major voice for alternatives and options systems. Richard Kammann popularized the argument for alternatives in a vivid and much-quoted passage:

> Imagine a town where every family is assigned arbitrarily to one local doctor by a ruling of the board of health. Imagine that the board of health assigns families only on the basis of the shortest distance from the home to the doctor's office. Imagine, finally, that when a family complains that the assigned doctor is not helping one of its ailing members, the board of health replies: "Sorry, no exceptions to doctor assignments."
>
> If this sounds like a totalitarian nightmare, it also is a description of the way school boards assign children to schools and teachers. . . .[6]

The idea of choice in public schooling received a considerable boost with the appearance in 1974 of a new interpretive history of American education, David Tyack's *The One Best System*.[7] Tyack's book led many to question the assumption that there is one best way to keep school: a single best set of aims for all, an ideal curriculum, one best set of instructional methods, one best way to organize and administer schools and to prepare teachers. Tyack greatly extended the discussion of alternative forms of schooling and lent legitimacy to a fledgling movement.

Supporters of alternatives in education were quick to point out that the notion is highly consistent with the principles of a democratic society, a pluralistic culture, the need for community involvement in education, the need for institutional self-renewal in schools, and the need for financial austerity. This broadly based rationale—which appeared in the first issue of the ICOPE bulletin, *Changing Schools*[8]—suggests something of the scope of the appeal of alternatives. They have a remarkable capacity to respond to a wide spectrum of concerns.

From these beginnings 10 years ago, public alternative schools have grown from 100 or so in 1970 to more than 10,000 today. Alternatives are found in 80% of the nation's larger school districts (those enrolling 25,000 or more students), and they have begun to appear even in the smallest districts: One out of every five districts enrolling fewer than 600 students now claims one or more alternatives. An estimated three million U.S. youngsters are currently enrolled in alternative programs.[9]

What are they like, these alternative schools that have proliferated at such a rapid rate across the U.S.? Generalizations are difficult because the alternatives represent institutionalized diversity. Some are clearly linked to their forebears—the free schools and freedom schools of the 1960s. Many seem marked by an informality rarely found in other schools. Alternative schools tend to rely on close personal relationships instead of rules as the basis for social organization and control within the school. Charismatic leadership tends to play a larger role than do formal principles of role and function. The curriculum is chosen from a wider range of knowledge and life than is the case in other schools, and it may be pursued in novel ways and in unusual settings. I must also add, however, that one of the fastest-growing types of alternatives during the past five years has been the so-called fundamentalist or back-to-basics program, which relies heavily on formality, deference to authority, traditional curriculum, and such instructional strategies as drill, recitation, and rote learning.

Alternative schools have changed markedly in both mood and tone within the past decade. Many of the spiritual progeny of the free schools, for example, were heavily concerned with the existential *angst* of all participants. There was much talk about being free to do your own thing without having someone else's trip laid on. But many other early alternatives simply emphasized some degree of freedom from standard school procedures and requirements in order to proceed with a more substantial education. Programs of the first sort tended to deemphasize cognitive learning, but some remarkable scholarship emerged from alternatives of the second variety.

The values and goals of the early alternative schools were typically quite individualistic and private—rarely oriented toward increased group consciousness or commonality. But programs emphasizing group awareness and responsibility and seeking to build a deliberate sense of community began to appear in the mid-1970s. (Greta Pruitt, who has worked extensively with alternative schools in California, finds insufficient group orientation a continuing feature of alternatives—giving rise to the quite plausible possibility that patterns and emphases may be regional in character.[10])

The early emphasis on collective decision making via participatory democracy has become less pronounced. One comparative study of alternative school evaluations lists the satisfactory carrying out of group decision making as a common problem.[11] On the other hand, an early sympathetic analyst—himself a director of an alternative school—suggested that, unless alternative schools struck a compromise on participatory democracy, they would probably run into trouble. His suggestion was to limit student involvement to certain key decisions and to seek genuine involvement in those.[12] However, even in the absence of much collective decision making, most alternative schools share an emphasis on the freedom and authority over one's person that Allen Graubard urged in his book, *Free the Children*. It is, in effect, the power of the veto: No youngster should be forced to do what he or she is determined to reject.[13]

In at least one respect—the commitment these schools engender from all within them, students and staff alike—the decade has not changed alternative schools, except perhaps to intensify that commitment. The devotion of the youngsters is strange and wondrous to behold. Incredible as it may seem, they are uniformly eager to testify on behalf of their school.

Because of the limited amount of systematic research to date, the success secrets of alternatives cannot yet be recounted with much assurance. There have been interpretive analyses, particularly of organizational structures and processes, e.g., interaction patterns, decision making, and operative values. And there have been case studies and a number of evaluations; almost all public school alternatives are required annually to document their effectiveness. These studies and evaluations enable us to state that alternative schools typically lead to greater academic achievement on the part of their students.[14] At least some alternatives send a substantially higher percentage of their graduates on to college than do comparable schools in the same district; the only inquiries to date suggest that alternative school graduates may outperform the others in college. Such results assume special significance in view of the fact that so many alternative education students begin as poorly motivated underachievers. A great deal of other evidence also indicates that alternative schools have a clear and positive effect on their students' attitudes toward school and on their attitudes toward themselves. Most critically, so far as success in school is concerned, students in alternative schools come to experience a heightened sense of control over their own lives.

Systematic evidence involving larger samples and comparative groups should soon be available. David Mann at the Institute for Social Research of the University of Michigan has just finished a study of the effects of alternative schools on the behavior of disruptive students. James Coleman's current longitudinal study of secondary education includes 30 alternative schools, and a broad participative inquiry intended as a contemporary analogue to the Eight-Year Study is now under way. So current knowledge about the dynamics and outcomes of alternative schools should soon find firmer footing.

One of the reasons for the rapid proliferation of alternative schools is surely the fact that many groups with disparate agendas have seen alternatives as the means to achieve their own purposes. Youngsters who hate school have regarded alternatives as a much more satisfactory arrangement. (In Plainview, New York, for example, a group of high school students met for more than a year and then presented a detailed formal proposal to the board of education for the alternative they had designed.) Teachers seeking a practicable way to individualize instruction have looked to alternatives, as have teachers who feel as locked in and restricted by conventional school practices as many students. And school administrators, leaders, and policy makers have looked to alternatives as a way to effect reform in education. For some, the goal was nothing less than the humanizing of the entire system. The turbulent Sixties taught some harsh lessons about the change process, showing that would-be reformers had simply been barking up the wrong tree. They had sought substantial change by modifying a single facet of the school—curriculum or methods or teacher deployment or scheduling arrangements. They failed to appreciate the school's capacity to absorb and co-opt and defuse. Analysts began to conclude that realistic hopes for improvement would have to focus on the whole institutional structure—the social organization and its culture or climate. Many saw alternative schools as just the mechanism for introducing different institutional arrangements and climates. In fact, some perceived alternatives as the key to institutional renewal[15]—renewal on a continuing basis, since demands for a new alternative and diminished interest in an existing one would be the means whereby the system could reform itself.

The last 10 years have witnessed an expansion of the mission of alternative schools, which accounts in considerable part for their growing popularity. Student disaffection has been evident throughout the decade in the forms of school vandalism and violence, high truancy and dropout rates. The earliest evaluations showed clearly that alternatives are an extraordinarily effective solution to these problems. Agencies interested in delinquency and juvenile crime prevention quickly came to see alternative schools as an answer. As school desegregation difficulties intensified, it appeared that attractive alternatives—magnet schools—might draw youngsters from various neighborhoods on a voluntary basis. (This was the crux of Judge Arthur Garrity's plan for Boston.) In the inner cities, where feelings of powerlessness and disenfranchisement were widespread, policy analysts saw alternatives as a way of bestowing immediate empowerment.

The growth of the alternative school movement was further stimulated by the growing critique of education and the increasing pressures on schools to better serve each and every youngster. Declining test scores and plummeting public confidence combined to increase the pressures on schools. Many came to see alternatives as a means of tailoring educational programs—content, approach, structure, climate—to the specific needs of different groups. Particularly in school districts with heterogeneous populations, teachers and administrators have looked to alternatives as a means of fitting education to particular sets of needs. Declining enrollments have further pressed administrators to search for programs that can deliver greater holding power and increased effectiveness in the interest of halting the flight to suburban and private schools.

The breadth of this appeal and the several distinct constituencies it creates may account for the early Establishment approval of alternatives—which began as a somewhat radical proposal pressed by dissidents. As I mentioned earlier, a number of major corporations and foundations aided the early free and freedom schools. The federal government helped launch a number of individual alternatives and sought, through two different programs, to encourage the development of systems of choice. State education departments have helped with various forms of assistance. Universities have been involved—notably through such efforts as ICOPE at Indiana University and the National Alternative Schools Program at the University of Massachusetts, which offered direct help of various sorts to alternative school staff members and students. More recently, units concerned with alternatives have been established at several other universities, including the Center for Educational Alternatives at California State University/Fullerton and the Center for the Study of Educational Alternatives at Hofstra University in Hempstead, New York. Professional organizations of educators have demonstrated interest in alternatives by featuring them in their publications—although they have made relatively few commitments to aiding the movement. However, the continuing problem of public confidence in education and the resurgent voucher proposal may well serve to intensify the interest of professional organizations in alternatives. These groups may be coming to see, as one advocate put it, that "the development of alternative schools could well be the last, best chance for reforming public education."[16]

It would appear, then, that the growth of the last decade will continue and, indeed, has probably not yet reached its peak. The discovery phase is past, so the intense publicity given the movement during its formative years has cooled. Some alternative schools are closing as needs and interests change, but many more are opening. Last September, for example, Milwaukee doubled its alternatives for disaffected students—after just one year's trial of the program. Moreover, there are few signs that the pressures on public education are abating or that the public is willing to reduce its expectations. Indeed, with all of our talk of individualization—and our enactment of that arrangement into federal law in P.L. 94-142—we may soon discover that diversified programs for all may be the only practicable way of carrying out the law of the land.

---

1. See B. Frank Brown, "The Reform of Secondary Education," *NASSP Bulletin*, May 1974, p. 47; and Paul Nachtigal, *A Foundation Goes to School* (New York: Ford Foundation, 1972) and "Attempts to Change Education in the Sixties," *Changing Schools*, vol. 1, no. 2, p. 8.

2. Harvey Averch et al., *How Effective Is Schooling?* (Englewood Cliffs, N.J.: Educational Technology Press, 1974).

3. See, for example, Frank E. Armbruster, "The More We Spend, the Less Children Learn," *New York Times Magazine*, 28 August 1977, pp. 9-11 ff.

4. Denis P. Doyle, "The Politics of Choice: A View from the Bridge," in James S. Coleman et al., *Parents, Teachers, and Children* (San Francisco: Institute for Contemporary Studies, 1977) pp. 227-55.

5. Mario Fantini, *Public Schools of Choice* (New York: Simon and Schuster, 1973).

6. Richard Kammann, "The Case for Making Each School in Your District 'Different,'" *American School Board Journal*, January 1972, pp. 37, 38.

7. David B. Tyack, *The One Best System* (Cambridge, Mass.: Harvard University Press, 1974).

8. "The Age of Alternatives: A Developing Trend in Educational Reform," *Changing Schools*, 001 (n.d.), pp. 1-3.

9. Data are cited from Vernon Smith, "A Decade of Alternative Schools and What of the Future?," *NASSP Curriculum Report*, October 1978; and "A New Approach to Classroom Education," *U.S. News & World Report*, 10 September 1979.

10. Greta Pruitt, "Alternative Schools—Ten Years Later," *Changing Schools*, Summer 1978, p. 2.

11. Heather Doob, *Evaluations of Alternative Schools* (Arlington, Va.: Educational Research Service, 1977).

12. Jerry R. Fletcher, "The Implications of Alternative Schools for the Public Education System: The End of the Formal Institution?," *School and Community* (Paris: Organization for Economic Cooperation and Development, 1975), pp. 61-63.

13. See Allen Graubard, *Free the Children* (New York: Vintage Books, 1974), esp. Chap. 4.

14. The claims that follow come from one or more of three studies of evaluations: Robert Barr, Bruce Colston, and William Parrett, "The Effectiveness of Alternative Public Schools: An Analysis of Six School Evaluations," *Viewpoints in Teaching and Learning*, July 1977, pp. 1-30; Daniel Duke and Irene Muzio, "How Effective Are Alternative Schools? A Review of Recent Evaluations and Reports," *Teachers College Record*, February 1978, pp. 461-83; and Doob, op. cit.

15. Daniel L. Duke, "Challenge to Bureaucracy: The Contemporary Alternative School," *Journal of Educational Thought*, vol. 10, no. 1, pp. 34-48.

16. Robert D. Barr, "Editorial Reflections on Educational Reform," *Changing Schools*, 001 (n.d.), p. 9.

Public Alternative Schools and
The Future of Democracy
by Joe Nathan and Herbert Kohl

Mary Anne Raywid's April KAPPAN *article perpetuated several destructive myths about public alternative schools, claim the authors, who attempt to debunk those myths.*

We commend the *KAPPAN* and Vernon Smith for assembling, in the April 1981 issue, a fascinating collection of manuscripts that reviewed the history, philosophy, practice, and evaluation of public alternative schools. However, we must also take issue with a number of views presented by Mary Anne Raywid in her lead article, "The First Decade of Public School Alternatives." Raywid has written extensively about alternatives—usually with sensitivity and insight. But our disagreements are far more than intellectual quibbles.

We believe that the development and widespread adoption of the best public alternative school practices is vital for the survival of public education. Furthermore, our democracy depends on a strong, effective system committed to the education of all of our children—a commitment presently maintained only by public schools.

"History is a collection of myths agreed upon," wrote a perceptive critic. We believe Raywid's article perpetuates a number of destructive myths about public alternatives that give unwarranted assistance to those who oppose what many of us have worked so hard to develop over the last decade.

The first myth is the notion that most public alternative schools give students "the power of the veto: No youngster should be forced to do what he or she is determined to reject" (p. 552). Having worked for a total or more than 15 years in public alternative schools in the Midwest and Western U.S., visited more than 750 public alternatives throughout the country, and directed projects to help other districts design and implement alternatives, we can state with considerable confidence that *no* public alternative school that has survived more than two years gave students such a veto. Successful public alternative schools (of which there are hundreds) soon learned that they needed rules about behavior, attendance, graduation requirements, respecting rights of others, etc. For example, public alternatives would not tolerate the possession, use, or distribution of drugs on the school campus. Public alternatives have also developed important variations on traditional school practices, such as requiring demonstration of basic and applied competence in various areas before graduation.[1] As Barbara Case points out in the same issue in her excellent article, "Lasting Alternatives: A Lesson in Survival," "Alternatives flounder when they know with certainty only what they oppose but have no clear understanding of what they support" (p. 555).

Unquestionably, alternative public school students have had opportunities to help make, review, and revise many rules. Unquestionably, these students have had opportunities to learn in a variety of ways from community resources not often available to conventional school students. We must distinguish between giving students the opportunity to participate in sensible democratic decision making and endorsing the tyranny of any group in a school: students, community members, teachers, parents, or administrators.

Alternative schools have been committed to giving students and parents a voice, to having them help develop their own educational programs, and to taking student perceptions of bad educational practice seriously. At times this involves considerable discussion and negotiation of student, parent, and teacher priorities. Participation is the essence of learning to be a responsible citizen of a democracy. However, the negotiations in alternative schools have been over how to go about reading, for example, not about whether or not to learn to read.

To suggest that alternative public schools allow students to ignore rules they are "determined to reject" is not a misinterpretation or questionable analysis. It simply is not consistent with the facts and is a dangerous, destructive misstatement. It is the kind of sentence that will be quoted endlessly (and out of context) by opponents of public alternative schools.

Raywid puts forth another view that is inconsistent with facts when she describes the results of public alternative school evaluations. She presents the opinion that evaluation "of all of these programs resulted in the bitterly disappointing finding of 'no significant differences'" (p. 551). Space does not permit documentation and review of the more than 75 public alternative school evaluations with which we are personally familiar that describe statistically significant differences in attitude or achievement between matched groups of conventional and alternative school students. Interested readers should review, among others, Robert Horwitz's *Psychological Effects of Open Classroom Teaching on Primary School Children: A Review of the Research*[2], "Startling/Disturbing Research Supporting Educational Change," by Wayne Jennings and Joe Nathan[3]; *The Guinea Pigs After 20 Years*, by Margaret Willis[4]; a number of evaluations of public alternatives that have been identified as "carefully evaluated, proven innovations worthy of national replication"[5]; and Nathan's forthcoming dissertation.[6] The dissertation compares experiences and attitudes of students who graduated in 1979 from a traditional and a public alternative school in St. Paul, Minnesota.

A third myth that Raywid reinforces concerns the roots of public alternatives. The article suggests that the impetus for developing public alternatives came from members of the largely white, upper-middle-class "counterculture" of the 1960s who opposed the Vietnam war and technocratic development.

Mario Fantini and Vito Perrone have written helpful summaries of public alternative school histories that describe the contributions of the progressives of the early 1900s and of black and Native American activists who have pushed for greater human and civil rights for the last 50 years.[7] How can the contributions of Southern Citizenship Schools established during the early Sixties, of the American Indian Movement, and of Urban League Street Academies be wiped out? What of the recommendations of progressives such as John Dewey and George Counts for interdisciplinary learning, action-learning projects, advisor/advisee systems, and beginning instruction by building on students' interests? A comprehensive history of public alternative schools should not ignore the contributions of Francis Parker in the 1870s or the struggles of Calvin Stowe, Catharine Beecher, Elizabeth Peabody, Bronson Alcott, and other progressive educators of the 1830s and 1840s. A continuous tradition of what is loosely called alternative education has existed since the inception of the common school movement in the 1800s; the tradition has roots in the ideas of Benjamin Franklin, Benjamin Rush, Jean Jacques Rousseau, and others who saw self-discipline, the ability to make choices, and the thoughtful mastery of skills as keys to the development of democracy. We need to recognize the diversity of people who contributed to this progress.

Raywid also ignores another important part of the history of public alternative schools. In the early 1970s a split developed between community activists who started different schools because they felt U.S. society needed fundamental, comprehensive change to fulfill its dreams, and foundation and government officials who encouraged development of public alternatives to remove pressure from a system that was failing. Space does not permit adequate discussion of the take-over of the movement by professional educators. However, some community support for education and promising educational practices was sacrificed in the transition of power.

The experiences in Berkeley and Minneapolis form fascinating case studies of the professionalization of reform. Raywid says that the federal Experimental Schools Program "enabled Berkeley and Minneapolis to set up extensively differentiated educations to be available by choice" (p. 551). As Herbert Kohl explained in Fantini's *Public Schools of Choice*, the number of public alternatives in Berkeley actually declined because of the federal money and the restrictions entailed.[8] Moreover, the federal money enabled the Berkeley school district to take power away from individual school sites and to create a centralized alternative school bureaucracy staffed almost exclusively by people hostile to alternative education.

Those familiar with the Minneapolis federally funded Southeast Alternatives Project know how it frustrated many alternative school activists. A strong case can be made that the federal money enabled the district to resist for several years the establishment of public alternatives in sections of the city where multiracial groups of parents, students, and teachers were trying to develop them. Without making definitive judgments about the effect of federal money, we think it clear that the results are more complicated than the *KAPPAN* article suggests.

It is unfortunate that so many distortions and myths—which years ago hindered the development of progressive education and now restrict the progress of public alternative schools—are supported by Raywid's article. Alternative public schools provide a means of revitalizing public education through the participation of students, parents, community members, teachers, and administrators. Working together, community members have developed, carried out, and evaluated a variety of alternative programs. Many have produced remarkable benefits for young people and their teachers. Students have gained skills and confidence necessary to live in and contribute to their communities. Teachers have gained enormous satisfaction in their work.

Education for a democracy must satisfy four crucial conditions. It must be effective in teaching basic and applied skills; it must be accessible to all; it must be devoted to helping every child achieve his or her potential; and it must promote successful social interaction leading to respect, appreciation, and harmony among all members of society.

In practice, most private schools concern themselves only with the first of these four goals. Most private schools carefully select their students and do not admit those who fail to meet their admission standards. They have wide latitude to expel students. Having worked with numerous students who have been pushed out of private schools, we know that the schools use this power. Private programs need not be concerned about working successfully with a true cross section of students and helping *all* young people come to appreciate each other. In fact, private schools sometimes promote the fear of one group for another by threatening that, if their students do not behave, they will be sent to "unruly, undisciplined public schools." (Numerous parents have reported such comments to us.) We do not call for the closing of private schools but for the recognition of important differences between their mission and that of public schools.

Current efforts to dismantle the public schools must be understood as threats to the American ideals of equal opportunity, equal access to high-quality education, and equal justice for all. Now, as never before, the best of alternative school practices must be continued and expanded if public education is to survive.

When considering the question of public alternative schools, readers must consider one more issue: alternatives to what? Very few people are making a strong positive case for the conventional public schools. The best public alternatives have demonstrated that their students gain basic and applied skills necessary to function effectively in society. Many of the best public alternatives have brought together parents from different racial and socioeconomic backgrounds to plan and work for better lives for their children. These programs deserve to be models. Rather than retreat from public education altogether, we need to preserve what is effective in public education and expand it.

If we abandon the vision of providing a good education for *all* the children of *all* of our people, we must then face the frightening realization that we also have abandoned our belief in democracy. We refuse to forsake our faith in democratic education. Our experiences working in community-supported public alternative schools have been exhilarating, exhausting, and enormously rewarding. Alternative public education is neither easy nor elitist, but it can be excellent. We are confident that it is worth the struggle.

1. See Joe Nathan and Wayne Jennings, "Educational Bait-and Switch," *Phi Delta Kappan*, May 1978, p. 621.

2. Robert Horwitz, *Psychological Effects of Open Classroom Teaching on Primary School Children: A Review of the Research* (Grand Forks: University of North Dakota, 1976). The vast majority of studies included in this review were conducted in true alternative schools, that is, schools in which parents and students had chosen to participate.

3. Wayne Jennings and Joe Nathan, "Startling/Disturbing Research Supporting Educational Change," *Phi Delta Kappan*, March 1977, pp. 568-72.

4. Margaret Willis, *The Guinea Pigs After Twenty Years* (Columbus: Ohio State University Press, 1961). This fascinating study compared the attitudes and experiences of students who had chosen to attend one of the most famous of the schools in the Eight-Year Study with other groups of students.

5. See, for example, evaluations of the St. Paul (Minn.) Open School, High School in the Community in New Haven (Conn.), and the Alternative Learning Project in Providence (R.I.).

6. Joe Nathan, "A Comparison of Attitudes Toward High School Education Held by

Graduates of a Traditional and an Alternative Public School in St. Paul, Minnesota"
(Doctoral dissertation, University of Minnesota, 1981).

7. Mario Fantini, *Public Schools of Choice* (New York: Simon and Schuster, 1973); and
Vito Perrone, "A View of School Reform," in Ruth Dropkin and Arthur Tobier, *Roots
of Open Education in America* (New York: City College Center for Open Education,
1976), pp. 173-90.

8. Herbert Kohl, in Fantini, op. cit., pp. 250-52.

On Clarifying History:
A Response to Nathan and Kohl
by Mary Anne Raywid

Ms. Raywid attempts to resolve her differences with Messrs.
Nathan and Kohl. Their greatest disagreement, she suspects, may
lie in their differing approaches to history itself.

Joe Nathan and Herb Kohl have made an excellent addition to the collection of articles on alternative schools in the April *KAPPAN*. Among other things, they have offered a good case for the importance of alternative schools to the survival of public education and the importance, in turn, of public education to a democratic society. We are in extensive agreement on these matters; I appreciate their forceful framing of the case.

The appreciation is a bit one-sided, however, since Nathan and Kohl evidently find that my article in the April *KAPPAN* contains inaccuracies, distortions, and dangerous, destructive misstatements. They accuse me of perpetuating three myths about alternative schools.

The first myth concerns the question of whether alternative school students generally retain a veto. My report is accurate, I think, but it needs clarifying. Most important, whatever "veto" alternative students hold pertains to curriculum and content, *not* to rules governing behavior. I did not intend to suggest that any alternative school student can personally veto any school regulation by doing what he or she pleases. I agree emphatically that a right to "civil disobedience" has not been a feature of public alternative schools. But as I suggested—obviously elliptically—Allen Graubard urged that youngsters retain what amounts to a veto over what each one shall study. Graubard described with approval various alternative school efforts to stimulate students to learn what adults believe important. But he would not resort to simply *imposing* content on the unwilling learner. In effect, he counsels against trying to proceed by duress.° There seem at least two grounds for eschewing coercion. One is the fundamental respect for the person that many of the earliest, humanistically inspired alternative schools emphasized. Kohl's writing, as well as Graubard's, manifests this responsive, respectful regard for students as sentient creatures with distinctive purposes and feelings. Thus, while we can try to *influence*, we ought to avoid coercion. Most of the alternative school people I know reflect this position, and I would be surprised if Joe Nathan does not.

John Dewey elaborated a slightly different case with regard to the effective veto. He argued that unless the learner's interest can be captured and his or her thinking brought to bear on selected content, then cognitive learnings will be minimal and/or distorted and attitudinal learnings will be largely negative. Thus, for Dewey as well, if the teacher can find no way to present content X in a form that engages the intelligence of the learner, then the learner's withholding of interest is an effective veto—and the teacher is well advised to look further instead of resorting to sheer power to impose this content.

°See Allen Graubard, *Free the Children: Radical Reform and the Free School Movement* (New York: Vintage, 1972), Chapt. 4, esp. pp. 222-28.

The second myth Nathan and Kohl attribute to me is the claim that no evaluations of public alternative schools have been clearly positive. That is not my belief. Indeed, were that the case, all three of us might be hard pressed to defend our shared commitment to alternatives. There is indeed a substantial body of presumptive evidence of the effectiveness of public alternative schools. (The confusion here stemmed partly from an editorial change that I failed to spot and partly from a misreading by Nathan and Kohl: They equated my generalization about the government- and foundation-supported innovations of the Sixties with a claim about alternative schools. Actually, of course, by no means all of the innovations were alternatives.)

Third, Nathan and Kohl attribute to me the view that public alternative schools evolved solely from the counter-culture. I do not believe that they did. In fact, when discussing the roots of the alternatives movement I emphasize the distinction between "free" and "freedom" school forebears. Much of the "free" school ancestry is associated with the counter-culture, but the "freedom" school roots grew out of the social change efforts of civil rights activists. But my article did not attempt to deal with the *roots* or *backgrounds* of the public school alternatives that grew in the Seventies; I was trying to describe that growth and chronicle that decade.

Nathan and Kohl object to my omission of ideological connections extending back to progressive education and beyond. I distrust that kind of ideological history because of the distortions it can create. Although some alternative schools call to mind characteristics of progressive education (more so in the case of the St. Paul Open School, with which Nathan was connected, than is generally true), I find such connections more misleading than illuminating without a closer look at similarities and differences.

I believe that Nathan, Kohl, and I are actually in substantial agreement, but our greatest difference may lie in the doing of history. The primary purpose of my article was to trace the events associated with the burgeoning of public school alternatives—that is, to provide an institutional history. I do not disparage ideological history or the history of ideas (in fact, I probably turn to these more readily than to institutional history). But both the more general nature of the *KAPPAN*'s readership and the length specifications I was given recommended the focus on the more immediate causes of the events—and that is where I tried to stay.

I am pleased, however, that Nathan and Kohl have carried the discussion beyond my original confines. Obviously no author can be pleased at being misunderstood, but I *am* pleased with their concern about the nature of alternative schooling, and I am glad to have the opportunity to amend some statements that were evidently subject to misinterpretation. I agree with Joe Nathan and Herb Kohl that "alternative public schools provide a way . . . to revitalize our depressed public educational system." Finally, I share their conviction that efforts to that effect are well worth the struggle.

XIII
The Future

Introduction

T*he Rev. Walton Cole told this story at the 26th Biennial Council of Phi Delta Kappa in December 1958:*

> "The millenium is at hand. Man has invented everything that can be invented. He has done all he can do."
>
> These words were spoken by a bishop at a church gathering in 1870. They were challenged by the presiding officer, who suggested that a great invention would be made within the next 50 years.
>
> The bishop asked him to name such an invention.
>
> The reply: "I think man will learn to fly."
>
> The bishop replied that this was blasphemy. "Don't you know that flight is reserved to the angels?"
>
> The bishop was Milton Wright, father of Orville and Wilbur.°

There is a saying that if one is 25 years ahead of his time, he is a genuine prophet; if he is just five years ahead, he is a nuisance. Harold Shane, author of "Future Shock and the Curriculum" (October 1964) has made the transition, I think, from nuisance to prophet in the time between writing this article and producing "A Curriculum for the New Century," which heads the "Our Future" section of the January 1981 Diamond Jubilee KAPPAN.

"Future Shock and the Curriculum" was one of the first articles to be written by an American educator on predictions of the future as a force in education. Six years thereafter, Phi Delta Kappa commissioned Shane, as a pioneer futurist in education, to write The Educational Significance of the Future, *one of a series of PDK Educational Foundation monographs. Based on the author's study of futures planning for the U.S. commissioner of education, it has become a classic of its kind.*

William Van Til, one of America's truly distinguished leaders in educational thought, has written 28 KAPPAN columns, articles, and reviews. His column, "One Way of Looking At It," appeared regularly from 1971 until his retirement as Coffman Distinguished Professor of Education at Indiana State University, Terre Haute, in 1978. Among many memorable columns was one I was particularly relieved to get, for it meant that the author had recovered from food poisoning suffered in India while he was on a round-the-world trip. Van Til titled it "Calcutta: A Vision of the End of the World." It recorded

°*"What Man Knows Man's Limitations?," February 1958 KAPPAN, inside back cover.*

397

*his "future shock" upon recognizing what other major cities of the world may
be like if there is not "a colossal gathering of forces for caring and survival," as
he put it.*

*The Van Til column reprinted here appeared on the back cover of the
special 144-page Bicentennial issue of the KAPPAN in September 1976. It is a
good example of the genre of Janus-type futures articles that start from different assumptions.*

*R. Thomas Tanner represents the combination of scientific understand-
ing, environmental concern, and humanistic caring that should, I think, infuse
the teaching profession. Now a professor of environmental studies at Iowa
State University, Ames, he has written five KAPPAN feature articles, including one highly controversial piece, "The China Syndrome as a Teaching
Tool" (June 1979). It appeared only a month after the Three Mile Island
incident in Pennsylvania and became the first of a series of KAPPAN articles
related to education in the Nuclear Age, including my own interview with
physicist Ernest Sternglass titled "The Nuclear Radiation/SAT Decline Connection" (November 1979).*

*Tanner believes his first KAPPAN article, "The Science Curriculum: Un-
finished Business for an Unfinished Century" (March 1970) is of greatest
lasting interest. I agree.*

*William H. Boyer is professor of education and chairman of the
Department of Educational Foundations, University of Hawaii. When he
wrote "Education for Survival" (January 1971), he was teaching a course
titled "Education for a World Without War" at the university. It was based on
Boyer's concern about militarism, world order, and alternatives to armed
conflict. The article was his first attempt to develop a broader planning
theory to include ecological, social justice, and quality of life considerations.
He wanted to identify some ways of developing priorities during this period
in history, when much if not all of the human race is in peril from
thermonuclear and environmental threats.*

*Boyer says, "From the Seventies on, we will enter the planning phase of
human history. Unless schools teach people to participate intelligently in
planning, the decisions will be made by economic special interests or largely
unaccountable politicians." Most of his writing in the Seventies focused on
this problem, and his book called* Alternative Futures: Designing Social
Change *was published in 1975 as a text for high school and college students on
the topic of social planning.*

*During this period Boyer became one of the current breed of futurists. He
tried, however, to point out that "ad hocracy, the technofix, and the
deterministic beliefs often connected with market economics are among the
major traps to hinder creation of a better future." Many futurists have embraced these notions; others talk of "participation" as a panacea or make a
doctrine out of decentralization. Boyer's emphasis has been on identifying
the limits of natural systems and on identifying alternative political-eco-
nomic plans that maximize public participation to choose the best of such
integrated plans. "This means," he says, "putting people in charge of institutions and economic planning and probably requiring constitutional rights to a
sustainable life-support system. If the right to work in a socially useful, en-*

vironmentally responsible form of work is added, considerable change in American economic orthodoxies will result."

Boyer considers our current government largely reactionary, anti-ecological, lacking in commitment to economic justice, dedicated to increase in the arms race, and committed to maximum power for corporate capitalism. "The willingness of the public to support such obsolete politics is at least partly related to the lack of the kind of citizenship education appropriate to this period of history."

Among more than 30 articles and books, one of Boyer's most successful publications dealt with educability. Titled "Are Children Born Unequal?," it was first published in The Saturday Review *(19 October 1968) and was repeatedly reprinted in the U.S., Canada, and overseas. The State Department translated and sent it throughout the world. Widely used by ethnic groups, it had an impact on the "Jensen" nature-nurture debate; that debate now seems to be resolved in a manner consistent with Boyer's article.*

Neil Postman is an intellectual Marshall McLuhan, the late communications guru. I have chosen "The Day Our Children Disappear: Predictions of a Media Ecologist" (January 1981) as the final entry in this anthology because in it Postman joins a highly original view of emerging forms of communication (read education) with a delightful and informative writing style. I wish that all KAPPAN articles could be as intellectually stimulating.

Postman is professor of education, Department of Communication Arts and Science, New York University. His most recent book is Teaching as a Conserving Activity. *An excerpt from the book, "The First Curriculum: Comparing School and Television," appeared in the November 1979* KAPPAN. *It is a brilliant analysis of these competing learning systems.*

—SME

Future Shock and the Curriculum
by Harold G. Shane

Like culture shock among travelers, future shock takes its toll among educators. Here is a fascinating analysis of the "dizzying disorientation" caused by a premature collision with the future.

Most Americans who have traveled in Africa, Asia, or Latin America are aware of the phenomenon of *culture shock*. This is a psychosomatic reaction, often of considerable violence, that results from entanglement in the invisible web of a new and partly incomprehensible way of life. Explicitly, the shock comes from a sense of confusion that arises when the customs, language, and similar elements of an alien people fail to make sense in the context of the experiences transferred from the familiar cultural landscape through which one previously has learned to thread his way.[1]

Culture Shock and Future Shock

Persons who grow up in other cultures simply do not see and hear things as we do, and vice versa. Concepts of time, territorial or space rights, status, and so on are not only different, they may be in conflict. In an anthropologist's words, it is no longer valid to assume, "when two human beings are subject to the same 'experience,' [that] virtually the same data are being fed to the two control nervous systems and that the two brains record similarly."[2] To use an illustration, a Spaniard and a person from the U.S. do not see or "record" the same bullfight in the Madrid bull ring. The *Madrileño* identifies with the skilled matador and the American identifies with the doomed bull. Obviously, a similar sensory input leads to totally different reactions.

Just as many people from the U.S. are upset when residing overseas by the absence of familiar cultural clues and suffer culture shock, many Americans are beginning to suffer from *future shock*.[3] Future shock, like culture shock, is a condition marked by a decline in cognitive powers, misinterpretation of reality, and loss of the ability to communicate ideas with one's usual skill.

We have encountered the future so rapidly and with such violent changes in the ordered and familiar patterns of our way of life that we are suffering "the dizzying disorientation brought on by the premature arrival of the future."[4]

Many generations of change have been compressed into the span of 10 years, so brief a period that it is scarcely a single second on the clockface of history.[5] As a result, the changed social and scientific environment in which persons find themselves today is literally as strange, in many ways, as that in which the U.S. foreign aid worker or Peace Corps volunteer finds himself in an Indian village of the Andes, a Hausa tribe in Nigeria, or a center of Moslem life in West Pakistan.

The possible consequences of future shock for education are considerable. Let us first review the sources of the dislocation that seems to threaten the composure and effectiveness of individuals involved in educational leadership, research, and service.

Some Educational Sources of Future Shock

During the 1920s and 1930s the educational scene in the U.S. was a lively one. Changes were made in methods and materials, and periodical literature was full of stimulating ideas. Manuscript writing, the project method, teacher/pupil planning, social reconstruction through education, and a hundred similar proposals found strident supporters and dogged opponents.

Violent as the debates of the times became, however, no one seemed to be traumatized or even seriously upset as verbal warfare between conservative and liberal or between "subject-oriented" and "learner-oriented" forces enlivened commerce in the free market of educational ideas. Certainly, prior to the 1950s there was less uneasiness, less uncertainty, and less poorly concealed panic about the nature, the merit, and the speed of educational change than there is now.

No real future shock was experienced by educators of this era because adoption of these new practices—despite the debates they generated—was rarely rapid[6] and generally were *extensions* and *refinements* of familiar ideas, methods, and procedures rather than basic *changes* or *innovations* involving heretofore unfamiliar technologies or based on concepts with little or no precedent.

What, then, has recently happened *in* education and *to* education to bring on the "dizzying disorientation" caused by a premature collision with the future? Since around 1950 many educators have found themselves confronting new educational directions to which their past learning and experience simply do not transfer. For purposes of clarity, some examples need to be given to show how, in a very few years, the jolting educational changes of a long lifetime have been compressed into a 10-year interval:

● Education's casual and sometimes pious interest in the contributions of related disciplines got out of hand. Specialists outside of the teaching profession began to contribute more than the schools could readily assimilate in mathematics, cultural anthropology, linguistics, ethology,[7] sociology, biochemistry, and so on.

● Long-postponed implementation of civil rights legislation created many stresses.

● New interpretations of the role of higher education created issues as to its scope, purpose, and control as post-secondary education began moving toward virtual universalization.

● The educational power structure began to show signs of changing, particularly at the national level. (For example, the administration for one U.S. Office of Education function moved from an Ed.D. in administration to a Ph.D. in anthropology, and thence to a systems engineer formerly with a major U.S. corporation.)[8]

● After the future shock of Russia's Sputnik in 1957 and the questioning of U.S. education that it created, there was an unprecedented increase in the funding of education. This was an unsettling experience in itself; it further disturbed administrators because local choice in the deployment of the monies did not increase in proportion to the sums available.

● Both the concentration and overspill of population in U.S. cities were recognized as conspicuous problems, as were the new inner-city—megalopolitan inequities in educational opportunities.

● The "learning business" virtually exploded as the educational and financial possibilities of technology were recognized. Among those involved in new combines and novel ventures in educational technology: Time, Inc., G.E., I.B.M., Raytheon, C.B.S., R.C.A., Minnesota Mining and Manufacturing, et al.[9]

• Several years before Marshall McLuhan reported that TV was "retribalizing" U.S. children (and turning the world into a "global village"), it became apparent that there were unusual behavioral and intellectual mutations occurring among the young.[10] These inward changes seem to be one of many causes of nationwide "protest movements" among youth. The "phantom curriculum" created by mass media, the great unindexed body of data children acquire even before beginning kindergarten, has made education's clientele "different" in the span of a decade.

• Cybernetics—the realm of automatic control systems in mechanical electrical communication systems—is another great generator of future shock in education. Whether reflected in individualized computer programming for pupils or in complex information retrieval, such developments as computer-based instruction (CBI) and individually planned instruction (IPI), with the computer serving as a mediating agency, are an unnerving change to many teachers and create within them fears of falling into obsolescence.[11]

• New approaches and content in such fields as mathematics, science, and English instruction have placed teachers at all levels under heavy stress. The pressure at the moment is especially high in the field of English, where the introduction of so-called linguistic approaches, often based on incompletely developed theories and partially tested hypotheses, has created considerable confusion and disturbance among teachers.[12]

The 10 preceding examples illustrate how educators have been thrust from yesterday into tomorrow. They also show how future shock ensues when, in the face of so many rapid changes, one is deprived of familiar clues that hitherto have successfully guided his interaction with the environment.

Some Suggestions for Coping with Future Shock in Education

Although the new malady of future shock is disconcerting, care has been taken to avoid labeling it as "bad." Just as recovery from culture shock after a few disturbing months of residence in Bangkok or Cairo can herald an increase in one's wisdom and intercultural insight, so U.S. educators' exposure to a future they were not prepared to meet so soon could do a great deal to improve our schools. After all, much of the rest of the world also is meeting an even more unanticipated future head-on; why not the curricula in our schools? Consider the developing countries overseas that are attempting in 25 years to adapt certain processes of democratic government which, after nearly two centuries of experiment, remain in a condition of imperfect development even in our own land. Nor are many of these countries doing too badly in view of the odds imposed by tribal traditions, illiteracy, and myriads of similar problems.

What, specifically, promises to be good medicine with which to treat future shock in education? For one thing, it should be recognized that old and young educators vary in their need for therapy. The young ones merely need the right diet, the proper "care and feeding" that will enable them to work contributively in a newly arrived future. After all, tomorrow is not strange for those who belong to it. The beginning teacher today never knew the pre-TV world, was an infant when the day of the atom began in 1945, and hadn't finished elementary school when Sputnik orbited us into the space age a decade ago.

Our problem in preservice education and in graduate study, therefore, is to do whatever is necessary to avoid contaminating tomorrow's teachers with the future shock "fall-out" of our groundless personal fears and unfounded illusions about education. Our best, if not our only, treatment here is *preventive* medicine.

Now let us turn our thinking to the question of what can be found in the pharmacopoeia to remedy our malady. This includes treatment for philosophically blurred vision, curricular dyspepsia, and the temporary aphasia resulting from technical progress and accompanying social upheavals, which temporarily have exceeded both our grasp of change in education and our receptivity to it. I hope the following prescriptions are the result of good diagnoses.

1. Develop inservice education programs that face the future. Educational leadership needs to bring teachers' thinking into focus with respect to their tasks in the immediate future. This is important when we realize that some of the younger ones will still be influencing educational practices in 2015 A.D. Among examples of possible inservice practices are:

● Greatly liberalized leave policies to encourage teachers to re-educate and to retool themselves with respect to educational theory, content, and practice.

● New relationships with higher education such as visiting professorships awarded *by public schools* to college staff members, on loan from universities, to serve in local program development and inservice classes.

● Greater *informed* teacher participation in decision making that bears on rapid program change.

● Provision for teachers' short-term instruction in theory, in basic maintenance, and in the use of the products of the "learning business," possibly through resident study in plants producing new media.

● Experiments with salary differentials for specialized faculty assignments.

● "Residencies," following preservice education, during which beginning teachers are "phased in" to their work as part of educational terms in the schools.

● Much greater use of teacher exchange, especially among U.S. schools and within large districts, but including overseas schools.

2. Deliberately purchase imagination. We need to purchase imagination, to develop a breed of professionally respectable educators who have the skills of educational navigation plus the vision of scientific soothsayers. The schools need to buy top-flight brains, just as industry has. The schools also need individuals who are skilled in *change analysis* and in developing sound educational thrust into the 1970s and 1980s.

3. Reverse the traditional emphasis on the upper levels of education. From earliest times we have respected the important role of secondary and collegiate education. Available funds and status have gravitated to high schools and colleges, and elementary school faculty members have been left to wail, "But I'm only a second-grade teacher." It will help us to cope with the future if we literally reverse our educational priorities. While we have given lip service to the importance of early childhood, we have nevertheless provided a starvation diet for these formative years. We will move into the future in distinctly better order when teachers of the youngest are prepared (and rewarded) in the same manner as those who direct the work of doctoral candidates.[13]

4. *Recognize and alleviate the reasons for student protest movements.* Vehement student protests and demonstrations in almost every type of college and university (and in some secondary schools) have been one of the unsettling developments on U.S. campuses. *We need to recognize that the protest movement itself is a manifestation of future shock hitting students.* In the 1930s humane relationships and mutual respect were encouraged in class-rooms as teachers and young people alike stood bewildered by the depression and their shared misery.

World War II, the cold war, and Sputnik combined to usher in the present college-level shock waves of mechanization, standardization, automation: all inadvertent but effective ways of eroding security, the stimulation of discovery/inquiry, and self-identity.[14] A rehumanization of education with greater stress on individual*ity* rather than individual*ization* seems overdue.

5. *Conceive a model of a "lifetime curriculum"* It seems reasonable to conceptualize the idea of the lifetime curriculum as a useful means of diminishing future shock. The "lifetime curriculum" concept presupposes that the current rate of change will continue to crowd us, that world problems will by no means diminish, that a number of yesterday's arts and occupations will change or disappear, that the rate of knowledge accumulation will continue to increase, and that human beings will continue to fall somewhere short of perfection.

Under this set of circumstances, and assuming the continuation of trends such as those leading toward the leisure of an eight-month year for workers[15] and to the transfer of magnetic programmed tapes rather than of people to operate machines,[16] it seems reasonable for the schools to sponsor a lifetime of education. By the 1980s and 1990s this could become virtually an educational "conducted tour" or continuum of learning experience stretching from early childhood to old age for those who sought it. Let us turn in the next three topic headings to a more precise consideration of what form this proposal might take when phased into the educational environment.

6. *Design new comprehensive self-realization centers.* Highly effective tonic for diminishing *future* attacks of future shock probably can be found in the form of the Self-Realization or S-R center. This may be defined as a unified educational complex providing learning services for an entire population. What is, in the 1960s, labeled "elementary," "secondary," and "higher" education doubtless will be handled on a unitary or coordinated basis in such a complex. Such elements in our social infrastructure as recreation and health services, museums, conservatories, planeteria, and aquaria also might be administered and operated in the education center—at least until such a time as their functions are superseded by multidimensional simulation.

7. *Create the kinds of school organization that the future mandates.* Most discussions and proposals with direct relevance to the structure and administration of education have shown remarkably little long-range fore-sight. Concentration on the present is understandable and necessary.[17] At the same time, planning for the operation of schools likely to be needed in 1977—

not to mention 1997—should not be neglected. Public schools and universities need to begin to project ways to cultivate administrators adept in new ways of thinking and acting, since the young men and women who will provide our senior leadership for administration in 1997 are just now beginning to cast a speculative eye on preparation for this vocation.

Within the next few years we will need rapidly to develop the prototype for a combination scholar-scientist-senior administrator who is capable of orchestrating the activities of education centers serving clusters of people ranging from one million to 20 million or more in size and from 18 months to well over 100 years in age.[18] Such proposals are by no means science fiction. Indeed, major educational complexes already operating foreshadow this sort of emergent development. What we need is less haphazard drift and more deliberate planning of their design.

School organization likewise needs to develop a momentum that will carry it ahead. For at least a century educators have tried to devise organizational plans and structures that would facilitate instruction and temper the problem of human differences.[19] Most thinking that has been done thus far has concentrated on changes within the framework of basically *conventional* schools. The next evolutionary step in organizing schools to cope with individuality will not come in a conventional form at all.[20] Let us next examine three ideas that should help us to counter future shock. Each promises to be helpful in improving teaching methods and content.

8. *Phase in the cyborg unit.* A cyborg unit is a cooperative combination of machine and human *controlled by the latter.*[21] The word is derived by combining CYBernetic and ORGanic. Functionally speaking, a man with an artificial kidney is a cyborg. Within the next 10 years, as a result of meeting the future so quickly, we are almost certain to develop cyborg teams: teachers whom educational media and technology have extended almost beyond our present capacity to imagine.[22] We will begin to show signs of recovering from future shock when conventional school organization and school plant have been replaced by the S-R type of education center mentioned above: essentially one large teaching aid operated *with human values paramount* and in which man, media, and machines serve man.

Such a school would not be *centered* around media—*the school plant itself would be media* from which people of all ages and backgrounds would learn. The designing of learning, the retrieval of information, the encouragement of self-direction, the extension of experience for persons of all ages at any time of the year, and above all the consummately skillful low-pressure nurture and guidance of human development and questing would be the task of the cyborg-team teachers. Anything but a machine himself, such a teacher presumably would have no more than three class-contact hours during a "3-M day" in which man, media, and machine combined their input, guidance, and evaluative feedback to make learning meaningful for the individual learner in the quest for his personal goals.

The gradual phase-in of media and machines as hinted above is an excellent potential cure for future shock. Lest scoffers cry "science fiction," it is worth noting that by 1967 planning of educational resources of the sort described already had appeared in print for a proposed community of 100,000 contemplated near Phoenix, Arizona.[23]

9. *Learn how to annex content from other fields.* By the 1950s it was al-

ready clear that part of education's future shock stemmed from developments in content fields that, as in the case of the "new math" or "new science," reflected the trend toward curriculum change guided from outside the teaching profession.[24] Proper therapy to relieve this shock is self-evident. Education needs to seize the initiative and develop the brainpower and the means for methodically annexing the relevant content and tools or methods of promise created in related disciplines.

In effect this is a proposal that education not only plan to draw on materials from other fields to strengthen itself, but also that education bring into its ranks many more persons whose preparation combines educational *and* academic backgrounds.

10. *Apply the "Culture-centric Curriculum Change" concept.* Many approaches have been made to curriculum change—so many that the literature bristles with jargon and drips with slogans. None has proved to be a final answer. A promising and largely untried approach that augurs well for easing our progress into future changes is basing curriculum coordination and change on the analysis of culture as indirectly proposed by Trager and Hall.[25] Cultural anthropology holds much promise for helping educators to realize how the cultural backgrounds of mankind create major potential misunderstandings.

Humans are not turned into stereotypes by growing up under the influence of an alien culture or under U.S. subcultural influences—but neither is the superficial assumption that "all men are alike" an intellectually defensible one. In a world rapidly becoming a crowded global space ship as it spins into the future, we need to base the curriculum on the results of study-in-depth of the human clientele of the school.

The Far Side of the Great Watershed

There have been only a few great watersheds in history. Two of these mountainous divisions separating an outmoded past from a suddenly altered future were the development of printing and the onset of the Industrial Revolution. Mass media and cybernetics made the mid-twentieth century a third great watershed.

In the early 1800s, in response to the shock effect of the Industrial Revolution in Great Britain, a number of unemployed factory workers went berserk. Under the exhorting of a slow-witted Leicestershire mill worker, Ned Ludd, these "Luddites" smashed the power-driven looms that they felt had robbed them of their jobs. In education, as we move over to the far side of our twentieth-century watershed, it is important that we avoid similar panic patterns of behavior.

Let us demonize neither change nor machinery; let us recognize reality. We cannot change the history of education's collision with the future, but we can conceptualize and build better programs of instruction as we digest the meaning of new opportunities and responsibilities.

In the process, let us make a more determined effort to communicate clearly. This includes acknowledging that labeling or defining problems is not solving them, and that words are no substitute for action. And let us keep and increase our confidence in the cognitive powers of ourselves and others. This involves recognizing that the virtually untapped power of the human mind set free dwarfs the power of any machine—and that machines were created by men to serve men; not for men to serve, but for men to *use* in freeing that power of the mind.

---

1. Cross-cultural misunderstandings, confusion, and "shock" are simply and clearly discussed by the anthropological linguist, Edward T. Hall. Cf. his books, *The Silent Language* (Doubleday, 1959) and *The Hidden Dimension* (Doubleday, 1966).

2. Edward T. Hall, *The Hidden Dimension*. New York: Doubleday, 1966, p. 2.

3. Insofar as I can determine, the term *future shock* was coined by Alvin Toffler. See his "The Future as a Way of Life," *Horizons*, Summer, 1965.

4. *Ibid.*, p. 109.

5. The speed and scope of change are so great as to blur vision and memory. A good review and reminder of what happened in the 25 years between 1939 and 1964 can be found in John Brook's readable social history, *The Great Leap*. New York: Harper and Row, 1966. 382 pp.

6. Years ago, on the basis of a study of trends, Mort and Cornell concluded that it required from 75 to 100 years for an educational idea or theory to be translated into common practice. Cf. Paul Mort and Francis Cornell, *American Schools in Transition*. New York: Bureau of Publications, Teachers College, Columbia University, 1941, p. 49.

7. *Ethology*, a relatively new science, is not always listed in the dictionary. It is concerned with the precise, methodical study of innate, or inherited, animal behavior.

8. Cf. Peter Schrag, "Voices in the Classroom: Is There a New Establishment?" *Saturday Review*, Oct. 15, 1966, p. 87.

9. Cf. Henry Bern, "Wanted: Education Engineers," *Phi Delta Kappan*, January 1967, pp. 230-36.

10. Probably the best digest of McLuhanism and the "media impact" was written by one of his colleagues at Fordham University. Cf. John M. Culkin, S. J., "A Schoolman's Guide to Marshall McLuhan," *Saturday Review*, March 18, 1967.

11. Cf. John C. Flanagan, "Functional Education for the Seventies," *Phi Delta Kappan*, September, 1967, pp. 27-31.

12. For a recently published review and appraisal of developments, cf. Harold G. Shane, *Linguistics and the Classroom Teacher*. Washington, D.C.: The Association for Supervision and Curriculum Development, NEA, 1967. 120 pp.

13. Also cf. G. B. Leonard, "A Hopeful Look at Education in 2000 A.D.," *Educational Services Bulletin No. 21*, Arizona State University, pp. 9-23.

14. Biological research of a wide-ranging nature is confirming the importance of security, stimulation, and identity. Cf. the society of inward antagonism (or *noyau*) concept in J. J. Petter, "L'Ecologie et L'Ethologie des Lémuriens Malgache," *Memoires du Muséum National d'Histoire Naturelle*, Tome XXVII, Fascicule 1, Paris, 1962.

15. Ottino Caracciolo di Forino, "Some Reflections for 1986," *Business Horizons*, Spring, 1967, pp. 31-38.

16. *Ibid.*, p. 35. Signor di Forino anticipates that, once automated equipment (say in Africa) is installed, we will not need to send technicians to operate it. We will simply send programmed tapes which *replicate* their skills in operating the machines.

17. As one harassed administrator put it, "I don't celebrate *arrival* of the new year; I celebrate *survival* of the last year."

18. Life spans of 200 years or more are forecast for 2100 A.D., with the "human" body quite possibly—in its later years or due to injuries—composed of its present organic equipment plus, say, a mechanical heart, leg, liver, or lung. More and more we will find old age treated like a disease rather than as an inevitable fate.

19. A vintage article by Henry J. Otto relates in interesting retrospect the efforts made to organize schools to cope with individual differences between 1860 and 1930. Cf. references cited.

20. Two current research reports related to grouping, broadly conceived, anticipate the future. Cf. Miriam Goldberg, Harry Passow, and Joseph Justman, *The Effects of Ability Grouping.* New York: Teachers College Press, Columbia University; 1966. 254 pp. Also cf. H. A. Thelen, *Classroom Grouping for Teachability.* New York: John Wiley & Sons, Inc., 1967. 274 pp.

21. Cf. B. R. Joyce, *The Teacher and His Staff: Man Media and Machines.* Washington, D.C.: Center for the Study of Instruction, NEA, 1967.

22. It was Marshall McLuhan who said that all media work us over completely because they function as psychic or physical extensions of some human faculty. E.g., the wheel is an extension of our feet.

23. The learning center, one of comprehensive dimensions, proposed by G. B. Leonard, *ibid.,* p. 10 ff.

24. Cf. John Goodlad, *The Changing School Curriculum.* New York: Fund for the Advancement of Education, 1966. 122 pp.

25. Cf. Edward T. Hall, *ibid., et passim.*

Tricentennial Speech, 2076:
Two Versions
by William Van Til

Alternative Scenario One

Fellow citizens, how can we best sum up developments in education during the three centuries since 1776? In the first century we established the American democratic principle of universal free public education. In the second century we sought equal educational opportunity for all, and we began to adapt our schools to meet human needs, illuminate social realities, and clarify values in a pluralistic society. In the third century, 1976-2076, education came of age in the United States as we learned to educate all the people through life experiences.

Our predecessors who summoned the People's Congresses initiated in 2000 were scoffed at as utopians because of their ideas and beliefs, even as were the men who wrote the Declaration of Independence. But the proposals of the assemblages of thinkers in the Twenty-One Fields and the follow-up discussions by the world's people in the many meetings we call the Considerations may well have save mankind. Particularly crucial were the proposals of three People's Congresses, those on Environment, Energy, and Population, and the subsequent Considerations. Yes, the ratification of the work of the People's Congresses and Considerations proceeded slowly: The first ratification by a sovereign government was by New Zealand in 2038, and the final ratification by all nations of the world came in 2069. Yes, the recommendations of the People's Congresses had to be continually updated. But the fundamental principles established in the early twenty-first-century People's Congresses and modified in the Considerations have endured, even as have the principles of our U.S. Constitution established at the beginning of the nation. The die was cast for the Planet Earth, our new world state.

Before the year 2000, American education was divided on many issues. The People's Congress on Education in the first decade of the twenty-first century was one of the most quarrelsome and even rancorous of the Congresses in the Twenty-One Fields.

What turned the tide in education? Not the early agreements in the People's Congress on Education; those agreements were highly general and, indeed, quite tentative. What accounts for our achievement of lifelong continuous education through life itself is the *experience* people had in the subsequent Considerations. For the first time in history, the people had the opportunity to study, discuss, and act on problems vital to their lives. Leadership was expert and humane; every medium of communication was utilized; every social institution was employed in the extensive Considerations.

Children and youth in elementary and secondary schools were also deeply engaged in the Considerations of the Twenty-One Fields. During the decades of the Considerations, teachers learned that the skills needed for modern life could best be taught through study and action on life's problems, that academic disciplines could be drawn on in study of the interdisciplinary Twenty-One Fields, that both the school and the community must educate. Basically it was the experience of the Considerations that reformed the schools.

The Tricentennial challenge before us as educators of the Planet Earth in 2076 is to achieve equal educational opportunity for all infants, children, youth, and adults throughout the world, even as we achieved equal educational opportunity in the U.S.A. during the past century.

Alternative Scenario Two

Fellow citizens, how can we best sum up developments in education during the three centuries since 1776? Beguiled by the Jeffersonian ideal, we attempted at first to institute universal free public education. We ignored Hamilton's wisdom: "The people are turbulent and changing; they seldom judge or determine right." During the second century we managed to maintain a program of academic education despite progressive education proposals. In the last century, 1976-2076, we recognized that education should be a privilege of the meritocracy alone, for the masses require only training. The movement away from the sentimentalism of democratic education dates from 1984, when we made education after the age of 12 voluntary. The culmination came in 2067 when the social class structure was replaced by our present hereditary caste system.

Confronted by worldwide population expansion, the dwindling of world energy supplies, the threats of the Communists, and the demands of the Third World, our leaders established Fort America. Through our technological ingenuity and our military-industrial complex, we became independent of the rest of the world before the mid-twenty-first century. Education made a valiant contribution to Fort America. We trained the masses to carry out their simple tasks, closely defined through our behavioral objectives and accompanied by strict accountability. We educated the meritorious and scheduled them for the tasks demanded by national needs.

Without our highly specialized education, we would never have invented the perfect nuclear bomb, which effectively destroyed The Enemy without fallout within the continental United States. Our surpise attack on The Enemy resulted in the destruction of all industrialized areas in Europe, South America, Asia, and Africa. Years of secret planning preceded that historic Fourth of July weekend in 2055 when we totally destroyed The Enemy.

Since the successful War Against Mankind, we have made strides in our educational sorting and categorization. A century ago our sorting instruments, such as intelligence tests, were pitifully crude. But by strengthening and tightening social class categories, we have made our sorting system more effective. Then our value-free researchers and scientists developed genetic breeding processes and subservience drugs. Our magnificent caste system was achieved.

Now that we are importing slaves from the rural areas of the world in which the survivors among The Enemy live, we face a new challenge to our educational ingenuity. Can we institute programs which will train them to labor in the building of monuments to the memory of our leaders? Can we make sure that no subversive thoughts of revolution or democracy ever enter their dim minds? This is the great challenge to American education in this Tricentennial Year.

The Science Curriculum: Unfinished Business for an Unfinished Country

by R. Thomas Tanner

Mr. Tanner wants to build on past developments in the science disciplines through the inclusion of socially relevant themes. A socially concerned science educator himself, he describes some urgently needed themes related to the quality of our deteriorating environment. These, he argues, are the unfinished business of science education.

Tanner believes a multidisciplinary team approach involving social studies teachers and other educators is essential; we cannot depend upon science teachers alone.

Although the science curriculum has undergone a major overhaul in the past 13 years, portents of new and needed changes are already blowing in the wind. In this article, I shall 1) summarize the developments of the recent past, 2) suggest some work still left undone, and 3) propose ways in which educators from other curriculum areas may participate in effecting these changes.

In science education, a reform movement of considerable dimensions began in the mid-1950s and has achieved fruition in the form of the "alphabet soup" high school courses now familiar to most of us (by name at least): BSCS biology, PSSC physics, CHEMS and CBA chemistry, ESCP earth science, plus a host of elementary school projects. Whereas previous texts were written by individual science educators, the new curricular packages were developed by writing teams in which practicing scientists played a dominant role. The content was not just updated; more important, the curricula were organized around the basic concepts of inquiry and structure.

Inquiry is epistemological. Students were to engage in laboratory work that was genuinely investigative rather than verificational. They were to infer from their own data rather than memorize a rhetoric of conclusions. They were to study the reasoning of scientists in the evolution of scientific concepts rather than commit to memory the associated names and dates. The processes and not just the products of science were emphasized.

Structure is ontological. First, the science course was to represent genuine science and was not to be a catch-all for units in alcohol, smoking, narcotics, and the like. Second, and more fundamental, the science course was not to be a hodgepodge of discrete facts or a series of minicourses in physiology, anatomy, genetics, light, or mechanics; rather, it was to be given unity by a few overarching themes. For instance, the Biological Sciences Curriculum Study claimed nine themes as having guided its work throughout the writing of several texts and supporting materials. These themes include evolution, genetic continuity, and complementarity of structure and function, among others. The Earth Science Curriculum Project chose 10 themes, including universality of change, conservation of mass and energy in the universe, and uniformity of process as the key to understanding the past. The National Science Teachers Association prepared a much-debated list of seven "conceptual schemes" meant to guide future curricular efforts. The schemes are extremely broad generalizations regarding matter and energy; an example is,

"All matter is composed of units called fundamental particles; under certain conditions these particles can be transformed into energy and vice versa."

This article is not concerned with inquiry, nor does it question the structures (the themes) that have been developed in the several courses. Rather, I wish to suggest some additional themes. The subject matter developed during the past 13 years may very well constitute a much-improved curriculum in science per se, but it does not go very far beyond science concepts in exploring the societal implications of the scientific enterprise, the interactions of science with society, culture, and human values. Scientists and science educators are beginning to express grave concern over this deficiency in the new status quo of science education.[1,2,3] Having long been in complete concurrence with this view, I would like to describe three new themes, which are intended mainly to be suggestive and catalytic. I hope that a cross-disciplinary conference of scholars and educators may arrive at a more profound list in the near future.

These three themes all deal directly with technology and thus indirectly with basic sciences upon which technology is founded. (Science is the ongoing pursuit of basic principles of nature; technology is the concurrent application of these principles in developing new products and techniques. The layman often uses the term *science* when in fact he is referring to technology.) The themes:

Technology and Mankind: A Master-Servant Relationship?

Shall the technological revolution be directed by man for the greatest common good, or shall it sweep us all along toward an unplanned and unthinkable brave new world? Will man utilize technological possibilities "just because they are there," or will he weigh their assets against the sociocultural upheaval they instigate? Shall technology be used to aid in uplifting the minds of men, or shall mindless men be used to consume the surplus products of technology? These are the kinds of pressing questions our students should explore.

The chasm between Snow's two cultures widens; our folkways, laws, institutions, and traditional modes of thought fall further behind our technological advances and their use by industry; social discontinuities proliferate. Automation threatens employability, self-respect, and pride of craftsmanship, while organized labor can respond with little more than feather-bedding and hereditary privilege of union membership. Computers serve the interests of giant corporations while plaguing the individual with incorrect invoices, errorful records, and unresponsiveness to protest. The institutionalized uses of technology have created a populace with wealth, mobility, and free time, but the people are as yet uneducated for use of these benefits. Spaceships and peasants co-exist paradoxically within a single nation. Medical technology controls death, but laws still do not control birth. The weapons of complete and instant extinction are stockpiled as if they were only spears, rifles, or cannon.

It would appear that if ever we need a utopia, we need it now. To this end, it is somewhat encouraging to note the birth of futuristics, the study of the future. The Commission on the Year 2000, the World Future Society, and similar organizations are beginning to chart desirable and feasible futures, as answers to the darker dystopias of Orwell and Huxley. Despite the skepticism traditionally accorded utopian thinkers, we must surely place increasing but humanitarian control over the future, if we are to be assured of having one. To continue the practice of brinksmanship in these times is to invite either a bang or a whimper.

Tomorrow's Technology and Today's License

A common excuse for the exercise of greed, irresponsibility, and shortsightedness is that tomorrow's technology can clean up the resultant mess. Once it was easy to turn our backs on the fallacy and go West, leaving the scarred land behind, but now the frontier is gone (although the process is being repeated in "developing" nations). Nevertheless, we continue to act as if the frontier were still there. Business equates growth with progress, and the depletion of natural resources is euphemistically referred to as development of natural resources. Population growth causes or intensifies many dilemmas of the day: pollution in all its insidious forms, depletion of natural resources, famine, loss of identity and individual freedom, degradation of the environment, extinction of species, and even war and racism.

Yet technology is optimistically applied to these problems while population growth and economic irresponsibility are accepted or even lauded. Smog devices, desalination plants, floating cities, and high-yield food production methods lull the public into a blind faith in technology, but these are only temporary, stop-gap measures—they are Band-aids applied to a cancer. Similarly, there is a tendency to ascribe to the process of research powers far beyond its capacities. For instance, alarm at the impending extinction of the great whales is assuaged by the assurance that research is being applied to the problem, when it should be obvious that no amount of research will save anything in the absence of strictly enforced international whaling laws.

Implicit in all this is a charge for the educator: A society that has replaced an unquestioning faith in God with a hindsighted faith in science and technology has not made a very significant intellectual advance. Overfaith should be accorded the same derision as overkill.[4]

Man in Nature, Man over Nature

American man has traditionally considered nature to be opposed to his progress, and he has endeavored to conquer the natural world and its laws. This attitude, which we have inherited, has deep roots. From Europe's late Renaissance and Age of Reason, Western man brought to these shores the concept of progress through empiricism, in contrast with a former slavish acceptance of the fates. He said, "God helps those who help themselves." Here he found a wilderness that reinforced the attitude by yielding, albeit stubbornly, to his axe, rifle, and plow. At about the time that the frontier was disappearing, along with its opportunities for the common man, social Darwinism became the rationalization for industrial barons who conducted a highly successful "struggle for existence" against nature and against their fellow man. In this century, unionism has spread the wealth to many, and so the many have been cajoled into accepting the industrial revolution's continued battle against the natural world. Now, the technological revolution is succeeding the industrial revolution; it has already contributed to increasing the wealth a hundredfold and decreasing human physical effort by a similar order of magnitude.

This entire period, from Enlightenment to technological revolution, has been marked by a new faith in science as the means of comprehending and thus controlling the environment.

Equilibrium theories such as Festinger's cognitive dissonance give educators a reasonable explanation of attitudes through this historical progression. The frontiersman wrested his homestead from a resisting wilderness, the captain of industry fought "fang and claw" to the top, and this century's laborers endured wars and depression to claim their share of the bounty. As Festinger might note, they all placed high value on the fruits of their labors because of the effort expended and hardships suffered to obtain those fruits. Thus the concept of a struggle with nature was easily rationalized by all. By the same token, today's restless youth (as epitomized by *The Graduate*) who question the value of great material wealth may be doing so, in part, simply because they themselves did not have to strive for its acquisition. One of our jobs as educators is to bring them to question not just the love of material wealth but also the dangerous concomitant concept of man over nature.

What are the character and the danger of this attitude? Its character is obvious when man boasts of "conquering disease" (but conquers not his procreative urge), when his mineral resources are "ingeniously wrested from a reluctant earth," when he poses proudly with boot and rifle-butt planted atop the carcass of a "savage killer" (unresponsive to the plight of the "killer's" dwindling numbers and insensitive to the ironic self-condemnation of the expression). The attitude is sired by egocentrism and spawned of ignorance. Its danger has already been alluded to under Theme II, above; in brief, an infinitely expanding population can seek infinite material wealth for only a finite period of time, since it exists in a closed system: a planet with finite resources of space and material. Mother Earth is where it is (what's left of it). Those who assume that some day we will find our iron on Jupiter, our water on Mars, or our tranquillity in a distant solar system may be asking their posterity to pay the piper an impossible fee. Like it or not, we are *in* nature and it would behoove us to act that way; we can never be *over* nature. We must understand, even more profoundly than did Bacon, that "nature is only to be commanded by obeying her." If we insist upon making a fight of it, we must expect to lose.

A Proposal

As bleak a picture as these themes present, they should not be interpreted as despairing; rather, they represent that enlightened brand of pessimism that anticipates the worst and plans against it, knowing that the only surprises available to the optimist are unpleasant ones, happy surprises being the exclusive delight of the positive pessimist. Furthermore, there is some assurance to be gained when one notes the responsiveness of politicians to the growing grassroots sentiment for conservation issues, and the widespread dismay over the papal position on birth control. Finally, the themes set forth here certainly do not constitute the full range of societal understandings that citizens might appropriately possess; they are only some of the possible candidates for inclusion in the curriculum.

The science teacher is unlikely to possess all of the competencies necessary to deal adequately with these themes or with others dealing with the interplay of science, technology, and mankind. Furthermore, he may require the moral support of others in his school as he deals with possibly controversial issues. This suggests a unified high school course with a multidisciplinary team approach (and that is why this article is being directed to educators other than those in science).

Examples of some possible units and materials are in order. History and science teachers could examine the audacious new way in which man began to view his world during the late Renaissance and the Age of Reason, and the contributions of Copernicus, Galileo, and Bacon to the crossing of the Great Divide. The history teacher might deal with revolutions, the degree to which they are directed by men or, conversely, sweep men along in their course. Sociocultural revolutions such as the pastoral, agricultural, industrial, and technological could be compared and contrasted with political revolutions. The science and social science teacher could contribute to discussion of the technological revolution and its societal concomitants. Teachers of social science, history, and perhaps geography could develop the various concepts of man's place in nature held by us and by other peoples, including some of the Indian tribes that preceded us as the human stewards of the continent's resources. Examination of current legislation and government policies would constitute no small part of the curriculum. Political cartoons, such as the conservation gibes of Ding Darling and R. Cobb, would constitute an interesting source of material and a lively vehicle for discussion.

The English teacher could guide the study of contemporary utopian and dystopian novels such as *Lord of the Flies, Walden Two, Fahrenheit 451*, or *Anthem*, as well as brief consideration of earlier utopias such as those of Bacon or More. The University of Southern California film *THX 1138*, by George Lucas, provides a kind of cinematic little *Brave New World* in the light-show, McLuhanish, *cinema verité* form that seems to communicate to many of today's young people. (Incidentally, it was obviously no series of random events that saw these bleak societies conceived of in a century of science rather than in a previous era.) Fletcher Knebel's suspenseful novel, *Vanished*, illustrates the social concern of the scientific community today. Species threatened by the advance of man are considered touchingly in Bodsworth's *Last of the Curlews* and profoundly in Gary's *The Roots of Heaven*. The poetry of Jeffers and the philosophy of de Chardin suggest themselves, among a plethora of possibilities. Even some of the day's popular songs are appropriate.

The construction of such a new curriculum might best be accomplished by the team-writing approach used in creating the new science courses. Subject-matter scholars, professional educators, psychologists, school administrators, and classroom teachers would meet together to identify the students they are trying to reach, to state conceptual themes and subsumed objectives, to determine practicable schedules of teacher load and course organization, to effect pre-and inservice teacher training, and to direct the preparation of whatever materials are deemed appropriate—texts, films, exams, etc. The plan not only requires the two cultures to sit at table together, but to be joined there by newcomers from the space, oceanographic, environmental, information systems, and futuristic sciences.

Contemporary educators have often tended to embrace means that were either devoid of ends or connected by illogic to only the fuzziest of ends. The writing group would be charged with keeping sight of ends, both immediate and long-range. Some immediate goals must be the preparation of a curriculum that is resistant to degeneration into dogma, and that will not quickly be made obsolete by the very rapidity of change with which it will be concerned. Consideration of the former goal will necessarily include scrutiny of student evaluation, since objective testing for discrete and trivial facts is temptingly easy and therefore has always been highly contributory to the degeneration process.

A long-range goal is suggested by Max Lerner in an essay written a few years ago: Youth need be instilled with an élan, a "feeling of commitment and of being on fire, a sense of mission . . . of our country still being unfinished, a sense of the authentic revolutionary tradition which is in our history."[5] The youthful unrest that has subsequently become so evident surely constitutes, in part at least, an expression of or search for élan. As a necessary direction for the release of its energies, I submit for consideration the following national purpose: *America should take the lead in establishing and maintaining a varied environment that offers maximum freedom of choice to mankind and to its individual members, everywhere and in perpetuity.* This goal has been discussed elsewhere, along with its implications for our current concepts of economic growth and progress.[6]

This goal should be made explicit for the students in this curriculum. It should be capable of stimulating and directing their élan for some time to come: We are still very far from its achievement.

---

1. Fred W. Fox, "A Better Climate for Science." Eugene, Ore.: Oregon State University, 1968 (mimeographed).

2. Fred W. Fox, "Forces Influencing Education: Present and Future," in David P. Butts (ed.) *Designs for Progress in Science Education*, Austin: Science Education Center, University of Texas.

3. Paul DeHart Hurd, "The Scientific Enterprise and the Educated Citizen: An Unfinished Task." Paper presented at the meeting of the Kansas City, Missouri, Science Teachers, November 17, 1967.

4. A documented enumeration of our vast ecological problems is not within the scope of this article. These have been detailed at length in the popular press and in technical journals. The reader is referred to such periodicals as *BioScience, Natural History, Audubon,* and *The Living Wilderness,* and to the *Conservation Yearbooks* of the Department of the Interior. Stewart Udall's *The Quiet Crisis* (New York: Holt, Rinehart and Winston, 1963) and Paul Ehrlich's *The Population Bomb* (New York: Ballantine, 1968) are also recommended.

5. Max Lerner, "Humanist Goals," in Paul R. Hanna (ed.), *Education: An Instrument of National Goals.* New York: McGraw-Hill, 1962, pp. 105, 116.

6. R. Thomas Tanner, "Freedom and a Varied Environment," *The Science Teacher,* April, 1969, pp. 32-34.

Education for Survival
by William H. Boyer

Fear of the future increasingly corrodes modern life. We are beginning to sense the ways in which we have become locked into old institutional habits and their supporting mythologies, permitting technology and organizational technique to become the central determiners of social change. The tail usually wags the dog, and we do what is technologically possible, whether or not it is humanly desirable. Established systems become self-perpetuating and create their own goals, defining their own meaning of reality and progress. People are finally beginning to ask whether change is synonymous with progress or whether some change is destructive and even suicidal. Through our lack of qualitative standards we have often accepted all change as synonymous with social progress—the more the better. The gross national product is still the primary official indicator of national achievement. It lumps together the total dollar units of cigarette commercials and cancer therapy, automobile sales and mortuary fees, napalm and sulfa drugs.

The arrogant use of modern power has implications that are not only political and economic but ecological as well. Particularly in the West, where the Judeo-Christian traditions have flourished, man has encouraged himself to believe that he is above nature and that he can dictate to nature without showing respect for it. This arrogance is producing a dangerous ecological crisis to which the United States is the foremost contributor. The early rape and exploitation of seemingly boundless land and natural beauty still continues. The ugly consequences become more and more apparent. The beauty of irreplaceable giant redwood trees is increasingly denied to all future generations, as corporation profits and the chain saw continue to triumph over nature's ancient monuments. Lakes, streams, underground water, and even the oceans are headed rapidly toward pollution levels so high that they will be irreversible. In some areas of the United States, the air has become so polluted that it kills increasingly larger numbers of people as well as forests and vegetation. Increasingly, the birds that we don't see because of the smog are not there anyway, for our insecticides often hit wide of their mark. "Overkill" has become the symbol of our age.

Technology itself is not inherently evil, but when it develops without corresponding political, economic, and educational advances, a society becomes glutted with physical change unguided by integrated social planning. A society without control over change is a society with its future out of control. We are now at the dawn of a growing awareness that we must choose our destiny. The race is now on between catastrophe and more fundamental planning than we have ever engaged in.

Modern institutions, sustained by an immense amount of knowledge, paradoxically also require an abundance of ignorance to perpetuate them. Ignorance is the cement that continues to stabilize most contemporary institutions. Blindness to the ways in which old habits support intolerable levels of population, pollution, social inequality, and international violence is a prerequisite to the continuation of the world as it is.

Schools, also paradoxically, are usually one of the instruments for the perpetuation of ignorance. This is achieved primarily by isolating knowledge within separate compartments and by focusing on knowledge which is the least relevant, therefore meeting the traditional requirements of transmitting knowledge without disturbing the existing order. This is neither an intentional nor a stated goal of most schools; yet, by isolating students from the major problems of the world, the results are usually no less effective than if the goals were intended. Schools are usually so intertwined with the larger culture (educators often proclaim that enculturation is their main objective) that they often fail to see the dangers, even the suicidal consequences, of adjusting students to obsolete aspects of the culture.

Schools that fail to develop the capacity of students to participate intelligently in the control of their society not only emasculate them but alienate them from the dominant culture. Furthermore, this approach guarantees that social decision making is kept where it is—in the hands of a few who use such power to preserve the personal advantages enjoyed only by the decision-making elite. This process, which in the past has produced social injustice, now has brought us to the point where life on this planet cannot long continue without a new relationship of both man to man and man to nature. Therefore, students are engaged in a new quest for relevance.

A Definition of Relevance

There are a variety of current uses of the word "relevance," so I would like to suggest how relevance might be defined. This will lead to a proposal for planning a relevant future through education. Then I will focus particularly on planning for survival and suggest how all this applies to social studies.

I will define an education as being relevant when it has a vital connection to human life—either to the conditions that sustain life or to the conditions that give life meaning. An education that contributes to the knowledge of health, food production, nutrition, population control, and war prevention is the kind of education that can help sustain life. Education that provides knowledge of aesthetic, social, and religious quality is the kind that helps give meaning to life.

Relevance Through Planning

An education that is relevant must connect knowledge and social change so that the student becomes a causal agent in historical change. Such education should help him participate in the development of the future by directing him into the mainstream of human events, by giving him experience in making effective social decisions, and by illuminating the alternative choices and their consequences. The student should be taught to join others in cooperatively planning the future.

The essential data in all planning involves information about the direction of trends that permits likely forecasts of the future. This requires information about present conditions, historical data to plot the rate and direction of change, and projections based on locating present trends at some point in the distant future. Short-term prediction is more reliable than long-term prediction, and unexpected events may alter even short-term predictions. The purpose of planning is to minimize accidental change and to maximize intentional change. The motive for the entire enterprise is based on the unwillingness to continue what Michael Harrington has called our Accidental Century, a century that has been based on a faith in history and the marketplace and the belief that when you get into trouble you will inevitably come out smelling like roses.

Planning can occur through an elitist top-down system, or it can be based on bottom-up participation, the relative emphasis being reflective of an autocratic or democratic social philosophy. Specialists are needed in either system to provide accurate information about the consequences of alternative plans, but value judgments are necessary to define the kind of future to be planned. This role cannot be performed by a specialist. The failure of schools to help students become participants in planning processes virtually predetermines that social planning will be elitist, representing the values of those who have the power to affect social policy.

Some types of planning are already well developed, particularly in large industries. This type is well described in John Galbraith's book, *The New Industrial State*. But such planning is aimed either at anticipating trends and then adapting to them or else at manipulating the larger public into the acceptance of a goal that may serve the corporation at the expense of the larger public.

Government planning is similar, usually with even less anticipation of trends and more reliance on ad hoc crisis treatment. The manipulation of public consent is also well established, but government even includes a self-predatory addition where branches of government withhold information from other branches, each in an attempt to achieve its own special interest.

Virtually all current social planning is *expansive* planning, based on the anticipation of trends. We are told that certain kinds of jobs will be increasingly available in the next decade with the assumption that the enterprising citizen will prepare himself to become more marketable; but another kind of planning, which might be called *reconstructive* planning, assumes that what is needed is not mainly planning *for* the future, but planning *of* the future. The reconstructive planner does not assume that people need necessarily adjust to trends but rather that trends should be adjusted to people. Reconstructive planning requires integrative social planning—with the larger social unit being given priority. If it is a question of what is good for General Motors or what is good for the American people, the latter should have the overriding claim. If it is a matter of what is good for the United States or what is good for the human race, the human race should be given priority.

The difference between expansive national defense planning and reconstructive defense planning can be illustrated as follows: The effort to build ABMs and fallout shelters to protect against the radioactivity of World War III is an example of expansive planning. The Clark-Sohn plan for World Peace Through World Law, which is designed to *avert* cataclysmic war, is an example of reconstructive planning.

Areas of Planning

In order to teach planning, it is advisable to set up areas of study. Such classifying involves the danger of once again separating problems and neglecting their interrelatedness, but some problems are more urgent than others, at least from the standpoint of survival; so distinctions in the kinds of problems permits the appropriate allocation of energy and time. Planning areas might be usefully classified under problems of 1) social justice, 2) environmental quality, and 3) survival.

Social justice involves the study of human exploitation and plans to remedy such exploitation. *Environmental quality* involves planning which increases the desirability of living in a particular society. *Survival* planning minimizes the chances of unnecessary death.

If existence does precede essence, survival planning should be given central emphasis. This is the kind of ordering understood by Martin Luther King. In spite of his deep concern for increasing social justice, he saw that it would be no victory to achieve integration of radioactive corpses. He recognized the priority of the problems of international violence in the atomic age. It is this comparative perspective that must be cultivated if planning is to order energies toward the most important problems.

Statistics are necessary but are not sufficient for describing the consequences of trends. The *meaning* of a future can be illuminated by having some sense of what it would be like to live in a world suggested by particular trends. Futurist novels, plays—any dramatic and artistic form that provides vicarious experience of alternative futures are useful to the assessment of the desirability of living in such a world. That is why novels like *1984* and films like *On the Beach* and *Seven Days in May* make future possibilities real in a way that usually cannot be achieved by statistics. It is one thing to know what the statistical probabilities are for cigarette lung cancer. But many people require a more vivid and personal event (such as the death of Edward R. Murrow) to illustrate what the statistics mean.

Planning to Survive

Four major survival problems are cataclysmic war, uncontrolled population, resource depletion, and pollution of the biosphere on which human life depends. Projections in each of these three areas give little hope that mankind can long survive. If nothing is done to change trends in any of these areas, even short-range future survival chances are very low—most of the human race is not likely to survive this century. It is increasingly possible to predict the approximate time and place where autogenocide from overpopulation, pollution, and resource depletion will take place, but the war system is somewhat different. It combines the comparatively fixed probabilities of a mutual deterrence/mutual annihilation system. Estimates of the odds for the system failing range from 1% to 10% per year. Assuming that a 2% per year probability of mutual annihilation is an optimistic figure, the current war system itself is not likely to get most of the human race through the twentieth century.

The war system, however, may be one of the easier systems to reconstruct if enough people come to see that the atomic age has fundamentally transformed the meaning of national defense. Nations no longer have effective defense against nuclear arms; therefore, the national "defense" they have is largely in name only. Current defense systems are examples of institutions locked into the constraints and habits of expansive planning. To move to the level of reconstructive planning requires a careful examination of alternative forms of world order. By patterning our changes according to old habits, we merely add new technology to old pre-atomic systems, giving virtually no attention to reconstructive possibilities such as an international system of national defense.

Survival and the Social Studies Teacher

The social studies programs in most schools would be transformed if they included a commitment to futurist goals directed toward the development of a world with greater social justice, improved quality of the physical environment, and increased chances for human survival. Such a commitment would provide new criteria for the selection of subject matter. History would no longer be largely an antiquarian excursion into the particular events that have come to be a dreary part of the perennial puberty rites of American youth. History should not be ignored in futurist studies, but it should be selectively studied to understand current problems. History is *always* written and studied selectively, but instead of merely chronicling battles, it could examine them not only to find out what seemed to be the primary causes but to question whether better ways might have been used to resolve the conflict. Causes of historical events include not only the precipitating factors but also the structures that were *not* present. It is not only what people do that causes wars; it is also what they failed to do in the way of developing procedures, habits, norms, and political machinery for averting war. This use of *negative causality,* or what was ommitted in the system, can be an exceedingly useful concept for analyzing historical events for the purpose of planning a future that avoids some of the pitfalls of the past.

Clearly it will be necessary to reorient our study of history to focus on those events that are the most productive. In most current history texts, very little consideration is given to the bombing of Hiroshima and the political-military implications of the nuclear era. The Nuremburg trials, the Cuban missile crisis, and the Vietnam War can be used as case studies to raise questions about the need for new principles of international law and new peacekeeping systems. The assumptions on which American policy has been based, which include atomic threat systems and a mutual deterrence theory, are crucially in need of more critical examination.

Earlier, I suggested that the four main crisis areas are war, population, resource depletion, and pollution. In all these problems, a basic strategy is to explore alternative futures and then to make comparisons of alternative goals and strategies of change as a basis for commitment to social action. New information becomes necessary. In the case of teaching about population problems, demographic and birth control information is basic. In the case of pollution, the information describing trends, danger levels, and causes becomes basic. Understanding causes should include knowledge of the resistance to pollution control offered by organizations that have a vested interest in pollution, such as the automobile industry.

But knowledge of how to bring about change must go beyond the usual mere assimilation of facts and theory. It must include direct experience. For example, if high school students were to identify a problem of air or water pollution in their own community, they could inquire into the reasons for the problem. They may find there is a lack of appropriate legislation, or lack of monitoring and enforcement. Their findings could be used to illuminate the local needs. They would, at the minimum, obtain more understanding of the politics of pollution control, and at the maximum they would help effect actual changes. Futurist education must link theory and practice if the goal of teaching planning is to be really effective. It involves a change in the meaning of social education—away from competitive individual success, toward cooperative social action.

The basic model of reconstructive planning is not difficult to understand, but the task of reorienting a curriculum toward planning, even toward survival planning, is likely to be difficult because of the entrenched commitments to obsolete practices. The self-righteous autonomy of schools is a major obstacle. Psychologists have often defined intelligence as that which IQ tests measure, and the same quaint logic is often used by schools to define education as that which schools do. Without some outside theory of man, history, and the good life, schools have no outside standard of measurement and they easily commit a kind of Cartesian fallacy in which they say, "Schools are, therefore relevance exists." The most common traps include some of the following assumptions: 1) that state-adopted materials are necessarily relevant, 2) that the traditional content of social studies is necessarily relevant, 3) that the mass media concentrate on problems that are necessarily relevant, 4) that regents' examinations and college entrance requirements are necessarily relevant, 5) that materials prepared by university academicians are necessarily relevant. A reexamination of these assumptions may threaten the self-interest of existing bureaucracies, but may provide a breath of fresh air in the midst of the present educational stagnation.

Danger—University Ahead

The increased influence of universities on social studies curricula is a mixed blessing. To the unwary and the innocent, the university can be one more snare to trap the social studies teacher. When the university is treated as the citadel of the philosopher-king, a kind of tragic comedy can result—a case of the blind leading the blind. Theodore Roszak is even more critical:

> Until the recent rash of campus protest related to the Vietnam war, nothing has so characterized the American academic as a condition of entrenched social irrelevance, so highly developed that it would be comic if it were not sufficiently serious in its implications to stand condemned as an act of criminal delinquency. (*The Dissenting Academy*, p. 12)

"Criminal delinquency" is strong language, but a teacher who deprives his students of knowledge that might literally save his life could be said to be committing a type of criminal act. Universities often are Parkinsonian bureaucracies where words expand to fill the time available. They are often places to learn many reasons why nothing can be done—a kind of staging area for intellectual paralysis. A teacher who wants knowledge to be an instrument of action for helping people participate in social change will need to be aware that this is not the dominant meaning of knowledge in American universities. The academician carries an implicit theory of knowledge with him, and most academicians are not concerned with the kind of knowledge that makes futurist education possible.

The disciplinary compartmentalization of knowledge is one of the major traps, but even when knowledge becomes interdisciplinary, it is not necessarily relevant to the problems of our age. The new Fenton High School Social Studies Series is a case in point. The texts are more interdisciplinary and integrative than most texts, but the particular type of inquiry method that is used is aimed at inducting students into the language and problems of behavioral *science*. The mode of inquiry is analytic and scientific. If it were also philosophical and critical, it would move beyond description into normative questions—judgments about values and questions of what ought to be, not merely what has been and what is. This would make it more suitable for futurist study. As it stands, it encourages the kind of neutrality that characterizes most behavioral science. Education for planning requires the use of scientific inquiry skills, but it also requires movement toward commitment rather than toward neutrality—an instrumental use of knowledge rather than interest in scientific inquiry as an end in itself. But Fenton himself does have social goals in mind. He points out that the students who are successful with his curriculum are not learning merely as an end in itself; the material does serve other needs—it helps them "pass the College Board examinations." Middle-class "success" values once again take precedence over the more existential values of survival. What appears to be a new approach to social studies turns out not really to be an instrument of reform but only one more way of aiming at adaptive individual middle-class success in a society that desperately needs reconstruction. The Fenton series is typical of the academic traps that reinforce old social systems under the guise of reform.

So even what is called the "new social studies" can be a way of actually preserving old ideologies. This is achieved by ignoring the more fundamental problems of our age. If by contrast we give precedence to life rather than death, beauty rather than ugliness, human equality rather than exploitation, we can then use science to see if present practices are likely to lead in such a direction. Previous illustrations have focused on social studies, but futurism is applicable to all areas of the schools. Selective use of social science, natural science, and philosophy can then become integrated educational tools that help people learn the ecological limits of human action and learn to plan the best of possible worlds.

Conclusion

This is the first period in human history where man has the means to reflect not only on his social policies but also on the values that underlie them. His new capacity to engage in fundamental replanning, including intentional reconstruction of the culture itself, is the most important achievement of the twentieth century. This capacity is not yet being realized, yet no institution can be more useful than the schools in helping to bring this new knowledge to the general citizenry. But to do so schools must extricate themselves from many of their old habits and avoid merely trying to adapt the young to a world gone by. Schools are inextricably involved in social change, either because of what they do or what they fail to do. In an age when relevant education is desperately urgent, the ritualistic trivia and bureaucratic games that occupy most schools are not merely a waste of time but a form of pathology.

There are some old values, such as maximum freedom of choice, that are still important, but schools must *illuminate the next context* in which choices must be made. They should help students identify trends that are sucidal and also those that perpetuate social injustice and exploitation. Then the job is to collectively design optimum futures, first focusing on classes, next on schools expanding local communities, the nation, and a new world order. Such planning should include implementing and testing effective strategies for change.

If people were less alienated from the forces of social change, more aware of the problems of common survival, and more accustomed to cooperating to create the future, we could then be optimistic about the future. Schools have a crucial survival role: They can either continue to reinforce pathological trends or else by reconstructing themselves they can help divert history from the suicidal path on which it is now embarked.

The Day Our Children Disappear: Predictions of a Media Ecologist
by Neil Postman

The modern media—especially television—are a disaster for our youth, Mr. Postman argues. Will they in the end turn out to be a great blessing?

I am aware that in addressing the question of the future of education, one can write either a "good news" or a "bad news" essay. Typically, a good news essay presents readers with a problem, then proceeds to solve it (more or less). Readers usually find such essays agreeable, as well they should. A good news essay gives us a sense of potency and control, and a really *good* "good news" essay shows us how to employ our imaginations in confronting professional issues. Although I have not yet seen the other essays in this special *KAPPAN*, I feel sure that most of them are of the good news type, solid and constructive.

A bad news essay, on the other hand, presents readers with a problem— and ends (more or less). Naturally, readers find such essays disagreeable, since they engender a sense of confusion and sometimes hopelessness. Still, they have their uses. They may, for example, help us understand some things that need explaining. Let me tell you, then, that while I hope my remarks will be illuminating, you must prepare yourself for an orthodox—even classical— bad news essay. I wish it could be otherwise, because I know my temperament to be more suited to optimism than to gloom and doom. But I write as a person whose academic interests go by the name of media ecology. Media ecology is the study of the effects of communications technology on culture. We study how media affect people's cognitive habits, their social relations, their political biases, and their personal values. And in this capacity I have almost nothing optimistic to write about, for, if I am to respect the evidence as I understand it, I am bound to say that the effects of modern media—especially television—have been and will probably continue to be disastrous, especially for our youth. What I intend to do here is describe in some detail one important respect in which this is the case and explain how it occurred. As is the custom in bad news essays, I shall offer no solution to this problem— mainly because I know of none.

Before proceeding, I must express one bit of "good news" about what I shall be saying. It is to be understood that when I speak of some development as "disastrous," I mean that it is disastrous from my very limited point of view. Obviously, what appears disastrous to me may be regarded as marvelous by others. After all, I am a New Yorker, and most things appear to me disastrous. But even more to the point, what may appear disastrous at one historical moment may turn out to be marvelous in a later age. There are, in fact, many historical instances of someone's correctly predicting negative effects of a medium of communication but where, in the end, what appeared to be a disaster turned out to be a great advance.

The best example I know of concerns the great Athenian teacher, Socrates, who feared and mocked the written word, which in his time was beginning to be used for many purposes and with great frequency. But not by him. As you know, Socrates wrote no books, and had it not been for Plato and Xenophon, who did, we would know almost nothing about him. In one of his most enduring conversations, called the *Phaedrus*, Socrates gives three reasons why he does not like writing. Writing, he says, will deprive Athenians of their powerful memories, for if everything is written down there will be no need to memorize. Second, he says that writing will change the form of education. In particular, it will destroy the dialectic process, for writing forces students to follow an argument rather than participate in it. And third, Socrates warns that writing will change concepts of privacy and the meaning of public discourse; for once you write something down, you never know whose eyes will fall upon it—those for whom it is intended, perhaps, but just as likely those for whom it is not intended. Thus, for Socrates, the widespread use of writing was, and would be, a cultural disaster. In a sense it was. For all of Socrates' predictions were correct, and there is no doubt that writing undermined the oral tradition that Socrates believed to be the most suitable mode for expressing serious ideas, beautiful poetry, and authentic piety. But Socrates did not see what his student, Plato, did: that writing would create new modes of thought altogether and provide new and wonderful uses for the intellect—most especially what today we call *science*.

So without intending to suggest an unsupportable comparison, I write as a Socrates-like character, prophesying that the advent of the television age will have the direst outcome. I hope that among you there is a Plato-like character who will be able to see the television age as a blessing.

In order for me to get to the center of my argument as quickly as possible, I am going to resist the temptation to discuss some of the fairly obvious effects of television, such as its role in shortening our students' attention span, in eroding their capacity to handle linguistic and mathematical symbolism, and in causing them to become increasingly impatient with deferred gratification. The evidence for these effects exists in a variety of forms—from declining SAT scores to astronomical budgets for remedial writing classes to the everyday observations of teachers and parents. But I will not take the time to review any of the evidence for the intellectually incapacitating effects of television. Instead, I want to focus on what I regard as the most astonishing and serious effect of television. It is simply this: Television is causing the rapid decline of our concept of childhood. I choose to discuss this because I can think of nothing that is bound to have a more profound effect on our work as educators than that our children should disappear. I do not mean, of course, that they will physically disappear. I mean that the *idea* of children will disappear.

If this pronouncement, on first hearing, seems implausible, let me hasten to tell you that the idea of childhood is not very old. In fact, in the Western world the idea of childhood hardly existed prior to the 16th century. Up until that time children as young as 6 and 7 were not regarded as fundamentally different from adults. As far as historians can tell, the language of children, their dress, their games, their labor, and the legal rights were the same as those of adults. It was recognized, of course, that children tended to be smaller than adults, but this fact did not confer upon them any special status; there were certainly no special institutions for the nurturing of children. Prior to the 16th century, for example, there were no books on child rearing or, indeed, any books about women in their role as mothers. Children, to take another example, were always included in funeral processions, there being no reason anyone could think of to shield them from knowledge of death. Neither did it occur to anyone to keep a picture of a child if that child lived to grow to adulthood or had died in infancy. Nor are there any references to children's speech or jargon prior to the 17th century, after which they are found in abundance. If you have ever seen 13th- or 14th-century paintings of children, you will have noticed that they are always depicted as small adults. Except for size, they are devoid of any of the physical characteristics we associate with childhood, and they are never shown on canvas alone—that is, isolated from adults. Such paintings are entirely accurate representations of the psychological and social perceptions of children prior to the 16th century. Here is how the historian J. H. Plumb puts it:

> There was no separate world of childhood. Children shared the same games with adults, the same toys, the same fairy stories. They lived their lives together, never apart. The coarse village festivals depicted by Breughel, showing men and women besotted with drink, groping for each other with unbridled lust, have children eating and drinking with the adults. Even in the soberer pictures of wedding feasts and dances, the children are enjoying themselves alongside their elders, doing the same things.

Barbara Tuchman, in her marvelous book about the 14th century titled *A Distant Mirror*, puts it more succinctly: "If children survived to age 7, their recognized life began, more or less as miniature adults. Childhood was already over."

Now the reasons for this are fairly complicated. For one thing, most children did *not* survive; their mortality rate was extraordinarily high, and it is not until the late 14th century that children are even mentioned in wills and testaments—an indication that adults did not expect them to be around very long. In fact, probably because of this, in some parts of Europe children were treated as neuter genders. In 14th-century Italy, for example, the sex of a child who had died was never recorded.

Certainly, adults did not have the emotional commitment to children that *we* accept as normal. Phillipe Aries, in his great book titled *Centuries of Childhood*, remarks that the prevailing view was to have several children in order to keep a few; people could not allow themselves to become too attached to something that was regarded as a probable loss. Aries quotes from a document that records a remark made by the neighbor of a distraught mother of five young children. In order to comfort the mother, the neighbor says, "Before they are old enough to bother you, you will have lost half of them, or perhaps all of them."

We must also not forget that in a feudal society children were often regarded as mere economic utilities, adults being less interested in the character and intelligence of children than in their capacity for work. But I think the most powerful reason for the absence of the idea of childhood is to be found in the communication environment of the Dark and Middle Ages. Since most people did not know how to read, or did not *need* to know how to read, a child became an adult—a fully participating adult—when he or she learned how to speak. Since all important social transactions involved face-to-face oral communication, full competence to speak and hear—which is

usually achieved by age 7—was the dividing line between infancy and adulthood. There was no intervening stage, because none was needed—until the
middle of the 15th century. At that point an extraordinary event occurred that
not only changed the religious, economic, and political face of Europe but
also created our modern idea of childhood. I am referring, of course, to the invention of the printing press. And because in a few minutes you will, perhaps,
be thinking that I am claiming too much for the power of modern media,
especially TV, it is worth saying now that no one had the slightest inkling in
1450 that the printing press would have such powerful effects on our society
as it did. When Gutenberg announced that he could manufacture books, as he
put it, "without the help of reed, stylus, or pen but by wondrous agreement,
proportion, and harmony of punches and types," he did not imagine that his
invention would undermine the authority of the Catholic Church. Yet less
than 80 years later Martin Luther was in effect claiming that, with the Word of
God on everyone's kitchen table, Christians did not require the Papacy to
interpret it for them. Nor did Gutenberg have any inkling that his invention
would create a new class of people: namely, children. Or more specifically,
male children, for there is no doubt that boys were the first class of specialized children.

How was this accomplished? Simply by the fact that, less than a hundred
years after Gutenberg's invention, European culture became a reading culture; i.e., adulthood was redefined. One could not become an adult unless he
or she knew how to read. In order to experience God, one had to be able,
obviously, to read the Bible, which is why Luther himself translated the Bible
into German. In order to experience literature, one had to be able to read
novels and personal essays, forms of literature that were wholly created by
the printing press. Our earliest novelists—for example, Richardson and
Defoe—were themselves printers. Montaigne, who invented the essay,
worked hand in hand with a printer, as did Thomas More when he produced
what may be called our first science fiction novel—his *Utopia*. Of course, in
order to learn science one not only had to know how to read but, by the
beginning of the 17th century, one could read science in the vernacular—that
is, in one's own language. Sir Francis Bacon's *The Advancement of Learning*,
published in 1605, was the first scientific tract an Englishman could read in
English. And of course one must not forget the great Dutch humanist,
Erasmus, who, understanding the meaning of the printing press as well as
anyone, wrote one of the first books of etiquette for the instruction of young
men. He said of his book, "As Socrates brought philosophy from heaven to
earth, so I have led philosophy to games and banquets." (By the way,
Erasmus dedicated the book to his publisher's son, and the book includes
advice and guidance on how to convert prostitutes to a moral life.)

The importance of books on etiquette should not be overlooked. As
Norman Elias shows in his book titled *The Civilizing Process*, the sudden
emergence in the 16th century of etiquette books signifies that one could no
longer assume that children knew everything adults knew—in other words,
the separation of childhood from adulthood was under way.

Alongside all of this, Europeans rediscovered what Plato had known
about learning to read: namely, that it is best done at an early age. Since
reading is, among other things, an unconscious reflex as well as an act of
recognition, the habit of reading must be formed in that period when the

brain is still engaged in the task of acquiring oral language. The adult who learns to read after his or her oral vocabulary is completed rarely becomes a fluent reader.

What this came to mean in the 16th century is that the young had to be separated from the rest of the community to be taught how to read—that is, to be taught how to function as an adult. This meant that they had to go to school. And going to school was the essential event in creating childhood. The printing press, in other words, created the idea of school. In fact, school classes originated to separate students according to their capacities as readers, not to separate them according to age. That came later. In any event, once all of this occurred it was inevitable that the young would be viewed as a special class of people whose minds and character were qualitatively different from those of adults. As any semanticist can tell you, once you categorize people for a particular purpose, you will soon discover many other reasons why they should be regarded as different. We began, in short, to see human development as a series of stages, with childhood as a bridge between infancy and adulthood. For the past 350 years we have been developing and refining our concept of childhood, this with particular intensity in the 18th, 19th, and 20th centuries. We have been developing and refining institutions for the nurturing of children; and we have conferred upon children a preferred status, reflected in the special ways we expect them to think, talk, dress, play, and learn.

All of this, I believe, is now coming to an end. And it is coming to an end because our communication environment has been radically altered once again—this time by electronic media, especially television. Television has a transforming power at least equal to that of the printing press and possibly as great as that of the alphabet itself. It is my contention that, with the assistance of other media such as radio, film, and records, television has the power to lead us to childhood's end.

Here is how the transformation is happening. To begin with, television presents information mostly in visual images. Although human speech is heard on TV and sometimes assumes importance, people mostly *watch* television. What they watch are rapidly changing visual images—as many as 1,200 different shots every hour. This requires very little conceptual thinking or analytic decoding. TV watching is almost wholly a matter of pattern recognition. The *symbolic form* of television does not require any special instruction or learning. In America, TV viewing begins at about the age of 18 months; by 30 months, according to studies by Daniel Anderson of the University of Massachusetts, children begin to understand and respond to TV imagery. Thus there is no need for any preparation or prerequisite training for watching TV. Television needs no analogue to the McGuffey *Reader*. And, as you must know, there is no such thing, in reality, as children's programming on TV. Everything is for everybody. So far as symbolic form is concerned, "Charlie's Angels" is as sophisticated or as simple to grasp as "Sesame Street." Unlike books, which vary greatly in syntactical and lexical complexity and which may be scaled according to the ability of the reader, TV presents information in a form that is undifferentiated in its accessibility. And that is why adults and children tend to watch the same programs. I might add, in case you are thinking that children and adults at least watch at different times, that according to Frank Mankiewicz's *Remote Control*, approximately 600,000 children watch TV between midnight and two in the morning.

To summarize: TV erases the dividing line between childhood and adulthood for two reasons: first, because it requires no instruction to grasp its form; second, because it does not segregate its audience. It communicates the same information to everyone simultaneously, regardless of age, sex, race, or level of education.

But it erases the dividing line in other ways as well. One might say that the main difference between an adult and a child is that the adult knows about certain facets of life—its mysteries, its contradictions, its violence, its tragedies—that are not considered suitable for children to know. As children move toward adulthood we reveal these secrets to them in what we believe to be a psychologically assimilable way. But television makes this arrangement quite impossible. Because television operates virtually around the clock—it would not be economically feasible for it to do otherwise—it requires a constant supply of novel and interesting information. This means that all adult secrets—social, sexual, physical, and the like—must be revealed. Television forces the entire culture to come out of the closet. In its quest for new and sensational information to hold its audience, TV must tap every existing taboo in the culture: homosexuality, incest, divorce, promiscuity, corruption, adultery, sadism. Each is now merely a theme for one or another television show. In the process each loses its role as an exclusively adult secret.

Some time ago, while watching a TV program called "The Vidal Sassoon Show," I came across the quintessential example of what I am talking about. Vidal Sassoon is a famous hairdresser whose TV show is a mixture of beauty hints, diet information, health suggestions, and popular psychology. As he came to the end of one segment of the show in which an attractive woman had demonstrated how to cook vegetables, the theme music came up and Sassoon just had time enough to say, "Don't go away. We'll be back with a marvelous new diet and, then, a quick look at incest." Now, this is more—much more—than demystification. It is even more than the revelation of secrets. It is the ultimate trivialization of culture. Television is relentless in both revealing and trivializing all things private and shameful, and therefore it undermines the moral basis of culture. The subject matter of the confessional box and the psychiatrist's office is now in the public domain. I have it on good authority that, shortly, we and our children will have the opportunity to see commercial TV's first experiments with presenting nudity, which will probably not be shocking to anyone, since TV commercials have been offering a form of soft-core pornography for years. And on the subject of commercials—the 700,000 of them that American youths will see in the first 18 years of their lives—they too contribute toward opening to youth all the secrets that once were the province of adults—everything from vaginal sprays to life insurance to the causes of marital conflict. And we must not omit the contributions of news shows, those curious entertainments that daily provide the young with vivid images of adult failure and even madness.

As a consequence of all of this, childhood innocence and specialness are impossible to sustain, which is why children have disappeared from television. Have you noticed that all the children on television shows are depicted as merely small adults, in the manner of 13th- or 14th-century paintings? Watch "The Love Boat" or any of the soap operas or family shows or situation comedies. You will see children whose language, dress, sexuality, and interests are not different from those of the adults on the same shows. Like the paintings of Breughel, the children *do* everything the adults do and are shielded from nothing.

And yet, as TV begins to render invisible the traditional concept of childhood, it would not be quite accurate to say that it immerses us in an adult world. Rather, it uses the material of the adult world as the basis for projecting a new kind of person altogether. We might call this person the adult-child. For reasons that have partly to do with TV's capacity to reach everyone, partly to do with the accessibility of its symbolic form, and partly to do with its commercial base, TV promotes as desirable many of the attitudes that we associate with childishness: for example, an obsessive need for immediate gratification, a lack of concern for consequences, an almost promiscuous preoccupation with consumption. TV seems to favor a population that consists of three age groups: on the one end, infancy; on the other, senility; and in between, a group of indeterminate age where everyone is somewhere between 20 and 30 and remains that way until dotage descends. In *A Distant Mirror*, Tuchman asks the question, Why was childishness so noticeable in medieval behavior, with its marked inability to restrain any kind of impulse? Her answer is that so large a proportion of society was in fact very young in years. Half the population was under 21; a third under 14. If we ask the same question about our own society, we must give a different answer, for about 65% of our population is over 21. We are a nation of chronological grown-ups. But TV will have none of it. It is biased toward the behavior of the child-adult.

In this connection, I want to remind you of a TV commercial that sells hand lotion. In it we are shown a mother and daughter and challenged to tell which is which. I find this to be a revealing piece of sociological evidence, for it tells us that in our culture it is considered desirable that a mother should not look older than her daughter, or that a daughter should not look younger than her mother. Whether this means that childhood is gone or adulthood is gone amounts to the same thing, for if there is no clear concept of what it means to be an adult, there can be no concept of what it means to be a child.

In any case, however you wish to phrase the transformation that is taking place, it is clear that the behavior, attitudes, desires, and even physical appearance of adults and children are becoming increasingly indistinguishable. There is now virtually no difference, for example, between adult crimes and children's crimes; in many states the punishments are becoming the same. There is also very little difference in dress. The children's clothing industry has undergone a virtual revolution within the past 10 years, so that there no longer exists what we once unambiguously recognized as children's clothing. Eleven-year-olds wear three-piece suits to birthday parties; 61-year-old men wear jeans to birthday parties. Twelve-year-old girls wear high heels; 42-year-old men wear sneakers. On the streets of New York and Chicago you can see grown women wearing little white socks and imitation Mary Janes. Indeed, among the highest-paid models in America are 12- and 13-year-old girls who are presented as adults. To take another case: Children's games, once so imaginatively rich and varied and so emphatically inappropriate for adults, are rapidly disappearing. Little League baseball and Peewee football, for example, are not only supervised by adults but are modeled in their organization and emotional style on big league sports. The language of children and adults has also been transformed so that, for example, the idea that there may be words that adults ought not to use in the presence of children now seems faintly ridiculous. With TV's relentless revelation of all adult secrets, language secrets are difficult to guard, and it is not inconceivable to me that in the near future we shall return to the 13th- and 14th-century situation in which no words were unfit for a youthful ear. Of course, with the assistance of modern contraceptives, the sexual appetite of both adults and children can be satisfied without serious restraint and without mature understanding of its meaning. Here TV has played an enormous role, since it not only keeps the entire population in a condition of high sexual excitement but stresses a kind of egalitarianism of sexual fulfillment: Sex is transformed from a dark and profound mystery to a product that is available to everyone—like mouthwash or underarm deodorant.

In the 2 November 1980 *New York Times Magazine*, Tuchman offered still another example of the homogenization of childhood and adulthood. She spoke of the declining concept of quality—in literature, in art, in food, in work. Her point was that, with the emergence of egalitarianism as a political and social philosophy, there has followed a diminution of the idea of excellence in all human tasks and modes of expression. The point is that adults are *supposed* to have different tastes and standards from those of children, but through the agency of television and other modern media the differences have largely disappeared. Junk food, once suited only to the undiscriminating palates and iron stomachs of the young, is now common fare for adults. Junk literature, junk music, junk conversation are shared equally by children and adults, so that it is now difficult to find adults who can clarify and articulate for youth the difference between quality and schlock.

It remains for me to mention that there has been a growing movement to recast the legal rights of children so that they are more or less the same as those of adults. The heart of this movement—which, for example, is opposed to compulsory schooling—resides in the claim that what has been thought to be a preferred status for children is instead only an oppression that keeps them from fully participating in the society.

All of this means, I think, that our culture is providing fewer reasons and opportunities for childhood. I am not so single-minded as to think that TV alone is responsible for this transformation. The decline of the family, the loss of a sense of roots (40 million Americans change residence every year), and the elimination, through technology, of any significance in adult work are other factors. But I believe that television creates a communication context which encourages the idea that childhood is neither desirable nor necessary—indeed, that we do not need children. I said earlier, in talking about childhood's end, that I did not mean the physical disappearance of the children. But in fact that, too, is happening. The birthrate in America is declining and has been for a decade, which is why schools are being closed all over the country.

This brings me to the final characteristic of TV that needs mentioning. The *idea* of children implies a vision of the future. They are the living messages we send to a time we will not see. But television cannot communicate a sense of the future or, for that matter, a sense of the past. It is a present-centered medium, a speed-of-light medium. Everything we see on television is experienced as happening *now*, which is why we must be told, in language, that a videotape we are seeing was made months before. The grammar of television has no analogue to the past and future tenses in language. Thus it amplifies the present out of all proportion and transforms the childish need for immediate gratification into a way of life. And we end up with what Christopher Lasch calls "the culture of narcissism"—no future, no children, everyone fixed at an age somewhere between 20 and 30.

Of course I cannot know what all of this means to you, but my own position, I'm sure, is clear. I believe that what I have been describing is disastrous—partly because I value the charm, curiosity, malleability, and innocence of childhood, which is what first drew me to a career in education, and partly because I believe that adults need, first, to be children before they can be grown-ups. For otherwise they remain like TV's adult-child all their lives, with no sense of belonging, no capacity for lasting relationships, no respect for limits, and no grasp of the future. But mainly I think it is disastrous because it makes problematic the future of school, which is one of the few institutions still based on the assumption that there are significant differences between children and adults and that adults therefore have something of value to teach children.

So my bad news essay comes down to these questions: In a world in which children are adults and adults children, what need is there for people like ourselves? Are the issues we are devoting our careers to solving being rendered irrelevant by the transforming power of our television culture? I devoutly hope your answers to these questions are more satisfactory than mine.

Epilogue

As I indicated in the introduction, my inclination was to include another 100 or so articles in this volume. If this one proves popular, perhaps I will try another book next year. In the meantime, here are the names of some authors whose work I desperately wanted to include but couldn't for space reasons:

Louis E. Alley, Benjamin Bloom, David W. Brison, Jere E. Brophy (with Thomas L. Good), William C. Budd (with Charles Harwood), Meyer Cahn, Roald Campbell, Walter W. Cook, Diane Divoky, Robert W. Cole, Henry Steele Commager, Lee Conway, Walter R. Coppedge, Audrey C. Cohen, James B. Conant, Lee Cronbach, Joe Cronin, Patricia Cross, Justice William O. Douglas, Daniel L. Duke (with Adrienne M. Meckel), Don Emblen, Arthur Schlesinger, Jim Enochs, Thorwald Esbensen, Chester E. Finn, Jr., James D. Finn, John H. Fischer, Michael Fischler, Paul Fleisher, N. L. Gage, David K. Gast, Nancy Gayer, George Gerbner, J. W. Getzels (with P. W. Jackson), Bentley Glass, Ira Glasser, Allan Glatthorn (with Joseph E. Ferderbar), Egon G. Guba, James W. Guthrie (with Thomas C. Thomas), Don Haefele, Paul Hanna (interviewing Arnold Toynbee), William D. Hedges, Theodore Hesburgh, Banesh Hoffman, Florence Howe, Frank Hunnes, H. Thomas James, James Jarrett, F. Washington Jarvis, Joseph Junell, Joseph Katz (with Nevitt Sanford), John F. Kennedy, James K. Kent, Herbert J. Klausmeier, Ivor Kraft, Ruth Love, Alvin D. Loving, Stan Luxenberg, Michael Marien, Kenneth McIntyre, James A. Mecklenburger, Patricia Michaels, Stanley Milgram, Bartley B. Nourse, Jr., Ellis Page, Franklin Parker, Raymond P. Perkins, Laurence J. Peter, Philip H. Phenix, Jan Phillips, Gerald Read, George Reavis, Donald R. Reich, Jerry Robbins (with Thomas A. Teeter), Vincent R. Rogers, Robert N. Rowe, Kevin Ryan (with David Purpel), David Selden, Robert Sidwell, B. F. Skinner, Robert H. Snow, George Stoddard, Gordon Swanson, Harold Taylor, Ruskin Teeter, M. Donald Thomas (with Margaret Richards), Sidney Trubowitz, William Clark Trow, Charles Tyson, Mimi Warshaw, Thayer S. Warshaw, W. W. Wayson, Edgar Bruce Wesley, Burton White (with John Brademas, Wilson Riles, and Raymond Moore), Beverly Wood, and Richard Wynn.

—SME